GUIDE TO THE WRITING PROCESS

CHOOSING
Purpose and Audience

COLLECTING

Observing

Sensory details
Comparisons and images
Changes
What is not there

Remembering

Specific scenes
Changes and conflicts
Connections between past
  and present

Investigating

Asking questions
Interviews
Questionnaires
Library research

SHAPING

Chronological order
Spatial order
Comparison/contrast
Definition
Example

Focusing and narrowing
  subject
Introductions
Body paragraphs
Conclusions

Casual analysis
Process analysis
Dialogue
Image
Voice and persona

DRAFTING

Planning
Re-reading
Talking

Reconsidering purpose
  and audience

Starting at the beginning
Starting at the middle
Writing non-stop
Stopping when you know
  what comes next

REVISING AND EDITING

Major Changes

Changing purpose or audience
Collecting new information, ideas, evidence,
  examples
Reshaping paragraphs or reorganizing an essay
Choosing a new point of view

Minor Changes

Revising sentences, transitions, word choice
Editing for grammar, punctuation, usage
Proofreading for spelling and mechanics

The Prentice Hall Guide for
College Writers

The Prentice Hall Guide for
College Writers

Second Edition

Stephen Reid

Colorado State University

PRENTICE HALL, Englewood Cliffs, New Jersey 07632

Library of Congress Cataloging-in-Publication Data

Reid, Stephen
    The Prentice Hall guide for college writers / Stephen Reid. — 2nd
ed.
      p.   cm.
    Includes index.
    ISBN 0-13-721986-5
    1. English language—Rhetoric.   I. Title.
PE1408.R424   1992
808'.042—dc20   91-25886
                                              CIP

Acquisitions Editor: *Tracy Augustine*
Development Editor: *Kate Morgan*
Editorial/production supervision: *Jordan Ochs*
Cover and interior design: *Sue Behnke*
Copy editor: *Elizabeth Torjussen*
Cover art: *Nantucket © 1991 Thomas McKnight*
Prepress buyer: *Herb Klein*
Manufacturing buyer: *Patrice Fraccio*

 © 1992, 1989 by Prentice-Hall, Inc.
A Simon & Schuster Company
Englewood Cliffs, New Jersey 07632

Printed in the United States of America
10 9 8 7 6 5 4 3 2 1

ISBN 0-13-721986-5

Prentice-Hall International (UK) Limited, *London*
Prentice-Hall of Australia Pty. Limited, *Sydney*
Prentice-Hall Canada Inc., *Toronto*
Prentice-Hall Hispanoamericana, S.A., *Mexico*
Prentice-Hall of India Private Limited, *New Delhi*
Prentice-Hall of Japan, Inc., *Tokyo*
Simon & Schuster Asia Pte. Ltd., *Singapore*
Editora Prentice-Hall do Brasil, Ltda., *Rio de Janeiro*

BRIEF CONTENTS

CONTENTS

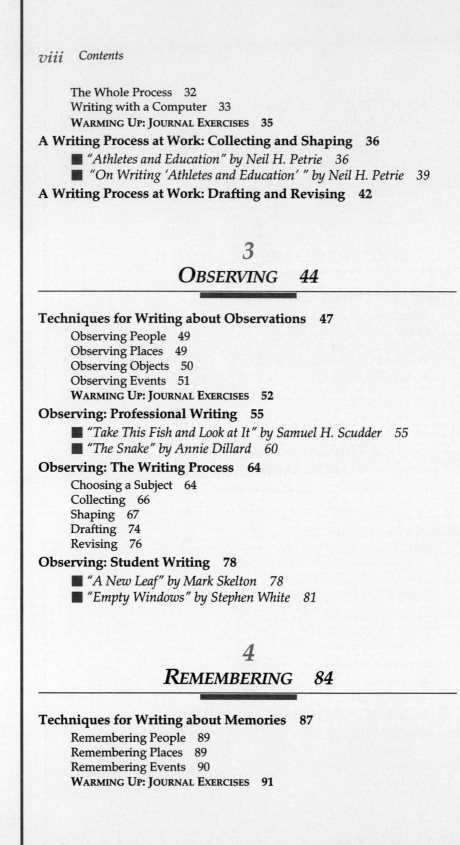
3

OBSERVING   *44*

4

REMEMBERING   *84*

5

INVESTIGATING   **124**

6

EXPLAINING 176

7

EVALUATING 222

10
WRITING A RESEARCH PAPER   372

11
RESPONDING TO LITERATURE   434

APPENDIX: WRITING UNDER PRESSURE   472

HANDBOOK   484

PREFACE

Every writer learns that a piece of writing, once published and sent on its way, acquires its own identity. It stands by itself, virtues and shortcomings plainly obvious. During the past two years, I relearned that lesson each time I visited composition classes in which teachers were using *The Prentice Hall Guide for College Writers*. Although I attended these classes in order to offer our graduate teaching assistants some teaching tips, I discovered that I was the learner, and the teachers and students my best critics.

Sometimes I watched students respond to assignments and reading selections just as I had hoped. For example, once I observed one of our teachers discuss a remembering selection, "The Boy's Desire," by Richard Rodriguez. At first, several young men in the room struggled to distance themselves from this selection, refusing to believe that a male writer might actually admit to wanting a doll for Christmas. After reconciling the students to the subject and the confessional tone, however, the teacher then encouraged students to explore how key imagery—the Sacramento fog and the closet door—evokes the haze of memory and effort to remember. By the end of the period, students were applying some of Rodriguez's strategies to their own drafts, sharpening specific scenes, adding sensory detail, developing key images, and focussing on a single idea.

Sometimes, however, I discovered my selections created unexpected problems. In another class, during a discussion of Edward Abbey's "The Damnation of a Canyon," a group of students attacked Abbey and the teacher, saying that Abbey's essay was **not** a good model of argumentation. They claimed that Abbey did not argue reasonably or represent opposing points of view fairly. Were they supposed to use Abbey's emotional tactics in their own essays? Why, in fact, did the teacher assign this essay? Fortunately, the teacher remained poised and commended students for noticing that Abbey's arguments were not always fair or reasonable. She then asked students to identify the passages in question and discuss how—given his purpose and audience—Abbey should change his essay. Although the discussion was fruitful, I decided that the students were right. They should have a clearer model of traditional argumentation. As a result of this discussion, then, I chose to leave Abbey's essay, but to encourage students to examine Abbey's tone and argumentative tactics more critically. To balance

Abbey's inflammatory tactics, I now precede it with Stephen Jay Gould's reasoned argument in "Darwin's Middle Road."

All of the changes and additions to the second edition of *The Prentice Hall Guide for College Writers* have been prompted by experiences such as these and by feedback I have received from teachers and students across the country. The second edition retains its emphasis on the writer's processes and on purposes for writing. It retains a clear cognitive sequence to the chapters. It retains strong support for students, with journal entries, collecting and shaping strategies, and revision tips. It retains its diverse and interesting professional selections and continues to feature student writing.

The most notable additions to the second edition include the following:

Seven additional full-length professional essays. Authors added are Annie Dillard, Stephen Jay Gould, Helen Keller, Robert Kiely, Jonathan Kozol, David Quammen, and Gloria Steinem.

Responding to Literature: This chapter features strategies for critical reading and writing, contains two short fiction pieces by Kate Chopin and Eudora Welty, and concludes with two student essays.

Writing Under Pressure. This appendix shows students how to analyze their audience, understand key terms in a question, make a sketch outline, and practice writing beforehand. Included are sample impromptu essays in history and biology with the instructors' actual comments and grades.

AIE Teaching Tips. The teaching tips in the Annotated Instructor's Edition are expanded to include suggestions in six new areas: Collaborative Activities, Critical Reading, Diversity Issues, Peer Response, and Write-to Learn suggestions. In addition, a box with integrated Research Tips has been added to chapters six through nine.

AIE Teaching Guide with Research Articles. Available with the text is a teaching manual with guidelines for designing writing assignments, sequencing class activities, using critical reading strategies, organizing collaborative projects, conducting peer response groups, and responding to student writing are now expanded in a separate volume that includes key articles on composition research and pedagogy.

OVERVIEW OF THE TEXT

An Introduction to Myths and Rituals for Writing. Chapter 1, "Writing Myths and Rituals," discounts some common myths about college writing courses, introduces the notion of writing rituals, and outlines the variety of journal writing used throughout the text. Rituals are crucial for all writers but especially so for novice writers; effective rituals are simply those behavioral strategies that complement the cognitive strategies of the writing process. Illustrating a variety of possible writing rituals are quotations from a dozen professional writers on the nature of writing. These short quotations continue throughout the book, reminding students that writing is not some magical process, but a madness that has a method to it, a love that is built from labor, and a learning that is born of reading, thinking, observing, remembering, discussing, and writing.

An Orientation to Rhetorical Situation and to Writing Processes. Chapter 2, "Purposes and Processes for Writing," bases the writing process in the rhetorical situation (writer, subject, purpose, text, and audience). It restores the writer's intent or purpose (rather than a thesis sentence or a rhetorical strategy) as the driving force during the writing process. It demonstrates how meaning evolves from a variety of recursive, multidimensional, and hierarchical activities that we call the writing process. Finally, it reassures students that, since individual writing and learning styles differ, they will be encouraged to discover and articulate their own processes from a range of appropriate possibilities.

Aims and Purposes for Writing. The text then turns to specific purposes and assignments for writing. Chapters 3 through 5 ("Observing," "Remembering," "Investigating") focus on invention strategies. These chapters illustrate how writing to learn is a natural part of learning to write. Writing to learn—through observing, discovering, expressing, remembering, and investigating—is central to the sequence of purposes that structures this text. To promote learning, these chapters introduce three important sources of feelings, ideas, and information necessary for any writing: *observing* people, places, events and objects; *remembering* people, places, and events; and *investigating* information and ideas through interviews, surveys, and written sources. Although in each of these chapters students write essays intended for definite audiences, the emphasis in these early chapters is on invention strategies and on writer-based purposes for writing. This text includes expressive and transactional elements in every assignment, but the direction of the overall sequence of assignments is from the more personal forms of discourse to the more public forms.

Chapters 6 through 9 (Explaining, Evaluating, Problem Solving, and Arguing) are built on subject- and audience-based purposes. The sequence in these chapters moves the student smoothly from exposition to argumentation (acknowledging the obvious overlapping), building on the skills and cognitive strategies of the previous chapters. The teacher may, in fact, use chapters

6 through 9 as a minicourse in argument, teaching students how to develop and argue claims of fact, claims of cause and effect, claims about values, and claims about solutions or policies.

Research Chapter. Chapter 10 (Writing a Research Paper) draws on all the skills and cognitive strategies presented in the first nine chapters. Research papers are written for a purpose and audience too, but the writing process is much more extended. This chapter helps students select and plan their projects, use the library, evaluate and document sources, record their progress, and test ideas in a research log—learning all the while to integrate the information they gather with their own experiences and ideas.

Responding to Literature. Chapter 11 guides students through the writing of interpretative essays, using many of the critical reading tips, invention techniques, and shaping strategies practiced in the earlier chapters. This chapter contains two short fiction works and two student essays (one with process materials).

Writing Under Pressure. This appendix offers concise and practical advice for writing short impromptu essays and includes actual student samples of essays written in biology and history courses.

Optional Handbook. The Prentice Hall Guide for College Writers is available with a handbook (standard edition) or without (shorter edition). The focus of the handbook is on solving the problems writers encounter during editing and proofreading.

Special Features. This text has several other features that are particularly noteworthy:

Journal or daybook writing is integral to this text, helping writers "warm-up" for each assignment, practice various invention and shaping strategies, and improve their reading skills.

Writing strategies (process analysis, comparison-contrast, definition, classification, causal analysis) are treated both as invention and as shaping strategies. More importantly, they are *integrated into each chapter as part of the writing process.*

Nearly a hundred short quotations by novelists, poets, essayists, researchers, and teachers illustrate key ideas from each chapter. In addition to their bits of advice, these authors' voices personalize for the inexperienced writer a larger community of writers who are still struggling with the same problems each student faces.

Professional and student writing appear in each chapter. One student essay (complete with invention notes, rough draft, and final draft) illustrates a writing process appropriate for that particular purpose and audience.

Assignments for each chapter are intentionally general so that students can develop or explore their own interests. Teachers can, of course, tailor the writing to class or programmatic needs. Throughout the text, journal assignments and suggested topics emphasize *cross-curriculum* dimensions: students are continually encouraged to write about what they are studying and learning in other courses.

The Annotated Instructor's Edition integrates teaching tips and citations for relevant research into the text for easy reference.

The most obvious feature of this text is the cyclical, selfcontained structure for each chapter. In place of the traditional modes and strategies approach, the invention-arrangement-style organization, or the sentence-paragraph-essay structure, this text presents a sequence of purposes and assignments and then supports the students' efforts with appropriate invention strategies and arrangement schemes. The result is a flexible and easy-to-use text. Teachers can concentrate on those chapters most relevant to their program and their students. For some chapters, teachers may ask students to write only journal entries or portfolio assignments; for other chapters, teachers may require complete essays and thorough revisions.

Good writing teachers, however, don't teach a text or a course; they teach students. They help writers learn to read, write, think, learn and communicate more effectively, with greater range and variety, and with greater understanding of writers' techniques and readers' expectations. It is my hope that this text supports those activities.

ACKNOWLEDGMENTS

This textbook builds on the work of hundreds of teachers and researchers. Its most obvious and immediate debts are to James Kinneavy, Frank D'Angelo, Donald Murray, Rise Axelrod and Charles Cooper, Jeanne Fahnestock and Marie Secor, Linda Flower and John Hayes, Maxine Hairston, and James Moffett. But beyond those are many other writers whose theories and practices contribute to this textbook: David Bartholomae, Ann Berthoff, Wayne Booth, James Britton, Kenneth Bruffee, Hugh Burns, Richard Coe, Robert Connors, Edward Corbett, Peter Elbow, Caroline Eckhardt and David Stewart, Janet Emig, Richard Fulkerson, Toby Fulwiler, George Hillocks, Richard Larson, Stephen Toulmin, Lynn Troyka, Joseph Williams, William Zeiger, and Robert Zoellner.

In addition, the following teachers offered excellent advice about changes and additions for the second edition: Sarah Liggett, Duane Roen, Stuart Brown, Bob Mayberry, Dr. Mary Ann Wilson, and Richard P. Batteiger.

For the expert crew at Prentice Hall, I am especially grateful. Phil Miller, a fine editor and friend, enthusiastically supported this text from the first day. Kate Morgan and Tracy Augustine exercised their excellent editorial judgment and continually buoyed my spirits. Jordan Ochs provided editorial guidance.

Finally, I wish to thank my family for their continued patience and active support: Joy, Shelley, and Michael.

THE NEW YORK TIMES and PRENTICE HALL are sponsoring A CONTEMPORARY VIEW: a program designed to enhance student access to current information of relevance in the classroom.

Through this program, the core subject matter provided in the text is supplemented by a collection of time-sensitive articles from one of the world's most distinguished newspapers, THE NEW YORK TIMES. These articles demonstrate the vital, ongoing connection between what is learned in the classroom and what is happening in the world around us.

To enjoy the wealth of information of THE NEW YORK TIMES daily, a reduced subscription rate is available. For information, call toll-free: 1-800-631-1222.

PRENTICE HALL and THE NEW YORK TIMES are proud to co-sponsor A CONTEMPORARY VIEW. We hope it will make the reading of both textbooks and newspapers a more dynamic, involving process.

ACKNOWLEDGMENTS

The Prentice Hall Guide for
College Writers

1 | WRITING MYTHS AND RITUALS

Grandma Moses
Catching the Thanksgiving Turkey
Copyright 1989, Grandma Moses Properties
Co., New York

One myth about writing I have believed my whole life is that "good writers are born, not made." My attitude when beginning this writing course was one of apprehension and dread. I wondered if I *could* improve my writing, or if I was destined to receive B's and C's on every essay for the rest of my life. This writing class has given me concrete examples and suggestions for improvement—not just grammar or essay maps. The free writing is such a great help that whenever I'm stuck I immediately turn to my ten-minute free writing to open up blocked passages. Once I get past my writer's block, I see that I can be a good writer. □

For me, the most effective writing ritual is to gather up all of my stuff—legal pad and pencil, notes, dictionary, and thesaurus—and get on my bike, ride to campus, and set myself up in the art lounge in the student center. During the week, I'll do this in the evening after dinner. On a weekend I go anytime from 10 A.M. to midnight. I don't write effectively at home because there are always distractions. Some people will be moving around and I'll go see who they are and what they're doing, or I'll go get a cup of coffee or a piece of toast, or I'll snap on the TV, ignoring that tiny voice inside saying, "Get busy—you have to get this done!" So what makes the art lounge better? Simple—no distractions. I can lay out all of my stuff, get a cup of coffee, and go to work. All around me people are doing the same thing, and somehow all of those hardworking people are an encouragement. The art lounge is always quiet, too—quieter than the library—and it doesn't smell like the library. □

A writer is someone who writes, that's all.

—Gore Vidal, novelist and social commentator

I've always disliked words like inspiration. *Writing is probably like a scientist thinking about some scientific problem or an engineer about an engineering problem.*

—Doris Lessing, author of essays and fiction, including The Golden Notebook

I always worked until I had something done and I always stopped when I knew what was going to happen next. That way I could be sure of going on the next day.

—Ernest Hemingway, journalist and novelist, author of The Old Man and the Sea

As you begin a college writing course, you need to get rid of some myths about writing that you may have been packing around for some time. Don't allow misconceptions to ruin a good experience.

MYTH: "Good writers are born, not made. A writing course really won't help my writing."

FACT: *Writers acquire their skills the same way athletes do—through practice and hard work.* There are very few "born" writers. Most writers—even professional writers and journalists—are not continually inspired to write. In fact, they often experience "writer's block," the stressful experience of staring helplessly at a piece of paper, unable to think or to put words down on paper. A writing course will teach you how to cope with your procrastination, anxiety, lack of "inspiration," and false starts by focusing directly on solving the problems that occur during the writing process.

MYTH: "Writing courses are just a review of boring grammar and punctuation. When teachers read your writing, the only thing they mark is that stuff, anyway."

FACT: *Learning and communicating—not grammar and punctuation—come first in college writing courses.* Knowledge of grammar, spelling, punctuation, and usage is essential to editing, but it is secondary to discovering ideas, thinking, learning, and communicating. In a writing course, students learn to revise and improve the content and organization of each other's writing, and then they help each other edit for grammar, punctuation, or spelling errors.

MYTH: "College writing courses are really 'creative writing,' which is not what my major requires. If I wanted to be another Shakespeare and write poetry, I'd change my major."

FACT: *Writing courses emphasize rhetoric, not poetry.* Rhetoric involves practicing the most effective means or strategies for informing or persuading an audience. All writing—even technical or business writing—is "creative." Deciding what to write, how to write it, how best to get your reader's attention, and how to inform or persuade your reader requires creativity and imagination. Every major requires the skills that writing courses teach: exploring new ideas, learning concepts and processes, communicating with others, and finding fresh or creative solutions to problems.

MYTH: "Writing courses are not important in college or the real world. I'll never have to write, anyway."

FACT: *Writing courses do have a significant effect on your success in college, on the job, and in life.* Even if you don't have frequent, formal writing assignments in other courses, writing improves your note taking, reading comprehension, and thinking skills. When you do have other written tasks or assignments, a writing course teaches you to *adapt* your writing to a variety of different purposes and audiences—whether you are writing a lab report in biology, a letter to an editor, a complaint to the Better Business Bureau, a proposal for an urban project, or a memorandum to your boss. Taking a writing course helps you express yourself more clearly, confidently, and persuasively—a skill that comes in handy whether you're writing a philosophy essay, a job application, or a love letter.

The most important fact about writing is that *you are already a writer.* You have been writing for years. A writer is someone who writes, not just someone who writes a nationally syndicated newspaper column, publishes a bestseller, or wins a Pulitzer Prize. To be an effective writer, you don't have to earn a million dollars; you just have to practice writing enough to know its personal benefits for you and its value for others.

WARM-UP EXERCISE: FREEWRITING

Right now, put this book aside and take out pencil or pen and a piece of paper. Use this free exercise (private, unjudged, ungraded) to remind yourself that you are already a writer. Time yourself for five minutes. Write on the first thing that comes to mind—*anything whatsoever.* Write *nonstop.* Keep writing even if you have to write, "I can't think of anything to say. This feels stupid!" When you get an idea, pursue it.

When five minutes is up, stop writing and reread what you have written. Whether you write about the weather or a more interesting topic, freewriting is an excellent way to warm up, to get into the habit of writing, and to establish a writing ritual.

WRITING FITNESS: RITUALS AND PRACTICE

Writing is no more magic or inspiration than any other human action you admire: figure skating at the Olympics, rebuilding a car engine, cooking a gourmet meal, or acting in a play. Behind every human

Writing is [like] making a table. With both you are working with reality, a material just as hard as wood. Both are full of tricks and techniques. Basically very little magic and a lot of hard work are involved. . . . What is a privilege, however, is to do a job to your own satisfaction.

—*Gabriel Garcia Marquez, Nobel Prize-winning author of* One Hundred Years of Solitude

achievement are many unglamorous hours of practice—working and sweating, falling flat on your face, and picking yourself up again. You can't learn to write just by reading some chapters in a textbook or by memorizing other people's advice. You need help and advice, but you also need practice. Consider the following parable about a Chinese painter:

> A rich patron once gave money to the painter Chu Ta, asking him to paint a picture of a fish. Three years later, when he still had not received the painting, the patron went to Chu Ta's house to ask why the picture was not done. Chu Ta did not answer but dipped a brush in ink and with a few strokes drew a splendid fish. "If it is so easy," asked the patron, "why didn't you give me the picture three years ago?" Again, Chu Ta did not answer. Instead, he opened the door of a large cabinet. Thousands of pictures of fish tumbled out.

Most writers develop little rituals that help them practice their writing. A ritual is a *repeated pattern of behavior* that provides structure, security, and a sense of progress to the one who practices it. Creating your own writing rituals and making them part of your regular routine will help reduce that dreaded initial panic and enable you to call upon your writing process with confidence when you need it.

Place, Time, and Tools

Some writers work best in pen and ink, sprawled on their beds in the afternoon, with a pet snoozing on the blankets nearby. Others rely upon 8 A.M., a hard chair, a clean table, and a handful of Number 2 pencils sharpened to needle points, or upon the blinking amber or green light of a word processor at midnight. Legal-sized pads help some writers produce, while others feel motivated by a spiral notebook with a picture of a mountain stream on the cover. Only you can determine which place, time, and tools give you the best support as a writer.

The place where you write is extremely important. If you are writing in a computer lab, you have to adapt to that place, but if you write a draft in longhand, on a typewriter, or on your own word processor, you can choose the place yourself. In selecting a place, keep the following tips in mind:

Writers are notorious for using any reason to keep from working: overresearching, retyping, going to meetings, waxing the floors—anything.

—*Gloria Steinem, editor of* Ms. Magazine

- *Keep distractions minimal.* Some people simply can't write in the kitchen, where the refrigerator is distractingly close, or in a room that has a TV in it. On the other hand, a public place—a library, an empty classroom, a cafeteria—can be fine as long as the activity does not disturb you.

- *Control interruptions.* If you can close the door to your room and work without interruptions, fine. But even then, other people often assume that you want to take a break when *they* do. So choose a place where *you* can decide when it's time to take a break.

- *Have access to notes, journal, textbooks, sources, and other materials.* If the place is totally quiet but you don't have room to work or you don't have access to important notes or sources, you still may not make much progress. Whatever you need—a desk to spread your work out on, access to notes and sources, a pencil sharpener—make sure your place has it.

The time of day you write and the tools you write with can also affect your attitude and efficiency. Some people like to write early in the morning, before their busy day starts; others like to write in the evening, after classes or work. Whatever time you choose, try to write *regularly*—at least three days a week—at about the same time. If you're trying to get in shape by jogging, swimming, or doing aerobics, you wouldn't exercise for five straight hours on Monday and then take four days off. Writing, like exercise, requires regular practice and conditioning.

Your writing tools—pen, pencil, paper, legal pads, four- by six-inch notecards, notebooks, computer—should also be comfortable for you. Some writers like to make notes with pencil and paper and write their draft on a computer; some like to do all their composing on the computer. As you try different combinations of tools, be aware of how you feel and whether your tools make you more effective. If you feel comfortable, it will be easier to establish rituals that lead to regular practice.

Rituals are important because they help you with the most difficult part of writing—getting started. So use your familiar place, time, and tools to trick yourself into getting some words down on paper. Your mind will devise clever schemes to avoid writing those first ten words—watching TV, balancing your checkbook, drinking some more coffee, or calling a friend and whining together about all the writing you have to do. But if your body has been through the ritual before, it

FRANK AND ERNEST ®by Bob Thaves   Reprinted by permission of NEA, Inc.

will walk calmly to your favorite place, where all your tools are ready, bringing the mind kicking and screaming all the way. Then, after you get the first ten words down, the mind will say, "Hey, this isn't so bad—I've got something to say about that!" And off you'll go.

Each time you perform your writing ritual, the *next* time you write will be that much easier. Soon, your ritual will let you know: *"This is where you write. This is when you write. This is what you write with."* No fooling around. Just writing.

Energy and Attitude

I am by nature lazy, sluggish and of low energy. It constantly amazes me that I do anything at all.

—*Margaret Atwood has managed to produce numerous books of fiction and poetry.*

Since I began writing I have always played games . . . . I have a playful nature; I have never been able to do things because it is my duty to do them. If I can find a way to do my duty by playing a game, then I can manage.

—*Maria Irene Fornes, Obie Award-winning playwright*

Once you've tricked yourself into the first ten words, you need to keep your attitude positive and your energy high. When you see an intimidating wall starting to form in front of you, don't ram your head into it; figure out a way to sneak around it. Try these few tricks and techniques:

- *Start anywhere, quickly.* No law says that when you sit down to write a draft, you have to "begin at the beginning." If the first sentence is hard to write, begin with the first thoughts that come to mind. Or begin with a good example from your experience. Use that to get you going; then come back and rewrite your beginning after you've figured out what you want to say.

- *Write the easiest parts first.* Forcing yourself to start a piece of writing by working on the hardest part first is a sure way to make yourself hate writing. Take the easy way in. If you can't get your thesis to come out right, jot down more examples. If you can't think of examples, go back to brainstorming.

- *Keep moving.* Once you've plunged in, write as fast as you can— whether you are scribbling ideas out with a pencil or hitting the keys of a typewriter or a computer. Maintain your momentum. Reread if you need to, but then plunge ahead.

- *Quit when you know what comes next.* When you do have to quit for the day, stop at a place where you know what comes next. Don't drain the well dry; stop in the middle of something you know how to finish. Make a few notes about what you need to do next and circle them. Leave yourself an easy place to get started next time.

One of the most important strategies for every writer is to *give yourself a break from the past and begin with a fresh image.* In many fields—mathematics, athletics, art, engineering—some people are late bloomers. Don't let that C or D you got in English back in the tenth grade hold you back now like a ball and chain. Imagine yourself cutting the chain and watching the ball roll away for good. Now you are free to start fresh with a clean slate. Your writing rituals should include only positive images about the writer you are right now and realistic expectations about what you can accomplish.

- *Visualize yourself writing.* Successful athletes know how to visualize a successful tennis swing, a basketball free throw, or a baseball swing. When you are planning your activities for the day, visualize yourself writing at your favorite place. Seeing yourself doing your writing will enable you to start writing more quickly and maintain a positive attitude.

- *Discover and emphasize the aspects of writing that are fun for you.* Emphasize whatever is enjoyable for you—discovering an idea, getting the organization of a paragraph to come out right, clearing the unnecessary words and junk out of your writing. Concentrating on the parts you enjoy will help you make it through the tougher parts.

- *Set modest goals for yourself.* Don't aim for the stars; just work on a sentence. Don't measure yourself against some great writer; be your own yardstick. Compare what you write to what *you* have written before.

- *Congratulate yourself for the writing you do.* Writing is hard work; you're using words to create ideas and meanings literally out of nothing. So pat yourself on the back occasionally. Keep in mind the immortal words of comedian Steve Martin, the original Wild and Crazy Guy: "I think I did pretty well, considering I started out with nothing but a bunch of blank paper."

Keeping a Journal

Many writers keep some kind of notebook in which they write down their thoughts for later use. Some writers call it a journal, a place for their day-to-day thoughts. Other writers call it a daybook, a place to record ideas, collected information, possible outlines, titles, questions—anything related to the process of writing, thinking, and learning. Scientists and social scientists keep daily logs in which they record data or describe behavior. The word "journal" is the general term referring to "a place for daily writing." Whatever you call it, it should become part of your writing ritual. In it should go all kinds of writing. Bits and pieces of experience or memory that might come in handy later. Reactions to what you're reading. A log of the problems you face as you write. Memorable sayings or quotations. Short sum-

"I carry a journal with me almost all the time. . . ."

—*Ntozake Shange, author of the play,* For Colored Girls Who Have Considered Suicide When the Rainbow is Enuf

"The most valuable writing tool I have is my daybook. . . . I write in my lap, in the living room or on the porch, in the car or an airplane, in meetings at the university, in bed, or sitting down on a rock wall during a walk. . . . It is always a form of talking to myself, a way of thinking on paper.

—Donald Murray, journalist, author of books and essays about writing

maries of what you're reading in your classes. Your journal is a place to practice, a closet where all your "fish paintings" go.

For maximum flexibility, your journal should be a loose-leaf notebook, so you can add, take out, or rearrange materials. Some writers, though, prefer a spiral notebook, a manila folder with pockets, or a computer disk. Whatever format you choose, make sure that you feel comfortable with it.

As the following list indicates, there are many kinds of journal entries.

- *Warm-up writing.* Writing, like any other kind of activity, improves when you loosen up, stretch, get the kinks out, practice a few lines. Any daybook or journal entry gives you a chance to warm up.

- *Collecting and shaping exercises.* Some journal entries will help you collect information by observing, remembering or investigating people, places, events, or objects. You can also record quotations or startling statistics for a future writing topic. Other entries will give you a chance to practice organizing your information. Strategies of development, such as comparison/contrast, definition, classification, process analysis, and casual analysis will help you discover and shape ideas.

- *Practice in writing for a specified audience.* In some entries, you need to play a role, to imagine you are in a specific situation and writing for a defined audience. For example, you might write a letter of application to a college admissions officer or a letter to your employer asking for a week's vacation.

- *Identifying and solving writing problems.* Your journal is also the place to keep a log, a running account of your writing plans and problems. The log helps you record your progress and identify and solve problems as they occur.

- *Summarizing, responding, and recording vocabulary entries.* A journal is an excellent place to summarize articles for other courses, respond to class discussions, or record definitions of words you look up in the dictionary.

- *Imitating styles of writers.* Use the journal to copy passages from writers you like or practice imitating their style.

- *Free journal entries.* Use your journal to record ideas, reactions to people on campus, events in the news, conversations after classes or work, or just your private thoughts.

For most journal entries, try to let your ideas flow easily. Don't stop to fix spelling or punctuation. Focus on your train of thought.

Below is a sample of a free journal entry. The author decided to write about a bumper sticker she saw, but the more she wrote, the more it suggested related ideas to her.

Although Ciccarello never wrote an essay about that bumper sticker, the theme of being an individual and wanting to make the world a better place was an undercurrent in several of her essays. Articulating these questions helped her discover what she wanted to write about.

I just bought a bumper sticker, white writing on black that reads, "are we having fun yet?" It struck me as funny. The purpose of that bumper sticker for those who display it is to make a statement about a way of life. Are we having fun yet? It conveys a sense of dissatisfaction at the way life is supposed to be. It's an attitude. Why does it have to be structured the way it is? Does everyone have to fit in? Is this it? Is this all? Are we having fun yet? Are we supposed to be? When do I get get to do what I want to do? Why don't things go my way? Can't I play by my own rules?

That seems like a lot of "message" in one little saying, but when I read it for the first time, that's what it brought to my mind. So, I was part of the audience. I think a lot of people, especially young people are the intended audience for this sticker. Young people who are still idealistic; who think that maybe there is still time to change the world. Young people who are brought into a society they didn't organize and if they had, it would have been done differently. Young people, who want to be individuals when they "grow up", not just another nameless faceless joe blow on the street. Are we having fun yet? When is it our turn to run the show?

— Terri Ciccarello

WARMING UP: JOURNAL EXERCISES

Choose three of the exercises below and write for ten minutes on each. Date and number each entry.

1. Make an "authority" list of activities, subjects, ideas, places, people, or events you already know something about. List as many topics as you can. If your reaction is, "I'm not really an *authority* on anything," then imagine you've met someone from another school, state, country, or historical period. Relative to that audience, what are you an "authority" on?

2. Choose one activity, sport, or hobby that you do well and that others might admire you for. In the form of a letter to a friend, describe the steps or stages of the process through which you acquired that skill or ability.

3. In two or three sentences, answer the following question: "I have trouble writing because . . ."

4. In a few sentences, answer the following question: "In my previous classes and from my own writing experience, I've learned that the three most important rules about writing are . . ."

5. Describe your own writing rituals. *When, where,* and *how* do you write best?

6. Write an open journal entry. Describe events from your day, images, impressions, bits of conversation—anything that catches your interest. Read the following essay by Roy Hoffman for possible ideas for open journal entries.

ON KEEPING A JOURNAL

Roy Hoffman

In a Newsweek On Campus *essay, Roy Hoffman describes his own experience, recording events and trying out ideas just as an artist doodles on a sketch pad. Your own journal entries about events, images, descriptions of people, and bits of conversation will not only improve your writing but will also become your own personal time capsule, to dig up and reread in the year 2010.*

Wherever I go I carry a small notebook in my coat or back pocket for thoughts, observations and impressions. As a writer I use this notebook as an artist would a sketch pad, for stories and essays, and as a sporadic journal of my comings and goings. When I first started keeping notebooks, though, I was not yet a professional writer. I was still in college.

I made my first notebook entries in the summer of 1972, just after my freshman year, in what was actually a travel log. A buddy and I were setting out to trek from our Alabama hometown to the distant tundra of Alaska. With unbounded enthusiasm I began: "Wild, crazy ecstasy wants to wrench my head from my body." The log, written in a university composition book, goes on to chronicle our adventures in the land where the sun never sets, the bars never close and the prepipeline employment prospects were so bleak we ended up taking jobs as night janitors.

When I returned to college that fall I had a small revelation: the world around me of libraries, quadrangles, Frisbees and professors was as rich with material for my journals and notebooks as galumphing moose and garrulous fishermen.

These college notebooks, which built to a pitch my senior year, are gold mines to me now. Classrooms, girlfriends, cups of coffee and lines of poetry—from mine to John Keats's—float by like clouds. As I lie beneath these clouds again, they take on familiar and distinctive shapes.

Though I can remember the campus's main quadrangle, I see it more vividly when I read my description of school on a visit during summer break: "the muggy, lassitudinal air . . . the bird noises that can not be pointed to, the summer emptiness that grows emptier with a few students squeaking by the library on poorly oiled bicycles." An economics professor I fondly remember returns with less fondness in my notebooks, "staring down at the class with his equine face." And a girl I had a crush on senior year, whom I now recall mistily, reappears with far more vitality as "the ample, slightly-gawky, whole-wheat, fractured object of my want gangling down the hall in spring heat today."

When, in reading over my notebooks, I am not peering out at quadrangles, midterm exams, professors or girlfriends, I see a portrait of my parents and hometown during holidays and occasional weekend breaks. Like a wheel, home revolves, each turn regarded differently depending on the novel or political essay I'd been most influenced by the previous semester.

Mostly, though, in wandering back through my notebooks, I meet someone who could be my younger brother: the younger version of myself. The younger me seems moodier, more inquisitive, more fun-loving and surprisingly eager to stay up all night partying or figuring out electron orbitals for a 9 a.m. exam. The younger me wanders through a hall of mirrors of the self, writes of "seeing two or three of myself on every corner," and pens long meditations on God and society before scribbling in the margin, "what a child I am." The younger me also finds humor in trying to keep track of this hall of mirrors, commenting in ragged verse.

> I hope that one day
> Some grandson or cousin
> Will read these books,
> And know that I was
> Once a youth
> Sitting in drugstores with
> Anguished looks.
> And poring over coffee,
> And should have poured
> The coffee
> Over these lines.

I believe that every college student should attempt to keep some form of notebook, journal or diary. A notebook is a secret garden in which to dance, sing, muse, wander, perform handstands, even cry. In the privacy of this little book, you can make faces, curse, turn somersaults and ask yourself if you're *really* in love. A notebook or journal is one of the few places you can call just your own.

. . . Journal writing suffers when you let someone, in your mind, look over your shoulder. Honesty wilts when a parent, teacher or friend looms up in your imagination to discourage you from putting your *true* thoughts on the page. Journal writing also runs a related hazard: the dizzying suspicion that one day your private thoughts, like those of Samuel Pepys or Virginia Woolf, will be published in several volumes and land up required reading for English 401. How can you write comfortably when the eyes of all future readers are upon you? Keep your notebooks with the abandon of one who knows his words will go up in smoke. Then you might really strike fire a hundred years or so from now if anyone cares to pry.

By keeping notebooks, you improve your writing ability, increasing your capacity to communicate both with yourself and others. By keeping notebooks, you discover patterns in yourself, whether lazy ones that need to be broken or healthy ones that can use some nurturing. By keeping notebooks, you heighten some moments and give substance to others: even a journey to the washateria offers potential for some offbeat journal observations. And by keeping notebooks while still in college, you chart a terrain that, for many, is more dynamically charged with ideas and discussions that the practical, workaday world just beyond. Notebooks, I believe, not only help us remember this dynamic charge, but also help us sustain it.

Not long ago, while traveling with a friend in Yorktown, Va., I passed by a time capsule buried in the ground in 1976, intended to be dug up in 2076. Keeping notebooks and journals is rather like burying time capsules into one's own life. There's no telling what old rock song, love note, philosophical complaint or rosy Saturday morning you'll unearth when you dig up these personal time capsules. You'll be able to piece together a remarkable picture of where you've come from, and may well get some important glimmers about where you're going.

2 PURPOSES AND PROCESSES FOR WRITING

E. K. F. Von Gekhardt
The Students
Super Stock

As a Chinese American woman growing up in America, you decide to write about the difficulty of living in two cultures. You recall how, during your childhood, you rebelled against your mother when she insisted that you learn about your Chinese heritage. You remember how much you hated your Chinese school and how embarrassed you were that your mother could not speak English properly. As you grew older, however, you realized the price you paid for your assimilation into American culture. After discussing this conflict with your friends, you decide to describe your experiences to others who share your experiences or who may want to know what you learned. At that point, you write an autobiographical account of your experiences and send it to a metropolitan newspaper. □

A veteran smoker, you have become increasingly irritated at the nonsmoking regulations that have appeared in restaurants, businesses, and other public places. And it's not just the laws that are irritating, but it's the attitude of people who assume a holier-than-thou attitude, who presume that what's good for them should be good for you. The nonsmoking laws seem to give people license to censure your behavior while totally ignoring their own offensive behavior: polluting the atmosphere with hydrocarbons, fouling the aquifers with fertilizers, and generally corrupting the social air with odors of false superiority. So after one particularly memorable experience, you write a letter to the editor of the local paper, intending not only to express your own frustration but also to satirize those smug do-gooders. □

First and foremost I write for myself. Writing has been for a long time my major tool for self-instruction and self-development.

—Toni Cade Bambara, *author of* The Salt Eaters

How do I know what I think until I see what I say?

—E. M. Forster, *author of* A Passage to India

The writing for this course (and the structure of this textbook) starts with the premise that effective communication begins with learning, and learning results—at least in part—from your written efforts *to make connections and see relationships* between your own observations and experience, and the written or collected knowledge of others. There are three important sources for learning, writing, and communication:

- Observing and describing the world around you
- Remembering and drawing on your own experiences
- Investigating knowledge in books and other people

Writing, as a means of learning and communicating, begins with what you see and have experienced, and then connects with what you're reading in texts, hearing in lectures, finding out at work, or learning from friends and family.

FREEWRITING: INVENTORY OF YOUR WRITING

Before you read further in this chapter, take out a pen or pencil and a piece of paper and inventory what you have written in the last year or two. Brainstorm a list of everything you can think of: grocery lists, letters, wedding invitations, reports, school essays, notes to friends, applications for jobs, memos to your boss. Then for *one* of your longer writing projects, jot down several sentences describing the situation that called for that piece of writing—*when* you did it, *whom* you wrote it for, *what* its purpose was, *where* you wrote it, and *how* you went about writing it.

Most good writing has a personal dimension. It may be about the writer personally or it may address a subject or an idea the writer cares about. It begins with honesty, curiosity, inquiry, and vulnerability. Good writers assert themselves, knowing that they are vulnerable to other people's criticism. They take risks—sometimes writing on subjects they don't completely understand—knowing that is one way to actively engage the information that threatens to overwhelm them. By continually probing and learning, being honest with themselves, and accepting the risks, writers can use their writing to teach themselves and their readers.

WRITING FOR MYSELF

Russell Baker

For many years, Russell Baker wrote humorous essays for The New York Times, *but before that, he was just a writer, someone who wrote about his experiences, what he was learning or was curious about, or what he found amusing or absurd. In this selection from his autobiography,* Growing Up, *Russell Baker describes how bored he was with writing "compositions" until he finally found a topic which he had some experience with and some interest in. The essay he wrote for his composition class, on the art of eating spaghetti, taught Baker an important truth: Writers should write honestly about topics that are important—even fun—for them.*

The notion of becoming a writer had flickered off and on in my head since the Belleville days, but it wasn't until my third year in high school that the possibility took hold. Until then I'd been bored by everything associated with English courses. I found English grammar dull and baffling. I hated the assignments to turn out leaden, lackluster paragraphs that were agonies for teachers to read and for me to write. The classics thrust on me to read seemed as deadening as chloroform.

When our class was assigned to Mr. Fleagle for third-year English I anticipated another grim year in that dreariest of subjects. Mr. Fleagle was notorious among City students for dullness and inability to inspire. He was said to be stuffy, dull, and hopelessly out of date. To me he looked to be sixty or seventy and prim to a fault. He wore primly severe eyeglasses, his wavy hair was primly cut and primly combed. He wore prim vested suits with neckties blocked primly against the collar buttons of his primly starched white shirts. He had a primly pointed jaw, a primly straight nose, and a prim manner of speaking that was so correct, so gentlemanly, that he seemed a comic antique.

I anticipated a listless, unfruitful year with Mr. Fleagle and for a long time was not disappointed. Late in the year we tackled the informal essay. Mr. Fleagle distributed a homework sheet offering us a choice of topics. None was quite so simpleminded as "What I Did on My Summer Vacation," but most seemed to be almost as dull. I took the list home and dawdled until the night before the essay was due. Sprawled on the sofa, I finally faced up to the grim task, took the list out of my notebook, and scanned it. The topic on which my eye stopped was "The Art of Eating Spaghetti."

This title produced an extraordinary sequence of mental images. Surging up out of the depths of memory came a vivid recollection of a night in Belleville when all of us were seated around the supper table—Uncle Allen, my mother, Uncle Charlie, Doris, Uncle Hal—and Aunt Pat served spaghetti for supper. Spaghetti was an exotic treat in those days. Neither Doris nor I had ever eaten spaghetti, and none of the adults had enough experience to be good at it. All the good humor of Uncle Allen's house reawoke in my mind as I recalled the laughing arguments we had that night about the socially respectable method for moving spaghetti from plate to mouth.

Suddenly I wanted to write about that, about the warmth and good feeling of it, but I wanted to put it down simply for my own joy, not for Mr. Fleagle. It was a moment I wanted to recapture and hold for myself. I wanted to relive the pleasure of an evening at New Street. To write it as I wanted, however, would violate all the rules of formal composition I'd learned in school, and Mr. Fleagle would surely give it a failing grade. Never mind. I would write something else for Mr. Fleagle after I had written this thing for myself.

When I finished it the night was half gone and there was no time left to compose a proper, respectable essay for Mr. Fleagle. There was no choice next morning but to turn in my private reminiscence of Belleville. Two days passed before Mr. Fleagle returned the graded papers, and he returned everyone's but mine. I was bracing myself for a command to report to Mr. Fleagle immediately after school for discipline when I saw him lift my paper from his desk and rap for the class's attention.

"Now, boys," he said. "I want to read you an essay. This is titled, 'The Art of Eating Spaghetti.' "

And he started to read. My words! He was reading my words out loud to the entire class. What's more, the entire class was listening. Listening attentively. Then somebody laughed, then the entire class was laughing, and not in contempt and ridicule, but with openhearted enjoyment. Even Mr. Fleagle stopped two or three times to repress a small prim smile.

I did my best to avoid showing pleasure, but what I was feeling was pure ecstasy at this startling demonstration that my words had the power to make people laugh. In the eleventh grade, at the eleventh hour as it were, I had discovered a calling. It was the happiest moment of my entire school career. When Mr. Fleagle finished he put the final seal on my happiness by saying, "Now that, boys, is an essay, don't you see. It's—don't you see—it's of the very essence of the essay, don't you see. Congratulations, Mr. Baker."

PURPOSES FOR WRITING

Getting a good grade, making a million dollars, or contributing to society may be among your reasons or motives for writing. However, as a writer, you also have more specific *purposes* for writing to help you make key decisions about content, structure, or style. When your main purpose is to express your feelings, you may write a private entry in your journal. When your main purpose is to explain how your sales promotion increased the number of your company's customers, you may write a factual report to your boss. When your main purpose is to persuade others to see a movie you like, you may write a review for the local newspaper. In each case, the intended use or impact of what you write helps determine what you write and how you write it.

> *The writer may write to inform, to explain, to entertain, to persuade, but whatever the purpose there should be, first of all, the satisfaction of the writer's own learning. . . .*
>
> —*Donald Murray, teacher and Pulitzer Prize-winning journalist*

Writer-Based Purposes

Because writing is, or should be, for yourself first of all, everything you write involves at least some purpose that *benefits* you. Of course, *expressing yourself* is a fundamental purpose of all writing. Without the satisfaction of expressing your thoughts, feelings, reactions, knowledge, or questions, you might not make the effort to write in the first place. A closely related purpose is *learning:* Writing helps you discover what you think or feel, simply by using language to identify and compose your thoughts. Writing not only helps you form ideas, but actually promotes *observing* and *remembering.* If you write down what you observe about people, places, or things, you can actually "see" them more clearly. Similarly, if you write down facts, ideas, experiences, or reactions to your readings, you will remember them longer. Writing and rewriting facts, dates, definitions, impressions, or personal experiences will improve your powers of recall on important occasions such as examinations and job interviews.

Subject- and Audience-Based Purposes

Although some writing is intended only for yourself—such as entries in a diary, lists, class notes, reminders—much of your writing will be read by others, by those readers who constitute your "audience." You may write to *inform* others about a particular subject—to tell them about the key facts, data, feelings, people, places, or events. Or you may write to *explain* to your readers what something means, how it works, or why it happens. You may write to *persuade* others to believe

> *I think writing is really a process of communication. . . . It's the sense of being in contact with people who are part of a particular audience that really makes a difference to me in writing.*
>
> —*Sherley Ann Williams, poet, critic, and novelist*

or do something—to convince others to agree with your judgment about a book, record, or restaurant, or to persuade them to take a certain class, vote for a certain candidate, or buy some product you are advertising. You may write to *explore* ideas and "truths," to examine how your ideas have changed, to ask questions that have no easy answers, and then to share your thoughts and reflections with others. You may write to *entertain*—as a primary purpose in itself or as a purpose combined with informing, explaining, persuading, or exploring. Whatever your purposes may be, good writing both teaches *and* pleases. Your readers will learn more, remember more, or be more convinced when your writing contains humor, wit, or imaginative language.

Combinations of Purposes

In many cases, you write with more than one purpose in mind. Purposes may appear in combinations, connected in a sequence, or actually overlapping. Initially you may take notes about a subject to learn and remember, but later you may want to inform others about what you have discovered. Similarly, you may begin by writing to express your feelings about a movie that you loved or that upset you; later, you may wish to persuade others to see it—or not to see it. Purposes can also contain each other, like Chinese boxes, or overlap, blurring the distinctions. An explanation of how an automobile works will contain information about that vehicle. An attempt to persuade someone to buy an automobile may contain an explanation of how it handles and information about its body style or engine. Usually writing to persuade others will contain explanations and basic information, but the reverse is not necessarily true; you can write simply to give information, without trying to persuade anyone to do anything.

Subject, Purpose, and Thesis

The *thesis, claim,* or *main idea* in a piece of writing is related to your purpose. As a writer, you usually have a purpose in mind that serves as a guide while you gather information about your subject and think about your audience. As you collect and record information, impressions, and ideas, however, you gradually narrow your subject to a specific topic, and thus clarify your purpose. You bring your purpose into sharper and sharper focus—as if progressing on a target from the outer circles to the bull's-eye—until you have narrowed your purpose down to a central *thesis*. The thesis is the dominant idea, explanation, evaluation, or recommendation you want to impress upon your readers.

The following examples illustrate how a writer moves from a general subject, guided by purpose, to a specific thesis or claim.

Subject	Purpose	Thesis, Claim, or Main Idea
Childhood experiences	To *express* your feelings and *explain* how one childhood experience was important.	The relentless competition between me and my sisters distorted my easygoing personality.
Heart disease	To *inform* readers about relationships between Type A personalities and heart attacks.	Type A personalities do not necessarily have an abnormally high risk of suffering heart attacks.
AIDS	To *persuade* readers not to quarantine AIDS victims.	Children afflicted with AIDS should not be prevented from attending school.

PURPOSE AND AUDIENCE

Writing for yourself is relatively easy, since you already know your audience and can make spontaneous judgments about what is essential and what is not. When your purpose is to communicate to other readers, however, you need to *analyze your audience*. Anticipating what your readers know and need to know, what they are interested in, and what their beliefs or attitudes are will make your writing more effective. As you write for different readers, you will select different kinds of information, organize it in different ways, or write in a more formal or less formal style.

FREEWRITING: WRITING FOR DIFFERENT AUDIENCES

Before you read further, get a pen or pencil and several sheets of paper, and do the following exercise.

1. For your eyes only, write about what you did at a recent party. Write for four minutes.

2. On a second sheet of paper, describe for the members of your writing class what you did at this party; you will read it aloud to the class. Stop after four minutes.

3. On a third sheet of paper, write a letter to one of your parents describing what you did at the party. Stop after four minutes.

Audience Analysis

If you are writing to communicate to other readers, analyzing your probable audience will help you answer some basic questions:

- How much information or evidence is enough? What should I assume my audience already knows? What should I not tell them? What do they believe? Will they readily agree with me or will they be antagonistic?

- How should I organize my writing? How can I get my reader's attention? Can I just describe my subject and tell a story or should I analyze everything in a logical order? Should I put my best examples or arguments first or last?

- Should I write informally, with simple sentences and easy vocabulary, or should I write in a more elaborate or specialized style, with technical vocabulary?

Analyze your audience by considering the following questions. As you learn more about your audience, the possibilities for your own role as a writer will become clearer.

1. *Audience profile.* How narrow or broad is your audience? Is it a *narrow and defined* audience—a single person, such as your Aunt Mary, or a group with clear common interests, such as the zoning board in your city or the readers of *Organic Gardening?* Is it a *broad and diverse* audience: educated readers who wish to be informed on current events, American voters as a whole, or residents of your state? Do your readers have identifiable roles? Can you determine their age, sex, economic status, ethnic background, or occupational category?

2. *Audience-subject relationship.* Consider what your readers *know* about your subject. If they know very little about it, you'll need to explain the basics; if they already know quite a bit, you can get right to more difficult or complex issues. Also estimate their probable *attitude* toward this subject. Are they likely to be sympathetic or hostile?

3. *Audience-writer relationship.* What is your relationship with the readers? Do you know each other personally? Do you have any-

thing in common? Will your audience be likely to trust what you say or will they be skeptical about your judgments? Are you the expert on this particular subject and the reader a novice? Or are you a novice and your reader the expert? (If you're a novice writing to an expert, absolute honesty and careful reliance on evidence will help win you a hearing.)

4. *Writer's role.* To communicate effectively with your audience, you should also consider your own role or perspective. Of the many roles that you could play (friend, big sister or brother, student of psychology, music fan, employee of a fast-food restaurant, and so on), choose one that will be effective for your purpose and audience. If, for example, you are writing to sixth-graders about nutrition, you could choose the perspective of a concerned older brother or sister, but your writing might be more effective if you assume the role of a person who has worked in fast-food restaurants for three years and knows what goes into hamburgers, French fries, and milkshakes.

Writers may write to a real audience, or they may create an audience. Sometimes the relationship between writer and reader is real (sister writing to brother), and so the writer starts with a known audience and writes accordingly. Sometimes, however, writers begin writing and gradually discover or create an audience in the process of writing. Knowing the audience guides the writing, but the writing may create an audience as well.

The Writing Situation

Taken together, the writer's purpose or aim, the subject, and the probable audience (whether yourself or others) define the *writing situation*. Sometimes an instructor or employer assigns you a specific writing situation. At other times, you construct a situation yourself from scratch.

The components of the writing situation—subject, purpose, thesis, and audience—are so interrelated that a change in one may affect the other three. As you write, therefore, you do not always follow a step-by-step order. You may begin, for example, with a specific audience on which you wish to make an impression; as you analyze the audience, you decide what subject and purpose would be most appropriate. You may start with an interesting subject but no clear sense of purpose or audience. Or you may be asked to write for a certain audience, and the needs and expectations of that audience may lead you to discover or modify your purpose or subject.

Subject, purpose, thesis, and audience are all modified, reconsidered, and revised as you write.

The following examples illustrate how subject, purpose, and audience combine to define a writing situation.

> In response to a request by an editor of a college recruiting pamphlet, a student decides to write an essay explaining the advantages of the social and academic life at his university. According to the editor, the account needs to be realistic, but it should also promote the university. It shouldn't be too academic and stuffy, since the college catalogue itself contains all the basic information, but it should give high school seniors a flavor of college life. The student decides to write a narrative account of his most interesting experiences during his first week at college.

> A student majoring in journalism reads about correspondents', accounts of restrictions during the Persian Gulf conflict. The military limited reporters to carefully controlled "pools," and during the ground offensive, television journalists' tapes were mysteriously delayed or lost until after the ground war was over. Following a class debate on the public's right to know versus the military's need to maintain secrecy in times of war, the student investigates specific incidents to see if the military exercised unnecessary or excessive censorship. The student researches these incidents and reports her findings in a letter to her congressional representative, asking for a further investigation of certain cases of alleged censorship.

PURPOSE AND AUDIENCE IN TWO ESSAYS

The two short essays that follow appeared as columns in newspapers. Both relate the writer's own experiences. They are similar in form but have different purposes and appeal to different kinds of readers. As you read each essay, decide which essay you find more interesting—and why.

THE STRUGGLE TO BE AN ALL-AMERICAN GIRL

Elizabeth Wong

It's still there, the Chinese school on Yale Street where my brother and I used to go. Despite the new coat of paint and the high wire fence, the school I knew 10 years ago remains remarkably, stoically the same.

Every day at 5 p.m., instead of playing with our fourth- and fifth-grade friends or sneaking out to the empty lot to hunt ghosts and animal bones, my brother and I had to go to Chinese school. No amount of kicking, screaming, or pleading could dissuade my mother, who was solidly determined to have us learn the language of our heritage.

Forcibly, she walked us the seven long, hilly blocks from our home to school, depositing our defiant tearful faces before the stern principal. My only memory of him is that he swayed on his heels like a palm tree, and he always clasped his impatient twitching hands behind his back. I recognized him as a repressed maniacal child killer, and knew that if we ever saw his hands we'd be in big trouble.

We all sat in little chairs in an empty auditorium. The room smelled like Chinese medicine, and imported faraway mustiness. Like ancient mothballs or dirty closets. I hated that smell. I favored crisp new scents. Like the soft French perfume that my American teacher wore in public school.

Although the emphasis at the school was mainly language— speaking, reading, writing—the lessons always began with an exercise in politeness. With the entrance of the teacher, the best student would tap a bell and everyone would get up, kowtow, and chant, "sing san ho," the phonetic for "How are you, teacher?"

Being ten years old, I had better things to learn than ideographs copied painstakingly in lines that ran right to left from the tip of a *moc but*, a real ink pen that had to be held in an awkward way if blotches were to be avoided. After all, I could do the multiplication tables, name the satellites of Mars, and write reports on "Little Women" and "Black Beauty." Nancy Drew, my favorite book heroine, never spoke Chinese.

The language was a source of embarrassment. More times than not, I had tried to disassociate myself from the nagging loud voice that followed me wherever I wandered in the nearby American supermarket outside Chinatown. The voice belonged to my grandmother, a fragile woman in her seventies who could outshout the best of the street vendors. Her humor was raunchy, her Chinese rhythmless, patternless. It was quick, it was loud, it was unbeautiful. It was not like the quiet, lilting romance of French or the gentle refinement of the American South. Chinese sounded pedestrian. Public.

In Chinatown, the comings and goings of hundreds of Chinese on their daily tasks sounded chaotic and frenzied. I did not want to be thought of as mad, as talking gibberish. When I spoke English, people nodded at me, smiled sweetly, said encouraging words. Even the people in my culture would cluck and say that I'd do well in life. "My, doesn't she move her lips fast," they would say, meaning that I'd be able to keep up with the world outside Chinatown.

My brother was even more fanatical than I about speaking English. He was especially hard on my mother, criticizing her, often cruelly, for her pidgin speech—smatterings of Chinese scattered like chop suey in her conversation. "It's not 'What it is,' Mom," he'd say in exasperation. "It's 'What *is* it, what *is* it, what *is* it!" Sometimes Mom might leave out an occasional "the" or "a," or perhaps a verb of being. He would stop her in mid-sentence: "Say it again, Mom. Say it right." When he tripped over his own tongue, he'd blame it on her: "See, Mom, it's all your fault. You set a bad example."

After two years of writing with a *moc but* and reciting words with multiples of meanings, I finally was granted a cultural divorce. I was permitted to stop Chinese school.

I thought of myself as multicultural. I preferred tacos to egg rolls; I enjoyed Cinco de Mayo more than Chinese New Year.

At last, I was one of you; I wasn't one of them.

Sadly, I still am.

I'M OK, BUT YOU'RE NOT

Robert Zoellner

The American novelist John Barth, in his early novel, *The Floating Opera,* remarks that ordinary, day-to-day life often presents us with embarrassingly obvious, totally unsubtle patterns of symbolism and meaning—life in the midst of death, innocence vindicated, youth versus age, etc.

The truth of Barth's insight was brought home to me recently while having breakfast in a lawn-bordered restaurant on College Avenue near the Colorado State University campus. I had asked to be seated in the smoking section of the restaurant—I have happily gone through three or four packs a day for the past 40 years.

As it happened, the hostess seated me—I was by myself—at a little two-person table on the dividing line between the smoking and non-smoking sections. Presently, a well-dressed couple of advanced years, his hair a magisterial white and hers an electric blue—you know, the sort of couple for whom wearing Reagan buttons would be an act of total redundancy—were seated in the non-smoking section five feet away from me.

It was apparent within a minute that my cigarette smoke was bugging them badly, and soon the husband leaned over and asked me if I would please stop smoking. As a chronic smokestack, I normally comply, out of simple courtesy, with such requests. Even an addict such as myself can quit for as long as 20 minutes.

But his manner was so self-righteous and peremptory—he reminded me of Lee Iacocca boasting about Chrysler—that the promptings of original sin, always a problem with me, took over. I quietly pointed out that I was in the smoking section—if only by five feet—and that that fact meant that I had met my social obligation to non-smokers. Besides, the idea of morning coffee without a cigarette was simply inconceivable to me—might as well ask me to vote Republican.

The two of them ate their eggs-over-easy in hurried and sullen silence, while I chain-smoked over my coffee. As well as be hung for a sheep as a lamb, I reasoned. Presently they got up, paid their bill, and stalked out in an ambiance of affronted righteousness and affluent propriety.

And this is where John Barth comes in. They had parked their car—a diesel Mercedes—where it could be seen from my table. And in the car, waiting impatiently, was a splendidly matched pair of pedigreed poodles, male and female.

Both dogs were clearly *in extremis,* and when the back door of the car was opened, they made for the restaurant lawn in considerable haste. Without ado (no pun intended), the male did a doo-doo that would have done credit to an animal twice his size, and finished off with a leisurely, ruminative wee-wee. The bitch of the pair, as might be expected of any well-brought-up female of Republican proclivities, confined herself to a modest wee-wee, fastidious, diffident, and quickly executed.

Having thus polluted the restaurant lawn, the four of them marshalled their collective dignity and drove off in a dense cloud of blue smoke—that lovely white Mercedes was urgently in need of a valve-and-ring job, its emission sticker an obvious exercise in creative writing.

As I regretfully watched them go—after all, the four of them had made my day—it seemed to me that they were in something of a hurry, and I uncharitably wondered if the husband was not anxious to get home in order to light the first Fall fire in his moss-rock fireplace, or apply the Fall ration of chemical fertilizer to his doubtlessly impeccable lawn, thus adding another half-pound of particulates to the local atmosphere and another 10 pounds of nitrates and other poisons to the regional aquifers. But that, of course, is pure and unkindly speculation.

In any case, the point of this real-life vignette, as John Barth would insist, is obvious. The current controversy over public smoking in Fort Collins is a clear instance of selective virtue at work, coming under the rubric of, what I do is perfectly OK, but what you do is perfectly awful.

QUESTIONS FOR WRITING AND DISCUSSION

1. For *both* essays, answer the following question (choose only one adjective to describe your main reaction to each essay): "When I finished the _____ [Wong, Zoellner] essay, I was _____ [intrigued, bored, amused, irritated, curious, confused, or _____] because _____. Explain your choice of adjectives in one or two sentences.

2. Referring to specific passages, explain the purpose and state the thesis or main point of each essay.

3. What personality or role does each writer project? Drawing from evidence in the essay, describe what you think both writers would be like if you met them.

4. Both of these essays appeared in newspapers. What kind of reader would find each essay interesting? What kind of reader would *not* enjoy each essay? For each essay, find examples of specific sentences, word choices, vocabulary, experiences, or references to culture or politics that would appeal to one reader but perhaps irritate some other reader.

5. These two essays are similar in form (they are both informal essays, narrating personal experiences and explaining what each writer discovered or learned), but there are differences in structure and style. What differences do you notice in the way each essay begins and concludes, in the order of the paragraphs, and in vocabulary or style of the sentences?

I don't see writing as communication of something already discovered, as 'truths' already known. Rather, I see writing as a job of experiment. It's like any discovery job; you don't know what's going to happen until you try it.

—William Stafford, teacher, poet, and essayist

PROCESSES FOR WRITING

Processes for writing vary from one writer to the next and from one writing situation to the next, but most writers can identify four basic stages, or dimensions, of their writing process: *collecting, shaping, drafting,* and *revising*. The writing situation may precede these stages—particularly if you are assigned a subject, purpose, audience, and form. Usually, however, you continue to narrow your subject, clarify your purpose, meet the needs of your audience, and modify your form as you go through the stages of your writing process.

Collecting

Writers gather and record facts, impressions, opinions, and ideas that are relevant to their subject, purpose, and audience. Mark Twain, author of *Adventures of Huckleberry Finn*, once observed that if you attempt to carry a cat around the block by its tail, you'll gain a whole lot of information about cats that you'll never forget. You may collect such firsthand information, or you may rely on the data, experience, or expertise of others. Collecting involves observing, remembering, imagining, thinking, reading, listening, writing, investigating, talking, taking notes, and experimenting. Collecting also involves thinking about the relationships among the collected bits of information.

Shaping

Writers focus and organize the facts, examples, and ideas that they have collected into the recorded, linear form that is written language. When a hurricane hits the Gulf Coast, residents of Texas, Louisiana, Mississippi, Alabama, and Florida are likely to collect an enormous amount of data in just a few hours. Rain, floods, tree limbs snapping in the wind, unboarded windows shattering, sirens blaring—all of these events occur nearly simultaneously. If you try to write about such devastation, you need to *narrow your focus* (you can't describe everything that happened) and *organize the information* (you can't describe all of your experiences at the same time).

A chronological order is just one of the shapes a writer may choose to develop and organize experience. Such shaping strategies also help writers *collect* additional information and ideas. Reconstructing a chronological order, for example, may suggest for you some additional details—perhaps a wet, miserable-looking dog running through the heavy downpour—that you might not otherwise have remembered.

Drafting

At some point, writers actually write down a rough version of what will evolve into the finished piece of writing. Drafting processes vary widely from one writer to the next. Some writers prefer to reread their collecting and shaping notes, find a starting point, and launch themselves—figuring out what they want to say as they write it. Other writers start with a plan—a mental strategy, a short list, or an outline—of how they wish to proceed. Whatever approach you use in your draft, write down as much as possible, so you can see whether the information is clear, whether your overall shape expresses and clarifies your purpose, and whether the content and organization meet the needs and expectations of the audience.

Revising

When writers revise a rough draft, they literally "resee" their subject—and then modify the draft to fit the new vision. Revision is more than just tinkering with a word here and there; revision leads to larger changes—new examples or details, a different organization, or a new perspective. You accomplish these changes by adding, deleting, substituting, or reordering words, sentences, and paragraphs. Although revision begins the moment you get your first idea, most revisions are based on the reactions or anticipated reactions of the audience to your draft. You often play the role of audience yourself by putting the draft aside and rereading it later when you have some distance from your writing. Wherever you feel readers might not get your point, you revise to make it clearer. You may also get feedback from readers in a class workshop, suggesting that you collect more or different information, alter the shape of your draft to improve the flow of ideas, or clarify your terminology. As a result of your rereading and your readers' suggestions, you may change your thesis or write for an entirely different audience. Revising also includes *editing* to improve word choice, grammar, usage, or punctuation and *proofreading* for typos and other surface errors.

The writing process is not linear, moving smoothly in one direction from start to finish. It is messy, recursive, convoluted, and uneven. Writers write, plan, revise, anticipate, and review throughout the writing process. . . .

—*Maxine Hairston, teacher and author of articles and textbooks on writing*

We must and do write each our own way.

—*Eudora Welty, novelist and essayist*

The Whole Process

In practice, a writer's process rarely follows the simple, consecutive order that these stages or dimensions suggest. The writing process is actually *recursive:* It begins at one point, goes on to another, comes back to the first, jumps to the third, and so forth. A stage may last hours or only a second or two. While writing a letter to a friend, you may collect, shape, revise, and edit in one quick draft, while a research paper may require repeated shaping over a two-week period. As writers draft, they may correct a few mistakes or typos, but they may not proofread until many days later. In the middle of reorganizing an essay, writers often reread their draft, go back and ask more questions, and collect more data. Even while editing, writers may throw out several paragraphs, collect some additional information, and draft a new section.

In addition to the recursive nature of the writing process, keep in mind that writing often occurs during every stage, not just during drafting and revising. During collecting, you will be recording information and jotting down ideas. During shaping, you will be writing out trial versions that you may use later when you draft or revise. Throughout the writing process, you use your writing to modify your subject, purpose, audience, and form.

The most important point to keep in mind is that the writing process is *unique* to each writer and to each writing situation. What works for one writer may be absolutely wrong for you. Some writers compose nearly everything in their heads. Others write only after discussing the subject with friends or drawing diagrams and pictures. During the writing process, you need to experiment with several collecting, shaping, and drafting strategies to see what works best for you and for that particular piece of writing. As long as your process works, however, it's legitimate—no matter how many times you backtrack and repeat stages. When you are struggling with a piece of writing, remember that numerous revisions are a normal part of the writing process—even for most professionals.

Circling back over what you have already written—to sharpen your thesis, improve the organization, tighten up a paragraph, or add specific details to your examples—is likely to be the most time-consuming, yet worthwhile, part of your writing process. Most professional writers testify to the necessity and value of writing numerous drafts. When you are reworking a piece of writing, scrawling revisions over what you had hoped would be your finished product, remember, as Nobel laureate Isaac Bashevis Singer once pointed out, "the wastepaper basket is the writer's best friend."

Writing with a Computer

This is the computer age, and most writers, once they get over the initial shock of learning word-processing programs, welcome the new technology. Computers and word processors assist in the writing process by eliminating the time-consuming task of typing out a new draft each time you want to produce a clean, professional-looking copy. In addition, computers can help you collect, discover, or remember ideas and then help you shape, draft, revise, and edit a piece of writing. At your command, a word-processing program will add, move, or delete a letter, word, sentence, or whole paragraph. In its fluidity, the word processor is remarkably adaptive to the way our minds go about the process of writing—collecting a tidbit and adding it to a paragraph here, taking out a wrong word there, trying out a new sentence and deleting it if it doesn't flow, experimenting with phrasing and language, or chucking something into a "wastebasket" file (for retrieval, in case you change your mind tomorrow).

Some computer programs do more than simply respond to your commands: They interact with you by asking questions and

For better or worse, less of me will remain unsaid because of the speed and ease and even intimacy of computer-assisted writing.

—*Peter R. Stillman, teacher and essayist*

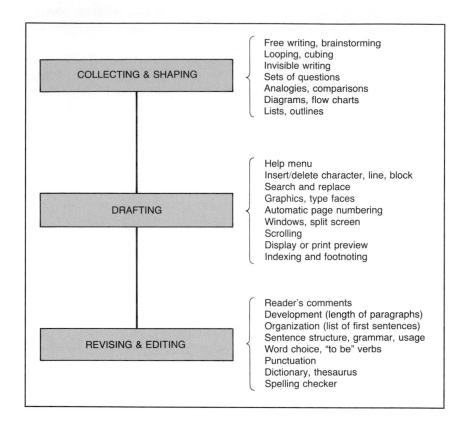

COLLECTING & SHAPING
- Free writing, brainstorming
- Looping, cubing
- Invisible writing
- Sets of questions
- Analogies, comparisons
- Diagrams, flow charts
- Lists, outlines

DRAFTING
- Help menu
- Insert/delete character, line, block
- Search and replace
- Graphics, type faces
- Automatic page numbering
- Windows, split screen
- Scrolling
- Display or print preview
- Indexing and footnoting

REVISING & EDITING
- Reader's comments
- Development (length of paragraphs)
- Organization (list of first sentences)
- Sentence structure, grammar, usage
- Word choice, "to be" verbs
- Punctuation
- Dictionary, thesaurus
- Spelling checker

making suggestions. As writing teachers and computer programmers anticipate problems you may have with writing on a computer, they add instructional elements to word processors. These computer-assisted instruction (CAI) programs provide specialized assistance with particular problems that writers regularly face at each stage of the writing process. At this time, no single CAI program has all of the features diagrammed in the following figure, but all of these features are available in different systems. Some of the most interesting programs prompt you with questions or advice; give you a model, form, or "template" to work from; and react to what you have already written with further questions—or with an elaborate analysis of your writing style and your possible errors in usage, grammar, or punctuation. The old "garbage in, garbage out" adage about computers has a new twist with these CAI programs. You may begin by putting garbage in, but the machine can help you process and transform the garbage into something palatable—perhaps even something delicious.

WARMING UP: JOURNAL EXERCISES

The following exercises will help you practice the topics covered in this chapter. In addition, you may discover a subject for your own writing. Choose three of the following entries, and write for ten minutes on each.

1. Reread your "authority" list from Chapter 1. Choose one of those subjects and then explain your *purpose* and a possible *audience* for whom you could write on that subject.

2. Find a sample of writing from a magazine or newspaper article, an advertisement, a letter, or from graffiti on walls. What is the purpose of that writing? Who is the intended audience? Why is the writing effective or ineffective?

3. Read Neil Petrie's essay and postscript at the end of this chapter. Then find the best paper you've written during the past year or two and write a "postscript" for it. Describe (a) what the writing situation was, (b) your purpose, and (c) the process you used to write it.

4. If you have already been given a writing assignment in another course, explain the *purpose* and the intended *audience* for that assignment. What might be your *process* for writing that essay?

5. During the first week of the term, one of your friends, Mark Lindstrom, is in an accident and is hospitalized. While still under the effects of anesthesia, he scribbles the following note for you to mail to his parents.

   Dear Mom and Dad,

   I arrived here last week. The trip was terrible. Dr. Stevens says that my leg will be better soon. My roommate is very strange. The police say my money is gone forever.

   Please send $1,500 to my new address right away.

   Thanks!

   Your loving son Mark

   Since you were at the accident and can fill in the details, you decide to explain everything to Mark's parents. Write a short letter to them. Next, write a paragraph to your best friend that describes what happened to Mark.

6. Write an open-journal entry. Writing for yourself, describe one event from your week that upset or angered you. What did you learn from this event?

A WRITING PROCESS AT WORK: COLLECTING AND SHAPING

ATHLETES AND EDUCATION

Neil H. Petrie

In the following essay that appeared in The Chronicle of Higher Education, *Neil H. Petrie argues that colleges have a hypocritical attitude toward student-athletes. Although most universities claim that their athletes—both male and female—are in college to get a good education, in reality, the pressures on athletes compromise their academic careers. The problem, Petrie argues, is not the old cliché that jocks are dumb, but that the endless hours devoted to practice or spent on road trips drain even the good student-athletes' physical and mental energies. Colleges point with pride to a tiny number of athletes who become professionals, but much more frequently the collegiate system encourages athletes to settle for lower grades and incomplete programs. In far too many cases, athletes never graduate. These are the students that, as Petrie says, "the system uses and then discards after the final buzzer."*

I have spent all my adult life in academe, first as a student and then as a professor. During that time I have seen many variations in the role of intercollegiate athletics in the university, and I've developed sharply split opinions on the subject. On one hand, I despise the system, clinging as it does to the academic body like a parasite. On the other hand, I feel sympathy and admiration for most of the young athletes struggling to balance the task of getting an education with the need to devote most of their energies to the excessive demands of the gym and the field.   (1)

My earliest experiences with the intrusion of athletics into the classroom came while I was still a freshman at the University of Colorado. While I was in my English professor's office one day, a colleague of hers came by for a chat. Their talk turned to the football coach's efforts to court the favor of the teachers responsible for his gladiators by treating them to dinner and a solicitous discussion of the academic progress of the players. I vividly recall my professor saying, "He can take me out to dinner if he wants, but if he thinks I'll pass his knuckleheads just because of that, he'd better think again."   (2)

Later, as a graduate teaching fellow, a lecturer, and then an assistant professor of English, I had ample opportunity to observe a Division I university's athletics program. I soon discovered that the prevailing stereotypes did not always apply. Athletes turned out to be as diverse as any other group of students in their habits, tastes, and abilities, and they showed a wide range of strategies for coping with the stress of their dual roles.   (3)

Some of them were poor students. An extreme example was the All-American football player (later a successful pro) who saw college only as a step to a six-figure contract and openly showed his disdain for the educational process. Others did such marginal work in my courses that I got the feeling they were daring me to give them D's or F's. One woman cross-country star, who almost never attended my composition class, used to push nearly illiterate essays under my office door at odd hours.   (4)

Yet many athletes were among the brightest students I had. Not so surprising, when you consider that, in addition to physical prowess, success in athletics require intelligence, competitive drive, and dedication—all qualities that can translate into success in the classroom as well as on the field. The trouble is that the grinding hours of practice and road trips rob student athletes of precious study time and deplete their reserves of mental and physical energy. A few top athletes have earned A's; most are content to settle for B's or C's, even if they are capable of better.   (5)

The athletes' educational experience can't help being marred by their numerous absences and divided loyalties. In this respect, they are little different from the students who attempt to go to college while caring for a family or working long hours at an outside job. The athletes, however, get extra help in juggling their responsibilities. Although I have never been bribed or threatened and have never received a dinner invitation from a coach, I am expected to provide extra time and consideration for athletes, far beyond what I give other students.   (6)

Take the midterm grade reports, for example. At my university, the athletic department's academic counselor sends progress questionnaires to every teacher of varsity athletes. While the procedure shows admirable concern for the academic performance of athletes, it also amounts to preferential treatment. It requires teachers to take time from other teaching duties to fill out and return the forms for the athletes. (No other students get such progress reports.) If I were a cynic it would occur to me that the athletic department might actually be more concerned with athletes' eligibility than with their academic work.   (7)

Special attendance policies for athletes are another example of preferential treatment. Athletes miss a lot of classes. In fact, I think the road trip is one of the main reasons that athletes receive a deficient education. You simply can't learn as much away from the classroom and the library as on the campus. Nevertheless, professors continue to provide make-up tests, alternative assignments, and special tutoring sessions to accommodate athletes. Any other student would have to have been very sick or the victim of a serious accident to get such dispensations.   (8)

It is sad to see bright young athletes knowingly compromise their potential and settle for much less education than they deserve. It is infuriating, though, to see the ones less gifted academically exploited by a system that they do not comprehend and robbed of any possible chance to grow intellectually and to explore other opportunities.   (9)

One specific incident illustrates for me the worst aspects of college athletics. It wasn't unusual or extraordinary—just the all-too-ordinary case of an athlete not quite good enough to make a living from athletics and blind to the opportunity afforded by the classroom.   (10)

I was sitting in my office near the beginning of a term, talking to a parade of new advisees. I glanced up to see my entire doorway filled with the bulk of a large young man, whom I recognized as one of our basketball stars from several seasons ago who had left for the pros and now apparently come back.   (11)

Over the next hour I got an intensive course on what it's like to be a college athlete. In high school, John had never been interested in much outside of basketball, and, like many other indifferent students, he went on to junior college on an athletic scholarship. After graduating, he came to the university, where he played for two more years, finishing out his eligibility. He was picked in a late round of the N.B.A. draft and left college, but in the end he turned out to be a step too slow for the pros. By that time he had a family to support, and when he realized he could never make a career of basketball, he decided to return to college.   (12)

We both knew that his previous academic career hadn't been particularly focused, and that because of transferring and taking minimum course loads during the basketball season, he wouldn't be close to a degree. But I don't think either one of us was prepared for what actually emerged from our examination of his transcripts. It was almost as if he had never gone beyond high school. His junior-college transcript was filled with remedial and non-academic courses.   (13)

Credit for those had not transferred to the university. Over the next two years he had taken a hodgepodge of courses, mostly in physical education. He had never received any advice about putting together a coherent program leading to a degree. In short, the academic side of his college experience had been completely neglected by coaches, advisers, and, of course, John himself.   (14)

By the time we had evaluated his transcripts and worked out a tentative course of study, John was in shock and I was angry. It was going to take him at least three years of full-time study to complete a degree. He thanked me politely for my time, picked up the planning sheets, and left. I was ashamed to be a part of the university that day. Why hadn't anyone in the athletic department ever told him what it would take to earn a degree? Or at least been honest enough to say, "Listen, we can keep you eligible and give you a chance to play ball, but don't kid yourself into thinking you'll be getting an education, too."   (15)

I saw John several more times during the year. He tried for a while. He took classes, worked, supported his family, and then he left again. I lost track of him after that. I can only hope that he found a satisfying job or completed his education at some other institution. I know people say the situation has improved in the last few years, but when I read about the shockingly low percentages of athletes who graduate, I think of John.   (16)

Colleges give student athletes preferential treatment. We let them cut classes. We let them slide through. We protect them from harsh realities. We applaud them for entertaining us and wink when they compromise themselves intellectually. We give them special dorms, special meals, special tutors, and a specially reprehensible form of hypocrisy.   (17)

I can live with the thought of the athletes who knowingly use the college-athletics system to get their pro contracts or their devalued degrees. But I have trouble living with the thought of the ones whom the system uses and then discards after the final buzzer.   (18)

ON WRITING
"ATHLETES AND EDUCATION"

In the following postscript on his writing process, Neil Petrie describes why he wanted to write the paper, how he collected material to support his argument, and how he shaped and focused his ideas as he wrote. His comments illustrate how his purpose— to expose the hypocrisies of collegiate athletics—guided his writing of the essay. In addition, Petrie explains that other key questions affected the shape of his essay: how he should begin, where he should use his best example, and what words he should choose.

This essay has its origin, as all persuasive writing should, in a strongly held opinion. I'm always more comfortable if I care deeply about my subject matter. As a teacher, I hold some powerful convictions about the uneasy marriage of big-time athletics and higher education, and so I wanted to write an essay that would expose what I think are the dangers and hypocrisies of that system.

At the beginning of my essay, I wanted to establish some authority to lend credibility to my argument. Rather than gather statistics on drop-out rates of student athletes or collect the opinions of experts, I planned to rely on my own experiences as both a student and teacher. I hoped to convince my readers that my opinions were based on the authority of first-hand knowledge. In this introduction I was also aware of the need to avoid turning off readers who might dismiss me as a "jock hater." I had to project my negative feelings about the athletic system while maintaining my sympathy with the individual student athletes involved in that system. The thesis, then, would emerge gradually as I accumulated the evidence; it would be more implied than explicitly stated.

Gathering the material was easy. I selected a series of examples from my personal experiences as a college student and instructor, as well as anecdotes I'd heard from other instructors. Most of these stories were ones that I had shared before, either in private discussions with friends or in classrooms with students.

Shaping the material was a little tougher. As I began thinking about my examples and how to order them, I saw that I really wanted to make two main points. The first was that most colleges give preferential treatment to athletes. The second point was that, despite the extra attention, the success of the athlete's academic career is often ignored by all parties involved. Many of my examples, I realized, illustrated the varieties of pressures put upon both athletes and instructors to make sure that the students at least get by in class and remain eligible. These examples seemed to cluster together because they showed the frustrations of teachers and the reactions of athletes trying to juggle sports and academics. This group would make a good introduction to my general exposé of the system. But I had one more example I wanted to use that seemed to go beyond the cynicism of some athletes or the hypocrisy of the educators. This was the case of John, an athlete who illustrated what I thought were the most exploitative aspects of varsity athletics. I originally planned on devoting the bulk of my essay to this story and decided to place it near the end where it would make my second point with maximum emotional effect.

A two-part structure for the essay now emerged. In the first segment following my introductory paragraph, I gave a series of shorter examples, choosing to order them in roughly chronological order (paragraphs 2–4). I then moved from these specific details to a more general discussion of the demands placed upon both students and teachers, such as lengthy practice time, grade reports, road trips and special attendance policies. This concluded my description of the way the system operates (paragraphs 5–8).

Then it was time to shift gears, to provide a transition to the next part of my essay, to what I thought was my strongest example. I wanted the story of John to show how the system destroyed human potential. To do this, I needed to increase the seriousness of the tone in order to persuade the reader that I was dealing in more than a little bureaucratic boondoggling. I tried to set the tone by my word choice: I moved from words such as "sad," "compromise," and "settle" to words with much stronger emotional connotations such as "infuriating," "exploited," and "robbed," all in a single short transitional paragraph (paragraph 9).

I then introduced my final extended example in equally strong language, identifying it as a worst-case illustration (paragraph 10). I elaborated on John's story, letting the details and my reactions to his situation carry the more intense outrage that I was trying to convey in this second part of the essay (paragraphs 10–16). The first version that I tried was a rambling narrative that had an overly long recounting of John's high school and college careers. So I tightened this section by eliminating such items as his progress through the ranks of professional basketball and his dreams of million-dollar contracts. I also cut down on a discussion of the various courses of study he was considering as option. The result was a sharper focus on the central issue of John's dilemma: the lack of adequate degree counseling for athletes.

After my extended example, all that was left was the conclusion. As I wrote, I was very conscious of using certain devices, such as the repetition of key words and sentence patterns in paragraph seventeen ("We let them . . . We let them . . . We protect them . . . We applaud them . . . We give them . . .") to maintain the heightened emotional tone. I was also conscious of repeating the two-part structure of the essay in the last two paragraphs. I moved from general preferential treatment (paragraph 17) to the concluding and more disturbing idea of devastating exploitation (paragraph 18).

On the whole, I believe that this essay effectively conveys its point through the force of accumulated detail. My personal experience was the primary source of evidence, and that experience led naturally to the order of the paragraphs and to the argument I wished to make: that while some athletes knowingly use the system, others are used and exploited by it.

QUESTIONS FOR WRITING AND DISCUSSION

1. In your journal, describe how your extracurricular activities (athletics, jobs, clubs, or family obligations) have or have not interfered with your education. Recall *one specific incident* that illustrates how these activities affected your classwork—either positively or negatively.

2. Describe Petrie's audience and purpose for this essay. What sentences reveal his intended audience? What sentences reveal his purpose? What sentences contain his thesis, claim, or main idea? Do you agree with that thesis? Why or why not?

3. Reread Petrie's postscript. Based on his comments and on your reading of the essay, how does Petrie describe or label each of the following sections of his essay.
   paragraphs 1–4:
   paragraphs 5–8:
   paragraph 9:
   paragraphs 10–16:
   paragraphs 17–18:

4. Who do you think is most to blame for the situation that Petrie describes: The athletes themselves? The colleges for paying their scholarships and then ignoring them when they drop out? The students and alumni who pay to see their teams win?

5. Petrie does not explicitly suggest a solution to the problem he describes. Assume, however, that he has been asked by the president of his university to propose a solution. Write the letter that you think Petrie would send to the president.

A WRITING PROCESS AT WORK: DRAFTING AND REVISING

While drafting and revising, writers frequently make crucial changes in their ideas and language. The first scribbled sentences, written primarily for ourselves, are often totally different from what we later present to other people in a final, polished version. Take, for example, the final version of Abraham Lincoln's Gettysburg Address. It begins with the famous lines "Four score and seven years ago our fathers brought forth on this continent a new nation. . . ." But his first draft might well have begun, "Eighty-seven years ago, several politicians and other powerful men in the American Colonies got together and decided to start a new country. . . ." It is difficult to imagine that language ingrained in our consciousness was once drafted, revised, drafted again, and edited, as the author or authors added, deleted, reordered, and otherwise altered words, sentences, and ideas.

Carl Becker's study of the American Declaration of Independence assembles the early drafts of that famous document and compares them with the final version. Shown below is Thomas Jefferson's first draft, with revisions made by Benjamin Franklin, John Adams, and other members of the Committee of Five that was charged with developing the new document.

Thomas Jefferson's Rough Draft of the Opening Sentences of the Declaration of Independence

When in the course of human events it becomes necessary for a ~~one~~ people to ~~advance from that subordination in which they have hith-~~ *dissolve the political bonds which have connected them with another, and to* ~~erto remained, &~~ to assume among the powers of the earth the *separate and equal* ~~equal & independent~~ station to which the laws of nature & of nature's god entitle them, a decent respect to the opinions of mankind requires that they should declare the causes which impel them to ~~the change~~ *the separation*.

We hold these truths to be ~~sacred & undeniable~~ *self-evident;* that all men are created equal ~~& independent~~; that *they are endowed by their Creator with* ~~from that equal creation they de-~~ ~~rive in rights~~ *rights; that* inherent & inalienable *these* among ~~which~~ are ~~the preserva-~~ ~~tion of~~ life, ~~&~~ liberty, & the pursuit of happiness. . . .

The Final Draft of the Opening Sentences of the Declaration of Independence, as Approved on July 4, 1776.

When in the Course of human events, it becomes necessary for one people to dissolve the political bands, which have connected them with another, and to assume among the powers of the earth, the separate and equal station to which the Laws of Nature and of Nature's God entitle them, a decent respect to the opinions of mankind requires that they should declare the causes which impel them to the separation.

We hold these truths to be self-evident, that all men are created equal, that they are endowed by their Creator with certain unalienable Rights, that among these are Life, Liberty and the pursuit of Happiness.

QUESTIONS FOR WRITING AND DISCUSSION

1. Describe your reaction to the "rough draft" of the Declaration of Independence. Where did it seem strange or make you feel uncomfortable?

2. Select one change in a sentence that most improved the final version. Explain how the revised wording is more effective.

3. Find one change in a word or phrase that constitutes an alteration in *meaning* rather than just a choice of "smoother" or more appropriate language. How does this change affect the meaning?

4. Upon rereading this passage from the Declaration of Independence, one reader wrote, "I was really irritated by that 'all *men* are created equal' remark. The writers were white, free, well-to-do, Anglo-Saxon, mostly Protestant males discussing *their own* 'unalienable rights.' They sure weren't discussing the 'unalienable rights' of female Americans or of a million slaves or of nonwhite free Americans!" Revise the passage from the Declaration of Independence using this person as your audience.

3 | *OBSERVING*

Leonardo daVinci
Mona Lisa (detail).
Louvre Museum, Paris

In the far corner of a friend's living room is a lighted aquarium. Instead of water, the aquarium has a few inches of white sand, a dish of water, and a small piece of pottery. When you ask about the aquarium, your friend excitedly says, "You mean you haven't met Nino?" In a matter of seconds, you have a small, tannish-brown snake practically in your lap, and your friend is saying, "This is Nino. She—or he—is an African sand boa." You imagined that all boa constrictors were those huge snakes that suffocated and then swallowed babies. "Actually, Nino is very shy. She prefers to burrow in the sand." The snake is fascinating. It is only fifteen inches long, with a strong, compact body and a stub tail. Before it burrows into your coat pocket, you observe it closely so you can describe this miniature boa to your younger brother who loves all kinds of snakes. ☐

In the physics laboratory, you're doing an experiment on light refraction. You need to observe how light rays bend as they go through water, so you take notes describing the procedure and the results. During each phase of the experiment, you observe and record the angles of refraction. The data and your notes will help you write up the lab report that is due next Monday. ☐

My task . . . is, by the power of the written word, to make you hear, to make you feel—it is, before all, to make you see.

—*Joseph Conrad, author of* Heart of Darkness *and other novels*

Seeing is of course very much a matter of verbalization. Unless I call my attention to what passes before my eyes, I simply won't see it.

—*Annie Dillard, naturalist and author of* Pilgrim at Tinker Creek

Observing is essential to good writing. Whether you are writing in a journal, doing a laboratory report for a science class, dashing off a memo at work, or writing a letter to the editor of a newspaper, keen observation is essential. Writing or verbalizing what you see helps you discover and learn more about your environment. Sometimes your purpose is limited to yourself: You observe and record to help you understand your world or yourself better. At other times, your purpose extends to a wider audience: You want to share what you have learned with others, to help them learn as well. No matter who your audience is or what your subject may be, however, your task is to *see* and to help your readers *see*.

Of course, observing involves more than just "seeing." Good writers draw on all their senses: sight, smell, touch, taste, hearing. In addition, however, experienced writers also notice what is absent, or *not* there. The smell of food that should be coming from the kitchen but isn't. A friend who usually is present but now is absent. The absolute quiet in the air that precedes an impending storm. Writers should also look for *changes* in their subject—from light to dark, from rough to smooth, from bitter to sweet, or from noise to sudden silence. Good writers learn to use their previous *experience* and their *imagination* to draw comparisons and create images. Does a sea urchin look and feel like a pincushion with the pins stuck in the wrong way? Does the room feel as cramped and airless as the inside of a microwave oven? Finally, good writers write from a specific *point of view* or role: a student describing basic laws of physics or an experienced worker in a mental health clinic describing the clientele.

Depending on the purpose and the audience, writing from observation can be relatively *objective,* as when you record what is actually, demonstrably there; or it can be more *subjective,* as when you suggest how you feel, think, or react to a subject. A writer might describe a bicycle objectively as "a secondhand 1984 blue 10-speed Trek, with a 23-inch frame, 27-inch wheels, a Sun Tour DL derailleur, SR crank, and Dia Compe brakes." A writer might need to communicate that objective information to a prospective buyer or an employee in a cycle repair shop. On the other hand, the writer may wish to communicate the bicycle's subjective feel—how easily it pedals or how it flows like water down the street. In most situations, however, good writers describe their subject both objectively and subjectively. They use some objectivity for accuracy and specific detail and some subjectivity to suggest the value or relevance of the subject in a human environment.

The key to effective observing is to *show* your reader the person, place, event, or object through *specific detail*. Good description allows the reader to draw general conclusions based on specific detail. Rather than just telling a reader, "This bicycle has good technical components," the writer should *show* or describe how it feels as she rides it. If your reader is going to learn from your observations, you need to give the *exact details that you learned from,* not just your conclusions or generalizations. Even in writing, experience is the best teacher, so use specific details to communicate the feel, the data, the sights and sounds and smells. Whether you are a tourist describing the cliff dwellings at Mesa Verde, a salesperson analyzing consumer preferences for your boss, a physicist presenting data on a new superconducting material to other physicists, or a social worker putting together the details of a child abuse case, your first task is to recreate the experience, to show your readers, to make them *see.*

FREEWRITING: OBSERVING

Before reading further in this chapter, do this exercise. Close your eyes and relax. Then turn your head slightly up, down, or to the right or left. Open your eyes and focus on the first thing you see. Write nonstop for five minutes, describing this thing in as much sensory detail as possible. After five minutes, stop writing. Now move closer. If possible, pick the thing up, turn it over, touch it, shake it, smell it, and reexamine it. Then write for five more minutes, nonstop, describing everything else you noticed.

TECHNIQUES FOR WRITING ABOUT OBSERVATIONS

The short passages that follow all use specific techniques for observing people, places, objects, or events. Some emphasize objective detail; some recreate subjective reactions or feelings. In all the passages, however, the writer *narrows* or *limits* the scope of the observation and selects specific details that add up to some *dominant idea.* The dominant *idea* reflects the writer's purpose for that particular audience. As you read the excerpts, notice how the authors use the following six techniques for writing a vivid observation:

> *. . . Not that it's raining, but the feel of being rained upon.*
>
> —E. L. Doctorow, author of Ragtime *and other novels*

- **Giving sensory details (sight, sound, smell, touch, taste).** Also include *actual dialogue* and *names of things* where appropriate. Good writers often *zoom in* on crucial details.
- **Using comparisons and images.** To help readers visualize the unfamiliar (or see the commonplace in a new light), writers often draw comparisons and use evocative images.

- **Describing what is not there.** Sometimes keen observation requires stepping back and noticing what is absent, what is not happening, or who is not present.
- **Noting changes in the subject's form or condition.** Even when the subject appears static—a landscape, a flower, a building—good writers look for evidence of changes, past or future: a tree being enveloped by tent worms, a six-inch purple-and-white iris that eight hours earlier was just a green bud, a sandstone exterior of a church being eroded by acid rain.
- **Writing from a distinct point of view.** Good writers assume a distinct role; in turn, their perspective helps clarify what they observe. A lover and a botanist, for example, see entirely different things in the same red rose. *What* is seen depends on *who* is doing the seeing.
- **Focusing on a dominant idea.** Good writers focus on those details and images that clarify the main idea or discovery. The discovery often depends on the *contrast* between the writer's expectations and the reality.

These six techniques are illustrated in the following two paragraphs by Karen Blixen, who wrote *Out of Africa* under the pen name Isak Dinesen. A Danish woman who moved to Kenya to start a coffee plantation, Blixen knew little about the animals in Kenya Reserve. In this excerpt from her journals, she describes a startling change that occurred when she shot a large lizard, an iguana.

Role: A Newcomer to the Reserve

In the Reserve I have sometimes come upon the Iguana, the big lizards, as they were sunning themselves upon a flat stone in a riverbed. They are not pretty in shape, but nothing can be imagined more beautiful than their coloring. They shine like a heap of precious stones or like a pane cut out of an old church window. When, as you approach, they swish away, there is a flash of azure, green and purple over the stones, the color seems to be standing behind them in the air, like a comet's luminous tail.

Comparisons and Images
Sensory Details
Comparisons and Images

Once I shot an Iguana. I thought that I should be able to make some pretty things from his skin. A strange thing happened then, that I have never afterwards forgotten. As I went up to him, where he was lying dead upon his stone, and actually while I was walking the few steps, he faded and grew pale, all color died out of him as in one long sigh, and by the time that I touched him he was grey and dull like a lump of concrete. It was the live impetuous blood pulsating within the animal, which had radiated out all that glow and splendor. Now that the flame was put out, and the soul had flown, the Iguana was as dead as a sandbag.

Changes in Condition

Sensory Detail

What Is Not There
Dominant Idea: Now Colorless and Dead

Observing People

Observing people—their dress, facial features, body language, attitudes, behavior, skills, quirks, habits, and conversation—is a pastime we all share. When writers describe a person, however, they zero in on specific details that fit an overall pattern or impression. In an *Esquire* magazine article, Joseph Nocera profiles Steven Jobs, the cocreator of the Apple and Macintosh computers, ex-chairman of the board of Apple Computer, and now head of Next, Inc., another Silicon Valley firm. All of Nocera's details reinforce his dominant idea that Steven Jobs is a temperamental boy genius.

> With personal computers so ubiquitous today, you tend to forget that the industry is still barely ten years old; the Apple II, the machine that began it all, was unleashed upon an unsuspecting world in 1977. You forget, that is, until you sit in a room full of people who have built them and realize how young they are. Jobs himself is only thirty-one. If anything, he looks younger. He is lithe and wiry. He is wearing faded jeans (no belt), a white cotton shirt (perfectly pressed), and a pair of brown suede wing-tipped shoes. There is a bounce to his step that betrays a certain youthful cockiness; the quarterback of your high school football team used to walk that way. His thin, handsome face does not even appear to need a daily shave. And that impression of eternal youth is reinforced by some guileless, almost childlike traits: by the way, for instance, he can't resist showing off his brutal, withering intelligence whenever he's around someone he doesn't think measures up. Or by his almost willful lack of tact. Or by his inability to hide his boredom when he is forced to endure something that doesn't interest him, like a sixth grader who can't wait for class to end.

Role: Writer Is an Outsider, Looks Objectively at Jobs, Is Probably Older Dominant Idea: Youth

Sensory Detail: Visual Description

Comparison and Image What Is Not There: Facial Hair

What Is Not There: Tact

Comparison

Observing Places

In the following excerpt from *Brown Girl, Brownstones,* Paule Marshall creates a catalog of the sights, sounds, and smells of a Brooklyn street during the Great Depression of the 1930s. In this paragraph, she records a typical Saturday night on Fulton Street: the bright lights, the clamorous street activity, the mixed odors of foods, and the faces of the street people. The specific details contribute to the overall idea of the street's vibrant, chaotic energy.

> Unlike Chauncey Street, Fulton Street this summer Saturday night was a whirling spectrum of neon signs, movie marquees, bright-lit store windows and sweeping yellow streamers of light from the cars. It was canorous voices, hooted laughter and curses ripping the night's warm cloak; a welter of dark faces and gold-etched teeth; children crying high among the fire escapes of the tenements; the subway rumbling below; the unrelenting wail of a blues spilling from a bar; greasy counters and

fish sandwiches and barbecue and hot sauce; trays of chitterlings and hog maws and fat back in the meat stores; the trolley's insistent clangor; a man and woman in a hallway bedroom, sleeping like children now that the wildness had passed; a drunken woman pitching along the street; the sustained shriek of a police car and its red light stabbing nervously at faces and windows. Fulton Street on Saturday night was all beauty and desperation and sadness.

Compare Marshall's portrait of the clamorous activity on Fulton Street with Wendell Berry's tranquil description of a barn on a family farm. Berry, author of *The Unsettling of America* and other books on America's agricultural crisis, gives us a simple but effective portrait of Elmer Lapp's Place. Since one of Berry's purposes is to argue that the family farm is worth saving, the details he selects create a positive dominant idea about farm life.

The thirty cows come up from the pasture and go one by one into the barn. Most of them are Guernseys, but there are also a few red Holsteins and a couple of Jerseys. They go to their places and wait while their neck chains are fastened. And then Elmer Lapp, his oldest son, and his youngest daughter go about the work of feeding, washing, and milking.

In the low, square room lighted by a row of big windows, a radio is quietly playing music. Several white cats sit around waiting for milk to be poured out for them from the test cup. Two collie dogs rest by the wall, out of the way. Several buff Cochin bantams are busily foraging for whatever waste grain can be found in the bedding and in the gutters. Overhead, fastened to the ceiling joists, are many barn swallow nests, their mud cups empty now at the end of October. Two rusty-barrelled .22 rifles are propped in window frames, kept handy to shoot English sparrows, and there are no sparrows to be seen. Outside the door a bred heifer and a rather timeworn pet jenny are eating their suppers out of feed boxes. Beyond, on the stream that runs through the pasture, wild ducks are swimming. The shadows have grown long under the low-slanting amber light.

Observing Objects

In observing an inanimate object such as a cookie, Paul Goldberger brings his special point of view, as an architecture critic for *The New York Times*, to his description. He totally ignores the cookie's taste, ingredients, and calories, focusing instead on the architectural relationships of function and form. Goldberger's architectural perspective helps focus his observations, creating a dominant idea for each passage.

Sugar Wafer (Nabisco)

There is no attempt to imitate the ancient forms of traditional, individually baked cookies here—this is a modern cookie through and through. Its simple rectangular form, clean and pure, just reeks of mass production and modern technological methods. The two wafers, held together by the sugar-cream filling, appear to float, and the Nabisco trademark, stamped repeatedly across the top, confirms that this is a machine-age object.

Fig Newton (Nabisco)

This, too, is a sandwich but different in every way from the Sugar Wafer. Here the imagery is more traditional, more sensual even; a rounded form of cookie dough arcs over the fig concoction inside, and the whole is soft and pliable. Like all good pieces of design, it has an appropriate form for its use, since the insides of Fig Newtons can ooze and would not be held in place by a more rigid form. The thing could have had a somewhat different shape, but the rounded tip is a comfortable, familiar image, and it's easy to hold. Not a revolutionary object but an intelligent one.

Observing Events

Observing events requires weaving specific details of people, place, and object into some chronological order, as in the following account of a rhythm-and-blues performance by artist Bobby "Blue" Bland. The paragraph, taken from Peter Guralnick's *Lost Highway: Journeys and Arrivals of American Musicians*, demonstrates how vivid, specific details (names of singers, description of barefoot dancing, titles of songs, actual dialogue and lyrics) create a dominant idea: a single night's performance blurs into an endless series of one-night stands.

> Every night it is exactly the same. The band, a brass-heavy ten pieces with dilapidated reading stands that say "Mel Jackson/MFs Bobby Bland's Revue," does a desultory thirty-minute set. Then Burnett Williams, singer, valet, bus driver, and all-around good fellow, swings affably into a succession of Al Green numbers and current soul hits. The band plays dispiritedly behind him; even the bandleader, Mel Jackson, has disappeared from the stand; but Burnett always works up a sweat, finishing out his segment with shoes kicked off, doing the barefoot to the strains of "Love and Happiness." This invariably cracks up Mel Jackson, who reappears precisely at this point, dapper, diminutive, very much in charge. His eyes gleam and dart skittishly about the room as he laughs out loud, proclaims, "That boy doing some barefooting!" and gives Burnett a soul slap and quick little hug as the warm-up singer departs from the stage, his shoes held delicately aloft. Then it's Show Time, Ladies and Gentlemen, a Young Man Who Needs No Introduction, he'll Take Care of You, Further on Up the Road, won't let you Cry No More, cause when you Cry Cry Cry he just wants to Turn On Your Lovelights, well he's a Good-Time Charlie, and You're the One (That He Adores), but now The Feeling is Gone and he's Two steps From the Blues. The string of hits becomes a litany, a numbing incantation. Audience talk becomes louder and more distracted, and then Bobby "Blue" Bland appears, big, shambling, sleepy-eyed, a cigarette between his fingers, tongue licking at the edge of his lips. He plays aimlessly for a moment with the microphone, his eyes cast upwards as if for inspiration, the band kicks off, and that smooth, mellow, almost horn-like voice slides in among the three trumpets, trombone, and saxophone (guitar, bass, two drummers, and occasionally a piano round out the band). "I pity the fool / I pity the fool that falls in love with you. . . ." It is ten-thirty, and Bobby "Blue" Bland is just going to work.

For Godsake, keep your eyes open. Notice what's going on around you.

William Burroughs, novelist

WARMING UP: JOURNAL EXERCISES

The following topics will help you practice close, detailed observation and may possibly suggest a subject for your observing assignment. Read the following exercises and then write on the three that interest you the most. If another interesting idea occurs to you, write a "free" entry about it.

1. Go to a public place (library, bar, restaurant, hospital emergency room, gas station, laundromat, park, shopping mall, hotel lobby, police station, beach, skating rink, beauty salon, city dump, tennis court, church, etc.). Sit and observe everything around you. Use your pencil to help you see, both by drawing sketches and by recording sensory details in words. What do you see that you haven't noticed before? Then *narrow* your attention to a single person, *focus* on a restricted place, or *zoom in* on a single object. What do you see that you haven't noticed before?

2. Buy a piece of fruit or a vegetable. An apple, orange, pear, carrot, or onion will do, but if possible find a persimmon, pawpaw, mango, pineapple, guava, pomegranate, lime, coconut, passion fruit, artichoke, cauliflower, broccoli, jicama, bok choy, or rutabaga. Sit down somewhere and look at it. Record your impressions. Hold it close to your ear and shake it. Record your impressions. Scrape your fingernail over its surface. Rub it against your cheek. Record your impressions. Close your eyes and lick it all over. Record your impressions. Scratch the surface with a utensil. Then close your eyes and smell it. Record your impressions. Peel it or take it apart. Describe what it looks like now. Take a bite out of it. Record your impressions.

3. Find a place where people (your friends or strangers) are talking (over lunch, at a bar, at a party). For ten or fifteen minutes, record the conversation word for word. To keep friends from being self-conscious, tell them that you're doing homework. If you're eavesdropping on strangers, be as inconspicuous as possible. Your purpose is to record as much of the dialogue as possible, with the pauses, interruptions, *uh*'s and *er*'s, unfinished sentences, slang—everything *exactly* as you hear it.

4. Go to a private place that is away from the rush of everyday life (a field, a lake, a grove of trees, a hill, a desert, a seashore, or even an oasis in the city that is quiet and peaceful). Sit for a few minutes until you are accustomed to the quiet and the silence. Then observe the place around you and describe what is happening. You'll have to be attentive, noticing the little things, minor events, or subtle changes. Record your observations.

5. Working with one other student in your class, visit a place that you would like to observe. Bring a snapshot or video camera. Take a series of pictures and write a three-minute commentary to accompany your pictures. Your pictures and commentary should explain, for other members of your class, something that you *discovered* about this place.

6. "Obnoxious," the dictionary says, means "highly disagreeable, offensive, irritating, odious." Describe the most obnoxious person you know by giving at least two detailed examples of his or her obnoxious behavior. Or do just the reverse: Tell how the most obnoxious person you know would describe you.

7. Go to a gallery, studio, or museum where you can observe sculpture, paintings, or other works of art. Choose one work of art and draw it. Then describe it as fully as possible. Return to the gallery the next day, reread your first description, observe the artwork again, and add details you didn't notice the first time.

8. In a class you are taking, record in detail the dress, habits, mannerisms, nervous tics, speech, and gestures of the teacher. After describing the teacher in detail, choose a *single word* that expresses your dominant idea about him or her. Circle the details in your description that reinforce this dominant idea.

9. As you sit in a lecture class, restaurant, student lounge, library, department store, airport, or bar, describe the three or four most common *types* of people you observe there. In a class, for example, you might describe the Fanatic Scribbler, the Whisperer, and the Sleeper. In a department store, you might describe *types* of shoppers: the Look-but-Never-Buy Customer, the Complainer/Whiner, the Price-Haggler, and the Bet-You-Can't-Fit-Me Buyer. Describe their behavior using specific details.

10. Visit a local park. Pretend that you are a landscape architect, a photographer, a bird-watcher, an entomologist, an engineer building a road, a jogger, or a mother with two small children. Describe what you see. Now choose another role—you're a social worker, a woman alone in a park at night, a person without a home, a Secret Service agent assigned to protect the President of the United States, a Saint Bernard, or a sixth-grader just out of school for the day. Describe what you see.

Reread both descriptions. Compare them. Briefly, explain how and why they are similar or dissimilar.

11. Observe the behavior of one person in your dorm, house, or apartment as he or she gets ready for a date on Friday or Saturday night. Record how this person gets ready, noting the clothes, conversation about prospective dates or companions, and appearance of the person as he or she leaves for the evening. Explain what you learned by observing such behavior.

OBSERVING: PROFESSIONAL WRITING

TAKE THIS FISH AND LOOK AT IT

Samuel H. Scudder

In this essay, Samuel H. Scudder (1837–1911), an American entomologist, narrates his early attempts at scientific observation. Scudder recalls how a famous Swiss naturalist, Louis Agassiz, taught him to learn by observing closely, carefully, and repeatedly. Agassiz, a professor of natural history at Harvard, taught his students that both factual details and general laws are important. "Facts are stupid things," he said, "until brought into connection with some general law." Scudder, writing about his studies under Agassiz, suggests that repeated observation can help us connect facts or specific details with general laws. The essay shows us what Scudder learned: To help us see, describe, and connect, "a pencil is one of the best of eyes."

It was more than fifteen years ago that I entered the laboratory of Professor Agassiz, and told him I had enrolled my name in the Scientific School as a student of natural history. He asked me a few questions about my object in coming, my antecedents generally, the mode in which I afterwards proposed to use the knowledge I might acquire, and, finally, whether I wished to study any special branch. To the latter I replied that, while I wished to be well grounded in all departments of zoology, I purposed to devote myself specially to insects.   (1)

"When do you wish to begin?" he asked.   (2)

"Now," I replied.   (3)

This seemed to please him, and with an energetic "Very well!" he reached from a shelf a huge jar of specimens in yellow alcohol.

"Take this fish," he said, "and look at it; we call it a haemulon; by and by I will ask what you have seen."   (4)

With that he left me, but in a moment returned with explicit instructions as to the care of the object entrusted to me.   (5)

"No man is fit to be a naturalist," said he, "who does not know how to take care of specimens."   (6)

I was to keep the fish before me in a tin tray, and occasionally moisten the surface with alcohol from the jar, always taking care to replace the stopper tightly. Those were not the days of ground-glass stoppers and elegantly shaped exhibition jars; all the old students will recall the huge neckless glass bottles with their leaky, wax-besmeared corks, half eaten by insects, and begrimed with cellar dust. Entomology was a cleaner science than ichthyology, but the example of the Professor, who had unhesitatingly plunged to the bottom of the jar to produce the fish, was infectious; and though this alcohol had a "very ancient and fishlike smell," I really dared not show any aversion within these sacred precincts, and treated the alcohol as though it were pure water. Still I was conscious of a passing feeling of disappointment, for gazing at a fish did not commend itself to an ardent entomologist. My friends at home, too, were annoyed when they discovered that no amount of eau-de-Cologne would drown the perfume which haunted me like a shadow.   (7)

In ten minutes I had seen all that could be seen in that fish, and started in search of the Professor—who had, however, left the Museum; and when I returned, after lingering over some of the odd animals stored in the upper apartment, my specimen was dry all over. I dashed the fluid over the fish as if to resuscitate the beast from a fainting fit, and looked with anxiety for a return of the normal sloppy appearance. This little excitement over, nothing was to be done but to return to a steadfast gaze at my mute companion. Half an hour passed—an hour—another hour; the fish began to look loathsome. I turned it over and around; looked it in the face—ghastly; from behind, beneath, above, sideways, at three-quarters' view—just as ghastly. I was in despair; at an early hour I concluded that lunch was necessary; so, with infinite relief, the fish was carefully replaced in the jar, and for an hour I was free.   (8)

On my return, I learned that Professor Agassiz had been at the Museum, but had gone, and would not return for several hours. My fellow-students were too busy to be disturbed by continued conversation. Slowly I drew forth that hideous fish, and with a feeling of desperation again looked at it. I might not use a magnifying-glass; instruments of all kinds were interdicted. My two hands, my two eyes, and the fish: it seemed a most limited field. I pushed my finger down its throat to feel how sharp the teeth were. I began to count the scales in the different rows, until I was convinced that was nonsense. At last a happy thought struck me—I would draw the fish; and now with surprise I began to discover new features in the creature. Just then the Professor returned.   (9)

"That is right," said he; "a pencil is one of the best of eyes. I am glad to notice, too, that you keep your specimen wet, and your bottle corked."   (10)

With these encouraging words, he added: "Well, what is it like?"   (11)

He listened attentively to my brief rehearsal of the structure of parts whose names were still unknown to me: the fringed gill-arches and movable operculum; the pores of the head, fleshy lips and lidless eyes; the lateral line, the spinous fins and forked tail; the compressed and arched body. When I finished, he waited as if expecting more, and then, with an air of disappointment:

"You have not looked very carefully; why," he continued more earnestly, "you haven't even seen one of the most conspicuous features of the animal, which is plainly before your eyes as the fish itself; look again, look again!" and he left me to my misery.   (12)

I was piqued; I was mortified. Still more of that wretched fish! But now I set myself to my task with a will, and discovered one new thing after another, until I saw how just the Professor's criticism had been. The afternoon passed quickly; and when, towards its close, the Professor inquired:

"Do you see it yet?"   (13)

"No," I replied, "I am certain I do not, but I see how little I saw before."   (14)

"That is next best," said he, earnestly, "but I won't hear you now; put away your fish and go home; perhaps you will be ready with a better answer in the morning. I will examine you before you look at the fish."   (15)

This was disconcerting. Not only must I think of my fish all night, studying, without the object before me, what this unknown but most visible feature might be; but also, without reviewing my discoveries, I must give an exact account of them the next day. I had a bad memory; so I walked home by Charles River in a distracted state, with my two perplexities.   (16)

The cordial greeting from the Professor the next morning was reassuring; here was a man who seemed to be quite as anxious as I that I should see for myself what he saw.   (17)

"Do you perhaps mean," I asked, "that the fish has symmetrical sides with paired organs?"   (18)

His thoroughly pleased "Of course! of course!" repaid the wakeful hours of the previous night. After he had discoursed most happily and enthusiastically—as he always did—upon the importance of this point, I ventured to ask what I should do next.   (19)

"Oh, look at your fish!" he said, and left me again to my own devices. In a little more than an hour he returned, and heard my new catalogue.   (20)

"That is good, that is good!" he repeated; "but that is not all; go on"; and so for three long days he placed that fish before my eyes, forbidding me to look at anything else, or to use any artificial aid. "Look, look, look," was his repeated injunction.   (21)

This was the best entomological lesson I ever had—a lesson whose influence has extended to the details of every subsequent study; a legacy the Professor had left to me, as he has left it to so many others, of inestimable value, which we could not buy, with which we cannot part.   (22)

A year afterward, some of us were amusing ourselves with chalking outlandish beasts on the Museum blackboard. We drew prancing starfishes; frogs in mortal combat; hydra-headed worms; stately crawfishes, standing on their tails, bearing aloft umbrellas; and grotesque fishes with gaping mouths and staring eyes. The Professor came in shortly after, and was as amused as any at our experiments. He looked at the fishes.   (23)

"Haemulons, every one of them," he said; Mr. ——— drew them."   (24)

True; and to this day, if I attempt a fish, I can draw nothing but haemulons.   (25)

The fourth day, a second fish of the same group was placed beside the first, and I was bidden to point out the resemblances and differences between the two; another and another followed, until the entire family lay before me, and a whole legion of jars covered the table and surrounding shelves; the odor had become a pleasant perfume; and even now, the sight of an old, six-inch worm-eaten cork brings fragrant memories.   (26)

The whole group of haemulons was thus brought in review; and, whether engaged upon the dissection of the internal organs, the preparation and examination of the bony framework, or the description of the various parts, Agassiz's training in the method of observing facts and their orderly arrangement was ever accompanied by the urgent exhortation not to be content with them.   (27)

"Facts are stupid things," he would say, "until brought into connection with some general law."   (28)

At the end of eight months, it was almost with reluctance that I left these friends and turned to insects; but what I had gained by this outside experience has been of greater value than years of later investigation in my favorite groups.   (29)

VOCABULARY

In your journal, write down the meanings of the following words.

- my *antecedents* generally   (1)
- all departments of *zoology*   (1)
- *entomology* was a cleaner science than *ichthyology*   (7)
- dared not show any *aversion*   (7)
- to an *ardent* entomologist   (7)
- to *resuscitate* the beast   (8)
- instruments of all kinds were *interdicted*   (9)
- movable *operculum*   (12)
- I was *piqued*   (13)
- this was *disconcerting*   (16)
- with my two *perplexities*   (16)
- his repeated *injunction*   (21)
- *hydra-headed* worms   (23)
- the urgent *exhortation*   (27)

QUESTIONS FOR WRITING AND DISCUSSION

1. Without looking again at the essay, write down what you found most memorable about the essay. What parts seemed most vivid? Explain.

2. As a reader of Scudder's essay, apply his technique of *repeated observation* to this essay. Read the essay a second time, carefully, looking for techniques of writing observations. Use a pencil to help you read, by underlining or making brief notes. What do you notice on the *second* reading that you did not see on the first?

3. What is the purpose of this essay? To *inform* us about fish? To *explain* how to learn about fish? To *persuade* us to follow Professor Agassiz's method? To *entertain* us with his college stories? What is the primary purpose, in your estimation?

4. Describe the intended audience for this essay. Which *sentences* most clearly address the intended audience?

5. "Facts are stupid things," Agassiz says, "until brought into connection with some general law." Reread paragraph 8. What is the "general law," or, in this case, the *dominant idea* created by the

specific details describing Scudder's first session with his fish? Are his descriptive details objective, subjective, or a combination of both? Explain.

THE SNAKE

Annie Dillard

Annie Dillard was born in Pittsburgh in 1945 and received her B.A. and M.A. degrees from Hollins College. She has published a book of poetry, Tickets for a Prayer Wheel *(1974), columns and essays for* Living Wilderness, Harpers, *and the* Atlantic, *and several books, including* Pilgrim at Tinker Creek *(1984),* An American Childhood *(1987), and* A Writing Life *(1989). In the following selection from* Pilgrim at Tinker Creek, *Dillard carefully observes a snake, a poisonous copperhead, as it lies on a sandstone quarry ledge at twilight. To her surprise, a mosquito alights on the snake and goes about its business of drilling through the scaly skin and sucking the snake's blood. Observing this bizarre episode, Dillard wonders about the laws of biological survival: "A little blood here, a chomp there, and still we live, trampling the grass? Must everything whole be nibbled?"*

There was a snake at the quarry with me tonight. It lay shaded by cliffs on a flat sandstone ledge above the quarry's dark waters. I was thirty feet away, sitting on the forest path overlook, when my eye caught the dark scrawl on the rocks, the lazy sinuosity that can only mean snake. I approached for a better look, edging my way down the steep rock cutting, and saw that the snake was only twelve or thirteen inches long. Its body was thick for its length. I came closer still, and saw the unmistakable undulating bands of brown, the hourglasses: copperhead.   (1)

I never step a foot out of the house, even in winter, without a snakebite kit in my pocket. Mine is a small kit in rubber casing about the size of a shotgun shell; I slapped my pants instinctively to fix in my mind its location. Then I stomped hard on the ground a few times and sat down beside the snake.   (2)

The young copperhead was motionless on its rock. Although it lay in a loose sprawl, all I saw at first was a camouflage pattern of particolored splotches confused by the rushing speckles of light in the weeds between us, and by the deep twilight dark of the quarry pond beyond the rock. Then suddenly the form of its head emerged from the confusion: burnished brown, triangular, blunt as a stone ax. Its head and the first four inches of its body rested on airy nothing an

inch above the rock. I admired the snake. Its scales shone with new-
ness, bright and buffed. Its body was perfect, whole and unblemished.
I found it hard to believe it had not just been created on the spot, or
hatched fresh from its mother, so unscathed and clean was its body, so
unmarked by any passage.   (3)

Did it see me? I was only four feet away, seated on the weedy
cliff behind the sandstone ledge; the snake was between me and the
quarry pond. I waved an arm in its direction: nothing moved. Its low-
forehead glare and lipless reptile smirk revealed nothing. How could I
tell where it was looking, what it was seeing? I squinted at its head,
staring at those eyes like the glass eyes of a stuffed warbler, at those
scales like shields canted and lapped just so, to frame an improbable,
unfathomable face.   (4)

Yes, it knew I was there. There was something about its eyes,
some alien alertness . . . what on earth must it be like to have scales
on your face? All right then, copperhead. I know you're here, you
know I'm here. This is a big night. I dug my elbows into rough rock
and dry soil and settled back on the hillside to begin the long business
of waiting out a snake.   (5)

The only other poisonous snake around here is the timber rattler,
Crotalus horridus horridus. These grow up to six feet long in the mountains, and as big as your thigh. I've never seen one in the wild; I don't
know how many have seen me. I see copperheads, though, sunning in
the dust, disappearing into rock cliff chinks, crossing dirt roads at twilight. Copperheads have no rattle, of course, and, at least in my experience, they do not give way. You walk around a copperhead—if you
see it. Copperheads are not big enough or venomous enough to kill
adult humans readily, but they do account for far and away the greatest number of poisonous snakebites in North America: there are so
many of them, and people, in the Eastern woodlands. It always interests me when I read about new studies being done on pit vipers; the
team of herpetologists always seems to pick my neck of the woods for
its fieldwork. I infer that we have got poisonous snakes as East Africa
has zebras or the tropics have orchids—they are our specialty, our
stock-in-trade. So I try to keep my eyes open. But I don't worry: you
have to live pretty far out to be more than a day from a hospital. And
worrying about getting it in the face from a timber rattler is like worrying about being struck by a meteorite: life's too short. Anyway, perhaps the actual bite is painless. . . .   (6)

The copperhead in front of me was motionless; its head still
hung in the air above the sandstone rock. I thought of poking at it
with a weed, but rejected the notion. Still, I wished it would do something. Marston Bates tells about an English ecologist, Charles Elton,
who said, with his Britishness fully unfurled, "All cold-blooded ani-

mals . . . spend an unexpectedly large proportion of their time doing nothing at all, or at any rate nothing in particular." That is precisely what this one was doing.   (7)

I noticed its tail. It tapered to nothingness. I started back at the head and slid my eye down its body slowly: taper, taper, taper, scales, tiny scales, air. Suddenly the copperhead's tail seemed to be the most remarkable thing I had ever seen. I wished I tapered like that somewhere. What if I were a shaped balloon blown up through the tip of a finger?   (8)

Here was this blood-filled, alert creature, this nerved rope of matter, really here instead of not here, splayed soft and solid on a rock by the slimmest of chances. It was a thickening of the air spread from a tip, a rush into being, eyeball and blood, through a pin-hole rent. Every other time I had ever seen this rock it had been a flat sandstone rock over the quarry pond; now it hosted and bore this chunk of fullness that parted the air around it like a driven wedge. I looked at it from the other direction. From tail to head it spread like the lines of a crescendo, widening from stillness to a turgid blast; then at the bulging jaws it began contracting again, diminuendo, till at the tip of its snout the lines met back at the infinite point that corners every angle, and that space once more ceased being a snake.   (9)

While this wonder engaged me, something happened that was so unusual and unexpected that I can scarcely believe I saw it. It was ridiculous.   (10)

Night had been rising like a ground vapor from the blackened quarry pool. I heard a mosquito sing in my ear; I waved it away. I was looking at the copperhead. The mosquito landed on my ankle; again, I idly brushed it off. To my utter disbelief, it lighted on the copperhead. It squatted on the copperhead's back near its "neck," and bent its head to its task. I was riveted. I couldn't see the mosquito in great detail, but I could make out its lowered head that seemed to bore like a well drill through surface rock to fluid. Quickly I looked around to see if I could find anyone—any hunter going to practice shooting beer cans, any boy on a motorbike—to whom I could show this remarkable sight while it lasted.   (11)

To the best of my knowledge, it lasted two or three full minutes; it seemed like an hour. I could imagine the snake, like the frog sucked dry by the giant water bug, collapsing to an empty bag of skin. But the snake never moved, never indicated any awareness. At last the mosquito straightened itself, fumbled with its forelegs about its head like a fly, and sluggishly took to the air, where I lost it at once. I looked at the snake; I looked beyond the snake to the ragged chomp in the hillside where years before men had quarried stone; I rose, brushed myself off, and walked home.   (12)

Is this what it's like, I thought then, and think now: a little blood here, a chomp there, and still we live, trampling the grass? Must everything whole be nibbled? Here was a new light on the intricate texture of things in the world, the actual plot of the present moment in time after the fall: the way we the living are nibbled and nibbling—not held aloft on a cloud in the air but bumbling pitted and scarred and broken through a frayed and beautiful land.   (13)

VOCABULARY

In your journal, write down the meanings of the following words:

- the lazy *sinuosity* (1)
- *undulating* bands (1)
- team of *herpetologists* (6)
- *splayed* soft and solid (9)
- lines of a *crescendo* (9)
- *diminuendo* (9)
- in time after the *fall* (13)

QUESTIONS FOR WRITING AND DISCUSSION

1. If you have ever seen a snake or reptile up close, describe it (and your experience) in a paragraph.

2. Using only the details and description provided by Dillard, write a paragraph describing and characterizing the copperhead. Now, compare the paragraph you wrote in question 1 (above) with the details that Dillard gives. What does she describe that you did not? What did you notice that she doesn't?

3. Reread Dillard's essay, annotating for sensory details, images, descriptions of what is not there, and changes in her subject. Cite two specific examples (phrases or sentences) for each of these four observing techniques. Which of these techniques does she use most frequently? Which does she use most effectively?

4. In addition to observing her subject, Dillard describes herself and her relationship to the snake. Find three specific instances in the essay of this strategy. If she omitted these descriptions of herself, would her essay be more effective? Explain.

5. Observing essays focus on a discovery, a dominant idea, or a perceived general law. In Scudder's essay, Professor Agassiz

says, "Facts are stupid things until brought into connection with some general law." What "facts" does Dillard observe? What general law does she perceive? In which sentences does Dillard *connect* observed facts with her general law or dominant idea?

OBSERVING: THE WRITING PROCESS

ASSIGNMENT FOR OBSERVING

Do a piece of writing in which you observe a specific person, place, object, or event. Your goal is to show how specific, observed details create *dominant ideas* about the person, place, object, or event. Your initial purpose is to use your writing to help you observe, discover, and learn about your subject; your final purpose will be to show your reader what you have seen and learned.

Important: Repeated observation is essential. Choose some limited subject (a person or small group of people, a specific place, a single object or animal, or a recurring event) that *you can reobserve over a period of several days during your writing process.*

Choosing a Subject

If one of your journal entries suggested an interesting subject, try the collecting and shaping strategies. If none of those exercises caught your interest, consider the following ideas:

- Think about your current classes. Do you have a class with a laboratory—chemistry, physics, biology, engineering, animal science, horticulture, industrial sciences, physical education, social work, drawing, pottery—in which you have to make detailed observations? Use this assignment to help you in one of those classes: Write about what you observe and learn during one of your labs.

- Seek out a new place on campus that is off your usual track. Check the college catalog for ideas about places you haven't yet seen: a theater where actors are rehearsing, a greenhouse, a physical education class in the martial arts, a studio where artists are working, a computer laboratory, or an animal research center. Or visit a class you wouldn't take for credit. Observe, write, and learn about what's there and what's happening.

- Get a copy of the Yellow Pages for your town or city. Open to a page at random and place your finger on the page. If it lands on

"Write about dogs!"

an advertisement for a nearby store, take your notebook there for a visit. Describe the chocolate mousse at a restaurant, an expensive wine at a liquor store, a new car at a dealership, a headstone at a burial-monument company, a twelve-string guitar at a music shop—whatever you would like to learn about through careful observation.

As you write on your subject, consider a tentative audience and purpose. Who might want to know what you learn from your observations? What do you need to explain? What will readers already know? Jot down tentative ideas about your subject, audience, and purpose. Remember, however, that these are not cast in concrete. You may discover some new idea, focus, or angle as you write.

Collecting

We don't take in the world like a camera or a set of recording devices. The mind is an agent, not a passive receiver. . . . The active mind is a composer and everything we respond to, we compose.

—Ann Berthoff, author and teacher

Once you have chosen a subject for your essay, from your journal or elsewhere, begin collecting information. Depending on your purpose, your topic, even your personal learning preferences, some activities will work better than others. However, you should *practice* all of these activities to determine which is most successful for you and your topic. During these collecting activities, go back and *reobserve your subject*. The second or third time you go back, you may see additional details or more actively understand what you're seeing.

Sketching   Begin by *drawing* what you see. A pen or pencil can be "the best of eyes," as Scudder's essay demonstrates. Your drawing doesn't have to be great art to suggest other details, questions, or relationships that may be important. Try to narrow and focus on one limited subject and draw it in detail, instead of trying to cover a wide range of objects.

Brad Parks, a student in a writing class, decided to visit an Eskimo art display at a local gallery. As part of his observing notes, he drew the following sketches of Eskimo paintings. As he drew, he made notes in the margins of his sketches and zoomed in for more detail on one pair of walruses.

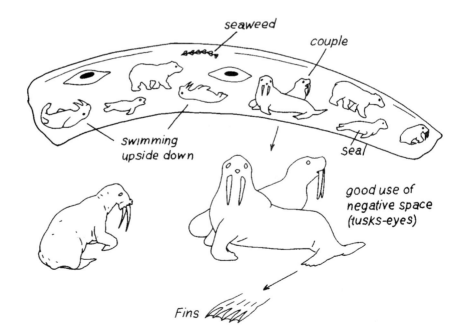

Taking Double-Entry Notes   Taking notes in a double-entry format is a simple but effective system for recording observed details. Draw a vertical line down the middle of a page in your journal. On the left-hand side, record bits of description and sensory details. On the right-hand side, jot down your reactions, thoughts, or ideas. Observed details on the left-hand side should be as *objective* as possible; comments on the right-hand side will be more *subjective*, noting your impressions, reactions, comparisons, images, as well as additional questions and ideas.

Sensory Details, Facts, Data	Impressions, Reactions, Ideas, Questions
size, color, shape, sounds, smell, touch, taste, actions, behavior	impressions, associations, feelings, reactions, ideas, images, comparisons, related thoughts, questions

Answering Questions   To help you describe the person, place, object, or event, write a short response in your journal to each of the following questions:

- What exactly is it? Can you define this person, place, object, or event? If it's an object, are its parts related? Who needs it, uses it, or produces it?
- How much could it change and still be recognizable?
- Compare and contrast it. How is the person, place, thing, or event similar to or different from other comparable people, places, things, or events?
- From what points of view is it usually seen? From what point of view is it rarely seen?

Freewriting   Freewriting means exactly what it says. Write about your subject, nonstop, for five to ten minutes. Sometimes you may have to write, "I can't think of anything" or "This is really stupid," but keep on writing. Let your words and ideas suggest other thoughts and ideas. For observing, the purpose of freewriting is to let your *imagination* work on the subject, usually *after* you have observed and recorded specific details. Freewriting on your subject will develop more *associations* or *comparisons* for the right-hand side of your double-entry log, too. It should also help you to identify a dominant idea for your details.

Shaping

To begin the shaping process, consider your subject, purpose, and audience again. Has your purpose changed? Can you narrow your subject to a specific topic? Some of the answers you may know now; others you may not know until after you do your first draft. Jot down your current responses to the following questions:

Your audience is one single reader. I have found that sometimes it helps to pick out one person—a real person you know, or an imagined person and write to that one.

—*John Steinbeck, novelist*

- Subject: What is your general subject?
- Specific topic: What aspect of your subject are you interested in? Try to *narrow* your field or *limit* your focus.
- Purpose: Why is this topic interesting or important to you or to others? From what point of view will you be writing? What is the dominant idea you are trying to convey?
- Audience: Who are your readers? What are these readers like and why might they be interested in this topic? How can you direct your description of your subject to your particular audience?

With your answers to these questions in mind, you should experiment with several of the following shaping strategies. These strategies will organize your specific examples, but they may also suggest related ideas that might improve your description.

As you practice these strategies, try to *focus* your subject. In a profile of a person, for example, focus on key facial features or revealing habits or mannerisms. If you're writing about a place or an event, narrow the subject. Describe, for instance, the street at night, a spider spinning a web in a windowsill, a man in a laundromat banging on a change machine, a bird hovering in midair, a photograph, a fish. Write in depth and detail about a *limited* subject.

With a limited subject, a shaping strategy such as spatial order, classification, or comparison/contrast will organize all your specific details for your audience. The shaping strategies give you ways of seeing relationships among the many bits of your description and presenting them in an organized manner for your reader. Seeing these relationships will also help you discover and communicate the *dominant idea* to your reader.

COMPUTER TIPS: COLLECTING

1. Computers are perfectly tailored to freewriting. As you type, you don't have to hit a "Return" key, since the text file keeps expanding as long as your ideas are flowing. You never have a dull pencil or run out of paper.

2. If your computer has split-screen capability, do your double-entry log on the computer. On a computer, you can expand any one point as much as you like, without having to write in the margins or on the back of a page.

3. Answering questions can be an excellent stimulus for writing. On the computer, you can keep writing and adding details if one question turns out to be especially appropriate for your subject.

4. Try *invisible writing.* If you are freewriting and you find that you keep stopping to fix spelling or sentence errors as you write, turn down the contrast on the screen and then type as you normally would. At first, writing with a blank screen in front of you will seem a bit strange. As you practice, however, you will become more comfortable. Invisible writing imitates the spontaneous process of thinking to yourself, without the distraction of typos or misspelled words. After you are finished writing, turn up the contrast and read what you have written.

Spatial Order Spatial order is a simple way to organize your descriptive details. Choose some sequence—left to right, right to left, bottom to top—and describe your observed details in that sequence. In the following description of his "trashed" dorm room, Dale Furnish, a student who was the victim of a prank, uses spatial order. The italicized words illustrate the spatial order.

> As I walked in the door, I could hardly believe that this scene of destruction used to be my room. *Along the left hand wall,* nearly hiding my desk and mirror, was a pile of beer cans and bottles, paper cups and old crumpled newspapers. The small window *on the far wall* was now covered with the mattress of the bed, and the frame of the bunk bed stood on end. The clothes closet, *to the right of the window,* looked as though it were a giant washing machine which had just gone through spin cycle—clothes were plastered all over, and only four hangers remained, dangling uselessly on the pole. *On the right wall,* where the bed had been, was the real surprise. Tied to the heating pipe was a mangy looking sheep. I swear. It was a real sheep. As I looked at it, it turned to face me and loudly and plaintively said, "Baaaa." *Behind me,* in the hall, everyone began laughing. I didn't know whether to laugh or cry.

Chronological Order Chronological order is simply the time sequence of your observation. The above description of a dorm room contains chronological order as well as spatial order. The observer enters the room, looks at the left wall, then looks at the far window, and finally looks at the sheep. After the sheep cries "baaa," the people in the hall begin laughing.

Since it is impossible to describe everything at once, many observations follow a chronological order. In the following passage, Gregory Allen, writing from his point of view as a five-foot-six-inch-tall guard on a basketball team, describes sights, sounds, and his feelings during a pickup game. The italicized words emphasize the chronological order.

> The game *begins.* The guy checking me is about 6' 1", red hair, freckles, and has no business on the court. He looks slow, *so* I decide to run him to tire him. I dribble twice, pump fake, and the guy goes for it, thinking that he's going to block this much smaller guy's shot. *Then* I leap, flick my wrist, and the ball glides through the air and flows through the net with a swish as the net turns upside down. I come down and realize that I have been scratched. *Suddenly,* I feel a sharp pain as sweat runs into the small red cut. I wipe the blood on my shorts and *continue playing* the game. *After* that first play, I begin to hear the common song of the game. There's the squeak of the high-top Nike sneakers, the bouncing ball, the shuffle of feet. *Occasionally,* I hear "I'm open!" "Pass the ball!" "Augghh!" And *then,* "Nice play, man!"

Comparison/Contrast   If what you've observed and written about your subject so far involves seeing similarities or differences, you may be able to use comparison/contrast as a shaping strategy—either for a single paragraph or for a series of paragraphs. The following two paragraphs, for example, are taken from Albert Goldman's biography of Elvis Presley, entitled *Elvis.* In these paragraphs, Goldman's dominant idea depends on the striking contrast between what he finds on the front lawn of Graceland, the rock star's mansion in Memphis, and what he notices when he steps through the front door.

> Prominently displayed on the front lawn is an elaborate crèche. The stable is a full-scale adobe house strewn with straw. Life-sized are the figures of Joseph and Mary, the kneeling shepherds and Magi, the lambs and ewes, as well as the winged annunciatory angel hovering over the roof beam. Real, too, is the cradle in which the infant Jesus sleeps.
>
> When you step through the ten-foot oak door and enter the house, you stop and stare in amazement. Having just come from the contemplation of the tenderest scene in the Holy Bible, imagine the shock of finding yourself in a *whorehouse!* Yet there is no other way to describe the drawing room of Graceland except to say that it appears to have been lifted from some turn-of-the-century bordello down in the French Quarter of New Orleans. . . . The room is a gaudy melange of red velour and gilded tassels, Louis XV furniture and porcelain bric-a-brac, all informed by the kind of taste that delights in a ceramic temple d'amour housing a miniature Venus de Milo with an electrically simulated waterfall cascading over her naked shoulders.

Reexamine your collecting notes about your subject. If there are striking similarities or differences between the two parts or aspects of your subject, perhaps a comparison or contrast structure will organize your details.

Classification   Classifying people, events, or things by *types* may provide a shape you can use for a paragraph or a whole essay. In the following paragraph from "Speedway," an essay on racing at the Indianapolis 500, cultural critic Paul Fussell categorizes spectators into three social classes: the middle classes, or "middles"; the high proletarians, or "high proles"; and the "uglies."

> I'd say the people can be divided into three social classes: the middles, who on race day tend, in homage to the checkered flag, to dress all in black and white and who sit in reserved seats; the high proles, who watch standing or lolling in the infield, especially at the turns, "where the action is"; and the uglies, the overadvertised, black-leathered, beer-sodden, pot-headed occupiers of that muddy stretch of ground in the infield at the first turn, known as the Snake Pit. These are the ones who, when girls pass, spiritlessly hold up signs reading "Show Us Your T— s." The uglies are sometimes taken to be the essence of Indy, and they are the people who, I think Frank Deford has in mind when he speaks of "barbarians." But they are not the significant Indy audience. The middle class is, all those people arriving at the Speedway in cars bearing Purdue and Indiana State stickers.

Classification is often a useful method of shaping description. To see if it is appropriate for your subject, ask "What types do you observe?" The answer may lead to categories or types you hadn't observed, and the categories may provide a shape you can adopt.

Definition   Definition is the essence of observation. Defining a person, place, or object requires stating its exact meaning and describing its basic qualities. Literally, a definition sets the boundaries, indicating, for example, how an apple is distinct from an orange, or how a canary is different from a sparrow. Definition, however, is a catchall term for a variety of strategies. It uses classification and comparison as well as description. It often describes a thing by negation, by saying what it is not. Sidney Harris, a columnist for many years for the *Chicago Daily News*, defines a "jerk" by referring to several types of people ("boob," "fool," "dope," "bore," "egotist," "nice person," "clever person") and then compares or contrasts these terms to show, for example, where "jerk" leaves off and "egotist" begins. Harris also defines by negation, saying that a jerk has no grace and is tactless. The result, when combined with a description of qualities he has observed in jerks, is definition.

> Thinking it over, I decided that a jerk is basically a person without insight. He is not necessarily a fool or a dope, because some extremely clever persons can be jerks. In fact, it has little to do with intelligence as we commonly think of it; it is, rather, a kind of subtle but persuasive aroma emanating from the inner part of the personality.

I know a college president who can be described only as a jerk. He is not an unintelligent man, or unlearned, nor even unschooled in the social amenities. Yet he is a jerk *cum laude,* because of a fatal flaw in his nature—he is totally incapable of looking into the mirror of his soul and shuddering at what he sees there.

A jerk, then, is a man (or woman) who is utterly unable to see himself as he appears to others. He has no grace, he is tactless without meaning to be, he is a bore even to his best friends, he is an egotist without charm. All of us are egotists to some extent, but most of us—unlike the jerk—are perfectly and horribly aware of it when we make asses of ourselves. The jerk never knows.

At this stage in the writing process, you have already been defining your subject simply by describing it. But you may want to use a deliberately structured definition, as Sidney Harris does, to shape your observations.

Simile, Metaphor, and Analogy   Simile, metaphor, and analogy create vivid word pictures or *images* by making *comparisons.* These images may take up only a sentence or two, or they may shape several paragraphs.

- A *simile* is a comparison using "like" or "as": A is like B. "George eats his food like a vacuum cleaner."

- A *metaphor* is a direct or implied comparison suggesting that A *is* B: "At the dinner table, George is a vacuum cleaner."

- An *analogy* is an extended simile or metaphor that builds a point-by-point comparison into several sentences, a whole paragraph, or even a series of paragraphs. Writers use analogy to explain a difficult concept, idea, or process by comparing it with something more familiar or easier to understand.

   If the audience knows about engines but has never seen a human heart, for example, a writer might use an analogy to explain that a heart is like a simple engine, complete with chambers or cylinders, intake and exhaust valves, and hoses to carry the fuel and the exhaust.

   As an illustration of simile and metaphor, notice how Joseph Conrad, in the following brief passage from *Heart of Darkness,* begins with a simile and then continues to build on his images throughout the paragraph. Rather than creating a rigid structural shape for his details (as classification or comparison/contrast would do), the images combine and flow like the river he is describing.

> Going up that river was like travelling back to the earliest beginnings of the world, when vegetation rioted on the earth and the big trees were kings. An empty stream, a great silence, an impenetrable forest. The air was warm, thick, heavy, sluggish. There was no joy in the brilliance of

sunshine. The long stretches of the waterway ran on, deserted, into the gloom of overshadowed distances. On silvery sandbanks hippos and alligators sunned themselves side by side. The broadening waters flowed through a mob of wooded islands; you lost your way on that river as you would in a desert, and butted all day long against shoals, trying to find the channel, till you thought yourself bewitched and cut off for ever from everything you had known once—somewhere—far away—in another existence perhaps.

An analogy helps shape the following paragraph by Carl Sagan, author of *The Dragons of Eden* and *Cosmos*. To help us understand a difficult concept, the immense age of the Earth (and, by comparison, the relatively tiny span of human history), Sagan compares the life-time of the universe to something simple and familiar: the calendar of a single year.

> The most instructive way I know to express this cosmic chronology is to imagine the fifteen-billion year lifetime of the universe . . . com-pressed into the span of a single year. . . . It is disconcerting to find that in such a cosmic year the Earth does not condense out of interstellar matter until early September; dinosaurs emerge on Christmas Eve; flow-ers arise on December 28th; and men and women originate at 10:30 P.M. on New Year's Eve. All of recorded history occupies the last ten seconds of December 31; and the time from the waning of the Middle Ages to the present occupies little more than one second.

Consider whether a good analogy would help you shape one or more paragraphs in your essay. Ask yourself: "What is the most diffi-cult concept or idea I'm trying to describe?" Is there an extended point-by-point comparison, an analogy, that would clarify it?

Title, Introduction, and Conclusion   Depending on your purpose and audience, you may want a *title* for what you're writing. At the minimum, titles—like labels—should accurately indicate the contents in the package. In addition, however, good titles capture the reader's interest with some catchy phrasing or imaginative language—to make the reader want to "buy" the package. Writing primarily for himself, Mark Skelton uses a simple label, "A New Leaf," for his description which appears at the end of this chapter. Samuel H. Scudder's title, however, is both a good label (the essay is about looking at fish) and has catchy phrasing: "Take This Fish and Look at It." If a title is appropriate for your observation, write out several possibilities in your journal.

Introductions should set up the context for the reader—*who, what, when, where,* and *why*—so that readers can orient themselves. Depending on the audience and purpose, introductions can be very brief, pushing the reader quickly into the scene, or they can take more time, easing readers into the setting: "It was more than fifteen years ago that I entered the laboratory of Professor Agassiz . . . ," Scudder begins, giving us background information and context. Stephen White, in his essay about Mesa Verde at the end of this chapter, begins more mysteriously: "It is difficult for me to say exactly what it was that drew me to this solitary place. . . ." White doesn't tell his reader that he's talking about Mesa Verde until the second paragraph. Mark Skelton, writing primarily for himself, however, is content with an abrupt beginning: "My potted plant sits on my desk at home."

Conclusions should bring the observation to a close, giving a sense of completeness. Conclusions depend upon a writer's purpose and audience, but they tend to be of two types or have two components: a *summary* and a *reference* to the introduction. Scudder summarizes his dominant idea that his experiences were of great value, and he also refers back to the introduction: "At the end of eight months, it was almost with reluctance that I left these friends and turned to insects. . . ." Mark Skelton concludes by reemphasizing the dominant idea of his description: the plant is really a family of leaves.

As you work on shaping strategies and drafting, make notes about possible titles, appropriate introductions, or effective conclusions for your written observations.

Drafting

Reread Journal Entries and Notes From Collecting and Shaping
Before you start drafting, review your material so you aren't writing cold. Stop and reread everything you've written on your subject. You're not trying to memorize particular sentences or phrases; you're just getting it all fresh in your mind, seeing what you still like and discarding details that are no longer relevant.

Reobserve Your Subject   If necessary, go back and observe your subject again. One more session may suggest an important detail or idea that will help you get started writing.

Reexamine Purpose, Audience, Dominant Idea, and Shape
After all your writing and rereading, you may have some new ideas about your purpose, audience, or dominant idea. Take a minute to jot these down in your journal. Remember that your specific details should *show* the main point or dominant idea, whether you state it explicitly or not.

Next, if the shaping strategies suggested an order for your essay, use it to guide your draft. You may, however, have only your specific details or a general notion of the dominant idea you're trying to communicate to your reader. In that case, you may want to begin writing and work out a shape or outline as you write.

COMPUTER TIPS: COLLECTING AND SHAPING

Transfer the following shaping strategies directly to your computer file. After you have done that, reread your journal or collecting notes, adding your details in the blank parts. If the shaping strategy is appropriate for your subject and purpose, you may generate more details and, at the same time, organize your ideas. On the computer, play with the possibilities for each shaping strategy.

1. **Spatial Order.** Enter a series of transition words in your file, and then complete the sentences, noting what you saw. For example, for a line-of-sight description, enter:

   From where I was sitting, at first I saw . . .
   As I raised my eyes just slightly . . .
   Only a few feet ahead was . . .
   Beyond that, I noticed . . .
   Finally, I saw . . .

2. **Chronological Order.** Enter a series of transition words, filling in the necessary details after each prompt: First . . . Next . . . After that . . . Then . . . Shortly thereafter . . . Soon . . . At last . . .

As you add details, you are actually shaping a trial version.

3. **Comparison/Contrast.** Enter the subjects (A and B) and then enter your observations. As you write, you will be experimenting with a possible structure for your observations.

   Subject A _____
       Observations about point one . . .
                            point two . . .
                            point three . . .
   Subject B _____
       Observations about B and similarities/differences
       between A and B on point one . . .
                            point two . . .
                            point three . . .

4. **Classification.** List the types within a single group that you observe, and then add your observed details about each.

   First type:_____.   Observing details: _____.
   Second type:_____.   Observing details: _____.
   Third type:_____.   Observing details: _____.

As you add details, you will be testing your subject to see if classification is appropriate.

*The idea is to get the
pencil moving quickly.*

—*Bernard Malamud,
novelist*

Drafting With the above notes as a guide, you are ready to start drafting. Work on establishing your ritual: Choose a comfortable, familiar place with the writing tools you like. Make sure you'll have no interruptions. Try to write nonstop. If you can't think of a word, put a dash. If you can't remember how to spell a word, *don't* stop to look it up now—keep writing. Write until you reach what feels like the end. If you do get stuck, *reread* your last few lines or some of your writing process materials. Then go back and pick up the thread. Don't stop to count words or pages. You should shoot for more material than you need, since it's usually easier to cut material later, when you're revising, than to add more if you're short.

Revising

*All the stuff you see
back there on the floor is
writing I did last week
that I have to rewrite
this week.*

—*Ernest J. Gaines, author of*
The Autobiography of Miss
Jane Pittman

Gaining Distance and Objectivity Revising, of course, has been going on since you put your first sentence down on paper. You've changed ideas, thought through your subject again, and reobserved your person, place, object, or event. After your rough draft is finished, your next step is to revise, to *resee* the whole thing. But before you do, you need to let it sit at least twenty-four hours, to get away from it for a while, to gain some distance and perspective. Relax. Congratulate yourself.

About the time you try to relax, however, you may get a sudden temptation—even an overwhelming urge—to have someone else read it, immediately! Usually, it's better to resist that urge. Chances are, you will want to have someone else read it either because you're bubbling with enthusiasm and you want to share it or else because you're certain that it's all garbage and you want to hear the bad news right away. Most readers will not find it either as great as you hope it is *or* as awful as you fear it is. As a result, their offhand remarks may seem terribly insensitive or condescending. In a day or so, however, you'll be able to see your writing more objectively: Perhaps it's not great yet, but it's not hopeless, either. At that point, you're ready to get some feedback and start your revisions.

Rereading and Responding to Your Readers When you've been away from the draft for a while, you are better able to see the whole piece of writing. Start by rereading your own draft and making marginal notes. Don't be distracted by spelling errors or typos; concentrate on the quality of the details and the flow of the sentences. Focus on the overall effect you're creating, see if your organization still makes sense, and check to make sure that all the details support the dominant idea. If you have feedback from a workshop session, think about the comments and suggestions you've received. Depending on the reactions of your readers, you may need to change the point of view, add a few specific examples or some comparisons or images, fix the organization of a paragraph, reorder some details, delete some sentences, or do several of the above. Be prepared, however, to rewrite several paragraphs to help your readers really *see* what you are describing.

Guidelines for Revision   As you revise your essay, keep the following tips in mind:

- **Reexamine your purpose and audience.** Are you doing what you intended? If your purpose or audience has changed, what other changes do you need to make as you revise your draft?

- **Pay attention to the advice your readers give you, but don't necessarily make all the changes they suggest.** Ask them *why* something should be changed. Ask them specifically *where* something should be changed.

- **Consider your point of view.** Would changing to another point of view clarify what you are describing?

- **Consider your vantage point.** Do you have a bird's-eye view, or are you observing from a low angle? Do you zoom in for a close-up of a person or object? Would a different vantage point fit your purpose and audience?

- **Check to make sure you are using sensory details where appropriate.** Remember, you must *show* your reader the details you observe. If necessary, *reobserve* your subject.

- **Do all your details and examples support the *dominant idea?*** Reread your draft and omit any irrelevant details.

- **What is *not* present in your subject that might be important to mention?**

- **What *changes* occur in the form or function of your subject?** Where can you describe those changes more vividly?

- **Make comparisons if they will help you or your reader understand your subject better.** Similes, metaphors, or analogies may describe your subject more vividly.

- **Does what you are observing belong to a class of similar objects?** Would classification organize your writing?

- **Be sure to cue, or signal, your reader with appropriate transition words.** Transitions will improve the coherence or flow of your writing.

Spatial Order: on the left, on the right, next, above, below, higher, lower, farther, next, beyond

Chronological Order: before, earlier, after, afterward, thereafter, then, from then on, the next day, shortly, by that time, immediately, slowly, while, meanwhile, until, now, soon, within an hour, first, later, finally, at last

Comparison/Contrast: on one hand, on the other hand, also, similarly, in addition, likewise, however, but, yet, still, although, even so, nonetheless, in contrast.

> *I went for years not finishing anything. Because, of course, when you finish something you can be judged. . . .*
>
> —*Erica Jong, author of* Fear of Flying

- **Revise sentences for clarity, conciseness, emphasis, and variety.**

- **When you have revised your essay, edit your writing for correct spelling and appropriate word choice, punctuation, usage, and grammar.**

POSTSCRIPT ON THE WRITING PROCESS

When you've finished writing this assignment, do one final journal entry. Briefly, answer the following three questions:

1. What was the hardest part of this writing assignment for you?

2. What exercise, practice, strategy, or workshop was the "breakthrough" for you? What led you to your discovery or dominant idea?

3. State in one sentence your discovery or the dominant idea of your essay.

4. What did you learn about your writing ritual and process? What did you learn about observing?

OBSERVING: STUDENT WRITING

A NEW LEAF

Mark Skelton

Mark Skelton decided to write a description of his potted plant, an impatiens, *which he kept in his room. His initial purpose was to learn, through careful scrutiny, exactly how the plant looked. Following Agassiz's advice, Skelton observed his plant on three different occasions, each time taking notes, drawing pictures, and then writing a draft. What follows are his notes from the first two observing sessions, his first draft, and then a revised version. As you read his drafts, notice how his focus changes as he zooms in closer for more detail. Look also for an interesting discovery he makes about his plant.*

Observing Notes

Observation 1
9:40 pm
2-4-88

* combination of light green and dark green
* shaped like a dog's head with ears sticking up
* about an inch and a half long
* crinkled appearance like someone wadded it up and then straightened it out
* can tell it's younger by the shiny appearance (shinier than the older leaves)
* deeper in color than the older leaves
* no brown tips or yellow spots like the old leaves that need to be cut off
+ no smell
* top is smooth
* underneath is rough because of the little veins)
* characteristics of each half are different (like fingerprints)
* shape is symmetrical

left side
more light green color
less dark green

right side
more dark green color
less light green

Observation 2
3:00 pm
2-5-88

* small dust particles dull some of the shine
* hidden beneath the large leaves like a shy child behind his mother's leg
* tilted more toward the sun nourishing its growth
* supported by a long stem which looks too skiny to hold it up
* veins which are not visible on the top side can be seen running like a spiderweb on the underneath side
* if held in your fingertips and wedged gently a small popping sound is made from the small bulges in the surface as they pop in and out
* light green color running through the middle looks like the shape of a ~~beyond with its dead and the a pair of tips~~ maple leaf
* ~~it~~ The light green runs along the main veins which are larger.

First Draft

My Potted Plant

My potted plant is not a particularly spectacular specimen but it at least brightens up my otherwise surgically practical room. The plant is about eighteen inches high and is planted in a two-gallon pot made of wooden slats held together with a pair of brass rings. The plant is a light green, similar to the green of a Cox's apple. It has one solitary pink flower perched delicately on the end of one limb. The flower is only about half an inch in diameter and has six petals centered around a white middle. The plant is densely leafed with various sizes of oval shaped leaves. It has no hard, woody, sections of stem but rather a soft, watery stem. When it needs water, it droops like a marathon runner overcome with exhaustion, gasping for breath. During the summer, the plant springs to life, and several tiny, bright flowers appear, randomly decorating its foliage like distant stars in the night sky. Occasionally it sheds its leaves and is left barren for a number of days until it returns to its normal perkiness.

Revised Version

A NEW LEAF

A potted plant sits on my desk at home. It is not a particularly spectacular specimen, but it adds a human touch to my otherwise surgically sterile room. The plant, called an *impatiens* or a Busy Lizzie, is about eighteen inches high and sits in a two-gallon pot made from several slats of wood held together with a pair of brass rings. The plant is light green, similar to the green of a Cox's apple. Nestled among all of the larger, more mature leaves of the plant is a sign of new growth: a young leaf. Like a small, shy child peering from behind his mother's leg, this inch-and-a-half baby leaf is just barely visible. At first appearance the shape of this combined greenish-yellow and deep green leaf looks like a dog's head, with its ears sticking straight up. Up the center of the leaf runs a larger vein the width of a straight pin, separating the leaf into two symmetrically-shaped sides, each looking like a wafer-thin orange slice. Because of its youth, the new leaf has not fully straightened out, and it looks like a piece of wadded up paper that has been flattened out. Shinier and a deeper green than the older leaves, this young leaf has no brittle brown tips and is dulled by only a few minute dust particles. A smooth top, like that of a vinyl seat cover, hides the rougher texture found underneath, and the waxy surface repels water just like a slicker on a rainy day. Supporting this dog-eared leaf is a very slender, deep green stem that looks as if it has to struggle to support the leaf. Due to phototropism, the fragile-looking stem leans towards the beam of morning sunlight like wheat bending in a breeze. The leaf gives off no apparent smell, but because of its youthful appearance, a feeling of springtime fills the air in my room. Hidden there among the duller, more mature leaves of the plant, the new leaf looks remarkably like a young child in a family. In fact, the rest of the *impatiens'* leaves do support this young leaf, giving their energy to the new growth. This family of leaves, a plant, goes quietly about its business of generating new life, brightening my room. All I have to do is notice.

QUESTIONS FOR WRITING AND DISCUSSION

1. *Without looking again at either draft,* describe what you remember about this plant. List all the details you can remember. Reread your list of details and then look again at the drafts: From which version did you remember the details?

2. Of the six strategies for observing discussed at the beginning of this chapter, which does Skelton use? Which are most effective? Which are least effective?

3. What does Skelton learn or discover while observing his plant? Where in the revised draft does he reveal his discovery? Do his images lead naturally to this discovery? What details or images would you suggest *adding* or *deleting* in order to sharpen the focus or dominant idea of the paragraph?

EMPTY WINDOWS

Stephen White

In this essay, Stephen White describes both what his senses tell him and what he can only imagine about the Anasazi, the ancient Native Americans who more than a thousand years ago built the cliff dwellings at Mesa Verde in southwestern Colorado. Writing about those empty dwellings with their darkened windows, White says, "Perhaps there lurks, behind every blackened window, a certain unexplainable something we can never understand."

It is difficult for me to say exactly what it was that drew me to this solitary place and held me here, virtually entranced, the entire day. It's the silence, maybe, or the empty houses perched precariously on the canyon wall below me. Or, could it be the knowledge that something seemingly nonexistent does indeed exist?   (1)

I awoke this morning with a sense of unexplainable anticipation gnawing away at the back of my mind, that this chilly, leaden day at the Mesa Verde would bring something new and totally foreign to any of my past experiences. It was a sensation that began to permeate my entire being as I sat crouched before my inadequate campfire, chills running up my spine. Chills which, I am certain, were due not entirely to the dreary gray of a winter "sunrise."   (2)

It had been my plan to travel the so-called Ruins Road early today, and then complete my visit here, but as I stopped along the road and stood scanning the opposite wall of the canyon for ruins, I felt as if some force had seized control of my will. I was compelled to make my way along the rim.   (3)

Starting out upon the rock, I weaved in and out repeatedly as the gaping emptiness of the canyon and the weathered standstone of the rim battled one another for territory. At last arriving here, where a narrow peninsula of canyon juts far into the stone, I was able to peer back into the darkness of a cave carved midway in the vertical wall opposite, within whose smoke blackened walls huddle, nearly unnoticeable, the rooms of a small crumbled ruin.   (4)

They are a haunting sight, these broken houses, clustered together down in the gloom of the canyon. It presents a complete contrast to the tidy, excavated ruins I explored yesterday, lost within a cluster of tourists and guided by a park ranger who expounded constantly upon his wealth of knowledge of excavation techniques and archaeological dating methods. The excavated ruins seemed, in comparison, a noisy, almost modern city, punctuated with the clicking of camera shutters and the bickering of children. Here it is quiet. The silence is broken only by the rush of the wind in the trees and the trickling of a tiny stream of melting snow springing from ledge to ledge as it makes its way down over the rock to the bottom of the canyon. And this small, abandoned village of tiny houses seems almost as the Indians left it, reduced by the passage of nearly a thousand years to piles of rubble through which protrude broken red adobe walls surrounding ghostly jet black openings, undisturbed by modern man.   (5)

Those windows seem to stare back at me as my eyes are drawn to them. They're so horribly empty, yet my gaze is fixed, searching for some sign of the vitality they must surely have known. I yearn for sounds amidst the silence, for images of life as it once was in the bustling and prosperous community of cliff dwellers who lived here so long ago. It must have been a sunny home when the peaceful, agrarian Anasazi, or ancient ones, as the Navajo call them, lived and dreamed their lives here, wanting little more than to continue in their ways and be left alone, only to be driven away in the end by warring people with whom they could not contend.   (6)

I long to hear, to see, and to understand, and though I strain all my senses to their limits, my wishes are in vain. I remain alone, confronted only by the void below and the cold stare of those utterly desolate windows. I know only an uneasy sensation that I am not entirely alone, and a quick, chill gust gives birth once again to that restless shiver tracing its path along the length of my spine.   (7)

As a gray afternoon fades into a gray evening, I can find neither a true feeling of fear nor one of the quiet serenity one would expect to experience here. It is comforting for me to believe that it was the explorer in me which brought me here, to feel that I was lured to stand above this lonely house by that same drive to find and explore the unknown which motivated the countless others who have come here since seeking knowledge and understanding of the ancient people of the "Green Table." Yet as I begin the journey back to my car and the security of an evening fire, I remain uncomfortably unconvinced.   (8)

Perhaps the dreariness of a cloudy day united with my solitude to pave a mental pathway for illusion and mystery. Or perhaps all homes are never truly empty, having known the multitude of experience which is human life. Perhaps there lurks, behind every blackened window, a certain unexplainable something we can never understand. I know only that the Indian has long respected these places and given them wide berth, leaving their sanctity inviolate.   (9)

QUESTIONS FOR WRITING AND DISCUSSION

1. Describe a similar experience you have had with an empty room or vacant house. White says that "perhaps all homes are never truly empty, having known the multitude of experience which is human life." Based on your experience, do you agree with him?

2. Through his description, what did White help you "see" about the Anasazi and their cliff dwellings? What did you learn?

3. Of the basic techniques for observing—using sensory detail, comparisons, and images; describing what is not there; noting changes; and writing from a clear point of view—which ones does White use most effectively? Cite an example of each technique from his essay.

4. In which paragraphs does White use each of the following shaping strategies: spatial order, chronological order, comparisons or contrasts, and simile, metaphor, or analogy? Which strategies did you find most effective in organizing the experience for you as a reader?

4 | REMEMBERING

Georges Seurat
Sunday Afternoon on the Island of La Grande Jatte (detail).
The Art Institute of Chicago, Helen Birch Bartlett Memorial Collection

This morning you accidentally ran into a certain person you knew several years ago, and for several hours you've been in a bad mood. You called your best friend, but no one answered the phone. You went to class and then for your usual jog, but you pooped out after only half a mile. You even watched a game show on television in the middle of the afternoon and ate half a bag of potato chips, but you still felt lousy. "Why do I always react this way when I see that person?" you yell at the television. But the television has no reply. So you grab some paper and begin scrawling out every memory you have of your experiences with the person you ran into this morning, hoping to understand your feelings. □

You and several co-workers have formed a committee to draft a report for your company's vice-president in charge of personnel. You have grievances about workload, pay scale, daily procedures, and the attitudes of supervisors. Your report needs to recommend changes in current policies. The committee decides that each person will contribute part of the report by describing actual incidents that have had negative effects on efficiency and human relations. You decide to describe a day last June when your immediate supervisor expected you to learn a new word-processing system and at the same time meet a 3:00 P.M. deadline for a thirty-seven-page budget analysis. □

For me the initial delight is in the surprise of remembering something I didn't know I knew.

—Robert Frost, poet

The fact is that there's no understanding the future without the present, and no understanding where we are now without a glance, at least, to where we have been.

—Joyce Maynard, columnist and author of Looking Backward: A Chronicle of Growing Up Old in the Sixties

The human brain is a pack rat: Nothing is too small, obscure, or mundane for the brain's collection. Bits and pieces in the collection may seem useless, but they may be important. Often the brain collects and discards information without regard to our wishes. Out of the collection may arise, with no warning, the image of windblown whitecaps on a lake you visited more than five years ago, the recipe for Uncle Joe's incomparable chili (which you needed last week), or even the right answer to an exam question you've been staring at for the past fifteen minutes.

Remembering is sometimes easy, sometimes difficult. Often careful concentration yields nothing, while the most trivial occurrence—an old song on someone else's car radio, the acrid smell of diesel truck exhaust, the face of a stranger—will trigger a flood of recollections. Someone tells a story and you immediately recall incidents, funny or traumatic, from your own life. Some memories, however, are nagging and troublesome, keeping you awake at night, daring you to deal with them. You pick at these memories. . . . Why are they so important? You write about them, usually to probe that mystery of yesterday and today. Sights, sounds, or feelings from the present may draw you to the past, but the past leads, just as surely, back to the present.

Direct observations are important to learning and writing, but so are your memories, experiences, and stories. You may write an autobiographical account of part of your life or you may recall a brief event, a person, or a place just as an example to illustrate a point. Whatever form your writing from memory takes, however, your initial purpose is to remember information and experiences so you can understand yourself and your world. The point is not to write fiction, but to practice drawing on your memories and to write vividly enough about them so that you and others can discover and learn.

The value of remembering lies exactly here: Written memories have the power to teach you and, through sympathy with your readers, to inform or convince them as well. At first, you may be self-conscious about sharing your personal memories. But as you reveal these experiences, you realize that your story is worth telling—not because you're such an egotist, but because sharing experiences helps everyone learn.

FREEWRITING: FIRST MEMORIES

Turn to a blank page in your journal or open a computer file. What are your earliest memories? Choose one particular event. How old were

Time passes and the past becomes the present. . . . These presences of the past are there in the center of your life today. You thought . . . they had died, but they have just been waiting their chance.

—Carlos Fuentes, essayist, dramatist, and diplomat

you? What was the place? Who were the people around you? What happened? Write nonstop for ten minutes.

TECHNIQUES FOR WRITING ABOUT MEMORIES

Writing vividly about memories includes all the skills of careful observing, but it adds additional techniques that are described below. Not all writing about memories uses all five techniques, but often one or two of them will transform a lifeless or boring account into an effective narrative.

- **Using *detailed observation* of people, places, and events.** Writing vividly about memories requires many of the skills of careful observation. Give *actual dialogue* where appropriate.

- **Creating specific scenes set in time and space.** *Show* your reader the actual events, don't just *tell* about events. Narrate specific incidents as they actually happened. Avoid monotonously summarizing events or presenting just the conclusions (for instance, "those experiences really changed my life").

- **Noting *changes, contrasts,* or *conflicts*.** Changes in people or places, contrasts between two different memories or between memories of expectations and the reality, or conflicts between people or ideas will often lead to the meaning or importance of a remembered person, place, or event.

- **Making *connections* between past events, people, or places and the present.** The main idea of a narrative often grows out of the changes and conflicts or arises from the *connections* you make between past and present.

- **Discovering and focusing on a main idea.** A remembering essay is not a random narrative of the writer's favorite memories. A narrative should have a clear main point, focus on a main idea, or make a discovery. The essay should clearly show *why* the memories are important.

Using details, creating scenes, noting conflicts, making connections between past and present, and focusing on a main idea are all important techniques, but you should also keep several other points in mind. Normally, you should write in the *first person,* using "I" or "we" throughout the narrative. Usually, you will write in *past tense,* but sometimes you may wish to lend immediacy to the events by retelling them in the *present tense,* as though they are happening now. Finally, you may stick with a straightforward *chronological order*, or you may begin near the end and use a *flashback* to tell the beginning of the story.

The key to effective remembering, though, is to get beyond *generalities and conclusions* about your experiences ("I had a lot of fun—those days really changed my life") to *specific incidents set in time and place* which *show* how and why those days changed your life. The specific incidents should show your *main point* or *dominant idea*.

The following passage by Andrea Lee began as a journal entry during a year she spent in Moscow and Leningrad following her graduation from college. She then combined these firsthand observations with her memories and published them in a collection called *Russian Journal*. She uses first person and, frequently, present tense as she describes her reactions to the sights of Moscow. In these paragraphs, she weaves observations and memories together to show her main idea: The contrast between American and Russian advertising helped her understand both the virtues and the faults of American commercialism.

Specific Scene

In Mayakovsky Square, not far from the Tchaikovsky Concert Hall, a big computerized electric sign sends various messages flashing out into the night. An outline of a taxi in green dots is accompanied by the words: "Take Taxis—All Streets are Near." This is replaced by multicol-

Detailed Observation

ored human figures and a sentence urging Soviet citizens to save in State banks. The bright patterns and messages come and go, making this one of the most sophisticated examples of advertising in Moscow. Even on chilly nights when I pass through the square, there is often a little group of Russians standing in front of the sign, watching in fasci-

Connections Past and Present

nation for five and ten minutes as the colored dots go through their magical changes. The first few times I saw this, I chuckled and recalled an old joke about an American town so boring that people went out on weekends to watch the Esso sign.

Contrast

Advertising, of course, is the glamorous offspring of capitalism and art: why advertise in a country where there is only one brand, the State brand, of anything, and often not enough even of that? There is nothing here comparable to the glittering overlay of commercialism that

Main Idea

Americans, at least, take for granted as part of our cities; nothing like the myriad small seductions of the marketplace, which have led us to expect to be enticed. The Soviet political propaganda posters that fill up a small part of the Moscow landscape with their uniformly cold red

Detailed Observation

color schemes and monumental robot-faced figures are so unappealing that they are dismissable.

Connections Past and Present

I realize now, looking back, that for at least my first month in Moscow, I was filled with an unconscious and devastating disappointment. Hardly realizing it, as I walked around the city, I was looking for the constant

Contrast and Change

sensory distractions I was accustomed to in America. Like many others my age, I grew up reading billboards and singing advertising jingles;

Main Idea

my idea of beauty was shaped—perniciously, I think—by the models with the painted eyes and pounds of shining hair whose beauty was accessible on every television set and street corner.

Remembering People

In the following passage from the introduction to *The Way to Rainy Mountain*, N. Scott Momaday remembers his grandmother. Details of place and event are recreated, too, but the primary focus is on the character of his grandmother as revealed in several *specific*, recurring actions. Momaday does not give us generalities about his feelings (for instance, "I miss my grandmother a lot, especially now that she's gone"); instead, he begins with specific memories of scenes that show how he felt.

> Now that I can have her only in memory, I see my grandmother in the several postures that were peculiar to her: standing at the wood stove on a winter morning and turning meat in a great iron skillet; sitting at the south window, bent above her beadwork, and afterwards, when her vision failed, looking down for a long time into the fold of her hands; going out upon a cane, very slowly as she did when the weight of age came upon her; praying. I remember her most often at prayer. She made long, rambling prayers out of suffering and hope, having seen many things. I was never sure that I had the right to hear, so exclusive were they of all mere custom and company. The last time I saw her she prayed standing by the side of her bed at night, naked to the waist, the light of a kerosene lamp moving upon her dark skin. Her long, black hair, always drawn and braided in the day, lay upon her shoulders and against her breasts like a shawl. I do not speak Kiowa, and I never understood her prayers, but there was something inherently sad in the sound, some merest hesitation upon the syllables of sorrow. She began in a high and descending pitch, exhausting her breath to silence; then again and again—and always the same intensity of effort, of something that is, and is not, like urgency in the human voice. Transported so in the dancing light among the shadows of her room, she seemed beyond the reach of time. But that was illusion; I think I knew then that I should not see her again.

Remembering Places

In the following passage from *Farewell to Manzanar*, Jeanne Wakatsuke Houston remembers the place in California where, as Japanese Americans, her family was imprisoned during World War II. As you read, look for specific details and bits of description that convey her main idea:

> In Spanish, Manzanar means "apple orchard." Great stretches of Owens Valley were once green with orchards and alfalfa fields. It has been a desert ever since its water started flowing south into Los Angeles, some-

time during the twenties. But a few rows of untended pear and apple trees were still growing there when the camp opened, where a shallow water table had kept them alive. In the spring of 1943 we moved to block 28, right up next to one of the old pear orchards. That's where we stayed until the end of the war, and those trees stand in my memory for the turning of our life in camp, from the outrageous to the tolerable.

Papa pruned and cared for the nearest trees. Late that summer we picked the fruit green and stored it in a root cellar he had dug under our new barracks. At night the wind through the leaves would sound like the surf had sounded in Ocean Park, and while drifting off to sleep, I could almost imagine we were still living by the beach.

Remembering Events

In "The Boy's Desire," Richard Rodriguez recalls a particular event from his childhood that comes to mind when he remembers Christmas. In his memory, he sorts through the rooms in his house on 39th street in Sacramento, recalling old toys: a secondhand bike, games with dice and spinning dials, a jigsaw puzzle, and a bride doll. In this passage, Rodriguez describes both the effort to remember and the memory itself, the one memory that still "holds color and size and shape." Was it all right, he wonders, that a boy should have wanted a doll for Christmas?

> The fog comes to mind. It never rained on Christmas. It was never sharp blue and windy. When I remember Christmas in Sacramento, it is in gray: The valley fog would lift by late morning, the sun boiled haze for a few hours, then the tule fog would rise again when it was time to go into the house.

> The haze through which memory must wander is thickened by that fog. The rooms of the house on 39th Street are still and dark in late afternoon, and I open the closet to search for old toys. One year there was a secondhand bike. I do not remember a color. Perhaps it had no color even then. Another year there were boxes of games that rattled their parts—dice and pegs and spinning dials. Or perhaps the rattle is of a jigsaw puzzle that compressed into an image . . . of what? of Paris? a litter of kittens? I cannot remember. Only one memory holds color and size and shape: brown hair, blue eyes, the sweet smell of styrene.

> That Christmas I announced I wanted a bride doll. I must have been seven or eight—wise enough to know not to tell anyone at school, but young enough to whine out my petition from early November.

> My father's reaction was unhampered by psychology. A shrug—*"Una muñeca?"*—a doll, why not? Because I knew it was my mother who would choose all the presents, it was she I badgered. I wanted a bride doll! "Is there something else you want?" she wondered. No! I'd make

clear with my voice that nothing else would appease me, "We'll see," she'd say, and she never wrote it down on her list.

By early December, wrapped boxes started piling up in my parents' bedroom closet, above my father's important papers and the family album. When no one else was home, I'd drag a chair over and climb up to see . . . Looking for the *one*. About a week before Christmas, it was there. I was so certain it was mine that I punched my thumb through the wrapping paper and the cellophane window on the box and felt inside—lace, two tiny, thin legs.

I got other presents that year, but it was the doll I kept by me. I remember my mother saying I'd have "to share her" with my younger sister—but Helen was four years old, oblivious. The doll was mine. My arms would hold her. She would sleep on my pillow.

And the sky did not fall. The order of the universe did not tremble. In fact, it was right for a change. My family accommodated itself to my request. My brother and sisters played round me with their own toys. I paraded my doll by the hands across the floor.

The other day, when I asked my brother and sisters about the doll, no one remembered. My mother remembers. "Yes," she smiled. "One year there was a doll."

The closet door closes. (The house on 39th Street has been razed for a hospital parking lot.) The fog rises. Distance tempts me to mock the boy and his desire. The fact remains: One Christmas in Sacramento I wanted a bride doll, and I got one.

WARMING UP: JOURNAL EXERCISES

The following topics will help you practice writing about your memories. Read all of the following exercises, and then write on three that interest you the most. If another idea occurs to you, write a free entry about it.

1. Select one moment in your past that changed your life or showed you how your life had already changed. What was the event? What were you like before it and afterward?

2. Go through old family photographs and find one of yourself, taken at least five years ago. Describe the person in the photograph—what he or she did, thought, said, or hoped. How is that person like or unlike the person you are now?

Some very small incident that takes place today may be the most important event that happens to you this year, but you don't know that when it happens. You don't know it until much later.

—*Toni Morrison, author of* Song of Solomon *and other novels*

3. Remember a place, a sanctuary, where you used to go to be alone. What was it like? When did you go there? Have you been back there recently? If so, how had it (or you) changed?

4. Remember the first job you had. How did you get it, and what did you do? What mistakes did you make? What did you learn? Were there any humorous or serious misunderstandings between you and others?

5. You and a friend are trading stories about sensitive times in your lives. You want to tell a story about a particularly embarrassing or sensitive moment, but you don't want your friend's sympathy. So you decide to tell the story through some imaginary person. You change a few details about the story so your friend won't recognize you, but the basic story is still yours. Using the third person, write the story you'd tell your friend.

6. Pick a favorite record from your collection and play one track of it. As you listen, write down the associations or memories that come to mind. What were you doing when you first heard the song? What other people, places, or events does it remind you of?

7. Reread your freewriting exercise from the beginning of this chapter. Then call members of your family and interview them for their memories of this incident. How does what you actually remember differ from what your family has told you about that incident? Revise your first memory to incorporate additional details provided by your family.

8. Go to a restaurant, cafeteria, or grocery store and find some specific food—fruit, cereal, soup, soda, meat, vegetable, or dessert—something that you either loved or absolutely detested but haven't eaten in years. Eat this food and then record the associations or memories that come to mind. What did you used to do when you ate this food? Who was there when you ate it? Where were you when you ate it?

9. At some point in the past you may have faced a conflict between what was expected of you—by parents, friends, family, coach, or employer—and your own personality or abilities. Describe one occasion when these expectations seemed unrealistic or unfair. Was the experience entirely negative or was it, in the long run, positive?

REMEMBERING: PROFESSIONAL WRITING

THE DAY LANGUAGE CAME INTO MY LIFE

Helen Keller

At the age of eighteen months, Helen Keller (1880–1968) lost her sight and hearing as a result of a serious illness. During the next five years of her childhood, Helen Keller became increasingly wild and unruly as she struggled against her dark and silent world. In "The Day Language Came Into My Life," Keller remembers how, at age seven, her teacher Anne Sullivan arrived and taught her the miracle of language. After learning sign language and Braille, Helen Keller began her formal schooling and—with continued help from Anne Sullivan—eventually graduated with honors from Radcliffe College. In her adult years, Helen Keller became America's best-loved ambassador for the blind and disabled. She met nearly every American president, traveled to dozens of countries to speak on behalf of blind and deaf people, and wrote several books, including The Story of My Life *(1903),* The World I Live In *(1908), and* Midstream: My Later Life *(1930). The story of Anne Sullivan's teaching is told in William Gibson's Pulitzer Prize-winning play,* The Miracle Worker.*

The most important day I remember in all my life is the one on which my teacher, Anne Mansfield Sullivan, came to me. I am filled with wonder when I consider the immeasurable contrast between the two lives which it connects. It was the third of March 1887, three months before I was seven years old.   (1)

On the afternoon of that eventful day, I stood on the porch, dumb, expectant. I guessed vaguely from my mother's signs and from the hurrying to and fro in the house that something unusual was about to happen, so I went to the door and waited on the steps. The afternoon sun penetrated the mass of honeysuckle that covered the porch and fell on my upturned face. My fingers lingered almost unconsciously on the familiar leaves and blossoms which had just come forth to greet the sweet southern spring. I did not know what the future held of marvel or surprise for me. Anger and bitterness had preyed upon me continually for weeks and a deep languor had succeeded this passionate struggle.   (2)

Have you ever been at sea in a dense fog, when it seemed as if a tangible white darkness shut you in, and the great ship, tense and anxious, groped her way toward the shore with plummet and sounding-line, and you waited with beating heart for something to happen? I was like that ship before my education began, only I was without compass or sounding-line and had no way of knowing how near the harbor was. "Light! give me light!" was the wordless cry of my soul, and the light of love shone on me in that very hour.   (3)

I felt approaching footsteps. I stretched out my hand as I supposed to my mother. Someone took it, and I was caught up and held close in the arms of her who had come to reveal all things to me, and, more than all things else, to love me.   (4)

The morning after my teacher came she led me into her room and gave me a doll. The little blind children at the Perkins Institution had sent it and Laura Bridgman had dressed it; but I did not know this until afterward. When I had played with it a little while, Miss Sullivan slowly spelled into my hand the word "d-o-l-l." I was at once interested in this finger play and tried to imitate it. When I finally succeeded in making the letters correctly I was flushed with childish pleasure and pride. Running downstairs to my mother I held up my hand and made the letters for doll. I did not know that I was spelling a word or even that words existed; I was simply making my fingers go in monkeylike imitation. In the days that followed I learned to spell in this uncomprehending way a great many words, among them *pin, hat, cup* and a few verbs like *sit, stand* and *walk*. But my teacher had been with me several weeks before I understood that everything has a name.   (5)

One day, while I was playing with my new doll, Miss Sullivan put my big rag doll into my lap also, spelled "d-o-l-l" and tried to make me understand that "d-o-l-l" applied to both. Earlier in the day we had had a tussle over the words "m-u-g" and "w-a-t-e-r." Miss Sullivan had tried to impress it upon me that "m-u-g" is *mug* and that "w-a-t-e-r" is *water*, but I persisted in confounding the two. In despair she had dropped the subject for the time, only to renew it at the first opportunity. I became impatient at her repeated attempts and, seizing the new doll, I dashed it upon the floor. I was keenly delighted when I felt the fragments of the broken doll at my feet. Neither sorrow nor regret followed my passionate outburst. I had not loved the doll. In the still, dark world in which I lived there was no strong sentiment or tenderness. I felt my teacher sweep the fragments to one side of the hearth, and I had a sense of satisfaction that the cause of my discomfort was removed. She brought me my hat, and I knew I was going out into the warm sunshine. This thought, if a wordless sensation may be called a thought, made me hop and skip with pleasure.   (6)

We walked down the path to the well-house, attracted by the

fragrance of the honeysuckle with which it was covered. Some one was drawing water and my teacher placed my hand under the spout. As the cool stream gushed over one hand she spelled into the other the word *water*, first slowly, then rapidly. I stood still, my whole attention fixed upon the motions of her fingers. Suddenly I felt a misty consciousness as of something forgotten—a thrill of returning thought; and somehow the mystery of language was revealed to me. I knew then that "w-a-t-e-r" meant the wonderful cool something that was flowing over my hand. The living word awakened my soul, gave it light, hope, joy, set it free! There were barriers still, it is true, but barriers that could in time be swept away.   (7)

I left the well-house eager to learn. Everything had a name, and each name gave birth to a new thought. As we returned to the house every object which I touched seemed to quiver with life. That was because I saw everything with the strange, new sight that had come to me. On entering the door I remembered the doll I had broken. I felt my way to the hearth and picked up the pieces. I tried vainly to put them together. Then my eyes filled with tears; for I realized what I had done, and for the first time I felt repentance and sorrow.   (8)

I learned a great many new words that day. I do not remember what they all were; but I do know that *mother, father, sister, teacher* were among them—words that were to make the world blossom for me, "like Aaron's rod, with flowers." It would have been difficult to find a happier child than I was as I lay in my crib at the close of that eventful day and lived over the joys it had brought me, and for the first time longed for a new day to come.   (9)

VOCABULARY

In your journal, write the meaning of the following words:

- I stood on the porch, *dumb* (2)
- a deep *languor* (2)
- with *plummet* and *sounding-line* (3)
- no strong *sentiment* (6)
- like *Aaron's rod* (9)

QUESTIONS FOR WRITING AND DISCUSSION

1. Write for five minutes, recalling your earliest memories with reading, speaking, or writing. Focus on *one specific incident*. How old were you? Where were you? What were you reading or writing?

2. Helen Keller's books have been translated into more than fifty languages. Explain why you believe her story, as illustrated in this essay, has such universal appeal.

3. In paragraph 3, Keller uses an analogy to explain her feelings and her state of mind before language opened her life. Identify the extended comparison. What "difficult concept" does Keller explain through her analogy?

4. In paragraph 8, Keller says, "Everything had a name, and each name gave birth to a new thought." Use examples of the *names* of things from your own life to explain what Keller means.

5. Contrast Keller's actions and feelings before she discovers language to her actions and feeling afterward. In addition to learning words, how do her feelings and personality change?

6. A century ago, when Helen Keller was learning to read and speak, people who were blind and deaf were classified by the law as idiots. Describe one experience you have had with a disabled person. Based on that experience, explain how Americans' attitudes toward people with some disability have (or have not) improved.

BEAUTY: WHEN THE OTHER DANCER IS THE SELF

Alice Walker

Alice Walker is the author of the Pulitzer Prize-winning novel The Color Purple *(1983), but she has written other works of fiction and poetry, including* Love and Trouble: Stories of Black Women *(1973),* Meridian *(1976), and* Revolutionary Petunias and Other Poems *(1973). "Beauty: When the Other Dancer Is the Self" originally appeared in* Ms. *magazine and was revised and published in her collection of essays* In Search of Our Mother's Gardens *(1983). Walker, a former editor of* Ms., *refers in this essay to Gloria Steinem and an interview published in* Ms. *entitled, "Do You Know This Woman? She Knows You— A Profile of Alice Walker." As you read the essay reprinted below, consider Walker's purpose: Why is she telling us—total strangers—about a highly personal and traumatic event that shaped her life?*

It is a bright summer day in 1947. My father, a fat, funny man with beautiful eyes and a subversive wit, is trying to decide which of his eight children he will take with him to the county fair. My mother, of course, will not go. She is knocked out from getting us ready: I hold my neck stiff against the pressure of her knuckles as she hastily completes the braiding and then beribboning of my hair.   (1)

My father is the driver for the rich old white lady up the road. Her name is Miss Mey. She owns all the land for miles around, as well as the house in which we live. All I remember about her is that she once offered to pay my mother thirty-five cents for cleaning her house, raking up piles of her magnolia leaves, and washing her family's clothes, and that my mother—she of no money, eight children, and a chronic earache—refused it. But I do not think of this in 1947. I am two-and-a-half years old. I want to go everywhere my daddy goes. I am excited at the prospect of riding in a car. Someone has told me fairs are fun. That there is room in the car for only three of us doesn't faze me at all. Whirling happily in my starchy frock, showing off my biscuit polished patent leather shoes and lavender socks, tossing my head in a way that makes my ribbons bounce, I stand, hands on hips, before my father. "Take me, Daddy," I say with assurance, "I'm the prettiest!"   (2)

Later, it does not surprise me to find myself in Miss Mey's shiny black car, sharing the backseat with the other lucky ones. Does not surprise me that I thoroughly enjoy the fair. At home that night I tell all the unlucky ones about the merry-go-round, the man who eats live chickens, and the abundance of Teddy bears, until they say: that's enough, baby Alice. Shut up now, and go to sleep.   (3)

It is Easter Sunday, 1950. I am dressed in a green, flocked scalloped-hem dress (handmade by my adoring sister Ruth) that has its own smooth satin petticoat and tiny hot-pink roses tucked into each scallop. My shoes, new T-strap patent leather, again highly biscuit polished. I am six years old and have learned one of the longest Easter speeches to be heard in church that day, totally unlike the speech I said when I was two: "Easter lilies / pure and white / blossom in / the morning light." When I rise to give my speech I do so on a great wave of love and pride and expectation. People in the church stop rustling their new crinolines. They seem to hold their breath. I can tell they admire my dress, but it is my spirit, bordering on sassiness (womanishness), they secretly applaud.   (4)

"That girl's a little *mess*," they whisper to each other, pleased.   (5)

Naturally I say my speech without stammer or pause, unlike those who stutter, stammer, or, worst of all, forget. This is before the word "beautiful" exists in people's vocabulary, but "Oh, isn't she the *cutest* thing!" frequently floats my way. "And got so much sense!" they gratefully add . . . for which thoughtful addition I thank them to this day.   (6)

It was great fun being cute. But then, one day, it ended.   (7)

I am eight years old and a tomboy. I have a cowboy hat, cowboy boots, checkered shirt and pants, all red. My playmates are my brothers, two and four years older than I. Their colors are black and green, the only difference in the way we are dressed. On Saturday nights we all go to the picture show, even my mother; Westerns are her favorite kind of movie. Back home, "on the ranch," we pretend we are Tom Mix, Hopalong Cassidy, Lash LaRue (we've even named one of our dogs Lash LaRue); we chase each other for hours rustling cattle, being outlaws, delivering damsels from distress. Then my parents decide to buy my brothers guns. These are not "real" guns. They shoot "BBs," copper pellets my brothers say will kill birds. Because I am a girl, I do not get a gun. Instantly I am relegated to the position of Indian. Now there appears a great distance between us. They shoot and shoot at everything with their new guns. I try to keep up with my bow and arrows.   (8)

One day while I am standing on top of our makeshift "garage"—pieces of tin nailed across some poles—holding my bow and arrow and looking out toward the fields, I feel an incredible blow in my right eye. I look down just in time to see my brother lower his gun.   (9)

Both brothers rush to my side. My eye stings, and I cover it with my hand. "If you tell," they say, "we will get a whipping. You don't want that to happen, do you?" I do not. "Here is a piece of wire," says the older brother, picking it up from the roof; "say you stepped on one end of it and the other flew up and hit you." The pain is beginning to start. "Yes," I say. "Yes, I will say that is what happened." If I do not say this is what happened, I know my brothers will find ways to make me wish I had. But now I will say anything that gets me to my mother.   (10)

Confronted by our parents we stick to the lie agreed upon. They place me on a bench on the porch and I close my left eye while they examine the right. There is a tree growing from underneath the porch, that climbs past the railing to the roof. It is the last thing my right eye sees. I watch as its trunk, its branches, and then its leaves are blotted out by the rising blood.   (11)

I am in shock. First there is intense fever, which my father tries to break using lily leaves bound around my head. Then there are chills: my mother tries to get me to eat soup. Eventually, I do not know how, my parents learn what has happened. A week after the "accident" they take me to see a doctor. "Why did you wait so long to come?" he asks, looking into my eye and shaking his head. "Eyes are sympathetic," he says. "If one is blind, the other will likely become blind too."   (12)

This comment of the doctor's terrifies me. But it is really how I look that bothers me most. Where the BB pellet struck there is a glob of whitish scar tissue, a hideous cataract, on my eye. Now when I stare at people—a favorite pastime, up to now—they will stare back. Not at the "cute" little girl, but at her scar. For six years I do not stare at anyone because I do not raise my head.   (13)

Years later, in the throes of a mid-life crisis, I ask my mother and sister whether I changed after the "accident." "No," they say, puzzled. "What do you mean?"   (14)
What do I mean?   (15)

I am eight, and for the first time, doing poorly in school, where I have been something of a whiz since I was four. We have just moved to the place where the "accident" occurred. We do not know any of the people around us because this is a different county. The only time I see the friends I knew is when we go back to our old church. The new school is the former state penitentiary. It is a large stone building, cold and drafty, crammed to overflowing with boisterous, ill-disciplined children. On the third floor there is a huge circular imprint of some partition that has been torn out.   (16)
"What used to be here?" I ask a sullen girl next to me on our way past it to lunch.   (17)
"The electric chair," says she.   (18)
At night I have nightmares about the electric chair, and about all the people reputedly "fried" in it. I am afraid of the school, where all the students seem to be budding criminals.   (19)
"What's the matter with your eye?" they ask, critically.   (20)
When I don't answer (I cannot decide whether it was an "accident" or not), they shove me, insist on a fight.   (21)
My brother, the one who created the story about the wire, comes to my rescue. But then brags so much about "protecting" me, I become sick.   (22)
After months of torture at the school, my parents decide to send me back to our old community to my old school. I live with my grandparents and the teacher they board. But there is no room for Phoebe, my cat. By the time my grandparents decide there *is* room, and I ask for my cat, she cannot be found. Miss Yarborough, the boarding teacher, takes me under her wing, and begins to teach me to play the piano. But soon she marries an African—a "prince," she says—and is whisked away to his continent.   (23)
At my old school there is at least one teacher who loves me. She is the teacher who "knew me before I was born" and bought my first baby clothes. It is she who makes my life bearable. It is her presence that finally helps me turn on the one child at the school who continually calls me "one-eyed bitch." One day I simply grab him by his coat

and beat him until I am satisfied. It is my teacher who tells me my mother is ill.   (24)

My mother is lying in bed in the middle of the day, something I have never seen. She is in too much pain to speak. She has an abscess in her ear. I stand looking down on her, knowing that if she dies, I cannot live. She is being treated with warm oils and hot bricks held against her cheek. Finally a doctor comes. But I must go back to my grandparents' house. The weeks pass, but I am hardly aware of it. All I know is that my mother might die, my father is not so jolly, my brothers still have their guns, and I am the one sent away from home.   (25)

"You did not change," they say.   (26)

Did I imagine the anguish of never looking up?   (27)

I am twelve. When relatives come to visit I hide in my room. My cousin Brenda, just my age, whose father works in the post office and whose mother is a nurse, comes to find me. "Hello," she says. And then she asks, looking at my recent school picture which I did not want taken, and on which the "glob" as I think of it is clearly visible, "You still can't see out of that eye?"   (28)

"No," I say, and flop back on the bed over my book.   (29)

That night, as I do almost every night, I abuse my eye. I rant and rave at it, in front of the mirror. I plead with it to clear up before morning. I tell it I hate and despise it. I do not pray for sight. I pray for beauty.   (30)

"You did not change," they say.   (31)

I am fourteen and baby-sitting for my brother Bill who lives in Boston. He is my favorite brother and there is a strong bond between us. Understanding my feelings of shame and ugliness, he and his wife take me to a local hospital where the "glob" is removed by a doctor named O. Henry. There is still a small bluish crater where the scar tissue was, but the ugly white stuff is gone. Almost immediately I become a different person from the girl who does not raise her head. Or so I think. Now that I've raised my head, I win the boyfriend of my dreams. Now that I've raised my head, I have plenty of friends. Now that I've raised my head, classwork comes from my lips as faultlessly as Easter speeches did, and I leave high school as valedictorian, most popular student and *queen*, hardly believing my luck. Ironically, the girl who was voted most beautiful in our class (and was) was later shot twice through the chest by a male companion, using a "real" gun, while she was pregnant. But that's another story in itself. Or, is it?   (32)

"You did not change," they say.   (33)

It is now thirty years since the "accident." A beautiful journalist comes to visit and to interview me. She is going to write a cover story for her magazine that focuses on my last book. "Decide how you want to look on the cover," she says. "Glamorous, or whatever."   (34)

Never mind "glamorous," it is the "whatever" that I hear. Suddenly all I can think of is whether I will get enough sleep the night before the photography session: if I don't, my eye will be tired and wander, as blind eyes will.   (35)

At night in bed with my lover I think up reasons why I should not appear on the cover of a magazine. "My meanest critics will say I've sold out," I say. "My family will now realize I write scandalous books."   (36)

But what's the real reason you don't want to do this?" he asks.   (37)

"Because in all probability," I say in a rush, "My eye won't be straight."   (38)

"It will be straight enough," he says. Then, "Besides, I thought you'd made your peace with that."   (39)

And I suddenly remember that I have.   (40)

I remember:

I am talking to my brother Jimmy, asking if he remembers anything unusual about the day I was shot. He does not know I consider that day the last time my father, with his sweet home remedy of cool lily leaves, "chose" me, and that I suffered and raged inside because of this. "Well," he says, "all I remember is standing by the side of the highway with Daddy, trying to flag down a car. A white man stopped, but when Daddy said he needed somebody to take his little girl to the doctor, he drove off."   (41)

I remember:

I am in the desert for the first time. I fall totally in love with it. I am so overwhelmed by its beauty, I confront for the first time, consciously, the meaning of the doctor's words years ago: "Eyes are sympathetic. If one is blind, the other will likely become blind too." I realize I have dashed about the world madly, looking at this, looking at that, storing up images against the fading of the light. *But I might have missed seeing the desert!* The shock of that possibility—and gratitude for over twenty-five years of sight—sends me literally to my knees. Poem after poem comes—which is perhaps how poets pray.

On Sight

I am so thankful I have seen
The Desert
And the creatures in the desert
And the desert Itself.

The desert has its own moon
Which I have seen
With my own eye
There is no flag on it.

Trees of the desert have arms
All of which are always up
That is because the moon is up
The sun is up
Also the sky
The stars
Clouds
None with flags.
If there *were* flags, I doubt
the trees would point.
Would you? (42)

But mostly, I remember this:

I am twenty-seven, and my baby daughter is almost three. Since her birth I have worried over her discovery that her mother's eyes are different from other people's. Will she be embarrassed? I wonder. What will she say? Every day she watches a television program called "Big Blue Marble." It begins with a picture of the earth as it appears from the moon. It is bluish, a little battered-looking, but full of light, with whitish clouds swirling around it. Every time I see it I weep with love, as if it is a picture of Grandma's house. One day when I am putting Rebecca down for her nap, she suddenly focuses on my eye. Something inside me cringes, gets ready to try to protect myself. All children are cruel about physical differences, I know from experience, and that they don't always mean to be is another matter. I assume Rebecca will be the same.   (43)

But no-o-o-o. She studies my face intently as we stand, her inside and me outside her crib. She even holds my face maternally between her dimpled little hands. Then, looking every bit as serious and lawyerlike as her father, she says, as if it may just possibly have slipped my attention: "Mommy, there's a *world* in your eye." (As in, "Don't be alarmed, or do anything crazy.") And then, gently, but with great interest: "Mommy, where did you *get* that world in your eye?"   (44)

For the most part, the pain left then. (So what if my brothers grew up to buy even more powerful pellet guns for their sons and to carry real guns themselves. So what if a young "Morehouse man" once nearly fell off the steps of Trevor Arnett Library because he thought my eyes were blue.) Crying and laughing I ran to the bathroom, while Rebecca mumbled and sang herself off to sleep. Yes indeed, I realized, looking into the mirror. There *was* a world in my eye. And I saw that it was possible to love it; that in fact, for all it had taught me, of shame and anger and inner vision, I *did* love it. Even to see it drifting out of orbit in boredom, or rolling up out of fatigue, not to mention floating back at attention in excitement (bearing witness, a friend has called it), deeply suitable to my personality, and even characteristic of me.   (45)

That night I dream I am dancing to Stevie Wonder's song "Always" (the name of the song is really "As," but I hear it as "Always"). As I dance, whirling and joyous, happier than I've ever been in my life, another bright-faced dancer joins me. We dance and kiss each other and hold each other through the night. The other dancer has obviously come through all right, as I have done. She is beautiful, whole and free. And she is also me.   (46)

VOCABULARY

In your journal, write the meaning of the following words.

- a *subversive* wit   (1)
- rustling their new *crinolines*   (4)
- Eyes are *sympathetic*   (12)
- a hideous *cataract*   (13)
- *boisterous*, ill-disciplined children   (16)
- bearing *witness*   (45)

QUESTIONS FOR WRITING AND DISCUSSION

1. Why does Alice Walker share this story with us? What memories from your own life did her story trigger? Write them down.
2. What does Walker discover or learn about herself? As a reader, what did you learn about your own experiences by reading this essay?
3. Reread the essay, looking for examples of the following techniques for writing about memories: (1) using detailed observations; (2) creating specific scenes; (3) noting changes, contrasts,

or conflicts; and (4) seeing relationships between past and present. In your opinion, which of these techniques does she use most effectively?

4. What is Walker's main idea in this autobiographical account? State it in your own words. Where in the essay does she state it most explicitly?

5. How many scenes or episodes does Walker retell? List them according to her age at the time. Explain how each episode relates to her main idea.

6. Walker also uses images of sight and blindness to organize her essay. The story begins with a description of her father who has "beautiful eyes" and ends with her dancing in her dream to a song by Stevie Wonder. Catalogue the images of sight and blindness from each scene or episode. Explain how, taken together, these images reinforce Walker's main idea.

7. Walker writes her essay in the present tense, and she uses italics to emphasize ideas and to indicate the difference between past thoughts and events and the present. List the places where she uses italics. Explain how the italicized passages reinforce her main point.

REMEMBERING: THE WRITING PROCESS

ASSIGNMENT FOR REMEMBERING

Write an essay about an important person, place, and/or event in your life. Your purpose is to recall and then use specific examples that *recreate* this memory and *show why* it is so important to you.

As you begin writing, assume that you are writing for yourself or for a small audience of good friends who are interested in your life. Let your writing recreate the experience vividly enough so that your readers can see the main idea that you wish to convey.

Choosing a Subject

If one of the journal entries suggested a possible subject, try the collecting and shaping strategies below. If none of those exercises led to an interesting subject, consider the following ideas:

- Interview (in person or over the phone) your parents, a brother or sister, or a close friend. What events or experiences do they remember that were important to you?

- Get out a map of your town, city, state, or country and spend a few minutes doing an inventory of places you have been. Make a list of trips you have taken, with dates and years. Which of those places is the most memorable for you?

- Dig out a school yearbook and look through the pictures and the inscriptions that your classmates wrote. Whom do you remember most clearly? What events do you recall most vividly?

- Go to the library and look through news magazines or newspapers from five to ten years ago. What were the most important events of those years? What do you remember about them? Where were you and what were you doing when these events occurred? Which events had the largest impact on your life?

- Choose an important moment in your life, but write from the *point of view* of another person—a friend, family member, or stranger who was present. Let this person narrate the events that happened to you.

  Note: Avoid choosing overly emotional topics such as the recent death of a close friend or family member. If you are too close to your subject, responding to your reader's revision suggestions may be difficult. Ask yourself if you can emotionally distance yourself from that subject. If you received a C for that essay, would you feel devastated?

Collecting

Once you have chosen a subject for your essay, try the following collecting strategies:

Memory is more indelible than ink.

—Anita Loos, author of Kiss Hollywood Goodbye

Brainstorming Brainstorming is merely jotting down anything and everything that comes to mind that is remotely connected to your subject: words, phrases, images, or complete thoughts. You can brainstorm by yourself or in groups, with everyone contributing ideas and one person recording them.

Looping Looping is a method of controlled freewriting that generates ideas and provides focus and direction. Begin by freewriting about your subject for eight to ten minutes. Then pause, reread what you have written, and *underline* the most interesting or important idea in what you've written so far. Then, using that sentence or idea as your starting point, write for eight to ten minutes more. Repeat this cycle, or "loop," one more time. Each loop should add ideas and details from some new angle or viewpoint, but overall you will be focusing on the most important ideas you discover.

Being accused of theft— interrogated by police

The police stopped after we hit them with snowballs

Gordon Sapp sat on my head after school

Finding the treasure

Falling out of a tree

The great ice storm and broken trees

Childhood Memories

The Saturday hiking club

The rusted machete

My sister cut her leg one night – 6 stitches

Playing kick-the-can summer evenings

Catching fireflies for 1¢ each

Catching jumping spiders in the basement

Trying to kill a snapping turtle w/a .22 rifle

Clustering   Clustering is merely a visual scheme for brainstorming and free-associating about your topic. It can be especially effective for remembering because it helps you sketch relationships among your topics and subtopics. Your sketch of these ideas helps you see relationships between ideas or get a rough idea about an order or shape you may wish to use.

Shaping

First, reconsider your purpose; perhaps it's clearer or more definite since your journal entry. In your journal, jot down tentative answers for the following. If you don't have an answer, go on to the next question.

- *Subject:* What is your general subject?
- *Specific Topic:* What aspect of your subject are you interested in?
- *Purpose:* Why is this topic interesting or important to you or your readers?
- *Main idea:* What might your main idea be?
- *Audience:* For whom are you writing this? What is your reader like, and why might he or she be interested in this topic?

Narrow and focus your subject. If you're going to write just a three-page essay, don't try to cover everything in your life. Focus on one person, one episode, one turning point, one day, even one *part* of one day, and do that in depth and detail.

As you start your shaping activities, use the observing strategies discussed in Chapter 2. *Spatial order* may help you shape your description of a place you are remembering; *classification* or *definition* can shape the people, places, or events you remember. *Similes, metaphors,* and *analogies* will make your writing more vivid, and they may also suggest a shape or help you develop your subject.

In addition, use the following strategies for shaping written memories. Try each strategy to see if it works for your subject. Some strategies may not be appropriate, but others will work naturally, suggesting ways to shape and develop your writing.

Chronological Order   If you are writing about remembered events, you will probably use some form of chronological order. Try making a *chronological list of the major scenes or events.* Then go through the list, deciding what you will emphasize by telling about it in detail and what you will pass over quickly. Normally, you will be using a straightforward chronological order, but you may wish to use a flashback, starting in the middle or near the end and then returning to tell the beginning. In his paragraph about a personal relationship, for example, student writer Gregory Hoffman begins the story at the most dramatic point, returns to tell how the relationship began, and then concludes the story.

> Her words hung in the air like iron ghosts. "I'm pregnant," she said as they walked through the park, the snow crackling beneath their feet. Carol was looking down at the ground when she told him, somewhat ashamed, embarrassed and defiant all at once. Their relationship had only started in September, but both had felt the uneasiness surrounding them for the past months. She could remember the beginning so well and in such favor, now that the future seemed so uncertain. The all-night conversations by the bay window, the rehearsals at the university theatre—where he would make her laugh during her only soliloquy, and most of all the Christmas they had spent together in Vermont. No one else had existed for her during those months. Yet now, she felt duped by her affections—as if she had become an absurd representation of a tragic television character. As they approached the lake he put his arm around her, "Just do what you think is best, babe. I mean, I think you know how I feel." At that moment, she knew it was over. It was no longer "their" decision. His hand touched her cheek in a benedictorial fashion. The rest would only be form now. Exchanging records and clothes with an aside of brief conversation. She would see him again, in the market or at a movie, and they would remember. But like his affection in September, her memory of him would fade until he was too distant to see.

Comparison/Contrast   Although you may be comparing or contrasting people, places, or events from the past, you will probably also be comparing or contrasting the past to the present. You may do that at the beginning, noting how something in the present reminds you of a past person, place, or event. You may do it at the end, as Andrea Lee does in *Russian Journal.* You may do it at the beginning and the end, as Richard Rodriguez does in "The Boy's Desire." You may even contrast past and present throughout, as Alice Walker does in "Beauty: When the Other Dancer Is the Self." Comparing or contrasting the past with the present will often clarify the dominant idea of your own essay.

Image   Sometimes a single mental picture or recurring image will shape a paragraph or two in an essay. Consider how novelist George Orwell, in his essay "Shooting an Elephant," uses the image of a puppet or dummy to describe his feeling at a moment when he realized that, against his better judgment, he was going to have to shoot a marauding elephant in order to satisfy a crowd of two thousand Burmese who had gathered to watch him. The italicized words emphasize the recurring image.

> Suddenly I realized that I should have to shoot the elephant after all. The people expected it of me and I had got to do it; I could feel their *two thousand wills pressing me forward,* irresistibly. And it was at this moment, as I stood there with the rifle in my hands, that I first grasped the hollowness, the futility of the white man's dominion in the East. Here was I, the white man with his gun, standing in front of the unarmed native crowd—*seemingly the leading actor* of the piece; but in reality I was only an absurd *puppet pushed to and fro* by the will of those yellow faces behind. I perceived in this moment that when the white man turns tyrant it is his own freedom that he destroys. He becomes a sort of *hollow, posing dummy,* the *conventionalized figure* of a sahib. For it is the condition of his rule that he shall spend his life in trying to impress the "natives" and so in every crisis he has got to do what the "natives" expect of him. He *wears a mask,* and his face grows to fit it. I had got to shoot the elephant. I had committed myself to doing it when I sent for the rifle. *A sahib has got to act like a sahib;* he has got to appear resolute, to know his own mind and do definite things.

Voice and Tone   When you have a personal conversation with someone, the way you look and sound—your body type, your voice, your facial expressions and gestures—communicates a sense of personality and attitude, which in turn affects how the other person reacts to what you say. In written language, you don't have those gestures, expressions, or the actual sound of your voice, but you can still create the sense that you are talking directly to your listener.

The term *voice* refers to a writer's personality as revealed through language. Writers may use emotional, colloquial, or conversational language to communicate a sense of personality. Or they may use abstract, impersonal language to conceal their personality or to lend an air of scientific objectivity. *Tone* is a writer's attitude toward the subject. The attitude may be positive or negative. It may be serious, humorous, honest, or ironic; it may be skeptical or accepting; it may be happy, frustrated, or angry. Often voice and tone overlap, and together they help us hear a writer talking to us. In the following passage, we hear student writer Kurt Weekly talking to us directly; we hear a clear, honest voice telling the story. His tone is not defensive or guilty: He openly admits he has a "problem."

> Oh no, not another trash day. Everytime I see all those trash containers, plastic garbage bags and junk lined up on the sidewalks, it drives me crazy. It all started when I was sixteen. I had just received my driver's license and the most beautiful Ford pick-up. It was Wednesday as I remember and trashday. I don't know what happened. All of a sudden I was racing down the street swerving to the right, smashing into a large green Hefty trashbag filled with grass clippings. The bag exploded, and grass clippings and trash flew everywhere. It was beautiful and I was hooked. There was no stopping me.
>
> At first I would smash one or two cans on the way to school. Then I just couldn't get enough. I would start going out the night before trashday. I would go down the full length of the street and wipe out every garbage container in sight. I was the terror of the neighborhood. This was not a bad habit to be taken lightly. It was an obsession. I was in trouble. There was no way I could kick this on my own. I needed help.
>
> I received that help. One night after an evening of nonstop can smashing, the Arapahoe County Sheriff Department caught up with me. Not just one or a few but the whole department. They were willing to set me on the right path, and if that didn't work, they were going to send me to jail. It was a long, tough road to rehabilitation, but I did it. Not alone. I had the support of my family and the community.

Persona   Related to voice and tone is the *persona,* the "mask" that a writer can put on. Sometimes in telling a story about yourself you may want to speak in your own "natural" voice. At other times, however, you may change or exaggerate certain characteristics in order to project a character different from your "real" self. Writers may project themselves as braver and more intelligent than they really are. Or they may create a persona who is more foolish or clumsy than they really are, to create a humorous effect. This persona can shape a whole passage. James Thurber, a master of autobiographical humor, uses a persona—along with his chronological narrative—to shape his account of a frustrating botany class.

> I passed all the other courses that I took at my university, but I could never pass botany. This was because all botany students had to spend

several hours a week in a laboratory looking through a microscope at plant cells, and I could never see through a microscope. I never once saw a cell through a microscope. This used to enrage my instructor. He would wander around the laboratory pleased with the progress all the students were making in drawing the involved and, so I am told, interesting structure of flower cells, until he came to me. I would just be standing there. "I can't see anything," I would say. He would begin patiently enough, explaining how anybody can see through a microscope, but he would always end up in a fury claiming that I could too see through a microscope but just pretended that I couldn't. "It takes away from the beauty of flowers anyway," I used to tell him. "We are not concerned with beauty in his course," he would say. "We are concerned solely with what I may call the mechanics of flars." "Well," I'd say, "I can't see anything." "Try it just once again," he'd say, and I would put my eye to the microscope and see nothing at all, except now and again a nebulous milky substance—a phenomenon of maladjustment. You were supposed to see a vivid, restless clockwork of sharply defined plant cells. "I see what looks like a lot of milk," I would tell him. This, he claimed, was the result of my not having adjusted the microscope properly, so he would readjust it for me, or rather, for himself. And I would look again and see milk.

I finally took a deferred pass, as they called it, and waited a year and tried again. (You had to pass one of the biological sciences or you couldn't graduate.) The professor had come back from vacation brown as a berry, bright-eyed, and eager to explain cell-structure again to his classes. "Well," he said to me, cheerily, when we met in the first laboratory hour of the semester, "we're going to see cells this time, aren't we?" "Yes, sir," I said. Students to the right of me and to the left of me and in front of me were seeing cells; what's more, they were quietly drawing pictures of them in their notebooks. Of course, I didn't see anything.

"We'll try it," the professor said to me, grimly, "with every adjustment of the microscope known to man. As God is my witness, I'll arrange this glass so that you see cells through it or I'll give up teaching. In twenty-two years of botany, I—" He cut off abruptly for he was beginning to quiver all over, like Lionel Barrymore, and he genuinely wished to hold onto his temper; his scenes with me had taken a great deal out of him.

So we tried it with every adjustment of the microscope known to man. With only one of them did I see anything but blackness or the familiar lacteal opacity, and that time I saw, to my pleasure and amazement, a variegated constellation of flecks, specks, and dots. These I hastily drew. The instructor, noting my activity, came back from an adjoining desk, a smile on his lips and his eyebrows high in hope. He looked at my cell drawing. "What's that?" he demanded, with a hint of a squeal in his voice. "That's what I saw," I said. "You didn't, you didn't, you didn't!" he screamed, losing control of his temper instantly, and he bent over and squinted into the microscope. His head snapped up. "That's your eye!" he shouted. "You've fixed the lens so that it reflects! You've drawn your eye!"

Dialogue   Dialogue, which helps to *recreate* people and events rather than just tell about them, can become a dominant form and thereby shape your writing. You could possibly write a whole scene using nothing but dialogue, recreating an actual conversation. More often, however, writers use dialogue occasionally for dramatic effect. In the account of his battle with the microscope, Thurber uses dialogue in the last two paragraphs to dramatize the conclusion.

> "We'll try it," the professor said to me, grimly, "with every adjustment known to man. As God is my witness, I'll arrange this glass so that you see cells through it or I'll give up teaching. In twenty-two years of teaching botany, I—". . . "What's that?" he demanded. . . . "That's what I saw," I said. "You didn't, you didn't, you didn't!" he screamed. . . . "You've fixed the lens so that it reflects! You've drawn your eye!"

Title, Introduction, and Conclusion   In your journal, sketch out several possible *titles* you might use. You may want a title that is merely an accurate label, such as *Russian Journal* or "The Boy's Desire," but you may prefer something less direct that gets your reader's attention. For example, student writer Todd Petry uses the title, "The Wind Catcher," for his essay about his hat that appears at the end of this chapter. As a reader, what do you think about the title, "Beauty: When the Other Dancer Is the Self," that Alice Walker uses for her essay?

COMPUTER TIPS: COLLECTING AND SHAPING

1. To help generate similes, metaphors, or a recurring image you can use for your piece of writing, try the following exercise. Open a new file or access the file for your remembering essay. Complete the following sentence using one word from the following list. You may write more than one sentence if necessary.

   The _____ is
       (the person, place, or event you are describing)

(like)(unlike) _____
           (choose word from list)

because _____
       (finish sentence)
1. machine, computer, mixer
2. birth, death
3. cat, tiger, cockroach
4. tree, flower, seed
5. sunrise, darkness, cloud
6. sailboat, sports car, locomotive
7. sledgehammer, pulley, key
8. actor, trained seal, parrot
9. love, hatred

    Example: Hitting trash cans as I drove my car down the street was like being a giant high-speed *mixer*—in my rearview mirror, I could see grass clippings whirling in the air, blending with cereal boxes, milk cartons, wrappers, and bits of paper trash.

    The sentences you write may make sense or they may seem silly or outrageous, but these connections and free associations may lead to an image or an idea you can use in your account. The computer will allow you to write as much or as little as you need for each item.

2. If you are remembering an event, test your essay to see if a **flashback** might work. Open a file and brainstorm a list of specific incidents within the event that you want to write about. Arrange this list in chronological order. Now, use your MOVE feature to reorder the events in the list to create a flashback effect. Choose one crucial incident *near* the end and move it to the top of the list. See if you could begin your story at this point and then flash back to tell earlier incidents. You can then conclude your story with the incidents at the end of the list.

Introductions or beginning paragraphs take several shapes. Some plunge the reader immediately into the action, as Gregory Hoffman does, and then later fill in the scene and context. Others are more like Kurt Weekly's, announcing the subject—trash cans—and then taking the reader from the present to the past, to the beginning of the story: "It all started when I was sixteen. . . ." At some point, however, readers do need to know the context—the *who, what, when,* and *where* of your account.

Conclusions, similarly, are of several types. In some, writers will return to the present and discuss what they have learned, as Andrea Lee does in *Russian Journal.* Some writers end with an image or even a dream, as Alice Walker does in her essay. Some writers conclude with a dramatic moment, as James Thurber does, or with an emotional scene, as student writer Brooke Selby does in her essay on Kit Carson that appears at the end of this chapter. But many writers will try to tie the conclusion back to the beginning, as Richard Rodriguez does at the end of "The Boy's Desire": "The closet door closes . . . the fog rises." In your journal, experiment with several possibilities until you find one that works for your subject.

Drafting

When you have experimented with the above shaping strategies, reconsider your purpose, audience, and main idea. Have they changed? In your journal, reexamine the notes you made before the shaping activities. If necessary, revise your statements about purpose, audience, or main idea based on what you have actually written.

I start at the beginning, go on to the end, then stop.

Gabriel Garcia Marquez

Working from your journal material and from your collecting and shaping activities, draft your essay. It is important *not* to splice different parts together or just recopy and connect segments, for they may not fit or flow together. Instead, reread what you have written, and then start with a clean sheet of paper. If you're working on a computer file, you can start with your list of events or one of your best shaping strategies and expand that file as you draft. Concentrate on what you want to say, and write as quickly as possible.

To avoid interruptions, choose a quiet place to work. Follow your own writing rituals. Try to write nonstop. If you cannot think of the right word, put a line or a dash, but keep on writing. When necessary, go back and reread what you have previously written.

I always know the ending; that's where I start.

Toni Morrison

Revising

Revising begins, of course, when you get your first idea and start collecting and shaping. After you have a draft and some feedback from other readers, however, you need to distance yourself and objectively reread what you have written. Especially for this remembering essay, make sure your memories are *recreated* on paper. Don't be satisfied with suggesting incidents that merely trigger your own memories: You must *show* the people and events vividly for your reader.

Guidelines for Revision

- **Reexamine your purpose and audience.** Are you doing what you intended?

- **Revise to make the main idea of your account clearer.** You don't need a "moral" to the story or a bald statement saying "This is why this person was important," but the reader should know clearly why you wanted to write about that memory.

- **Revise to clarify the important *relationships* in your story.** Consider relationships between past and present, between you and the people in your story, between one place and another place, between one event and another event.

- **Close and detailed observation is crucial.** *Show,* don't just tell. Can you use any of the collecting and shaping strategies for observing discussed in Chapter 3?

- **Revise to show crucial changes, contrasts, or conflicts more clearly.** Keller's and Walker's essays illustrate how *conflict* and *change* are central to an effective remembering essay. See if their strategies will work in your essay.

- **Have you used a straight chronological order?** If it works, keep it. If not, would another order be better? Should you begin in the middle and do a flashback? Do you want to move back and forth from present to past or stay in the past until the end?

- **If you are using a chronological order,** cue your reader by occasionally using transitional words to signal changes:

    then, when, first, next, last, before, after, while, as, sooner, later, initially, finally, yesterday, today

- **Be clear about point of view.** Are you looking back on the past, viewing the events from the present? Are you using the point of view of yourself as a child or at some earlier point in your life? Are you using the point of view of another person or object in your story?

- **What are the key images in your account?** Should you add or delete an image to show the experience more vividly?

- **What voice are you using?** Does it support your purpose? If you are using a persona, is it appropriate for your audience and purpose?

- **Revise sentences to improve clarity, conciseness, emphasis, and variety.** (See handbook.)

The difference between the right word and the nearly right word is the same as that between lightning and the lightning bug.

—Mark Twain, *author of* The Adventures of Huckleberry Finn

■ **When you are relatively satisfied with your draft, edit for correct spelling, appropriate word choice, punctuation, and grammar.** (See handbook.)

POSTSCRIPT ON THE WRITING PROCESS

After you finish writing, revising, and editing your essay, you will want to breathe a sigh of relief and turn it in. But before you do, think about what problems you solved as you wrote this essay. *Remember:* One of your goals in this course is to discover your style of writing or composing. What approaches work best for you? And, just as important, what doesn't work? Take a few minutes to answer the following questions:

1. Collecting and shaping. Which strategies helped you remember incidents most quickly and clearly? What strategies most helped you to focus and organize your essay? What problems were you unable to solve?

2. Drafting and revising. What problems did you run into during your drafting? Where did you go back and reshape or redraft portions? Where did your workshop advice help most?

3. Was the writing process you used effective for this essay? Why or why not? Assuming that you had the *same* amount of time to work on this essay, what would you do differently?

4. Rereading your essay, what do you like best about your essay? What parts of your essay still need work? What would you change if you had another day to work on this assignment?

REMEMBERING: STUDENT WRITING

THE WIND CATCHER

Todd Petry

Todd Petry decided to write about his cowboy hat, observing it in the present and thinking about some of the memories it brought back. His notes, his first short draft paragraphs, and his revised version demonstrate how observing and remembering work together naturally: The details stimulate memories, and memories lead to more specific details.

<u>NOTES AND DETAILS</u>

<u>DETAILS</u>	<u>MORE SPECIFIC DETAILS</u>
Gray	Dirty, dust coated, rain stained cowdung color
Resistol	The name is stained and blurred
Size 7 3/8	
Diamond shape	Used to be diamond shape, now battered, looks abandoned
4" brim	Front tipped down, curled up in back
1" sweat band	blackish
5 yrs. old	still remember the day I bought it
4x beaver	
What it is not:	it is unlike a hat fresh out of the box.
What it compares to:	point of crown like the north star like a pancake with wilted edges battered like General Custer's hat
What I remember:	the day I bought the hat a day at Pray Mesa

First Draft

The Wind Catcher

The other day while I was relaxing in my favorite chair and listening to Ian Tyson, I happened to notice my work cowboy hat hanging on the wall. Now I look at that old hat no less than a dozen times a day without too much thought, but on that particular day, my eyes remained fixed on it and my mind went to remembering.

I still remember I had $100 cash in my pocket the day I went hat shopping. The local tack, feed, and western wear CO-OP was my first and only stop. Finding a hat to meet my general specifications was no big deal. I wanted a gray Resistol, size 7 3/8, with a 4-inch brim and diamond shaped crown. From there on, though, my wants became very particular. I took 30 minutes to find the one that had the right fit, and five times that long to come to terms with the hat shaper. Boy, but I was one proud young fellow the next day when I went to school sporting my new piece of head gear. I've had that windcatcher five years through rough times, but in a way, it really looks better now, without any shape, dirty, and covered with dust and cowdung.

Revised Version

THE WIND CATCHER

The other day while I was relaxing in my favorite chair and listening to Ian Tyson, I happened to notice my work cowboy hat hanging on the wall. Now I look at that old hat no less than a dozen times a day without too much thought, but on that particular day, my eyes remained fixed on it and my mind went to remembering.   (1)

I was 15 years old and had $100 cash in my pocket the day I went hat shopping 5 years ago. The local tack, feed, and western wear CO-OP was my first and only stop. Finding a hat to meet my general specifications was no big deal. I wanted a gray 4X Resistol, size 7 3/8, with a 4-inch brim and diamond shaped crown. I wanted no flashy feathers or gaudy hatbands, which in my mind were only for pilgrims. From there on, though, my wants became very particular. I took 30 minutes to find the one that had the right fit, and five times that long to come to terms with the hat shaper. Boy, but I was one proud young fellow the next day when I went to school sporting my new piece of head gear.   (2)

About that time, Ian Tyson startled me out of my state of reminiscence by singing "Rose in the Rockies," with that voice of his sounding like ten cow elk cooing to their young in the springtime. As I sat there listening to the music and looking at that old hat, I had to chuckle to myself because that wind catcher had sure seen better days. I mean it looked rode hard and put up wet. The gray, which was once as sharp and crisp as a mountain lake, was now faded and dull where the sun had beat down. Where the crown and brim met, the paleness was suddenly transformed into a gritty black which ran the entire circumference of the hat. This black was unlike any paint or color commercially available, being made up of head sweat, dirt, alfalfa dust, and powdered cow manure. Water blemishes from too much rain and snow mottled the brim, adding to the colors' turbidity. Inside the crown and wherever the slope was less than ninety degrees, dust had collected to hide the natural color even more.   (3)

After awhile, my attention lost interest in the various colors and began to work its way over the hat's shape, which I was once so critical of. General Custer's hat itself could not have looked worse. All signs of uniformity and definite shape had disappeared. The diamond shaped crown, which was once round and smooth, now bowed out on the sides and had edges as blunt as an orange crate. The point, which once looked like the North Star indicating the direction, now was twisted off balance from excessive right hand use. Remembering last spring, how I threw that hat in the face of an irate mother cow during calving, I had to chuckle again. Throwing that hat kept my horse and me out of trouble but made the "off balance look" rather permanent. As I looked at the brim, I was reminded of a three-day-old pancake with all its edges wilted. The back of that brim curled upward like a snake ready to strike, and the front had become so narrow and dipped, it looked like something a dentist would use on your teeth.   (4)

For probably half an hour I sat looking at the wear and tear on that ancient hat. Awhile back, I remember, I decided to try to make my old hat socially presentable by having it cleaned and blocked, removing those curls and dips and other signs of use. However, when a hat shop refused to even attempt the task, I figured I'd just leave well enough alone. As I scanned my eyes over the hat, I noticed several other alterations from its original form, such as the absent hat band which was born off in the brush on Pray Mesa and the black thread that drew together the edges of a hole in the crown. However, try as I

might, I could not for the life of me see where any character had been
lost in the brush, or any flair had been covered with cowdung.   (5)

QUESTIONS FOR WRITING AND DISCUSSION

1. Close observation often leads to specific memories. In the opening paragraph of the revised version of his essay, Todd Petry
   says that "on that particular day, my eyes remained fixed on it
   and my mind went to remembering." He then recalls the time
   when he was fifteen years old and bought his hat. Identify two
   other places where observation leads Petry to remember specific
   scenes from the past.

2. Petry chose "The Wind Catcher" as the title for his essay. Reread
   the essay and then brainstorm a list of five other titles that might
   be appropriate for this short essay. Which title do you like best?

3. Where does Petry most clearly express the main idea of his
   essay? Write out the main idea in your own words.

KIT CARSON

Brooke Selby

*In the following essay, Brooke Selby remembers an Easter
reunion that turned out to be a celebration of life in a small western town. As she wrote, Selby says, she tried to "paint a prose
portrait of a place which always held an almost spiritual 'special-
ness' for my family. I closed my eyes and tried to recall actual
snapshots from the day; I used those mental images as I searched
for the words to describe it."*

The town of Kit Carson is often omitted from Colorado maps. One
sees just a glimpse from the highway, a square cluster of peeling white
frame houses and dingy brown buildings, long bathed in the eastern
Colorado dust. To the two hundred and eighty persons who call Kit
Carson their home, it is the very center of existence, but to outsiders it
is a curious, tattered remnant from farming days: a slow-moving,
wind-blown apparition from the past.   (1)

The highway bisects Kit Carson, seeming almost an incongruity
amidst the time-worn face of the town. The only motel lies on the
northernmost edge, gaudy and commercial amidst the waving plains
grasses. From the road one catches a glimpse of a one room museum,

an old red brick drug store, some tired stone churches, rusted screen doors which lead into the musty quiet of the few surviving shops, some deserted buildings with splintered boards nailed across the windows . . . all this in a rapid blur like an old newsreel, flashed by too quickly to grasp any more than a vague impression of deteriorating quiet. Yet from the road, one sees also black windmills, the sentinels of surrounding farms, and huge fields, opulent with crops, so that one knows that there are those who still prosper in this town.   (2)

My mother was fifteen years old when she left Kit Carson. Times were hard and the farm's livelihood was not dependable enough to support a family of five, so they moved to Denver, with high hopes that an invention of my grandfather's would open the door to new prosperity and financial security. Yet in leaving Kit Carson, they left behind something which became to them a symbol of childhood, a place where innocence was not outdated, where the pace of life still permitted one time to be alone and to dream, and where one could go to escape when the pressures of job and existence became too overbearing. Even now, the mention of Kit Carson evokes nostalgic memories and a burning, longing homesickness among my mother and her brother and sister. The three have all instilled in their children the same sacred image of the town, the same craving to go home, to return to times less strenuous and demanding. It is a different sort of world—although not untouched by the insensitive and often callous times we live in, it remains still a sanctuary, where one can walk out onto the prairie, breathe as deeply as possible, and feel a rare sense of complete inner peace, as if even miracles are possible and God not far away.   (3)

There are those who cling yet to the town, like children clutching at their mother's skirts, certain that life elsewhere would be only a tarnished replica of life in Kit Carson. My great-grandparents are among these, their beings intricately woven within the fibers of the town's foundation. My great-grandfather will brook no criticism, disapproval, or even hinted dissatisfaction with his town, for it is "God's country" and "those big cities simply aren't fit for even animals to make their home." Outwardly, we scoff at Kit Carson's backwardness; inwardly we all feel its pull, yet we long for an actual confirmation of its magic, to prove to ourselves that it is not simply a land of dreams never realized. Easter brought us closer to this wish.   (4)

We left early that Sunday morning, being unable to afford the time to go for the entire weekend. There was just the slightest hint of winter's last lingering sighs, as we sleepily crawled into our car. The sun seemed indecisive, resolving first to stretch its healing arms out toward the dormant earth, but then withdrawing its offer, as if uncertain that the spring had truly yet arrived.   (5)

We spoke little on the trip, all caught up, I think, in our own thoughts and early morning sleepiness. We were restless, anticipating the celebration which lay ahead of us, as over fifty relatives gathered to mark my great-grandparents' sixtieth wedding anniversary. I stared lazily out the window, fixing my gaze on the telephone poles careening down the road, and struggling desperately against the fuzzy blanket of sleep which kept falling over my head.   (6)

We were met in Kit Carson with a warm and loving welcome, immediately swallowed up in the overflowing concern oozing from each corner of the crowded house. The house was afire with conversation, exclamations, greetings issued to new arrivals, fantastic smells drifting out from the kitchen, and love tumbling from and between every person. Naturally, the occasion centered on my great-grandparents, who beamed proudly at the house filled with their family and loved ones. Both were beautifully dressed for the day. My great-grandmother resembled a velvet, pale pink rose, fragile and perhaps a little faded, yet with pride's stiff spine keeping her ever strong. Great-grandpa was filled with nervous energy, rushing from one group to another and beaming so joyously that an ache rose inside of me at the thought that perhaps soon a photograph would be our only tangible recollection of that grin.   (7)

The day passed quickly in a blur of flashcubes, singing around the piano, and endless hugs, some from people I couldn't place. The afternoon was winding down, and many were beginning to talk of starting the drives back to their respective homes, when a young cousin ran into the house, shouting to my great-uncle that he should come outside immediately. He disappeared into the back, but shortly, two more young cousins came racing in, both eager to be the first to shout the news. My great-uncle, another romanticist, had several years earlier purchased ten buffalo and set them to graze upon his land, in an attempt to return that which rightfully belonged to the earth. Now one of the buffalo was having a baby and the young cousins were impatient that everyone should come to see.   (8)

Although a couple of the adults were skeptical at first, the house grew quiet as everyone streamed into the back. My uncle confirmed that one of the buffalo was indeed calving and that the wait would not be long. At first, we all stood, gazing out over the fence into the pasture, laughing and joking about the coincidence of the birth on Easter. Soon, however, we were all caught up in the drama unfolding in front of us. It was a loud silence, so full was it of anticipation and unspoken thought.   (9)

When a buffalo is in labor, it is on its own. As in the days of the early West, no veterinarian can make its task easier. To come near the animal would be to invite death for oneself or the newborn. It was soon apparent, however, that the mother buffalo was in serious trouble, and we stood in somber silence, voicing whispered prayers for the animals. It was as though a physical bond had those of us on the hillside tightly glued together, for we were straining as one, with frustration at our inability to aid the animals. My uncle paced nervously, almost certain that the birth was to be breech, for it appeared that the small calf's legs were emerging first. We waited what seemed an eon, squinting against the descending sun, and shivering from the slight breeze.   (10)

It was hard to distinguish calf from mother when it began to appear, for from the distance it looked almost as one. Suddenly, though, my uncle gave a shout, and we could see the tiny calf was born and was standing, leaning its weight against its mother. As one, we all began to cheer and shout and talk in hushed voices about the miracle we had just witnessed. We began to vie with one another for the selection of an appropriate name, and dozens of suggestions were tossed out. Finally, one aunt cried that we should christen it "Resurrection," in light of the occasion and its close brush with death.   (11)

Again quieted, we straggled back into the house and the prairie once more grew silent. I was the last to return inside and turned for one last glimpse of the newborn creature. In the twilight, the little calf was outlined against the prairie sky, still standing wobbly-kneed and shaky against the big mother buffalo. As I turned back around to return to the house, I saw spring's first flower, poking its head through the earth at the side of the building, and I was overwhelmed with the magnitude of what had just occurred. Kit Carson had confirmed its holiness, its magical potential as a place where miracles do not cease with growing up. I swallowed the lump in my throat and went inside.   (12)

QUESTIONS FOR WRITING AND DISCUSSION

1. Selby's essay is very much about human feelings and emotions. Stop and think for a moment. What specific feelings did you have as you read the essay?

2. Reread paragraphs 1 and 2. In terms of the rest of the essay, why does Selby spend so much time describing the *town* of Kit Carson for the reader? Is it necessary, or could it be deleted? Explain.

3. In writing about the remembered people, places, or events, writers should make the main idea obvious without overstating it. What sentences contain the main point Selby tries to make?

(How does paragraph 5, for example, contribute to that thesis?) In your opinion, is Selby's thesis stated too obviously, not stated clearly enough, or given just the proper emphasis?

4. Good writers do not rush a story. They carefully set up the scene, let events develop, and take the time to tell the most important events. Reread this essay. Where do you notice Selby keeping a steady pace, refusing to rush her story?

5. Choose the best paragraph in this essay and copy it into your journal. When you have finished copying the paragraph, reread it. What is it about the sentences that makes them effective?

5 | INVESTIGATING

Bill Martin
Abalone Shells
Courtesy of the artist

Your boss at the local self-service gas station where you work wants to expand the station's range of convenience items. Currently, you sell only snacks, such as soda pop, candy, and ice cream. Your boss asks you to find out what is sold at other gas-station convenience stores. Next, she wants you to design a survey for your customers, asking which items they would like to have the station carry. After tabulating questionnaires from thirty-five customers, you write a short report for the boss outlining what the competition stocks, how you designed your questionnaire, and what the responses from your customers indicate. □

While watching joggers running in the park one day, you notice their straining muscles, their labored breathing, and the grimaces etched on their faces. Why, you wonder, do people go through the pain of running? Does it have a physical or a psychological benefit? Or can it even become an addiction for those people who *have* to run every day? You decide to investigate this question in runners' magazines and professional journals and then interview a few serious runners to determine their motives and the effects running has on them, both physically and psychologically. The results of your report, you hope, will prove interesting to those who run as well as to those who merely watch others run. □

When you stop learning, stop listening, stop looking and asking questions, always new questions, then it is time to die.

—Lillian Smith, civil rights activist, journalist, author of Killers of the Dream

As the free press develops, the paramount point is whether the journalist, like the scientist or scholar, puts truth in the first place or in the second.

—Walter Lippmann, journalist and author

Investigating begins with questions. What causes the greenhouse effect? How does illiteracy affect a person's life? How does rape affect the lives of women in America? How is AIDS transmitted? How do TV rating systems work? How do colleges recruit applicants? What can you find out about a famous person's personality, background, and achievements? At what age do children first acquire simple mathematical abilities? What kind of employee is most likely to be promoted? Why are sunsets yellow, then orange, red, and finally purple?

Investigating also carries an assumption that probing for answers to such questions—by observing and remembering, reading sources, interviewing key people, or conducting surveys—will uncover truths not generally known or accepted. As you dig for information, you learn *who, what, where,* and *when.* You may even learn *how* and *why.*

The purpose of investigating is to uncover or discover facts, opinions, and reactions for yourself and then to *report* that information to other people who want to know. A report strives to be as objective and informative as possible. It may summarize other people's judgments, but it does not editorialize. It may represent opposing viewpoints or arguments, but it does not argue for one side or the other. A report is a window on the world, allowing readers to see the information for themselves.

FREEWRITING: INVESTIGATING YOUR OWN EXPERTISE

If you haven't done so already, write a personal "authority" list, naming subjects about which you have some expertise or information. Consider your hobbies, academic interests, occupational skills, friends and family members, social problems, community concerns, art, sports, travel, animals, films, TV shows, and so forth. Jot down a few words or phrases indicating what you know about each item on your list. Emphasize *what* or *who* it is, *how* it happens or *how* to do it, and *when* or *where* it happens. Since one of these topics may develop into an essay for this course, spend at least fifteen minutes on this exercise.

TECHNIQUES FOR INVESTIGATIVE WRITING

Curiosity is my natural state and has led me headlong into every worthwhile experience . . . I have ever had.

—*Alice Walker, author of* The Color Purple

Investigative writing begins with asking questions and finding informed sources: published material, knowledgeable people, or both. In most cases, collecting information in an investigation requires the ability to use a library and then to summarize, paraphrase, and quote key ideas accurately from other people's writing. In addition, personal interviews are often helpful or necessary. For an investigation, you might talk to an expert or an authority, an eyewitness or participant in an event, or even the subject of a personality profile. Finally, you may wish to survey the general public to determine opinions, trends, or reactions. Once you have collected your information, you must then present your findings in a written form suitable for your audience, with clear references in the text to the sources of your information.

Investigative writing uses the following techniques:

- **Beginning with an interesting title and a catchy lead sentence or paragraph.** The first few sentences arouse your readers' *interest* and focus their attention on the subject.

- **Giving background information by answering relevant *who, what, when, where,* and *why* questions.** Answering the *reporter's "Wh" questions* ensures that readers have sufficient information to understand your report.

- **Stating the main idea, question, or focus of the investigation.** The purpose of a report is to convey information as *clearly* as possible. Readers shouldn't have to guess the main idea.

- **Summarizing or quoting information from written or oral sources; citing sources in the text.** Quote *accurately* any statistics, data, or sentences from your sources. Cite authors and titles.

- **Writing in a readable and interesting style appropriate for the intended audience.** Clear, direct, and readable language is essential in a report. Use graphs and charts as appropriate.

The following reports illustrate three common types of investigative writing: the summary of a single book or article, the investigation of a controversial issue (using multiple sources), and the profile of a person. The three types may overlap (an investigation of a controversial issue may contain a personality profile, for instance), and all three types may use summaries of written material, questionnaires, and interviews. Some investigative reports are brief, intended to be only short news items, while others are full-length features.

The intended audience for each report is often determined by the publication in which the report appears: *Psychology Today* assumes that its readers are interested in personality and behavior; *Discover* magazine is for readers interested in popular science; and readers of *Ms.* magazine expect coverage of contemporary issues concerning women.

Summary of a Book Article

The following report from *Psychology Today* by journalist Jeff Meer summarizes information taken from an article by Charlene L. Muehlenhard and Melaney A. Linton that appeared in *Journal of Counseling Psychology*. Although the *Psychology Today* report summarizes only that one article, it demonstrates several key features of an investigative report.

Attention-Getting Title

Date Rape: Familiar Strangers

Lead-In Paragraph

By now, everyone knows the scenario. Boy meets girl, they go to a party, get drunk, return to his apartment, and he forces her to have sex.

Focus of Investigation or Report

Most people assume that date rape occurs on a first or second date between relative strangers. But new research supports a different conclusion: The individuals involved generally know each other fairly well.

Who, What, Where Questions Answered

Summary of Results

Psychologist Charlene L. Muehlenhard and undergraduate Melaney A. Linton asked more than 600 college men and women about their most recent dates, as well as their worst experience with "sexual aggression"—any time a woman was forced to participate in acts, ranging from kissing to intercourse, against her will. More than three quarters of the women and more than half of the men admitted to having an experience with sexual aggression on a date, either in high school or in college. And nearly 15 percent of the women and 7 percent of the men said they had intercourse against the woman's will.

Summary of Results

The researchers found that when a man initiated the date, drove to and from and paid for the date, sexual aggression was more likely. They also found that if both people got drunk (at a party, for example) and "parked," or found themselves in the man's dorm room or apartment, the date was more likely to end with the women being forced to perform against her wishes. Men and women who thought of themselves as having traditional values and those who were more accepting of violence were also more likely to have been involved in date rape.

Summary of Results

But contrary to what one might expect, date rape and sexual aggression were much more likely to happen between partners who knew each other. On average, students said they had known the partner almost a year before the incident. "If women were more aware of this, they might

Quotation

be less surprised and more prepared to deal with sexual aggression by someone they know well," Muehlenhard says.

Summary

She points out that communication is often a big problem on dates during which there is sexual aggression. Both men and women reported that the man had felt "led on" during such dates. Men said that women desired more sexual contact on these dates than had others on previous dates. Women said that they had desired less sexual contact than usual.

Muehlenhard believes that a direct approach, such as a woman saying   *Quotation*
"I don't want to do anything more than kiss," might clear up confusion better than simply saying "No."

Investigation of a Controversial Issue

A slightly longer report on "Type A" and "Type B" behavior, appearing in *Science85,* also illustrates the key features of investigating and reporting. In this article, John Tierney examines how two studies have called into question a frequent presumption: aggressive, impatient, and inflexible "Type A" men are prime candidates for heart attacks.

Type A's: Maybe Now You Can Relax

A quick summary for the Type A reader who doesn't have time to read this whole article:

Two new studies find that someone with a Type A personality—impatient, competitive, aggressive, easily angered—does not have an abnormally high risk of suffering a heart attack. These results are surprising and controversial. Some researchers speculate that it's safe to be Type A as long as you're not hostile.

Now, for the leisurely Type B still reading, some background. In the last several years, the Type A person has had plenty to worry about—not that this is unusual, of course. The Type A *always* has plenty to worry about. But only recently did the medical establishment add to his woes. Most researchers ignored the theory about A and B personality types long after it was proposed in 1959 by cardiologists Meyer Friedman and Ray Rosenman. The theory wasn't officially sanctioned until 1981, when the American Heart Association reviewed evidence of a disproportionate rate of heart disease among Type A's. It decided that Type A behavior should be classified as a risk factor for heart disease.

Last year Friedman further convinced the establishment with a study in which victims of heart attacks were trained to relax. These men were told to drive in slow highway lanes, pick out the longest line at the bank, play a game to lose, set aside time for doing nothing. Compared with a control group, the men who modified their Type A behavior suffered only half as many nonfatal heart attacks. Friedman, concluding that Type A behavior is the primary cause of heart disease, wrote, "We *know* now beyond any doubt what we suspected before."

But this year new doubts have arisen. A team led by Robert B. Case, a cardiologist at St. Luke's-Roosevelt Hospital Center in New York, analyzed the personalities of 516 heart attack victims and then monitored their health for up to three years. "We fully expected that the people who scored highest in Type A traits would have more heart attacks and die sooner," says Case. "Then we analyzed the data and found no relationship at all." This study impresses many researchers, but it's also been faulted because of how it measured Type A personalities. The subjects were asked to fill out a questionnaire about their habits and traits—whether they found it difficult to make time for a haircut, for instance, or whether they were more hard driving than their colleagues at work. This same questionnaire has been used in the past to link Type A's and heart disease (and it's cited approvingly by the American Heart Association), but some insist that Type A traits can only be measured accurately in an interview. Friedman and Rosenman say that it's crucial for an interviewer to observe telltale signs of Type A behavior, such as speaking rapidly, interrupting often, jiggling knees, clenching a fist, or grimacing.

But another study, scheduled for publication this fall, used interviews and also produced negative results. Richard Shekelle, an epidemiologist at the University of Texas, and colleagues studied 3,110 middle-aged men who had not suffered a heart attack but were considered prime candidates because of their blood pressure, cholesterol level, or cigarette smoking. Interviewers rated the men as Type A or Type B. Within eight years of the interviews, 129 of the men had heart attacks, and 62 died. There was no pattern: Type B's were just as likely to be stricken as Type A's.

It's possible, as many critics claim, that the interviewers weren't skilled at identifying Type A behavior. "But the fact remains," says Shekelle, "that several investigators are not finding an association of Type A behavior and heart disease, and we have to reassess the conventional wisdom." Both he and Case suspect the problem may lie in the definition of Type A. "It's too diffuse," Case says. "We're indebted to Friedman and Rosenman for pointing the way, but the time has come to focus on specific characteristics of behavior that are dangerous."

On hostility, for instance. Duke University internist Redford Williams and University of Maryland psychologist Theodore Dembroski recently found that a person's level of hostility and cynicism is a better predictor of heart disease than his overall level of Type A behavior. . . . "The kind of person at risk is someone who generally feels that other people are not to be trusted—that they'll lie and cheat if they can get away with it," says Williams. "It's the kind of person who, when an elevator doesn't come up from the floor below, immediately assumes people downstairs are holding up the elevator out of sheer inconsideration." This theory is gaining favor with scientists, although it does seem to provoke hostility in the fathers of Type A theory. "You can't dissect a human—you can't isolate hostility from other Type A traits," says Rosenman. Adds Friedman, "It's awfully hard to find a hostile man who isn't impatient. And an impatient man eventually gets hostile."

Any Type A who reads this far must be frustrated. Whom to believe? Is it really necessary to slow down? Perhaps the most soothing advice comes from Dembroski: "I suspect the danger is not a matter of being hard driving, hard working, quick to do things. It's how you go about it—whether or not you're hostile. Don't let things get to you."

Profile of a Person

The following passage is a profile of a person—a biographical sketch intended to give a sense of the person's appearance, behavior, character, and accomplishments. These paragraphs are part of a profile of Oprah Winfrey written by journalist Joan Barthel that appeared in *Ms.* magazine.

Here Comes Oprah!

A profile of Oprah Winfrey is not just the story of a survivor, though she obviously is one: besides that bottom-line day five years ago [when she wrote a suicide note], she's survived early adolescent years so troubled that she became a runaway and was nearly placed in a juvenile detention home.

Nor is it just a success story of a black woman who's made it in the white man's world of network television, though she's done that, too. At 19, she was anchoring the news in Nashville—the first woman, the first black. She worked for seven years in Baltimore, first paying her dues as a TV street reporter, "hating every minute of it," especially when she was required to ask a woman who'd just lost her children and her house in a fire how she felt. (When she didn't have the heart to do that piece, her boss told her to get it or lose her job. She came back to the studio with the story and, on the air live, apologized for it.) She did everything she was told, including trying to remake herself. "They told me my nose was too wide, my hair too thick and long, and they sent me to a place in New York to get my first perm. I felt the lotion burning my skull, and I kept saying, 'Excuse me, this is beginning to burn a little.' They kept saying, 'Oh, just a few more minutes.'" Within a week all her hair had fallen out. "You learn a lot about yourself when you're bald," she says now.

Nor is it even a rags-to-riches tale, though her dazzling condominium apartment (marble floors, four baths, including one with a gold swan as the tub faucet and another with adjoining sauna) is a glamorous world apart from the Milwaukee housing project where she spent part of her childhood. "I don't think of myself as a poor deprived ghetto girl who made good," she declares. "I think of myself as somebody who from an early age knew I was responsible for myself, and I *had* to make good."

Knowing did not always mean doing, though. Which is why a profile of Oprah Winfrey is, mostly, a look at a woman in process.

WARMING UP: JOURNAL EXERCISES

The following exercises will help you practice investigative writing. Read all of the following exercises and then, in your journal, write on three that interest you the most. One of these exercises may suggest an idea for your investigating essay.

1. Skim through your journal entries from the observing or remembering chapters. Is there some experience, memory, or observation you could investigate by doing additional reading or interviewing? Choose one subject and list the *questions* your investigation would answer.

2. Start a "curiosity" list. Make a list of subjects you are interested in and would like to know more about.

3. Page through the notebooks and texts from another course you are currently taking. What subjects mentioned in that class or referred to in the text might you investigate? Make a list of topics for investigation that would help you in that course. During that class, jot down any other suggestions that occur to you. The topics should not be an essay already assigned in that course, but they could relate to relevant background reading.

4. An editor for the college newspaper has asked you to report on typical student activities on campus using your own activities during one calendar week from the school year. Select a recent week and write a summary of your activities.

5. Find a recent issue of a magazine you like to read—*Time, Science Digest, Ebony, Newsweek, Sports Illustrated, Ms., Rolling Stone, Playboy, Glamour, Jet, New Yorker,* and so forth. Your purpose is to determine current trends in magazine advertising. Using only the full-page ads as your subject, collect at least three ads and take notes on their important features: use of color, design, personalities, sex appeal, slogans, technology, or whatever else recurs frequently. What conclusions can you draw from your investigations?

6. Next semester, you will be taking a course in your major field, but you aren't sure which professor you should pick. To investigate the differences among the teachers, interview several students who have taken this course from different professors. Prepare questions that encourage factual responses: How many papers or tests does the teacher require? What is the grade distribution? What textbook was required? What

was the reading or homework load? What were typical lecture topics? Was the teacher available outside of class?

7. As a member of the student governing board, your job is to solicit student opinions about some aspect of campus life that needs improving. Choose a subject such as dorms, classes, the library, parking, student clubs, the film or fine art series, or recreational opportunities. Then choose a question to focus your investigation and write a one-page questionnaire that you might distribute to students. (See the section on writing questionnaires in this chapter.)

8. Watch an investigative news show such as *60 Minutes* or *Nightline*, taking notes about the interviewer's techniques. Is there a sequence to the questions, from gentle and polite to critical or controversial? What information does the interviewer have *before* the interview? Can you tell which questions are planned or scripted and which are spontaneous? After taking notes on a show, explain what you think are the *three* most important tips for successful interviewing.

9. Interview a classmate for a 200- to 250-word "personality profile." Your object is to profile this person and *one* of his or her major interests. First, in your daybook, prepare questions you need to ask for biographical information. Then, in an eight- to ten-minute interview, ask questions about the person and about several topics from that person's "authority" list. After the interview, take two or three minutes to review your notes. At home, write up the results of your interview, which is to appear in your local or campus newspaper.

INVESTIGATING: PROFESSIONAL WRITING

THE TRIUMPH OF THE WHEEL

Lewis Grossberger

In this excerpt from an investigative piece that appeared in the December 1986 issue of Rolling Stone, *freelance writer Lewis Grossberger focuses on one question: Why has* Wheel of Fortune, *a television game show, become so popular that it has achieved cult status? In seeking an answer to this question, he considers several possibilities: Is it just an entertaining family game? Is its popularity due to Vanna White's skill in turning letters? Is its popularity a reflection of American cultural values? In the process of his investigation, Grossberger researches articles about the show's popularity, observes how* Wheel of Fortune *works, and interviews the show's key personalities.*

The first time I saw *Wheel of Fortune,* I thought it was a vapid piece of fluff that could appeal only to brain-dead TV zombies. Five minutes of this tedious dreck was all it took to waft me sleepward.   (1)

But the second time my reaction was different. The second time I realized—having been assigned meantime to write an article on the show that would bring a much-needed fee—that *Wheel of Fortune* was, in fact, a fascinating, deeply significant national phenomenon, the comprehension of which was essential to any proper understanding of our era.   (2)

Thank God I'm open-minded.   (3)

Soon I was wafting westward on an urgent sociophilosophical inquiry, clutching an envelope fat with press clippings that further impressed upon me the importance of my subject. *The Washington Post*'s TV critic said *Wheel* is watched by 42 million people a day. *Time* said *Wheel* is the highest-rated syndicated series in television history. *The New York Times* said *Wheel* is so popular it has become a dominant factor in TV scheduling, sometimes wreaking havoc with local and network news. *People* said that Vanna White has blond hair, weighs 107, measures 36-23-33 and adores greasy hamburgers from White Castle.   (4)

Vanna White is the hostess on *Wheel of Fortune,* which should not be confused with the master of ceremonies, who is Pat Sajak, although he is not called the MC but the host. Despite the fact that Vanna's function is mainly decorative and that she is rarely permitted to utter more than a parting "bye," she has become, *People* assured me, a bigger cult sensation than Paul Shaffer, Max Headroom or even Willard Scott.   (5)

The only thing the press failed to tell me was *why.*   (6)

Why a silly game show based on a simple children's spelling game and a cheezy carnival wheel so captivates the mightiest nation on earth. Now here was a journalistic challenge worthy of Murrow, of Woodward and Bernstein, perhaps even of the great Geraldo Rivera. Immune to the show's mysterious allure, I could operate with scientific detachment. By God, I would take up the gauntlet. I would find out why—or doze off trying.   (7)

"I swear on the grave of every game-show host who ever lived that I have no idea," said Pat Sajak.   (8)

Pat Sajak is overqualified for his job in that he is capable of wit. A former TV weatherman, he sounds a little like Bob Newhart and looks like . . . well, if Dick Clark went through that teleportation gizmo from *The Fly* and this time a chipmunk sneaked in, out would come Pat Sajak.   (9)

I talked with Pat Sajak in his dressing room and found him a personable and modest man who readily admits that game-show hosting "is kind of a dopey way to make a living." I talked as rapidly as possible. When I arrived at the NBC studios in fabled Burbank, the publicity lady who collected me said that the staff would be taping five half-hour shows that night and that I could examine Pat and Vanna only during the fifteen-to-twenty minute breaks between shows. She was very apologetic, but, you know, everyone wants them, it's so exhausting, we have to protect them. I groused a bit—journalistic reflex—but, in truth, it didn't matter. Both host and hostess had been asked to explain the *why* before. They never could.   (10)

"I mean, I know why it's successful," said Pat. "It's an easy game to play—you know, the people at home, unless you're a total moron, can generally solve the puzzles ahead of the people in the studio, so you feel kind of superior. It's a compelling game. You walk by the set and the puzzle's on and you tend to play along. But that just explains why it's a successful game show. Why it has gone beyond success to become—I don't know—part of the pop culture, I haven't the foggiest idea. I don't think anyone knows."   (11)

I assured him that I would know. Soon. For that was my quest. My Grail. He responded politely enough, but I could see he was skeptical. It seemed like we'd been talking only a few minutes when a pounding on the door commenced, and a voice demanded Pat's presence, and he went forth to hostify.   (12)

The *Wheel of Fortune* set looks like that of most Eighties game shows, decorated in feel-good Vegas Gaudy with bright splashes of color, flashing lights and revolving mounds of, as the announcer usually describes them, "fantastic prizes, fabulous and exciting merchandise." The studio audience of close to 200 well-behaved androids was stashed safely out of the way behind a sideline array of cameras, electronic gear, crew and staff.   (13)

The actual gaming consists of a word puzzle and, naturally, a wheel. Large, multicolored, divided into slim wedges, each marked with a different dollar amount, the wheel is set horizontally in front of the three contestants, so they can lean forward and spin it. By doing so, they may accumulate a dollar account to be later spent on prizes.   (14)

Between twirls, they take whacks at the word puzzle, which is basically that old childhood chestnut, hangman. The puzzle is mounted on a big vertical display board on a platform that's hauled on and off the set by crewmen at alarming speeds, usually with the coura-geous Vanna aboard. A display of blank tiles tells the contestants how many words and letters there are in a mystery phrase. As the contes-tants guess at the letters and Vanna rushes purposefully about, uncov-ering those correctly called out, the mystery phrase (usually some-thing as banal as "walking on air" or "curiosity killed the cat") gradually emerges until someone identifies it. The winner then may go shopping among the pricetagged prizes until his or her account is exhausted. At the end of the proceedings, the champion tackles a bonus-round puzzle for a grand prize.   (15)

During one break I was taken to meet the hostess. Vanna was in her dressing room, snacking from a take-out dish and wearing a snap-py off-the-shoulder number. (She changes costume and hairdo for each show.) She was very energetic and cheerful and was able to maintain, under close interrogation, not only that Vanna White was her real name but also that she had known four other Vannas while growing up in South Carolina.   (16)

A small-town girl, Vanna, who is not twenty-nine, drove to Hollywood in a U-Haul truck six years ago, because it was a child-hood dream. Hollywood, not trucks. After landing some bit parts in movies, she heard that *Wheel of Fortune* needed a new hostess, and she beat out 200 other young women, even though in her final on-air audi-tion she was so nervous her knees shook and she couldn't talk. Fortunately, speech was not a job qualification.   (17)

Laboring under the cloud of bimbosity imposed by the alternate-ly fawning and smirking media, Vanna told me what she always tells interviewers: "It's a lot harder than it looks. It really is."   (18)

It seemed to me the wrong tactic. Were I her media adviser, I'd counsel this approach: "Hey, I look great, I walk sexy. For this they pay me a hundred big ones and put me on the cover of *People*. I should turn them down? Is it my fault I live in a society that accentu-ates superficial values?   (19)

Too soon came the inevitable pounding, and Vanna vanished, leaving me back on the set, watching a woman named Ruth win a Toyota by guessing "League of Women Voters." I talked to a contes-tant from Fresno named Bill. Bill told me that his family watches *Wheel of Fortune* all the time and that he was so good at it his wife got after him to become a contestant. He did. But he hadn't won a Toyota, and he seemed a little tense.   (20)

I was not to meet *Wheel*'s biggest winner. Who is that? Why, Merv Griffin. Yes, the same Merv Griffin who has spent the last twen-ty-three years demonstrating what Johnny Carson would be like with-out jokes. Merv always did seem a bit dazed, as though his mind were on something else. Now we know what. Puzzles. It was Merv who invented *Wheel of Fortune*, hired Pat Sajak and Vanna White and still approves every single puzzle. It was Merv who recently sold Merv Griffin Enterprises, which produces *Wheel* (not to mention *Jeopardy* and *Dance Fever*) to Coca-Cola for—my fingers go numb as I type this—a reported $250 million. According to Tom Shales, TV critic for *The Washington Post*, Merv was rumored to have run around his office waving his quarter-of-a-billion-dollar check in the air, joking that he couldn't find anyone to cash it.   (21)

Puzzles. All this from puzzles. The man is a lifelong puzzle junkie. "You would think," said Sajak, "that a man who's worth $84 billion, or whatever he is, would have better things to do than make up puzzles—but he does. If you have lunch with Merv, the waiter comes over and says, 'May I take your order?' and Merv goes, 'Ooo! "May I take your order?" What a great puzzle!' and he writes it down."   (22)

People, we underestimated Merv Griffin. We dismissed him as some kind of welfare agency for the Gabor sisters. But Merv figured out what America wanted, and he provided it. And became very, very rich. Much too rich to talk to the likes of me. But Nancy Jones, *Wheel's* producer, a woman who actually has puzzle meetings with Merv, did. Her take on *why* was family. "It's a show the whole family can enjoy. Anybody from six to a hundred can watch *Wheel of Fortune*. They're gonna understand what's going on. You know, there are kids in college now that learned their ABC's by watching *Wheel*." Interesting, I thought, but not convincing. Not incisively all-encompassing. After all, there are plenty of family shows that don't have 42 million viewers.   (23)

If stats like 42 million or quarter of a billion haven't sufficiently defined the scope of *Wheel's* triumph for you, surely Pat Sajak's parking spot will. It was one away from Johnny Carson's. Now *that's* success. I discovered this when Pat gave me a lift back to my hotel, a nice gesture. But he voiced a depressing vision. "This could literally be a show that is never canceled," he said. "You know, my grandkid will be up there, spinning the wheel, saying silly things and putting on hair spray."   (24)

Considerably sobered, I retired and the next morning flew away. I'd already spent an evening on this investigation—in my view more than enough. Enroute to the airport, a chatty cabby pointed out an evocative sight: a new, exclusive real-estate development on a hill where, he said, the houses start at $1 million. The hill had previously served as a garbage dump, and the driver indicated a pumping station built to clear away the methane gas constantly seeping forth. So scarce is land in L.A. there had been no problem finding wealthy people to reside on top of Old Stinky.   (25)

Soon afterward I was on the plane, thinking about *Wheel of Fortune*, which, as always, acted as a soporific. I dreamed of the lovely

Vanna. She's in a terrific gold lamé jump suit, and she's starring in a big-budget disaster movie (a silent, oddly) about a gassy mountain threatening to explode and bury a nervous populace neck deep in putrid lava. Desperately trying to avert panic, Mayor Merv announces that the mountain, with its shining edifices concealing a rotten nether world, is merely a metaphor for an overly materialistic society, but then he whispers to me that only I can save the day—if I can complete this common, everyday phrase:

V__C__R_____S THR__LLS

Then Pat Sajak's grandkid spins the wheel. The pointer falls on BANKRUPT, and Swill Hill erupts, burying me neck deep in lethal sludge. I woke high over the Jersey swamps, and I had the answer. I knew *why*.   (26)

Vicariousness. *Wheel of Fortune* creates the illusion for the hard-working, treadmill-trotting Middle American yearner that he or she is in the big game. Viewers don't exactly identify with the contestants; they *become* the contestants.   (27)

Look at the elements of the show.   (28)

The Players: Wheel contestants are ordinary folk who serve as the viewers' surrogates. In the whoopee-cushion Seventies, game-show contestants screamed, bounced and wet themselves, but in the we-mean-business Eighties, Americans are cooler and less likely to appear in public dressed as yams. *Wheel* subtly de-emphasizes its contestants, who seem interchangeable. Pat introduces these undemonstrative, low-profile types with the briefest possible questioning, then the camera quickly moves off them and zooms in on the game. With the contestants relegated to the background, the viewer can put himself in their place and play. In your fantasy, you are the star.   (29)

The Game: Both games promise easy success, one through luck, the other skill. The wheel—hypnotic, alluring, symbolic of nearly everything—is luckier than a roulette wheel, since it can yield only two bad outcomes: BANKRUPT or LOSE A TURN. Any other spin wins. Nice odds. The word puzzle is simple but compelling—it gets easier as you play, because more letters fill in. As Pat Sajak noted, viewers often solve the puzzle before contestants. With the whole family watching, someone at home is almost bound to. The result: You feel happy, excited, superior. You're chalking up wins. You're on a roll.   (30)

The Payoff: During play, the wheel-whirling contestants (and, by extension, the viewers) are given credit. A nice touch. Who doesn't love credit? It's like betting on someone else's tab. And when you win, you don't win mere cash or some preordained prize. You go *shopping!* A brilliant touch. Shopping may be the ultimate thrill in this commod-

ity-crazed era, an actual addiction for some. And it doesn't hurt *Wheel* in the yuppie department, either. Merv himself once said, "It's like being let loose on Rodeo Drive." As the winner shops, the camera lovingly roves around the prize showcase, as though the viewers' own eyeballs have been let loose amid the VCRs, Isuzu pickups, Tahitian vacations and ceramic Dalmations. *Wheel*'s ambiance blends the organized excitement of the casino with the primal pull of the department store.   (31)

The Cast: Game-show hosts are permitters and forgivers. Their benign presence signals that it's okay to indulge your greed, just in case some shred of conscience or old-fashioned values intrudes to make you feel guilty for craving wealth without work. Pat Sajak is today's kind of authority figure: casual, low-key, jocular, even a bit irreverent. Dignified and well dressed, he could be a yuppie cleric, lawyer or doctor. He could switch jobs with Ronald Reagan and little would change.   (32)

And Vanna? Pat Sajak likes to say that Vanna's silence gives her a mysterious air. But there isn't any mystery. Her personality shines through without benefit of speech. She's a *cheerleader.* Your own personal cheerleader. Her most vital function is not really her letter turning (artistic though it is) but her clapping! She is forever clapping for the contestants (all of them—Vanna is impartial). When I asked if she'd been a cheerleader in high school, she said, "Of course. Who would have ever thought I'd still be a cheerleader?"   (33)

And that's *why.* Now you know. Let me just add, before taking a well-deserved nap, that I doubt that Merv and his minions set out to design *Wheel of Fortune* around the Big V Principle or analyzed the economy. I think they just happened, by instinct, experience—and good luck—to hit on a formula that would make it the state-of-the-art Eighties game show. A formula that sucks the viewer through the screen and into that dazzling dreamscape—Vanna's Nirvana—where he is transformed from a nullity, a hapless anonymous bozo, a nobody from nowhere, to the only being now worth being: a Winner. Someone possessed of wealth, luck and, maybe more important, television exposure. Someone, in short, who finally exists. You know, a big wheel.   (34)

VOCABULARY

In your journal, write the meanings of the following words.

- *vapid* piece of fluff (1)
- tedious *dreck* (1)
- take up the *gauntlet* (7)

- My *Grail* (12)
- well-behaved *androids* (13)
- *accentuates* superficial values (19)
- an *evocative* sight (25)
- acted as a *soporific* (26)
- *putrid* lava (26)
- shining *edifices* (26)
- rotten *nether* world (26)
- *vicariousness* (27)
- viewers' *surrogates* (29)
- *Wheel's ambiance* (31)
- *primal* pull (31)
- *benign* presence (32)
- Merv and his *minions* (34)
- Vanna's *Nirvana* (34)

QUESTIONS FOR WRITING AND DISCUSSION

1. Grossberg has several *purposes* in this article: *entertaining* readers; *informing* readers about Pat Sajak, Vanna White, the game show, and its reception in the media; and *explaining* why the show is so popular. Based on your own reading, which of these purposes did he accomplish most effectively? Which least effectively? Explain.

2. In collecting the information for this article, Grossberger used several kinds of sources: summaries or quotations from written material, information and quotations from interviews, and observations of people, places, and events. Find one example of each kind of source.

3. Reread the article. Then give paragraph numbers identifying the following parts of the essay (each part may have several paragraph numbers):

   Lead-in, catching the reader's interest   (_____)

   Main idea, thesis, or focus of investigation   (_____)

   Narrative of writer's investigative steps   (_____)

   Profile of key people   (_____)

   Observation of the set and the game   (_____)

   Analysis of the elements of the show   (_____)

   Conclusion   (_____)

4. As a freelance journalist, Grossberger creates a role, or persona, as he writes. Which specific passages most clearly reveal his real or assumed personality? Explain.

5. As the editor of *TV Guide,* you want to use an excerpt from Grossberger's article. To do so, you will need to cut this piece by two thirds and adapt it for the *TV Guide* audience. As you cut sections, consider your audience. How are readers of *TV Guide* likely to be different from the readers of *Rolling Stone?* (If you are not familiar with these magazines, look at current issues in your library.) What parts of this article will be most appealing to *TV Guide* readers?

THE HOMELESS AND THEIR CHILDREN

Jonathan Kozol

In his most famous book, Illiterate America *(1985), Jonathan Kozol says that because more than one third of America's adults are at least partially illiterate, we should organize a massive government and volunteer army to liberate people imprisoned by illiteracy. In "The Homeless and Their Children," taken from* Rachel and Her Children *(1988), Kozol investigates individual cases of poverty in a New York City welfare hotel. He uses his own observations and interview transcripts to demonstrate vividly the connection between illiteracy and poverty. Instead of arguing indignantly for literacy programs to save the lives of these poor and illiterate, however, Kozol simply reports the case of a single illiterate woman trying to raise her four children. The woman he calls Laura cannot decipher labels on products at the grocery store, cannot read notices from the welfare office, and cannot understand letters from the hospital warning of her children's lead poisoning.*

The Martinique Hotel, at Sixth Avenue and Thirty-second Street, is one of the largest hotels for homeless people in New York City. When I visited it, in December of 1985, nearly four hundred homeless families, including some twelve hundred children, were lodged in the hotel, by arrangement with the city's Human Resources Administration. One of the residents I spoke to at some length was an energetic, intelligent woman I'll call Kim. During one of our conversations, she mentioned a woman on the seventh floor who had seemingly begun to find her situation intolerable. Kim described this woman as "a broken stick," and offered to arrange for us to meet.   (1)

The woman—I will call her Laura, but her name, certain other names, and certain details have been changed—is so fragile that I find it hard to start a conversation when we are introduced, a few nights later. Before I begin, she asks if I will read her a letter from the hospital. The oldest of her four children, a seven-year-old boy named Matthew, has been sick for several weeks. He was tested for lead poisoning in November, and the letter she hands me, from Roosevelt Hospital, says that the child has a dangerous lead level. She is told to bring him back for treatment. She received the letter some weeks ago. It has been buried in a pile of other documents that she cannot read.   (2)

Although Laura cannot read, she knows enough about the dangers of lead to grasp the darker implications of this information. The crumbling plaster in the Martinique Hotel is covered with sweet-tasting paint, and children eat or chew chips of the paint as it flakes off the walls. Some of the paint contains lead. Children with lead poisoning may suffer loss of coordination or undergo convulsions. The consequences of lead poisoning may be temporary or long-lasting. They may appear at once or not for several years. This final point is what instills so much uneasiness; even months of observation cannot calm a parent's fear.   (3)

Lead poisoning, then, is Laura's first concern, but she has other problems. The bathroom plumbing has overflowed and left a pool of sewage on the floor. A radiator valve is broken, and every now and then releases a spray of scalding steam at the eye level of a child. A crib provided by the hotel appears to be unstable. A screw that holds two of its sides together is missing. When I test the crib with my hand, it starts to sway. There are four beds in the room, and they are dangerous, too. They have metal frames with unprotected corners, and the mattresses do not fit the frames; at one corner or another, metal is exposed. If a child has the energy or the playfulness to jump or turn a somersault or wrestle with a friend, and if he falls and strikes his head against the metal corner, the consequences can be serious. The week before, a child on the fourteenth floor fell in just this way, cut his forehead, and required stitches. Most of these matters have been brought to the attention of the hotel management; in Laura's case, complaints have brought no visible results.   (4)

All of this would be enough to make life difficult for an illiterate young woman in New York, but Laura has one other urgent matter on her hands. It appears that she has failed to answer a request for information from her welfare office, and, for reasons that she doesn't understand, she did not receive her benefits this week. The timing is bad; it's a weekend. The city operates a crisis center in the Martinique, where residents can go for food and other help, but today the crisis center is not open, so there's nobody around to tide her over with emergency supplies. Laura's children have been eating cheese and bread and peanut butter for two days. "Those on welfare," the

Community Service Society of New York said in a report published in 1984, may be suddenly removed from welfare rolls "for reasons unrelated to their actual need," or even to eligibility standards. Welfare workers in New York City call this practice "churning." Laura and her children are being churned.   (5)

The room is lighted by fluorescent tubes in a ceiling fixture. They cast a stark light on four walls of greenish paint smeared over with sludge draining from someone's plumbing on the floor above. In the room are two boys with dark and hollowed eyes and an infant girl. A third boy is outside and joins us later. The children have the washed-out look of the children Walker Evans photographed for "Let Us Now Praise Famous Men." Besides the four beds and the crib, the room contains two chairs, a refrigerator, and a television set, which doesn't work. A metal hanger serves as an antenna, but there is no picture on the screen. Instead, there is a storm of falling flakes and unclear lines. I wonder why Laura keeps it on. There are no table lamps to soften the fluorescent glare, no books, no decorations. Laura tells me that her father is of Panamanian birth but that she went to school in New York City. Spanish is her first language. I don't speak Spanish well. We talk in English.   (6)

"I cannot read," Laura says. "I buy the New York *Post* to read the pictures. In the grocery, I know what to buy because I see the pictures."   (7)

What of no-name products—generic brands, whose labels have no pictures but which could save her a great deal of money?   (8)

"If there are no pictures, I don't buy it," she says. "I want to buy pancakes, I ask the lady, 'Where's the pancakes?' So they tell me."   (9)

She points to the boys and says, "He's two. He's five. Matthew's seven. My daughter is four months. She has this rash." She shows me ugly skin eruptions on the baby's neck and jaw. "The carpets, they was filthy from the stuff, the leaks that come down on the wall. All my kids have rashes, but the worst she has it. There was pus all over. Somewhere here I have a letter from the nurse." She shuffles around but cannot find the letter. "She got something underneath the skin. Something that bites. The only way you can get rid of it is with a cream."   (10)

She finds the letter. The little girl has scabies.   (11)

Laura continues, "I have been living here two years. Before I came here, I was in a house we had to leave. There was rats. Big ones, they crawl on us. The rats, they come at night. They come into our house, run over my son's legs. The windows were broken. It was winter. Snow, it used to come inside. My mother lived with us before. Now she's staying at my grandma's house. My grandma's dying in the bed. She's sixty-five. My mother comes here once a week to do the groceries. Tomorrow she comes. Then she goes back to help my grandma.   (12)

"I know my name, and I can write my name, my children's names. To read, I cannot do it. Medicines, I don't know the instructions. I was living here when I was pregnant with Corinne. No, I didn't see no doctor. I was hungry. What I ate was rice and beans, potato chips and soda. Up to now this week we don't have food. People ask me, 'Can you help? Do you got this? Do you got that?' I don't like to tell them no. If I have something, I give it. This week, I don't got. I can read baby books—like that, a little bit. If I could read, I would read newspapers. I would like to know what's going on. Matthew, he tells me I am stupid. 'You can't read.' You know, because he wants to read. He don't understand what something is. I tell him, 'I don't know it. I don't understand.' People laugh. You feel embarrassed. On the street. Or in the store." She weeps. "There's nothing here."   (13)

Laura sweeps one hand in a wide arc, but I can't tell whether she means the gesture to take in the room or something more. Then she makes her meaning clear: "Everything I had, they put it on the sidewalk when I was evicted. I don't know if that's the law. Things like that—what is the law, what isn't? I can't read it, so I didn't understand. I lost everything I had. I sign papers. Somebody could come and take my children. They could come. 'Sign this. Sign that.' I don't know what it says. Adoption papers—I don't know. This here paper that I got I couldn't understand."   (14)

She hands me another letter. This one is from the management of the hotel: "This notice is to inform you that your rent is due today. I would appreciate your cooperation in seeing to it that you go to your center today." Another form that she hands me asks her to fill out the names and the ages of her children.   (15)

"Papers, documents—people give it to me. I don't know it: I don't understand." She pauses, and then says, "I'm a Catholic. Yes—I go two weeks ago to church. This lady say they have these little books that learn me how to spell. You see the letters. Put them together. I would like to read. I go to St. Francis' Church. Go inside and kneel—I pray. I don't talk to the priest. I done so many things—you know, bad things. I buy a bottle of wine. A bottle of beer. That costs a dollar. I don't want to say to God. I get a hundred and seventy-three dollars restaurant allowance. With that money I buy clothes. Food stamps, I get two hundred dollars. That's for groceries. Subway tokens I take out ten dollars. Washing machine, I do downstairs. Twenty-five dollars to dry and wash. Five dollars to buy soap. Thirty dollars twice a month."   (16)

Another woman at the Martinique calculates her laundry costs at my request, and they come out to nearly the same figure. These may be the standard rates for a midtown site. The difficulty of getting out and traveling to find lower prices, whether for laundromats or for groceries, cannot be overstated. Families at the Martinique are trapped in a commercial district.   (17)

I ask Laura who stays with the children when she does her chores.   (18)

"My mother keeps the children when I do the wash," she replies. "If she can't, I ask somebody on the floor. 'Give me three dollars. I watch your kids.' For free? Nothing. Everything for money. Everybody's poor."   (19)

Extending a hand, she says, "This is the radiator. Something's wrong." She shows me where the steam sprays out. I test it with my hand. "Sometimes it stops. The children get too close. Then it starts— like that! Leak is coming from upstairs down." I see the dark muck on the wall. "The window is broke. Lights broke." She points to the fluorescent tubes. They flicker on and off. "I ask them, 'Please, why don't you give me ordinary lights?' They don't do nothing. So it been two weeks. I go downstairs. They say they coming up. They never come. So I complain again. Mr. Tuccelli—Salvatore Tuccelli, the manager of the Martinique—said to come here to his office. Desks and decorations and a lot of pictures. It's above the lobby. So the manager was there. Mr. Tuccelli sat back in his chair. He had a gun. He had it here under his waist. You know, under his belt. I said, 'Don't show it to me if you isn't going to use it.' I can't tell what kind of gun it was. He had it in his waist. 'You are showing me the gun so I will be afraid.' If he was only going to show it, I would not be scared. If he's going to use it, I get scared.   (20)

"So he says, 'You people bring us trouble.' I said, 'Why you give my son lead poison and you didn't care? My child is lead-poisoned.' He said, 'I don't want to hear of this again.' What I answer him is this: 'Listen. People like you live in nice apartments. You got a home. You got TV. You got a family. You got children in a school that learn them. They don't got lead poison.'   (21)

"I don't know the reason for the guards. They let the junkies into the hotel. When my mother comes, I have to sign. If it's a family living good, they make it hard. If it's the drug dealers, they come in. Why they let the junkies in but keep away your mother? The guards, you see them taking women in the corner. You go down twelve-thirty in the night, they're in the corner with the girls. This is true. I seen it."   (22)

She continues, "How I know about the lead is this: Matthew sits there and he reaches his fingers in the plaster and he put it in his mouth. So I ask him, 'Was you eating it?' He says, 'Don't hit me. Yes, I was.' So then I took him to the clinic and they took the blood. I don't know if something happen to him later on. I don't know if it affects him. When he's older . . ."   (23)

I ask Laura why she goes to church.   (24)

"I figure: Go to church. Pray God. Ask Him to help. I go on my knees. I ask Him from my heart. 'Jesus Christ, come help me, please. Why do you leave me here?' When I'm lying down at night, I ask, 'Why people got to live like this?' On the street, the people stare at you when you go out of the hotel. People look. They think, I wonder how they live in there. Sometimes I walk out this door. Garbage all over in the stairs. When it's hot, a lot of bugs around the trash. Sometimes there are fires in the trash. I got no fire escape. You have to get out through the hall. I got no sprinkler. Smoke detector doesn't work. When I cook and food is burning, it don't ring. If I smoke, it starts to ring. I look up. I say, 'Why you don't work? When I need you, you don't work. I'm gonna knock you down.' I did!" She laughs.   (25)

There is a sprinkler system in the corridor. In 1987, the hotel management informed residents that the fire-alarm system was "inoperable."   (26)

I ask Laura if the older children are enrolled in school. Nodding at Michael, her middle son, she says, "This one doesn't go to school. He's five. I need to call tomorrow. Get a quarter. Then you get some papers. Then you got to sign those papers. Then he can start school.   (27)

"For this room I pay fifteen hundred dollars for two weeks. I don't pay. The welfare pays. I got to go and get it." The room, although it is undivided, was originally a two-room suite and is being rented at the two-room rate. "They send me this. I'm suppose to sign. I don't know what it is. Lots of things you suppose to sign. I sign it but I don't know what it is."   (28)

While we are talking, Matthew comes in and sits beside his mother. He lowers his eyes when I shake his hand.   (29)

Laura goes on, "Looking for a house, I got to do it." She explains that she's required to give evidence that she is searching for a place to live. "I can't read, so I can't use the paper. I get dressed. I put my makeup on. If I go like this, they look afraid. They say, 'They going to destroy the house!' You got to dress the children and look nice. Owners don't want homeless. Don't want welfare. Don't want kids. What I think? If they pay one thousand and five hundred dollars every two weeks, why not pay five hundred dollars for a good apartment?"   (30)

She hands me another paper. "Can you tell me what is this?"   (31)

It's a second letter from the hospital, telling her to bring her son for treatment.   (32)

She says, "Every day, my son this week, last week was vomiting.

Every time he eat his food, he throw it right back out. I got to take him to the clinic.   (33)

"Christmas, they don't got. For my daughter I ask a Cabbage Patch. For my boys I ask for toys. I got them stockings." She shows me four cotton stockings tacked to the wall with nothing in them. "They say, 'Mommy, there's no toys.' I say not to worry. 'You are going to get something.' But they don't. They don't get nothing. I could not afford. No, this isn't my TV. Somebody lended it to me. Christmas tree I can't afford. Christmas I don't spend it happy. I am thinking of the kids. What we do on Christmas is we spend it laying on the bed. If I go outside, I feel a little better. When I'm here, I see those walls, the bed, and I feel sad. If I had my own apartment, maybe there would be another room. Somewhere to walk. Walk back and forth."   (34)

I ask her, "How do you relax?"   (35)

"If I want to rest, relax, I turn out the light and lie down on the bed," she says. "When I met his father, I was seventeen." She says she knew him before she was homeless, when she lived in Brooklyn with her mother. He was working at a pizza parlor near her mother's home. "One night, he bought me liquor. I had never tasted. So he took me to this hallway. Then my mother say that what I did is wrong. So I say that I already did it. So you have to live with what you did. I had the baby. No. I did not want to have abortion. The baby's father I still see. When he has a job, he brings me food. In the summer, he worked in a flower store. He would bring me flowers. Now he don't have any job. So he don't bring me flowers."   (36)

She sweeps her hand in a broad arc and says again, "Nothing here. I feel embarrassed for the room. Flowers, things like that, you don't got. Pretty things you don't got. Nothing like that. No."   (37)

In the window is a spindly geranium plant. It has no flowers, but some of the leaves are green. Before I go, we stand beside the window. Blowing snow hits the panes and blurs the dirt.   (38)

"Some of the rooms high up, they got a view," Laura says. "You see the Empire State."   (39)

I've noticed this—seen the building from a window. It towers high above the Martinique.   (40)

"I talk to this plant. I tell him, 'Grow! Give me one flower!' He don't do it." Then, in an afterthought, "No pets. No. You don't got. Animals. They don't allow."   (41)

It occurs to me that this is one of the few places I have been except a hospital or a reform school where there are hundreds of children and virtually no pets. A few people keep cats illegally.   (42)

"I wish I had a dog," Laura says. "Brown dog. Something to hug."   (43)

VOCABULARY

In your journal, write the meanings of the following words.

- the darker *implications* (3)
- call this practice *"churning"* (5)
- ugly skin *eruptions* (10)
- girl has *scabies* (11)

QUESTIONS FOR WRITING AND DISCUSSION

1. Describe your intellectual and emotional reaction to Kozol's article. What information about the lives of the poor and illiterate did you already know? What information surprised you? How did Kozol's essay make you feel about this problem?

2. The purpose of an investigative report is to give information without editorializing or arguing for or against a solution. In which paragraphs does Kozol remain most objective and unemotional? Which sentences reveal Kozol's sympathy for Laura's situation? Does he avoid editorializing?

3. Reread the essay, marking those places where Laura's illiteracy causes her problems. Based on your notes, explain how her illiteracy (rather than her poverty) causes or magnifies her problems.

4. Describe the investigative techniques Kozol probably used to write his essay. In addition to his interviews with Laura, what were his other probable sources of information?

5. According to the information provided by Kozol, what support does the welfare system provide Laura and her children? How does the welfare system encourage Laura to improve her life? List three changes you believe the welfare system should make to solve Laura's problems and make her more self-sufficient.

6. On your next trip to the grocery store, see which products would appeal to an illiterate person. List the items (and their prices) you might buy, based on the pictures on the labels. Write a paragraph describing your findings. Is Kozol correct in assuming that Laura pays too much for her groceries?

INVESTIGATING: THE WRITING PROCESS

ASSIGNMENT FOR INVESTIGATING

Choose a subject to investigate: one aspect of a current social or political policy, a scientific discovery or principle, a historical event, a profile of a controversial public figure, or perhaps just an ordinary event, person, process, or place that you find interesting. Your initial purpose should be to discover or learn about your subject. Then, with a specific audience in mind, report your findings. A report presents the information that you find; it should not argue for or against any idea or plan. With the final copy of your investigative report, you must turn in photocopies of any sources you have summarized or cited, notes from your interview(s), and/or copies of questionnaires that you used.

Choosing a Subject

If one of your journal topics does not suggest a subject for your investigation, consider the following ideas. If you have a subject, go on to the collecting and shaping strategies.

- Write an investigation of some aspect of your favorite hobby. No matter what the subject is, you will find several magazines in the library devoted to it: fashion, cars, rock-climbing, music, cooking, fly fishing, photography, scuba diving, interior decorating, health foods, and so on. Find several magazines and browse through them. Based on what you find in the magazines, interview and/or survey other people interested in this subject. Focus your survey or interview on one specific aspect of this topic.

- At the place where you work, investigate how something does or does not work, research how the business (or your part of the business) is organized, do a profile of a co-worker, or survey your customers to find out what they like best or least about your store or company.

- Choose some idea, principle, process, or theory discussed in a class you are currently taking. Begin by interviewing classmates, graduate students, or a professor about how to investigate the history, development, or personalities behind this idea. With information from the interview, continue your investigation in the library, looking in appropriate magazines, books, or journals. As you read, focus your question on one *narrow* or *specific* area.

- Go back to your remembering essay. Do other people remember the person, place, or event? If so, interview one or more of them, either in person or on the phone. How do their recollections of the subject differ from yours? After investigating what happened from other points of view, rewrite your remembering essay to include their perspectives and memories.

Collecting

The collecting strategies discussed in Chapters 3 and 4 (brainstorming, looping, mapping, sketching, taking double-entry notes) may be useful as you collect ideas. Other strategies particularly useful for investigating are suggested below. Try each of these collecting strategies for your subject.

Had I known the answer to any of these questions, I would never have needed to write.

—*Joan Didion, essayist and novelist*

Asking Questions Asking the *right questions* is crucial to investigative writing. Sets of questions (often called *heuristics*) will help you narrow and focus your subject and tailor your approach to the expectations or needs of your audience. You don't know what information you need to collect until you know what questions your investigation needs to answer.

1. The "reporter's" or the familiar "Wh" questions are one basic heuristic:

    Who? What? When? Where? Why?

    Asking these questions of a topic ensures that you're not leaving out any crucial information. If, for example, you are investigating recreational opportunities in your city or on campus, you might ask the following questions to focus your investigation (remember to ask the *negative* version of each question, too):

    - *Whom* is the recreation for?
    - *Who* runs the programs?
    - *Who* is excluded from the programs?
    - *Who* pays for the programs?

    - *What* is the program?
    - *What* sports are included in the program?
    - *What* sports are not included?
    - *What* is the budget for these programs?

    - *When* are these opportunities available or not available?

    - *Where* do the activities take place?
    - *Where* are they restricted?

- *Why* are these programs offered?
- *Why* are certain activities not offered?
- *Why* have activities been changed?

These questions might lead you to focus your investigation on the scheduling, on why soccer has been excluded, or on why participants are charged a fee for one class or program but not for another.

2. The classical "topics" provide a second set of questions for an investigation.

Definition: What is it?

Comparison: What is it like or unlike?

Relationship: What caused it? What are its consequences?

Testimony: What has been said or written about it?

These questions can be used in conjunction with the reporter's questions to focus an investigation. Applied to the topic on recreational opportunities, the questions might be as follows:

Definition: What activities exist?

How can the activities be described, classified, or analyzed?

Comparison: What are similarities or differences with other programs?

Relationship: What caused these programs to be offered?

What causes people to use or avoid these activities?

What are the consequences of these programs?

Testimony: What do students think about these activities?

What do administrators think?

What have other schools done?

What does research show?

What proverbs or common sayings apply here?

These two sets of questions will *expand* your information, helping you collect facts, data, examples, and ideas—probably more than you can use in a short essay. Once you have all of this information, you can then *narrow* your topic.

Using the Library   Knowing how to use a library is crucial for most investigations. For this essay you will not need to do exhaustive research on your topic, but you may need some background information, statistics, or information about current research, public opinion trends, or recent discoveries. Chapter 10, "Writing a Research Paper," will answer your research questions in more depth, but you can get information quickly in a library by using a few key sources.

- *Ask librarians for assistance.*   Every library has librarians stationed at information desks, checkout counters, or reference desks whose job is to answer your questions. Be sure to ask for their advice when you need it. Since frustration is the number-one enemy of research projects, ask for assistance *early* in your investigation. The best procedure is simply to explain your project—what you intend to do and have done so far—and ask for advice or help. *There are no stupid questions in a library.*

COMPUTER TIP: COLLECTING

Create a new file on the computer and enter the "Wh" questions or the questions derived from the classical topics. Then leave a few lines between each question so you have room to write and answer each question. Some of your answers may generate only a sentence or two, but others may lead to several sentences or paragraphs. Since these questions often relate to the shaping strategies discussed later in this chapter, you will be collecting ideas and at the same time shaping and drafting a trial version of part of your investigative essay.

- *Acquaint yourself with the basic sources of information in the library.* Most libraries offer group tours that familiarize their users with the location of the following:

    The card catalogue or online catalogue

    Basic references such as encyclopedias, almanacs, and dictionaries

    Biographical reference sources:
    Current Biography
    Dictionary of American Biography

Notable American Women
Who's Who in America

Frequently used magazine or periodical indexes:
The Readers' Guide to Periodical Literature
Applied Science and Technology Index
Social Sciences and Humanities Index
The New York Times Index

Computer access systems:

Many of these, such as searches of the ERIC system, DIALOG, and others, are relatively expensive and are intended for major research projects. Sometimes, however, libraries provide free computer searches of newspapers and magazines. One popular system, INFOTRAK, will search articles under key headings and print out a list of relevant articles.

Using Written Sources

- *Make photocopies of relevant articles.* The small amount of money you spend on copies will enable you to reread articles if necessary, quote or paraphrase from them accurately, and cite them accurately as references. (The money you spend is also excellent antifrustration insurance, in case you return to the library stacks and discover that someone else has checked out your magazine or book.) On your photocopies, be sure to write source information: magazine or book title, author, publisher, date and place of publication, volume, and page numbers. For this investigative report, remember that you must turn in photocopies of any pages of articles or books you refer to or cite.

- *Make notes and summaries from your photocopied sources.* As you collect information from photocopied sources, jot down key facts, ideas, and direct quotations from the source. For every note you take, record the author, title, publishing information, and page numbers of your source. You may *paraphrase* another writer's ideas, examples, sentences, or short passages by writing them in your own words. Use *direct quotation* when words or phrases in a source are more striking than your paraphrase might be. You may edit a direct quotation by (1) deleting any irrelevant or unnecessary words or phrases by using ellipsis points (three spaced periods . . .) to indicate the deleted words and by (2) inserting your own words in square brackets [ ] if you need to clarify a quoted passage. Otherwise, the words within the quotation marks must *accurately* reproduce the original: No altered spellings, changed words, or rephrasings are allowed.

- *Avoid plagiarism.* Use quotation marks whenever you quote more than a word or two from your source. Paraphrase in your own words rather than stringing together phrases and sentences written by someone else. Give credit for ideas, facts, and language by citing your sources. In informal investigative writing, you may simply mention the author and title of written sources, citing page numbers of direct quotations in parentheses. (All formal research papers and some investigative essays cite sources in full in a "Works Cited" section at the end. See Chapter 11, "Writing a Research Paper," for more details.)

Summarizing   A *summary* is a concise explanation of the main and supporting ideas in a passage, report, essay, book, or speech. It is usually written in the present tense. It identifies the author and title of the source; it may refer to the context or the actual place where the study took place; it contains the passage's main ideas; and it may quote directly a few forceful or concise sentences or phrases. It will *not* usually cite the author's examples. A *paraphrase* usually expresses all the information in the passage—including examples—in your own words. Summary, paraphrase, and direct quotation often occur together as you use sources.

The following passage is a concise summary of Lewis Grossberger's article, *The Triumph of the Wheel:*

> In his *Rolling Stone* article, "The Triumph of the Wheel," Lewis Grossberger investigates why the television game show *Wheel of Fortune* has become so popular. Grossberger describes the workings of the game show, interviews the show's personalities (Pat Sajak and Vanna White) on location, describes Merv Griffin's role as producer and puzzle-maker for the show, and explains his own theory about why the show has reached the status of a "cult sensation."
>
> *Source, Author, Title Focus of Article*
>
> *Summary of Article's Main Ideas*

> *Wheel of Fortune* is popular, Grossberger contends, because it gives its viewers a vicarious sense of participating in the excitement of solving a puzzle and winning thousands of dollars' worth of merchandise. The show's contestants are not stars, so the viewers at home can imagine that they are the contestants. The game itself involves a simple roulette wheel and the puzzles are easy to solve, giving home viewers a sense of accomplishment and superiority. The selection of prizes after the contestant has solved the puzzle similarly allows viewers to shop, vicariously, with the winner. Finally the show's personalities are familiar, people-next-door types: Pat Sajak is low-key and occasionally humorous; Vanna White is the show's bouncy cheerleader. *Wheel of Fortune,* Grossberger concludes, is a state-of-the-art show that "sucks the viewer . . . into that dazzling dreamscape—Vanna's Nirvana—where he [or she] is transformed from a nullity, a hapless anonymous bozo . . . [into] the only being now worth being: a Winner."
>
> *Article's Thesis*
>
> *Summary of Points That Support the Article's Thesis*
>
> *Direct Quotation from Article*

Citing Sources in Your Text As you collect information, you need to note authors, titles of books or magazines, dates of publication, publishers, and page numbers to give proper credit to your sources. For some journalistic writing, you may need to cite only the author, the title of your source, or both:

> *Time* said that *Wheel* is the highest-rated syndicated series in television history.

> According to Tom Shales, TV critic for *The Washington Post,* Merv was rumored to have run around his office waving his quarter-of-a-billion-dollar check in the air, joking that he couldn't find anyone to cash it.

According to the MLA (Modern Language Association) format, formal in-text citation requires that the author and page numbers be given, usually in parentheses, at the end of the sentence (Grossberger 24–25). If the author of the article you are citing is not known, use a shortened title *(Wheel 27).*

> *Wheel of Fortune* viewers are "transformed from a nullity, a hapless anonymous bozo . . . [into] the only being now worth being: a Winner" (Grossberger 28).

If you refer to the author in the sentence introducing him or her, indicate just the page numbers in parentheses.

> Grossberger implies that, by and large, viewers of *Wheel of Fortune* are a bunch of bozos (28).

For additional information on formal, in-text citation, consult Chapter 10, " Writing a Research Paper."

Interviewing After you have done some initial research, interviews are a logical next step. Remember that the more you know about the subject (and the person you're interviewing), the more productive the interview will be. In planning an interview, keep the following steps in mind.

1. Make an *appointment* with the person you wish to interview. Although you may feel hesitant or shy about calling someone for an interview, remember that most people are flattered that someone else is interested in them and wants to hear their opinions or learn about their area of expertise.

2. Make a *list of questions,* in an appropriate *sequence,* that you can ask during the interview. The interview itself will generate additional topics, but your list will jog your memory if the interview gets off the track. Begin with relatively objective or factual questions and work your way, gradually, to the more subjective questions or controversial issues. Phrase your questions, if possible, so that they require more than a yes or no answer.

3. Begin the interview by introducing yourself and describing your investigation. Keep *your* biases or opinions out of the questions. Be sure to *listen* carefully and ask follow-up questions: "What information do you have on that? What do the statistical studies suggest? In your opinion, do these data show any trends? What memorable experiences have you had relating to this topic?" Like a dog with a good bone, a reporter doesn't drop a topic until the meat's all gone.

4. During the interview, *take notes,* and, if appropriate, use a tape recorder to ensure accuracy. Don't hesitate to ask your interviewee to repeat or clarify a statement. Remember: People want you to get the facts right and quote them accurately. Especially if you're doing a personality profile, describe notable features of your interviewee: hair color, facial features, stature, dress, gestures, nervous habits, and details about the room or surroundings. Finally, don't forget to ask your interviewee for additional

leads or sources. At the conclusion of the interview, express your thanks and ask if you can check with him or her later, if necessary, for additional details or facts.

5. Immediately after the interview, go over your notes. If you recorded the interview, listen to the tape and transcribe important responses. List other questions you may still have.

Writing Questionnaires   Questionnaires are useful when you need to know the attitudes, preferences, or opinions of a large group of people. If you are surveying customers in your business, you may discover that 39 percent of those surveyed would prefer that your business stay open an additional hour, from 5 P.M. to 6 P.M. If you are surveying students to determine their knowledge of geography, you might discover that only 8 percent can correctly locate Beirut on a map of the Middle East. The accuracy and usefulness of a survey depend on the kinds of questions you ask, on the number of people you survey, and on the sample of people you select to respond to your questionnaire.

Open questions are easy to ask, but the answers can be difficult to interpret. If, for example, you want to survey customers at a department store where you work, you might ask questions requiring a short written response:

- What is your opinion of the service provided by clerks at Macy's?
- What would make your shopping experience at Macy's more enjoyable?

These questions may give you interesting—and often reliable—responses, but the results may be difficult to tabulate. Open-ended questions are often valuable in initial surveys because they can help you to determine specific areas or topics for further investigation.

Closed questions are more typical than open-ended questions in surveys. They limit the responses so you can focus on a particular topic and accurately tabulate the responses. Below are several types of closed questions:

- *Yes/No* questions: Have you shopped at Macy's in the last three months?

  _____   Yes

  _____   No

- *Multiple Choice:* How far did you travel to come to Macy's?

  _____   0–5 miles

  _____   5–10 miles

_____ 10–15 miles

_____ Over 15 miles

How would you characterize the salespeople at Macy's?

_____ Exceptionally helpful

_____ Helpful

_____ Indifferent

_____ Occasionally rude

_____ Usually rude

- *Checklists:* Which departments at Macy's do you usually visit?

  _____ Women's Wear

  _____ Sporting Goods

  _____ Children's Wear

  _____ Lingerie

  _____ Men's Wear

  _____ Household Goods

- *Ranking Lists:* Rank the *times* you prefer to shop (1 indicates most convenient time, 2 indicates slightly less convenient, and so on).

  _____ 9 A.M. to 11 A.M.

  _____ 11 A.M. to 1 P.M.

  _____ 1 P.M. to 4 P.M.

  _____ 4 P.M. to 8 P.M.

As you design, administer, and use your questionnaire, keep the following tips in mind:

- Limit and focus your questions so respondents can fill out the questionnaire quickly.

- Avoid loaded or biased questions. For example, don't ask, "How do you like the high-quality merchandise in Macy's sports department?"

- At the top of your questionnaire, write one or two sentences describing your study and thanking participants.

- Pretest your questionnaire by giving it to a few people. Based on their oral and written responses, focus and clarify your questions.

- Use a large sample group. Thirty responses will give you more accurate information about consumer attitudes than will three responses.

- Make your sample as *random* or as evenly representative as possible. Don't survey customers on only one floor, in only one department, or at only one time of day.

- Be sure to include a copy of your questionnaire with your article or essay.

Note: If you intend to do a formal study using questionnaires, check your library for additional sources to help you design and administer statistically reliable surveys.

Shaping

As you begin shaping your material, reconsider your purpose and audience. Limit your subject to create a *narrowed* and *focused* topic. Don't try to cover everything; focus on the *most interesting questions and information*. Take the time to write out a statement of your topic, key questions, purpose, and audience. Then try the following strategies.

But for whom have I tried so steadfastly to communicate? Who have I worried over in this writing? Who is my audience?

—*Cherrie Moraga, social critic and poet*

Inverted Pyramid   A common form for reports, especially in journalism, is the *inverted pyramid*. The writer begins with a succinct but arresting title, opens the story with a sentence or short paragraph that answers the reporter's "Wh" questions, and then fills in the background information and details in order of importance, from the *most important* to the *least important*.

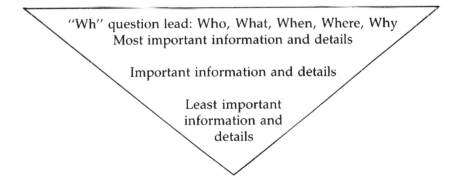

Writers use the inverted pyramid when concrete information and the convenience of the reader are most important. The advantage of the inverted pyramid is that a hurried reader can quickly gather the most important information and determine whether the rest of the story is worth reading. The disadvantage is that some details or information may be scattered or not presented in a clear sequence. In investigative writing, therefore, writers often supplement the inverted pyramid with other forms of development: chronological order, definition, classification, or comparison/contrast.

Chronological Order   Often, writers present their information in the order in which they discovered it, enabling the reader to follow the research as though it were a "whodunit." In this format, you set forth the key questions for the investigation and then describe the steps in *your* investigation, from your earliest questions or clues to your final explanation or resolution.

Lewis Grossberger uses the chronology of his own investigation to shape his article about *Wheel of Fortune*. The following sentences—most of them appearing at the beginning of paragraphs—illustrate how he uses chronological order to shape his account:

> The first time I saw *Wheel of Fortune,* I thought it was a vapid piece of fluff. . . .
>
> But the second time my reaction was different.
>
> Soon I was wafting westward on an urgent sociophilosophical inquiry. . . .
>
> Now here was a journalistic challenge. . . . By God, I would take up the gauntlet. I would find out why—or doze off trying.
>
> When I arrived at the NBC studios in fabled Burbank, the publicity lady who collected me said. . . .
>
> During one break I was taken to meet the hostess. Vanna was in her dressing room . . . .
>
> Too soon came the inevitable pounding, and Vanna vanished. . . .
>
> Considerably sobered, I retired and the next morning flew away.
>
> Soon afterward I was on the plane, thinking about *Wheel of Fortune,* which, as always, acted as a soporific.
>
> I woke high over the Jersey swamps, and I had the answer. I knew *why.*

As an alternative, you may want to use a chronological analysis of the *history* of a particular subject to shape your investigative writing. Notice the signals for chronological order that structure John Tierney's report on Type A behavior in American males:

> Most researchers ignored the theory about A and B personality types long after it was proposed in 1959. . . . The theory wasn't

officially sanctioned until 1981, when the American Heart Association reviewed evidence. . . .

Last year Friedman further convinced the establishment with a study in which victims of heart attacks were trained to relax.

But this year new doubts have arisen. A team led by Robert B. Case . . . analyzed the personalities of 516 heart attack victims. . . .

But another study, scheduled for publication this fall, used interviews and also produced negative results.

Definition   Definitions are central to investigating and reporting, whether they shape only a sentence or two, or several paragraphs. Grossberger uses informal definition to shape one paragraph in his article that explains the meaning of the word "vicariousness," the condition of imagined participation in another person's experience or emotions:

> Vicariousness. *Wheel of Fortune* creates the illusion for the hard-working, treadmill-trotting Middle American yearner that he or she is in the big game. Viewers don't exactly identify with the contestants; they *become* the contestants.

Comparison and Contrast   Comparison and contrast are as essential to investigating and reporting as they are to observing and remembering. Consider how Lance Morrow uses comparison to shape the opening paragraphs of a *Time* magazine essay on AIDS. In this essay, entitled "The Start of a Plague Mentality," Morrow notes the similarities between attitudes created by a plague 200 years ago and contemporary attitudes toward AIDS.

> An epidemic of yellow fever struck Philadelphia in August 1793. Eyes glazed, flesh yellowed, minds went delirious. People died, not individually, here and there, but in clusters, in alarming patterns. A plague mentality set in. Friends recoiled from one another. If they met by chance, they did not shake hands but nodded distantly and hurried on. The very air felt diseased. People dodged to the windward of those they passed. They sealed themselves in their houses. The deaths went on, great ugly scythings. . . .
>
> In the past four years, some 6,000 people have died of AIDS in the U.S. From a statistical point of view, AIDS is not a major plague. Still, one begins to detect a plague mentality regarding the disease and those who carry it.

Analysis   In the process of investigating any subject, writers frequently use analysis to organize or shape their writing. Analysis simply involves dividing a whole into its parts. In the process of analyzing *why* the *Wheel of Fortune* is successful, for example, Grossberger devotes one paragraph to each of the four main elements of the show: the players, the game itself, the payoff, and the cast. Ask yourself, "What are the major components of my subject?" The answer may lead to some new ideas about your subject and may, as well, create a shape to help organize your material.

Additional Shaping Strategies Other shaping strategies, discussed in previous chapters, may be useful for your investigation, too. *Classifying people, places, or things* may help organize your investigation. *Simile, metaphor, or analogy* may develop and shape parts of your article. Even in investigative reporting, writers may create an identifiable *persona* or adopt a humorous *tone.* In the examples of reports given earlier in this chapter, John Tierney, Jeff Meer, and Joan Barthel assume a reporter's objective persona and use a serious, straightforward tone. In contrast, Lewis Grossberger establishes a humorous persona and tone. He admits that *Wheel* is "tedious dreck" and is "soporific," he makes fun of Vanna when she says that turning the letters is a "lot harder than it looks," and he even recounts his own weird dream about Old Stinky.

Title, Introduction, and Conclusion Especially in an investigative report, a catchy title is important to help get your reader's interest and attention. Jot down several ideas for titles now and add to that list *after* you've drafted your essay.

In your introductory paragraph(s), answering the "Wh" questions will help focus your investigation. Or you may wish to use a short *narrative.* Grossberger, for example, begins his article by describing how he became interested in his investigation: "The first time I saw *Wheel of Fortune,* I thought it was a vapid piece of fluff. . . ." Joan Barthel begins her article with stories from Oprah Winfrey's life, pointing out that her profile "is not just the story of a survivor, though she obviously is one. . . ." Other types of lead-ins, such as a short *description,* a *question,* a *statement of a problem,* a *startling fact* or *statistic,* or an arresting *quotation,* may get the reader's interest and focus on the main idea you wish to investigate.

The conclusion should resolve the question or questions posed in the investigation, summarize the most important information (useful primarily for long or complicated reports), and give the reader a sense of completion or closure, often by picking up an idea, fact, quotation, narrative, or bit of description used in the introduction. Grossberger's conclusion, for example, mentions the formula used in *Wheel of Fortune,* reiterates the idea that viewers of *Wheel* want to be winners, and puns on the title of the show: "You know, a big wheel."

Some writers like to have a title and know how they're going to start a piece of writing before they begin drafting. However, if you can't think of the perfect title or introduction, begin drafting and continue working on the title, introduction, and the conclusion after the first draft.

Drafting

Before you begin a first draft, reconsider your purpose in writing, and further focus your questions, sense of audience, and shaping strategies.

All good writing is swimming under water and holding your breath.

—*F. Scott Fitzgerald, author of* The Great Gatsby

The actual drafting of an investigative essay requires that you have all your facts, data statistics, quotations, summaries, and notes from interviews or results of surveys ready to use. Organize your notes, decide on an overall shaping strategy, or write a sketch outline. In investigative writing, a primary danger is postponing writing too long, in the mistaken belief that if you read just one more article or interview just one more person, you'll get the information you need. At some point, usually *before* you feel ready, you must begin writing. (Writers rarely feel they know enough about their subject, but deadlines require them to begin.) Your main problem, you'll quickly discover, will be having too much to say rather than not enough. If you have too much, go back to your focusing questions and see whether you can narrow your topic further.

COMPUTER TIP: TITLES, INTRODUCTIONS, AND CONCLUSIONS

Often your best ideas for snappy titles, good lead-ins, or smooth conclusions will come while you're working on something else—collecting material, practicing shaping strategies, or even drafting a trial version. If your computer can copy material from one file and place it in another file (or even transfer it to the end of your file), try making copies of interesting examples, quotations, facts, and bits of narrative or description. You may use these in the body of your essay, or you might want to use them in an introduction or conclusion. After you draft your essay, you can then see which examples, facts, and so forth you want for the main part of your essay and which might make a good title, lead-in, or conclusion.

Revising

Guidelines for Revision As you add, delete, substitute, or rearrange materials, keep the following tips in mind:

- **Reexamine your purpose and audience:** Are you doing what you intended? You should be *reporting* your findings; you should *not* be arguing for or against any idea.

- **Is the form of your essay or report responsive to audience needs and expectations?** Use samples of other writing for your audience (from newspapers, magazines, journals, and so on) as models.

- **Can you add any of your own observations or experiences to the investigation?** Remember that your own perceptions and experiences are also relevant data.

- **Review the reporter's "Wh" questions.** Are you providing your readers relevant information *early* in the report and also catching their interest with a key statistic, fact, quotation, example, question, description, or short narrative?

- **Recheck your summaries, paraphrases, or direct quotations.** Are they accurate, and have you cited these sources in your text?

- **Use signals, cues, and transitions to indicate your shaping strategies:**

  Chronological Order: before, then, afterward, next, soon, later, finally, at last

  Comparison/Contrast: likewise, similarly, however, yet, even so, in contrast

  Analysis: first, next, third, fourth, finally

- **Revise sentences for directness, clarity, and conciseness.** Avoid unnecessary passive voice. See your handbook for guidance.

- **Edit your report for appropriate word choice, usage, and grammar.** Check your writing for problems in spelling and punctuation.

We are all apprentices at a craft where no one ever becomes a master.

—Ernest Hemingway, novelist

POSTSCRIPT ON THE WRITING PROCESS

While the process of writing the investigative essay is still fresh in your mind, answer the following questions in your journal.

1. What sources of information (articles, books, interviews, surveys) were most helpful in your investigation? Explain.

2. Most researchers discover that the more they learn, the more they still need to know about their subject. If you had more time to work on this essay, which sources would you investigate further?

3. What was the most difficult problem you had to solve during your collecting, shaping, drafting, and revising? What helped you most as you tried to solve this problem (further reading, additional writing, advice from peers, and so on)? Explain.

4. What was the single most important thing you learned about investigating as you wrote this paper?

5. What do you like best about the final version of your investigative report?

INVESTIGATING: STUDENT WRITING

SEE DICK RUN, RUN DICK RUN, WHY, WHY, WHY?

Jan Peterson

Jan Peterson, a jogger herself, decided to investigate why jogging is so popular. She read several articles from popular magazines such as Runner's World *and also found a relevant article in a technical journal,* Research Quarterly for Exercise and Sport. *Then she interviewed several joggers to profile their jogging behavior and attitudes. Shown below are notes from one of the articles she read, questions and notes from one interview, her first rough draft, and the revised version.*

Notes from an Article

Notes from a photocopy of Albert Mehrabian and Marijke Flynne Bekken, "Temperament Characteristics of Individuals Who Participate in Strenuous Sports," Research Quarterly for Exercise and Sport, *1986, Vol. 57, No. 2, pp 160-166.*

In their article, Mehrabian and Bekken found that "those who participate in strenuous sports regularly and intensively are healthier psychologically than the general population" (163). Psychological health in this case was composed of dominance, pleasantness and a relaxed attitude. The authors also addressed the question of whether certain personality types gravitate towards certain types of sports, or whether certain sports activities seem to create certain temperament characteristics. They concluded that certain people gravitate towards certain types of sports (164). (Some of the language here was too technical – PFO scales and formulas.) Also important: "Relaxed temperament is thus associated with low fear and low anxiety levels and high tolerance for discomfort and pain. Further, it is associated with the ability to delay gratification; to endure discomfort, stress, and pain to achieve desired results; and to cope with stressful situations or activities" (164). The most important conclusion of the paper appeared to be "that athletes are healthier psychologically than the general population" (165).

Questions for an Interview

1. How long have you been running?
2. Why did you start running?
3. Is running a personal thing – do you run alone or in a group?
4. Have your reasons for running changed over the years?
5. Do you experience a "runner's high"?
6. How do you feel after you run?
7. How do you feel when you don't run?
8. What do you think about when you run?
9. Do you compete at running?

Notes from an Interview

This runner started running in high school on cross country team — took up running again in 1979. Started running because he liked it and wanted to be on the track team - but wasn't good enough to compete in shorter distances. He now runs to stay in shape, relax and relieve stress. However, he is unusual in that he enjoys several types of exercise – social forms – such as basketball where there is much more interaction between team members Running relaxes him while he runs and those feelings of relaxation last long after the run ends. Not a "runner's high," as such. Things don't seem to bother him as much. He isn't extremely competitive – except with himself – he keeps track of his timed distances and tries to improve. He says he might have been an addicted runner had he started earlier.

First Draft

Question: Why do people run?

Audience: General, readers of a local newspaper possibly

Purpose: To report psychological effects of running

See Jane Run—Run, Jane, Run—Run, Run, Run

Why have so many thousands of people taken up a pastime lately which so closely resembles torture? You don't see runners or joggers smiling as they dash by you. What you see instead are painful grimaces etched into tight faces, and intense looks of concentration. What exactly is it that motivates these fanatics devoted to such misery and self-abuse?   (1)

According to Bruce Tuckman, author for *Runner's World* magazine, running can be "good medicine for bad moods." Tuckman says running has often been used as a treatment for clinical depression because "it incubates feelings of control, discipline, and self-worth in people who may have been feeling ineffectual." However, he also points out the possible dangers of developing a running addiction. This condition occurs in someone who depends too much on the good feelings provided by running, and is manifested in a person who can't and won't quit running.   (2)

I interviewed one such person, who wishes to remain anonymous. Although he claims he is not addicted to running, I have suspicions to the contrary. Two days after a serious accident with a chainsaw in which he received 20 stitches in the middle of his shin, he attempted to hobble through his usual 6 mile course. The pain admittedly got to him, so he decided to wait 2 more days to try again. His repeated stressing of the injured leg resulted in a lump the size of a walnut on his shin bone. Perhaps he is not a total addict, as he did give up his passion for a few days, but I would surmise that addiction is just a matter of degree. Why is this person so dedicated to this form of self-abuse?   (3)

It has been demonstrated that running causes biochemical as well as physiological changes in the body. In the past, endorphins, which are the body's naturally occurring opiates, were suspected to be at high levels in runners. But researchers were unable to detect a correlation between endorphins and runner's feelings of euphoria often known as a "runner's high." However, recently another drug has gained attention as a mood enhancer—the hormone noradrenaline. Tuckman claims that runners have higher levels of noradrenaline than do nonrunners.   (4)

However, the editors of *The Complete Runner* claim that the calming effect produced from running has its roots in our heredity.

Our ancestors had only two options in how to react to threats: fight—that is stand their ground and club each other (or that growling saber-toothed tiger), or flight—that is run away from the apparent danger. Options for dealing with stress today are no longer so clear cut. If our boss threatens us, we can't very well punch him or her, or run away. Instead we are forced to stand there and just take the verbal abuse—somehow internalizing the stress. But, we still must deal with the stress. Some of us deal with stress by numbing the effects with drugs or alcohol. Others have come to depend upon strenuous exercise, such as running, for our tension releaser. This perhaps sounds strange—because when you run you tense your muscles and it would appear that the very act of tensing muscles would inhibit tension release. However, recent research reported by the editors of *The Complete Runner* has revealed that "relaxation is most pronounced after muscular work."   (5)

Revised Version

SEE DICK RUN. RUN, DICK, RUN. WHY, WHY, WHY?

Why have so many thousands of people taken up a pastime lately that so closely resembles self-abuse? You don't often see runners or joggers smiling as they trot past you-what you see instead are painful grimaces etched into tight faces and intense looks of concentration. What motivates these fanatics? What sort of satisfaction could they possibly be deriving from such agony? Or are they perhaps all just a bunch of masochists?   (1)

People of all ages, shapes, and sizes have started running by the droves. You see them everywhere-at the park, downtown, on college campuses, at the beach, and in the mountains. Even more strange is the fact that once they start running, many of them won't, or *can't* quit. Now, I can understand the reasons why most people start a program of running—reasons such as wanting to lose weight or wanting to get into shape. What I fail to comprehend is why people continue to run after they find out what kind of pain is involved in the sport.   (2)

Reasons for running are as varied and diverse as people are. One runner interviewed for this article claimed to have started running in high school. He said he joined the cross country track team because he wanted to be a runner, but he was unable to compete effectively in shorter distance events. Now, however, he runs to stay in shape, relax, and relieve stress. A second interviewed runner began running in high school as well—also on the cross country team. However, he ran only to be in better shape for his true love, wrestling. He says he runs now to stay in shape and keep his sanity.   (3)

Runners may claim that running promotes sanity, but in fact there are both positive and negative psychological effects of running. In a recent *Runner's World* article entitled "Brighter Days," Bruce Tuckman explains that running can be "good medicine for bad moods." Tuckman says running has often been used as a treatment for clinical depression because "it incubates feelings of control, discipline, and self-worth in people who may have been feeling ineffectual." However, he also points out the possible dangers of developing a running addiction. This condition occurs in someone who depends too much on the good feelings provided by running and is manifested by a person who can't and won't quit running.   (4)

One of the runners I interviewed provided a vivid example of the negative effects of running addiction. This person had an unfortunate encounter with a chain saw while cutting firewood. As a result of their rather abrupt meeting, he ended up with approximately twenty stitches in the middle of his shin. Two days after the accident occurred, he attempted to hobble through his usual six mile course. Crazy, you say? Not according to his philosophy—the more you use your body, the faster it heals! The result of this madness is a lump the size of a walnut in the middle of his shin, and a leg that still gives him problems. And he claims he runs just to stay in shape and keep his sanity—what sanity?   (5)

Recent research has suggested that addiction to running may be caused, at least in part, by certain physiological or biochemical changes in the body. In the past, endorphins (the body's naturally occurring opiates) were suspected to be at high levels in runners. Researchers, however, were unable to detect a correlation between endorphins and runners' feelings of euphoria (often known as "runner's high"). Another mood-enhancing drug has gained attention more recently—the hormone noradrenaline. Tuckman claims runners have higher levels of noradrenaline than nonrunners.   (6)

However, the editors of *The Complete Runner* argue that the calming effect produced by running has its roots in our heredity. Our ancestors had only two options for handling threats: fight (stand your ground and club each other) or flight (run away from that sabre-toothed tiger that thinks you might make a scrumptious meal). Options for dealing with stress today are no longer so clear cut. If your boss threatens you, you can't very well retaliate with a club. It probably wouldn't look too good if you ran away, either. So what are your choices? Stand there and internalize the stress, go home later and throw down a couple of martinis, yell at the wife and kids, and fall asleep watching television. This behavior, however, seems only to dull the tension rather than relieve it. The urges to fight or flee remain bottled up inside, and the stress is not alleviated. The only way we can release our stress and really relax is by voluntary muscular work. As the editors of *The Complete Runner* say, "Running offers one of the few chances left to get our feet on the ground—for the sake of our heads."   (7)

Runners may be addicted psychologically or physiologically, but the result, some experts think, is positive. Albert Mehrabian and Marijke Bekken, writing in the *Research Quarterly for Exercise and Sport*, conclude that "those who participate in [running] regularly and intensively are healthier psychologically than the general population." These authors found that athletes in general have more dominant and pleasant temperaments than nonathletes. They also equated a relaxed temperament with those who run or exercise regularly. They defined "relaxed temperament" to be associated with "low fear and low anxiety levels and high tolerance for discomfort and pain. Further, it is associated with the ability to delay gratification; to endure discomfort, stress, and pain to achieve desired results; and to cope with stressful situations or activities." Do you suppose that the "chainsaw jogger" I interviewed may have a little more sanity than I previously gave him credit for? Maybe I'd better go put on my running shoes!   (8)

QUESTIONS FOR WRITING AND DISCUSSION

1. One purpose of an investigative report is to give readers information. Without looking back at Peterson's revised article, recall the information you got from it. Were you confused at some points in the article? Explain.

2. What information, ideas, or quotations does Peterson pick up from the article notes and interview to use in her revised version? Was there anything else she should have used but didn't?

3. Which shaping strategies discussed in this chapter does Peterson use to organize the revised version of her article? Referring to paragraph numbers, identify two important shaping strategies.

4. Compare Peterson's first draft with her revised version. Find one change in content (added or deleted facts, examples, quotations). Is the change an improvement over the first draft? Find one change in shaping or organization (look particularly at transitions in the opening sentences of paragraphs). Is the revision an improvement? Finally, find one change in wording in a sentence. Does the rewording improve the clarity or appropriateness of the sentence? Explain.

WHAT WILL THEY ADVERTISE NEXT?

Kevin Tobey

After seeing a television advertisement for condoms, Kevin Tobey decided to investigate the arguments for and against the use of such advertising on television. During his investigation, he read current newspaper and magazine accounts and conducted a survey of his own. He didn't want his essay to editorialize or argue for one side or the other; he simply wanted to discover the various arguments so he could be informed—and inform others—about this highly controversial issue.

During a commercial break appearing in the middle of NBC's "The Cosby Show," three commercials appear on the airwaves. You sit through them so that you can see the conclusion of "Cosby," but do not really pay attention to their content as you think about all of the things you have to do tomorrow. The first commercial passes by, almost unnoticed, as a television family seems surprised to learn that the prime rib they just ate was from a Swanson's frozen dinner. The second advertisement shows an obnoxious white bear making a free-fall dive into a pile of sheets that are now "Snuggly Soft" due to new and improved Snuggle fabric softener. Suddenly, a commercial for Trojan brand condoms practically knocks you out of your chair as your attention is quickly drawn back to the television. This scenario may seem far-fetched, but these ads are appearing on commercial television as we move into a new era of contraceptive advertisements.   (1)

Are such advertisements appropriate for television audiences? Should condoms be openly advertised in print media such as newspapers and magazines? Questions such as these are creating a heated debate among station managers, publishers, church clergy, and various citizen's organizations throughout the nation. The purpose of this paper is not to say whether or not contraceptive advertisements are appropriate for general audiences, but just to present both the pros and cons of such advertisements so that readers can make an informed decision.   (2)

PROS:

Ten years ago, condom displays were neatly tucked away behind pharmacy counters, but today they are arranged in bright, attractive displays that are accessible to everyone. There are several reasons for this sudden change. The most important factor is that condoms are effective in preventing the spread of the AIDS virus and several other sexually transmitted diseases such as herpes, chlamydia, and gonorrhea—according to a *Denver Post* article, "Public Interest in Condoms Stirs Debate." With AIDS outbreaks reaching epidemic proportions, something needs to be done to curb the spreading of the disease, and the use of condoms may be a partial solution. Recently, the *Denver Post* quoted Surgeon General C. Everett Koop as saying that although condoms cannot provide complete protection from the transmission of the AIDS virus, "it's the only thing we have in the way of a barrier."   (3)

Another argument suggests that condom advertisements should be carried by the media because the media glorifies sexual activity in a wide variety of soap operas, sit-coms, and television series. These people reason that the media is partially responsible for making sex seem so "safe," and therefore has the responsibility to show how people should protect themselves from health hazards which may be brought about by sexual activity.   (4)

In order to sample public opinion of college students, I conducted an informal survey involving sixteen dormitory residents at Colorado State University. Fourteen respondents favored contraceptive advertisements on T.V. and in the print media, while only two opposed them. The major stipulation placed on such advertisements was that they should not be shown before 10:00 p.m. (See Appendix A.)   (5)

Finally, many parents feel that education on birth control devices may be able to reverse the trend toward teenage pregnancies. In a debate reported in the *Denver Post*, Joyce Weinstein, the mother of both college and high school-age children said, "People are afraid to say teenagers in high school have sex. But they do. It's normal. So let's teach our kids to take care of themselves [through education]."   (6)

CONS:

On the other side of this issue are those who oppose condom advertisements. Several church leaders, for example, oppose contraceptive advertisements because the use of birth control devices is contrary to their religious beliefs. They also argue that such advertisements could lead to sexual promiscuity because of the high visibility and increased accessibility of the products. In addition, in the survey I conducted, these arguments seemed accurate as almost half (seven) of the people I polled thought that such advertisements will lead to more promiscuous activity.   (7)

Others argue that such advertisements may reach the wrong audience. For example, young children watching television may be exposed to such advertisements before they are capable of making informed decisions about whether the products should or should not be advertised on commercial television.   (8)

A third argument against condom advertisements stems from the feeling that they may lead to a very competitive and commercialized business, with condom manufacturers arguing about whose product is the "best." In my own survey, six of the sixteen respondents agreed with this argument and felt that specific brand names should not be mentioned in advertisements.   (9)

A final argument against contraceptive advertisements claims that they violate the freedom of parents, schools, and churches to teach children about contraceptives. They say that contraceptive advertisements would force people to watch the commercials—unless they change the channel or turn off the television.   (10)

There is no question that this debate will continue to be controversial. Station managers have been placed in the middle of the conflict, as they decide whether contraceptive advertisements should be aired on television. Some stations do carry the advertisements after 10 p.m., while others are still contemplating such a drastic change in station policies. Viewer input will help to decide the fate of such commercials. However, if as viewers and citizens we are to respond in an informed way, we must be able to see the serious arguments on both sides of the issue.   (11)

Appendix A

This survey was conducted over a three day period in the dormitory. Respondents were all college students; nine were men, seven were women.

1. Should contraceptives be advertised on television?
   A. Yes   (14)
   B. No   (2)
2. If yes, what time should such commercials appear?
   A. Anytime   (0)
   B. 9:00 a.m.—3:00 p.m.   (0)
   C. Prime time—after 7:00 p.m.   (4)
   D. After 10:00 p.m.   (12)
   E. After midnight   (0)

3. Should contraceptives be advertised in the print media (i.e. newspapers and magazines)?

   A. Yes   (15)

   B. No   (0)

   C. Other (specify) " Yes, if no specific brand names are used."   (1)

4. Should specific brand names be mentioned?

   A. Yes   (10)

   B. No   (6)

5. Do you think that contraceptive advertisements will lead to more promiscuity?

   A. Yes   (6)

   B. No   (10)

QUESTIONS FOR WRITING AND DISCUSSION

1. Which arguments do you agree with? Are you aware of any arguments—for either side—that Tobey does not mention?

2. If you were helping Tobey revise his questionnaire, what suggestions would you make?

3. Reread suggestions for lead-ins in this chapter. Which type of lead-in does Tobey use? Is it effective?

4. What shaping strategies help Tobey organize his report? Using the paragraph numbers, explain where he uses each strategy.

5. Tobey intends his audience to be anyone who watches television or reads newspapers or magazines. In your estimation, how well does he succeed in addressing that general audience? Is his information too complex, too simple, or about right? Cite one example from the report to support your answer. Is his tone too objective, too emotional, or about right? Cite one example to support your answer.

6 | EXPLAINING

Henry O. Tanner
The Banjo Lesson
Hampton University Museum. Photo by Mike Fischer

You have decided to quit your present job, so you write a note to your boss giving thirty days' notice. In response, your boss asks you, during your last few weeks at work, to write a three-page job description to help orient the person who will replace you. The job description should include a list of your current duties as well as advice to your replacement on how to execute these duties most efficiently. To write the description, you record your daily activities, look back through your calendar, comb through your records, and brainstorm a list of everything you do. As you write up the description, you include specific examples and illustrations of your typical responsibilities. □

As a gymnast and dancer, you gradually become obsessed with losing weight. You start skipping meals, purging the little food you do eat, and lying about your eating habits to your parents. Before too long, you weigh less than seventy pounds, and your physician diagnoses your condition: **anorexia nervosa**. With advice from your physician and counseling from a psychologist, you gradually begin to control your disorder. To explain to others what anorexia is, how it is caused, and what its effects are, you write an essay in which you explain your ordeal, alerting other readers to the potential dangers of uncontrolled dieting. □

Become aware of the two-sided nature of your mental make-up: one thinks in terms of the connectedness of things, the other thinks in terms of parts and sequences.

Gabriel Lusser Rico, author of Writing the Natural Way

What [a writer] knows is almost always a matter of the relationships he establishes, between example and generalization, between one part of a narrative and the next, between the idea and the counteridea that the writer sees is also relevant.

Roger Sale, author of On Writing

Explaining and demonstrating relationships is a frequent purpose for writing. Explaining goes beyond investigating the facts and reporting information; it analyzes the component parts of a subject and then shows how the parts fit in relation to one another. Its goal is to clarify for a particular group of readers *what* something is, *how* it happened or should happen, and/or *why* it exists or occurs.

Explaining begins with *analysis:* You divide a thing or phenomenon (object, person, place, feeling, belief, event, process, or cause) into its various parts. Explaining how to learn to play the piano, for example, begins with an analysis of the parts of the learning process: playing scales, learning chords, getting instruction from a teacher, sight reading, and performing in recitals. Explaining why two automobiles collided at an intersection begins with an analysis of the contributing factors: what the intersection looked like, how many cars were involved, whether the drivers were sober or intoxicated, and what the condition of each vehicle was. Then you bring the parts together and show their *relationships:* You show how practicing scales on the piano fits into the process of learning to play the piano, or you demonstrate why one small factor—such as a faulty turn signal—combined with other factors to cause an automobile accident.

How much emphasis you give to the *analysis* of the object or phenomenon and how much time you spend explaining *relationships* of the parts depends on your purpose, subject, and audience. If you want to explain how a flower reproduces, for example, you may begin by identifying the important parts, such as the pistil and stamen, that most readers need to know about before they can understand the reproductive process. However, if you are explaining the process to a botany major who already knows the parts of a flower, you might spend more time discussing the key operations in pollination or why some flowers cross-pollinate and others do not. In any effective and clear explanation, analyzing parts and showing relationships must work together for that particular group of readers.

Expository writing, or writing to explain, should be as clear as possible, since its purpose is to teach the reader. In doing that, however, explanations are more than organized pieces of information. Expository writing contains information that is focused by your point of view, by your experience, and by your reasoning powers. Thus, your explanation of a thing or phenomenon makes a point or has a thesis: This is the *right* way to define "happiness." This is how one *should* bake lasagne or do a calculus problem. These are the *most important* reasons why the senator from New York was elected. To make your explanation clear, you show what you mean by using specific support—facts, data, examples, illustrations, statistics, comparisons, analogies, and images. Your thesis is a general assertion about the relationships of the specific parts; the support helps your reader identify the parts and see the relationships. Expository writing teaches the reader by alternating between generalizations and specific examples.

FREEWRITING: EXPLAINING A CUSTOM

Before you read further in this chapter, take out a pencil or pen and a piece of paper and do this exercise. Imagine that you have just met a person from the Australian outback who knows little about American civilization or culture. This person asks you to explain a popular American custom—a sport, a holiday, an example of "polite manners," a typical entertainment activity, or a political practice. Your object is to explain the custom as clearly as you can. Since you do not want to appear foolish, you try to make American behavior appear as reasonable as possible. Write for ten minutes, explaining this custom.

TECHNIQUES FOR EXPLAINING

The main thing I try to do is write as clearly as I can.

—*E. B. White, journalist and co-author of* Elements of Style

Explaining requires first that you assess your subject and your audience. You will need to draw on your own observations and memories about this subject, but you may also need to do some reading or interview an expert. As you consider your subject, keep in mind that an explanation (involving both analysis and showing relationships) focuses on *what, how,* or *why,* but it may involve all three. Below are five important techniques for writing clear explanations.

- **Getting the reader's attention and stating the thesis.** Devise an accurate but interesting *title.* Use an attention-getting *lead-in.* State the *thesis* clearly.

- **Defining key terms and describing *what* something is.** Analyze and *define* by describing, comparing, classifying, and giving examples.

- **Identifying the steps in a process and showing *how* the steps relate to the overall process.** Describe how something should be done or how something typically happens.

- **Describing causes and effects and showing *why* certain causes lead to specific effects.** Analyze how several causes lead to a single effect or show how a single cause leads to multiple effects.

- **Supporting explanations with specific evidence.** Use descriptions, examples, comparisons, analogies, images, facts, data, or statistics to *show* what, how, or why.

In *Spirit of the Valley: Androgyny and Chinese Thought,* psychologist Sukie Colgrave illustrates many of these techniques as she explains an important concept from psychology: the phenomenon of "projection." Colgrave explains how we "project" attributes missing in our own personality onto another person—especially someone we love.

Explaining What:
Definition
Example

Explaining Why:
Effects of Projection

Explaining How: The
Process of Freeing
Ourselves from
Dependency

A one-sided development of either the masculine or feminine principles has [an] unfortunate consequence for our psychological and intellectual health: it encourages the phenomenon termed "projection." This is the process by which we project onto other people, things, or ideologies, those aspects of ourselves which we have not, for whatever reason, acknowledged or developed. The most familiar example of this is the obsession which usually accompanies being "in love." A person whose feminine side is unrealised will often "fall in love" with the feminine which she or he "sees" in another person, and similarly with the masculine. The experience of being "in love" is one of powerful dependency. As long as the projection appears to fit its object nothing awakens the person to the reality of the projection. But sooner or later the lover usually becomes aware of certain discrepancies between her or his desires and the person chosen to satisfy them. Resentment, disappointment, anger and rejection rapidly follow, and often the relationship disintegrates. . . . But if we can explore our own psyches we may discover what it is we were demanding from our lover and start to develop it in ourselves. The moment this happens we begin to see other people a little more clearly. We are freed from some of our needs to make others what we want them to be, and can begin to love them more for what they are.

Explaining *What*

Explaining *what* something is or means requires showing the relationship between it and the class of beings, objects, or concepts to which it belongs. *Formal definition,* which is often essential in explaining, has three parts: the thing or term to be defined, the class, and the distinguishing characteristics of the thing or term. The thing being defined can be concrete, such as a turkey, or abstract, such as democracy.

Thing or Term		Class	Distinguishing Characteristics
A turkey	is a	bird	that has brownish plumage and a bare, wattled head and neck; it is widely domesticated for food

Democracy	is	government	by the people, exercised direct-ly or through elected represen-tatives

Frequently, writers use an *extended definition* when they need to give more than just the formal definition. An extended definition may explain the word's etymology or historical roots, describe sensory characteristics of the term (how it looks, feels, sounds, tastes, smells), identify its parts, indicate how something is used, explain what it is not, provide an example of it, and/or note similarities or differences between this term and other words or things. The following extended definition of "democracy" begins with the etymology and then explains—using analysis, comparison, illustration, and description—what democracy is and what it is not:

> Since democracy is government of the people, by the people, and for the people, a democratic form of government is not fixed or static. Democracy is dynamic; it adapts to the wishes and needs of the people. The term "democracy" derives from the Greek word *demos,* meaning "the common people," and *-kratia,* meaning "strength or power" used to govern or rule. Democracy is based on the notion that a majority of people creates laws and then everyone agrees to abide by those laws in the interest of the common good. In a democracy, people are not ruled by a king, a dictator, or a small group of powerful individuals. Instead, people elect officials who use the power temporarily granted to them to govern the society. For example, the people may agree that their government should raise money for defense, so the officials levy taxes to support an army. If enough people decide, however, that taxes for defense are too high, then they request that their elected officials change the laws or they elect new officials. The essence of democracy lies in its responsiveness: Democracy is a form of government in which laws and lawmakers change as the will of the majority changes.

Formal Definition

Description: What Democracy Is

Etymology: Analysis of the Word's Roots

Comparison: What Democracy Is Not

Example

Formal Definition

Figurative expressions—vivid word pictures using simile, metaphor, or analogy—can also explain what something is. During World War II, the Writer's War Board asked E. B. White (author of *Charlotte's Web* and many *New Yorker* magazine essays) to provide an explanation of democracy. Instead of giving a formal definition or etymology, White responded with a series of imaginative comparisons showing the *relationship* between various parts of American culture and the concept of democracy:

> Surely the Board knows what democracy is. It is the line that forms on the right. It is the don't in Don't Shove. It is the hole in the stuffed shirt through which the sawdust slowly trickles; it is the dent in the high hat. Democracy is the recurrent suspicion that more than half of the people are right more than half of the time. It is the feeling of privacy in the voting booths, the feeling of communion in the libraries, the feeling of

vitality everywhere. Democracy is the score at the beginning of the ninth. It is an idea which hasn't been disproved yet, a song the words of which have not gone bad. It's the mustard on the hot dog and the cream in the rationed coffee. Democracy is a request from a War Board, in the middle of a morning in the middle of a war, wanting to know what democracy is.

Explaining *How*

Explaining *how* something should be done or how something happens is usually called *process analysis.* One kind of process analysis is the "how-to" explanation: how to cook a turkey, how to tune an engine, or how to get a job. These recipes or directions are *prescriptive:* You typically explain how something *should* be done. In a second kind of process analysis, you explain how something happens or typically is done—without being directive or prescriptive. In a *descriptive* process analysis, you explain how some natural or social process typically happens: how cells split during mitosis, how hailstones form in a cloud, how students react to the pressure of examinations, or how political candidates create their public images. In both prescriptive and descriptive explanations, however, you are analyzing a process—dividing the sequence into its parts or steps—and then showing how the parts contribute to the whole process.

Cookbooks, automobile repair manuals, instructions for assembling a toy or appliance, and self-improvement books are all examples of *prescriptive* process analysis. Writers of recipes, for example, begin with an analysis of the ingredients and the steps in preparing the food. Then they carefully explain how the steps are related, how to avoid problems, and how to serve their mouth-watering concoction. Farley Mowat, naturalist and author of *Never Cry Wolf*, gives his readers the following detailed—and humorous—recipe for creamed mouse. Mowat became interested in this recipe when he decided to test the nutritional content of the wolf's diet. "In the event that any of my readers may be interested in personally exploiting this hitherto overlooked source of excellent animal protein," Mowat writes, "I give the recipe in full."

Souris à la Crème

Ingredients:

One dozen fat mice	Salt and pepper
One cup white flour	Cloves
One piece sowbelly	Ethyl alcohol

Skin and gut the mice, but do not remove the heads; wash, then place in a pot with enough alcohol to cover the carcasses. Allow to marinate for about two hours. Cut sowbelly into small cubes and fry slowly until most of the fat has been rendered. Now remove the carcasses from the alcohol and roll them in a mixture of salt, pepper and flour; then place in frying pan and sauté for about five minutes (being careful not to allow the pan to get too hot, or the delicate meat will dry out and become tough and stringy). Now add a cup of alcohol and six or eight cloves. Cover the pan and allow to simmer slowly for fifteen minutes. The cream sauce can be made according to any standard recipe. When the sauce is ready, drench the carcasses with it, cover and allow to rest in a warm place for ten minutes before serving.

Explaining "how" something happens or is typically done uses a *descriptive* process analysis. It requires showing the chronological relationship between one idea, event, or phenomenon and the next— and it depends on close observation. In *Lives of the Cell*, biologist and physician Lewis Thomas explains that ants are like humans: they are individuals, but they can also act together to create a social organism. Although exactly how ants communicate remains a mystery, Thomas explains how they combine to form a thinking, working organism.

> [Ants] seem to live two kinds of lives: they are individuals, going about the day's business without much evidence of thought for tomorrow, and they are at the same time component parts, cellular elements, in the huge, writhing, ruminating organism of the Hill, the nest, the hive. . . .
>
> A Solitary ant, afield, cannot be considered to have much of anything on his mind; indeed, with only a few neurons strung together by fibers, he can't be imagined to have a mind at all, much less a thought. He is more like a ganglion on legs. Four ants together, or ten, encircling a dead moth on a path, begin to look more like an idea. They fumble and shove, gradually moving the food toward the Hill, but as though by blind chance. It is only when you watch the dense mass of thousands of ants, crowded together around the Hill, blackening the ground, that you begin to see the whole beast, and now you observe it thinking, planning, calculating. It is an intelligence, a kind of live computer, with crawling bits for its wits.
>
> At a stage in the construction, twigs of a certain size are needed, and all the members forage obsessively for twigs of just this size. Later, when outer walls are to be finished, thatched, the size must change, and as though given new orders by telephone, all the workers shift the search to the new twigs. If you disturb the arrangement of a part of the Hill, hundreds of ants will set it vibrating, shifting, until it is put right again. Distant sources of food are somehow sensed, and long lines, like tentacles, reach out over the ground, up over walls, behind boulders, to fetch it in.

Explaining *Why*

"Why?" may be the question most commonly asked by human beings. We are fascinated by the reasons for everything we experience in life. We ask questions about natural phenomena: Why is the sky blue? Why does a teakettle whistle? Why do some materials act as superconductors? We also find human attitudes and behavior intriguing: Why is chocolate so popular? Why do some people hit small leather balls with big sticks and then run around a field stomping on little white pillows? Why are America's farms economically depressed? Why did the United States go to war in Vietnam?

Explaining *why* something occurs can be the most fascinating—and difficult—kind of expository writing. Answering the question "why" usually requires analyzing *cause-and-effect relationships,* but the causes may be too complex or intangible to identify precisely. We are on comparatively secure ground when we ask *why* about physical phenomena than can be weighed, measured, and replicated under laboratory conditions. Under those conditions, we can determine cause and effect with precision. Fire, for example, has three *necessary* and *sufficient* causes: combustible material, oxygen, and ignition temperature. Without each of these causes, fire will not occur (each cause is "necessary"); these three causes are, taken together, enough to cause fire (all three are "sufficient"). The cause-and-effect relationship, in this case, can be illustrated by an equation:

Cause 1	+	Cause 2	+	Cause 3	=	Effect
(Combustible material)		(Oxygen)		(Ignition temperature)		(Fire)

Analyzing both necessary and sufficient causes is essential to explaining an effect. You may say, for example, that wind shear (an abrupt downdraft in a storm) "caused" an airplane crash. In fact, wind shear may have *helped* cause the crash (been necessary), but by itself wind shear was not the total (sufficient) cause of the crash: An airplane with enough power may be able to overcome wind shear forces in certain circumstances. An explanation of the crash is not complete until you analyze the full range of necessary *and* sufficient causes, which may include wind shear, lack of power, mechanical failure, and even pilot error.

Sometimes, explanations for physical phenomena are beyond our analytical powers. Astrophysicists, for example, have good theoretical reasons for believing that black holes cause gigantic gravitational whirlpools in outer space, but they have difficulty explaining why black holes exist—or whether they exist at all.

In the realm of human cause and effect, determining causes and effects can be as tricky as explaining why black holes exist. Why do some children learn math easily, while others fail? What effect does failing at math have on a child? What are necessary and sufficient causes for divorce? What are the effects of divorce on parents and children? You may not be able to explain all the causes or effects of something, but you should not be satisfied until you have considered a wide range of possible causes and effects. Even then, you need to qualify or modify your statements, using such words as "might," "usually," "often," "seldom," "many," or "most," and then giving as much support and evidence as you can.

In the following paragraphs, Jonathan Kozol, a critic of America's educational system and author of *Illiterate America,* explains the multiple effects of a single cause: illiteracy. Kozol supports his explanation by citing specific ways that illiteracy affects the lives of people.

Illiterates cannot read the menu in a restaurant.

They cannot read the cost of items on the menu in the *window* of the restaurant before they enter.

Illiterates cannot read the letters that their children bring home from their teachers. They cannot study school department circulars that tell them of the courses that their children must be taking if they hope to pass the SAT exams. They cannot help with homework. They cannot write a letter to the teacher. They are afraid to visit in the classroom. They do not want to humiliate their child or themselves. . . .

Many illiterates cannot read the admonition on a pack of cigarettes. Neither the Surgeon General's warning nor its reproduction on the package can alert them to the risks. Although most people learn by word of mouth that smoking is related to a number of grave physical disorders, they do not get the chance to read the detailed stories which can document this danger with the vividness that turns concern into determination to resist. They can see the handsome cowboy or the slim Virginia lady lighting up a filter cigarette; they cannot heed the words that tell them that this product is (not "may be") dangerous to their health. Sixty million men and women are condemned to be the unalerted, high-risk candidates for cancer. . . .

Illiterates cannot travel freely. When they attempt to do so, they encounter risks that few of us can dream of. They cannot read traffic signs and, while they often learn to recognize and to decipher symbols, they cannot manage street names which they haven't seen before. The same is true for bus and subway stops. While ingenuity can sometimes help a man or woman to discern directions from familiar landmarks, building, cemeteries, churches, and the like, most illiterates are virtually immobilized. They seldom wander past the streets and neighborhoods they know. Geographical paralysis becomes a bitter metaphor for their entire existence. They are immobilized in almost every sense we can imagine. They can't move up. They can't move out. They cannot see beyond.

WARMING UP: JOURNAL EXERCISES

The following exercises will help you practice writing explanations. Read all of the following exercises and then write on the three that interest you most. If another idea occurs to you, write a free entry about it.

1. Choose a term or concept from a course you are taking and explain what it means or is. Assume that your audience is someone who is not enrolled in that class.

2. Imitating E. B. White's short "definition" of democracy, use imaginative comparisons to write a short definition—serious or humorous—of one of the following words: "freedom," "adolescence," "mathematics," "politicians," "parents," "misery," "higher education," "luck," or a word of your own choice.

3. Novelist Ernest Hemingway once defined courage as "grace under pressure." Using this definition, explain how you or someone you know showed this kind of courage in a difficult situation.

4. When asked what jazz is, Louis Armstrong replied: "Man, if you gotta ask you'll never know." If you know quite a bit about jazz, explain what Armstrong meant. Or choose a familiar subject to which the same remark might apply. What can be "explained" about that subject and what cannot?

5. Observe the behavior of people in some specific place—at a party, in a cafeteria, at a sporting event, on the street, in a supermarket or department store, on buses or trains, or at the beach. After observing the variety of behavior, "explain" the people you find there by classifying them into types.

6. Choose a skill you've acquired (for example, playing a musical instrument, operating a machine, playing a sport, drawing, counseling others, driving in rush-hour traffic, dieting) and explain to a novice how he or she can acquire that skill. Reread what you've written. Then write another version addressed to an expert. What parts can you leave out? What must you add?

7. At your place of work, you've just hired a substitute to fill in for you for one day. Write a note to that person explaining what he or she should do and how to do it.

8. Three-year-old children are insatiably curious. They ask any older person around them a never-ending series of "why" questions. Imagine you are going for a walk in a familiar place with a three-year-old. What questions might the child ask you about either strange or commonplace things or occurrences? Select one "why" question. First write out an explanation of that question for another adult. Then write your explanation for the three-year-old.

9. Anger can come so suddenly and swiftly that sometimes we are unaware that, like other emotions, it has causes. When we become angry with someone, we usually assume that the other person's attitudes or actions are sufficient cause. Often, however, our anger has other causes that may be related to our experiences on that particular day or in the past. Choose one particular time when you were angered by someone. Then, in two separate lists, *analyze* what this person did to make you angry, but also what you had been doing or worrying about before your angry outburst. Review these two lists and explain which combination of causes were necessary and sufficient to cause your sudden anger.

EXPLAINING : PROFESSIONAL WRITING

IS SEX NECESSARY?
VIRGIN BIRTH AND OPPORTUNISM
IN THE GARDEN

David Quammen

In this selection from Natural Acts: A Sidelong View of Science and Nature *(1985), David Quammen uses his skills as a novelist and biology watcher to describe the mysterious sex life of the aphid. In the process of explaining how and why aphids reproduce, he humorously informs his readers about cloning and genetic evolution. Beginning with his catchy title—a reference to James Thurber and E. B. White's satire* Is Sex Necessary?*— Quammen teases his readers into the private world of those "little nebbishy sap-sucking insects." As Quammen admits, he is not a scientist but someone who haunts libraries and snoops on other* *people's field trips, "asking too many foolish questions and occasionally scribbling notes." Quammen's conversational tone, witty style, and natural curiosity immediately engage readers who might fall asleep over a biology textbook. Quammen has also written a spy thriller,* The Zolta Configuration *(1983); published a second collection of essays on science,* The Flight of the Iguana *(1988); and written a regular column for* Outside *magazine.*

Birds do it, bees do it, goes the tune. But the songsters, as usual, would mislead us with drastic oversimplifications. The full truth happens to be more eccentrically nonlibidinous: Sometimes they *don't* do it, those very creatures, and get the same results anyway. Bees of all species, for instance, are notable to geneticists precisely for their ability to produce offspring while doing *without.* Likewise at least one variety of bird—the Beltsville Small White turkey, a domestic dinner-table model out of Beltsville, Maryland—has achieved scientific renown for a similar feat. What we are talking about here is celibate motherhood, procreation without copulation, a phenomenon that goes by the technical name *parthenogenesis.* Translated from the Greek roots: virgin birth.   (1)

And you don't have to be Catholic to believe in this one.   (2)

Miraculous as it may seem, parthenogenesis is actually rather common throughout nature, practiced regularly or intermittently by at least some species within almost every group of animals except (for reasons still unknown) dragonflies and mammals. Reproduction by virgin females has been discovered among reptiles, birds, fishes, amphibians, crustaceans, mollusks, ticks, the jellyfish clan, flatworms, roundworms, segmented worms; and among insects (notwithstanding those unrelentingly sexy dragonflies) it is especially favored. The order Hymenoptera, including all bees and wasps, is uniformly parthenogenetic in the manner by which males are produced: Every male honeybee is born without any genetic contribution from a father. Among the beetles, there are thirty-five different forms of parthenogenetic weevil. The African weaver ant employs parthenogenesis, as do twenty-three species of fruit fly and at least one kind of roach. The gall midge *Miastor* is notorious for the exceptionally bizarre and grisly scenario that allows its fatherless young to see daylight: *Miastor* daughters cannibalize the mother from inside, with ruthless impatience, until her hollowed-out skin splits open like the door of an overcrowded nursery. But the foremost practitioners of virgin birth—their elaborate and versatile proficiency unmatched in the animal kingdom—are undoubtedly the aphids.   (3)

Now no sensible reader of even this book can be expected, I realize, to care faintly about aphid biology *qua* aphid biology. That's just asking too much. But there's a larger rationale for dragging you aphid-ward. The life cycle of these little nebbishy sap-sucking insects, the very same that infest rose bushes and house plants, not only exemplifies *how* parthenogenetic reproduction is done; it also very clearly shows *why*.   (4)

First the biographical facts. A typical aphid, which feeds entirely on plant juices tapped off from the vascular system of young leaves, spends winter dormant and protected, as an egg. The egg is attached near a bud site on the new growth of a poplar tree. In March, when the tree sap has begun to rise and the buds have begun to burgeon, an aphid hatchling appears, plugging its sharp snout (like a mosquito's) into the tree's tenderest plumbing. This solitary individual aphid will be, necessarily, a wingless female. If she is lucky, she will become sole founder of a vast aphid population. Having sucked enough poplar sap to reach maturity, she produces—by *live birth* now, and without benefit of a mate—daughters identical to herself. These wingless daughters also plug into the tree's flow of sap, and they also produce further wingless daughters, until sometime in late May, when that particular branch of that particular tree can support no more thirsty aphids. Suddenly there is a change: The next generation of daughters are born with wings. They fly off in search of a better situation.   (5)

One such aviatrix lands on an herbaceous plant—say a young climbing bean in some human's garden—and the pattern repeats. She plugs into the sap ducts on the underside of a new leaf, commences feasting destructively, and delivers by parthenogenesis a great brood of wingless daughters. The daughters beget more daughters, those daughters beget still more, and so on, until the poor bean plant is encrusted with a solid mob of these fat little elbowing greedy sisters. Then again, neatly triggered by the crowded conditions, a generation of daughters are born with wings. Away they fly, looking for prospects, and one of them lights on, say, a sugar beet. (The switch from bean to beet is fine, because our species of typical aphid is not inordinately choosy.) The sugar beet before long is covered, sucked upon mercilessly, victimized by a horde of mothers and nieces and granddaughters. Still not a single male aphid has appeared anywhere in the chain.   (6)

The lurching from one plant to another continues; the alternation between wingless and winged daughters continues. But in September, with fresh tender plant growth increasingly hard to find, there is another change.   (7)

Flying daughters are born who have a different destiny: They wing back to the poplar tree, where they give birth to a crop of wingless females that are unlike any so far. These latest girls know the meaning of sex! Meanwhile, at long last, the starving survivors back on that final bedraggled sugar beet have brought forth a generation of males. The males have wings. They take to the air in quest of poplar trees and first love. *Et voilà.* The mated females lay eggs that will wait out the winter near bud sites on that poplar tree, and the circle is thus completed. One single aphid hatchling—call her the *fundatrix*—in this way can give rise in the course of a year, from her own ovaries exclusively, to roughly a zillion aphids. (8)

Well and good, you say. A zillion aphids. But what is the point of it?   (9)

The point, for aphids as for most other parthenogenetic animals, is (1) exceptionally fast reproduction that allows (2) maximal exploitation of temporary resource abundance and unstable environmental conditions, while (3) facilitating the successful colonization of unfamiliar habitats. In other words the aphid, like the gall midge and the weaver ant and the rest of their fellow parthenogens, is by its evolved character a galloping opportunist.   (10)

This is a term of science, not of abuse. Population ecologists make an illuminating distinction between what they label *equilibrium* and *opportunistic* species. According to William Birky and John Gilbert, from a paper in the journal *American Zoologist:* "Equilibrium species, exemplified by many vertebrates, maintain relatively constant population sizes, in part by being adapted to reproduce, at least slowly, in most of the environmental conditions which they meet. Opportunistic species, on the other hand, show extreme population fluctuations; they are adapted to reproduce only in a relatively narrow range of conditions, but make up for this by reproducing extremely rapidly in favorable circumstances. At least in some cases, opportunistic organisms can also be categorized as colonizing organisms." Birky and Gilbert also emphasize that "The potential for rapid reproduction is the essential evolutionary ticket for entry into the opportunistic life style."   (11)

And parthenogenesis, in turn, is the greatest time-saving gimmick in the history of animal reproduction. No hours or days are wasted while a female looks for a mate; no minutes lost to the act of mating itself. The female aphid attains sexual maturity and, bang, she becomes automatically pregnant. No waiting, no courtship, no fooling around. She delivers her brood of daughters, they grow to puberty and, zap, another generation immediately. If humans worked as fast, Jane Fonda today would be a great-grandmother. The time saved to parthenogenetic species may seem trivial, but it is not. It adds up dizzyingly: In the same time taken by a sexually reproducing insect to complete three generations for a total of 1,200 offspring, an aphid (assuming the *same* time required for each female to mature, and the *same* number of progeny in each litter), squandering no time on courtship or sex, will progress through six generations for an extended family of 318,000,000.   (12)

Even this isn't speedy enough for some restless opportunists. That matricidal gall midge *Miastor*, whose larvae feed on fleeting eruptions of fungus under the bark of trees, has developed a startling way to cut further time from the cycle of procreation. Far from waiting for a mate, *Miastor* does not even wait for maturity. When food is abundant, it is the *larva*, not the adult female fly, who is eaten alive from inside by her own daughters. And as those voracious daughters burst free of the husk that was their mother, each of them already contains further larval daughters taking shape ominously within its own ovaries. While the food lasts, while opportunity endures, no *Miastor* female can live to adulthood without dying of motherhood.   (13)

The implicit principle behind all this nonsexual reproduction, all this hurry, is simple: Don't argue with success. Don't tamper with a genetic blueprint that works. Unmated female aphids, and gall midges, pass on their own gene patterns virtually unaltered (except for the occasional mutation) to their daughters. Sexual reproduction, on the other hand, constitutes, by its essence, genetic tampering. The whole purpose of joining sperm with egg is to shuffle the genes of both parents and come up with a new combination that might perhaps be more advantageous. Give the kid something neither Mom nor Pop ever had. Parthenogenetic species, during their hurried phases at least, dispense with this genetic shuffle. They stick stubbornly to the gene pattern that seems to be working. They produce (with certain complicated exceptions) natural clones of themselves.   (14)

But what they gain thereby in reproductive rate, in great explosions of population, they give up in flexibility. They minimize their genetic options. They lessen their chances of adapting to unforeseen changes of circumstance.   (15)

Which is why more than one biologist has drawn the same conclusion as M. J. D. White: "Parthenogenetic forms seem to be frequently successful in the particular ecological niche which they occupy, but sooner or later the inherent disadvantages of their genetic system must be expected to lead to a lack of adaptability, followed by eventual extinction, or perhaps in some cases by a return to sexuality."   (16)

So it *is* necessary, at least intermittently (once a year, for the aphids, whether they need it or not), this thing called sex. As of course you and I knew it must be. Otherwise surely, by now, we mammals and dragonflies would have come up with something more dignified.   (17)

VOCABULARY

In your journal, write the meanings of the following words.

- more eccentrically *nonlibidinous* (1)
- *celibate* motherhood (1)
- the technical name *parthenogenesis* (1)
- exceptionally *bizarre* (3)
- *qua* aphid biology (4)
- the *vascular* system (5)
- begun to *burgeon* (5)
- One such *aviatrix* (6)
- an *herbaceous* plant (6)
- a galloping *opportunist* (10)
- That *matricidal* gall midge (13)
- natural *clones* of themselves (14)
- particular ecological *niche* (16)

QUESTIONS FOR WRITING AND DISCUSSION

1. Write for five minutes describing your response to Quammen's essay. Did you enjoy reading it? Did you think Quammen was being too cute? Describe what you learned from the essay. Which biological terms or concepts were difficult or unfamiliar?

2. According to Quammen, what are the genetic advantages and disadvantages of parthenogenesis in the animal kingdom?

3. Quammen's essay illustrates how writers typically combine definition, process analysis, and causal analysis in a single essay. Identify paragraphs where he *defines* key terms. Which paragraphs explain the stages in the *process* of parthenogenesis? (What are the major stages?) Which paragraphs explain the positive and negative *effects* of parthenogenesis?

4. Describe the intended audience for Quammen's essay. Where does Quammen directly address his readers? Where does Quammen cue his readers about what he intends to discuss? Find examples of the following audience cues: thesis sentence, essay map, paragraph hooks, transition words, and summaries of major points.

5. Describe Quammen's tone (his attitude toward his subject) in this essay. Cite two passages that illustrate this tone. Describe

Quammen's voice (his personality as projected in the essay). Cite two passages that reveal his voice. Based on your description, are his tone and voice appropriate for the subject and the audience?

6. In paragraph 3, Quammen says that the gall midge's skin "splits open like the door of an overcrowded nursery." Find two other similes or images in his essay. Are his images vivid? Are they appropriate?

7. Anthropomorphism is the attribution of human motivation and behavior to nonhuman objects or species. Where is Quammen anthropomorphic in his essay? Is his humanizing of aphids entertaining or effective? Explain your answer, based on your perception of his intended purpose and audience.

TO DISPEL FEARS OF LIVE BURIAL

Jessica Mitford

In this selection from The American Way of Death, *Jessica Mitford illustrates the kind of investigative journalism (some call it muckraking) she has perfected. Other works by Mitford include* The Trial of Dr. Spock *(1969),* Kind and Unusual Punishment: The Prison Business *(1973), and* Poison Penmanship *(1979), a collection of articles. In "To Dispel Fears of Live Burial," Mitford explains what embalming is, shows how the process works, and suggests why funeral directors and the public agree to the whole affair. If writing exposition means the "act of exposing" as well as offering explanation, then Mitford is definitely writing "expository" prose. The exposure is so revealing, in fact, that we are shocked by what we learn. As we read her essay, we begin to wonder about causes. Why doesn't the public know more about the funeral industry? Why are we so ignorant in these matters? Are we, as consumers, getting what we really want—and deserve?*

Embalming is indeed a most extraordinary procedure, and one must wonder at the docility of Americans who each year pay hundreds of millions of dollars for its perpetuation, blissfully ignorant of what it is all about, what is done, how it is done. Not one in ten thousand has any idea of what actually takes place. Books on the subject are extremely hard to come by. They are not to be found in most libraries or bookshops.   (1)

In an era when huge television audiences watch surgical operations in the comfort of their living rooms, when, thanks to the animated cartoon, the geography of the digestive system has become familiar territory even to the nursery school set, in a land where the satisfaction of curiosity about almost all matters is a national pastime, the secrecy surrounding embalming can, surely, hardly be attributed to the inherent gruesomeness of the subject. Custom in this regard has within this century suffered a complete reversal. In the early days of American embalming, when it was performed in the home of the deceased, it was almost mandatory for some relative to stay by the embalmer's side and witness the procedure. Today, family members who might wish to be in attendance would certainly be dissuaded by the funeral director. All others, except apprentices, are excluded by law from the preparation room.   (2)

A close look at what does actually take place may explain in large measure the undertaker's intractable reticence concerning a procedure that has become his major *raison d'être*. Is it possible he fears that public information about embalming might lead patrons to wonder if they really want this service? If the funeral men are loath to discuss the subject outside the trade, the reader may, understandably, be equally loath to go on reading at this point. For those who have the stomach for it, let us part the formaldehyde curtain. . . .   (3)

The body is first laid out in the undertaker's morgue—or rather, Mr. Jones is reposing in the preparation room—to be readied to bid the world farewell.   (4)

The preparation room in any of the better funeral establishments has the tiled and sterile look of a surgery, and indeed the embalmer-restorative artist who does his chores there is beginning to adopt the term "dermasurgeon" (appropriately corrupted by some mortician-writers as "demi-surgeon") to describe his calling. His equipment, consisting of scalpels, scissors, augers, forceps, clamps, needles, pumps, tubes, bowls and basins, is crudely imitative of the surgeon's, as is his technique, acquired in a nine- or twelve-month post-high-school course in an embalming school. He is supplied by an advanced chemical industry with a bewildering array of fluids, sprays, pastes, oils, powders, creams, to fix or soften tissue, shrink or distend it as needed, dry it here, restore the moisture there. There are cosmetics, waxes and paints to fill and cover features, even plaster of Paris to replace entire limbs. There are ingenious aids to prop and stabilize the cadaver: a Vari-Pose Head Rest, the Edwards Arm and Hand Positioner, the Repose Block (to support the shoulders during the embalming), and the Throop Foot Positioner, which resembles an old-fashioned stocks.   (5)

Mr. John H. Eckels, president of the Eckels College of Mortuary Science, thus describes the first part of the embalming procedure: "In the hands of a skilled practitioner, this work may be done in a comparatively short time and without mutilating the body other than by slight incision—so slight that it scarcely would cause serious inconvenience if made upon a living person. It is necessary to remove the blood, and doing this not only helps in the disinfecting, but removes the principal cause of disfigurements due to discoloration." (6)

Another textbook discusses the all-important time element: "The earlier this is done, the better, for every hour that elapses between death and embalming will add to the problems and complications encountered. . . ." Just how soon should one get going on the embalming? The author tells us, "On the basis of such scanty information made available to this profession through its rudimentary and haphazard system of technical research, we must conclude that the best results are to be obtained if the subject is embalmed before life is completely extinct—that is, before cellular death has occurred. In the average case, this would mean within an hour after somatic death." For those who feel that there is something a little rudimentary, not to say haphazard, about this advice, a comforting thought is offered by another writer. Speaking of fears entertained in early days of premature burial, he points out, "One of the effects of embalming by chemical injection, however, has been to dispel fears of live burial." How true; once the blood is removed, chances of live burial are indeed remote. (7)

To return to Mr. Jones, the blood is drained out through the veins and replaced by embalming fluid pumped in through the arteries. As noted in *The Principles and Practices of Embalming,* "every operator has a favorite injection and drainage point —a fact which becomes a handicap only if he fails or refuses to forsake his favorites when conditions demand it." Typical favorites are the carotid artery, femoral artery, jugular vein, subclavian vein. There are various choices of embalming fluid. If Flextone is used, it will produce a "mild flexible rigidity. The skin retains a velvety softness, the tissues are rubbery and pliable. Ideal for women and children." It may be blended with B. and G. Products Company's Lyf-Lyk tint, which is guaranteed to reproduce "nature's own skin texture . . . the velvety appearance of living tissue." Suntone comes in three separate tints: Suntan; Special Cosmetic Tint, a pink shade "especially indicated for female subjects"; and Regular Cosmetic Tint, moderately pink. (8)

About three to six gallons of dyed and perfumed solution of formaldehyde, glycerin, borax, phenol, alcohol and water is soon circulating through Mr. Jones, whose mouth has been sewn together with a "needle directed upward between the upper lip and gum and brought out through the left nostril," with the corners raised slightly "for a more pleasant expression." If he should be bucktoothed, his teeth are cleaned with Bon Ami and coated with colorless nail polish.

His eyes, meanwhile, are closed with flesh-tinted eye caps and eye cement. (9)

The next step is to have at Mr. Jones with a thing called a trocar. This is a long, hollow needle attached to a tube. It is jabbed into the abdomen, poked around the entrails and chest cavity, the contents of which are pumped out and replaced with "cavity fluid." This done, and the hole in the abdomen sewn up, Mr. Jones's face is heavily creamed (to protect the skin from burns which may be caused by leakage of the chemicals), and he is covered with a sheet and left unmolested for a while. But not for long—there is more, much more, in store for him. He has been embalmed, but not yet restored, and the best time to start the restorative work is eight to ten hours after embalming, when the tissues have become firm and dry. (10)

The object of all this attention to the corpse, it must be remembered, is to make it presentable for viewing in an attitude of healthy repose. "Our customs require the presentation of our dead in the semblance of normality . . . unmarred by the ravages of illness, disease or mutilation," says Mr. J. Sheridan Mayer in his *Restorative Art.* This is rather a large order since few people die in the full bloom of health, unravaged by illness and unmarked by some disfigurement. The funeral industry is equal to the challenge: "In some cases, the gruesome appearance of a mutilated or disease-ridden subject may be quite discouraging. The task of restoration may seem impossible and shake the confidence of the embalmer. This is the time for intestinal fortitude and determination. Once the formative work is begun and affected tissues are cleaned or removed, all doubts of success vanish. It is surprising and gratifying to discover the results which may be obtained." (11)

The embalmer, having allowed an appropriate interval to elapse, returns to the attack, but now he brings into play the skill and equipment of sculptor and cosmetician. Is a hand missing? Casting one in plaster of Paris is a simple matter. "For replacement purposes, only a cast of the back of the hand is necessary; this is within the ability of the average operator and is quite adequate." If a lip or two, a nose or an ear should be missing, the embalmer has at hand a variety of restorative waxes with which to model replacements. Pores and skin texture are simulated by stippling with a little brush, and over this cosmetics are laid on. Head off? Decapitation cases are rather routinely handled. Ragged edges are trimmed, and head joined to torso with a series of splints, wires and sutures. It is a good idea to have a little something at the neck—a scarf or a high collar—when time for viewing comes. Swollen mouth? Cut out tissue as needed from inside the lips. If too much is removed, the surface contour can easily be restored by padding with cotton. Swollen necks and cheeks are reduced by removing tissue through vertical incisions made down each side of the neck. "When the deceased is casketed, the pillow will hide the suture incisions . . . as an extra precaution against leakage, the suture may be painted with liquid sealer." (12)

The opposite condition is more likely to present itself—that of emaciation. His hypodermic syringe now loaded with massage cream, the embalmer seeks out and fills the hollowed and sunken areas by injection. In this procedure the backs of the hands and fingers and the under-chin area should not be neglected. (13)

Positioning the lips is a problem that recurrently challenges the ingenuity of the embalmer. Closed too tightly, they tend to give a stern, even disapproving expression. Ideally, embalmers feel, the lips should give the impression of being ever so slightly parted, the upper lip protruding slightly for a more youthful appearance. This takes some engineering, however, as the lips tend to drift apart. Lip drift can sometimes be remedied by pushing one or two straight pins through the inner margin of the lower lip and then inserting them between the two front upper teeth. If Mr. Jones happens to have no teeth, the pins can just as easily be anchored in his Armstrong Face Former and Denture Replacer. Another method to maintain lip closure is to dislocate the lower jaw, which is then held in its new position by a wire run through holes which have been drilled through the upper and lower jaws at the midline. As the French are fond of saying, *il faut souffrir pour être belle.* (14)

If Mr. Jones has died of jaundice, the embalming fluid will very likely turn him green. Does this deter the embalmer? Not if he has intestinal fortitude. Masking pastes and cosmetics are heavily laid on, burial garments and casket interiors are color-correlated with particular care, and Jones is displayed beneath rose-colored lights. Friends will say "How well he looks." Death by carbon monoxide, on the other hand, can be rather a good thing from the embalmer's viewpoint: "One advantage is the fact that this type of discoloration is an exaggerated form of a natural pink coloration." This is nice because the healthy glow is already present and needs but little attention. (15)

The patching and filling completed, Mr. Jones is now shaved, washed and dressed. Cream-based cosmetic, available in pink, flesh, suntan, brunette and blond, is applied to his hands and face, his hair is shampooed and combed (and, in the case of Mrs. Jones, set), his hands manicured. For the horny-handed son of toil special care must be taken; cream should be applied to remove ingrained grime, and the nails cleaned. "If he were not in the habit of having them manicured in life, trimming and shaping is advised for better appearance—never questioned by kin." (16)

Jones is now ready for casketing (this is the present participle of the verb "to casket"). In this operation his right shoulder should be depressed slightly "to turn the body a bit to the right and soften the appearance of lying flat on the back." Positioning the hands is a matter of importance, and special rubber positioning blocks may be used. The hands should be cupped slightly for a more lifelike, relaxed appearance. Proper placement of the body requires a delicate sense of balance. It should lie as high as possible in the casket, yet not so high that the lid, when lowered, will hit the nose. On the other hand, we are cautioned, placing the body too low "creates the impression that the body is in a box."   (17)

Jones is next wheeled into the appointed slumber room where a few last touches may be added—his favorite pipe placed in his hand or, if he was a great reader, a book propped into position. (In the case of little Master Jones a Teddy bear may be clutched.) Here he will hold open house for a few days, visiting hours 10 a.m. to 9 p.m.   (18)

VOCABULARY

In your journal, write the meaning of the following words.

- *docility* of Americans   (1)
- *intractable reticence* concerning a procedure   (3)
- *raison d'être* [reason for being]   (3)
- *loath* to discuss the subject   (3)
- *rudimentary* and haphazard system (7)
- *somatic* death   (7)
- left *unmolested* for a while   (10)
- splints, wires and *sutures*   (12)
- that of *emaciation*   (13)
- *il faut souffrir pour être belle* [one must suffer in order to be beautiful]   (14)
- died of *jaundice*   (15)

QUESTIONS FOR WRITING AND DISCUSSION

1. What word best describes your initial reaction to this article: disgust, nausea, confusion, anger, surprise, amazement, disbelief, or some other word? Explain your reaction.

2. Funeral directors all over the country were outraged when *The American Way of Death* appeared. What passages from this selection would most likely anger them—and why?

3. Do you believe Mitford's *purpose* in this essay was just to inform us about the embalming procedure? To explain how and why it happens? To persuade us to some belief or action? What parts of the essay illustrate her purpose(s) most clearly? (Refer to paragraph numbers.)

4. The contrast between appearance and reality is a recurring theme in this essay—the lifelike appearance of the embalmed and prepared body versus the reality of death. Where in the essay is this contrast most obvious?

5. Mitford's essay illustrates organization by process analysis—her explanation of *how* the embalming process occurs. List the major steps in the embalming process. (Refer to paragraph numbers for each step.) What references to time or sequence does she use for transitions at the beginning of the paragraphs?

6. Without doing a thorough investigation, Mitford could not have learned enough to write this explanation of embalming. What books, journals, or interviews does she refer to in her essay? What direct quotations does she use?

7. Describe the *persona* Mitford projects in this essay. What is her *tone* or attitude toward the subject? Is she writing from the perspective of a sympathetic observer of the funeral industry or of one hostile to its pretensions? Where in the essay is her tone most obvious?

EXPLAINING: THE WRITING PROCESS

ASSIGNMENT FOR EXPLAINING

Explain *what* something means or is, *how* it should be done or how it occurs, and/or *why* something occurs. Choose from your personal experiences, talents, or interests or choose from ideas, concepts, theories, or strategies you are learning in other courses. Your purpose is to explain something as clearly as possible for your audience by analyzing, showing relationships, and demonstrating with examples, facts, illustrations, data, or other information.

Choosing a Subject

If one of your journal entries suggested a possible subject, go on to the collecting and shaping strategies. If you still need an interesting subject, consider the following suggestions:

You can write about anything, *and if you write well enough, even the reader with no intrinsic interest in the subject will become involved.*

—*Tracy Kidder, novelist*

- Reread your authority list or the most interesting journal entries from previous chapters. Do they contain an idea that you might define or explain, a process suitable for a how-to explanation, or causes or effects you could analyze and explain for a certain audience?
- Brainstorm a list of the five most important things you've done in the last three years. Focus on one thing, event, or idea. Now imagine that your audience is someone like you, only three years younger. Explain this topic.
- Reread your notes from another class that has an upcoming examination. Select some topic, idea, principle, process, famous person, or event from the text or your notes. Investigate other texts, popular magazines, or journals for information on that topic. If appropriate, interview someone or conduct a survey. Explain this principle or process to a member of your writing class.

Collecting

Questions   Once you have a tentative subject and audience in mind, consider which of the following will be your *primary* focus (all three may be relevant):

- *What* something means or is
- *How* something occurs or is done (or should be done)
- *Why* something occurs or what its effects are

To explain *what* something is, jot down answers to each of the following questions. The more you can write on each question, the more details you'll have for your topic.

- What are its class and distinguishing characteristics?
- What is its etymology?
- How can you describe it?
- What examples can you give?
- What are its parts or its function?
- What is it similar to or what is it *not?*
- What figurative comparisons apply?
- How can it be classified?
- Which of the above is most useful to your audience?

To explain *how* something occurs or is done, answer the following questions:

- What are the component parts or steps in the whole process?
- What is the exact sequence of steps or events?
- Are several of the steps or events related?
- If steps or events were omitted, would the outcome change?
- Which steps or events are most crucial?
- Which steps or events does your audience most need to know?

To explain *why* something occurs or what its effects are, consider:

- Which are the necessary or sufficient causes?
- Which causes are remote in time and which are immediate?
- What is the order or sequence of the causes, or do the causes occur simultaneously?
- What are the effects, and do they occur in a sequence or simultaneously?
- Do the causes and effects occur in a "chain reaction"?
- Is there an action or situation that would have prevented the effect?
- Are there comparable things or events that have similar causes or effects?
- Which causes or effects need special clarification for your audience?

Branching   Often, *branching* can help you visually analyze your subject. Start with your topic and then subdivide each idea into its component parts. The resulting analysis will help generate ideas, and it may also suggest ways to shape an essay.

Branching can also take the form of a tree, with a main trunk for the subject and separate branches for each of the subtopics. For her essay on effective job hunting, Lisa Walters put her information in a tree diagram.

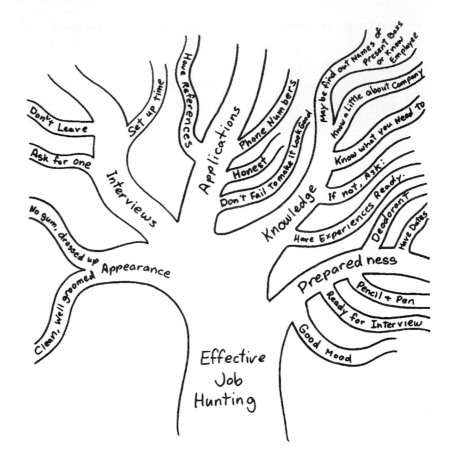

Observing If you can observe your subject, then draw it, describe it, or take careful notes. Which senses can you use to describe it: sight, sound, touch, smell, taste? If it is a scientific experiment you can reproduce or a social situation you can reconstruct, go through it again and observe carefully. As you observe it, put yourself in your readers' shoes: What do you need to explain to them?

Remembering Your own experience and memory are essential for explaining. *Freewriting, looping,* and *clustering* may all generate detailed information, good examples, and interesting perspectives that will make your explanation clearer and more vivid. (See Chapter 4 for an explanation of looping and clustering.)

Investigating Use sources available in the library, textbooks containing relevant information, or interviews with teachers, participants, or experts. Interview your classmates about their own subjects for this essay: Someone else's subject may trigger an idea you can write about or suggest a fresh approach to the subject you have already chosen.

RESEARCH TIPS

Review your topic for research possibilities. Four research strategies are direct *observation*, use of *memories* and personal experience, *field research* (including interviews and surveys), and *library research*. (See Chapter 5, pp. 156–159, for interview and survey techniques. See Chapter 10, pp. 407–424 on Using and Documenting Sources.) Tips to remember: Make *photocopies* of all sources you plan to cite in your essay. When you make copies, be sure to *write all relevant information* on the photocopies, such as author, date, publisher, place of publication, journal title, and volume numbers. When you cite sources in the text, be sure to *introduce* your sources. (See pp. 409–410.) Make sure your direct quotations are *accurate* word-for-word transcriptions.

Shaping

As you collect information and generate ideas from your collecting activities, be sure to *narrow* and *focus* your subject into a topic suitable for a short essay. You will not be able to cover everything you've read, thought, or experienced about your subject. Choose the most interesting ideas—for you and for your audience—and shape, order, and clarify those ideas. In addition to *spatial order* and *comparison/contrast*, which are discussed in Chapters 3 and 4, one of the following shaping strategies may help you organize your essay.

Definition and Classification An essay explaining *what* something means or is can be shaped using a variety of definition strategies or by classifying the subject.

Definition itself is not a single organizing strategy; it encompasses a variety of strategies that may be useful in shaping your essay: description, analysis of parts or function, comparison/contrast, development by examples, or figures of speech such as simile, metaphor, and analogy.

Classification, on the other hand, is a single strategy that can organize a paragraph or a whole essay quickly. Observers of human behavior love to use classification. Grocery shoppers might be classified by types: racers (the ones who seem to have just won forty-five

Readers may be strangers who have no immediate reason to care about your writing. They want order, clarity, and stimulation. . . .

—Elizabeth Cowan Neeld, teacher and author

seconds of free shopping and run down the aisles, filling their carts as fast as possible), talkers (the ones whose phone must be out of order because they stand in the aisles gossiping forever), penny-pinchers (who always have their calculators out and read the unit price labels for everything), party shoppers (who camp out in the junk food aisles, filling their carts with potato chips, dip, candy, peanuts, and drink mixers), and dawdlers (who leave their carts crosswise in the aisles while they read twenty-nine different soup-can labels). You can write a sentence or two about each type, or devote a whole paragraph to explaining a single type.

Example   Development by example can effectively illustrate what something is or means, but it can also help explain how or why something happens. Usually, an example describes a specific incident, located at a certain place and occurring at a particular time, that *shows* or *demonstrates* the main idea. In the following paragraph from *Mediaspeak*, Donna Woolfolk Cross explains what effects soap operas can have on addicted viewers. This paragraph is developed by several examples—some described in detail, others referred to briefly.

> Dedicated watchers of soap operas often confuse fact with fiction. . . . Stars of soap operas tell hair-raising stories of their encounters with fans suffering from this affliction. Susan Lucci, who plays the promiscuous Erica Kane on "All My Children," tells of a time she was riding in a parade: "We were in a crowd of about 250,000 traveling in an antique open car moving ver-r-ry slowly. At that time in the series I was involved with a character named Nick. Some man broke through, came right up to the car and said to me, 'Why don't you give *me* a little bit of what you've been giving Nick?'" The man hung onto the car, menacingly, until she was rescued by the police. Another time, when she was in church, the reverent silence was broken by a woman's astonished remark, "Oh, my god, Erica prays!" Margaret Mason, who plays the villainous Lisa Anderson in "Days of Our Lives," was accosted by a woman who poured a carton of milk all over her in the supermarket. And once a woman actually tried to force her car off the Ventura Freeway.

Voice and Tone   Writers also use voice and tone to shape and control a whole passage, often in combination with other shaping strategies. In the following paragraph, Toni Bambara, author of *The Salt Eaters* and numerous short stories, explains *what* being a writer is all about. This paragraph is shaped both by a single extended example and by Bambara's voice talking directly to the reader.

> When I replay the tapes on file in my head, tapes of speeches I've given at writing conferences over the years, I invariably hear myself saying— "A writer, like any other cultural worker, like any other member of the

community, ought to try to put her/his skills in the service of the community." Some years ago when I returned south, my picture in the paper prompted several neighbors to come visit. "You a writer? What all you write?" Before I could begin the catalogue, one old gent interrupted with—"Ya know Miz Mary down the block? She need a writer to help her send off a letter to her grandson overseas." So I began a career as the neighborhood scribe—letters to relatives, snarling letters to the traffic chief about the promised stop sign, nasty letters to the utilities, angry letters to the principal about that confederate flag hanging in front of the school, contracts to transfer a truck from seller to buyer, etc. While my efforts have been graciously appreciated in the form of sweet potato dumplings, herb teas, hair braiding, and the like, there is still much room for improvement—"For a writer, honey, you've got a mighty bad hand. Didn't they teach penmanship at that college?" Another example, I guess of words setting things in motion. What goes around, comes around, as the elders say.

Chronological Order and Process Analysis   Using chronological order for a *how* explanation creates a process analysis. Jessica Mitford's explanation of embalming illustrates how chronological order or process analysis can shape a whole essay. Notice how the beginnings of several body paragraphs use transitions that *signal* to the reader the chronological order of the embalming process:

> The body is *first* laid out in the undertaker's morgue. . . .   (4)

> Mr. John H. Eckels . . . describes the *first part* of the embalming procedure. . . .   (6)

> *To return* to Mr. Jones, the blood is drained out through the veins. . . .   (8)

> The *next step* is to have at Mr. Jones with a thing called a trocar.   (10)

> The embalmer, *having allowed an appropriate interval to elapse, returns* to the attack. . . .   (12)

> The patching and filling *completed,* Mr. Jones is *now* shaved, washed and dressed.   (16)

> Jones is *now* ready for casketing. . . .   (17)

> Jones is *next* wheeled into the appointed slumber room. . . .   (18)

Causal Analysis   In order to explain *why* something happens or what the effects of something are, writers often use one of the following three patterns of cause and effect to shape their material:

$$\text{Cause 1} + \text{Cause 2} + \text{Cause 3} \ldots + \text{Cause } n \rightarrow \text{Effect}$$

In the case of fire, discussed earlier in this chapter, we know that three causes lead to a single effect. The causes do not occur in any special sequence; they all need to be present at the same time. For historical events, however, we usually list the causes in chronological order.

Sometimes one cause has several effects. In that case, we reverse the pattern:

Cause → Effect 1 + Effect 2 + Effect 3 . . . + Effect *n*

An explanation of the collapse of the economy following the stock market crash of 1929, for example, might follow this pattern. The crash (itself a symptom of other causes) led to a depreciated economy, widespread unemployment, bankruptcy for thousands of businesses, foreclosures on farms, and so forth. An essay on the effects of the crash might devote one or two paragraphs to each effect.

In the third pattern, causes and effects form a pattern of chain reactions. One cause leads to an effect that then becomes the cause of another effect, and so on:

Cause 1 → Effect 1 (Cause 2) → Effect 2 (Cause 3) → Effect 3

We could analyze events in the Middle East prior to the Persian Gulf War as a series of actions and reactions, in which each effect becomes the cause of the next effect in the chain of skirmishes, car bombings, air raids, terrorist hijackings, and kidnappings. An essay on the chain reaction of events in the Middle East might have a paragraph or two on each of the links in this chain.

Introduction, Paragraph Transitions and Hooks, and Body Paragraphs The *introduction* to an explaining essay—whether one paragraph or several—usually contains the following features:

- *Lead-in:* Some example, description, statistic, startling statement, short narrative, or quotation to get the reader's interest *and* focus on the topic you will explain
- *Thesis:* Statement of main idea; a "promise" to the reader that the essay fulfills
- *Essay Map:* A sentence, or part of a sentence, that *lists* (in the order in which the essay discusses them) the main subtopics for the essay

In her essay on *anorexia nervosa* at the end of this chapter, Nancie Brosseau's introductory paragraph has all three features:

Lead-In: Startling Statement	I knew my dieting had gotten out of hand, but when I could actually see the movement of my heart beating beneath my clothes I knew I was in trouble. At first, the family doctor reassured my parents that my rapid weight loss was a "temporary phase among teenage girls." However,
Description	when I, at 14 years old and 5′ 0″ tall, weighed in at 63 pounds, my doctor changed his diagnosis from "temporary phase" to "anorexia nervosa." Anorexia nervosa is the process of self-starvation that affects

over one hundred thousand young girls each year. Almost six thousand of these girls die every year. Anorexia nervosa is a self-mutilating disease that affects its victim both physically and emotionally. (1)

The *essay map* is contained in the phrase "both physically and emotionally": The first half of the essay discusses the *physical* effects of anorexia nervosa; the second half of the essay explains the *emotional* effects. Like a road map, the essay map helps the reader anticipate what topics the writer will explain.

Transition words and *paragraph hooks* are audience cues that help the reader shift from one paragraph to the next. These connections between paragraphs help the reader see the relationship of the various parts. *Transition words*—"first," "second," "next," "another," "last," "finally," and so forth—signal your reader that a new idea or a new part of the idea is coming up. In addition to transition words, writers often tie paragraphs together by using a key *word* or *idea* from a previous paragraph in the opening sentence of the following paragraph to "hook" the paragraphs together. The following paragraphs from Mitford's essay illustrate how transition words and paragraph hooks work together to create smooth connections between paragraphs.

About three to six gallons of a dyed and perfumed solution of formaldehyde, glycerin, borax, phenol, alcohol and water is soon circulating through Mr. Jones. . . . If he should be bucktoothed, his teeth are cleaned with Bon Ami and coated with colorless nail polish. His eyes, meanwhile, are closed with flesh-tinted eye caps and eye cement. (9)

The *next step* is to have at Mr. Jones with a thing called a trocar. . . . This done, and the hole in the abdomen sewn up, Mr. Jones's face is heavily creamed . . . and he is covered with a sheet and left unmolested for a while. But not for long—there is more, much more, in store for him. He has embalmed, but not yet restored, and the best time to start the restorative work is eight to ten hours after embalming, when the tissues have become firm and dry. (10)

Transition: "next step"
Hook: "Mr. Jones"

The object of all this attention to the corpse, it must be remembered, is to make it presentable for viewing in an attitude of healthy repose. . . . The funeral industry is equal to the challenge: "In some cases, the gruesome appearance of a mutilated or disease-ridden subject may be quite discouraging. The task of restoration may seem impossible and shake the confidence of the embalmer. . . . Is is surprising and gratifying to discover the results which may be obtained." (11)

Hooks: "this attention," "corpse"

The embalmer, having allowed an appropriate interval to elapse, returns to the attack, *but now* he brings into play the skill and equipment of sculptor and cosmetician. Is a hand missing? Casting one in plaster of Paris is a simple matter. . . .

Hooks: "embalmer," "attack"
Transition: "but now"

Body paragraphs in expository writing are the main paragraphs in an essay, excluding any introductory, concluding, or transition paragraphs. They often contain the following features:

- *Topic sentence:* To promote clarity and precision, writers often use topic sentences to announce the main idea of the paragraph. This main idea should be clearly related to the writer's thesis. A topic sentence usually occurs early in the paragraph (first or second sentence) or at the end of the paragraph.
- *Unity:* To avoid confusing readers, writers focus on a single idea for each paragraph. Writing unified paragraphs helps writers— and their readers—concentrate on one point at a time.
- *Coherence:* To make their writing flow smoothly from one sentence to the next, writers supplement their shaping strategies with coherence devices: repeated key words, pronouns referring to key nouns, and transition words.

The following body paragraph from Jessica Mitford's essay, "To Dispel Fears of Live Burial," illustrates these features. The paragraph begins with a topic sentence; it has unity because it focuses on a single idea (positioning the lips) and it uses transitions, pronouns, and repeated key words to promote coherence.

Topic Sentence
Pronoun: "They"
Repeated Key Words:
"Lips," "Embalmer"

Transition: "However"

Repeated Key Word:
"Lip"

Transition: "Another"

Positioning the lips is a problem that recurrently challenges the ingenuity of the embalmer. Closed too tightly, they tend to give a stern, even disapproving expression. Ideally, embalmers feel, the lips should give the impression of being ever so slightly parted, the upper lip protruding slightly for a more youthful appearance. This takes some engineering, *however,* as the lips tend to drift apart. Lip drift can sometimes be remedied by pushing one or two straight pins through the inner margin of the lower lip and then inserting them between the two front upper teeth. If Mr. Jones happens to have no teeth, the pins can just as easily be anchored in his Armstrong Face Former and Denture Replacer. *Another* method to maintain lip closure is to dislocate the lower jaw, which is then held in its new position by a wire run through holes which have been drilled through the upper and lower jaws at the midline. As the French are fond of saying, *il faut souffrir pour être belle.*

Drafting

Before you begin drafting, reconsider your purpose and audience. What you explain depends on what your audience needs to know or what would demonstrate or show your point most effectively.

As you work from an outline or from an organizing strategy, remember that all three questions— *what, how,* and *why*—are interrelated. If you are writing about causes, for example, an explanation of *what* the topic is and *how* the causes function may also be necessary to explain your subject clearly. As you write, balance your sense of plan and organization with a willingness to pursue ideas that you discover as you write. You need to have a plan, but you should be ready to change course if you discover a more interesting idea or angle.

Revising

Since clarity is the number-one goal in explaining, concentrate on making yourself perfectly clear, on illustrating with examples where your reader might be confused, and on signaling the relationship of the parts of your essay to your reader.

I wish he would explain his explanation.

—*Lord Byron, poet*

Guidelines for Revision

- **Compare your thesis sentence with what you say in your conclusion.** You may have a clearer statement of your thesis near the end of your paper. Revise your original thesis sentence to make it clearer, more focused, or more in line with what your essay actually says.

- **Explaining means** *showing* **and** *demonstrating* **relationships.** Be sure to follow general statements with *specific examples, details, facts, statistics, memories, dialogues,* or other *illustrations.*

- **In a formal definition, be sure to include the class of objects or concepts to which the term belongs.** Avoid ungrammatical writing, such as "Photosynthesis is *when* plants absorb oxygen," or "The lymphatic system is *where* the body removes bacteria and transports fatty cells."

- **Avoid introducing definitions with "Webster says. . . ."** Instead, read definitions from several dictionaries and give the best or most appropriate definition.

- **Remember that you can modify the dictionary definition of a term or concept to fit your particular context.** For example, to you, "heroism" may mean having the courage to *say* what you believe, not just to endanger your life through selfless actions.

- **Don't mix categories when you are classifying objects or ideas.** If you are classifying houses *by floor design* (ranch, bilevel, split level, two story), don't bring in other categories, such as passive solar, which could be incorporated into any of those designs.

- **In explaining** *how* **something occurs or how it should be done, be sure to indicate to your audience which steps are** *most important.*

- **In cause-and-effect explanations, avoid** *post hoc* **fallacies.** (The term comes from the Latin phrase *post hoc, ergo propter hoc:* "after this, therefore because of this.") Just because Event B occurred after Event A does not mean, necessarily, that A caused B. If, for example, statistics show that traffic fatalities in your state actually declined after the speed limit on interstate highways was increased, you should not conclude that higher speeds actually caused the reduction in fatalities. Other causes—increased radar patrols, stiffer drunk-driving penalties, or more rigorous vehicle-maintenance laws—may have been responsible for the reduction.

- **As you revise to sharpen your meaning or make your organization clearer, use appropriate transitional words and phrases to signal the** *relationship among the various parts of your subject.*

COMPUTER TIPS: EDITING

Most word-processing programs have a built-in dictionary or spell check to catch your spelling errors and typos. Too often, however, writers rely on their spell check to catch *all* their errors. While spell checkers are a useful editing aid, don't rely on them to proofread.

As you proofread, check for words that are spelled correctly but used incorrectly, such as affect/effect or principal/principle. Second, look for "computos," errors that frequently occur while drafting and revising on a computer. Check for *omissions*, for words or phrases mistakenly deleted. Similarly, look for *word doubles*, or repetitions created by failing to delete a word or phrase. Finally, check for *shifts* in sentence construction or phrasing. Don't expect spell checkers to catch these problems.

One effective proofreading strategy is to reduce the margins on your text and display it in narrow columns. Often, errors that you may have overlooked will suddenly pop out at you. See, for example, if you can find the errors in the following text display:

> Most word-processing programs have a dictionary to check for catch your spelling errors and typos. Although a spell-checking program may site obvious spelling errors but then miss an embarrassing error. The program cannot advice you to fix a word a word that is spelled correctly. You have to except responsibility for it's limitations. Reformatting your text in narrow columns may enable you to see problems see problems the spell checker misses.

To signal relation in time: before, meanwhile, later, soon, at last, earlier, thereafter, afterward, by that time, from then on, first, next, now, presently, shortly, immediately, finally

To signal similarity: likewise, similarly, once again, once more

To signal difference: but, yet, however, although, whereas, though, even so, nonetheless, still, on the other hand, on the contrary

To signal consequences: as a result, consequently, therefore, hence, for this reason

---

POSTSCRIPT ON THE WRITING PROCESS

Before you hand in your essay, reflect on your writing and learning process. In your journal, spend a few minutes answering each of the following questions:

1. What writing rituals did you use as you wrote this essay? Describe how, when, and where you did most of your writing.

2. What caused you the most difficulty with this essay? How did you solve the problem—or attempt to solve it? What parts are you still least satisfied with?

3. What are the best parts of your paper? Refer to specific paragraphs—what do you like most about them?

4. What was the most important thing you learned about writing or your writing process as you wrote this paper?

EXPLAINING: STUDENT WRITING

"THE POLICE WERE CALLING ME NAMES": AN EXPLANATION OF HARD-CORE PUNK ROCK

Dennis Alexander

Dennis Alexander's essay on hard-core punk rock explains what punk rock is, but he uses definition and analysis to make his own point: Punk rock, despite its detractors, is a legitimate form of music.

Alexander's Postscript on His Writing Process

When I was thinking about this paper, I wanted to write a cause-and-effect type of paper, but I couldn't seem to come up with any ideas I wanted to write on. Then one night I ordered a pizza and a really punked-out guy delivered it. I was playing some hard core and he said something about how few people understand it. This gave me my idea for the paper. I wanted to express the idea that punk was a real and legitimate form of music, so I spent some time looking up words in the dictionary, defining terms and finding the right words. I listened to a lot of music. This was harder than it sounds, going verse by verse to figure out the lyrics. I also listened to 180 minutes of interview tape from a radio interview with various hard-core artists. Then, after some brainstorming and outlining, I finally came up with a good thesis. When I had enough evidence to give good support to my thesis and also explain about punk, I wrote my essay and revised it.

Notes for Outline

Explaining Essay –
Support thesis and answer questions: (What is punk)
(Why it is)
(Who)

Legit   or Viable

Sanctioned   workable and likely to
by law   survive or to have real
or Custom   meaning, pertinence, relevance

Conforming
to or abiding by
standards,
principles

Thesis: Hardcore Punk is a viable Musical
Alternative

* ~~It is~~ alternative music
~~Fast Beat~~
Revival of Old Rock
New Raw Rock & Roll
Not New Wave
Fast Beat
Or satiric of other music

Its definition: Combination of vocal
and instrumental sounds or tones
in varying melody, harmony, rhythm,
and timbre so as to form structurally
complete and emotionally expressive
compositions.
Fast Beat, Back Beat 180 Beats/Min
Not as many chords, melody

(margin, rotated:) It is music / It is alternative / It is viable

* It is alternative

 - Revival of Old Rock
 - New Rock & Roll, Fun
 - Satirical of other music/lifestyles
 - Not New Wave

* It is viable
 - it is workable
  - provides for change
  - doesn't later to like
 - Likely to survive
  - survived since origin in
  early 70's in England
  - Brought to USA

 - Has meaning, pertinence, relevance
  - Commentary on war
  - political statement
  - social statement
  - draws attention to community
  problems (landlords, police)
  or social issues, war, politics,
  religion, poverty, social
  welfare, police)

First Draft

Purpose: To explain that hardcore is a viable musical

alternative

Audience: General, but especially young people who like music but may not like hard core—probably because they don't understand it.

Hard Core

What you need boy is a holiday in Cambodia
Where you'll kiss ass or crack.
Sweat for the price of your life
With a bowl of rice as a snack.

—The Dead Kennedys

"Fresh Fruit for Rotting Vegetables"

Musical tastes vary as much as the people who like music. In any record store in America, it is not uncommon to find rock, country, and classical albums for sale. It is uncommon for a typical record store to have a variety of hard-core punk rock records for sale. This is unusual considering that hard—core is a viable musical alternative.   (1)

Some people think that punk is not music. Webster's dictionary defines music as combinations of vocal and instrumental sounds or tones in varying melody, harmony, rhythm and timbre so as to form structurally complete and emotionally expressive compositions. Hard-core punk fits this definition. Having developed from rock music in the early 70's punk inherited its rhythm and beat. The melody and harmony in rock and punk are also similar although punk has a much harsher, distorted sound. It is structurally complete and expresses a variety of emotions. Hard-core may or may not sound as pleasant to the ear as other socially accepted forms of music. But this does not disqualify it as music.   (2)

Most of all the other forms of music are accepted as legitimate. They conform and abide by socially accepted standards and customs. Because punk does not, it provides an alternative. It does not fit into other categories, it is non-conformist music. The names of common groups express this: The Germs, The Dead Kennedys, The Suicidal Tendencies, Two Sounds of Liberty (T.S.O.L.). In some ways, punk tries to revive old rock and roll into new raw rock. In other ways, punk music attempts to satirize other musical forms and the lifestyles they represent. Most importantly, punk is not new wave music. In the words of a singer from The Germs: "There was never any such thing as new wave. New wave was the polite thing to say when you were trying to explain you were not into the boring old rock but you didn't dare say punk because you were afraid to get kicked out of the f——party." Because of the large difference between musical styles, punk is an excellent alternative.   (3)

Despite its differences, hard-core is a viable form of music. It is workable. It can evolve and change. Because of its base on nonconformity, it easily provides for change and does not cater to sentiment. Punk is likely to survive. From its roots in the late 60's it has prospered, spread and is stronger than ever. Hard-core punk also has meaning, pertinence, and relevance. It often provides a satirical social comment.   (4)

Punk highlights social problems by advocating crude solutions. Such satirically oriented songs are: "Kill the Poor," and "Lets lynch a Landlord" by ————. Punk music is not afraid to hide opinion, in fact it is made blatantly clear. This opinion can be on such issues as war, religion and politics. Opinion is expressed in lyrics like "Army, Navy, Airforce, or Jail" and "President Reagan can shove it" by T.S.O.L. In these ways, punk draws attention to community and social problems and reaffirms Americans' right to free speech. It is, therefore, viable. (5)

Because Hard core punk is a viable musical alternative there is no reason that it should be subject to undue discrimination or censorship. Just because it does not fit some people's idea of "good taste," it should not be cleared from the shelves. Hard-core punk is legitimate music that belongs on the shelves of music stores. (6)

Revised Version

"THE POLICE WERE CALLING ME NAMES": AN EXPLANATION OF HARD-CORE PUNK ROCK

I sat in my dorm room waiting for a pizza to be delivered. The Dead Kennedys blasted out through my stereo speakers. "What is that shit?" someone asked as he walked by with his fingers in his ears. The pizza guy finally arrived and walked into my room wearing combat boots, chains, spiked leather and a black and blonde mohawk. His foot tapped to the beat as I paid for the pie. He looked me over from my Levis jacket to my cowboy boots and said, "You listen to the D.K.? Way cool man!" Looking back on this incident, I think that the reaction of the pizza guy was normal while the attitudes of the dorm residents were narrow-minded. Hard-core punk rock is, in fact, a viable musical alternative. (1)

Is hard-core punk really music or is it just so much loud noise? Perhaps we need to define what music is. Music is a combination of vocal and instrumental sounds or tones that vary in melody, harmony, rhythm and timbre. The sounds should form a structurally complete and emotionally expressive composition. Hard-core punk fits this definition. Having developed from rock in the late 60s, punk inherited its rhythm and beat. The melody and harmony in rock and punk are also similar, although punk has a much harsher, distorted sound. It is also structurally complete and expresses a variety of emotions. Hard-core may or may not sound as pleasing to the ear as other socially accepted forms of music, but this does not disqualify it as music.   (2)

Almost all of the other forms of music, such as country, rock, and classical, are accepted as legitimate. They conform to and abide by socially accepted standards and customs. Because punk does not, it provides an alternative. It does not fit into other categories; it is non-conformist music. The names of common groups express their non-conformity: "The Germs," "The Dead Kennedys," the "Suicidal Tendencies," "Religious Vomit," and "Two Sounds of Liberty." In some ways, punk tries to revive old music into new raw rock (Dead Kennedys, "Rawhide"). In other ways, punk attempts to satirize other musical forms and the lifestyles they represent. The Dead Milkmen do this in "Bitching Camaro" when they say, "Don't forget to buy your Motley Crue T-shirts, all proceeds go to get their lead singer out of jail." Most importantly punk is not new wave music. In the words of a singer for The Germs, "There was never any such thing as new wave. It was the polite thing to say when you were trying to explain that you were not into the boring old rock, but you did not dare say punk because you were afraid to get kicked out of the f——— party." Because of the noticeable difference in musical styles, punk is an excellent musical alternative.   (3)

Despite its differences from rock, hard-core is a viable form of music. Let us consider some of the terms related to viability: ability to evolve, survivability, and relevance. Punk can evolve and change. Because of its basis in nonconformity, it easily provides for change and does not cater to fixed norms or sentiments. Punk is likely to survive. From its roots in the late 60s it has prospered and is stronger than ever. Hard-core punk also has meaning and relevance. It often provides a satirical social comment. Punk highlights social problems by advocating crude solutions. Such satirically oriented songs are "Kill the Poor" and "Let's Lynch a Landlord" by the Dead Kennedys. Punk music is not afraid to hide its opinion on relevant matters such as politics, war, religion, and human rights. Opinion is expressed in lyrics such as "Army, Navy, Air Force or jail" and "President Reagan can shove it." In these ways punk draws attention to community and social problems and reaffirms the right to free speech. It is, therefore, viable.   (4)

Whether people like hard-core rock or not, it is a viable musical alternative. It is a musical version of the freedom of speech guaranteed by our constitution. Punk music is an expression of feelings just like the pizza deliveryman expresses his feelings through his mohawk and chains. So the next time you hear some punk music, don't plug your ears or slam the door. Listen to it as though it were real music: it is.   (5)

QUESTIONS FOR WRITING AND DISCUSSION

1. Compare Alexander's first and revised drafts. Cite two specific changes that improved his revised version.

2. Alexander explains what punk music is, but he also takes a stand: He wants to convince his readers that it is a legitimate form of music. Where in his essay does he explain most clearly what punk music is? Where does he try to convince you that it is legitimate?

3. Assume that Alexander wants your advice before writing a third draft of this essay. What part of the writing process should he concentrate on: (1) collecting additional information and examples to clarify his explanation or make his thesis more convincing; (2) improving the organization, transitions, and coherence; or (3) editing sentences for grammar, punctuation, and clarity? Support your choice by citing a specific place that needs improvement.

ANOREXIA NERVOSA

Nancie Brosseau

In her essay on anorexia nervosa, Nancie Brosseau writes from her own experience, explaining what anorexia nervosa is and what its effects are. Her essay succeeds not only because it is organized clearly, but also because it is so vivid and memorable. Her explanation shows, using specific details, the effects of anorexia on her life.

I knew my dieting had gotten out of hand, but when I could actually see the movement of my heart beating beneath my clothes I knew I was in trouble. At first, the family doctor reassured my parents that my rapid weight loss was a "temporary phase among teenage girls." However, when I, at 14 years old and 5′ 0″ tall, weighed in at 63 pounds, my doctor changed his diagnosis from "temporary phase" to "anorexia nervosa." Anorexia nervosa is the process of self-starvation that affects over one hundred thousand young girls each year. Almost six thousand of these girls die every year. Anorexia nervosa is a self-mutilating disease that affects its victim both physically and emotionally.   (1)

As both a gymnast and a dancer, I was constantly surrounded by lithe, muscular people, all of them extremely conscious about their weight. Although I wasn't overweight to begin with, I thought that if I lost five to ten pounds I would look, feel, dance, and tumble better. I figured the quickest way to accomplish this was by drastically limiting my intake of food. By doing this, I lost ten pounds in one week and gained the approval of my peers. Soon, I could no longer control myself and ten pounds turned into twenty, twenty into forty, and so on, until I finally ended up weighing 58 pounds. (2)

Several serious health problems bombarded me, and it's a wonder I'm still alive. Because my body was receiving no nourishment at all, my muscles and essential organs, including my heart, liver, kidneys, and intestines, started to compensate by slowly disintegrating. My body was feeding on itself! As my weight plummeted, my circulation grew increasingly worse. My hands, feet, lips and ears took on a bluish-purple tint, and I was constantly freezing cold. My hair started to fall out and my whole body took on a very skeletal appearance. My eyes appeared to have sunken into my face, and my forehead, cheekbones, and chin protruded sharply. My wrists were the largest part of my entire arm, as were my knees the widest part of my legs. My pants rubbed my hips raw because I had to wear my belts at their tightest notch to keep them up. I would force myself to vomit as soon as possible if I was forced to eat. The enamel on my teeth started to be eaten away by the acid in the vomit, and my lips cracked and bled regularly. I stopped menstruating completely because I was not producing enough estrogen. Instead of improving my skills as a dancer and a gymnast, I drastically reduced them because I was so weak. One time, while executing a chain of back handsprings, I broke all five fingers on one hand and three on the other because my bones had become so brittle. My doctor realized the serious danger I was in and told me I either had to see a psychologist or be put in the hospital. I chose to see a psychologist, and she helped me sort out the emotional aspects of anorexia which in turn solved the physical problems. (3)

The emotional problems associated with anorexia nervosa are equally disastrous to the victim's health. Self-deception, lying, and depression are three examples of the emotions and actions an anorexic often experiences. During my entire bout with anorexia, I deceived myself into thinking I had complete control over my body. Hunger pains became a pleasant feeling, and sore muscles from over-exercising just proved to me that I still needed to lose more weight. When my psychologist showed me pictures of girls that were of normal weight for my age group, they honestly looked obese to me. I truly believed that even the smallest amount of food would make me extremely fat. (4)

Another problem, lying, occurred most often when my parents tried to force me to eat. Because I was at the gym until around eight o'clock every night, I told my mother not to save me dinner. I would come home and make a sandwich and feed it to my dog. I lied to my parents every day about eating lunch at school. For example, I would bring a sack lunch and sell it to someone and use the money to buy diet pills. I always told my parents that I ate my own lunch. I lied to my doctor when he asked if I was taking an appetite suppressant. I had to cover one lie with another to keep from being found out, although it was obvious that I was not eating by looking at me.   (5)

Still another emotion I felt, as a result of my anorexia, was severe depression. It seemed that, no matter how hard I tried, I kept growing fatter. Of course, I was getting thinner all the time, but I couldn't see that. One time, I licked a postage stamp to put on a letter and immediately remembered that there was 1/4 of a calorie in the glue on the stamp. I punished myself by doing 100 extra situps every night for one week. I pinched my skin until it bruised as I lay awake at night because I was so ashamed of the way I thought I looked. I doomed myself to a life of obesity. I would often slip into a mood my psychologist described as a "blue funk." That is, I would become so depressed, I seriously considered committing suicide. The emotional instabilities associated with anorexia nervosa can be fatal.   (6)

Through psychological and physical treatment, I was able to overcome anorexia nervosa. I still have a few complications today due to anorexia, such as dysmenorrhea (severe menstrual cramps), and the tendency to fast. However, these problems are minute compared to the problems I would have had if I hadn't received immediate help. Separately, the physical and emotional problems that anorexia nervosa create can greatly harm its victim. However, when the two are teamed together, the results are deadly.   (7)

QUESTIONS FOR WRITING AND DISCUSSION

1. Without looking back at this essay, jot down the specific examples that you found most memorable in this essay. How would you describe these examples: tedious and commonplace, eye-opening, shocking, upsetting, persuasive? Explain.

2. Identify the thesis statement and essay map. Referring to paragraph numbers, show how the essay map sets up the organization of the essay.

3. Reread the opening sentences of each body paragraph. Identify one opening sentence that creates a smooth transition from the previous paragraph. Identify one opening sentence in which the transition could be smoother. Revise this sentence to improve the transition by using a paragraph hook.

4. In this essay, Brosseau defines anorexia nervosa, explains its physical and emotional effects (and hints at its causes), and analyzes the process of the disorder, from its inception to its cure. Identify passages that illustrate each of these strategies: definition, cause-and-effect analysis, process analysis.

7 | *EVALUATING*

Honoré Daumier
The Print Collector
Philadelphia Museum of Art. Purchased: W.P. Wilstach Collection

In a letter to your parents, you explain that you are considering transferring to a different school for the following year. You have some misgivings about your decision to change, but after listing your criteria and ranking them in order from most to least important, you are convinced you're making the right choice. In the letter, you explain your decision, based on your criteria, and ask that your parents continue to support your education. ☐

At your business, you and a group of your co-workers decide to organize a week-long ocean cruise to several Caribbean ports of call. Your task is to find out which company offers the best group package. You begin by collecting information and brochures from local travel agencies, reading travel magazines, and talking to people who have either taken cruises or organized them. You rank several package deals on the basis of total cost, shipboard accommodations and entertainment, and variety of ports of call. Based on your investigation, you rate the strengths and weaknesses of the top three travel companies for your group to consider. ☐

When we evaluate, we have in mind . . . an ideal of what a good thing—pianist, painting, or professor—should be and do, and we apply that ideal to the individual instance before us.

—Jeanne Fahnestock and Marie Secor, authors of A Rhetoric of Argument

Purpose and craftsmanship—ends and means—these are the keys to your judgment.

—Marya Mannes, journalist and social commentator

Hardly a day passes when we do not express our likes or dislikes. We constantly pass judgment on people, places, objects, events, ideas, and policies in the world around us. "Sue is a wonderful person." "Bob's game was fantastic today." "The food in this cafeteria is horrible." "That movie we saw Saturday night ought to get an Oscar nomination for best picture.'" "The seat-belt law is a bad piece of legislation." "The Vietnam War was a national tragedy." At the same time, we are constantly exposed to the opinions of our friends, family members, teachers, and business associates. And, of course, the media barrages us with claims about products, famous personalities, and candidates for public office.

A claim or opinion, however, is not an evaluation. Your reaction to a person, a sports event, a meal, a movie, or a public policy becomes an evaluation only when you support your value judgment with clear standards and specific evidence. Your goal in evaluating something is not only to express your viewpoint, but also to persuade others to accept your judgment. You convince your readers by indicating the standards for your judgment and then supporting that judgment with evidence: "The food in this cafeteria is horrible [your claim]. I know that not all cafeteria food tastes great, but it should at least be sanitary [one standard of judgment]. Yesterday, I had to dig a piece of green mold out of the meatloaf, and just as I stuck my fork into the green salad, a large black roach ran out [evidence] ."

Most people interested in a subject agree that certain standards are important—for example, that a cafeteria be clean and pest-free. The standards that you share with your audience are the *criteria* for your evaluation. You convince your readers that something is good or bad, ugly or beautiful, tasty or nauseating by analyzing your subject in terms of the criteria. For each separate criterion, you support your judgment with specific *evidence:* descriptions, statistics, testimony, or examples from your personal experience. If your readers agree that your standards or criteria are appropriate, and if you supply detailed evidence, your readers should be convinced. They will take your evaluation seriously—and think twice about eating at that dirty, roach-infested cafeteria.

FREEWRITING : EVALUATING

Choose one of the following subjects: an art object, painting, or poster in your room; a book, sports performance, or television program you have seen within the last twenty-four hours; a brand-name product you have used today; or the actions of a friend, family member, or teacher you observed today. Timing yourself for fifteen minutes, write an evaluation of your subject for an audience consisting of several close acquaintances.

TECHNIQUES FOR WRITING EVALUATIONS

It is as hard to find a neutral critic as it is a neutral country in a time of war.

—*Katherine Anne Porter, novelist and short story writer*

Any writing that requires a *value judgment* uses the techniques of evaluating—whether you're writing about consumer products or services, works of art, or performances of people. Effective evaluations use the following techniques:

- **Stating an *overall claim* about your subject.** This statement serves as the *thesis* for your evaluation.
- **Describing the person, place, object, event, service, or performance being evaluated.** Readers need basic information—*who, what, when,* and *where*—to form a clear judgment.
- **Clarifying the *criteria* for your evaluation.** A criterion is a standard of judgment that most people interested in your subject agree is important. A criterion serves as a yardstick against which you measure your subject.
- **Stating a *judgment* for each criterion.** The overall claim is based on your judgment of each separate criterion.
- **Supporting each judgment with *evidence*.** This can include detailed description, facts, examples, testimony, and statistics.

In the following evaluation of a Chinese restaurant in Washington, DC, journalist and critic Phyllis C. Richman illustrates the main features of an evaluation:

Hunan Dynasty

215 Pennsylvania Ave. SE. 546-6161
Open daily 11 A.M. to 3 P.M. for lunch, 3 P.M. to 10 P.M. for dinner, until 11 P.M. on Friday and Saturday.
Reservations suggested for large parties.
Prices for lunch: appetizers $2 to $4.50, entrees $4.75 to $6.50; for dinner, appetizers $1 to $13.95 (combination platter), entrees $6.75 to $18.
Complete dinner with wine or beer, tax and tip about $20 a person.

Information & Description

Chinese restaurants in American were once places one went just to eat. Now one goes to dine. There are now waiters in black tie, cloths on the tables and space between those tables, art on the walls and decoratively carved vegetables on the plate—elegance has become routine in Chinese

Description

restaurants. What's more, in Chinese restaurants the ingredients are fresh (have you ever found frozen broccoli in a Chinese kitchen?), and the cooking almost never sinks below decent. . . . And it is usually moderately priced. In other words, if you're among unfamiliar restaurants and looking for good value, Chinese restaurants now are routinely better than ever.

Overall Claim
Criterion #1: Attractive
Setting
Judgment: Attractive,
Graceful
Evidence

The Hunan Dynasty is an example of what makes Chinese restaurants such reliable choices. A great restaurant? It is not. A good value? Definitely. A restaurant to fit nearly any diner's need? Probably.

First, it is attractive. There are no silk tassels, blaring red lacquer or Formica tables; instead there are white tablecloths and subtle glass etchings. It is a dining room—or dining rooms, for the vastness has been carved into smaller spaces—of gracefulness and lavish space.

Criterion #2: Good
Service
Judgment: Often Expert

Evidence

Criterion #3: Good
Main Dishes

Second, service is a strong priority. The waiters look and act polished, and serve with flourishes from the carving of a Peking duck to the portioning of dishes among the diners. I have found some glitches—a forgotten appetizer, a recommendation of two dishes that turned out nearly identical—but most often the service has been expert. . . .

Judgment: Good But
Not Memorable

Evidence

As for the main dishes, don't take the "hot and spicy" asterisks too seriously, for this kitchen is not out to offer you a test of fire. The peppers are there, but not in great number. And, like the appetizers, the main dishes are generally good but not often memorable. Fried dishes—and an inordinate number of them seem to be fried—are crunchy and not greasy. Vegetables are bright and crisp. Eggplant with hot garlic sauce is properly unctuous; Peking duck is as fat-free and crackly-skinned as you could hope (though pancakes were rubbery). And seafoods—shrimp, scallops, lobster—are tenderly cooked, though they are not the most full-flavored examples of those ingredients.

Criterion #3 Cont'd
Judgment: Sometimes
Bad
Evidence

I have found only one dismal main dish in a fairly broad sampling: lemon chicken had no redeeming feature in its doughy, greasy, overcooked and underseasoned presentation. Otherwise, not much goes wrong. Crispy shrimp with walnuts might be preferable stir-fried rather than batter-fried, but the tomato-red sauce and crunchy walnuts made a good dish. Orange beef could use more seasoning but the coating was nicely crusty and the meat tender. . . .

Overall Claim
Restated

So with the opening of the Hunan Dynasty, Washington did not add a stellar Chinese restaurant to its repertoire, but that is not necessarily what the city needed anyway. Hunan Dynasty is a top-flight neighborhood restaurant—with good food, caring service and very fair prices—that is attractive enough to set a mood for celebration and easygoing enough for an uncomplicated dinner with the family after work.

Evaluating Commercial Products or Services

Writers frequently evaluate commercial products or services. Consumer magazines test and rate every imaginable product or service—from cars and dishwashers to peanut butter and brokerage houses. Guidebooks evaluate tourist spots, restaurants, colleges, and hunting lodges. Specialty magazines such as *Modern Photography, Road and Track, Skiing,* and *Byte* often rate products and services of interest to their readers. To qualify as evaluation—and not just advertising—the authors and the publishers must maintain an independent status, uninfluenced by the companies of the products or services they judge.

Consider, first, the following "evaluation" of a wine, found on a bottle of Cabernet Sauvignon:

> "This Cabernet Sauvignon is a dry, robust, and complex wine whose hearty character is balanced by an unusual softness."

This evaluative language is so vague and esoteric that it may mean very little to the average consumer who just wants some wine with dinner. *Dry:* How can a liquid be dry? *Robust:* Does this refer to physique? *Soft:* Wine is not a pillow, though it might put you to sleep. *Complex:* Are they describing a wine or conducting a psychological analysis? While an independent evaluator may legitimately use these terms for knowledgeable wine drinkers, this particular description suggests that the wine is anything the buyer would like it to be—dry yet robust, hearty but at the same time soft. Apparently, the writer's purpose here is not to evaluate a product but to flatter readers who imagine themselves connoisseurs of wine. In fact, such readers are just being conned by slick language.

In the following report on the Yugo, *Consumer Reports* illustrates a popular format for a more objective evaluation of a consumer product. In this brief excerpt, the editors present the criteria, the evidence, and their judgments. Clearly, this is not the language of advertising or uncritical promotion.

How Much Car for $3990?

> An unusual new import, the *Yugo GV,* arrived in the U.S. last August. It's a tiny car—a couple of feet shorter than the *Chevrolet Chevette*—made in Yugoslavia by Zavodi Crvena Zastava (Red Flag Works). But the most unusual thing about it is the advertised price—$3990. The price quickens the pulse at a time when the average car sells for nearly $12,000 and a similar-sized car, the Japanese-made *Chevrolet Sprint,* sells for about $5570.
>
> Can you really buy a *Yugo* for $3990?
>
> No. Dealer preparation, included in the base price of most other cars, is $90 extra, and the destination charge is $299. If you add the official *Yugo* stereo radio with two speakers and a cassette player for $265, you have a $4644 automobile.
>
> Well, what's wrong with a *Yugo* for $4644? We'll let our test results speak for themselves.

Engine and Transmission

Acceleration. All-out acceleration from a standstill was adequate, but the *Yugo* struggled and strained to climb highway grades in high gear. Our 0-60 mph run took 18.5 seconds.

Transmission. Easily the worst we've encountered in years. The shifter was very imprecise and often balky. The sloppy shift linkage made it hard to tell which gear you were in.

Economy. Well below what you'd expect from a small car with such a small engine. Figure on averaging about 32 mpg. (The *Chevrolet Sprint*, a Japanese minicar, averages about 50 mpg). Cruising range is only about 250 miles.

Ride and Noise

Ride. Snappy and jerky on back roads, and harsh and busy even on expressways. But the *Yugo* took large bumps in stride. When the car carried its full recommended load—770 pounds—its ride softened just a bit.

Noise. Tiring. The small engine churned and buzzed on the highway. Coarse pavement increased the noise considerably. Wind noise, especially from the closed front vent windows, was also obtrusive.

Seating Accommodations

Driving position. Extremely awkward. The non-tilt steering wheel is too high, too far away, and too horizontal, and the steering column is angled toward the right. The pedals are too close to one another, and the intrusive wheel housing makes a very poor foot rest.

Rear seating. Unsuitable for adults. Six footers have to bow their head penitently and wrap their knees around the front seat back. The overly erect seatback forces passengers to slouch forward in a fetal tuck with all their weight on the base of their spine.

Our *Yugo* was a sorry sample indeed. We noted 21 defects attributable to sloppy assembly or incomplete dealer preparation. Oil dripped from the engine and coated the underbody as we drove. When it contacted the hot exhaust system, the car filled with acrid smoke. . . . The brakes squealed, and every so often they dragged so badly that we could barely coax the car to 45 mph on level pavement.

Recommendations

Is low price sufficient justification for buying the Yugo? We don't think so. Overall, the *Yugo* scored below every other small car we've tested in recent years. It's heavy for its size, and though its tiny engine revs willingly enough, it delivers weak performance and unimpressive fuel economy. Handling was competent and braking was very effective, but comfort, ride, shifting, heating, and the design of the controls were below par.

Evaluating Works of Art

Evaluations of commercial products and services tend to emphasize usefulness, practicality, convenience, and cost. Evaluations of works of art, on the other hand, focus on form, color, texture, design, balance, image, or theme. Even the phrase "appreciating a work of art" suggests that we are making a value judgment, though usually not one based on money. Through evaluation, writers teach us to appreciate all kinds of art: paintings, sculpture, photographs, buildings, antique cars or furniture, novels, short stories, essays, poems, and tapestries. A Dior fashion, a quilt, a silverware pattern, even an old pair of jeans might be evaluated primarily on aesthetic rather than practical grounds.

In the following selection, art critic Mark Stevens evaluates Francisco Goya's painting "The Third of May, 1808." This painting depicts the execution of Spanish hostages by Napoleon's forces, in retaliation for an attack by a mob on the previous day. As Stevens explains, Goya does not portray the doomed hostages as heroic martyrs; instead, he tries to show the horrors of war and death. In doing that, Stevens believes, Goya "told the truth: what happened on the third of May was a butchering."

> The iconography, the color and light, the composition—all contribute to the power of this picture. Its most impressive aspect, in my view, is that Goya . . . transformed the conventions of hope into those of despair. This makes the horror all the greater, for we can see what we have lost, in addition to what we have. In the background, for example, the spire of the church is a dark, dim reminder, certainly not a cause for hope. The cruelty of the execution, which takes place in a melodramatic light, reminds us of acts of martyrdom—but without the traditional promise of heavenly reward.

> Of course, the outstretched arms of the central figure also recall the Crucifixion, and the man's hands bear stigmata. However, the traditional religious gesture of acceptance—the outstretched arms of Christ—has here been turned into an expression of outrage, terror and meaninglessness. What is the victim saying? There is nothing he can say, for his situation is one in which neither faith nor reason matter. His outflung arms are mirrored by those of the corpse in the foreground: such is the promise of resurrection. The corpse itself is perhaps the most truthful ever painted, for its exhibits the unbearable banality, the crumpled emptiness of death.

> The men around the central victim display a variety of other reactions to their fate, none noble. One looks heavenward, but his expression is groveling. The praying man cannot raise his eyes. A third hides his face, as do the victims who await execution. Goya's use of light enhances their horror. The light contains no spiritual overtone, but rather emanates from a common lantern; an intense glow is cast on the small, grisly scene, but it cannot pierce the dark reaches. This light—glaring, without delicacy, lurid, almost artificial—seems peculiarly modern. . . .

Goya: *The Third of May 1808* (Museo Prado)

Goya: *The Third of May 1808 (detail)* (Museo Prado)

In addition to his brilliant use of light and shade, which isolates the central figure, Goya used several other formal devices to make his point. He employed sweeping diagonal lines to scissor the picture into sharp, claustrophobic spaces. He foreshortened the corpse, so that the body seems to draw toward the viewer. (It almost looks as though the dead man is bidding the viewer welcome.) Otherwise, Goya has positioned the figures so that the viewer, curiously, is placed on the side of the executioners. You and I, observing, are implicated in mankind's folly.

Evaluating Performances

Evaluating live, recorded, or filmed performances of people in sports, dance, drama, debate, public meetings or lectures, and music may involve practical criteria, such as the prices of tickets to sports events or rock concerts, but there are also aesthetic criteria related to people and their performances. In film evaluations, for example, the usual criteria are good acting and directing, entertaining or believable story or plot, memorable characters, dramatic special effects, and so forth. In the following paragraphs from her review of *Star Wars*, critic Judith Crist both describes and evaluates this classic space adventure.

"Feel Good" Film

> The era of the "feel good" movie, launched by *Cousin, Cousine* and *Rocky,* is upon us—with *Star Wars* to offer lavish, glittering, and nostalgic confirmation thereof.
>
> It is fitting that *Star Wars* is the creation of George Lucas, whose last film, in 1973, was that utterly charming re-creation of an adolescent yesterday, *American Graffiti.* This time the thirty-two-year-old writer-director has recreated the fantasies of a childhood soaked in adventure fictions, ranging from the respectability of Camelot and Oz to the trashery of comic strips and Saturday-afternoon serials. The last have provided the format for his chivalric science-fiction tale: he is giving us that very special Saturday when the printed prologue (appropriately moving off screen into the vast beyond) brings us up to date on the rebellion against the evil Galactic Empire and plunks us down into the final series of misadventures that will precede the breathtaking triumph of good over evil and the comforting assurance that the good will flourish happily ever after. Do children of all ages ask for anything more?
>
> The plot is simply a series of chases, captures, and escapes as the good guys set out to rescue the princess—yes, it is Princess Leia Organa (Carrie Fisher), the sweet-faced, lush-figured, feisty leader of the rebellion, who has fallen into the hands of the vile, führer-like Grand Moff Tarkin (Peter Cushing) and his black knight, Lord Darth Vader (David Prowse behind the armor, given voice by James Earl Jones), aboard their super-Pentagonish space station, Death Star. As familiar-but-gussied-up as the villains are the good guys: Luke Skywalker (Mark Hamill), a

blond, blue-eyed farm boy and crack pilot recruited by Ben "Obi-Wan" Kenobi (Alec Guinness), a hermit, last of the Jedi Knights, who believed in "the force" (as in "may the force be with you"), a belief that constituted "the old religion"; Han Solo (Harrison Ford), a hotshot pilot and mercenary who proves himself trueblue; Chewbacca, Solo's first mate, a gigantic, monkeylike creature who purrs and growls and bears a striking resemblance to the Cowardly Lion; and two Mutt-and-Jeff-like robots, See Threepio (C3PO), a gold-plated Tin Man programmed for diplomatic missions and therefore British-accented and prissy, and Artoo-Detoo (R2D2), a round little machine stuffed with data and given to chirps and burbles.

There are memorable moments along the way and a simply whiz-bang dazzle of battling space ships for a climax, with the happy ending all it should be. The joy of it all is that everyone is playing it straight, no bogging down in messages or monoliths on the one hand, no camping it up on the other. It is simply a triumph of creativity and technology by masters thereof, people who very obviously delight in doing what only the medium of film can do in the creation of magic. They are all listed at the end of the film and well deserve the applause you'll find yourself giving them—before you exit with that satisfied Saturday-afternoon-at-the-movies smile that feels so good.

Warming Up: Journal Exercises

The following exercises will help you practice writing evaluations. Read all of the following exercises and then write on the three that interest you most. If another idea occurs to you, write a free entry about it:

1. Choose the best of the courses you are currently taking. To persuade a friend to take it, evaluate the course, the teacher, or both. What criteria and evidence would you select to persuade your friend?

2. Evaluate an object related to one of your hobbies or special interests—stereo or video equipment, water or snow skiis, a cooking appliance or utensil, diving or hiking equipment, photography or art equipment, ranching or farming apparatus, fishing rods or reels, some part of a car, or computers. Write an evaluation for an audience similar to the readers of *Consumer Reports*, following the format of that magazine.

3. Oscar Wilde once said that a cynic is someone "who knows the price of everything but the value of nothing." Describe a

situation in which some person's words or actions illustrated that he or she fit Wilde's definition of a cynic.

4. You are a sales manager for the *Yugo*. You have just read *Consumer Reports'* article on the automobile, and you're extremely upset. Write the magazine a letter (which you hope it will have the courtesy to publish) refuting its assessment by pointing out how the report was inaccurate and unfair. As you write the letter, consider what criteria the report omitted, how the magazine overemphasized trivial features, or how the information was flawed.

5. Listen carefully in several classes for your teachers' evaluations of ideas, historical or contemporary events, famous people, or important policies or laws. Take notes and then write a short analysis of one teacher's evaluation: What are the criteria and evidence?

6. Evaluate a TV show that you find particularly irritating, boring, or insipid, but which you find yourself watching occasionally anyway. Watch the show, taking notes about scenes, characters, dialogue, and plot. Write a critique of the show for other students in this class.

7. To gather some information for yourself about a possible job or career, interview a person in your prospective field about his or her job or profession. Focus your questions on the person's opinions and judgments about this career. What criteria does this person use to judge it? What other jobs serve as a good basis for comparison? What details from this person's daily routine support the judgments?

8. At your place of work, evaluate one of your products or services. Write down the criteria and evidence your business might use to determine whether it is a "good" product or service. Then list the criteria and evidence that your customers or patrons probably use. Are these two sets of criteria and evidence identical? Explain.

9. Choose a piece of modern art (painting, drawing, poster, sculpture, ceramics, and so forth). Describe and evaluate it for an audience that is indifferent or possibly even hostile toward contemporary art. Explain why your readers should appreciate this particular art object.

10. Read James Gorman's essay "Man, Bytes, Dog." Imitating Gorman's essay, write a comparative evaluation of two dissimilar things.

MAN, BYTES, DOG

James Gorman

Many people have asked me about the Cairn Terrier. How about memory, they want to know. Is it I.B.M.-compatible? Why didn't I get the I.B.M. itself, or a Kaypro, Compaq, or Macintosh? I think the best way to answer these questions is to look at the Macintosh and the Cairn head on. I almost did buy the Macintosh. It has terrific graphics, good word-processing capabilities, and the mouse. But in the end I decided on the Cairn, and I think I made the right decision.

Let's start out with the basics:

MACINTOSH:

      Weight (without printer): 20 lbs.

      Memory (RAM): 128 K

      Price (with printer): $3,090

CAIRN TERRIER:

      Weight (without printer): 14 lbs.

      Memory (RAM): Some

      Price (without printer): $250

Just on the basis of price and weight, the choice is obvious. Another plus is that the Cairn Terrier comes in one unit. No printer is necessary, or useful. And—this was a big attraction to me—there is no user's manual.

Here are some of the other qualities I found put the Cairn out ahead of the Macintosh:

PORTABILITY: To give you a better idea of size, Toto in "The Wizard of Oz" was a Cairn Terrier. So you can see that if the young Judy Garland was able to carry Toto around in that little picnic basket, you will have no trouble at all moving your Cairn from place to place. For short trips it will move under its own power. The Macintosh will not.

RELIABILITY: In five to ten years, I am sure, the Macintosh will be superseded by a new model, like the Delicious or the Granny Smith. The Cairn Terrier, on the other hand, has held its share of the market with only minor modifications for hundreds of years. In the short term, Cairns seldom need servicing, apart from shots and the odd worming, and most function without interruption during electrical storms.

COMPATIBILITY: Cairn Terriers get along with everyone. And for communications with any other dog, of any breed, within a radius of three miles, no additional hardware is necessary. All dogs share a common operating system.

SOFTWARE: The Cairn will run three standard programs, SIT, COME, and NO , and whatever else you create. It is true that, being microcanine, the Cairn is limited here, but it does load the programs instantaneously. No disk drives. No tapes.

Admittedly, these are peripheral advantages. The real comparison has to be on the basis of capabilities. What can the Macintosh and the Cairn do? Let's start on the Macintosh's turf—income-tax preparation, recipe storage, graphics, and astrophysics problems:

	Taxes	Recipes	Graphics	Astrophysics
Macintosh	yes	yes	yes	yes
Cairn	no	no	no	no

At first glance it looks bad for the Cairn. But it's important to look beneath the surface with this kind of chart. If you yourself are leaning toward the Macintosh, ask yourself these questions: Do you want to do your own income taxes? Do you want to type all your recipes into a computer? In your graph, what would you put on the x axis? The y axis? Do you have any astrophysics problems you want solved?

Then consider the Cairn's specialties: playing fetch and tug-of-war, licking your face, and chasing foxes out of rock cairns (eponymously). Note that no software is necessary. All these functions are part of the operating system:

	Fetch	Tug-of-War	Face	Foxes
Cairn	yes	yes	yes	yes
Macintosh	no	no	no	no

Another point to keep in mind is that computers, even the Macintosh, only do what you tell them to do. Cairns perform their functions all on their own. Here are some of the additional capabilities that I discovered once I got the Cairn home and housebroken:

WORD PROCESSING: Remarkably, the Cairn seems to understand every word I say. He has a nice way of pricking up his ears at words like "out" or "ball." He also has highly tuned voice-recognition.

EDUCATION: The Cairn provides children with hands-on experience at an early age, contributing to social interaction, crawling ability, and language skills. At age one, my daughter could say "Sit," "Come," and "No."

CLEANING: This function was a pleasant surprise. But of course cleaning up around the cave is one of the reasons dogs were developed in the first place. Users with young (below age two) children will still find this function useful. The Cairn Terrier cleans the floor, spoons, bib, and baby, and has an unerring ability to distinguish strained peas from ears, nose, and fingers.

PSYCHOTHERAPY: Here the Cairn really shines. And remember, therapy is something that computers have tried. There is a program that makes the computer ask you questions when you tell it your problems. You say, "I'm afraid of foxes." The computer says, "You're afraid of foxes?"

The Cairn won't give you that kind of echo. Like Freudian analysts, Cairns are mercifully silent; unlike Freudians, they are infinitely sympathetic. I've found that the Cairn will share, in a nonjudgmental fashion, disappointments, joys, and frustrations. And you don't have to know BASIC.

This last capability is related to the Cairn's strongest point, which was the final deciding factor in my decision against the Macintosh—user-friendliness. On this criterion, there is simply no comparison. The Cairn Terrier is the essence of user-friendliness. It has fur, it doesn't flicker when you look at it, and it wags its tail.

EVALUATING: PROFESSIONAL WRITING

THE GETTYSBURG ADDRESS

Abraham Lincoln

Abraham Lincoln's Gettysburg Address, delivered as part of a memorial ceremony at the Gettysburg, Pennsylvania, battlefield in 1863, is a classic speech in American history. Brevity is surely one of its virtues—it is only 268 words long—but it is an excellent speech for other reasons as well. Gilbert Highet, a scholar and teacher of Latin and Greek for many years at Columbia University, describes the events leading up to the speech, the speech itself, and its reception by the audience and in the nation's leading newspapers. Highet claims that the Gettysburg Address is "one of the greatest speeches in all history." Read Lincoln's Gettysburg Address—aloud if possible—and then read Highet's evaluation. Do you agree with Highet's judgment?

Fourscore and seven years ago our fathers brought forth upon this continent a new nation, conceived in liberty, and dedicated to the proposition that all men are created equal.

Now we are engaged in a great civil war, testing whether that nation, or any nation so conceived and so dedicated, can long endure. We are met on a great battlefield of that war. We have come to dedicate a portion of that field as a final resting place for those who here gave their lives that that nation might live. It is altogether fitting and proper that we should do this.

But in a larger sense we cannot dedicate, we cannot consecrate, we cannot hallow this ground. The brave men, living and dead, who struggled here, have consecrated it far above our poor power to add or detract. The world will little note, nor long remember, what we say here, but it can never forget what they did here. It is for us the living, rather, to be dedicated here to the unfinished work which they who fought here have thus far so nobly advanced. It is rather for us to be here dedicated to the great task remaining before us, that from these honored dead we take increased devotion to that cause for which they gave the last full measure of devotion; that we here highly resolve that these dead shall not have died in vain; that this nation, under God, shall have a new birth of freedom; and that government of the people, by the people, and for the people, shall not perish from the earth.

THE GETTYSBURG ADDRESS

Gilbert Highet

Fourscore and seven years ago. . . .   (1)

These five words stand at the entrance to the best-known monument of American prose, one of the finest utterances in the entire language, and surely one of the greatest speeches in all history. Greatness is like granite: it is molded in fire, and it lasts for many centuries. . . .   (2)

The dedication of the graveyard at Gettysburg was one of the supreme moments of American history. The battle itself had been a turning point of the war. On the 4th of July 1863, General Meade repelled Lee's invasion of Pennsylvania. Although he did not follow up his victory, he had broken one of the most formidable aggressive enterprises of the Confederate armies. Losses were heavy on both sides. Thousands of dead were left on the field, and thousands of wounded died in the hot days following the battle. At first, their burial was more or less haphazard; but thoughtful men gradually came to feel that an adequate burying place and memorial were required. These were established by an interstate commission that autumn, and the finest speaker in the North was invited to dedicate them. This was the scholar and statesman Edward Everett of Harvard. He made a good speech—which is still extant: not at all academic, it is full of close strategic analysis and deep historical understanding.   (3)

Lincoln was not invited to speak, at first. Although people knew him as an effective debater, they were not sure whether he was capable of making a serious speech on such a solemn occasion. But one of the impressive things about Lincoln's career is that he constantly strove to *grow*. He was anxious to appear on that occasion and to say something worthy of it. (Also, it has been suggested, he was anxious to remove the impression that he did not know how to behave properly—an impression which had been strengthened by a shocking story about his clowning on the battlefield of Antietam the previous year.) Therefore when he was invited he took considerable care with his speech. He drafted rather more than half of it in the White House before leaving, finished it in the hotel at Gettysburg the night before the ceremony (not in the train, as sometimes reported), and wrote a fair copy next morning.   (4)

There are many accounts of the day itself, 19 November 1863. There are many descriptions of Lincoln, all showing the same curious blend of grandeur and awkwardness, or lack of dignity, or—it would be best to call it humility. In the procession he rode horseback: a tall lean man in a high plug hat, straddling a short horse, with his feet too near the ground. He arrived before the chief speaker, and had to wait patiently for half an hour or more. His own speech came right at the end of a long and exhausting ceremony, lasted less than three minutes, and made little impression on the audience. In part this was because they were tired, in part because (as eyewitnesses said) he ended almost before they knew he had begun, and in part because he did not speak the Address, but read it, very slowly, in a thin high voice, with a marked Kentucky accent, pronouncing "to" as "toe" and dropping his final R's.   (5)

Some people of course were alert enough to be impressed. Everett congratulated him at once. But most of the newspapers paid little attention to the speech, and some sneered at it. The *Patriot and Union* of Harrisburg wrote, "We pass over the silly remarks of the President; for the credit of the nation we are willing . . . that they shall no more be repeated or thought of"; and the London *Times* said, "The ceremony was rendered ludicrous by some of the sallies of that poor President Lincoln," calling his remarks "dull and commonplace." The first commendation of the Address came in a single sentence of the Chicago *Tribune,* and the first discriminating and detailed praise of it appeared in the Springfield *Republican,* the Providence *Journal,* and the Philadelphia *Bulletin*. However, three weeks after the ceremony and then again the following spring, the editor of *Harper's Weekly* published a sincere and thorough eulogy of the Address, and soon it was attaining recognition as a masterpiece.   (6)

At the time, Lincoln could not care much about the reception of his words. He was exhausted and ill. In the train back to Washington, he lay down with a wet towel on his head. He had caught smallpox. At that moment he was incubating it, and he was stricken down soon after he re-entered the White House. Fortunately it was a mild attack, and it evoked one of his best jokes: he told his visitors, "At last I have something I can give to everybody."   (7)

He had more than that to give to everybody. He was a unique person, far greater than most people realize until they read his life with care. The wisdom of his policy, the sources of his statesmanship—these were things too complex to be discussed in a brief essay. But we can say something about the Gettysburg Address as a work of art.   (8)

A work of art. Yes: for Lincoln was a literary artist, trained both by others and by himself. The textbooks he used as a boy were full of difficult exercises and skillful devices in formal rhetoric, stressing the qualities he practiced in his own speaking: antithesis, parallelism, and verbal harmony. Then he read and reread many admirable models of thought and expression: the King James Bible, the essays of Bacon, the best plays of Shakespeare. His favorites were *Hamlet, Lear, Macbeth, Richard III,* and *Henry VIII,* which he had read dozens of times. He loved reading aloud, too, and spent hours reading poetry to his friends. (He told his partner Herndon that he preferred getting the sense of any document by reading it aloud.) Therefore his serious speeches are important parts of the long and noble classical tradition of oratory which begins in Greece, runs through Rome to the modern world, and is still capable (if we do not neglect it) of producing masterpieces.   (9)

The first proof of this is that the Gettysburg Address is full of quotations—or rather of adaptations—which give it strength. It is partly religious, partly (in the highest sense) political: therefore it is interwoven with memories of the Bible and memories of American history. The first and the last words are Biblical cadences. Normally Lincoln did not say "fourscore" when he meant eighty; but on this solemn occasion he recalled the important dates in the Bible—such as the age of Abraham when his first son was born to him, and he was "fourscore and six years old." Similarly he did not say there was a chance that democracy might die out: he recalled the somber phrasing in the Book of Job—where Bildad speaks of the destruction of one who shall vanish without a trace, and says that "his branch shall be cut off; his remembrance shall perish from the earth." Then again, the famous description of our State as "government of the people, by the people, for the people" was adumbrated by Daniel Webster in 1830 (he spoke of "the people's government, made for the people, made by the people, and answerable to the people") and then elaborated in 1854 by the abolitionist Theodore Parker (as "government of all the people, by all the people, for all the people").   (10)

Analyzing the Address further, we find that it is based on a highly imaginative theme, or group of themes. The subject is—how can we put it so as not to disfigure it?—the subject is the kinship of life and death, that mysterious linkage which we see sometimes as the physical succession of birth and death in our world, sometimes as the contrast, which is perhaps a unity, between death and immortality. The first sentence is concerned with birth:

> Our *fathers brought forth* a *new* nation, *conceived* in liberty.

The final phrase but one expresses the hope that

> this nation, under God, shall have a *new birth* of freedom.

And the last phrase of all speaks of continuing life as the triumph over death. Again and again throughout the speech, this mystical contrast and kinship reappear: "those who *gave their lives* that that nation might *live,*" "the brave men *living* and *dead,*" and so in the central assertion that the dead have already consecrated their own burial place, while "it is for us, the *living,* rather to be dedicated . . . to the great task remaining." The Gettysburg Address is a prose poem; it belongs to the same world as the great elegies, and the adagios of Beethoven.   (11)

Its structure, however, is that of a skillfully contrived speech. The oratorical pattern is perfectly clear. Lincoln describes the occasion, dedicates the ground, and then draws a larger conclusion by calling on his hearers to dedicate themselves to the preservation of the Union. But within that, we can trace his constant use of at least two important rhetorical devices.   (12)

The first of these is *antithesis:* opposition, contrast. The speech is full of it. Listen:

The world will little	*note*		
nor long	*remember*	what *we say*	here
but it can never	*forget*	what *they did*	here

And so in nearly every sentence: "brave men, *living* and *dead*"; "to *add* or *detract.*" There is the antithesis of the Founding Fathers and men of Lincoln's own time:

> Our *fathers brought forth* a new nation. . . .
>
> now *we* are testing whether that nation . . . can *long endure.*

And there is the more terrible antithesis of those who have already died and those who still live to do their duty. Now, antithesis is the figure of contrast and conflict. Lincoln was speaking in the midst of a great civil war.   (13)

The other important pattern is different. It is technically called *tricolon*—the division of an idea into three harmonious parts, usually of increasing power. The most famous phrase of the Address is a tricolon:

> government of the people
>> by the people
>> for the people

The most solemn sentence is a tricolon:

> we cannot dedicate
>
> we cannot consecrate
>
> we cannot hallow   this ground.

And above all, the last sentence (which has sometimes been criticized as too complex) is essentially two parallel phrases, with a tricolon growing out of the second and then producing another tricolon: a trunk, three branches, and a cluster of flowers. Lincoln says that it is for his hearers to be dedicated to the great task remaining before them. Then he goes on,

> that from these honored dead

—apparently he means "in such a way that from these honored dead"—

> we take increased devotion to that cause.

Next, he restates this more briefly:

> that we here highly resolve. . . .

And now the actual resolution follows, in three parts of growing intensity:

> that these dead shall not have died in vain
>
> that this nation, under God, shall have a new birth of freedom

and that (one more tricolon)

> government of the people
>> by the people
>> for the people
>
> shall not perish from the earth.

Now, the tricolon is the figure which, through division, emphasizes basic harmony and unity. Lincoln used antithesis because he was speaking to a people at war. He used the tricolon because he was hoping, planning, praying for peace.   (14)

No one thinks that when he was drafting the Gettysburg Address, Lincoln deliberately looked up these quotations and consciously chose these particular patterns of thought. No, he chose the theme. From its development and from the emotional tone of the entire occasion, all the rest followed, or grew—by that marvelous process of choice and rejection which is essential to artistic creation. It does not spoil such a work of art to analyze it as closely as we have done; it is altogether fitting and proper that we do this: for it helps us to penetrate more deeply into the rich meaning of the Gettysburg Address, and it allows us the very rare privilege of watching the workings of a great man's mind.   (15)

VOCABULARY

In your journal, write down the meanings of the following words.

- *fourscore* and seven   (1)
- more or less *haphazard*   (3)
- is still *extant*   (3)
- wrote a *fair* copy   (4)
- *discriminating* and detailed praise   (6)
- a sincere and thorough *eulogy*   (6)
- formal *rhetoric*   (9)
- classical tradition of *oratory*   (9)
- Biblical *cadences*   (10)
- was *adumbrated* by Daniel Webster   (10)
- the *abolitionist* Theodore Parker   (10)
- *mystical* contrast and kinship   (11)
- *consecrated* their own burial place   (11)
- the great *elegies*   (11)
- the *adagios* of Beethoven   (11)
- the tricolon is the *figure*   (14)

QUESTIONS FOR WRITING AND DISCUSSION

1. Imagine that you are the mother of a soldier—actually just a fifteen-year-old boy—who died in battle at Gettysburg. You have been against the war from the start. You stand patiently throughout the long ceremony, but after listening to Lincoln's comments, you still believe your son died in vain. Write a short letter to Lincoln, responding to his address.

2. Read Lincoln's Gettysburg Address aloud. From your own point of view, do you agree with the original newspaper reports that found the speech "dull and commonplace," do you agree with

Gilbert Highet's high praise, or are your judgments mixed? Brainstorm a list of *your* positive and negative reactions to this speech. Then write one sentence expressing your overall impression.

3. List the *criteria* Highet uses to evaluate Lincoln's Gettysburg Address. Then, following each criterion, jot down examples of the support or evidence he gives. Which criteria and supporting examples do you find *least* convincing? Which are *most* convincing? Explain.

4. Highet evaluates Lincoln's speech, but he also evaluates Lincoln himself. List the criteria he uses and cite the support he gives for his judgments.

5. Identify the following structural elements in Highet's essay. For each item, indicate the appropriate paragraph number or numbers:

   - Lead-in:

   - Thesis or overall claim:

   - Background description, information about Lincoln and Gettysburg:

   - Criterion #1: judgment and evidence:

   - Criterion #2: judgment and evidence:

   - Criterion #3: judgment and evidence:

   - Conclusion:

ARMAGEDDON, COMPLETE AND UNCUT

Robert Kiely

In his article on Stephen King's The Stand, *Robert Kiely follows a book review format. Kiely's purpose, therefore, is partly to assess the novel's strengths and weaknesses, but partly to describe the novel in detail for his readers. Just as Gilbert Highet includes several paragraphs describing Lincoln's delivery of the Gettysburg Address, so Kiely devotes over half of his review to summarizing (and interpreting) King's novel. Readers of* The New York Times Book Review, *where Kiely's article appeared, certainly expect in-depth information about characters, plot, and themes in the unabridged version of* The Stand. *Kiely's overall judgment, that the novel's immensity is a source of both strengths and weaknesses, is stated directly and illustrated in the plot summary. An English professor at Harvard University, Kiely has published dozens of books and articles on authors such as Edgar Allan Poe, George Eliot, Charles Dickens, James Joyce, Virginia Woolf, D. H. Lawrence, and Thomas Pynchon.*

The Stand

The Complete and Uncut Edition.
By Stephen King.
Illustrated. 1,153 pp. New York:
Doubleday. $24.95.

What is longer than "Moby-Dick," "War and Peace" or "Ulysses"? If you guessed the Bible or the Manhattan telephone book, you would not be wrong (though there are small-print Bibles that are under a thousand pages). There are, of course, other longer books, but not many are novels and few of those have been able to sustain a hold on the popular imagination. "The Stand," unabridged and 1,153 pages long, may prove the exception.   (1)

In 1978, Stephen King, the author of "Carrie" and "The Shining," published "The Stand" and almost immediately added thousands of new readers to his already huge following. At that time, Mr. King's publishers thought the book would be better and certainly more salable if it were cut—in fact, cut by 500 pages, nearly half of its original length. Now the novel has been reissued with the missing 150,000 words reinstated, plus a preface by the author and 12 black-and-white illustrations by Bernie Wrightson.   (2)

It might seem unfair or irrelevant to dwell on size when assessing a novel, yet in this case it is impossible to do otherwise. One simply cannot ignore the bulk of this volume. Besides, a preoccupation with size and weight, particularly an American preoccupation with size and weight, is, as Mr. King insists, central to "The Stand." As it is linked with images of the land, of the spaciousness and diversity and opportunity of the nation, this is a familiar American theme. Mr. King has not only read his Melville but also his Whitman and Dos Passos. Like his predecessors, Mr. King is aware that there is menace as well as promise in the immensity of the United States. What appears modern (or post-modern) in Mr. King is that both the menace and the promise have been tainted by a cheap tedium, a repetition of bravado and monotony of violence. This is not another book about a still raw, untried, half-hidden America, but a nation exposed over and over to itself, as in an enormous mirror, part trite situation comedy, part science fiction, part cop show. In "The Stand," Mr. King comes across as the people's Thomas Pynchon. His characters are "toilers in the vinyl vineyards," just plain folks who drink Gatorade and V8 but who also may happen to have jobs on top secret Government installations in the barren recesses of Nevada.   (3)

The general outline of the plot is fairly simple. An accident occurs in an Army lab doing research on biological warfare. A virus breaks through the isolation barrier and rapidly causes the death of nearly everyone working in the plant. There is one survivor, however, who walks past the failed security apparatus, races home to his wife and child, bundles them into the car and speeds toward the Texas border. By the time they reach a gas station in Texas, he is very ill and his wife and daughter have died a horrible death that leaves their bodies bloated, blackened and stinking.   (4)

Of course, the handful of people at the gas station are also contaminated and they, in turn, pass on the virus to others in a macabre chain of association that is described in loving detail, like a parody of the circulation of money (the perennial bad penny) or a mammoth game of pin the tail on the donkey. From Texas to Maine, Los Angeles to New York, in a gruesome variation on the refrain of "This Land Is Your Land," the superflu spreads, causing its victims at first merely to sniffle and sneeze but soon after to expire in paroxysms of pain and burning fever. (The AIDS epidemic had not been identified when Mr. King originally wrote this book. What in 1978 might have looked like a fantastic exaggeration, in 1990 still appears statistically exaggerated but, sadly, not so fantastic).   (5)

Hundreds of pages of text are devoted to vignettes—some poignant, nearly all disgusting—of Americans in all regions and walks of life being stopped in the tracks of their ordinary existence by the dread and incurable disease. Two things make Mr. King's rendering of this phenomenon peculiar, one might almost say original. The first is the sheer number of cases reported and described. At first, you read along expecting things to change, a cure to be found, an escape to be discovered, but after 300 or more pages it becomes clear that variations on one theme—not progress—are the novelist's plan.   (6)

The second thing that makes these vignettes, and indeed the entire novel, peculiar is that the characters and situations are virtually all reproductions of American cultural icons. "L.A. Law" meets "The Wizard of Oz"; "On the Road" meets "The Grapes of Wrath"; "Rebel Without a Cause" meets "Walden"; Li'l Abner gets lost in the House of Usher; Huck Finn finds Rambo. The New England we see is Norman Rockwell's; the West is John Wayne's. They are often pointed out, lest the reader miss them. "She looked like a woman from an Irwin Shaw novel" or "It's like Bonnie and Clyde" are common interjections from the narrator and the characters. At the same time, neither comic parody nor a Joycean complexity is at work here. The reproduction of the familiar seems instead a kind of corporate raid, a literary equivalent of a megamonopoly in which the new owner parades brand names to show off the extent and importance of the newly purchased domain.   (7)

Everything is processed through a gigantic American meat grinder. Just as foreign monuments become a "Leaning Tower of Pizza" or "the Forbidden City Cafe," so the names and words of writers from other parts of the world are reproduced, respelled and repronounced. An admiring general turns Yeats into Yeets: "He said that things fall apart. He said the center doesn't hold. I believe he meant that things get flaky. . . . That's what I believe he meant. Yeets knew that sooner or later things get . . . flaky around the edges even if he didn't know anything else.   (8)

The few healthy characters seem not just to have survived the plague; they have also survived a rough-and-tumble translation from another medium. There is a Woody Allen look- and sound-alike: a New York songwriter with a sassy mother, who nags and pampers her successful and neurotic son during one of his rare visits home. There is a Jane Fonda character from Maine who is gutsy, beautiful, bursting with aerobic energy and slightly pregnant. And there is the hero, a strong, silent Texan, an amalgam of Gary Cooper and Kevin Costner. When the virus eventually peters out, after having done away with what appears to be most of the population, these and a few others gradually converge on the road, with their battered motorcycles, jalopies, slick sports cars and stolen bicycles, or just tramp exhaustedly from empty town to empty town in search of life and some place to start over.   (9)

Boulder, Colo., turns out to be the point of convergence for these friendly and cinematically familiar survivors and some dozens of others like them. No sooner do they find one another than they begin planning a government. Someone suggests a meeting in which they all ratify the Declaration of Independence, the United States Constitution and the Bill of Rights. Another objects that this is unnecessary since "we're all Americans." But, it is quickly explained, government is really an *"idea,"* and the reality of a democracy no longer exists: "The President is dead, the Pentagon is for rent, nobody is debating anything in the House or the Senate except maybe for the termites and the cockroaches."   (10)

It is all too shockingly and heavy-handedly clear that such statements—literally accurate within the plot of the novel—could (like the deadly virus) serve as metaphors for the dangerous and deplorable state of things in this country. However, rather than analysis or narrative development, there is a prophetic and programmatic explanation: a satanic figure, who has gathered his evil forces in Las Vegas, Nev. (where else?), has been haunting the American dream with fearful nightmares. He must be stopped. A few hand-picked heroes, macho males from "Butch Cassidy and the Sundance Kid" or "The Longest Day," scramble over dangerous, desolate terrain to get him, but are saved the trouble when he and his minions melt, like the Wicked Witch of the West, in a nuclear accident.   (11)

In short (well, not so short), this is the book that has everything—adventure, romance, prophecy, allegory, satire, fantasy, realism, apocalypse, etc., etc. Even Roger Rabbit gets mentioned. "The Stand" does have some great moments and some great lines. A desperate character trying to save his mother reaches an answering machine: "This is a recording made at Mercy General Hospital. Right now all of our circuits are busy." And there is a wonderful description of "mankind's final traffic jam." But the overall effect is more oppressive than imposing.   (12)

In many ways, this is a book for the 1990's, when America is beginning to see itself less and less in the tall image of Lincoln or even the robust one of Johnny Appleseed and more and more as a dazed behemoth with padded shoulders. Americans seemed delighted but in an odd way humiliated when Vaclav Havel, a tiny man from a small country, entered the great halls of Congress and delivered an uninflated Jeffersonian address. "The Stand," complete and uncut, is about the padded shoulders and the behemoth and the humiliation. Unfortunately, it also reproduces at length all the empty excesses that it appears to deplore.   (13)

VOCABULARY

In your journal, write the meanings of the following words.

- a *preoccupation* with size   (3)
- a cheap *tedium*   (3)
- *macabre* chain   (5)
- *paroxysms* of pain   (5)
- some *poignant*   (6)
- cultural *icons*   (7)
- comic *parody*   (7)
- an *amalgam*   (9)
- point of *convergence*   (10)
- *allegory, satire,* fantasy, realism, *apocalypse*   (12)
- appears to *deplore*   (13)

QUESTIONS FOR WRITING AND DISCUSSION

1. If you have read a novel by Stephen King, write a one-paragraph review of that work. Refer to the major characters, outline the plot, and support one or two judgments about the novel's strengths and weaknesses.

2. Kiely says his purpose is to "assess" the novel. Reread his article, noting words or phrases that indicate his evaluation of the strengths and weaknesses of *The Stand*. List Kiely's positive and negative judgments.

3. Locate a copy of a recent *New York Times Book Review*. First, list at least five books reviewed in that issue. Then, photocopy and read one book review. Based on your inspection of that issue and your reading of one article, profile the *audience* for that periodical. (Bring your photocopy and notes to class for discussion.)

4. Identify and list Kiely's cues about the organization of his review. What words and phrases signal or promise the reader that a new idea or section is coming?

5. Many of Stephen King's fans are younger people who are not readers of *The New York Times Book Review*. Select three or four paragraphs from Kiely's article and rewrite them for a high school or college audience. Assume that this revision will appear in a campus newspaper.

EVALUATING: THE WRITING PROCESS

ASSIGNMENT FOR EVALUATING

With a specific audience in mind, evaluate a product or service, a work of art, or a performance. (Choose a subject that is **reobservable**—that you can revisit or review as you write your essay.) Select criteria appropriate for your subject and audience. Collect evidence to support or determine a judgment for each criterion.

I love criticism so long as it's unqualified praise.

—*Noel Coward, playwright and songwriter*

Choosing a Subject

If you have already settled on a possible subject, try the collecting and shaping strategies below. If you have not found a subject, consider the following ideas:

- Evaluating requires some expertise about a particular person, performance, place, object, or service. You generate expertise not only through experience but also through writing, reading, and rewriting. Review your authority list from Chapter 5. Which of those subjects could you evaluate? Reread your journal entries on observing and investigating. Did you observe or investigate some person, place, or thing that you could write about again, only this time for the purpose of evaluating it?

- Comparing and contrasting leads naturally to evaluation. For example, compare two places you've lived, two friends, or two jobs. Compare two newspapers for their coverage of international news, local features, sports, or business. Compare two famous people from the same profession. Compare your expectations about a person, place, or event with the reality. The purpose of your comparison is to determine, for a specific audience, which is "better," based on the criteria you select and the evidence you find.

Collecting

Once you have a tentative subject and audience in mind, ask the following questions to focus your collecting activities:

- Can you narrow, restrict, or define your subject to focus your paper?
- What *criteria* will you use to evaluate your subject?
- What *evidence* might you gather? As you collect evidence, focus on three questions:

  What *comparisons* can you make between your subject and similar subjects?

  What are the *uses* or *consequences* of this subject?

  What *experiments* or *authorities* might you cite for support?

- What initial *judgments* are you going to make?

Observing   Observation and description of your subject are crucial to a clear evaluation. In most cases, your audience will need to know *what* your subject is before they can understand your evaluation.

- Examine a place or object repeatedly, looking at it from different points of view. Take notes. Describe it. Draw it if appropriate. Analyze its component parts. List its uses. Which senses does it appeal to—sight, sound, touch, smell, taste? If you are comparing your subject to other similar subjects, observe them carefully. Remember: The second or third time you observe your subject, you will see even more key details.
- If you are evaluating a person, collect information about this person's life, interests, abilities, accomplishments, and plans for the

future. If you are able to observe the person directly, describe his or her physical features, write down what he or she says, and describe the person's environment.

- If you are evaluating a performance or an event, a tape recording or videotape can be extremely useful. If possible, choose a concert, film, or play on tape, so you can stop and review it where necessary. If a tape recording or videotape is not available, attend the performance or event twice.

Making notes in a *three-column log* is an excellent collecting strategy for evaluations. Using the following example from Phyllis Richman's evaluation of the Hunan Dynasty restaurant, list the criteria, judgments, and evidence for your subject.

SUBJECT: HUNAN DYNASTY RESTAURANT

Criteria	Judgment	Evidence
Attractive setting	Graceful	No blaring red-lacquer tables White tablecloths Subtle glass etchings
Good service	Often expert	Waiters serve with flourishes Some glitches, such as a forgotten appetizer

Remembering You are already an authority on many subjects, and your personal experiences may help you evaluate your subject. Try *freewriting, looping, branching,* or *clustering* your subject to help you remember relevant events, impressions, and information. In evaluating appliances for consumer magazines, for example, reporters often use a product over a period of months, recording data, impressions, and experiences. Those experiences and memories are then used to support the criteria and judgments. Evaluating a film often requires remembering similar films you have liked or disliked. An evaluation of a great athlete may include your memories of previous performances. A vivid narrative of those memories can help convince an audience that a performance is good or bad.

Investigating All evaluations involve some degree of formal or informal investigation as you probe the characteristics of your subject and then seek evidence to support your judgments.

USING THE LIBRARY

Check the library for information on your subject, for ideas about how to design and conduct an evaluation of that subject, for possible criteria, for data in evaluations already performed, and for a sense of different possible audiences. In its evaluation of chocolate-chip cookies, for example, *Consumer Reports* magazine suggests criteria and outlines procedures. The magazine rated some two-dozen popular store-bought brands, as well as four "boutique" or freshly baked varieties, on "strength of chocolate flavor and aroma, cookie and chip texture, and freedom from sensory defects." When the magazine's evaluators faced a problem sampling the fresh cookies in the lab, they decided to move the lab: "We ended up loading a station wagon with scoresheet, pencils, clipboards, water containers, cups, napkins . . . and setting off on a tasting safari to shopping malls."

GATHERING FIELD DATA

You may want to supplement your personal evaluation with a sample of other people's opinions by using *questionnaires* or *interviews*. (See Chapter 5.) If you are rating a film, for example, you might give people leaving the theater a very brief *questionnaire*, asking for their responses on key criteria relating to the movie they just saw. If you are rating a class, you might want to *interview* several students in the class to support your claim that the class was either effective or ineffective. The interviews might also give you some specific examples—descriptions of their experiences that you can then use as evidence to support your judgments.

Shaping

The shaping strategies you have used in previous essays may be helpful, but the strategies that follow are particularly appropriate for shaping evaluations.

Analysis by Criteria   Often, evaluations are organized by criteria. You decide which criteria are appropriate for the subject and audience, and then you use those criteria to outline the essay. Your first few paragraphs of introduction establish your thesis or overall claim and then give background information: what the subject is, why you are evaluating it, what the competition is, and how you gathered your data. Then you order the criteria according to some plan: chronological order, spatial order, order of importance, or another logical sequence. Phyllis Richman's evaluation of the Hunan Dynasty restaurant follows the criteria pattern:

- Introductory paragraphs: *information* about the restaurant (location, hours, prices), general *description* of Chinese restaurants today, and *overall claim:* The Hunan Dynasty is reliable, a good value, and versatile.
- Criterion #1/Judgment: Good restaurants should have an attractive setting and atmosphere / Hunan Dynasty is attractive.
- Criterion #2/Judgment: Good restaurants should give strong priority to service / Hunan Dynasty has, despite an occasional glitch, expert service.
- Criterion #3/Judgment: Restaurants that serve moderately priced food should have quality main dishes / Main dishes at Hunan Dynasty are generally good but not often memorable. [Most important criterion, the quality of the main dishes, is saved for last.]

COMPUTER TIP: COLLECTING AND SHAPING

Open a file for your evaluating essay and write a list of possible criteria for your subject. Select the most important criteria for your audience and leave some space between each category.

> Background information or description:
> Criteria #1:
> > Judgment:
> > Evidence:
> Criteria #2:
> > Judgment:
> > Evidence:
> Criteria #3:
> > (continue)

Then *freewrite* for five minutes on the background information and on each criterion, putting down all the data or evidence you have read, observed, or can remember about your subject. As you accumulate evidence, state your judgment for each criterion. When you have a judgment and evidence for each criteria, try *ranking* your criteria. Which of these criteria is most or least important for your audience? Try arranging them in various orders. The word processor will help you "see" how the different orders will look to your readers.

- Concluding paragraphs: Hunan Dynasty is a top-flight neighborhood restaurant.

Comparison and Contrast   Many evaluations compare two subjects in order to demonstrate why one is preferable to another. Books, films, restaurants, courses, music, writers, scientists, historical events, sports—all can be evaluated using comparison and contrast. In evaluating two oriental restaurants, for example, student writer Chris Cameron uses a comparison-and-contrast structure to shape her essay. In the following body paragraph from her essay, Cameron compares two restaurants, the Unicorn and the Yakitori, on the basis of her first criterion—an atmosphere that seemed authentically oriental.

> Of the two restaurants, we preferred the authentic atmosphere of the Unicorn to the cultural confusion at the Yakitori. At first impression, the Yakitori looked like a converted truck-stop, sparsely decorated with a few bamboo slats and Japanese print fabric hanging in slices as Bruce Springsteen wailed loudly in the ears of the customers. The feeling at the Unicorn was quite the opposite as we entered a room that seemed transported from Chinatown. The whole room had a red tint from the light shining through the flowered curtains, and the place looked truly authentic from the Chinese patterned rug on the wall to the elaborate dragon on the ceiling. Soft oriental music played as the customers sipped tea from small porcelain cups and ate fortune cookies.

Cameron used the following *alternating* comparison-and-contrast shape for her whole essay:

- Introductory paragraph(s)

  Thesis: Although several friends recommended the Yakitori, we preferred the Unicorn for its more authentic atmosphere, courteous service, and well-prepared food.

- Authentic atmosphere: Yakitori vs. Unicorn
- Courteous service: Yakitori vs. Unicorn
- Well-prepared food: Yakitori vs. Unicorn
- Concluding paragraph(s)

Cameron might have used a *block* comparison-and-contrast structure for her essay. In this organizational pattern, Cameron's outline would be as follows:

- Introductory paragraph(s)

  Thesis: Although several friends recommended the Yakitori, we preferred the Unicorn for its more authentic atmosphere, courteous service, and well-prepared food.

- The Yakitori: atmosphere, service, and food

- The Unicorn: atmosphere, service, and food as compared to the Yakitori
- Concluding paragraph(s)

Chronological Order   Writers often use a chronological order to organize their claims and criteria. In her review of *Star Wars*, for example, Judith Crist shapes her evaluation by following a natural chronological order:

1. Comments on Lucas's previous film, *American Graffiti*.
2. Review of the plot.
3. Evaluation of the climax of the film.
4. Comment on the viewer's good feelings at the end of the film.

Causal Analysis   Analyzing the *causes or effects* of a place, object, event, or policy can shape an entire evaluation. Works of art or performances, for example, often measure the *effect* on the viewers or audience. Mark Stevens claims that Goya's painting has several definite effects on the viewer; those specific effects become the evidence that supports the claim.

- Criterion #1/Judgment: The iconography, or use of symbols, contributes to the powerful effect of this picture on the viewer.

  Evidence: The church as a symbol of hopefulness contrasts with the cruelty of the execution. The spire on the church emphasizes for the viewer how powerless the Church is to save the victims.

- Criterion #2/Judgment: The use of light contributes to the powerful effect of the picture on the viewer.

  Evidence: The light casts an intense glow on the scene, and its glaring, lurid, and artificial qualities create the same effect on the viewer that modern art sometimes does.

- Criterion #3/Judgment: The composition or use of formal devices contributes to the powerful effect of the picture on the viewer.

  Evidence: The diagonal lines scissor the picture into spaces that give the viewer a claustrophobic feeling. The corpse is foreshortened, so that it looks as though the dead man is bidding the viewer welcome.

Title, Introduction, and Conclusion   Titles of evaluative writing tend to be short and succinct, stating what product, service, work of art, or performance you are evaluating ("The Gettysburg Address," "Goya's *The Third of May, 1808*") or suggesting a key question or conclusion in the evaluation ("How Much Car for $3990?" "'Feel Good' Film").

Introductory paragraphs provide background information and description and usually give an overall claim or thesis. In some cases, however, the overall claim comes last, in a concluding "Recommendations" section, or in a final summary paragraph. If the overall claim appears in the opening paragraphs, the concluding paragraph may simply review the strengths or weaknesses, or just advise the reader: This *is* or *is not* worth seeing, reading, watching, doing, or buying.

RESEARCH TIP

Before you draft your evaluating essay, stop for a moment and *evaluate your sources* of information and opinion. If you are citing ideas or information from library articles, be skeptical. How reliable is your source? What do you know about the periodical's editorial slant or audience? Does the author have a particular bias? Be sure to *qualify* any biased or absolute statements you use from your sources. (See pp. 400–401 in Chapter 10 for additional ideas on evaluating written sources.)

If you cite observations or field sources (interviews, surveys), evaluate the information you collected. Does it reflect only one point of view? How is it biased? Are your responses in surveys limited in number or point of view? Remember: You may use sources that reflect a limited perspective, but *be sure to alert your readers to those limitations.* For example, you might say, "Obviously, these reactions represent only four viewers who saw this film, but . . ."or "Of course, the administrator wanted to defend this student program when he said . . ."

Drafting

With your criteria in front of you, your data or evidence at hand, and a general plan or sketch outline in mind, begin writing your draft. As you write, focus on your audience. If your evaluation needs to be short, you may have to use only those criteria that will appeal most effectively to your audience. As you write, check occasionally to be sure that you are including your key criteria. Some parts of the essay may seem forced or awkward as you write, but other parts will grow and expand as you get your thoughts on paper. As in other papers, don't stop to check spelling or worry about an occasional awkward

I have to stop being afraid of being wrong; I can't wait until everything is perfect before the work comes out. I don't have that kind of time.

—*Sherley Anne Williams, novelist and critic*

sentence. If you stop and can't get going, reread what you have written, look over your notes or sketch outline, and pick up the thread again.

Revising

I have rewritten—often several times—every word I have ever published. My pencils outlast their erasers.

—Vladimir Nabokov, novelist

Remember that revision is not just changing a word here or there or correcting occasional spelling errors. Make your evaluation more effective for your reader by including more specific evidence, changing the order of your paragraphs to make them clearer, cutting out an unimportant point, or adding a point that one of your readers suggests.

Guidelines for Revision   During your revision, keep the following tips in mind:

- **Criteria are *standards of value*.** They contain a category and a judgment, as in "good fuel economy," "reliability," or "powerful use of light and shade in a painting." Some categories, such as "price," have clearly implied judgment ("low price"), but make sure that your criteria refer implicitly or explicitly to a standard of value.

- **Examine your criteria from your audience's point of view.** Which criteria are most important in evaluating your subject? Will your readers agree that the criteria you select are indeed the most important ones? Will changing the order in which you present your criteria make your evaluation more convincing?

- **Be sure to include supporting evidence for each criterion.** Without any data or support, your evaluation will be just an opinion that will not persuade your reader.

- **Avoid overgeneralizing in your claims.** If you are evaluating only three software programs, you cannot say that Lotus 1-2-3 is the best business program around. You can say only that it is the best among the group or the best in the particular class you measured.

- **Unless your point is humor or irony, compare subjects that belong in the same class.** Comparing a Yugo to a BMW is absurd because they are not similar cars in terms of cost, design, or purpose.

- **If you need additional evidence to persuade your readers, review the questions at the beginning of the "Collecting" section of this chapter.** Have you addressed all the key questions listed there?

- **If you are citing other people's data or quoting sources, check to make sure your summaries and data are accurate.**

- *Signal* **the major divisions in your evaluation to your reader using clear transitions, key words, and paragraph hooks.** At the beginning of new paragraphs or sections in your essay, let your reader know where you are going.
- **Revise sentences for directness and clarity.**
- **Edit your evaluation for correct spelling, appropriate word choice, punctuation, usage, and grammar.**

POSTSCRIPT ON THE WRITING PROCESS

When you finish writing your essay, compare what you were trying to do with what you actually wrote. In your journal, complete the following sentences:

1. In my evaluation, I wanted to convince my reader that _____ [your subject] was really _____ [good, bad, and so on] because _____ [explain].
2. My main problem in writing this essay was _____. Explain.
3. I tried to solve this problem by _____ [observing the subject more closely, reading more about my subject or interviewing others, brainstorming for personal memories, reorganizing the draft, letting the draft sit for two days, taking the advice of readers, other]. Explain.
4. The part I still like best about my evaluation is _____. Explain.

EVALUATING: STUDENT WRITING

TWELVE STRINGS

Craig Flickinger

Craig Flickinger wrote his evaluation essay about a twelve-string guitar he wanted to buy. Like most consumers, he wanted the best guitar he could afford on his limited budget. Rather than just rate several twelve-string guitars, however, Flickinger says he tried "to take the audience chronologically through my investigation and discoveries about twelve-string guitars—in an entertaining way." After collecting information from friends and music stores, he recorded his notes from his observing, remembering, and investigating activities.

Collecting Notes

Subject: Twelve-string guitars -- which one to buy? Or what can I afford?

Criteria: Tone quality
Playability
Price
Materials and workmanship

Evidence: Visited the store, talked to my friends about which brand is best.

Comparisons: The Martin, Guild, Aria, Alvarez, Sigma Martin

Authorities: My music teacher, my friend Bill, salespeople?

Claims: Guild and Martin are the best, but I still don't know which one I'll get.

Observing

In the store, the Guild was so easy to play it almost played itself. Jumping for richness of sound -- Sigma Martin and Aria weren't good, Alvarez a bit better. For tone quality, Guild and Martin were superior. The quality of workmanship on all the guitars seemed, to me, very good. On the warranties, Martin and Guild have the best and the longest warranties. Prices were shockingly high (rounded to the nearest $50): Martin -- $800, Guild $900, Alvarez $500, Aria $450, Sigma Martin $350. All the stores had financing.

Remembering

The very first time I heard a 12-string I was really hooked. It sounded like a whole band. I remember Bill and I were playing, and he played "The Eagle and the Hawk" on a 12-string. It sounded like an entire orchestra, like church bells. I remember talking him into borrowing it, pleading with him. I played tug-of-war with Bill for the guitar. I couldn't keep my hands off it -- I must have played "The Eagle and the Hawk" about a hundred and fifty times.

Investigating

What am I evaluating? 12-string guitar. Do I have to explain it any further than that? If I'm writing for people like me who want to buy one but haven't started looking, then I don't have to explain what a 12-string is. What is it like or unlike? It's unlike a 6-string. It's like a band. The additional strings add a upper range of sound -- and volume. The important consequences are that it may cost $900, and I might go out of my mind if I don't buy the Guild.

Yesterday. Bill, my friend, has given me advice, as has my old music instructor who always liked the Guild. The salespeople have opinions, but I always get the feeling they're secretly trying to sell me a particular

brand. Maybe they were doing bait-and-switch, telling me I could get a good guitar for $350, and then leading me over to the Guild which played like a dream, and then casually saying -- "Oh, this may be a <u>little</u> out of your price range (it was $900!) -- but you <u>might</u> like it." She knew that once I played it, I would never be satisfied with the Sigma Martin.

Using the library / field data. most of my investigation has been in the field. I like to trust my own hands and ear when it comes to judging playing ease or tone quality.

First Draft

I have been playing the six-string guitar for ten years. Playing the six string has brought me great pleasure, but recently, I was introduced to a new facet of guitar playing—the twelve-string. A few friends and I decided to take advantage of a beautiful sunny day a couple of months ago, so we brought our guitars outside and had a jam session. My friend Bill suggested that we start off with "The Eagle and the Hawk." I agreed to play it, but I wasn't too crazy about it. After all, he always suggests "The Eagle and the Hawk," and it always sounds the same-awful. But this time was different. I could hear a deep, rich sound, like church bells ringing around my head. Bill had brought his twelve-string.

I talked him into letting me borrow it that afternoon and I played "The Eagle and the Hawk" about a hundred and fifty times. I decided to get a twelve-string guitar after playing tug of war with Bill for his guitar. Just what kind of twelve string should I get, though? Bill's was really nice, but he told me how expensive it was as we were playing tug of war. In order to make a good decision, I decided to shop at guitar stores and ask friends with twelve string guitars. I decided to base my judgments on the Martin, Sigma Martin, Guild, Aria and Alvarez, using the following criteria: cost, playability, tone quality, and service (guarantee).

I was shocked by the cost. Mountain Music store carried an average Martin for eight hundred dollars and a Guild for about nine hundred dollars. They had an Aria for four-hundred and fifty dollars. I was especially attracted, though, to the cost of their Sigma Martin twelve-string for three hundred and fifty dollars. Appleway had an Alvarez for about five hundred dollars. Financing was available.

For playing ease, I tried the Aria and found it adequate. The strings were spaced somewhat widely apart and the neck was somewhat wide. The Sigma Martin was about the same, and the action (height of the strings) was a bit higher. Bill's Alvarez had a medium width neck, somewhat thinner than the Sigma Martin. I played another friend's Martin and found it easier than the Sigma Martin, Aria, and Alvarez. At another store, Prosound, I tried a Guild. I remembered my guitar instructor telling me once, "Guild is about the easiest twelve-string to play. You can't beat it for comfort." As I played a Guild that the saleswoman handed me, I could not argue with what my instructor had told me. The Guild was by far the easiest to play. In fact, the Guild almost played itself. I felt that all I was doing was tickling it!

Overall, I was impressed the most with Guild and Martin. The Martin excelled in tone quality and the Guild was the easiest to play. They both offer good service and guarantee. Dollar for dollar, I feel that Guild and Martin are the best investments. However, dollar for dollar, the Sigma Martin looks attractive. I guess I will just keep saving my money and continue window shopping.

Revised Version

TWELVE STRINGS

I have been playing the six-string guitar for ten years. Playing the six-string has brought me great pleasure, but recently I was introduced to a new facet of guitar playing—the twelve-string. A few friends and I decided to take advantage of a beautiful sunny day a couple of months ago by bringing our guitars outside and having a jam session. Bill, a friend of mine, suggested that we start off with "The Eagle and the Hawk," so I agreed to play the tune, but I wasn't too crazy about it. After all, he always suggests "The Eagle and the Hawk," and it always sounds the same—awful. But this time was different. As he started to play, I heard a deep, rich sound, like church bells, ringing around my head. Bill had brought his twelve-string guitar.   (1)

I convinced him to let me borrow it that afternoon. I must have played "The Eagle and the Hawk" about a hundred and fifty times. After playing tug of war with Bill for his guitar, I decided to get a twelve-string of my own. Just what kind of twelve-string should I get, though? Bill's was really nice, but while we were playing, he told me how expensive it was. In order to make a good decision, I decided to ask my friends and test several guitars at stores. Using four criteria—cost, playability, tone quality, and warranty—I narrowed my choices to five guitar brands: Martin, Sigma Martin, Guild, Aria, and Alvarez.   (2)

First of all, I was shocked by the cost. I went into Appleway Music and asked the salesman for a really good twelve-string under two hundred dollars. He told me to go down the street a few blocks and into a store called K-Mart. The salesman said that good, new twelve-string guitars can't be found for under three hundred dollars. I was now tempted to go to K-Mart, but I have never cared much for plastic guitars with Elvis painted all over them. So I decided to make a trek to a number of guitar stores and price comparable models of different brands.   (3)

Mountain Music store carried an average Martin for eight hundred dollars and a Guild for about nine hundred dollars. They had an Aria for four hundred and fifty dollars. I was especially attracted, though, to the cost of their Sigma Martin twelve-string for three hundred and fifty dollars. Appleway had an Alvarez for about five hundred. To help ease the shock, both stores accepted trade-ins and had financing.   (4)

After swallowing the prices of the different brands, I was afraid to touch them to determine their playability. However, the salesman at Mountain Music assured me that it was all right. I tried the Aria and found it adequate. The strings were spaced widely apart and the neck was also uncomfortably wide. The Sigma Martin was about the same, and the action (determined primarily by the height of the strings) was a bit higher. Bill's Alvarez, which I had already played, had a medium-width neck, somewhat thinner than the Sigma Martin and the Aria. The strings were spaced nicely apart and were relatively easy to press down. The next guitar I tested, a Martin which belonged to a friend, was a little bit easier to play than the Sigma Martin, Aria, and Alvarez. It was, though, harder to slide up and down the fret board. In order to compare these guitars with the Guild, I went to a third store, Prosound. As I walked into the store and asked to play their Guild, I remembered my guitar instructor telling me once, "The Guild is the easiest twelve-string to play. You can't beat it for comfort." As I played a Guild that the saleswoman handed me, I could not argue with what my instructor had told me. The Guild was by far the easiest twelve-string to play. In fact, the Guild almost played itself. I felt that all I was doing was tickling it!   (5)

And the Guild poured forth beautiful music. The tone quality was deep and rich, and it sustained its sound for a long time. In fact, my instructor said that both Guild and Martin are superior in their tone quality and in their ability to sustain their sound and stay in tune. A friend who is a guitarist and a music major claims that Martins get better with their age. She says that apparently the wood mellows out and adjusts to a fuller sound. I did wonder, though, as I petted her dog Martin, if this was actual fact or just an owner's bias. Since I own a Martin six-string, however, I was already impressed with the sound quality and their ability to stay in tune. As far as Sigma Martin goes, I talked with a friend and owner of Guzzardo Music (in my home town of Rockford, Illinois) who said that the Sigma Martin tone quality is good, but it does not match the fullness of the Guild or the Martin. He told me about an excellent way to test for a guitar's richness of sound. Thumping the face board with your finger should produce a reverberation or echo inside the guitar. With the best guitars, you can do this even near the edge of the face board—and all around the edges—without losing the mellow sound. I found this to be true with the Guild and Martin. The Sigma Martin and Aria, however, muffled my thumps at about three-quarters of the way back from the bridge, showing less sound capability. The Alvarez was slightly better than the Sigma Martin and the Aria, both in sound quality and ability to hold a tune. (Bill says that he can play "The Eagle and the Hawk" six times in a row without having to adjust the pegs!) Overall, the Alvarez had significantly better sound than the Sigma Martin and the Aria, but there was an even greater difference between the Alvarez and the two best guitars, the Guild and the Martin.   (6)

The warranties of the five guitars seemed to parallel the tone quality rankings of the five guitars. Martin and Guild stand by their materials and workmanship one hundred percent. They have the longest warranties and provide quick, convenient service. Sigma Martin, which manufactures its guitars in Japan, takes more time for repairs—often over a month. Alvarez and Aria stand by their workmanship and offer quality service. However, their warranties were not as good as that offered on either the Guild or the Martin. Overall, I found that the strength of the guarantees parallel the quality of workmanship and materials—and, of course, the price.   (7)

I was impressed by the quality of all the guitars as I looked at cost, ease of playing, tone quality, and warranties. The highest ranking had to go to the Guild and Martin—the Guild excelled slightly in playability, but the Martin had the best tone quality. They both offer good service and a strong warranty. Dollar for dollar, the Guild and the Martin are the best investments. However, dollar for dollar, I can afford only a Guild or Martin kazoo! So the Sigma Martin looks attractive. I guess I will just keep saving my money and continue window shopping. In the mean time, I'll keep requesting "The Eagle and the Hawk" by Bill and his twelve-string.   (8)

Questions for Writing and Discussion

1. Flickinger tries to take his reader through his search for the best guitar "in an entertaining way." Where is he most successful at keeping your attention by using a sense of humor? Where is his evaluation least entertaining? Explain.

2. Flickinger decided early in his writing process that he didn't need to explain what a twelve-string guitar is. Do you agree with his decision?

3. In what paragraph is the evidence in support of a criterion most effective? Least effective? Explain.

4. Underline the essay map and circle two examples of paragraph hooks or transitions between body paragraphs that tie paragraphs together. Find one paragraph hook that could be smoother and rewrite it.

"THE BIG CHILL"

Kent Y'Blood

In his review of The Big Chill, *Kent Y'Blood writes a compact evaluation of the film for a campus newspaper audience. Film review writers often need to walk a tightrope: They should give*

*the basic information about key characters and plot—without
revealing too much about the story; they should analyze and evaluate the film—without so much analysis that the reader is bored.
As you read the essay, decide how successful Y'Blood is at both
informing yet entertaining the reader.*

"The Big Chill" is an actor's film in the very best sense. It's no easy
task to create eight major characters we can care about immediately
without resorting to some form of cinematic stereotyping, but director
Lawrence Kasdan does it. We meet eight individuals whose stories of
fading youthful optimism are familiar in many ways. These characters
are not mere representatives of those stories but living, breathing people in a psychological comedy.   (1)

And what a dark comedy it is. Death pervades every scene, and
not just the death of The Movement, or the death of Revolutionary
Ideals, or the death of The Spirit of a Generation. Those generalizations have little place here. "The Big Chill" is about a real, particular
death: that of Alex Marshall, permanent dropout, college friend of
Sam, Sarah, Michael, Nick, Harold, Meg and Karen. He committed
suicide in Harold's and Sarah's house where he was staying with his
young girlfriend Chloe. The old friends, who haven't seen much of
each other in years, regroup for his funeral and all decide to spend a
weekend at Harold's and Sarah's house in Georgia to try to sort out
their confusion over Alex's act.   (2)

At the beginning of the film, Kasdan packs plenty of character
information into a relatively short space so that we get to know the
people well. As they make their various ways to the funeral, spread
out across the country as they are, we begin to learn about them. Sam
(Tom Berenger) lines up four miniature vodka bottles on his airplane
tray and charms the stewardess out of just one more. Nick (William
Hurt) empties out a collection of pills on the seat of his Porsche,
downs a couple, and the car roars out ahead of the camera. We get
glimpses of the other characters intercut with shots of a man dressing
in a pinstripe suit and white shirt, all to the tune of Marvin Gaye's "I
Heard It Through the Grapevine." Kasdan ends this scene with a
shocker. As a sewn-up wrist is slipped beneath a white cuff, we realize it was Alex's corpse we saw being dressed. This combination of
expository information with emotionally powerful action is superb
movie making, and Kasdan does not let down after the promise of this
opening sequence.   (3)

At the funeral itself, we learn more about the principals. Michael
(Jeff Goldblum) obviously wants more than comfort from Chloe (Meg
Tilly). Harold (Kevin Kline) intones a eulogy and breaks down as
he remembers "there was something about Alex that was too good

for this world." His wife Sarah (Glen Close) weeps but holds together admirably. Throughout the film, all the characters are true to our first impressions of them, but are not mechanically programmed to act predictably. They can still surprise us, and they all do. Later, when the characters get assigned their bedrooms, we get a glimpse of their luggage. Knowing who brings the economy-size bottle of Maalox, who the TV script and a volume of Kafka, and who has many pairs of designer men's underwear just adds that much more to our sense of who each of these people is. It is a weekend of talk, but the talk is supplemented by what we've observed about these people, so the dialogue doesn't have to carry all the weight in the film.   (4)

When they do talk, the chat is brilliant. Their sentiment is constantly undercut by jokes that don't weaken their emotions, just complicate them. When Beth rises to play Alex's favorite song on the organ at the funeral (Rolling Stones' "You Can't Always Get What You Want"), it is simultaneously funny and heartbreaking. The friends collectively try to work out how they failed Alex, how they failed their younger selves by becoming successful and rich, and how the people they were became the people they are.   (5)

"The Big Chill" is beautifully edited, masterfully acted, and has a script that has more depth than anything I've seen in a long time. The film directly confronts such tough themes as the endurance of friendship, the question of suicide, isolation, meaninglessness—and all to the '60s music of the Temptations, Smokey Robinson, and the Rascals. That's what I call a good movie.   (6)

QUESTIONS FOR WRITING AND DISCUSSION

1. Profile yourself as a typical reader for this review: Give your age, note whether you frequently go to movies, describe the kinds of films you enjoy, describe your attitude toward music or events from the sixties, and indicate whether or not you have seen *The Big Chill*. With these notes, come to class prepared to discuss whether or not Y'Blood's review succeeded. Did it make you want to see the movie? If you've seen the film already, was his evaluation convincing? Was it entertaining?

2. Y'Blood's writing process materials are not reproduced here, but how do you imagine that he collected all the information and supporting evidence for his review? Describe a plausible sequence for his collecting activities.

3. In his review, Y'Blood emphasized Lawrence Kasdan's skills in directing this film. If he had chosen to focus on one particular

actor's performance (for example, William Hurt's performance as Nick) or on the relationship of the songs to the story, however, how would that have changed the review? For practice, rewrite the opening paragraph of this review, focusing either on one principal actor or on the sixties songs.

8 | PROBLEM SOLVING

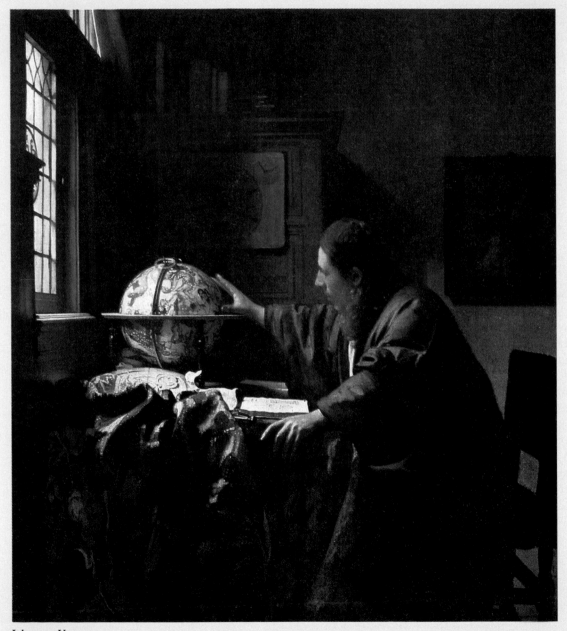

Johannes Vermeer
The Astronomer
Musee du Louvre, c. 1991 Reunion des Musees Nationaux, Paris

Trying to take notes in your Psych I lecture class—along with 250 other students—you realize you are completely lost and confused. So you raise your hand to ask a question, but the professor keeps on talking, throwing out more new terms and examples. You look at your neighbor, who just shrugs and keeps on writing. After class, when you think about how hard you've worked to pay your tuition, you realize you deserve better classes for your money. The problem, you decide, is in the large lecture format—there are just too many students for the teacher to answer questions and explain difficult concepts. So you decide to write a letter to the head of the psychology department (with a copy for the dean of arts and sciences) outlining the problems with this class and proposing that Psychology I be taught in classes no larger than fifty. Where the administrators get additional teachers, you decide, is their responsibility. You argue that, as administrators, it is their duty to give quality education the highest priority. □

Last year, when you took a new job, you decided to choose an independent health insurance company instead of enrolling in your employer's group plan. But after investigating coverages, rates, and discounts with several companies, you discover that premiums are sky high—primarily because of the expenses of a few policyholders. You decide that it is unfair that people who have good health records—who eat well, get regular exercise, drive prudently, and don't drink or smoke—should pay the health costs of those who don't take care of themselves. None of the companies you call, however, will give you more than a small nonsmoker discount. You decide to write a letter to the president of one of the insurance companies proposing that rates be based directly and equitably on health profiles and lifestyles. Since it is in the company's self-interest to have fewer medical claims, they should offer significantly lower rates to those who do take care of themselves. □

This country has more problems than it should tolerate and more solutions than it uses.

—Ralph Nader, consumer rights advocate

Whenever life doesn't seem to give an answer, we create one.

—Lorraine Hansberry, author of A Raisin in the Sun

W e don't have to look diligently for problems in our lives. They have a habit of seeking us out. It seems that if something can go wrong, it will. Countries are fighting each other, the environment is polluted, unemployment is too high, prejudice is still rampant, television shows are too violent, sports are corrupted by drugs and money, education is too impersonal, and people drive so recklessly that you take your life in your hands every time you drive across town. Everywhere we look, someone else creates problems for us—from minor bureaucratic hassles to serious or life-threatening situations. (On rare occasions, we're part of the problem ourselves.)

If you write in order *to propose a solution* to some problem, you have no lack of subjects. First, however, you may well ask whether your problem is one that can be solved. As journalist Charles Dudley Warner once observed, "Everybody talks about the weather, but nobody does anything about it." For the short term, the weather is not a problem that has a solution. We can predict the weather (sometimes), experiment with cloud seeding, or prepare for the effects of hurricanes or blizzards, but wisdom dictates that we accept the weather that comes. For the long term, however, we know that ozone depletion and greenhouse warming are serious weather-related problems that need worldwide planning and cooperation.

If the problem can be solved, the difficult part is to propose a solution and then persuade others that your solution will, in fact, solve the problem—without creating new problems and without costing too much. Since your proposal may ask readers to take some action, vote in a certain way, or actually work for your proposal, make sure that your readers vividly perceive the problem and agree that your plan outlines the most logical and feasible solution.

FREEWRITING: PROBLEM SOLVING

Wishful-thinking Department: Assume that as a member of the student government, your organization has been given $10,000 to spend on a campus improvement project. Think of some campus problem that needs solving. Describe why it is a problem. Then outline your plan for a solution, indicating how you would spend the money to help solve the problem.

TECHNIQUES FOR PROBLEM SOLVING

Problem solving requires all your skills as a writer. You need to observe carefully to see if a problem exists. You may need to remember experiences that illustrate the seriousness of the problem. You need to investigate which solutions have worked or have not worked. You often have to explain what the problem is, and why or how your proposal would remedy the situation. You may need to evaluate both the problem and the alternative solutions. To help you identify the problem and convince your readers of the soundness of your proposal, keep the following techniques in mind:

You see things; and you say, "Why?" But I dream things that never were; and I say, "Why not?"

—*George Bernard Shaw, dramatist*

- **Identifying and understanding your** *audience.* If you want something done, fixed, changed, improved, subsidized, banned, reorganized, made legal or illegal, make sure that you are writing to the appropriate audience.

- **Demonstrating that a** *problem exists.* Some problems are so obvious that your readers will readily acknowledge them: nuclear weapons, war in the Middle East, acid rain in industrialized nations, and drug and alcohol abuse. Often, however, you must first convince your audience that a problem exists: Are food preservatives really a serious problem, or would eliminating them cause even more problems?

- **Proposing a** *solution* **that will solve the problem.** After convincing your readers that a serious problem exists, you must then propose a remedy, plan, or course of action that will eliminate or reduce the problem.

- **Convincing your readers that your proposal will work, that it is** *feasible,* **or that it is better than the** *alternative solutions.* You convince your readers by supporting your proposal with *reasons* and *evidence.*

Demonstrating That a Problem Exists

Proposals begin with a description of the problem. Demonstrating that the problem exists and is serious will make your readers more receptive to your plan for a solution. The following selection from Frank Trippett's *Time* magazine essay "A Red Light for Scofflaws" identifies a problem and provides sufficient examples to demonstrate that scofflawry is pervasive and serious enough to warrant attention. Even if we haven't been personally attacked while driving the Houston or Miami or Los Angeles freeways, Trippett convinces us that scofflawry—deliberately disobeying (scoffing at) laws—is serious. His vivid description makes us aware of the problem.

Demonstrating That a
Problem Exists

Law and order is the longest-running and probably the bestloved political issue in U.S. history. Yet it is painfully apparent that millions of
Americans who would never think of themselves as lawbreakers, let
alone criminals, are taking increasing liberties with the legal codes that
are designed to protect and nourish their society. Indeed, there are
moments today—amid outlaw litter, tax cheating, illicit noise, and
motorized anarchy—when it seems as though the scofflaw represents
the wave of the future. Harvard sociologist David Riesman suspects
that a majority of Americans have blithely taken to committing supposedly minor derelictions as a matter of course. Already, Riesman says,
the ethic of U.S. society is in danger of becoming this: "You're a fool if
you obey the rules."

Evidence: Authority

Evidence: Examples

The dangers of scofflawry vary wildly. The person who illegally spits
on the sidewalk remains disgusting, but clearly poses less risk to others
than the company that illegally buries hazardous chemical waste in an
unauthorized location. The fare beater on the subway presents less
threat to life than the landlord who ignores fire safety statutes. The most
immediately and measurably dangerous scofflawry, however, also happens to be the most visible. The culprit is the American driver, whose
lawless activities today add up to a colossal public nuisance. The hazards range from routine double parking that jams city streets to the
drunk driving that kills some 25,000 people and injures at least 650,000
others yearly.

Evidence: Statistics

The most flagrant scofflaw of them all is the red-light runner. The flout-
ing of stop signals has got so bad in Boston that residents tell an anec-
dote about a cabby who insists that red lights are "just for decoration."
The power of the stoplight to control traffic seems to be waning everywhere. In Los Angeles, red-light running has become perhaps the city's
most common traffic violation. In New York City, going through an
intersection is like Russian roulette. Admits Police Commissioner
Robert J. McGuire: "Today it's a 50-50 toss-up as to whether people will
stop for a red light." Meanwhile, his own police largely ignore the law-
breaking.

Evidence: Authority

The prospect of the collapse of public manners is not merely a matter of
etiquette. Society's first concern will remain major crime, but a foretaste
of the seriousness of incivility is suggested by what has been happening
in Houston. Drivers on Houston freeways have been showing an
increasing tendency to replace the rules of the road with violent outbreaks. Items from the Houston police department's new statistical category—freeway traffic violence: (1) Driver flashes high-beam lights at car
that cut in front of him, whose occupants then hurl a beer can at his
windshield, kick out his tail lights, slug him eight stitches worth. (2)
Dump-truck driver annoyed by delay batters trunk of stalled car ahead
and its driver with steel bolt. (3) Hurrying driver of 18-wheel truck
deliberately rear-ends car whose driver was trying to stay within
55 m.p.h. limit.

Evidence: Examples

Proposing a Solution
and Convincing Your Readers

Once you have vividly described the problem, you are ready to propose a solution and convince your readers. In "Making the Case for Full Employment," an article that appeared in *The Christian Century*, Marjorie Hope and James Young propose a solution to a problem that everyone recognizes: high unemployment. In the following excerpt from their proposal, the authors move quickly from the problem to their specific proposals—and the supporting evidence. Notice that the audience requires the authors to focus on how churches and church organizers can become part of the solution.

Following the U.S. Catholic bishops' call for full employment in their pastoral letter, "Economic Justice for All," they were often criticized as utopian. However, more recently there has been a flurry of interest in full employment on the part of economists, church leaders, sociologists, community organizers and others who see it as an achievable goal.

Proposal

Clergy, union organizers and ordinary citizens have witnessed the suffering and disorientation caused by changes in the world of work: the decline of unions, the migration of American industry to countries where labor costs are cheaper, the replacement of workers by technology, the influx of undocumented foreign workers willing to take jobs that pay below minimum wage, persistently high unemployment among blacks and Hispanics, and the growing numbers of women who labor for low pay. Around the world the gap between rich and poor is widening. Unemployment has reached crisis proportions in many countries that enjoyed prosperity and low unemployment in the '60s and early '70s. The need for concerted action is urgent.

Demonstrating That a Problem Exists

Evidence: List of Examples

Current advocates of full employment are calling not only for jobs for those people able to work but for jobs with decent pay and working conditions, for equal access to jobs and training opportunities, for improved education for the employed and the underemployed, and for jobs that respect the environment.

Proposal

Some of the specific proposals being advanced include the following:

- *Raising the minimum wage.* Michael Harrington suggests that the minimum wage be set somewhere around $5.00 an hour, and that the government guarantee a useful job to everyone who wants to work.

Proposal Specifics

- *Shortening the work week.* Frank Riessman, co-editor of the journal *Social Policy*, points out that in 1938, "revolutionary" legislation cut the work week to 40 hours. A new revolution is long overdue. A four-day work week would spread jobs around, give people time to learn skills needed to keep up with rapidly changing tech-

Advantages of Proposal

nology, and lessen tensions experienced by working parents who want to spend more time with their children.

Reason + Evidence

- *Special efforts to reach minorities.* Economist John Jeffries points out that although all workers are threatened by the labor crisis, reform efforts should emphasize narrowing the most glaring income gaps—those between males and females and between whites and people of color. The unemployment rate for blacks is well over twice that for whites; the rate for black youth generally exceeds 40 per cent.

Reason + Evidence

- *Government support for a radical extension of quality daycare and related family support services, with fees based on ability to pay.* Such action is necessary for improving the status of women, whose mean earnings when they work full-time come to only 63 percent of full-time earnings for men. Providing daycare, preschool and other social services would both lessen the psychological and economic burden of parents, and would create more jobs.

Feasibility: How to Make Proposal Work

- *A balance between public- and private-sector involvement.* In the past, say Frank Reissman and Sheila Collins, full employment initiatives have relied too heavily on direct job programs, inviting the criticism that they were just "make work" affairs and were pervaded by political favoritism. We could instead, like some European countries, subsidize hiring efforts by voluntary associations and private forms. Other approaches would include job vouchers for the unemployed and tax subsidies for corporations that create jobs in areas of high unemployment.

Advantages of Proposal

Evidence

Who would benefit from a coordinated full employment policy? Virtually all Americans. More jobs mean more tax dollars collected and fewer funds paid out in unemployment insurance and welfare. Studies show that an increase of 1 million jobs would reduce the federal deficit by $40 billion. Thus a national health plan and daycare program could be paid for with the revenue created by full employment.

Forging the political will to achieve full employment is an enormous task. Church groups that recognize full employment as a cornerstone of a just social order have limited resources. Hence mainline Protestant denominations have generally chosen to play the catalytic role of supporting local and regional coalitions of religious, labor and community groups. Through these alliances, and directly from the pulpit, they have attempted to educate their constituencies about the human damage wrought by joblessness and about the possibilities for a new policy, and they have provided financial support for community organizing.

Call to Action

The question confronting all of us is: do we have the political will to make full employment a reality?

WARMING UP: JOURNAL EXERCISES

The following exercises will help you practice problem solving. Read all of the following exercises and then write on the three that interest you most. If another idea occurs to you, write a free entry about it.

1. As a student assistant for a campus residence hall, you have just listened to the twenty-third student this week complain about noise in the hall. You decide to create a policy that will solve the problem, but before you can implement it, you must present your idea at a student resident-assistant meeting. Write out the proposal you will present to the other student assistants at that meeting.

2. Reread Frank Trippett's analysis of the scofflaw problem. Write a letter to the city council recommending a solution to *one* of the problems Trippett identifies—a solution that the city council has the power to implement.

3. Eldridge Cleaver once said, "You're either part of the solution or part of the problem." Examine one of your activities or pastimes—sports, shopping, cruising, eating, drinking, or even studying. How does what you do possibly create a problem, from someone else's point of view? Explain.

4. After being away from your high school for a while, you can see more clearly its specific problems. Brainstorm or freewrite about the most important problems students faced in your high school. Write a letter to the school principal, explaining one specific problem that could and should be solved. Then propose your solution.

5. "Let the buyer beware" is a time-honored maxim for all consumers. Unless you are vigilant, you can easily be ripped off. Write a letter to the Better Business Bureau explaining some consumer problem or rip-off you've recently experienced and suggest a solution that will prevent others from being exploited.

6. Changing the rules of some sports might make them more enjoyable, less violent, or fairer: introducing the 30-second clock in NCAA basketball, using TV instant replays in professional and college football and basketball, imposing stiffer fines for brawls in hockey games, requiring boxers to wear padded helmets, giving equal pay and media coverage for

God, give us grace to accept with serenity the things that cannot be changed, courage to change the things which should be changed, and the wisdom to distinguish the one from the other.

—Reinhold Niebuhr, author and theologian

women's sports. Choose a sport you enjoy as a participant or observer, identify and explain the problem you want to solve, and justify your solution in a letter to the editors of *Sports Illustrated*.

7. "I dream things that never were; and I say, 'Why not?'" Use this quotation from George Bernard Shaw as inspiration for a proposal which, as Shaw suggests, describes a utopian vision of *one small part* of your life.

8. Remember the last family quarrel or argument you had. What was the source of the problem? Just for yourself, write some notes on what could be done to improve the situation. Does the problem lie in "human nature," which probably can't be changed, or could the problem be easily solved by slight behavioral changes by family members? Explain.

PROBLEM SOLVING: PROFESSIONAL WRITING

SEX, LIES AND ADVERTISING

Gloria Steinem

Does America have complete freedom of the press? Do advertisers control the editorial policies of magazines? Most readers assume that magazines are free to print any article of interest to its readers. As Gloria Steinem's essay illustrates, however, advertisers can and do influence editorial policy by refusing to run their ads without accompanying articles supporting their industry and their products. Steinem cites examples of specific companies—Philip Morris, Clairol, Lionel, Pillsbury, American Express, Estée Lauder—who refused to advertise in Ms. *magazine without editorial changes in the magazine. Although* Ms. *eventually sidestepped the problem by going to an ad-free format, Steinem proposes changes that will pressure advertisers, readers, and magazine editors to reduce advertisers' control over the content of articles. A longtime editor of* Ms. *magazine, Gloria Steinem has written numerous articles on feminist issues and has published several books, including* Outrageous Acts and Everyday Rebellions *(1983),* Marilyn: Norma Jean *(1986), and* Bedside Book of Self-Esteem *(1989).*

About three years ago, as *glasnost* was beginning and *Ms.* seemed to be ending, I was invited to a press lunch for a Soviet official. He entertained us with anecdotes about new problems of democracy in his country. Local Communist leaders were being criticized in their media for the first time, he explained, and they were angry.   (1)

"So I'll have to ask my American friends," he finished pointedly, "how more *subtly* to control the press." In the silence that followed, I said, "Advertising."   (2)

The reporters laughed, but later, one of them took me aside: How *dare* I suggest that freedom of the press was limited? How dare I imply that his newsweekly could be influenced by ads?   (3)

I explained that I was thinking of advertising's media-wide influence on most of what we read. Even newsmagazines use "soft" cover stories to sell ads, confuse readers with "advertorials," and occasionally self-censor on subjects known to be a problem with big advertisers.   (4)

But, I also explained, I was thinking especially of women's magazines. There, it isn't just a little content that's devoted to attracting ads, it's almost all of it. That's why advertisers—not readers—have always been the problem for *Ms.* As the only women's magazine that didn't supply what the ad world euphemistically describes as "supportive editorial atmosphere" or "complementary copy" (for instance, articles that praise food/fashion/beauty subjects to "support" and "complement" food/fashion/beauty ads), *Ms.* could never attract enough advertising to break even.   (5)

"Oh, *women's* magazines," the journalist said with contempt. "Everybody knows they're catalogs—but who cares? They have nothing to do with journalism."   (6)

I can't tell you how many times I've had this argument in 25 years of working for many kinds of publications. Except as money-making machines—"cash cows" as they are so elegantly called in the trade—women's magazines are rarely taken seriously. Though changes being made by women have been called more far-reaching than the industrial revolution—and though many editors try hard to reflect some of them in the few pages left to them after all the ad-related subjects have been covered—the magazines serving the female half of this country are still far below the journalistic and ethical standards of news and general interest publications. Most depressing of all, this doesn't even rate an exposé.   (7)

If *Time* and *Newsweek* had to lavish praise on cars in general and credit General Motors in particular to get GM ads, there would be a scandal—maybe a criminal investigation. When women's magazines from *Seventeen* to *Lear's* praise beauty products in general and credit Revlon in particular to get ads, it's just business as usual.   (8)

When *Ms.* began, we didn't consider *not* taking ads. The most important reason was keeping the price of a feminist magazine low enough for most women to afford. But the second and almost equal reason was providing a forum where women and advertisers could talk to each other and improve advertising itself. After all, it was (and still is) as potent a source of information in this country as news or TV and movie dramas.   (9)

We decided to proceed in two stages. First, we would convince makers of "people products" used by both men and women but advertised mostly to men—cars, credit cards, insurance, sound equipment, financial services, and the like—that their ads should be placed in a women's magazine. Since they were accustomed to the division between editorial and advertising in news and general interest magazines, this would allow our editorial content to be free and diverse. Second, we would add the best ads for whatever traditional "women's products" (clothes, shampoo, fragrance, food, and so on) that surveys showed *Ms.* readers used. But we would ask them to come in *without* the usual quid pro quo of "complementary copy."   (10)

We knew the second step might be harder. Food advertisers have always demanded that women's magazines publish recipes and articles on entertaining (preferably ones that name their products) in return for their ads; clothing advertisers expect to be surrounded by fashion spreads (especially ones that credit their designers); and shampoo, fragrance, and beauty products in general usually insist on positive editorial coverage of beauty subjects, plus photo credits besides. That's why women's magazines look the way they do. But if we could break this link between ads and editorial content, then we wanted good ads for "women's products," too.   (11)

By playing their part in this unprecedented mix of *all* the things our readers need and use, advertisers also would be rewarded: ads for products like cars and mutual funds would find a new growth market; the best ads for women's products would no longer be lost in oceans of ads for the same category; and both would have access to a laboratory of smart and caring readers whose response would help create effective ads for other media as well.   (12)

I thought then that our main problem would be the imagery in ads themselves. Carmakers were still draping blondes in evening gowns over the hoods like ornaments. Authority figures were almost always male, even in ads for products that only women used. Sadistic, he-man campaigns even won industry praise. (For instance, *Advertising Age* had hailed the infamous Silva Thin cigarette theme, "How to Get a Woman's Attention: Ignore Her," as "brilliant.") Even in medical journals, tranquilizer ads showed depressed housewives standing beside piles of dirty dishes and promised to get them back to work.   (13)

Obviously, *Ms.* would have to avoid such ads and seek out the best ones—but this didn't seem impossible. *The New Yorker* had been selecting ads for aesthetic reasons for years, a practice that only seemed to make advertisers more eager to be in its pages. *Ebony* and *Essence* were asking for ads with positive black images, and though their struggle was hard, they weren't being called unreasonable.   (14)

Clearly, what *Ms.* needed was a very special publisher and ad sales staff. I could think of only one woman with experience on the business side of magazines—Patricia Carbine, who recently had become a vice president of *McCall's* as well as its editor in chief—and the reason I knew her name was a good omen. She had been managing editor at *Look* (really *the* editor, but its owner refused to put a female name at the top of his masthead) when I was writing a column there. After I did an early interview with Cesar Chavez, then just emerging as a leader of migrant labor, and the publisher turned it down because he was worried about ads from Sunkist, Pat was the one who intervened. As I learned later, she had told the publisher she would resign if the interview wasn't published. Mainly because *Look* couldn't afford to lose Pat, it *was* published (and the ads from Sunkist never arrived).   (15)

Though I barely knew this woman, she had done two things I always remembered: put her job on the line in a way that editors often talk about but rarely do, and been so loyal to her colleagues that she never told me or anyone outside *Look* that she had done so.   (16)

Fortunately, Pat did agree to leave *McCall's* and take a huge cut in salary to become publisher of *Ms.* She became responsible for training and inspiring generations of young women who joined the *Ms.* ad sales force, many of whom went on to become "firsts" at the top of publishing. When *Ms.* first started, however, there were so few women with experience selling space that Pat and I made the rounds of ad agencies ourselves. Later, the fact that *Ms.* was asking companies to do business in a different way meant our saleswomen had to make many times the usual number of calls—first to convince agencies and then client companies besides—and to present endless amounts of research. I was often asked to do a final ad presentation, or see some higher decision-maker, or speak to women employees so executives could see the interest of women they worked with. That's why I spent more time persuading advertisers than editing or writing for *Ms.* and why I ended up with an unsentimental education in the seamy underside of publishing that few writers see (and even fewer magazines can publish).   (17)

Let me take you with us through some experiences, just as they happened:

■ Cheered on by early support from Volkswagen and one or two other car companies, we scrape together time and money to put on a major reception in Detroit. We know U.S. carmakers firmly believe that women choose the upholstery, not the car, but we are armed with statistics and reader mail to prove the contrary: a car is an important purchase for women, one that symbolizes mobility and freedom.   (18)

But almost nobody comes. We are left with many pounds of shrimp on the table, and quite a lot of egg on our face. We blame ourselves for not guessing that there would be a baseball pennant play-off on the same day, but executives go out of their way to explain they wouldn't have come anyway. Thus begins ten years of knocking on hostile doors, presenting endless documentation, and hiring a full-time saleswoman in Detroit; all necessary before *Ms.* gets any real results.   (19)

This long saga has a semihappy ending: foreign and, later, domestic carmakers eventually provided *Ms.* with enough advertising to make cars one of our top sources of ad revenue. Slowly, Detroit began to take the women's market seriously enough to put car ads in other women's magazines, too, thus freeing a few pages from the hothouse of fashion-beauty-food ads.   (20)

But long after figures showed a third, even a half, of many car models being bought by women, U.S. makers continued to be uncomfortable addressing women. Unlike foreign carmakers, Detroit never quite learned the secret of creating intelligent ads that exclude no one, and then placing them in women's magazines to overcome past exclusion. (*Ms.* readers were so grateful for a routine Honda ad featuring rack and pinion steering, for instance, that they sent fan mail.) Even now, Detroit continues to ask, "Should we make special ads for women?" Perhaps that's why some foreign cars still have a disproportionate share of the U.S. women's market.   (21)

▪ In the *Ms.* Gazette, we do a brief report on a congressional hearing into chemicals used in hair dyes that are absorbed through the skin and may be carcinogenic. Newspapers report this too, but Clairol, a Bristol-Myers subsidiary that makes dozens of products—a few of which have just begun to advertise in *Ms.*—is outraged. Not at newspapers or newsmagazines, just at us. It's bad enough that *Ms.* is the only women's magazine refusing to provide the usual "complementary" articles and beauty photos, but to criticize one of their categories—*that* is going too far.   (22)

We offer to publish a letter from Clairol telling its side of the story. In an excess of solicitousness, we even put this letter in the Gazette, not in Letters to the Editors where it belongs. Nonetheless— and in spite of surveys that show *Ms.* readers are active women who use more of almost everything Clairol makes than do the readers of any other women's magazine—*Ms.* gets almost none of these ads for the rest of its natural life.   (23)

Meanwhile, Clairol changes its hair coloring formula, apparently in response to the hearings we reported.   (24)

■ Our saleswomen set out early to attract ads for consumer electronics: sound equipment, calculators, computers, VCRs, and the like. We know that our readers are determined to be included in the technological revolution. We know from reader surveys that *Ms.* readers are buying this stuff in numbers as high as those of magazines like *Playboy;* or "men 18 to 34," the prime targets of the consumer electronics industry. Moreover, unlike traditional women's products that our readers buy but don't need to read articles about, these are subjects they want covered in our pages. There actually *is* a supportive editorial atmosphere.   (25)

"But women don't understand technology," say executives at the end of ad presentations. "Maybe not," we respond, "but neither do men—and we all buy it."   (26)

"If women *do* buy it," say the decision-makers, "they're asking their husbands and boyfriends what to buy first." We produce letters from *Ms.* readers saying how turned off they are when salesmen say things like "Let me know when your husband can come in."   (27)

After several years of this, we get a few ads for compact sound systems. Some of them come from JVC, whose vice president, Harry Elias, is trying to convince his Japanese bosses that there is something called a women's market. At his invitation, I find myself speaking at huge trade shows in Chicago and Las Vegas, trying to persuade JVC dealers that showrooms don't have to be locker rooms where women are made to feel unwelcome. But as it turns out, the shows themselves are part of the problem. In Las Vegas, the only women around the technology displays are seminude models serving champagne. In Chicago, the big attraction is Marilyn Chambers, who followed Linda Lovelace of *Deep Throat* fame as Chuck Traynor's captive and/or employee. VCRs are being demonstrated with her porn videos.   (28)

In the end, we get ads for a car stereo now and then, but no VCRs; some IBM personal computers, but no Apple or Japanese ones. We notice that office magazines like *Working Woman* and *Savvy* don't benefit as much as they should from office equipment ads either. In the electronics world, women and technology seem mutually exclusive. It remains a decade behind even Detroit.   (29)

■ Because we get letters from little girls who love toy trains, and who ask our help in changing ads and box-top photos that feature little boys only, we try to get toy-train ads from Lionel. It turns out that Lionel executives *have* been concerned about little girls. They made a pink train, and were surprised when it didn't sell.   (30)

Lionel bows to consumer pressure with a photograph of a boy *and* a girl—but only on some of their boxes. They fear that, if trains are associated with girls, they will be devalued in the minds of boys. Needless to say, *Ms.* gets no train ads, and little girls remain a mostly unexplored market. By 1986, Lionel is put up for sale.   (31)

But for different reasons, we haven't had much luck with other kinds of toys either. In spite of many articles on child-rearing; an annual listing of nonsexist, multi-racial toys by Letty Cottin Pogrebin; Stories for Free Children, a regular feature also edited by Letty; and other prizewinning features for or about children, we get virtually no toy ads. Generations of *Ms.* saleswomen explain to toy manufacturers that a larger proportion of *Ms.* readers have preschool children than do the readers of other women's magazines, but this industry can't believe feminists have or care about children.   (32)

▪ When *Ms.* begins, the staff decides not to accept ads for feminine hygiene sprays or cigarettes: they are damaging and carry no appropriate health warnings. Though we don't think we should tell our readers what to do, we do think we should provide facts so they can decide for themselves. Since the antismoking lobby has been pressing for health warnings on cigarette ads, we decide to take them only as they comply.   (33)

Philip Morris is among the first to do so. One of its brands, Virginia Slims, is also sponsoring women's tennis and the first national polls of women's opinions. On the other hand, the Virginia Slims theme, "You've come a long way, baby," has more than a "baby" problem. It makes smoking a symbol of progress for women.   (34)

We explain to Philip Morris that this slogan won't do well in our pages, but they are convinced its success with some women means it will work with *all* women. Finally, we agree to publish an ad for a Virginia Slims calendar as a test. The letters from readers are critical— and smart. For instance: Would you show a black man picking cotton, the same man in a Cardin suit, and symbolize the antislavery and civil rights movements by smoking? Of course not. But instead of honoring the test results, the Philip Morris people seem angry to be proven wrong. They take away ads for *all* their many brands.   (35)

This costs *Ms.* about $250,000 the first year. After five years, we can no longer keep track. Occasionally, a new set of executives listens to *Ms.* saleswomen, but because we won't take Virginia Slims, not one Philip Morris product returns to our pages for the next 16 years.   (36)

Gradually, we also realize our naiveté in thinking we *could* decide against taking cigarette ads. They became a disproportionate support of magazines the moment they were banned on television, and few magazines could compete and survive without them; certainly not *Ms.*, which lacks so many other categories. By the time statistics in the 1980s showed that women's rate of lung cancer was approaching men's, the necessity of taking cigarette ads has become a kind of prison.   (37)

▪ General Mills, Pillsbury, Carnation, DelMonte, Dole, Kraft, Stouffer, Hormel, Nabisco: you name the food giant, we try it. But no matter how desirable the *Ms.* readership, our lack of recipes is lethal.   (38)

We explain to them that placing food ads *only* next to recipes associates food with work. For many women, it is a negative that works *against* the ads. Why not place food ads in diverse media without recipes (thus reaching more men, who are now a third of the shoppers in supermarkets anyway), and leave the recipes to specialty magazines like *Gourmet* (a third of whose readers are also men)?   (39)

These arguments elicit interest, but except for an occasional ad for a convenience food, instant coffee, diet drinks, yogurt, or such extras as avocados and almonds, this mainstay of the publishing industry stays closed to us. Period.   (40)

■ Traditionally, wines and liquors didn't advertise to women: men were thought to make the brand decisions, even if women did the buying. But after endless presentations, we begin to make a dent in this category. Thanks to the unconventional Michael Roux of Carillon Importers (distributors of Grand Marnier, Absolut Vodka, and others), who assumes that food and drink have no gender, some ads are leaving their men's club.   (41)

Beermakers are still selling masculinity. It takes *Ms.* fully eight years to get its first beer ad (Michelob). In general, however, liquor ads are less stereotyped in their imagery—and far less controlling of the editorial content around them—than are women's products. But given the underrepresentation of other categories, these very facts tend to create a disproportionate number of alcohol ads in the pages of *Ms.* This in turn dismays readers worried about women and alcoholism.   (42)

■ We hear in 1980 that women in the Soviet Union have been producing feminist *samizdat* (underground, self-published books) and circulating them throughout the country. As punishment, four of the leaders have been exiled. Though we are operating on our usual shoestring, we solicit individual contributions to send Robin Morgan to interview these women in Vienna.   (43)

The result is an exclusive cover story that includes the first news of a populist peace movement against the Afghanistan occupation, a prediction of *glasnost* to come, and a grass-roots, intimate view of Soviet women's lives. From the popular press to women's studies courses, the response is great. The story wins a Front Page award.   (44)

Nonetheless, this journalistic coup undoes years of efforts to get an ad schedule from Revlon. Why? Because the Soviet women on our cover *are not wearing makeup.*   (45)

■ Four years of research and presentations go into convincing airlines that women now make travel choices and business trips. United, the first airline to advertise in *Ms.*, is so impressed with the response from our readers that one of its executives appears in a film for our ad presentations. As usual, good ads get great results.   (46)

But we have problems unrelated to such results. For instance: because American Airlines flight attendants include among their labor demands the stipulation that they could choose to have their last names preceded by "Ms." on their name tags—in a long-delayed revolt against the standard, "I am your pilot, Captain Rothgart, and this is your flight attendant, Cindy Sue"—American officials seem to hold the magazine responsible. We get no ads.   (47)

There is still a different problem at Eastern. A vice president cancels subscriptions for thousands of copies on Eastern flights. Why? Because he is offended by ads for lesbian poetry journals in the *Ms.* Classified. A "family airline," as he explains to me coldly on the phone, has to "draw the line somewhere."   (48)

It's obvious that *Ms.* can't exclude lesbians and serve women. We've been trying to make that point ever since our first issue included an article by and about lesbians, and both Suzanne Levine, our managing editor, and I were lectured by such heavy hitters as Ed Kosner, then editor of *Newsweek* (and now of *New York Magazine*), who insisted that *Ms.* should "position" itself *against* lesbians. But our advertisers have paid to reach a guaranteed number of readers, and soliciting new subscriptions to compensate for Eastern would cost $150,000, plus rebating money in the meantime.   (49)

Like almost everything ad-related, this presents an elaborate organizing problem. After days of searching for sympathetic members of the Eastern board, Frank Thomas, president of the Ford Foundation, kindly offers to call Roswell Gilpatrick, a director of Eastern. I talk with Mr. Gilpatrick, who calls Frank Borman, then the president of Eastern. Frank Borman calls me to say that his airline is not in the business of censoring magazines: *Ms.* will be returned to Eastern flights.   (50)

▪ Women's access to insurance and credit is vital, but with the exception of Equitable and a few other ad pioneers, such financial services address men. For almost a decade after the Equal Credit Opportunity Act passes in 1974, we try to convince American Express that women are a growth market—but nothing works.   (51)

Finally, a former professor of Russian named Jerry Welsh becomes head of marketing. He assumes that women should be cardholders, and persuades his colleagues to feature women in a campaign. Thanks to this 1980s series, the growth rate for female cardholders surpasses that for men.   (52)

For this article, I asked Jerry Welsh if he would explain why American Express waited so long. "Sure," he said, "they were afraid of having a 'pink' card."   (53)

▪ Women of color read *Ms.* in disproportionate numbers. This is a source of pride to *Ms.* staffers, who are also more racially representative than the editors of other women's magazines. But this reality is obscured by ads filled with enough white women to make a reader snowblind.   (54)

Pat Carbine remembers mostly "astonishment" when she requested African American, Hispanic, Asian, and other diverse images. Marcia Ann Gillespie, a *Ms.* editor who was previously the editor in chief of *Essence*, witnesses ad bias a second time: having tried for *Essence* to get white advertisers to use black images (Revlon did so eventually, but L'Oréal, Lauder, Chanel, and other companies never did), she sees similar problems getting integrated ads for an integrated magazine. Indeed, the ad world often creates black and Hispanic ads only for black and Hispanic media. In an exact parallel of the fear that marketing a product to women will endanger its appeal to men, the response is usually, "But your [white] readers won't identify." (55)

In fact, those we are able to get—for instance, a Max Factor ad made for *Essence* that Linda Wachner gives us after she becomes president—are praised by white readers, too. But there are pathetically few such images. (56)

▪ By the end of 1986, production and mailing costs have risen astronomically, ad income is flat, and competition for ads is stiffer than ever. The 60/40 preponderance of edit over ads that we promised to readers becomes 50/50; children's stories, most poetry, and some fiction are casualties of less space; in order to get variety into limited pages, the length (and sometimes the depth) of articles suffers; and, though we do refuse most of the ads that would look like a parody in our pages, we get so worn down that some slip through. (See this issue's No Comment.) Still, readers perform miracles. Though we haven't been able to afford a subscription mailing in two years, they maintain our guaranteed circulation of 450,000. (57)

Nonetheless, media reports on *Ms.* often insist that our unprofitability must be due to reader disinterest. The myth that advertisers simply follow readers is very strong. Not one reporter notes that other comparable magazines our size (say, *Vanity Fair* or *The Atlantic*) have been losing more money in one year than *Ms.* has lost in 16 years. No matter how much never-to-be-recovered cash is poured into starting a magazine or keeping one going, appearances seem to be all that matter. (Which is why we haven't been able to explain our fragile state in public. Nothing causes ad-flight like the smell of nonsuccess.) (58)

My healthy response is anger. My not-so-healthy response is constant worry. Also an obsession with finding one more rescue. There is hardly a night when I don't wake up with sweaty palms and pounding heart, scared that we won't be able to pay the printer or the post office; scared most of all that closing our doors will hurt the women's movement. (59)

Out of chutzpah and desperation, I arrange a lunch with Leonard Lauder, president of Estée Lauder. With the exception of Clinique (the brainchild of Carol Phillips), none of Lauder's hundreds of products has been advertised in *Ms.* A year's schedule of ads for just three or four of them could save us. Indeed, as the scion of a family-owned company whose ad practices are followed by the beauty industry, he is one of the few men who could liberate many pages in all women's magazines just by changing his mind about "complementary copy."   (60)

Over a lunch that costs more than we can pay for some articles, I explain the need for his leadership. I also lay out the record of *Ms.*: more literary and journalistic prizes won, more new issues introduced into the mainstream, new writers discovered, and impact on society than any other magazine; more articles that became books, stories that became movies, ideas that became television series, and newly advertised products that became profitable; and, most important for him, a place for his ads to reach women who aren't reachable through any other women's magazine. Indeed, if there is one constant characteristic of the ever-changing *Ms.* readership, it is their impact as leaders. Whether it's waiting until later to have first babies, or pioneering PABA as sun protection in cosmetics, *whatever* they are doing today, a third to a half of American women will be doing three to five years from now. It's never failed.   (61)

But, he says, *Ms.* readers are not *our* women. They're not interested in things like fragrance and blush-on. If they were, *Ms.* would write articles about them.   (62)

On the contrary, I explain, surveys show they are more likely to buy such things than the readers of, say, *Cosmopolitan* or *Vogue.* They're good customers because they're out in the world enough to need several sets of everything: home, work, purse, travel, gym, and so on. They just don't need to read articles about these things. Would he ask a men's magazine to publish monthly columns on how to shave before he advertised Aramis products (his line for men)?   (63)

He concedes that beauty features are often concocted more for advertisers than readers. But *Ms.* isn't appropriate for his ads anyway, he explains. Why? Because Estée Lauder is selling "a kept-woman mentality."   (64)

I can't quite believe this. Sixty percent of the users of his products are salaried, and generally resemble *Ms.* readers. Besides, his company has the appeal of having been started by a creative and hardworking woman, his mother, Estée Lauder.   (65)

That doesn't matter, he says. He knows his customers, and they would *like* to be kept women. That's why he will never advertise in *Ms.*   (66)

In November 1987, by vote of the Ms. Foundation for Education and Communication (*Ms.*'s owner and publisher, the media subsidiary of the Ms. Foundation for Women), *Ms.* was sold to a company whose officers, Australian feminists Sandra Yates and Anne Summers, raised the investment money in their country that *Ms.* couldn't find in its own. They also started *Sassy* for teenage women.   (67)

In their two-year tenure, circulation was raised to 550,000 by investment in circulation mailings, and, to the dismay of some readers, editorial features on clothes and new products made a more traditional bid for ads. Nonetheless, ad pages fell below previous levels. In addition, *Sassy*, whose fresh voice and sexual frankness were an unprecedented success with young readers, was targeted by two mothers from Indiana who began, as one of them put it, "calling every Christian organization I could think of." In response to this controversy, several crucial advertisers pulled out.   (68)

Such links between ads and editorial content was a problem in Australia, too, but to a lesser degree. "Our readers pay two times more for their magazines," Anne explained, "so advertisers have less power to threaten a magazine's viability."   (69)

"I was shocked," said Sandra Yates with characteristic directness. "In Australia, we think you have freedom of the press—but you don't."   (70)

Since Anne and Sandra had not met their budget's projections for ad revenue, their investors forced a sale. In October 1989, *Ms.* and *Sassy* were bought by Dale Lang, owner of *Working Mother, Working Woman,* and one of the few independent publishing companies left among the conglomerates. In response to a request from the original *Ms.* staff—as well as to reader letters urging that *Ms.* continue, plus his own belief that *Ms.* would benefit his other magazines by blazing a trail—he agreed to try the ad-free, reader-supported *Ms.* you hold now and to give us complete editorial control. . . .   (71)

What could women's magazines be like if they were as free as books? as realistic as newspapers? as creative as films? as diverse as women's lives? We don't know.   (72)

But we'll only find out if we take women's magazines seriously. If readers were to act in a concerted way to change traditional practices of *all* women's magazines and the marketing of *all* women's products, we could do it. After all, they are operating on our consumer dollars; money that we now control. You and I could:

■ write to editors and publishers (with copies to advertisers) that we're willing to pay *more* for magazines with editorial independence, but will *not* continue to pay for those that are just editorial extensions of ads;

■ write to advertisers (with copies to editors and publishers) that we want fiction, political reporting, consumer reporting—whatever is, or is not, supported by their ads;

■ put as much energy into breaking advertising's control over content as into changing the images in ads, or protesting ads for harmful products like cigarettes;

   ▪ support only those women's magazines and products that take *us* seriously as readers and consumers.   (73)

   Those of us in the magazine world can also use the carrot-and-stick technique. For instance: pointing out that, if magazines were a regulated medium like television, the demands of advertisers would be against FCC rules. Payola and extortion could be punished. As it is, there are probably illegalities. A magazine's postal rates are determined by the ratio of ad to edit pages, and the former costs more than the latter. So much for the stick.   (74)

   The carrot means appealing to enlightened self-interest. For instance: there are many studies showing that the greatest factor in determining an ad's effectiveness is the credibility of its surroundings. The "higher the rating of editorial believability," concluded a 1987 survey by the *Journal of Advertising Research,* "the higher the rating of the advertising." Thus, an impenetrable wall between edit and ads would also be in the best interest of advertisers.   (75)

   Unfortunately, few agencies or clients hear such arguments. Editors often maintain the false purity of refusing to talk to them at all. Instead, they see ad salespeople who know little about editorial, are trained in business as usual, and are usually paid by commission. Editors might also band together to take on controversy. That happened once when all the major women's magazines did articles in the same month on the Equal Rights Amendment. It could happen again.   (76)

   It's almost three years away from life between the grindstones of advertising pressures and readers' needs. I'm just beginning to realize how edges got smoothed down—in spite of all our resistance.   (77)

   I remember feeling put upon when I changed "Porsche" to "car" in a piece about Nazi imagery in German pornography by Andrea Dworkin—feeling sure Andrea would understand that Volkswagen, the distributor of Porsche and one of our few supportive advertisers, asked only to be far away from Nazi subjects. It's taken me all this time to realize that Andrea was the one with a right to feel put upon.   (78)

   Even as I write this, I get a call from a writer for *Elle,* who is doing a whole article on where women part their hair. Why, she wants to know, do I part mine in the middle?   (79)

   It's all so familiar. A writer trying to make something of a nothing assignment; an editor laboring to think of new ways to attract ads; readers assuming that other women must want this ridiculous stuff; more women suffering for lack of information, insight, creativity, and laughter that could be on these same pages.   (80)

   I ask you: Can't we do better than this?   (81)

VOCABULARY

In your journal, write the meanings of the following words.

- *euphemistically* describes (5)
- rate an *exposé* (7)
- the usual *quid pro quo* (10)
- this *unprecedented* mix (12)
- *disproportionate* share (21)
- may be *carcinogenic* (22)
- an excess of *solicitousness* (23)
- seem *mutually exclusive* (29)
- realize our *naiveté* (37)
- the *stipulation* (47)
- *preponderance* of edit over ads (57)
- as the *scion* (60)
- threaten a magazine's *viability* (69)

QUESTIONS FOR WRITING AND DISCUSSION

1. Explain your response to Steinem's article. What problem does she describe? Do you agree that the problem is serious? What solutions does she offer? Do you believe her solutions will help solve the problem?

2. In context, explain what Steinem means by the italicized words or phrases in the following sentences. "On the other hand, the Virginia Slims theme, 'You've come a long way, *baby*,' has more than a 'baby' problem" (paragraph 34). "By the time statistics in the 1980s showed that women's rate of lung cancer was approaching men's, the necessity of taking cigarette ads *has become a kind of prison*" (paragraph 37). "'Sure,' he said, 'they were afraid of having a *"pink"* card'" (paragraph 53). "The myth that *advertisers simply follow readers* is very strong" (paragraph 58).

3. Profile the intended audience for Steinem's article. To support your profile, find at least three specific examples, references, or sentences in the essay directed toward that audience.

4. Beginning with paragraph 18, Steinem cites specific examples from her own experience to illustrate the problem. How many such examples or scenarios does she give? Which of these examples are most effective? Why are they effective?

5. In a sidebar to her article, Steinem says that magazines often have "editorial pages devoted to 'complementary copy'; to text or photos that praise advertised categories, instruct in their use, or generally act as extensions of ads." Her own survey reports the following statistics: *Glamour*, April 1990, contains 339 pages total but only 65 nonad or ad-related pages. (The remaining 274 pages are ads or "complementary copy.") *Vogue*, May 1990, has 319 pages total with just 38 nonad or ad-related pages. *Family Circle*, March 13, 1990, has a total of 180 pages, of which only 33 are nonad or ad-related. Survey a popular magazine: What is the ratio of pages of ads to pages of copy not ad-related? What conclusions can you draw from your survey?

6. Assume that you represent one of the companies cited in the essay that chose not to advertise in *Ms.* magazine. Write a response to Steinem's essay, to appear in the Letters to the Editor in *Ms.* magazine. Answer Steinem's charges and defend your company's decision.

THE AGONY MUST END

Paul Zimmerman

In a proposal written for Sports Illustrated, *sportswriter Paul Zimmerman describes the problems of injuries in the National Football League and then proposes his solutions. In his article, Zimmerman documents the seriousness of the problem by referring to actual players injured, interviewing NFL players, and citing information and statistics provided by the NFL, the trainers, and the Players Association. Then he proposes several major changes, discusses the costs, and examines the feasibility of his changes. Read his essay and see if you agree with his proposals. Notice that although Zimmerman is writing for a general audience of readers interested in football, he clearly hopes that the people responsible for making a decision will also read his proposal.*

They are the assassins waiting behind the door in a dark room. They are pro football's unpredictable—yet only too predictable—curse. Injuries. As the fractures, concussions and bruises that play havoc with America's No. 1 sport struck down 183 NFL starters in the first half of the season, medical reports like these became commonplace:

> Two defensive backs, Anthony Young of Indianapolis and Tim Lewis of Green Bay, damaged nerves in their necks while making fairly routine tackles. They will never make any more. To do so would be to risk paralysis.

On Oct. 26 the San Francisco 49ers fielded only 37 healthy players out of a possible 45 for their game with Green Bay.

Dallas running back Tony Dorsett, after nine relatively injury-free years, missed three of his first eight games this season and hobbled through three more on an ailing knee.

Two Kansas City Chiefs, linebacker Ken McAlister and wide receiver Anthony Hancock, underwent surgery after their knees buckled on artificial turf without having been hit.   (1)

"Injuries," says Philip Rosenthal, the assistant director of New York's Nicholas Institute of Sports Medicine and Athletic Trauma, "are inherent to football. It's the nature of the beast."   (2)

O.K., but where does it stop? When do we make the breakthrough and start reducing injuries? The average playing career, 4.6 years in 1983, is now 3.6 years. Speed has increased through natural selection and lighter equipment. Size has shown a natural gain, too, but it also has an unnatural side because of the anabolic steroids that are such a major part of the weight-training programs favored by a number of players.   (3)

Artificial turf abounds, and it's still as hated by the players as it was 21 years ago when the Houston Astrodome opened. Where's the end of it? Today's 240-pounder is a pumped-up 280, thanks to the steroids. In five years maybe he'll be 300, moving even faster, inflicting greater damage. Can medical science keep up with that? Or will the incidence of injury be even higher? It's time that the NFL takes a long look at the problem and steps in, before football becomes Rollerball.   (4)

Questionable and conflicting data from the league, the Players Association and the trainers make it hard to determine exact percentages on injuries and whether they're up a great deal, up only slightly or staying more or less level. One thing that's certain is that they're not declining, and this in itself is frightening. Modern equipment is supposedly safer, and rule changes meant to protect players from injuries have been adopted. Then why, in a world in which modern medicine has discovered how to transplant organs, are pro football players still getting hurt at the same rate as they were in the old days?   (5)

The medical breakthroughs in football have been curative, not preventive. For example, arthroscopic surgery can mend a wounded knee and have a player who once would have been out for the season back on the field in three weeks. Arthroscopy can diagnose a minute fracture that used to be called water on the knee. Medical science and the equipment people are in a race against the changing physics of pro football, and they're not winning. They can't gain any ground on the steroid labs, which are turning out bigger, artificially built-up athletes, who move at higher speeds on faster tracks, thanks to synthetic turf.

The result is higher-speed collisions by larger people, a ferocity of hitting never before seen in football or any other sport. (6)

Injuries are publicized most heavily when quarterbacks are hurt. The quarterback thrashing is a constant. NFL figures show that after eight weeks of the '84 season there had been 41 different starting quarterbacks, 12 getting the call because of injury. Last year the midseason numbers were 40 and 11; this year they are 44 and 14. (7)

So the damage goes on, week after week, year after year. What should be done? Steroids are a good place to start. Everybody hates them, everybody knows the long-range damage they can cause, and lots of players in the NFL use them—and don't admit it. (8)

"That's about right," Los Angeles Raider defensive end Howie Long says. "At least 50 percent of the big guys. The offensive line—75 percent. Defensive line—40 percent, plus 35 percent of the linebackers. I don't know about the speed positions, but I've heard they're used there, too." (9)

The dangers are threefold: No. 1, the long-range risks—cancers, urinary tract problems and other perils. No. 2, turning pro football games into a game for artificially created giants, able to inflict great damage by their sheer mass. Danger No. 3 is that the artificial bulk causes more insidious injuries—muscle pulls and tendon strains that won't go away. (10)

"Eighty percent of the time when a big guy tears a muscle, steroids are probably the reason why," Long says. "You put 50 pounds of muscle on a player, and he goes from a baggage carrier in the jungle to Tarzan, and he says, 'Wow, this is great!' But something has to give. You're putting too much muscle fiber on a body not designed for it." (11)

Trainers around the league are slowly starting to realize he might be right. "I look with suspicion on some of those injuries when you can't determine how they happened," Saints trainer Dean Kleinschmidt says. "Steroids do strange things to your body. When a guy is pumped up on steroids, there's always a weak link, maybe an Achilles, maybe a patellar tendon." (12)

Solution: Attack anabolic steroids at the league level. A tough project. There hasn't been much concern about the question until recently. Steroids are not illegal unless they are obtained without a prescription. Testing is expensive. Each test costs about $100. O.K., it's worth it. Two spot checks for each player, every year, will cost a club about 10,000. (13)

Any effective antisteroid effort must become part of the new Players Association contract. The program will certainly have more bite and greater impact if the NFLPA enters into a joint endorsement with the league. (14)

The Players Association has another duty to perform, if it wishes to do something about the injury problem. It has to take a serious position on artificial turf. Both the NFL-sponsored Stanford Research Institute International's 1974 study and the NCAA's 1982 study showed that the incidence of injury on synthetic turf was significantly higher than on grass. Since then, the NFL has offered no research to the contrary. Two weeks ago in Giants Stadium, the Jets lost two Pro Bowlers, noseguard Joe Klecko for a game and linebacker Lance Mehl for the season, because of noncontact injuries attributable to the artificial turf.   (15)

New, softer carpets, with better cushions, are more comfortable to fall on, but according to some people they also increase traction so that the cleats catch, causing knee injuries. "When the nap of the turf is new there's just too much traction," Cincinnati trainer Paul Sparling says. "Archie Griffin tried to cut once on new turf and his foot stuck so firmly that he tore up his abdominal muscles in addition to his leg. He was out for the year."   (16)

The players' general hatred of artificial turf is well documented. Very few of them like fake grass, but in the last two contract sessions, while elimination of synthetics was a blanket demand, it quickly became a throwaway issue in former executive director Ed Garvey's negotiating strategy when the heavy matters came up—like money. Note to current association director Gene Upshaw: Worker safety is a top priority for a responsible union. It's not a throwaway.   (17)

San Francisco coach Bill Walsh's idea of a joint player-management committee to examine the carpets every year and replace them when necessary, or at least to eliminate the more unsafe aspects, is a good one. If a particular field proves to be unsafe no matter what is done, then bring back the grass in that particular stadium—assuming it's outdoors (sad to say, grass won't grow properly in the domes). Make that a keynote demand at the contract talks.   (18)

Cheap shots cause injuries, too. It's a fact of life in football—always was, always will be. The problem is that the people responsible for the cheap shots are now so much better equipped to deliver the crippling blow—again, the size and speed factors. The NFL takes a curious approach to cheap shots—protect the quarterback, protect the head. The cosmetic approach. Granted, quarterbacks must be protected from late hits, out-of-bounds hits and general mayhem.   (19)

Consistency in officiating is the key. But why protect only the quarterback? How about the running back who gets teed up by two tacklers and finished off by a third one as Bengal fullback Bill Johnson was against the Steelers (he missed one game with a neck injury). That's the play that really needs the quick whistle.   (20)

The NFL's interpretation of anatomy is strange. Head shots are severely penalized, but the crippling blindsider to the knee is O.K., especially when linemen do it to each other. It's time to take intent into account. Deliberate attempts to maim must be punished, even in cases in which a blow to the head is not involved.   (21)

Solution: Pass a rule that says no cut-blocking unless you're face-up with a man. Clipping is illegal everywhere else on the field. It should be on the line, too.   (22)

But how about the illegal, career-ending type of injury? New Orleans safety Antonio Gibson put the Giants' Lionel Manuel out six weeks ago with a vicious knee shot in the end zone after a pass had sailed out of reach. No flag. No nothing. The intent? Well, you don't go to break up a pass at knee level, and there's nothing to be gained by a low tackle in the end zone. Instead of worrying about hands-to-the-face calls, this is the type of thing the NFL should go after.   (23)

Solution: Biblical justice. An eye-for-an-eye penalty. If a player puts someone out for a week with a blatantly illegal blow, suspend *him* for a week. If the other guy is out for a month, suspend the culprit for a month, a year for a year, a career for a career. Think about it. If you want to eliminate the really bad cheap shots, then hand out really tough punishment.   (24)

Drastic problems need bold solutions. I have this to say:

- To Gene Upshaw—get your union members a safe surface to play on. The owners won't do it; it's up to you. The membership deserves it.
- To [NFL Commissioner] Pete Rozelle—begin steroid testing right now. Get rid of the freak show in the NFL.
- To Art McNally—make sure your refs are working on the same page. Get them to recognize intent to maim and punish it accordingly.
- To the Competition Committee—no more clipping. Don't build up the passing stats at the sake of people's knees.
- To the owners—spend some dough to preserve careers. Too many are being cut short. Just ask all those guys with casts on their knees and arms.   (25)

VOCABULARY

In your journal, write the meanings of the following words.

- are *inherent* to football   (2)
- *anabolic steroids*   (3)
- the *incidence* of injury   (4)
- *arthroscopic* surgery   (6)
- more *insidious* injuries   (10)
- a *patellar* tendon   (12)

- *clipping* is illegal   (22)
- *blatantly* illegal blow   (24)

QUESTIONS FOR WRITING AND DISCUSSION

1. To convince their readers, proposal writers usually explain or document the problem, suggest solutions, examine the feasibility of their plan, and answer objections. Referring to paragraph numbers, indicate where Zimmerman uses each strategy to help convince his readers.

2. Explain your reaction to Zimmerman's proposal by answering the following questions: Which of Zimmerman's proposals is most realistic (or which changes have already taken place)? What alternatives for reducing injuries in football does he ignore? What is most unrealistic about his proposal?

3. Assume that you are one of the following: a football player, a fan, a referee, or an owner. Which of Zimmerman's proposals would you agree with? What objections would you raise about Zimmerman's proposals? Explain.

4. Writers of proposals usually adopt a reasonable tone. What sentences in this essay illustrate Zimmerman's tone most clearly? What word would you use to describe the tone in those sentences: reasonable, angry, humorous, impatient, confident, demanding? Would you use another word? Explain.

PROBLEM SOLVING: THE WRITING PROCESS

ASSIGNMENT FOR PROBLEM SOLVING

Select a problem that you believe needs a solution. Narrow and focus the problem and choose an appropriate audience. Describe the problem and, if necessary, demonstrate for your audience that the problem needs a solution. State your solution and justify it with reasons and evidence. Where appropriate, weigh alternative solutions, examine the feasibility of your solution, and answer objections to your solution.

Choosing a Subject

If one of your journal entries suggests a possible subject, try the collecting and shaping strategies below. If none leads to a workable subject, consider the following suggestions.

- Evaluating leads naturally into problem solving. Reread your journal entries and topic ideas for "evaluating." If your evaluation of your subject was negative, consider what would make your evaluation more positive. Based on your evaluation, write a proposal, addressed to the proper audience, explaining the problem and offering your solution.

- Organized groups are already trying to solve a number of national and international problems: homeless street people, illegal aliens, the slaughter of whales, acid rain, abuse of animals in scientific experiments, nuclear disarmament, drug and alcohol abuse, toxic-waste disposal, and so forth. Read several current articles on one of these topics. Then narrow the problem to one aspect that students or residents of your town could help to resolve. Write an essay outlining the problem

Drawing by Stevenson; © 1987 The New Yorker Magazine, Inc.

"I can't think of anything I have no problem with."

and proposing some *specific and limited* actions citizens could take.

- Employers are always looking for workers with initiative and good ideas. At your place of work, take ten minutes during a break and *observe* what's going on around you. Take notes over a span of several days. Even though people may be getting the job done, would different procedures or policies improve efficiency, safety, quality, or personal relations? Write a letter to your boss identifying the problem you've noticed and justifying your solution.

- Take an inventory of the personal problems you regularly face, day to day. List the things that cost unnecessary amounts of time or money, that cause fear in your life, that increase your frustration level, or that simply make you less happy or productive than you could be. Then compare your inventory with your classmate's or friend's list. If there are common problems, discuss whether or how these problems might be solved.

Collecting

With a possible subject and audience in mind, write out answers for each of the following topics. Remember that not all of these will apply to your subject; some topics will suggest very little, while others may prompt you to generate ideas or specific examples appropriate for your problem and solution. A hypothetical problem—large classes that hinder learning—illustrates how these topics may help you focus on your subject and collect relevant ideas and information.

Identify and focus on the specific problem. Answer the first four "Wh" questions:

- Who: A Psychology I professor; the Psychology department

- What: Psychology I class

- When: Spring semester (the structure of this class may be slightly different from previous semesters)

- Where: University of Michigan (large lecture classes at one school may be different from those at another college or university)

You may want to generalize about large lecture classes everywhere, but begin by identifying the specific problem at hand.

Demonstrate that the problem needs a solution. Map out the *effects* of a problem. (See the diagram.)

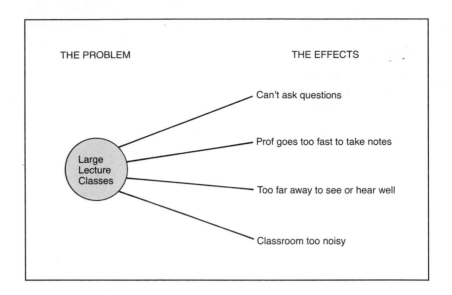

You may want to map out both *short-term effects* and *long-term effects*. Over the short term, large lecture classes prevent you from asking questions; over the long term, you may do poorly on an examination, get a lower grade in the class, lose interest in the subject, be unable to cope with your own and others' psychological problems, or end up in a different career or job.

Discover possible solutions. One strategy is to map out the *history* or the *causes* of the problem. If you can discover what caused the problem in the first place, you may have a possible solution. (See the diagram on the following page.)

A second strategy takes the imaginative approach. Brainstorm hypothetical cases by asking, "What if . . . ?"

"What if students petitioned the president of the university to abolish all lecture classes with enrollments over 100 students?" Would that work?

"What if students invited the professor to answer questions at a weekly study session?" Would the professor attend? Would students attend?

"What if students taught each other in a psychology class?" How would that work?

Evaluate possible solutions. Apply the "If . . . then . . ." test on each possible solution: Consider whether each proposal would

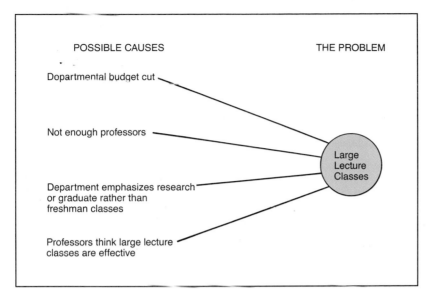

actually solve the problem;

meet criteria, such as cost effectiveness, practicality, ethicality, legality;

not create new problems.

"*If* classes were smaller, *then* students would learn more."

If classes were smaller, students might learn more, but a small class size does not necessarily guarantee greater learning.

Students might learn more, but do smaller classes meet other criteria? They are legal and ethical, but are they practical and cost effective?

Would smaller classes create new problems? Smaller classes might mean fewer upper-level course offerings. Is that a serious new problem?

Convince your readers. Support your proposed solutions by stating *reasons* and finding supporting *evidence.*

Reason: Smaller classes are worth the additional expense because students actually engage the material rather than just memorizing for exams.

Evidence: data from studies comparing large and small classes; personal testimony by students, interviews, or questionnaires; testimony or evidence from authorities on teaching.

Answer possible objections to your proposal. Every solution has a down side or possible drawbacks. You need to respond to the most important objections.

LIST DRAWBACKS

Small classes cost more.

Small classes might reduce course offerings.

Small classes might mean less money for research.

LIST YOUR RESPONSES

Good education does cost more. The University of Michigan has the reputation of an excellent undergraduate institution, and small classes would help it maintain quality education.

Perhaps some classes with low demand could be cut, but the necessary funds should not be taken out of upper-division classes for Psychology majors or research projects.

List possible steps for implementation. If appropriate, indicate the key steps or chronological sequence of your proposal.

1. Poll students and teachers of large lecture classes to confirm that the problem warrants attention.
2. Gather evidence from other colleges or universities on how they reduced class sizes.
3. Present results of polls and other evidence to the state legislature to request more funds.

Observing   As you gather evidence and examples, use your observation skills. If the problem is large lecture classes, attend classes and *observe* the behavior of students and professors. Are students distracted by noise? Can they ask questions? Does the professor talk too softly to be heard in the back row? Remember that *repeated* observation is essential. Observe your subject over a period of several days or weeks if necessary.

Remembering   Use *freewriting, looping,* or *clustering* to help you remember examples from your experience of the problem or of possible solutions. Brainstorm or freewrite about previous class sessions in Psychology I. Do looping or mapping on other small-enrollment classes: What made these classes effective or ineffective? What teaching strategies, projects, or small-group activities were possible in these classes that would not be possible in a class of 250 students?

Investigating   Use *the library* to find books or articles about the particular problem. Other writers may have offered solutions to your problem that you could consider. Articles may even suggest objections to your proposed solution that you need to answer.

Interview participants or authorities on the problem. The professor who is teaching your Psychology I class may have some ideas about a solution. Administrations—department chairs, deans, even the president—may agree to answer your questions and react to your possible solutions, so schedule an interview.

Design a questionnaire about your problem. Responses to questionnaires provide evidence that the problem is serious, immediate, and needs a solution. If the results of a questionnaire show that 175 of the 200 people in Psychology I who returned your questionnaire favored smaller sections, you can include that data in your letter to the head of the department and the dean of the college.

RESEARCH TIP

As you begin researching your problem, **don't** rush off to the library and start collecting articles. **Do** start by interviewing people who may know about your problem. Use your investigating skills to locate authorities and interview them. (See Chapter 5, pp. 156–57.) Find out what other people have already done to solve the problem—or why current solutions are not working. Interview a teacher who knows about the problem, a student who has firsthand experience with the problem, an owner of a local business, or the coordinator of a community service. Save your library research until you know what the problem really is and what is currently being done to correct it.

Shaping

Writers of proposals often do the following:

- Identify and demonstrate the problem
- Evaluate alternative solutions
- State a proposal
- Give reasons and evidence to support the proposal; answer objections, discuss feasibility and costs
- Indicate implementation or call for action

The best time for planning . . . is when you're doing the dishes.

—*Agatha Christie, mystery writer*

Not all problem-solving essays have all five elements, however. Some do not discuss feasibility or do not evaluate the alternative solutions. Zimmerman's proposal, for example, suggests only four important ways to solve the problem—without considering alternative solutions.

Outlines for Problem Solving The following patterns indicate four possible ways to organize a problem-solving essay. One of these patterns may help you organize your proposal:

PROBLEM-SOLUTION PATTERN

- **I.** Introduction
- **II.** The problem: identify and demonstrate
- **III.** The solution(s)
- **IV.** Answering possible objections, costs, drawbacks
- **V.** Conclusion: implementation plan; call to action

POINT-BY-POINT PATTERN

- **I.** Introduction
- **II.** The overall problem: identify and demonstrate
- **III.** One part of the problem, solution, evidence, answers to possible objections, feasibility
- **IV.** Second part of the problem, solution, evidence, answers to objections, feasibility
- **V.** Third part of the problem, solution, evidence, and so on
- **VI.** Conclusion: implementation; call to action

ALTERNATIVE PATTERN

- **I.** Introduction
- **II.** The problem: identify and demonstrate
- **III.** Alternative solution 1; why it's not satisfactory
- **IV.** Alternative solution 2; why it's not satisfactory
- **V.** Alternative solution 3; why it works best: evidence, objections, feasibility
- **VI.** Conclusion: implementation; call to action

STEP-BY-STEP PATTERN

- **I.** Introduction
- **II.** The problem: identify and demonstrate
- **III.** Plan for implementing the solution or how solution has worked in the past:
  - **A.** Step one: reasons and evidence showing why this step is necessary and feasible

    B. Step two: reasons and evidence showing why this step is necessary and feasible

    C. Step three: reasons and evidence showing why this step is necessary and feasible

IV. Conclusion

Causal Analysis   Causal analysis can be used to organize some paragraphs of a proposal. In arguing the benefits or advantages of a proposed solution, you are actually explaining the *effects* of your solution.

- The effects or advantages of smaller class sections in Psychology I would be greater student participation, fewer distractions, more discussion during lectures, and more individual or small-group learning.
- Shortening the work week to thirty-two hours would increase the number of jobs, reduce tensions for working parents, and give employees time to learn new skills.
- Eliminating steroid use among NFL athletes would reduce the impact of collisions and enable players to recover from injuries faster. Long-term effects of eliminating steroids would be to reduce incidence of cancers and urinary tract problems.

In each of these cases, each effect or advantage can become a separate point and, sometimes, a separate body paragraph.

Criteria Analysis   In some cases, the *criteria* for a good solution are clear. For example, feasibility, cost effectiveness, legality, and simplicity are criteria you can use to organize your proposal. If you work in a grocery store, for example, and are proposing to your manager a solution to stop the theft of grocery carts, you might defend your proposal (or answer possible objections) by discussing criteria that would appeal to him or her.

    Proposal: to reduce theft and damage of grocery carts by rewarding customers who return carts to the store with a token worth fifty cents toward any purchase of five dollars or more at the store.

- *Cost effectiveness.* Returned carts would not be damaged by cars in the parking lots. Each cart not stolen saves the store $250. The money saved on new carts would help meet costs of tokens. In addition, since most customers would return carts themselves, managers save the time and money required to return carts from the parking lot.

- *Feasibility.* Because the system is based on incentives to the customer, it would require only a place to return the carts and an attendant to give tokens to customers. In addition, this system has already been tried at another supermarket, with no special problems.

- *Promotion and advertising.* Tokens, like coupons from newspaper advertisements, would encourage customers to return to the store to redeem their tokens.

- *Simplicity.* The system would not require continual maintenance, nor would it penalize those customers who did not return their carts. Consumers who wished to save money could; others would leave their carts in the parking lot if they wished.

Chronological Order   If your proposal stresses the means of implementing your solution to a problem, you may organize several paragraphs or even an entire essay using a chronological order or step-by-step pattern.

A proposal to reduce boating accidents on a lake, for example, might involve a plan for educating boaters and enforcing regulations over a three-year period. The first year, notices about dangers might be posted at key docks. The second year, the county could pass a law requiring marinas to give a short instruction course for renters and set up voluntary classes on the lake for boat owners. Offenders might be given a warning and required to take a class. In the third year, offenders might face stiff fines for driving a boat recklessly.

A proposal to improve the reading skills of children might be justified by a series of coordinated steps, beginning by organizing seminars for teachers and PTA meetings to discuss possible solutions; establishing minimal reading requirements in grades K–6 that teachers and parents agree on; offering reading prizes; and organizing media coverage of students who participate in reading programs.

COMPUTER TIP: COLLECTING AND SHAPING

Choose one of the four outlines or patterns for problem solving presented in the *shaping* section that might work for your essay. Enter that pattern in your computer file, open up space between each heading, and type in ideas and information that you've collected. For example, if you choose pattern 1, enter the outline, and then add notes and information under the appropriate heading: Problem-Solution Pattern

I. Introduction

II. The problem: identify and demonstrate [Enter your ideas, information, statistics, and examples here.]

III. The solution(s) [Enter your ideas, information, statistics, and examples here.]

IV. Answering possible objections, costs, drawbacks [Enter your ideas, information, statistics, and examples here.]

V. Conclusion: implementation plan; call to action

This will give you a rough idea of a plan to use during drafting. After you have entered some information, however, you may decide to organize your essay using another pattern. If so, save the information you've entered and try another organizational pattern.

Drafting

Using your examples, recorded observations, reading, interviews, results from questionnaires, or your own experience, make a sketch outline and begin writing. As you write, let your own proposal and your intended audience guide you. In your first draft, get as much down as possible. Don't worry about spelling or awkward sentences. If you hit a snag, stop and read what you have written so far or reread your collecting-and-shaping notes.

Vigorous writing is concise.

—*William Strunk, Jr., author and teacher*

Revising

Use the following revising guidelines to identify areas for improving your draft. Even at this point, don't hesitate to collect additional information, if necessary, or reorganize your material. If a reader makes suggestions, reread your draft to see if those changes will improve your essay.

Guidelines for Revision

Have a classmate or someone who might understand your audience read your draft and play the devil's advocate. Have your reader pretend to be hostile to your solution and ask questions about alternative solutions or weaknesses in your own solution. Revise your proposal so that it answers any important objections.

Review your proposal for key elements. If you are missing one of the following, would adding it make your proposal more effective for your audience? Remember: Proposals do not necessarily have to have all of these elements. Develop the items that are most applicable to your proposal.

- Show that a problem exists and needs attention
- Evaluate alternative solutions
- Propose your solution
- Show that your solution meets certain criteria: feasibility, cost effectiveness, legality
- Answer possible objections
- Suggest implementation or call for action

Be sure that you *show* what you mean, using specific examples, facts, details, statistics, quotations from interviews or articles. Don't rely on general assertions.

Signal the major parts of your proposal with key words and transitions.

Avoid the following errors in logic and generalization.

- Don't commit an "either-or" fallacy. For example, don't say that "*either* we reduce class sizes *or* students will drop out of the university." There are more than two possible alternatives.
- Don't commit an *"ad hominem"* fallacy by arguing "to the man" rather than to the issue. Don't say, for example, that Paul Zimmerman's proposal would never work because he's never been a player and doesn't understand the issues.
- Test your proposal for "If . . . then . . ." statements. Does it really follow that "If we introduce tokens for grocery carts, then carts will never be stolen again?"
- Avoid overgeneralizing your solution. If all your research applies to solving problems in large lecture classes in psychology, don't assume that your solution will apply to classes in physics or physical education, for instance.

If you are citing data or quoting sources, check to be sure that your material is accurately cited.

Read your proposal aloud for flabby, wordy, or awkward sentences. Revise your sentences for clarity, precision, and forcefulness.

Edit your proposal for spelling, appropriate word choice, punctuation, usage, mechanics, and grammar. Remember that, in part, your form and audience help determine what is appropriate usage and mechanics.

POSTSCRIPT ON THE WRITING PROCESS

Before you turn in your essay, answer the following questions in your journal.

1. List the skills you used in writing this paper: observing people, places, or events; remembering personal experience; using questionnaires and interviews; reading written material; explaining ideas; or evaluating solutions. Which of these skills was most useful to you in writing this essay?

2. What was your most difficult problem to solve while writing this paper? Were you able to solve it yourself, or did your readers suggest a solution?

3. In one sentence, describe the most important thing you learned about writing while working on this essay.

4. What were the most successful parts of your essay?

PROBLEM SOLVING: STUDENT WRITING

NO PARKING

Kristy Busch, Steve Krause, and Keith Wright

Kristy Busch, Steve Krause, and Keith Wright worked together on a proposal to solve the parking problem at their university. They met several times to discuss the topic, select questions for the survey and interview, divide the research responsibilities, and determine who was going to draft each section. They agreed that Keith Wright would interview the director of parking management, and Kristy Busch and Steve Krause would survey students about the parking problem. After they collected their information, Wright drafted a first version of the section on the multilevel garage, Busch worked on the shuttle-bus proposal, and Krause wrote out the introduction and the rezoning proposal. Then they worked together to combine and revise their drafts, adding new information, reorganizing the paragraphs, and editing the final draft. Shown below are the questions for the interview, the results of the survey, the first draft of the introduction and rezoning proposal, and the revised draft of the entire proposal.

Interview

Interview Questions for Wes Westfall,
Director of Parking Management

1. Do you perceive a serious parking problem at CSU?
2. Do you think that students' arguments about lack of
"X" parking spaces along the dorms on the north
side of the campus are valid?
3. How many stickers for each zone are issued each
year? Do these numbers fluctuate?
4. Are you in favor of building a multi-level parking
facility?
Where would you build such a structure?
What would it cost? Is it feasible?
How long would it take to build?
5. Have you considered a shuttle-bus system
between Moby Gym and the central campus?
What would it cost? Is it feasible?
6. Is rezoning possible? Is it currently under
consideration? Would it solve the problem?
Is it feasible? What would it cost?

Parking Survey Results

1. Do you drive to CSU?

   Yes: 36

   Occasionally: 53

   No: 11

2. Does CSU need more parking for students?

   Yes: 62

   No: 38

3. Would rezoning close-in lots to eliminate dorm parking help?

   Yes: 78

   No: 22

4. Class (Fr., Soph., Jr., Sr., Other)

   Fr: 33

   Soph: 20

Jr:	22
Sr:	13
Other:	12

First Draft

If you drive to CSU, you may already know how hard it can be to find a parking place. If not then now would be a good time to make the changes necessary to accommodate more cars (before you start driving). Not only is the parking inadequate for the number of cars, but it is also poorly organized and poorly distributed among the groups who use it. A very common occurrence is being forced to park very far from the building where you need to go. Not only students are affected; faculty, staff, and visitors also have problems finding somewhere to park. For a visitor this is very distressing and certainly doesn't present an attractive first impression of CSU. It is clear that something will have to be done; what is unclear is exactly what would be the most practical and cost effective solution. First, and probably the most effective for the immediate future would be to rezone the existing parking to better accommodate the users. A shuttle-bus system could also be used; however this could be costly and would have to be used a lot to make it a practical investment. The ominous "multi-level parking facility" is a drastic last measure that we would have a lot of trouble paying for. [add closing sentence]

The most cost-effective and probably the most immediately effective would be a partial rezoning of existing parking. This year, the office of parking management sold 7,641 parking stickers for an available 6,238 spaces, a difference of 1,703. This means that there are a lot more stickers than places to park. Granted, all these people do not drive at the same time, but enough do to cause a problem. In poll taken this March, 78 percent of the people said that they would like to see the parking rezoned. In rezoning we should first look at the parking areas which are not full and determine why and then shift the zones in a way in which they will help. For example, the western sections of the "Z" lot at Moby Gym could be changed to "X" for those dorm dwellers. Then the close-in lots could be changed to "Z" for the commuting students. Or we could eliminate the metered parking and put "Z" parking in its place. Rezoning the lots would seem to be the easiest solution to the problem, but it cannot be permanent, since if this school survives it will inevitably grow.

Revised Version

NO PARKING

On Monday morning, Jennifer Martin left her apartment at 8:30 to drive to the Colorado State University campus, hoping to arrive on time for a test in her 9 A.M. sociology class. When she arrived at the student parking lot west of Aylesworth hall, there were no parking spots. So she began cruising up and down the lot, hoping that someone would soon pull out. As she drove slowly up and down the lanes, she muttered to herself and clenched her hands on the steering wheel. She did have a permit to park in the lot, but there were obviously more permits than spaces. About five minutes before class, a car pulled out of a place at the far end of the lot. She accelerated down the next lane, driving as fast as she could without running over other students, but just as she arrived, a green Ford Pinto cut in front of her and darted into the vacant space. She honked her horn and waved her fist, but the person got quickly out of the car and walked away. At this point, she realized that she had no choice. She wheeled into the area marked for motorcycles, parked her car, and raced for class. She was angry because she knew she was going to get a ticket even though she had a legal permit.   (1)

    If you drive to the CSU campus for classes, you have probably had a similar experience. But students are not the only ones who have parking problems on campus: faculty, staff, and visitors also have problems finding places to park. Especially for visitors, the overcrowded conditions don't present an attractive first impression of the campus. Clearly, something has to be done to improve parking facilities. After studying the problem, interviewing the director of parking management and polling one hundred students, we believe that there are three alternatives which the CSU administration should consider: building a multilevel parking facility, starting a shuttle-bus from remote lots, and rezoning the existing parking lots to better serve the users. (2)

A first possible solution to CSU's parking problem would be to build a multi-level parking facility. This sounds like a promising idea because it would allow more students, faculty, and staff to park over the same amount of ground space. CSU could build this facility at any of several locations. One place is on the west side of the Morgan Library, where the "A" parking zone—for faculty—is now. This location would provide parking convenient to classes, faculty offices, and the library. A second site would be the open parking lot west of Moby Gym. Although this location is further from classes, it would also be used during basketball games and concerts. A third location might be the large parking lot north of the Student Center. This too, like the library lot, would be close to classrooms and faculty offices. (3)

While these sites are all promising, we discovered that a multi-level parking facility has some serious drawbacks. Wes Westfall, manager of CSU parking, explained that there are several problems with these garages that most people don't consider. A first drawback to the parking garage is the expense. Westfall said that a multi-level garage would cost a minimum of $6,000 per parking space, raising the price of a parking permit from $30 to over $300. And that would be for a sticky piece of paper that still wouldn't guarantee a parking space for every car. Perhaps the president of the university could pay $300 a year, but most students can barely afford $30. (4)

A second drawback to a parking garage is that it doesn't last forever, and the maintenance costs can be considerable. Mr. Westfall has some frightening photographs of sections of strong, stable-looking concrete that has collapsed for no visible reason at all. One picture shows a whole garage leveled as though a good-sized bomb had hit it—nothing was left standing except for an occasional pillar here and there. Unless garages are carefully maintained, Westfall stated, they may not last over 20 years. The problem, he explained, lies in the rebarb (steel rods inside the concrete) that reinforces the concrete. Gas, oil, and anti-freeze from cars are gradually absorbed into the concrete, causing the rebarb to deteriorate and weaken the whole structure. The only way to check for this kind of damage, Westfall noted, is to use an expensive concrete X-ray machine. So even the maintenance for a garage can be an expensive proposition. (5)

The third and most serious problem, Westfall claims, is security. Parking garages can become just another place for sexual assault, drug trafficking, vandalism, and theft. Westfall commented that most garages have a monitor system and guards, but those precautions are not totally effective. By the time the guard detects a theft over the security system and arrives at the location, the thief has usually fled.

In addition, any security system adds to the already high costs of a parking facility. Clearly, the problems connected with a multi-level garage make it a last resort for solving the parking problems on campus.   (6)

A second alternative for solving the parking problems on the CSU campus is to use a bus shuttle service from the outlying "Z" lot at Moby Gym to the central campus. Students who responded to our survey frequently said that the lots on the perimeter of the campus were nearly empty, but they were too far away from the library and the classrooms. The shuttle would solve this problem by taking the following route: beginning at the Lory Student Center, the bus would head west down North Drive (along the residence halls) to the Moby Gym lot, and then stop and pick up drivers at both the north and south ends of the lot. It would then turn south onto Shields at the stoplight and turn east on South Drive, returning to central campus. This system would allow easier access to the core of the campus and, in return, put to full use the 539 parking spaces available in the Moby Gym parking lot. Of course, the shuttle, driver, and maintenance would cost money, so this solution would require a commitment from the university administration.   (7)

The most cost-effective solution would be a partial rezoning of the parking lots. This past year, the office of parking management sold 7,461 parking stickers for an available 6,238 spaces, a difference of 1,403. This means that they sold 1,403 more stickers than there are places to park. Not all people need to park at the same time, but enough do to cause a problem. Of the 100 students that we polled, 78 percent said that they would like to see the central campus lots rezoned. In this scheme, students parking their cars for long periods of time would use the outlying lots and commuting students, faculty, and staff would use the closer lots. For example, if we changed the western section of the outlying "Z" lot to "X" for those students living in the dorms, the parking spaces near the dorms along South Drive could be made available to those who have to drive everyday to campus to attend classes. Such rezoning seems to be the easiest and least expensive solution.   (8)

One main problem to overcoming CSU's parking problem is money. A multi-level parking facility would accommodate more cars per acre of ground space, yet it is the most expensive solution. The shuttle-bus system—which could still be implemented—is more economical, but it would require raising additional revenue, most likely by raising the price of parking stickers. We certainly recommend that the university try a shuttle system on an experimental basis to determine the exact costs and see whether the number of riders justifies the expense. Rezoning the lots, however, is clearly the least complicated and most economical solution. Signs could be changed during the summer months, and new maps and brochures printed in time for the beginning of fall semester. Our group proposes that the university rezone the lots at the end of this academic year and start planning for a shuttle bus and a garage to meet the need in future years. With more careful management of the close-in lots, the new parking stickers might be more than just a hunting license. A person with a permit might actually be able to arrive at a lot at 8:45 and still make that nine o'clock class.   (9)

QUESTIONS FOR WRITING AND DISCUSSION

1. After reading the revised version, look again at the questions for the interview and the survey. How would you advise the authors to modify either set of questions? What questions would you add? What questions would you change or delete? Explain.

2. Compare the introduction in the first draft with the introduction in the revised version. Which is more effective? Jot down an idea for a third introduction which the authors might consider.

3. Reread the revised version and *outline* the major parts of the proposal. Then compare that outline with the authors' initial outline, given below:

    I. Intro

    II. Rezoning proposal

    III. Shuttle-bus proposal

    IV. Multi-level garage proposal

    V. Conclusion

    Do you think that their revised plan for organizing the paper was an improvement? Explain.

4. Who is the intended audience for this proposal? What revisions would make this proposal appeal even more strongly to that audience? (During the planning stages of this essay, the authors decided to send this proposal to Wes Westfall, director of parking management. How do you think Westfall would react to this proposal, as it stands?)

WE CAN SAVE OUR NATIONAL PARKS— IF WE ACT NOW

Sarah Bates

You may have seen the film on TV news: hunters shooting help-less elk in wildlife preserves; buffalo being killed near Yellowstone National Park; foresters deliberately setting fires in national

*forests. Is this any way to protect our precious natural resources?
In her essay on saving our national parks, Sarah Bates identifies
a problem that foresters already recognize:* Protecting *the forest
will not necessarily* preserve *it. The solution, however, is more
difficult than it seems. If we cannot return a truly natural environment to the parks, how can we "manage" them in a natural
way? As you read Bates's essay, consider whether you agree with
her explanation of the problem and her proposed solution.*

Visiting a National Park can be relaxing, inspiring and rejuvenating,
but it can also be disturbing. Tear your eyes from the spectacular view
of Longs Peak as you drive into Rocky Mountain National Park, and
you will see starving elk, damaged meadows and dying forests. Our
Parks are growing old because we have mistakenly protected them
from natural processes, such as fire, predation, and insects. We
believed that we were saving these remnants of wild America, but
actually we have "protected" them to death. If we want to save our
National Parks, the National Park Service must change its management priorities to prevent overpopulation of animals and to restore
natural processes in the forests in order to prevent their stagnation
and "death" by old age. The Forest Service uses active management
(such as controlled fires, tree removal, and animal population control)
to maintain healthy, productive National forests. We can successfully
adapt such practices to fit the needs of our National parks. Above all,
we must act soon: our parks are dying of old age because we have
altered the forces in nature that keep them young and strong.   (1)

By tracing the history of our National Parks, we can understand
the problem and see why we need active management. In the early
part of this century, settlers exploited wildlife heavily, resulting in
near-extinction of many species. Therefore, several National Parks
were established by Congress primarily to save endangered animals:
Mount McKinley, Everglades, and Olympic (Ise 21). However, stricter
wildlife protection laws and improved wildlife management techniques resulted in greater populations of animals and overcrowding
in areas of high concentration, such as the Yellowstone elk herds
(Wauer and Supernaugh 12). Complicating the problem, the National
Park Service in the early part of this century adopted a policy of
aggressive predator elimination, thus reducing natural wildlife population control. Subsequently, elk and deer populations exploded in
many National Parks, resulting in severe damage to native vegetation.
Vigorous forest fire and insect suppression in the National Parks
throughout this century further altered the natural environment by
allowing forests to over-mature, without natural thinning processes.
Park managers thought that they were protecting the land, but actually they were removing important controls from the forest ecosystems.
Some wildlife biologists even warn that continuing this strict preser-

vation policy in the parks results in drastic changes in the environment, thus violating the Park Service goal of leaving these wild areas "unimpaired for future generations" (Leopold et al. 29). Clearly, we must act immediately if we want to pass down to our children and grandchildren the great legacy of our National Parks; we must step in and restore the natural processes which we have altered through our well-intentioned, but misguided, policies in the past.   (2)

In our attempt to restore natural processes to the National Parks, we encounter opposition from concerned park visitors, as well as Park Service personnel worried about adverse public reaction to management changes. Many visitors, unaware of the complicated web of relationships between different animals, become greatly disturbed when they see or hear of an animal being killed. For example, Yellowstone National Park elk herds suffer severe overpopulation problems. However, Park Service efforts in past years to reduce elk numbers through selective shooting met with emotional public outcry, forcing the shootings to stop. Similarly, National Park Service officials worry that other controversial management methods may threaten future public support for the National Parks (Wood 29). Some officials believe, however, that National Parks are not zoos, but rather areas in which native animal and plant life should be maintained in as natural a state as possible (Leopold et. al. 30). Visitors who do not understand good forestry practices believe that cutting down trees permanently harms the land and that all fires are bad (thanks, in part, to the overly-successful Smokey Bear campaign). Actually, fire helps restore wildlife habitat by opening up dense forest stands; cutting timber can achieve the same objective where controlled fire is unsafe or otherwise not feasible.   (3)

Park Service personnel worry that active management, such as direct herd reduction, will result in adverse publicity for the National Park Service. However, they do agree that some controls are necessary, so we must examine the alternatives. Although direct shooting of deer or elk is probably the most emotionally-charged option for reducing overpopulation, proposed reintroduction of natural predators, such as wolves, creates political conflicts as well. Ranchers living near National Parks fear that wandering wolves will kill their livestock. State wildlife agencies, who must compensate landowners for wildlife-related property damage, oppose predator reintroduction for the same reason (Moore 8). However, many biologists see predators as the "missing link" in park ecosystems and claim that their reintroduction will prove the most efficient, natural solution to overpopulated herds (Leopold et al. 38). Although some hunters propose limited public hunts in the parks, historian John Ise points out that such sport hunting would be incongruous with National Park Service principles and may be dangerous to park visitors (25). Live trapping and transplanting excess animals to other areas, a proposal which receives much public support, is also the most expensive and inconvenient control method. Dave Stevens, a Rocky Mountain National Park biologist, expresses the NPS view of this option: "It's too expensive. . . . Where would we put them?" (Moore 8).   (4)

We see the need, therefore, to revise our National Park management procedures. The NPS must overcome bureaucratic inertia and establish new goals for the parks. First, park biologists must complete ecological studies to determine historical conditions; data from the Forest Service should make this process relatively simple. Next, each National Park should draw up a management plan, stressing active techniques aimed at returning their area to its natural condition. These plans must include provisions for controlled fire, exotic species elimination and—where necessary—population control of animal herds. To make this effort work, the NPS should establish an advisory board under the Secretary of the Interior, to review management plans and suggest improvement. Thus, future NPS goals, strategies and management techniques will be consistent with our mandate to maintain the National Parks for future use. Furthermore, the NPS needs to improve its education programs, to ensure public support for park management.   (5)

In summary, the controversy over National Park management revolves around this question: what is our role in the natural environment of our National Parks? Some believe that we should take a "hands-off" approach, leaving nature to function as it always has, and presumably always will. However, I contend that we have always managed our parks, primarily through interference with natural processes such as fire and predation. Therefore, I believe that we have already created a role for ourselves in the Park environment; while we may find it necessary to alter our role, it would be ignorant to believe that our presence goes unfelt. Rather than leaving our National Parks to die of old age, I agree with the Conservation Foundation: "The National Park System should be a showcase for the proper stewardship of land, water and air" (3). We not only have a Congressional mandate to manage our parks; we also have an ethical responsibility to maintain or restore their natural qualities for future generations to enjoy. Thus, I propose that we establish a new advisory board to help the NPS develop and implement active management in the National Parks. We have the knowledge and the tools to save our parks; we need public support and professional guidance in order to begin. If we don't begin soon, we may lose our chance.   (6)

Works Cited

Conservation Foundation. *Proceedings of the Symposium: National Parks for the Future: The Next 100 Years.* Denver: Rocky Mountain Center on Environment, 1972.

Ise, John. *Our National Park Policy: A Critical History.* Baltimore: The Johns Hopkins Press, 1961.

Leopold, A. Starker, Stanley A. Cain, Clarence M. Cottain, Ira N. Gabrielson, and Thomas L. Kimball. "Wildlife Management in the National Parks." *Transactions of the Twenty-Eighth North American Wildlife Conference* 28 (1963): 28–45.

Moore, Nancy. "Rocky Mountain National Park Is Near Carrying Capacity." *Colorado Wildlife* Oct. 1984: 8.

Wauer, Roland H. and William R. Supernaugh. "Wildlife Management in the National Parks: An Historical Perspective." *National Parks* July–Aug. 1983: 12–17.

Wood, Pinckney. "The Elk Hunt Goes on at Grand Teton." *National Parks* Sept./Oct. 1984: 28–31.

QUESTIONS FOR WRITING AND DISCUSSION

1. In your own words, explain the problem that Bates sees in the national parks. Do you agree that this is, in fact, a problem? Why or why not?

2. Who is the intended audience for this essay? What changes might Bates make in her essay to address that audience more effectively? Explain.

3. Bates does not outline the drawbacks to her proposed solution. What feasibility problems—costs, time, and money required—might exist? Explain.

4. This proposal does not suggest a definite policy the National Park Service should follow. Instead, it outlines a *procedure* for determining what the correct policy should be. Should Bates recommend a specific policy? Explain.

5. Of the working outlines suggested in this chapter under *shaping,* which does Bates follow? Compare the structure of Bates's essay with the outline followed by Busch, Krause, and Wright in their essay on the parking problem. How do they differ? Which is more effective for you as a reader?

9 | *Arguing*

Howard Chandler Christy
Signing of the Constitution (detail)
Architect of the Capitol

After being cited for not wearing a seat belt while operating a motor vehicle, you decide that your rights have been violated. In order to write a convincing argument to your representative that seat-belt laws are unfair, you research current articles about the law and interview a law professor on the issue. You decide to claim that the seat-belt laws should be repealed because they are a fundamental violation of individual liberty. You believe that the opposing argument—that seat belts save lives and reduce insurance rates for everyone—is not relevant to the issue of individual liberty. Since your representative has supported seat-belt laws, you present both sides of the issue but stress the arguments supporting your viewpoint. □

In your job as research assistant for a state senator, you are asked to write a brief on the latest farm bill before the legislature. Your assignment is to present the arguments and evidence for and against this bill, and then recommend how the senator should vote. You interview the author of the bill, read the arguments for both sides, consult a legal assistant about several specific phrases in the bill, and talk to several farmers to discover how this bill would actually affect them. Then you condense your research and present your findings in the three-page format that the senator requires: two pages summarizing arguments for and against the bill, and one page outlining your recommendations. □

Give me liberty to know, to utter, and to argue freely according to conscience, above all liberties.

—John Milton, poet

Freedom of speech is established to achieve its essential purpose only when different opinions are expounded in the same hall to the same audience. . . . The opposition is indispensable.

—Walter Lippmann, journalist

When people argue with each other, they often become highly emotional or confrontational. Remember the last heated argument you had with a friend or family member—at the end of the argument, one person stomped out of the room, slammed the door, and didn't speak to the other for days. In the aftermath of such a scene, you felt angry with the other person and angry with yourself. Nothing was accomplished. Neither of you came close to achieving what you wanted when you began the argument. Rather than understanding each other's point of view and working out your differences, you effectively closed the lines of communication.

When writers construct an argument, however, they try, through reason and use of evidence, to avoid the emotional outbursts that often turn verbal arguments into displays of temper. Strong feelings may energize an argument—few of us make the effort to argue without an emotional investment in the subject—but written argument stresses a fair weighing of pros and cons. You advocate one position, but you keep the lines of communication open by acknowledging and evaluating opposing arguments. Because written arguments are public, they take on a civilized manner. They implicitly say, "Let's be reasonable about this. Let's look at the evidence for *both* sides. Let's not shout or fight; let's be as objective as we can."

As writers construct a written argument, they carefully consider the audience. Does the audience know about this controversy, or do they need background information? Do the readers hold the opposing viewpoint, or are they likely to listen to both sides and decide what to believe? What arguments will they find most persuasive? The written argument creates an atmosphere of reason, which encourages readers to examine their own views clearly and dispassionately. When successful, such argument convinces rather than alienates the audience: It changes people's minds or persuades them to adopt a recommended course of action.

FREEWRITING: ARGUING

Time yourself for fifteen minutes. Argue either for or against the following claim: "In college, all elective courses should be graded pass-fail." Brainstorm a list of reasons for and against your claim. Decide on an audience. Then choose the *two* best reasons for your claim and list evidence or describe specific examples from your personal experience that you could use to support each reason.

TECHNIQUES FOR WRITING ARGUMENT

A written argument is similar to a public debate—between attorneys in a court of law or members of Congress who represent different political parties. It begins with a *debatable* issue: Is this a good bill? Should we vote for it? In such debates, one person argues *for* a position or proposal, and the other person argues *against* it. The onlookers (the members of Congress, the jury, or the public) then decide what to believe or what to do. *Written argument imitates this situation by examining the opinions both for and against a position, and then advocating one of the positions or proposing a solution.* Written argument *evaluates* the conflicting positions and then uses reasons and evidence to support the writer's claim. The writer represents the opposing arguments, refutes them (if possible), and advocates his or her own position. A sound written argument uses the following techniques:

> *All writing . . . is propaganda for something.*
>
> —*Elizabeth Drew, writer and critic.*

- **Focusing on a** *debatable proposition or claim.* This claim becomes your thesis.

- *Analyzing the audience* **to determine what they already believe and how to convince them to believe or act on your thesis.**

- **Representing and evaluating the** *opposing points of view* **on the issue fairly and accurately.**

- **Arguing reasonably** *against the opposition and for your claim.* Support your claim with *evidence:* observations, facts, statistics, expert testimony, or personal examples.

In an article entitled "Active and Passive Euthanasia," James Rachels claims that active euthanasia may be defensible for patients with incurable and painful diseases. The following paragraphs from that article illustrate the key features of argument:

The distinction between active and passive euthanasia is thought to be crucial for medical ethics. The idea is that it is permissible, at least in some cases, to withhold treatment and allow a patient to die, but it is never permissible to take any direct action designed to kill the patient. This doctrine seems to be accepted by most doctors. . . .

Opposing Position

However, a strong case can be made against this doctrine. In what follows I will set out some of the relevant arguments, and urge doctors to reconsider their views on this matter.

Claim
Audience

To begin with a familiar type of situation, a patient who is dying of incurable cancer of the throat is in terrible pain, which can no longer be satisfactorily alleviated. He is certain to die within a few days, even if present treatment is continued, but he does not want to go on living for those days since the pain is unbearable. So he asks the doctor for an end to it, and his family joins in the request.

Argument for Claim
Example

Example

*Argument Against
Opposition*

Suppose the doctor agrees to withhold treatment, as the conventional doctrine says he may. The justification for his doing so is that the patient is in terrible agony, and since he is going to die anyway, it would be wrong to prolong his suffering needlessly. But now notice this. If one simply withholds treatment, it may take the patient longer to die, and so he may suffer more than he would if more direct action were taken and a lethal injection given. This fact provides strong reason for thinking that, once the initial decision not to prolong his agony has been made, active euthanasia is actually preferable to passive euthanasia, rather than the reverse. To say otherwise is to endorse the option that leads to more suffering rather than less, and is contrary to the humanitarian impulse that prompts the decision not to prolong his life in the first place.

Claims for Written Argument

The thesis of your argument is a claim that must be debatable. Opinions on both sides of the issue must have some merit. Claims for a written argument usually fall into one of four categories: claims of fact, claims about cause and effect, claims about value, and claims about solutions and policies. (A claim may occasionally fall into several categories or even overlap categories.)

Claims of Fact

- Grades do not measure intelligence or achievement.
- Polygraph tests do not accurately detect lies.
- Women face serious discrimination in the job market.

These claims are about matters of "fact" that are not easily measured or agreed upon. If I claimed that a Lhasa apso was an ancient Chinese ruler, you could check a dictionary and find out that I was wrong. A Lhasa apso is, in fact, a small Tibetan dog. There is no argument. But people do disagree about some supposed "facts": Do grades measure achievement? Are polygraph tests accurate? They also disagree about matters of "degree": Sexual discrimination exists in the marketplace, but is it "serious"? How prevalent and extreme are the economic inequities? What is "discrimination" anyway? *Definition* is a key to claims of fact: What do we mean by "detect lies"? Does "accurate" mean one hundred percent of the time? Ninety percent? Eighty percent? What does "serious discrimination" mean? Does the fact that female workers currently earn only sixty-seven cents for every dollar that male workers earn qualify as "serious discrimination"?

In an excerpt from *Crabgrass Frontier: The Suburbanization of the United States*, historian Kenneth T. Jackson argues that large shopping malls are not, as some boosters suggest, "taking the place of the old

central business district" in many cities. Instead, they are a new phenomenon, something that is almost the opposite of the old downtown
business centers. In the following two paragraphs, he makes a claim of
fact and then tries to convince us about the true nature of the mega-
mall.

> Boosters of such mega-malls argue that they are taking the place of the
> old central business districts and becoming the identifiable collecting
> points for the rootless families of the newer areas. As weekend and
> afternoon attractions, they have a special lure for teenagers, who often
> go there on shopping dates or to see the opposite sex. . . . They are also
> especially attractive to mothers with young children and to the elderly,
> many of whom visit regularly to get out of the house without having to
> worry about crime or inclement weather.

> In reality, even the largest malls are almost the opposite of downtown
> areas because they are self-contained and because they impose a unifor-
> mity of tastes and interests. They cater exclusively to middle-class tastes
> and contain no unsavory bars or pornography shops, no threatening-
> looking characters, no litter, no rain, and no excessive heat or cold. As
> Anthony Zube-Jackson has noted, their emphasis on cleanliness and
> safety is symptomatic of a very lopsided view of urban culture.

Claims About Cause and Effect

- Cigarettes cause lung cancer.
- Capital punishment does not deter violent crime.
- Rock music weakens the moral fiber of America's youth.

Unlike the claim "Grades affect admission to college," these
claims about cause and effect are debatable. The claim that cigarettes
cause lung cancer is, of course, less debatable than it was twenty years
ago, before the evidence demonstrating the link became overwhelming. The deterring effect of capital punishment is still an arguable
proposition with reasonable arguments on both sides. The argument
that rock music weakens the moral fiber of youth is certainly debatable; the writer would have to counter the argument that rock music
sometimes raises social consciousness and fights world hunger.

In a selection from her book, *The Plug-In Drug: Television,
Children, and the Family,* Marie Winn argues that television has a negative effect on family life. In her opening paragraphs, she sets forth
both sides of the controversy and then argues that the overall effect is
negative:

> Television's contribution to family life has been an equivocal one. For
> while it has, indeed, kept the members of the family from dispersing, it
> has not served to bring them *together*. By its domination of the time fam-
> ilies spend together, it destroys the special quality that depends to a

great extent on what a family *does,* what special rituals, games, recurrent jokes, familiar songs, and shared activities it accumulates.

"Like the sorcerer of old," writes Urie Bronfenbrenner, "the television set casts its magic spell, freezing speech and action, turning the living into silent statues so long as the enchantment lasts. The primary danger of the television screen lies not so much in the behavior it produces—although there is danger there—as in the behavior it prevents: the talks, the games, the family festivities and arguments through which much of the child's learning takes place and through which his character is formed. Turning on the television set can turn off the process that transforms children into people."

Yet parents have accepted a television-dominated family life so completely that they cannot see how the medium is involved in whatever problems they might be having. . . .

Claims About Value

- Boxing is a dehumanizing sport.
- The Ford Edsel is the ugliest automobile ever built in America.
- Toni Morrison is a great American novelist.

Claims about value lead to evaluative essays. All the strategies discussed in Chapter 7 apply here, with the additional requirement that you must counter opposing arguments. The argumentative essay that attempts to prove that boxing is dehumanizing must refute the argument that boxing is merely another form of competition that promotes athletic excellence. Arguing that Morrison is a great American novelist requires setting criteria for great American novels and then refuting critics who argue that Morrison's talent does not reach those standards.

In "College Is a Waste of Time and Money," teacher and journalist Caroline Bird argues that many students go to college simply because it is the "thing to do." For those students, Bird claims, college is not a good idea.

Nowadays, says one sociologist, you don't have to have a reason for going to college; it's an institution. His definition of an institution is an arrangement everyone accepts without question; the burden of proof is not on why you go, but why anyone thinks there might be a reason for not going. The implication is that an 18-year-old . . . should listen to those who know best and go to college.

I don't agree. I believe that college has to be judged not on what other people think is good for students, but on how good it feels to the students themselves.

I believe that people have an inside view of what's good for them. If a child doesn't want to go to school some morning, better let him stay at home, at least until you find out why. Maybe he knows something you don't. It's the same with college. If high-school graduates don't want to go, or if they don't want to go right away, they may perceive more clearly than their elders that college is not for them. It is no longer obvious that adolescents are best off studying a core curriculum that was constructed when all educated men could agree on what made them educated, or that professors, advisors, or parents can be of any particular help to young people in choosing a major or a career. High-school graduates see college graduates driving cabs and decide it's not worth going. College students find no intellectual stimulation in their studies and drop out.

Claims About Solutions or Policies

- Students with AIDS should be allowed to attend classes.

- The penalty for drunk driving should be a mandatory jail sentence and loss of driver's license.

- To reduce exploitation and sensationalism, the news media should not be allowed to interview victims of crime or disaster.

Claims about solutions or policies sometimes occur *along with* a claim of fact, cause and effect, or value. Because grades do not measure achievement (argue that this is a fact), they should be abolished (argue for this policy). Boxing is a dehumanizing sport (argue this claim of value); therefore, boxing should be banned (argue for this solution). Claims about solutions or policies involve all the strategies used for problem solving (see Chapter 8), but with special emphasis on countering opposing arguments: "Students with AIDS should be allowed to attend classes because attending school is their constitutional right and because AIDS is not transmitted by the kind of casual contact that occurs among schoolchildren."

In *When Society Becomes an Addict*, psychotherapist Anne Wilson Schaef argues that our society has become an "Addictive System" that has many characteristics in common with alcoholism and other addictions. Advertising becomes addictive, causing us to behave dishonestly. The social pressure to be "nice" can become addictive, causing us to lie to ourselves. Schaef argues that the solution for our social addictions begins when we face the reality of our dependency.

> We cannot recover from an addiction unless we first admit that we have it. Naming our reality is essential to recovery. Unless we admit that we are indeed functioning in an addictive process in an Addictive System, we shall never have the option of recovery. Once we name something, we own it. . . . Remember, to name the system as addict is not to condemn it: it is to offer it the possibility of recovery.

> Paradoxically, the only way to reclaim our personal power is by admitting our powerlessness. The first part of Step One of the AA [Alcoholics

Anonymous] Twelve-Step Program reads, "We admitted we were powerless over alcohol." It is important to recognize that admitting to powerlessness over an addiction is not the same as admitting powerlessness
as a person. In fact, it can be very power-full to recognize the futility of
the illusion of control.

Appeals for Written Argument

To support a claim and refute opposing arguments, writers use *appeals*
to the audience. Argument uses three important types of appeals: to
reason (logic and evidence support the claim), to *character* (the writer's
good character itself supports the claim), and to *emotion* (the writer's
expression of feelings about the issue may support the claim).
Effective arguments emphasize the appeal to reason but may also
appeal to character or emotion.

Appeal to Reason   An appeal to reason depends most frequently
on *inductive logic,* which is sometimes called the "scientific method."
Inductive logic draws a general conclusion from personal observation
or experience, specific facts, reports, statistics, testimony of authorities, and other bits of data.

Experience is the best teacher, we always say, and experience
teaches inductively. Suppose, using biologist Thomas Huxley's
famous example, you pick a green apple from a tree and take a bite.
Halfway through the bite you discover that the apple is sour and
quickly spit it out. But, you think, perhaps the next green apple will be
ripe and will taste better. You pick a second green apple, take a bite,
and realize it is just as sour as the first. You know that some apples—
like the Granny Smith—look green even when they're ripe, so you
take a bite out of a third apple. It is also sour. You're beginning to
draw a conclusion. In fact, if you taste a fourth or fifth apple, other
people may begin to question your intelligence. How many green
apples from this tree must you taste before you get the idea that all of
these green apples are sour?

Experience, however, may lead to the wrong conclusion. You've
tasted enough of these apples to convince *you* that all these apples are
sour, but will others think that these apples are sour? Perhaps you
have funny taste buds. You may need to ask several friends to taste
the apples. Or perhaps you are dealing with a slightly weird tree—in
fact, some apple trees are hybrids, with several different kinds of
apples grafted onto one tree. Before you draw a conclusion, you may
need to consult an expert, to be certain that your tree is a standard,
single-variety apple tree. If your friends and the expert also agree that
all of these green apples are sour, you may use your experience and

their testimony to reach a conclusion—and to provide evidence to make your argument more convincing to others.

In inductive logic, a reasonable conclusion is based on a *sufficient* quantity of accurate and reliable evidence, selected in a *random* manner to reduce human bias or take into account variation in the sample. The definition of "sufficient" varies, but generally the number must be large enough to convince your audience that your sample fairly represents the whole subject.

Let's take an example to illustrate inductive reasoning. Suppose you ask a student, one of fifty in a Psychology I class, a question of value: "Is Professor X a good teacher?" If this student says, "Professor X is the worst teacher I've ever had!" what conclusion can you draw? If you avoid taking the class based on a sample of one, you may miss an excellent class. So you decide to gather a *sufficient sample* by polling twenty of the fifty students in the class. But which twenty do you interview? If you ask the first student for a list of students, you may receive the names of twenty other students who also hate the professor. To reduce human or accidental bias, then, you choose a *random* method for collecting your evidence: As the students leave the class, you give a questionnaire to two out of every five students. If they all fill out the questionnaires, you probably have a *sufficient* and *random* sample.

Finally, if the responses to your questionnaire show that fifteen out of twenty students rate Professor X as an excellent teacher, what *valid conclusion* should you draw? You should not say, categorically, "X is an excellent teacher." Your conclusion must be restricted by your evidence and the method of gathering your evidence: "Seventy-five percent of the students polled in Psychology I believe that Professor X is an excellent teacher."

Most arguments use a shorthand version of the inductive method of reasoning. A writer makes a *claim* and then supports it with *reasons* and representative *examples* or *data*.

Claim:	Professor X is an excellent psychology teacher.
Reason #1:	Professor X is an excellent teacher because she gives stimulating lectures that students rarely miss.
	Evidence: Sixty percent of the students polled said that they rarely missed a lecture. Three students cited Professor X's lecture on "assertiveness" as the best lecture they'd ever heard.
Reason #2:	Professor X is an excellent teacher because she gives tests that encourage learning rather than sheer memorization.

Evidence: Seventy percent of the students polled said that Professor X's essay tests required thinking and learning rather than memorization. One student said that Professor X's tests always made her think about what she'd read. Another student said she always liked to discuss Professor X's test questions with her classmates and friends.

Appeal to Character   An appeal to your good character as a writer can also be important in argument. (The appeal to character is frequently called the "ethical" appeal because readers make a value judgment about the writer's character.) In a written argument, you show your audience—through your reasonable persona, voice, and tone—that you are a person who abides by moral standards that your audience shares: You have a good reputation, you are honest and trustworthy, and you argue "fairly."

A person's reputation often affects how we react to a claim, but also the *argument itself* should establish the writer's trustworthiness. You don't have to be an Eleanor Roosevelt or a Mahatma Gandhi to generate a strong ethical appeal for your claim. Even if your readers have never heard your name before, they will feel confident about your character if you are knowledgeable about your subject, present the pros and cons fairly, and support your own claim with sufficient, reliable evidence.

If your readers have reason to suspect your motives or think you may have something personal to gain from your argument, you may need to bend over backward to be fair. If you do have something to gain, lay your cards on the table. Declare your vested interest, but explain, for example, how your solution would benefit everyone equally. Similarly, you don't try to cover up or distort the opponents' arguments; you acknowledge the opposition's strong arguments and you refute the weak ones.

Appeal to Emotion   Appeals to emotion can be tricky because, as we have seen, when emotions come in through the door, reasonableness may fly out the window. Argument emphasizes reason, not emotion. We know, for example, how advertising plays on emotions, by means of loaded or exaggerated language or through images of famous or sexy people. Emotional appeals designed to *deceive* or *frighten* people or to *misrepresent* the virtues of a person, place, or object have no place in rational argument. But emotional appeals that illustrate a truth or movingly depict a reality are a legitimate and effective means of convincing your readers.

Combined Appeals   Appeals may be used in combination. Writers may appeal to reason and, at the same time, establish a trustworthy character and use legitimate emotional appeals. The following excerpt from Martin Luther King's "Letter from Birmingham Jail—April 16, 1963" illustrates all three appeals. He appeals to reason, arguing that, historically, civil rights reforms are rarely made without political pressure. He establishes his integrity and good character by treating the opposition (in this case, the Birmingham clergy) with respect and by showing moderation and restraint. Finally, he uses emotional appeals, describing his six-year-old daughter in tears and recalling his own humiliation at being refused a place to sleep. King uses these emotional appeals legitimately; he is not misrepresenting reality or trying to deceive his readers.

One of the basic points in [the statement by the Birmingham clergy] is that the action that I and my associates have taken in Birmingham is untimely. Some have asked: "Why didn't you give the new city administration time to act?" The only answer that I can give to this query is that the new Birmingham administration must be prodded about as much as the outgoing one, before it will act. We are sadly mistaken if we feel that the election of Albert Boutwell as mayor will bring the millennium to Birmingham. While Mr. Boutwell is a much more gentle person than Mr. Connor, they are both segregationists, dedicated to the maintenance of the status quo. I have hoped that Mr. Boutwell will be reasonable enough to see the futility of massive resistance to desegregation. But he will not see this without pressure from devotees of civil rights. My friends, I must say to you that we have not made a single gain in civil rights without determined legal and nonviolent pressure. Lamentably, it is an historical fact that privileged groups seldom give up their privileges voluntarily. Individuals may see the moral light and voluntarily give up their unjust posture; but, as Reinhold Niebuhr has reminded us, groups tend to be more immoral than individuals.

Appeal to Character and Appeal to Reason

Appeal to Reason

Evidence

We know through painful experience that freedom is never voluntarily given by the oppressor; it must be demanded by the oppressed. Frankly, I have yet to engage in a direct-action campaign that was "well timed" in the view of those who have not suffered unduly from the disease of segregation. For years now I have heard the word "Wait!" It rings in the ear of every Negro with piercing familiarity. This "Wait" has almost always meant "Never." We must come to see, with one of our distinguished jurists, that "justice too long delayed is justice denied."

Appeal to Character and Reason

We have waited for more than 340 years for our constitutional and God-given rights. . . . Perhaps it is easy for those who have never felt the stinging darts of segregation to say, "Wait." But when you have seen vicious mobs lynch your mothers and fathers at will and drown your sisters and brothers at whim; when you have seen hate-filled policemen curse, kick, and even kill your black brothers and sisters; when you see the vast majority of your twenty million Negro brothers smothering in

Appeal to Emotion Evidence

*Appeal to Emotion
Evidence*

an airtight cage of poverty in the midst of an affluent society; when you suddenly find your tongue twisted and your speech stammering as you seek to explain to your six-year-old daughter why she can't go to the public amusement park that has just been advertised on television, and see tears welling up in her eyes when she is told that Funtown is closed to colored children . . . when you take a cross-country drive and find it necessary to sleep night after night in the uncomfortable corners of your

*Appeal to Emotion
Evidence*

automobile because no motel will accept you; when you are humiliated day in and day out by nagging signs reading "white" and "colored"; when your first name becomes "nigger," your middle name becomes "boy" (however old you are) and your last name becomes "John" . . . —then you will understand why we find it difficult to wait. There comes a time when the cup of endurance runs over, and men are no longer willing to be plunged into the abyss of despair. I hope, sirs, you

Appeal to Character

can understand our legitimate and unavoidable impatience.

Rogerian Argument

Traditional argument presumes that the audience is not the opposition but a group of people who are relatively uninformed or undecided about the issue. Those with definite opposing views are a separate group of people, the writer's *adversaries.* The writer argues reasonably and fairly, but traditional argument becomes a kind of struggle or war as the writer attempts to "defeat" the arguments of the opposition. The purpose of the argument is to convince the undecided audience that the writer has "won a fight" and emerged "victorious" over the opposition.

In some arguments, however, the issues are particularly sensitive and the audience we are trying to persuade is, in fact, the opposition. In such cases, *Rogerian argument* —named after psychologist Carl Rogers—may be more effective than the traditional approach. Rogerian, or *nonthreatening* argument, opens the lines of communication by reducing conflict. When people's beliefs are attacked, they instinctively become defensive and strike back. As a result, the argument becomes polarized: The writer argues for a claim, the reader digs in to defend his or her position, and no one budges.

Crucial to Rogerian argument is the fact that convictions and beliefs are not abstract but reside in people. If people are to agree, they must be sensitive to each other's beliefs. Rogerian argument, therefore, contains a clear appeal to character. Rogerian argument uses reason and logic, but its primary goal is not to "win" the argument but to open the lines of communication. To do that, the writer must be sympathetic to different points of view and willing to modify his or her claims in response to the opposing arguments. Once the reader sees that the writer is open to change, the reader may become more flexible.

Once both sides are more flexible, a compromise position or solution becomes possible. As Rogers says, "This procedure gradually achieves a mutual communication. Mutual communication tends to be pointed toward solving a problem rather than toward attacking a person or group." Rogerian argument, then, imitates not a courtroom debate, but the mutual communication that may take place between two people. Whereas traditional argument intends to change the actions or the beliefs of the opposition, Rogerian argument works toward changes *in both sides* as a means of establishing common ground and reaching a solution.

If you choose Rogerian argument, remember that you must actually be willing to change your beliefs. Often, in fact, when you need to use Rogerian argument most, you may be least inclined to use it—simply because you are inflexible on that issue. If you are unwilling to modify your own position, your reader will sense your basic insincerity and realize that you are just playing a trick of rhetoric.

Rogerian argument is appropriate in a variety of sensitive or highly controversial situations. You may want to choose Rogerian argument if you are an employer requesting union members to accept a pay cut in order to help the company avoid bankruptcy. Similarly, if you argue to husbands that they should assume responsibility for half of the housework, or if you argue to Anglo-Americans that Spanish language and culture should play a larger role in public education, you may want to use a Rogerian strategy. By showing that you empathize with the opposition's position and are willing to compromise, you create a climate for mutual communication.

Rogerian argument makes a claim, considers the opposition, and presents evidence to support your claim, but in addition it avoids threatening or adversarial language and promotes mutual communication and learning. A Rogerian argument uses the following strategies:

- **Avoiding a *confrontational stance.*** Confrontation threatens your audience and increases their defensiveness. Threat hinders communication.

- **Presenting your *character* as someone who understands and can empathize with the opposition.** Show that you understand by restating the opposing position accurately.

- **Establishing *common ground* with the opposition.** Indicate the beliefs and values that you share.

- **Being willing to *change your views.*** Show where your position is not reasonable and could be modified.

- **Directing your argument toward a *compromise or workable solution.***

Note: An argument does not have to be either entirely adversarial or entirely Rogerian. You may use Rogerian techniques for the most sensitive points in an argument that is otherwise traditional or confrontational.

In his essay "Animal Rights Versus Human Health," biology professor Albert Rosenfeld illustrates several features of Rogerian argument. Rosenfeld argues that animals should be used for medical experiments, but he is aware that the issues are emotional and that his audience is likely to be antagonistic. In these paragaphs, Rosenfeld avoids threatening language, represents the opposition fairly, grants that he is guilty of specieism, and says that he sympathizes with the demand to look for alternatives. He indicates that his position is flexible: Most researchers, he says, are delighted when they can use alternatives. He grants that there is some room for compromise, but he is firm in his position that some animal experimentation is necessary for advancements in medicine.

States Opposing Position Fairly and Sympathetically

It is fair to say that millions of animals—probably more rats and mice than any other species—are subjected to experiments that cause them pain, discomfort, and distress, sometimes lots of it over long periods of time. . . . All new forms of medication or surgery are tried out on animals first. Every new substance that is released into the environment, or put on the market, is tested on animals. . . .

States Opposing Position Fairly

In 1975, Australian philosopher Peter Singer wrote his influential book called *Animal Liberation,* in which he accuses us all of "speciesism"—as reprehensible, to him, as racism or sexism. He freely describes the "pain and suffering" inflicted in the "tyranny of human over nonhuman animals" and sharply challenges our biblical license to exercise "dominion over the fish of the sea, and over the fowl of the air, and over every living thing that moveth upon the Earth."

Acknowledges Common Ground

Sympathetic to Opposing Position

Well, certainly we are guilty of speciesism. We do act as if we had dominion over other living creatures. But domination also entails some custodial responsibility. And the questions continue to be raised: Do we have the right to abuse animals? To eat them? To hunt them for sport? To keep them imprisoned in zoos—or, for that matter, in our households? Especially to do experiments on these creatures who can't fight back?

Suggests Compromise Position

Hardly any advance in either human or veterinary medicine—cure, vaccine, operation, drug, therapy—has come about without experiments on animals. . . . I certainly sympathize with the demand that we look for ways to get the information we want without using animals. Most investigators are delighted when they can get their data by means of tissue cultures or computer simulations. But as we look for alternative ways to get information, do we meanwhile just do without?

WARMING UP: JOURNAL EXERCISES

1. From the following list of "should" statements, choose *one* that relates to your experience and freewrite for ten minutes. When you finish your freewriting, state a *claim* and list arguments on both sides of the issue.

> Tuition should be free at state universities.
>
> Bicyclists should be subject to regular traffic laws, including DWI.
>
> Every citizen should carry a handgun.
>
> Unions should be abolished.
>
> NCAA football should have playoffs.
>
> High-quality child care should be available to all working parents at public expense.
>
> Computer literacy courses should be required at the college level.
>
> Police should carry mace, not guns.
>
> Fraternities and sororities should be forbidden to serve alcoholic beverages during rush.
>
> Students should work for one year between high school and college.
>
> Businesses should be required to provide free health insurance for all employees.
>
> Rock music should be rated and labeled, from "GP" to "X," as films are.
>
> Unsportsmanlike behavior in tennis should result in a match forfeit.
>
> Drug tests should be required for your job or at your school.
>
> Nonmajor courses should be graded pass/fail.
>
> Freshmen should be permitted to have cars on campus.

2. Controversial subjects depend as much on the audience as they do on the issue itself. Make a quick list of things you do every day—the kind of clothes you wear, the food you eat, the books you read, the friends you have, the ideas you discuss. For *one* of these activities, imagine a person who might find what you do immoral, illogical, unjust, or unhealthy. What claim might they make about your activity? What reasons or evidence might they use to argue that your activity should be abolished, outlawed, or changed? Write for five minutes arguing *their* point of view.

3. Television and television advertising are often the subject of much criticism, such as in Marie Winn's excerpt from "The Effects of Television on Family Life." Write a letter to Marie Winn, to your local or college newspaper, or to members of the PTA in your city defending the *positive* effects or value of television. Cite *one* particular program or commercial as an example.

4. Grades are important, but in some courses they get in the way of learning. Choose an actual course you have taken and write an open letter to the school administration, arguing for Credit/No Credit grading in that particular course. You intend to submit your letter to the campus newspaper.

5. News items often contain incidents that spark arguments about morality or justice. Choose one of the following incidents (or a recent controversial news story), and write out the arguments for or against the action taken in each case. (For more information on each of these incidents, check the *Readers' Guide* or ask a librarian to assist you.)

    —Intimidated by fear of muggings in the New York subway system, Bernard Goetz responds to his perception of a holdup by shooting four black teen-agers.

    —A Long Island judge sentences Cheryl Pierson, the victim of frequent and repeated rape and incest by her father, to six months in prison for conspiracy in the death of her father.

    —Fearing for the lives of their children, parents force school administrators in Florida to deny admission to three boys with AIDS. In response, a federal judge orders that they be admitted to their elementary school.

    —In response to threats of terrorist violence from a heavily armed radical group called MOVE, the Philadelphia police engage in "protective reaction" and bomb the barricaded headquarters of MOVE, starting a fire that leaves 260 people in the black neighborhood homeless.

6. Does the following cartoon from Gary Larson's "The Far Side" make a statement? Citing specific details from the cartoon, write a paragraph that explains the "point" of the cartoon (if there is one). (If "The Far Side" is not one of your favorites, choose another cartoon that makes a controversial point, and explain the "claim" it makes.)

ARGUING: PROFESSIONAL WRITING

DARWIN'S MIDDLE ROAD

Stephen Jay Gould

In his distinguished career as a spokesperson for the wonders of biology and the theory of evolution, Harvard professor Stephen Jay Gould has written dozens of scientific and popular articles and has published several collections of essays and award-winning books, including Ever Since Darwin *(1977),* The Panda's Thumb *(1980),* Hen's Teeth and Horse's Toes *(1983),* The Flamingo's Smile *(1985), and* Time's Arrow, Time's Cycle *(1987). "Science is not a heartless pursuit of objective information," Gould has said, "it is a creative human activity." That idea is clearly illustrated in "Darwin's Middle Road." Gould opens the essay with an episode from Homer's epic poem* The Odyssey. *At one point during his adventures, Odysseus must sail between two fearful dangers, between the horrible six-headed monster Scylla and the giant ocean whirlpool created by Charybdis. Odysseus' predicament dramatizes the focus of this essay.*

Gould's subject is the nature of scientific creativity and his central question is whether great scientific theories are based on purely inductive, data-driven research or whether they arise primarily from intuition, hunches, and flashes of genius. Gould's claim is that the theory of natural selection sprang from Darwin's unique blending of careful, inductive observation with reflection, intuition, and synthesis.

"We began to sail up the narrow strait lamenting," narrates Odysseus. "For on the one hand lay Scylla, with twelve feet all dangling down; and six necks exceeding long, and on each a hideous head, and therein three rows of teeth set thick and close, full of black death. And on the other mighty Charybdis sucked down the salt sea water. As often as she belched it forth, like a cauldron on a great fire she would seethe up through all her troubled deeps." Odysseus managed to swerve around Charybdis, but Scylla grabbed six of his finest men and devoured them in his sight—"the most pitiful thing mine eyes have seen of all my travail in searching out the paths of the sea."   (1)

False lures and dangers often come in pairs in our legends and metaphors—consider the frying pan and the fire, or the devil and the deep blue sea. Prescriptions for avoidance either emphasize a dogged steadiness—the straight and narrow of Christian evangelists—or an averaging between unpleasant alternatives—the golden mean of Aristotle. The idea of steering a course between undesirable extremes emerges as a central prescription for a sensible life.   (2)

The nature of scientific creativity is both a perennial topic of discussion and a prime candidate for seeking a golden mean. The two extreme positions have not been directly competing for allegiance of the unwary. They have, rather, replaced each other sequentially, with one now in the ascendency, the other eclipsed.   (3)

The first—inductivism—held that great scientists are primarily great observers and patient accumulators of information. For new and significant theory, the inductivists claimed, can only arise from a firm foundation of facts. In this architectural view, each fact is a brick in a structure built without blueprints. Any talk or thought about theory (the completed building) is fatuous and premature before the bricks are set. Inductivism once commanded great prestige within science, and even represented an "official" position of sorts, for it touted, however falsely, the utter honesty, complete objectivity, and almost automatic nature of scientific progress towards final and incontrovertible truth.   (4)

Yet, as its critics so rightly claimed, inductivism also depicted science as a heartless, almost inhuman discipline offering no legitimate place to quirkiness, intuition, and all the other subjective attributes adhering to our vernacular notion of genius. Great scientists, the critics claimed, are distinguished more by their powers of hunch and synthesis, than their skill in experiment or observation. The criticisms of inductivism are certainly valid and I welcome its dethroning during the past thirty years as a necessary prelude to better understanding. Yet, in attacking it so strongly, some critics have tried to substitute an alternative equally extreme and unproductive in its emphasis on the essential subjectivity of creative thought. In this, "eureka" view, creativity is an ineffable something, accessible only to persons of genius. It arises like a bolt of lightning, unanticipated, unpredictable and unanalyzable—but the bolts strike only a few special people. We ordinary mortals must stand in awe and thanks. (The name refers, of course, to the legendary story of Archimedes running naked through the streets of Syracuse shouting eureka [I have discovered it] when water displaced by his bathing body washed the scales abruptly from his eyes and suggested a method for measuring volumes.)   (5)

I am equally disenchanted by both these opposing extremes. Inductivism reduces genius to dull, rote operations; eurekaism grants it an inaccessible status more in the domain of intrinsic mystery than in a realm where we might understand and learn from it. Might we not marry the good features of each view, and abandon both the elitism of eurekaism and the pedestrian qualities of inductivism. May we not acknowledge the personal and subjective character of creativity, but still comprehend it as a mode of thinking that emphasizes or exaggerates capacities sufficiently common to all of us that we may at least understand if not hope to imitate.   (6)

In the hagiography of science, a few men hold such high positions that all arguments must apply to them if they are to have any validity. Charles Darwin, as the principal saint of evolutionary biology, has therefore been presented both as an inductivist and as a primary example of eurekaism. I will attempt to show that these interpretations are equally inadequate, and that recent scholarship on Darwin's own odyssey towards the theory of natural selection supports an intermediate position.   (7)

So great was the prestige of inductivism in his own day, that Darwin himself fell under its sway and, as an old man, falsely depicted his youthful accomplishments in its light. In an autobiography, written as a lesson in morality for his children and not intended for publication, he penned some famous lines that misled historians for nearly a hundred years. Describing his path to the theory of natural selection, he claimed: "I worked on true Baconian principles, and without any theory collected facts on a wholesale scale."   (8)

The inductivist interpretation focuses on Darwin's five years aboard the *Beagle* and explains his transition from a student for the ministry to the nemesis of preachers as the result of his keen powers of observation applied to the whole world. Thus, the traditional story goes, Darwin's eyes opened wider and wider as he saw, in sequence, the bones of giant South American fossil mammals, the turtles and finches of the Galapagos, and the marsupial fauna of Australia. The truth of evolution and its mechanism of natural selection crept up gradually upon him as he sifted facts in a sieve of utter objectivity.   (9)

The inadequacies of this tale are best illustrated by the falsity of its conventional premier example—the so-called Darwin's finches of the Galapagos. We now know that although these birds share a recent and common ancestry on the South American mainland, they have radiated into an impressive array of species on the outlying Galapagos. Few terrestrial species manage to cross the wide oceanic barrier between South America and the Galapagos. But the fortunate migrants often find a sparsely inhabited world devoid of the competitors that limit their opportunities on the crowded mainland. Hence, the finches evolved into roles normally occupied by other birds and developed their famous set of adaptations for feeding—seed crushing, insect eating, even grasping and manipulating a cactus needle to dislodge insects from plants. Isolation—both of the islands from the mainland and among the islands themselves—provided an opportunity for separation, independent adaptation, and speciation.   (10)

According to the traditional view, Darwin discovered these finches, correctly inferred their history, and wrote the famous lines in his notebook: "If there is the slightest foundation for these remarks the zoology of Archipelagoes will be worth examining; for such facts would undermine the stability of Species." But, as with so many heroic tales from Washington's cherry tree to the piety of Crusaders, hope rather than truth motivates the common reading. Darwin found the finches to be sure. But he didn't recognize them as variants of a common stock. In fact, he didn't even record the island of discovery for many of them—some of his labels just read "Galapagos Islands." So much for his immediate recognition of the role of isolation in the formation of new species. He reconstructed the evolutionary tale only after his return to London, when a British Museum ornithologist correctly identified all the birds as finches.   (11)

The famous quotation from his notebook refers to Galapagos tortoises and to the claim of native inhabitants that they can "at once pronounce from which Island any Tortoise may have been brought" from subtle differences in size and shape of body and scales. This is a statement of different, and much reduced, order from the traditional tale of finches. For the finches are true and separate species—a living example of evolution. The subtle differences among tortoises represent minor geographic variation within a species. It is a jump in reasoning, albeit a valid one as we now know, to argue that such small differences can be amplified to produce a new species. All creationists, after all, acknowledged geographic variation (consider human races), but argued that it could not proceed beyond the rigid limits of a created archetype.   (12)

I don't wish to downplay the pivotal influence of the *Beagle* voyage on Darwin's career. It gave him space, freedom and endless time to think in his favored mode of independent self-stimulation. (His ambivalence towards university life, and his middling performance there by conventional standards, reflected his unhappiness with a curriculum of received wisdom.) He writes from South America in 1834: "I have not one clear idea about cleavage, stratification, lines of upheaval. I have no books, which tell me much and what they do I cannot apply to what I see. In consequence I draw my own conclusions, and most gloriously ridiculous ones they are." The rocks and plants and animals that he saw did provoke him to the crucial attitude of doubt—midwife of all creativity. Sydney, Australia—1836. Darwin wonders why a rational God would create so many marsupials on Australia since nothing about its climate or geography suggests any superiority for pouches: "I had been lying on a sunny bank and was reflecting on the strange character of the animals of this country as compared to the rest of the World. An unbeliever in everything beyond his own reason might exclaim, 'Surely two distinct Creators must have been at work.'"   (13)

Nonetheless, Darwin returned to London without an evolutionary theory. He suspected the truth of evolution, but had no mechanism to explain it. Natural selection did not arise from any direct reading of the *Beagle's* facts, but from two subsequent years of thought and struggle as reflected in a series of remarkable notebooks that have been unearthed and published during the past twenty years. In these notebooks, we see Darwin testing and abandoning a number of theories and pursuing a multitude of false leads—so much for his later claim about recording facts with an empty mind. He read philosophers, poets, and economists, always searching for meaning and insight—so much for the notion that natural selection arose inductively from the *Beagle's* facts. Later, he labelled one notebook as "full of metaphysics on morals."   (14)

Yet if this tortuous path belies the Scylla of inductivism, it has engendered an equally simplistic myth—the Charybdis of eurekaism. In his maddeningly misleading autobiography, Darwin does record a eureka and suggests that natural selection struck him as a sudden, serendipitous flash after more than a year of groping frustration:

> In October 1838, that is, fifteen months after I had begun my systematic inquiry, I happened to read for amusement Malthus on Population, and being well prepared to appreciate the struggle for existence which

everywhere goes on from long-continued observation of the habits of animals and plants, it at once struck me that under these circumstances favorable variations would tend to be preserved, and unfavorable ones to be destroyed. The result of this would be the formation of new species. Here, then, I had at last got a theory by which to work.   (15)

Yet, again, the notebooks belie Darwin's later recollections—in this case by their utter failure to record, at the time it happened, any special exultation over his Malthusian insight. He inscribes it as a fairly short and sober entry without a single exclamation point, though he habitually used two or three in moments of excitement. He did not drop everything and reinterpret a confusing world in its light. On the very next day, he wrote an even longer passage on the sexual curiosity of primates.   (16)

The theory of natural selection arose neither as a workmanlike induction from nature's facts, nor as a mysterious bolt from Darwin's subconscious, triggered by an accidental reading of Malthus. It emerged instead as the result of a conscious and productive search, proceeding in a ramifying but ordered manner, and utilizing both the facts of natural history and an astonishingly broad range of insights from disparate disciplines far from his own. Darwin trod the middle path between inductivism and eurekaism. His genius is neither pedestrian nor inaccessible.   (17)

Darwinian scholarship has exploded since the centennial of the *Origin* in 1959. The publication of Darwin's notebooks and the attention devoted by several scholars to the two crucial years between the *Beagle's* docking and the demoted Malthusian insight has clinched the argument for a "middle path" theory of Darwin's creativity. Two particularly important works focus on the broadest and narrowest scales. Howard E. Gruber's masterful intellectual and psychological biography of this phase in Darwin's life, *Darwin on Man*, traces all the false leads and turning points in Darwin's search. Gruber shows that Darwin was continually proposing, testing, and abandoning hypotheses, and that he never simply collected facts in a blind way. He began with a fanciful theory involving the idea that new species arise with a prefixed life span, and worked his way gradually, if fitfully, towards an idea of extinction by competition in a world of struggle. He recorded no exultation upon reading Malthus, because the jigsaw puzzle was only missing a piece or two at the time.   (18)

Silvan S. Schweber has reconstructed, in detail as minute as the record will allow, Darwin's activities during the few weeks before Malthus (The Origin of the *Origin* Revisited, *Journal of the History of Biology*, 1977). He argues that the final pieces arose not from new facts in natural history, but from Darwin's intellectual wanderings in distant fields. In particular, he read a long review of social scientist and philosopher Auguste Comte's most famous work, the *Cours de philoso-*

phie positive. He was particularly struck by Comte's insistence that a proper theory be predictive and at least potentially quantitative. He then turned to Dugald Stewart's *On the Life and Writing of Adam Smith,* and imbibed the basic belief of the Scottish economists that theories of overall social structure must begin by analyzing the unconstrained actions of individuals. (Natural selection is, above all, a theory about the struggle of individual organisms for success in reproduction.) Then, searching for quantification, he read a lengthy analysis of work by the most famous statistician of his time—the Belgian Adolphe Quetelet. In the review of Quetelet, he found, among other things, a forceful statement of Malthus's quantitative claim—that population would grow geometrically and food supplies only arithmetically, thus guaranteeing an intense struggle for existence. In fact, Darwin had read the Malthusian statement several times before; but only now was he prepared to appreciate its significance. Thus, he did not turn to Malthus by accident, and he already knew what it contained. His "amusement," we must assume, consisted only in a desire to read in its original formulation the familiar statement that had so impressed him in Quetelet's secondary account.   (19)

In reading Schweber's detailed account of the moments preceding Darwin's formulation of natural selection, I was particularly struck by the absence of deciding influence from his own field of biology. The immediate precipitators were a social scientist, an economist, and a statistician. If genius has any common denominator, I would propose breadth of interest and the ability to construct fruitful analogies between fields.   (20)

In fact, I believe that the theory of natural selection should be viewed as an extended analogy—whether conscious or unconscious on Darwin's part I do not know—to the laissez faire economics of Adam Smith. The essence of Smith's argument is a paradox of sorts: if you want an ordered economy providing maximal benefits to all, then let individuals compete and struggle for their own advantages. The result, after appropriate sorting and elimination of the inefficient, will be a stable and harmonious polity. Apparent order arises naturally from the struggle among individuals, not from predestined principles or higher control. Dugald Stewart epitomized Smith's system in the book Darwin read:

> The most effective plan for advancing a people . . . is by allowing every man, as long as he observes the rules of justice, to pursue his own interest in his own way, and to bring both his industry and his capital into the freest competition with those of his fellow citizens. Every system of policy which endeavors . . . to draw towards a particular species of industry a greater share of the capital of the society than would naturally go to it . . . is, in reality, subversive of the great purpose which it means to promote.

As Schweber states: "The Scottish analysis of society contends that the combined effect of individual actions results in the institutions upon which society is based, and that such a society is a stable and evolving one and functions without a designing and directing mind." (21)

We know that Darwin's uniqueness does not reside in his support for the idea of evolution—scores of scientists had preceded him in this. His special contribution rests upon his documentation and upon the novel character of his theory about how evolution operates. Previous evolutionists had proposed unworkable schemes based on internal perfecting tendencies and inherent directions. Darwin advocated a natural and testable theory based on immediate interaction among individuals (his opponents considered it heartlessly mechanistic). The theory of natural selection is a creative transfer to biology of Adam Smith's basic argument for a rational economy: the balance and order of nature does not arise from a higher, external (divine) control, or from the existence of laws operating directly upon the whole, but from struggle among individuals for their own benefits (in modern terms, for the transmission of their genes to future generations through differential success in reproduction). (22)

Many people are distressed to hear such an argument. Does it not compromise the integrity of science if some of its primary conclusions originate by analogy from contemporary politics and culture rather than from data of the discipline itself? In a famous letter to Engels, Karl Marx identified the similarities between natural selection and the English social scene:

> It is remarkable how Darwin recognizes among beasts and plants his English society with its division of labor, competition, opening up of new markets, 'invention,' and the Malthusian 'struggle for existence.' It is Hobbes' *bellum omnium contra omnes* (the war of all against all).

Yet Marx was a great admirer of Darwin—and in this apparent paradox lies resolution. For reasons involving all the themes I have emphasized here—that inductivism is inadequate, that creativity demands breadth, and that analogy is a profound source of insight—great thinkers cannot be divorced from their social background. But the source of an idea is one thing; its truth or fruitfulness is another. The psychology and utility of discovery are very different subjects indeed. Darwin may have cribbed the idea of natural selection from economics, but it may still be right. As the German socialist Karl Kautsky wrote in 1902: "The fact that an idea emanates from a particular class, or accords with their interests, of course proves nothing as to its truth or falsity." In this case, it is ironic that Adam Smith's system of laissez faire does not work in his own domain of economics, for it leads to oligopoly and revolution, rather than to order and harmony. Struggle among individuals does, however, seem to be the law of nature. (23)

Many people use such arguments about social context to ascribe great insights primarily to the indefinable phenomenon of good luck. Thus, Darwin was lucky to be born rich, lucky to be on the *Beagle*, lucky to live amidst the ideas of his age, lucky to trip over Parson Malthus—essentially little more than a man in the right place at the right time. Yet, when we read of his personal struggle to understand, the breadth of his concerns and study, and the directedness of his search for a mechanism of evolution, we understand why Pasteur made his famous quip that fortune favors the prepared mind.   (24)

VOCABULARY

In your journal, write the meanings of the following words.

- in the *ascendency*   (3)
- is *fatuous*   (4)
- an *ineffable* something   (5)
- the *hagiography* of science   (7)
- the *nemesis* of preachers   (9)
- the *marsupial fauna* of Australia   (9)
- *speciation*   (10)
- British Museum *ornithologist*   (11)
- a created *archetype*   (12)
- *ambivalence* towards university life   (13)
- *metaphysics* on morals   (14)
- *serendipitous* flash   (15)
- the immediate *precipitators*   (20)
- an extended *analogy*   (21)
- *laissez faire* economics   (21)
- harmonious *polity*   (21)
- leads to *oligopoly*   (23)

QUESTIONS FOR WRITING AND DISCUSSION

1. In your own words, explain the two "extremes" of inductivism and eurekaism. Describe Darwin's middle path through these extremes.

2. In the course of his essay, Gould defines both "genius" and "natural selection." Identify sentences from the essay that describe or define these terms.

3. Argument begins with a debatable proposition or question. In your own words, state the question that Gould addresses. Identify the "pro" side of this argument (Gould's position) and the "con" side (the position Gould argues against).

4. Refutations of opposing positions must, in argument, be supported by evidence, testimony, facts, statistics, or other data. Find two paragraphs in which Gould refutes an opposing argument. List the evidence Gould provides in that paragraph. Which evidence best supports Gould's argument?

5. Gould has written a monthly column, "This View of Life," for *Natural History* magazine. Review a copy of *Natural History* and then profile Gould's intended audience. Where in "Darwin's Middle Road" does Gould appeal to this audience?

6. Gould popularizes his subjects without trivializing them. Compare Gould's essay with David Quammen's in Chapter 6. Assuming that your class is the target audience, which essay does the best job of informing this audience about the subject? Cite examples from each essay of vocabulary, sentence length, tone, organization, and content to support your evaluation.

ARGUING: PROFESSIONAL WRITING

THE DAMNATION OF A CANYON

Edward Abbey

"In wildness is the preservation of the world." Henry David Thoreau's words serve to introduce Edward Abbey's own nature ethic. Beginning with the classic Desert Solitaire *(1968) and including* The Monkey Wrench Gang *(1975),* Abbey's Road *(1979), and* Down the River *(1982), Abbey's writings celebrate the American West, its deserts, canyons, mountains, and rivers. But always in full view are Abbey's villains in the black hats: Industrialists, Bureaucrats, and Developers. And Dammers. In this selection, taken from* Beyond the Wall *(1984), Abbey contrasts the Eden that was Glen Canyon with the stagnant, lifeless waters of Lake Powell. Abbey's argument is shaped by a clear outline—his claim, his refutation of the opposing view, his analysis of consequences, and his solution—but also by Abbey's insistent, cranky, and passionate voice that echoes throughout the essay.*

There was a time when, in my search for essences, I concluded that the canyonland country has no heart. I was wrong. The canyonlands did have a heart, a living heart, and that heart was Glen Canyon and the golden, flowing Colorado River.   (1)

In the summer of 1959 a friend and I made a float trip in little rubber rafts down through the length of Glen Canyon, starting at Hite and getting off the river near Gunsight Butte—The Crossing of the Fathers. In this voyage of some 150 miles and ten days our only motive power, and all that we needed, was the current of the Colorado River.   (2)

In the summer and fall of 1967 I worked as a seasonal park ranger at the new Glen Canyon National Recreation Area. During my five-month tour of duty I worked at the main marina and headquarters area called Wahweap, at Bullfrog Basin toward the upper end of the reservoir, and finally at Lee's Ferry downriver from Glen Canyon Dam. In a number of powerboat tours I was privileged to see almost all of our nation's newest, biggest and most impressive "recreational facility."   (3)

Having thus seen Glen Canyon both before and after what we may fairly call its damnation, I feel that I am in a position to evaluate the transformation of the region caused by construction of the dam. I have had the unique opportunity to observe firsthand some of the differences between the environment of a free river and a powerplant reservoir.   (4)

One should admit at the outset to a certain bias. Indeed I am a "butterfly chaser, googly eyed bleeding heart and wild conservative." I take a dim view of dams; I find it hard to learn to love cement; I am poorly impressed by concrete aggregates and statistics in the cubic tons. But in this weakness I am not alone, for I belong to that ever-growing number of Americans, probably a good majority now, who have become aware that a fully industrialized, thoroughly urbanized, elegantly computerized social system is not suitable for human habitation. Great for machines, yes: But unfit for people.   (5)

Lake Powell, formed by Glen Canyon Dam, is not a lake. It is a reservoir, with a constantly fluctuating water level—more like a bathtub that is never drained than a true lake. As at Hoover (or Boulder) Dam, the sole practical function of this impounded water is to drive the turbines that generate electricity in the powerhouse at the base of the dam. Recreational benefits were of secondary importance in the minds of those who conceived and built this dam. As a result the volume of water in the reservoir is continually being increased or decreased according to the requirements of the Basin States Compact and the power-grid system of which Glen Canyon Dam is a component.   (6)

The rising and falling water level entails various consequences. One of the most obvious, well known to all who have seen Lake Mead, is the "bathtub ring" left on the canyon walls after each drawdown of water, or what rangers at Glen Canyon call the Bathtub Foundation. This phenomenon is perhaps of no more than aesthetic importance; yet it is sufficient to dispel any illusion one might have, in contemplating the scene, that you are looking upon a natural lake.   (7)

The utter barrenness of the reservoir shoreline recalls by contrast the aspect of things before the dam, when Glen Canyon formed the course of the untamed Colorado. Then we had a wild and flowing river lined by boulder-strewn shores, sandy beaches, thickets of tamarisk and willow, and glades of cottonwoods.   (8)

The thickets teemed with songbirds: vireos, warblers, mocking-birds and thrushes. On the open beaches were killdeer, sandpipers, herons, ibises, egrets. Living in grottoes in the canyon walls were swallows, swifts, hawks, wrens and owls. Beaver were common if not abundant: not an evening would pass, in drifting down the river, that we did not see them or at least hear the whack of their flat tails on the water. Above the river shores were the great recessed alcoves where water seeped from the sandstone, nourishing the semitropical hanging gardens of orchid, ivy and columbine, with their associated swarms of insects and birdlife.   (9)

Up most of the side canyon, before damnation, there were springs, sometimes flowing streams, waterfalls and plunge pools—the kind of marvels you can now find only in such small scale remnants of Glen Canyon as the Escalante area. In the rich flora of these laterals the larger mammals—mule deer, coyote, bobcat, ring-tailed cat, gray fox, kit fox, skunk, badger and others—found a home. When the river was dammed almost all of these things were lost. Crowded out—or drowned and buried under mud.   (10)

The difference between the present reservoir, with its silent sterile shores and debris choked side canyons, and the original Glen Canyon, is the difference between death and life. Glen Canyon was alive. Lake Powell is a graveyard.   (11)

For those who may think I exaggerate the contrast between the former river canyon and the present man-made impoundment, I suggest a trip on Lake Powell followed immediately by another boat trip on the river below the dam. Take a boat from Lee's Ferry up the river to within sight of the dam, then shut off the motor and allow yourself the rare delight of a quiet, effortless drifting down the stream. In that twelve-mile stretch of living green, singing birds, flowing water and untarnished canyon walls—sights and sounds a million years older and infinitely lovelier than the roar of motorboats—you will rediscover a small and imperfect sampling of the kind of experience that was taken away from everybody when the oligarchs and politicians condemned our river for purposes of their own.   (12)

Lake Powell, though not a lake, may well be as its defenders assert the most beautiful reservoir in the world. Certainly it has a photogenic backdrop of buttes and mesas projecting above the expansive surface of stagnant waters where the speedboats, houseboats and cabin cruisers play. But it is no longer a wilderness. It is no longer a place of natural life. It is no longer Glen Canyon. (13)

The defenders of the dam argue that the recreational benefits available on the surface of the reservoir outweigh the loss of Indian ruins, historical sites, wildlife and wilderness adventure. Relying on the familiar quantitative logic of business and bureaucracy, they assert that whereas only a few thousand citizens even ventured down the river through Glen Canyon, now millions can—or will—enjoy the motorized boating and hatchery fishing available on the reservoir. They will also argue that the rising waters behind the dam have made such places as Rainbow Bridge accessible by powerboat. Formerly you could get there only by walking (six miles). (14)

This argument appeals to the wheelchair ethos of the wealthy, upper-middle-class American slob. If Rainbow Bridge is worth seeing at all, then by God it should be easily, readily, immediately available to everybody with the money to buy a big powerboat. Why should a trip to such a place be the privilege only of those who are willing to walk six miles? Or if Pikes Peak is worth getting to, then why not build a highway to the top of it so that anyone can get there? Anytime? Without effort? Or as my old man would say, "By Christ, one man's just as good as another—if not a damn sight better." (15)

It is quite true that the flooding of Glen Canyon has opened up to the motorboat explorer parts of side canyons that formerly could be reached only by people able to walk. But the sum total of terrain visible to the eye and touchable by hand and foot has been greatly diminished, not increased. Because of the dam the river is gone, the inner canyon is gone, the best parts of the numerous side canyons are gone—all hidden beneath hundreds of feet of polluted water, accumulating silt, and mounting tons of trash. This portion of Glen Canyon— and who can estimate how many cubic miles were lost?—*is no longer accessible to anybody*. (Except scuba divers.) And this, do not forget, was the most valuable part of Glen Canyon, richest in scenery, archaeology, history, flora and fauna. (16)

Not only has the heart of Glen Canyon been buried, but many of the side canyons above the fluctuating waterline are now rendered more difficult, not easier, to get into. This because the debris brought down into them by desert storms, no longer carried away by the river, must unavoidably build up in the area where flood meets reservoir. Narrow Canyon, for example, at the head of the impounded waters, is already beginning to silt up and to amass huge quantities of driftwood, some of it floating on the surface, some of it half afloat beneath the surface. Anyone who has tried to pilot a motorboat through a raft of half-sunken logs and bloated dead cows will have his own thoughts on the accessibility of these waters. (17)

Second, the question of costs. It is often stated that the dam and its reservoir have opened up to the many what was formerly restricted to the few, implying in this case that what was once expensive has now been made cheap. Exactly the opposite is true.   (18)

Before the dam, a float trip down the river through Glen Canyon would cost you a minimum of seven days' time, well within anyone's vacation allotment, and a capital outlay of about forty dollars—the prevailing price of a two-man rubber boat with oars, available at any army-navy surplus store. A life jacket might be useful but not required, for there were no dangerous rapids in the 150 miles of Glen Canyon. As the name implies, this stretch of the river was in fact so easy and gentle that the trip could be and was made by all sorts of amateurs: by Boy Scouts, Camp Fire Girls, stenographers, schoolteachers, students, little old ladies in inner tubes. Guides, professional boatmen, giant pontoons, outboard motors, radios, rescue equipment were not needed. The Glen Canyon float trip was an adventure anyone could enjoy, on his own, for a cost less than that of spending two days and nights in a Page motel. Even food was there, in the water: the channel catfish were easier to catch and a lot better eating than the striped bass and rainbow trout dumped by the ton into the reservoir these days. And one other thing: at the end of the float trip you still owned your boat, usable for many more such casual and carefree expeditions.   (19)

What is the situation now? Float trips are no longer possible. The only way left for the exploration of the reservoir and what remains of Glen Canyon demands the use of a powerboat. Here you have three options: (1) buy your own boat and engine, the necessary auxiliary equipment, the fuel to keep it moving, the parts and repairs to keep it running, the permits and licenses required for legal operation, the trailer to transport it; (2) rent a boat; or (3) go on a commercial excursion boat, packed in with other sightseers, following a preplanned itinerary. This kind of play is only for the affluent.   (20)

The inescapable conclusion is that no matter how one attempts to calculate the cost in dollars and cents, a float trip down Glen Canyon was much cheaper than a powerboat tour of the reservoir. Being less expensive, as well as safer and easier, the float trip was an adventure open to far more people than will ever be able to afford motorboat excursions in the area now.   (21)

All of the foregoing would be nothing but a futile exercise in nostalgia (so much water over the dam) if I had nothing constructive and concrete to offer. But I do. As alternate methods of power generation are developed, such as solar, and as the nation establishes a way of life adapted to actual resources and basic needs, so that the demand for electrical power begins to diminish, we can shut down the Glen Canyon power plant, open the diversion tunnels, and drain the reservoir.   (22)

This will no doubt expose a drear and hideous scene: immense mud flats and whole plateaus of sodden garbage strewn with dead trees, sunken boats, the skeletons of long-forgotten, decomposing water-skiers. But to those who find the prospect too appalling, I say give nature a little time. In five years, at most in ten, the sun and wind and storms will cleanse and sterilize the repellent mess. The inevitable floods will soon remove all that does not belong within the canyons. Fresh green willow, box elder and redbud will reappear; and the ancient drowned cottonwoods (noble monuments to themselves) will be replaced by young of their own kind. With the renewal of plant life will come the insects, the birds, the lizards and snakes, the mammals. Within a generation—thirty years—I predict the river and canyons will bear a decent resemblance to their former selves. Within the lifetime of our children Glen Canyon and the living river, heart of the canyonlands, will be restored to us. The wilderness will again belong to God, the people and the wild things that call it home.   (23)

VOCABULARY

Look up the meanings of the following words.

- concrete *aggregates*   (5)
- *aesthetic* importance   (7)
- recessed *alcoves*   (9)
- *oligarchs* and politicians   (12)
- the wheelchair *ethos*   (15)
- richest in . . . *archaeology*   (16)
- preplanned *itinerary*   (20)
- a *drear* and hideous scene   (23)

QUESTIONS FOR WRITING AND DISCUSSION

1. Do you consider yourself an environmentalist—someone who is in favor of preserving wild rivers, designating wilderness areas, and forbidding mining, grazing, or the use of motorized vehicles in national parks? Or do you believe federal lands, parks, and rivers should serve multiple uses? Explain, using a state or national park you have visited to give specific examples.

2. Which of Abbey's arguments did you find most persuasive? Which were least persuasive? Are there opposing arguments which Abbey does not answer? Explain, *referring to your own beliefs* outlined above.

③ An argument contains a *claim, reasons* that support the claim or refute the opposition, and *evidence.*

What sentence or sentences best illustrate Abbey's overall claim or thesis for this essay? Does he make a claim of fact, value, cause, or solution—or some combination of these? Explain.

List the *reasons* Abbey gives to support his claim and refute the opposing arguments.

For *one* of his reasons, list the evidence, facts, examples, or testimony that Abbey gives.

4. Note passages where Abbey's *appeal to character* is evident. Where is he most reasonable? Where is he most cantankerous or even misanthropic? Are these facets of his character consistent with the persona portrayed in paragraph 5? In your judgment, does his appeal to character help or hurt his argument? Explain.

5. Cite one sentence in which Abbey uses an *emotional appeal.* Does this sentence make his argument more effective?

6. Assume you are the controller of the Glen Canyon dam. Write a short response to Abbey explaining why his solution—to "open the diversion tunnels, and drain the reservoir"—is absurd. Choose either an adversarial or a Rogerian strategy, whichever would work best for Abbey.

ARGUING: THE WRITING PROCESS

ASSIGNMENT FOR ARGUING

For this assignment, choose a subject that interests *you* or relates to *your own* experience. You may even choose a subject that you have already written about for this class. Then examine the subject for a debatable claim of fact, value, cause and effect, or policy which you could make about that subject. If the claim is arguable, you have a focus for your arguing paper. Analyze your probable audience to guide your argumentative strategy. (Avoid ready-made pro/con subjects such as abortion, drinking age, drugs, and euthanasia *unless* you have clear beliefs based on your own experience.)

Choosing a Subject

If a journal entry suggested a possible subject, do the collecting-and-shaping strategies. Otherwise, consider the following ideas:

- Review your journal entries from previous chapters and the papers you have already written for this class. Test these subjects for an arguable claim you could make, opposing arguments you could consider, and an appropriate audience for an argumentative piece of writing.

- Brainstorm possible ideas for argumentative subjects from the other courses you are currently taking or have taken. What controversial issues in psychology, art, philosophy, journalism, biology, nutrition, engineering, physical education, or literature have you discussed in your classes? Ask current or past instructors for possible controversial topics relating to their courses.

- Newspapers and magazines are full of controversial subjects in sports, medicine, law, business, and family. Browse through current issues looking for possible subjects. Check news items, editorials, and cartoons. Look for subjects related to your own interests, your job, your leisure activities, or your experiences.

- Interview your friends, family, or classmates. What controversial issues are affecting their lives most directly? What would they most like to change about their lives? What has irritated or angered them most in the past week?

You can write about anything, and if you write well enough, even the reader with no intrinsic interest in the subject will become involved.

—Tracy Kidder, novelist

Collecting

Narrowing and Focusing Your Claim   Narrow your subject to a specific topic and sharpen the focus of your topic by applying the "Wh" questions. If your subject is "grades" your responses might be as follows:

SUBJECT: GRADES

- *Who:* College students
- *What:* Letter grades
- *When:* Especially in freshman and sophomore years
- *Where:* Grades, especially in nonmajor courses
- *Why:* What purpose do grades in nonmajor courses serve?

Determine what claim or claims you want to make. Make sure that your claim is *arguable*. (Remember that claims can overlap; an argument may combine several related claims.)

CLAIM OF FACT:

- Letter grades exist. (Not arguable)
- Employers consider grades when hiring. (Slightly more arguable, but not very controversial)
- Grades do not measure learning. (Very arguable)

CLAIM ABOUT CAUSE OR EFFECT:

- Grades create anxiety for students. (Not very arguable)
- Grades actually prevent discovery and learning. (Arguable)

CLAIM ABOUT VALUE:

- Grades are not fair (Not very arguable: "fairness" can usually be determined)
- Grades are bad because they discourage individual initiative. (Arguable)
- Grades are good because they give students an incentive to learn. (Arguable)

CLAIM ABOUT A SOLUTION OR POLICY:

- Grades should be eliminated altogether. (Arguable—but difficult)
- Grades should be eliminated in humanities courses. (Arguable)
- Grades should change to pass/fail in nonmajor courses. (Arguable—and more practical)

Focusing and narrowing your *claim* helps determine what evidence you need to collect. Use your observing, remembering, and investigative skills to gather the evidence. *Note:* An argumentative essay should not be a mathematical equation that uses only abstract and impersonal evidence. *Your experience* can be crucial to a successful argumentative essay. Start by doing the *remembering* exercises. Your audience wants to know not only why you are writing on this particular *topic*, but also why the subject is of interest to *you*.

Remembering   Use *freewriting, looping, branching,* or *clustering* to recall experiences, ideas, events, and people who are relevant to your claim. If you are writing about grades, brainstorm about how *your* teachers used grades, how you reacted to specific grades in one specific class, how your friends or parents reacted, and what you felt or thought. These prewriting exercises will help you understand your claim and give you specific examples you can use for evidence.

Observing   If possible for your topic, collect data and evidence by observing, firsthand, the facts, values, effects, or possible solutions related to your claim. *Repeated* observation will give you good inductive evidence to support your argument.

Investigating   For most argumentative essays, some research or investigation is essential. Since it is difficult to imagine all the valid counterarguments, interview friends, classmates, family, co-workers, and authorities on your topic. From the library, gather books and articles that contain arguments in support of your claim. *Note:* As you do research in the library, make photocopies of key passages from relevant sources to hand in with your essay. If you cite sources from your research, list them on a "Work Cited" page following your essay. (See Chapter 11 for the proper format.)

Shaping

As you begin your shaping activities, reconsider your audience. Imagine one real person who might be among your readers. Is this person open-minded and likely to be convinced by your evidence? Does this person represent the opposing position? Would a Rogerian strategy be effective in this case? Reread your collecting notes and *underline* the reasons and evidence that would be most effective for this reader. After reconsidering your audience and rereading your collecting notes, try the shaping strategies below.

No one can write decently who is distrustful of the reader's intelligence, or whose attitude is patronizing.

—*E.B. White, essayist*

List of "Pro" and "Con" Arguments   Either on paper or in a computer file, write out your *claim* and then list the arguments for your position ("Pro") and the arguments for the opposing position ("Con"). After you have made the list, match up arguments by drawing lines, as indicated below. (On the computer file, move "Con" arguments so they appear directly opposite the corresponding "Pro" argument.)

CLAIM: Grades should be changed to pass/fail in nonmajor courses.

PRO	CON
Grades inhibit learning by putting too much emphasis on competition.	Grades actually promote learning by getting students to study as hard as possible.
Pass/fail grading encourages students to explore nonmajor fields.	Students should be encouraged to compete with majors. They may want to change majors and need to know if they can compete.
Grade competition with majors in the field can be discouraging.	
Some students do better without the pressure of grades; they need to find out if they can motivate themselves without grades, but they shouldn't have to risk grades in their major field to discover that.	If students don't have traditional grading, they won't take nonmajor courses seriously.

If some pro and con arguments "match," you will be able to argue against the con and for your claim at the same time. If some arguments do not "match," you will need to consider them separately. The outlines below suggest ways of organizing your pro and con arguments.

Outlines for Arguments   For more than two thousand years, writers and speakers have been trying to determine the most effective means to persuade audiences. One of the oldest outlines for a successful argument comes from classical rhetoric. The following six-part outline is intended as a guideline rather than a rigid list. Test this outline; see if it will work for *your* argument.

Introduction:	Announces subject; *gets audience's interest and attention;* establishes a trustworthy character for the writer
Narration:	Gives *background,* context, statement of problem, or definition
Partition:	States thesis or *claim,* outlines or *maps* out arguments
Argument:	Makes *arguments* and gives *evidence* for the claim or thesis
Refutation:	Shows why *opposing arguments* are not true or valid
Conclusion:	Summarizes arguments, suggests solution, *ties into the introduction or background*

Most arguments have these features, but not necessarily in this order. Some writers prefer to refute opposing arguments *before* giving the arguments in support of their claim. In cases where the con and pro arguments match, refuting an argument followed by the argument for your claim may work best. As you organize your own arguments, put your *strongest* argument last and your *weakest* argument either first or in the middle.

Since most short argumentative essays contain the introduction, narration, and partition all in a few introductory paragraphs, you may use the following abbreviated outlines for argument:

Outline #1	Intro (attention getter, background, claim or thesis, map)
	Your arguments
	Refute opposing arguments
	Conclusion
Outline #2	Intro
	Refute opposing arguments

Your arguments

Conclusion

Outline #3   Intro

Refute first opposing argument that matches your first argument

Refute second opposing argument that matches your second argument, and so on

Make your additional arguments

Conclusion

For Rogerian arguments, you can follow one of the above outlines, but the emphasis, tone, and attitude are different:

Introduction	Attention getter, background
	Claim (often downplayed to reduce threat)
	Map (often omitted)
	Appeal to character (crucial to Rogerian argument)
Opposing Arguments	State opposing arguments fairly
	Show where, how, or when those arguments may be valid; establish common ground
Your Arguments	State your position fairly
	Show where, how, or when your arguments are valid
Resolution	Present compromise position
	State your solution to the problem and show its advantages to both sides

COMPUTER TIP: SHAPING AND DRAFTING

If you already have your draft on a computer file, you can quickly move paragraphs around to change your outline. First, print a copy of your current draft. If, for example, you are using *Outline #1* (above), shift your paragraphs around to fit *Outline #2*, so that your arguments come last. Print a copy of this reorganized version. Read both versions, or have a reader compare both versions. Which is more effective?

Similarly, the computer will allow you to *reorder* your arguments. If you put your weakest argument first and your strongest last, perhaps you would like to see how the argument would read if you hid your weakest argument in the middle. Print a copy of your current draft, rearrange the paragraphs, and print a second copy for comparison.

In both cases, you will need to rewrite connections and transitions, but the computer can let you see how another sequence or organization might work with your paper. If you like your first version best, you can switch back in just a few seconds.

Developing Arguments   Think of your argument as a series of "because" statements, each supported by evidence, statistics, testimony, expert opinion, data, specific examples from your experience, or a combination of these.

THESIS OR CLAIM: Grades should be abolished in nonmajor courses

Reason #1	Because they may keep a student from attempting a difficult nonmajor course
	Statistics, testimony, data, examples, and so on
Reason #2	Because competition with majors in the field can be discouraging
	Statistics, testimony, data, examples, and so on
Reason #3	Because grades inhibit students learning in nonmajor fields
	Statistics, testimony, data, examples, and so on

You can develop each reason using a variety of strategies. The following strategies may help you generate additional reasons and examples.

Definition:	Define the crucial terms or ideas. (What do you mean by "learning?")
Comparison:	Compare the background, situation, context with another similar context. (What other schools have tried pass/fail grading for nonmajor courses? How has it worked?)
Process:	How does or should a change occur? (How do nonmajors become discouraged? How should a school implement pass/fail in grading?)

These strategies may help you develop an argument coherently and effectively. If several strategies are possible, consider which would be most effective for your *audience.*

RESEARCH TIP

When you draft your arguing essay, don't let your citations or direct quotations overpower your own argument. Two tactics will keep you in control of your argument:

First, "sandwich" your quotations. *Introduce* quotations by referring to the author, the source, and/or the author's study. *Follow* quotations with a sentence or two explaining how the author's evidence supports your argument. For examples, see paragraph 18 in Gould's essay and paragraphs 8 and 9 in the essay by student writer Jim Haas.

Second, keep your direct quotations *short.* If possible, reduce a long passage to one sentence and incorporate the quoted material in the flow of your own language. For example, in his essay at the end of the chapter, Haas writes,

> In fact, twenty-nine other countries have mandatory seat belt laws. "Where statistics are available," Transportation Secretary Dole says, "they show that highway deaths have declined by an average of 25 percent." (34)

Drafting   You will never know "enough" about the subject or have "enough" evidence. At some point, however, you must stop collecting and start your draft. The most frequent problem with drafting an argumentative essay is delaying the actual writing too long, until the deadline is too close.

For argumentative essays, start with a working order, sequence, or sketch an outline on paper or in your head. Additional examples and appeals to reason, character, or emotion may occur to you as you develop your argument or refute opposing arguments. In addition, if you have done some research, have your notes, photocopies of key data, statistics, quotations, and citations of authorities close at hand. As you write, you will discover that some information or arguments simply don't fit into the flow of your essay. Don't force arguments into your draft if they no longer seem to belong.

Revising

Argumentation is the most "public" of the purposes for writing. It requires that you become aware of many different points of view. You must counter the arguments of others and recognize the flaws in your own logic. Test your argument by having friends or classmates read it. Explain your claim, your focus, and your intended audience. Ask your readers to look for possible opposing arguments you need to counter, or weaknesses in your own argument or evidence. Were your appeals effective? Ask them if your argument should be more adversarial or more Rogerian.

Guidelines for Revision

- **When you finish your draft, reconsider your *audience*.** Persuading your audience requires that you tailor your reasons and evidence to your audience and situation. Do an audience analysis, and then reread your draft and make appropriate changes.

- **Ask a class member or friend to read your draft to determine the intended audience for your argument.** See which arguments your reader thinks would not be effective for your audience.

- **Ask your reader to tell you what kind of *claim* you are making, whether your arguments or counterarguments are logical, and whether your ethical or emotional appeals are effective for your audience.**

- **Which of your "because" arguments are most effective?** Which least effective? Should you change the outline or structure you initially chose?

- **Revise your draft to avoid fallacies or errors in reasoning.** Errors in logic create two problems: They can destroy your rational appeal and open your argument to a logical rebuttal, and they lessen your credibility—and thus reduce your appeal to your character. (Review the list below.)

- **Support your reasons with evidence: *data, facts, statistics, quotations, observations, testimony, statistics, or specific examples from your experience.*** Check your collecting notes once again for additional evidence to add to your weakest argument. Is there a weak or unsupported argument you should simply omit?

- **Signal the major arguments and counterarguments in your partition or map.** Between paragraphs, use clear transitions and paragraph hooks.

- **If you cite sources in your essay, check the *accuracy* of statis-

tics, quotations, and source references. (See Chapter 11 for proper format for in-text documentation and "Works Cited" page.)

- **Revise sentences to improve conciseness and clarity.**
- **Edit sentences for grammar, punctuation, and spelling.**

Revising Fallacies in Logic   *Hasty Generalization:* Conclusion not logically justified by sufficient or unbiased evidence. If your friend Mary tells you that Professor Paramecium is a hard grader because he gave her a 36 percent on the first biology test, she is making a hasty generalization. It may be *true*—Prof P. may *be* a difficult grader—but Mary's logic is not valid. She cannot logically draw that conclusion from a sample of one; the rest of the class may have received grades of between 80 and 100.

Post Hoc Ergo Propter Hoc: Literally, "after this, therefore because of this." Just because event B occurred after event A does not mean that A *necessarily* caused B. You washed your car in the morning, and it rained in the afternoon. Though we joke about how it always rains after we wash the car, there is, of course, no causal relationship between the two events. "I forgot to leave the porch light on when I went out last night, and someone robbed my house." Without further evidence, we cannot assume that the lack of light contributed to the robbery. A more obvious cause might be the back door you left unlocked.

The Genetic Fallacy: Arguing that the *origins* of a person, object, or institution determine its character, nature, or worth. Like the "post hoc" fallacy, the genetic fallacy is an error in causal relationships.

- John Hinckley couldn't possibly kill the President; after all, he came from a good home.
- This automobile was made in Detroit. It'll probably fall apart after 10,000 miles.
- He speaks with a funny oriental accent. He's really stupid, you know.
- He started Celestial Seasonings Herb Teas just to make a quick buck; it's just another phony yuppie product.

The second half of each statement *may* or *may not* be true; the logical error is in assuming that the origin of something will necessarily determine its worth or quality. Stereotyping is frequently caused by a genetic fallacy.

- *Begging the Question:* Loading the conclusion in the claim. Arguing that "pornography should be banned because it corrupts our youth" is a logical claim. However, saying that "filthy and corrupting pornography should be banned" is begging the question: the conclusion that the writer should prove (that pornography corrupts) is assumed in the claim. Other examples: "Those useless psychology classes should be dropped from the curriculum"; "Senator Swingle's sexist behavior should be censured by Congress"; "Everyone knows that our drug control program is a miserable failure." The writer must *prove* that the psychology classes are useless, that Senator Swingle is sexist, and that the drug program is a failure.

- *Circular Argument:* A sentence or argument that restates rather than proves. Thus, it goes in a circle: "President Reagan was a great communicator because he had that knack of talking effectively to the people." The terms in the beginning of the sentence ("great communicator") and the end of the sentence ("talking effectively") are interchangeable. The sentence ends where it started.

- *Either/Or:* An oversimplification that reduces alternatives to only two choices, creating a false dilemma. Statements such as "love it or leave it" attempt to reduce the alternatives to two. If you don't love your school, your town, or your country, you don't have to leave: A third choice is to change it and make it better. Proposed solutions frequently have an "either/or" fallacy: "Either we ban boxing or hundreds of young men will be senselessly killed." A third alternative is to change boxing's rules or equipment. "If we don't provide farmers with low-interest loans, they will go bankrupt." Increasing prices for farm products might be a better alternative.

- *Faulty Comparison or Analogy:* Basing an argument on a comparison of two things, ideas, events, or situations that are similar but not identical. Comparisons or analogies are often effective in argument, but they can hide logical problems. "We can solve the cocaine problem the same way we reduced the DWI problem: Attack it with increased enforcement and mandatory jail sentences." Although the situations are similar, they are not identical. The DWI solution will not necessarily work on drugs. An analogy is an extended comparison that uses something simple or familiar to explain something complex or less familiar. "Solving a mathematics problem is like baking a cake: You have to take it one step at a time. First you assemble your ingredients or your known data. . . . " Like baking, solving a problem does involve a process; unlike baking, however, mathematics is more exact. Changing the amount of flour in a recipe by 1 percent will not make the cake fall; changing a numeric value by 1 percent, however, may ruin the whole problem. The point, however, is *not* to avoid comparisons or analogies. Simply make sure that your conclusions are qualified; acknowledge the *differences* between the two things compared as well as the similarities.

- *Ad Hominem (literally, "to the man"):* An attack on the character of the individual or the opponent rather than his or her actual opinions, arguments, or qualifications. "Susan Davidson, the prosecuting attorney, drinks heavily. There's no way she can present an effective case." This is an attack on Ms. Davidson's character, rather than an analysis of her legal talents. Her record in court may be excellent.

- *Ad Populum (literally, "to the people"):* An emotional appeal to positive concepts (God, mother, country, liberty, democracy, apple pie) or negative concepts (communism, fascism, atheism) rather than a direct discussion of the real issue: "Those senators voting to reduce the defense budget are really communists at heart." "If you are a true American, you should be for tariffs to protect the garment industry."

- *Red Herring and Straw Man:* Diversionary tactics designed to avoid confronting the key issue. *Red Herring* refers to the practice of dragging a smelly fish across the trail to divert tracking dogs away from the real quarry. A "red herring" occurs when writers avoid countering an opposing argument directly: "Of course equal pay for women is an important issue, but I wonder whether women really want to take the responsibility that comes with higher paying jobs? Do they really want the additional stress?" this writer diverts attention away from the argument about equal pay to another issue, stress—thus, a "red herring." In the *Straw Man* diversion, the writer sets up an artificially easy argument to refute in place of the real issue. Former President Richard Nixon's famous "Checkers" speech is a good example. Accused of spending $18,000 in campaign gifts for personal use, Nixon described how he received Checkers, a little black-and-white spotted cocker spaniel dog. Since his daughter Tricia just loved this dog, Nixon decided to keep it. Surely, there's nothing wrong with that, is there? The "Checkers" argument is a "Straw Man" diversion: justifying his personal use of this gift is much easier than explaining how and why he spent the $18,000. Avoid "Red Herring" and "Straw Man" by either refuting an argument directly or acknowledging that it has some merit. Don't just change the subject.

POSTSCRIPT ON THE WRITING PROCESS

In your journal, answer the following questions.

1. Describe how your beliefs about your subject changed from the time you decided on your claim until you revised your essay. What caused the change in your views?

2. What opposing argument was most difficult to counter? Explain how you handled it.

3. Which was your strongest argument? Did you use logical appeals and evidence, or did you rely more on appeals to character or emotion? Explain.

4. How did your writing process for the argumentative essay change from previous essays? What steps or stages took longer? What stages did you have to go back and redo?

ARGUMENT: STUDENT WRITING

PROTECT YOURSELF—BUCKLE UP!

Jim Haas

Jim Haas decided to write his arguing paper about seat-belt laws, primarily because he had been in several accidents and had failed to fasten his own seat belt. He began collecting for this paper by writing a narrative of his own experience. Then, once he realized that he had a good subject, he read some articles in the library and clipped some stories from his home-town newspaper. Reproduced below are the narrative from his remembering exercise, a list of pro and con arguments, and the final draft.

Remembering Exercise

Nick, Milo, D.J. and I were on our way back from a bar in Mondamin, Iowa, where we had spent the previous six hours drinking brandy and beer. We were all riding in the cab of Nick's pickup and we were almost to Nick's house where our girlfriends were making dinner. Nick turned off the road and drove down by the irrigation canal adjacent to his farm. He thought it would be fun to turn off his lights and drive around in the darkness. We were driving in the blackness when we told him to turn his lights back on and he did so just in time for us to see the ground go out from underneath us. We had just driven off a twenty-five foot cliff. We hit nose first, then flipped over the top. We all escaped serious injury. Milo and D.J. were not injured at all, Nick had to have his thumb sewn back on because the roof smashed down on the steering wheel where he was holding on, and I hit the dashboard and the roof with my face and forehead. I had two black eyes and had to eat soup for the next week because I ripped apart the inside of my mouth.

I have been in two other automobile accidents and in all of them the vehicle I was riding in was totaled, but I escaped serious injury. I consider myself lucky, because many people have died in lesser accidents. I was not wearing a seat belt when any of the accidents occurred. I think if I had been wearing a seat belt, I might have been saved the pain of injury and the bother of filling out insurance forms.

List of Pro and Con Arguments

CLAIM: A mandatory seat belt law would save lives.

Pro	Con
Saves lives	Restricts freedom
Cut down on medical bills	Opens door for other laws which
Will reduce insurance costs	may restrict freedom
Saves money – will prevent manufacturers from using airbags, which will raise cost of automobiles.	Cannot be fairly enforced
	Costs money for inspecting seat belts to make sure they are working
Reduce taxes spent on government subsidized medical care	Seat belts will trap people in burning vehicles
	People can avoid injury by bracing themselves before a crash.

Revised Version

PROTECT YOURSELF–BUCKLE UP!

Two men were killed early Sunday morning in separate car accidents in El Paso County. Steven D. Carmichael, 29, of Palmer Lake was pronounced dead at 12:45 a.m. Sunday after a pickup he was driving went off the road. Carmichael, who was alone in the truck, was not wearing a seat belt. In the second accident . . . Joseph David Vasquez, 21, of 22105 Farmer Road, died of massive head and chest injuries after he was thrown from a pickup truck just east of Enoch Road. . . . Vasquez wasn't wearing a seat belt. (Hill 3)

All too often, unfortunately, articles like this one appear in newspapers across the country. Even more unfortunate is the fact that many of these traffic-related deaths could be prevented if more people in the United States would use their seat belts. This has prompted fourteen states, so far, to pass mandatory seat belt laws, requiring all persons in automobiles to use safety belts, or risk paying fines if they're caught not using them (Sundstrom 16). Mandatory seat belt laws are opposed in some states, but the law is a good idea to immediately reduce deaths on our highways and cut the social costs that accompany them.   (1)

U. S. Secretary of Transportation, Elizabeth Dole, states that "every year more than 40,000 persons are killed in auto accidents on our highways. . . . Car crashes are the leading cause of death of people up to [age] 34. For teenagers, car crash fatalities outnumber the next five causes of death combined" (33). These are sobering statistics, yet 85% of Americans still don't use the single most preventative measure to insure their survival in a car crash: seat belts (Horton 22).   (2)

Seat belts save lives. The Highway Users Federation says that because 15% of Americans use seat belts, 1800 lives are saved each year. They estimate that if 25% of all Americans used seat belts, 3,000 lives would be saved, and if 85% of Americans used seat belts, 9,600 human lives would be spared on our nation's highways each year (145). Philip Caldwell, Chairman of the Board at Ford Motor Company, explains: "Statistics show that in a typical auto accident, occupants restrained by standard safety belts have at least a 50% better chance of avoiding death or serious injury than those who are unrestrained" (38).   (3)

Many opponents of seat belt usage believe it is safer to be thrown from a car than to be trapped in it, but according to Virginia Tech behavioral psychologist E. Scott Geller, who has been studying the use of seat belts for over six years, "being thrown from a car is twenty-five times more lethal than being 'trapped.' The exceptions are widely publicized, and that perpetuates the myth" (Horton 22). A friend of mine who works on an ambulance and who has helped many victims of automobile crashes reminded me of the value of seat belts when he said that he had never unbuckled a dead body from a seat belt.   (4)

Other opponents are afraid that their car will end up underwater or on fire, and that they won't be able to escape. Actually the reverse is true. B. J. Campbell, director of Highway Safety Research Center at the University of North Carolina, tells us, "If you're wearing a [safety] belt, you've got a better chance of being conscious and not having your legs broken-distinct advantages in getting out of a dangerous situation" (Horton 22).　(5)

Another myth about auto accidents is addressed by Roslyn Kaiser of the National Highway Traffic Safety Administration (NHTSA). She points out that most people don't understand the dynamics of crashes: "They think they can save themselves by bracing with their arms. But a ten-mile-an-hour collision is equivalent to catching a two-hundred-pound bag of cement dropped from a second-story window" (Horton 22). I can attest to that. I've been in three automobile accidents in my lifetime, and all three were potentially life-threatening, but two of them really proved Kaiser's point. The first accident happened when a pickup truck I was riding in went over a twenty-five foot cliff. I was not wearing a seat belt, but I had braced myself against the seat by placing my hands against the dashboard. The moment before we hit (we hit front-end first, then flipped over), I had my arms locked straight against the dashboard, but when we hit, I don't remember my arms giving way. I don't even remember hitting the dashboard because it happened so quickly, but I did hit it, receiving two black eyes and two gashes inside my mouth.　(6)

My second accident also illustrated how helpless people are in an accident. I was a passenger in a 12-ton mobile drilling rig that rolled over while going about 50 miles per hour. I wasn't wearing a seat belt, and as the rig rolled over one and one-half times, I was thrown around like a rag doll. I received only minor injuries and was absent from work for only one week, but that accident impressed upon me how little control I had on the outcome of my life in such accidents. I definitely agree with Roger B. Smith, Chairman of general Motors, when he says, "The one sure way to achieve an immediate and dramatic reduction in accident injuries and fatalities is to get significantly more people to use the belt systems that are already in their cars" (35).　(7)

If one proves that seat belt usage saves lives, the next step is to find out how to increase their use. I think the mandatory seat belt law is the answer. The United States is not the first country to implement such a law. In fact, twenty-nine other countries have mandatory seat belt laws. "Where statistics are available," Transportation Secretary Dole says, "they show that highway deaths have declined by an average of 25 percent" (34). Lee Iacocca of Chrysler agrees:

> In France, the automobile accident death rate has dropped 25 percent after their belt law was passed. In Australia, nearly 90 percent of the people are buckling up. Right across the river from Detroit, the Province of Ontario has enjoyed similar success. Not one nation, state or territory

has repealed a belt use law once they've adopted it-because the laws work. (36)

Passing any kind of law is difficult, but the declining death rates indicate that the benefits from a mandatory seat belt law will be worth the effort.   (8)

Some people are against mandatory seat belt laws because they believe passive restraints and automatic seat belts would be more effective. Those people need to realize that passive restraints, alone, are not as effective. Anyone who does not want seat belts would just disconnect the automatic seat belt, and they would be left with very little protection. In addition, air bags are effective only in front-end collisions. Writing in the *National Safety News,* Phillip Caldwell says that "the air bag offers [only] supplemental protection. . . . The air bag offers added protection in frontal collisions at speeds greater than 12 to 15 miles per hour, but it does not provide protection, as safety belts do, in other kinds of accidents-like secondary collisions (after air bag deployment) and rollovers, or rear-end or side-impact collisions" (74). Dole, Iacocca, and Smith agree with Caldwell that safety belts are still the single most effective safety feature in the automotive industry, and they should not be substituted for, but supplemented with, air bags and other passive restraints.   (9)

The most serious argument against the mandatory seat belt law is that it infringes on an individual's freedom to choose whether or not he or she wishes to use the safety belt. People who take this position believe seat belt use should be a private, personal choice since it affects only the person who wears it. I once agreed with this view until I discovered that my choice affects all people in society. As Iacocca explains, "People who get injured because they don't use belts raise our taxes, increase our medical and hospitalization insurance, clog our courts, soak up social services for accident victims and survivors, and cause grief for friends and family. So the people who don't use belts because it hampers their freedom are already intruding on our freedom" (74).   (10)

Of course wearing seat belts would not eliminate these effects, but it would reduce them. A Michigan state legislator notes, "It is estimated that each traffic fatality costs the state and family about $333,000. Injuries and lost wages, caused by the nonuse of belts, cost society $2,500 per accident" (Goodman 12). There is overwhelming evidence that the nonuse of safety belts has a significant effect on most people in society who have to give up part of their earned wage to pay for other people's failure to protect themselves.   (11)

I think the heavy monetary cost that has to be absorbed by society as a result of death and injuries caused by the nonuse of seat belts, the loss of life itself, and the evidence that mandatory seat belt laws do reduce automobile fatalities are arguments that far outweigh any of the opposing arguments. Perhaps if our state had a seat belt law, I might have worn one and avoided the hospital costs and the days missed from work. More importantly, if Steven Carmichael and Joseph Vasquez had been required by law to wear seat belts, they might be alive today. Let's work together in an effort to reduce these tragic deaths on our nation's highways. Support the mandatory seat belt law, and in the meantime, protect your loved ones and protect yourself. Buckle up.   (12)

Works Cited

Caldwell, Philip. "A Rational Approach to Car-Occupant Protection." National Safety News Feb. 1985: 38, 74–75.

Goodman, Walter. "Fair Game-Reflections on Forced Buckling." New Leader 26 Nov. 1985: 12.

Highway Users Federation. "Buckle Up." Reader's Digest Dec. 1985: 145.

Hill, David. "Two Men Killed in Separate Accidents." Colorado Springs Sun 9 Dec. 1985: 3.

Horton, Elizabeth. "Why Don't We Buckle Up?" Science Digest Feb. 1985: 22.

Iacocca, Lee A. "Grass-Roots Pressure Can Make Restraints Mandatory." National Safety News Feb. 1985: 36, 74.

Smith, Roger B. "Built-in Protection Complements Passenger Restraints." National Safety News Feb. 1985: 35, 74.

Sundstrom, Geoff. "40 Percent Now Covered by Belt Laws." Automotive News 5 Aug. 1985: 16.

QUESTIONS FOR WRITING AND DISCUSSION

1. Does Haas make a claim of fact, value, cause and effect, policy, or some combination? Explain.

2. Were you convinced when you finished this essay? What evidence convinced you most? The personal experience? The statistics? The quotations from authorities? Explain.

3. Compare the version of Haas's personal experience in the remembering exercise with the account in the final version. What specific details were omitted in the final version? Would you recommend including them, leaving the final version the way it is, or condensing it even more? Explain.

4. Read the list of pro and con arguments. Which arguments were omitted from the essay? Were any added that were not on that original list? If you were writing the essay, which points would you include?

AIDS IN THE CLASSROOM

Rhonda Palsulich

Should AIDS patients be quarantined, as people with highly communicable diseases are, or should we think first of the constitutional rights and safety of the AIDS patient? In her essay, Rhonda Palsulich tries "to persuade others that isolation of school-aged AIDS victims is unnecessary and discriminatory." As you read the essay, see if you are persuaded by her arguments. Would a mother of school-aged children be persuaded?

Katie stands waiting for the school bus, eagerly anticipating the first day of second grade. She is excited about the same things as all the other seven-year-olds: her new school clothes, the prospect of new friends, new teachers, and novel experiences. She has worries, however, that other kids can never understand. Her past has been marred by bad health. Not only has she had to adapt to frequent and often painful visits to the hospital, but now she has been plagued by the grim misfortune of contracting AIDS through a contaminated blood transfusion. She must now face a limited and painful future. She also must endure the scorn and fear of her peers and others who do not understand the disease. She is destined to be treated like a leper, other students afraid to touch anything she has handled, afraid to even breathe the same air for fear of contracting the disease themselves. AIDS, which began as a disease limited to homosexuals and drug addicts, has now spread throughout the population, bringing with it a pervasive hysteria. AIDS now has the power to affect each member of society, either personally, through the acquaintance with an AIDS patient or through more indirect methods, such as policy decisions. Each person may soon have to decide what type of precautions and policies should be created to protect society against the threat of AIDS. One major arena is the public school system. There is a heated debate about whether school-aged AIDS patients should be allowed to attend school with uninfected children. My belief is that these afflicted children do not pose a sufficient threat to warrant their isolation.   (1)

Those who believe that there is a threat of the transmission of AIDS in the classroom environment cite a general lack of knowledge of all the causes of the disease as their primary defense. As Dr. Richard Restak, neurologist and bioethicist, said in an interview for *U.S. News* and *World Report,* "It seems each day, we're getting reassessments of how transmissible it [AIDS] is. My basic approach is until we get a better handle on this illness, we'd better be cautious" (50). He further elaborated that he thought special caution should be taken with very young children: "I'd be very concerned, especially about first and second graders scratching and biting and chewing each other's gum and sharing sandwiches and things like that" (50). However, the medical community has found little that would back up these fears. Another *U.S. News* article gives the testimonies of federal officials who claim that sexual activity, most often between homosexuals, and intravenous drug use are the primary causes of AIDS ("AIDS Spooks the Classroom," 7). These activities are definitely not significant in school-aged children. As Dr. Harold Jaffe, chief epidemiologist of the AIDS task force at the Center for Disease Control said, "Of all the AIDS cases reported in the past five years, not one resulted from sharing a residence, schoolroom or office with another AIDS patient" (Tanne 61).   (2)

The proponents of isolation policies for school-aged AIDS patients believe that the benefits to society as well as to the child with AIDS are justifications for the adoption of such policies. As Cathy Sherer, mother of two grade school children said, "I don't want to take a chance" ("AIDS Spooks the Classroom" 7). She voiced the sentiments of many who feel that any possibility of transmission justifies the institution of isolation policies. Also, as a recent *Newsweek* article states, in relation to one thirteen-year-old patient who is presently receiving private tutoring, "It would be best for the student, who could suffer psychological damage from harassment, to remain at home until a more accepting climate could be created" (Alter 25). These benefits to the student, however, are not great enough to outweigh the harm exacted by the adoption of isolation policies. Not only would children lose valuable education, but if these policies were enacted, the children would also lose their constitutional rights. Carol Levine, co-director of the Hastings Center Project, says that the civil rights of the AIDS patients are "the same as for every other citizen. There are no grounds for discriminating against such people in terms of insurance, employment, or access to public places" ("Should AIDS Victims Be Isolated?" 50).   (3)

Both the proponents and opponents of isolation policies agree about one instance when the child AIDS patient should not go to public schools. This instance is when the child is in the position of physical peril. As Fred Valentine, professor of medicine at New York University Medical Center, says of the AIDS patient, "You're more of a risk to him than he is to you. You might have a cold or some minor infection that would be very serious for him if he caught it, because he has no resistance" (Tanne 62). Those opposed to isolation policies still maintain, however, that the choice to take this risk should be left up to the patient, his parents, and his physicians. (4)

Do we have the right to take away Katie's constitutional rights? Is it our place to decide whether she should have the chance to lead a normal life? Just as we cannot imprison innocent people for crimes they did not commit, we cannot lock Katie away from society because she has had the misfortune of contracting a deadly disease. The medical community, those in our society who are the most informed on AIDS, has found little to support the isolation of AIDS patients such as Katie. Although there has been extensive world-wide research into the causes of AIDS, none of the researchers has found that casual contact between AIDS patients and uninfected people can lead to the transmission of AIDS. Therefore, unless Katie and others like her decide that the risks are too great, they should be allowed to lead a normal life, and a normal life must include, by rights, the chance to attend public schools. (5)

Works Cited

"As AIDS Spooks the Schoolroom." U.S. News and World Report 23 Sept. 1985: 7.

Alder, Jerry. "The AIDS Conflict." Newsweek 23 Sept. 1985: 18–24.

Alter, Jonathon. "Sins of Omission." Newsweek 23 Sept. 1985: 25.

Clark, Matt. "AIDS." Newsweek 12 August 1985: 20–27.

Gelman, David. "The Social Fallout From an Epidemic." Newsweek 12 August 1985: 28–29.

Tanne, Janice Hopkins. "AIDS: Is Anyone Safe?" Reader's Digest Feb. 1986: 60–64.

"Should AIDS Victims Be Isolated?" U.S. News and World Report 30 Sept. 1985: 50.

QUESTIONS FOR WRITING AND DISCUSSION

1. If you were Kathy Sherer, the mother referred to in this essay, how would you respond to Palsulich's argument? List several counterarguments you might make.

2. Referring to paragraph numbers, outline this essay. Which of the outlines suggested in the shaping section of this chapter does this essay most closely follow?

3. One person who read Palsulich's essay observed that the essay only *reviewed* the opposing positions and then stated her own position, rather than actually *arguing* against those positions and for her own position. Do you agree? If you do, does that make her essay less convincing? Explain.

10 | WRITING A RESEARCH PAPER

Raffaello
Scuola d'Atene
Scala / Art Resource

After reading Toni Morrison's *Song of Solomon* and talking with relatives about your own family tree, you decide to learn more about your ancestors—where they came from, what jobs they held, which ones were famous and which were not, and why they lived the lives they did. In the process, you hope to learn more about yourself and your immediate family. During your research, you read family records and letters, interview your parents and grandparents, check county records, and research genealogies in the library. You intend to write an investigative paper documenting not only what you find but the process of your search and the discoveries you make along the way. □

After spending two months in France living with a family and trying to understand their dinner conversation, you wonder why you—and other Americans—know so little about foreign languages. After reflecting on your inadequate background in French language and culture, you decide to investigate the current state of foreign language studies in the United States. During your research, you discover that Americans know very little about foreign languages and cultures simply because foreign languages are rarely required of students either in high school or in college. You decide to write a research paper that documents the current state of foreign language studies and demonstrates a need for a mandatory foreign language requirement for secondary schools. You hope it will persuade more students to study foreign languages and some schools to revise their requirements. □

Although the words "research paper" sound imposing to most people, research is really a natural and enjoyable part of our everyday experience, both outside and inside college classrooms. We pride ourselves on being good detectives—whether it's window-shopping for a good bargain, finding the hottest used sports car, asking co-workers for tips on the best Mexican food in town, or just browsing in a bookstore for something fun to read. Even in college classes, curiosity leads us to discover new ideas. Whenever we wonder about what causes ozone holes, why teen-agers commit suicide, what makes a computer program work, how artists turn clay into beautiful pottery, or what the national debt means, the seed for a research idea drops into our minds. At some point the idea becomes a question, takes root, and begins to grow. When that happens, we want to learn about something, to find out what others already know or don't know. Curiosity blooms into research when we'd rather discover the answers for ourselves instead of being handed an answer—an "answer" that may have the manufactured feel of a plastic flower.

The essays you have already written in this writing course have involved research, whether or not you called it by that name. The word "research" literally means "to seek out" or "to search again." All writing requires research. Your observing essay required you to "look again" at your subject in order to describe it well. For your remembering essay, you recalled special events from the past, researching your mind for memories. You have also investigated topics by searching in written documents and by doing surveys and interviews. You have explained, evaluated, argued, and even explored subjects using research. In short, you are already a researcher, with considerable experience in presenting the results of your research to a chosen audience. A research paper—sometimes called a term paper—is simply a more thorough and systematic extension of skills you have already practiced.

This chapter will show you how to write a research paper—preparing, locating sources, taking notes, collecting and shaping information, revising, and documenting your sources. As in other writing assignments, the process is recursive. Often, you will need to back up, collect new information, redraft parts of your paper, or refocus your subject during the writing process. At the end of this chapter, student writer Kate McNerny's paper, "Foreign Language Study: An American Necessity" illustrates the important features of a research paper. During the chapter, however, samples from her research log, bibliography, notes, drafts, and documentation illustrate various stages in one writer's process of writing a research paper.

FREEWRITING: RESEARCHING

In the library, find an issue of a magazine or newspaper published on or near the date and year of your birth. The issue may be on microfilm. Record the date and title of the newspaper or magazine. Browse through the issue, looking at headlines, articles, advertisements, editorials, comics, weather, sports, local news, and so forth. As you look through the issue, *record* any items, facts, or historical incidents that interest you. Photocopy one page that you find especially interesting. Explain why that page captured your attention.

TECHNIQUES FOR WRITING A RESEARCH PAPER

Like other kinds of writing, a research paper requires that you focus on a particular subject, develop a claim or thesis, and support your position with convincing evidence: background information, facts, statistics, descriptions, and other people's evaluations and judgments. The evidence you present in a research paper, however, is more detailed than that in an essay, and the sources must be cited in the text and documented at the end of the paper.

In a sense, a research paper is like a scientific experiment. **Your readers should be able to trace your whole experiment—to see what ideas and evidence you worked with, where you found them, and how you used them in your paper.** If readers have any questions about the information you've presented or the conclusions you've reached, they can start with your sources and recreate or check the "experiment" for themselves. If they want to investigate your subject further, your sources will guide their reading. As you write a research paper, keep the following techniques in mind:

- **Using *purpose, audience, and form* as your guides for writing.** Research is just a method of collecting and documenting ideas and evidence. Purpose, audience, and form should still direct your writing.

- **Finding *the best that has been written or said* about your subject.** Instead of trying to reinvent the wheel, discover what other people or writers already know or don't know, and then build on what they have learned.

- **Using sources to make *your* point.** As you gather information, you may revise your thesis in light of what you learn, but don't

Criticism [is] a disinterested endeavor to learn and propagate the best that is known and thought in the world.

—Matthew Arnold, poet and essayist

let the tail wag the dog. Don't allow the information to control you or your paper.

- *Documenting* **your sources, both in the text and at the end of the paper.** (Using ideas, information, or actual language from your sources without proper documentation is *plagiarism*.)

Using Purpose, Audience, and Form as Guides

Like any other kind of writing, research papers have a *purpose.* Reporting, explaining, evaluating, problem solving, and arguing are all purposes for a research paper. Purposes may appear in combinations, as in a paper that summarizes the current research and then proposes a solution to a current problem. Research papers are not just reports of other people's ideas or evidence, however. What you, the researcher, observe and remember and learn is important, too. Most subjects are not interesting until writers make them so. Your curiosity, your interests in the subject, your reason and intuition establish why the subject is worth researching in the first place—and why a reader would want to read the paper once it is finished.

Research papers have a defined *audience,* too. The subject you choose, the kind of research you do, the documentation format, the vocabulary and style you use—all should be appropriate for your selected audience. If you write a senior research paper in your major, you will write for a professor and for a community of people knowledgeable about your field. If you are a legal assistant or a junior attorney in a law firm, a superior may ask you to research a specific legal precedent. If you work for a manufacturer, a manager may assign you a research report on the sales and strategies of a competitor. Although your classmates and teacher will probably read the research paper you write for this class, you will ask them to role-play your audience. They will try to read your paper from the point of view of a defined audience—an employer, a politician, a nutritionist, an artist, an astronomer, or a senior law partner. Your instructor may, in fact, ask you to send your paper to some person or persons who actually are part of your audience.

Finally, your research paper will follow a *form* that fits your purpose and meets the expectations and needs of your audience. First, form is controlled by purpose. If you are writing a research paper evaluating some product or performance, your research paper may look like an evaluating paper, organized around your claims, criteria, judgments, and evidence. If you are writing a problem-solving paper, you will demonstrate the problem, propose a solution, and convince your readers that your proposal is necessary or will work. If you are writing a research paper arguing for a position or claim, you will present research showing both sides of the controversy and then try to convince your reader to believe or act on your claim. In each case, however, you will cite your sources in the body or text of your paper and include a list of your sources (a *bibliography*) at the end.

The *form* for your research paper is also affected by your intended audience. If you are researching new advances in sports medicine for an audience of experts or researchers, you may choose an elaborate form, with an abstract or summary of your ideas at the beginning, a section reviewing and evaluating current research, subsections for each of your main points with diagrams and charts, and an appendix with supplementary materials. If, however, you are writing primarily for jogging enthusiasts, your research paper may look more like an informal essay. Magazines and journals in the field illustrate a variety of appropriate forms for research papers. The student essay by Kate McNerny at the end of this chapter illustrates one form for research papers.

Finding the Best Sources

Accessing information from both published and unpublished sources is central to all research. To find good sources, you need to hone your detective skills. Unfortunately, Hollywood has promoted the myth that good detectives follow their suspects in high-speed car chases or through glamorous affairs. Of course, that's just fantasy. Detectives must do actual research—paperwork and legwork—to track down leads. Writers are, in a real sense, also detectives, constantly researching their own experiences and the experiences of others. Journalists, lawyers, psychologists, doctors, businesspeople, coaches, scientists, novelists—all sorts of people practice their skills in locating key bits of information and tracking down good leads.

Research combines careful planning with bits of good luck, mindless drudgery and moments of inspiration, many dead ends and a few rare discoveries. As coaches sometimes say, those who prepare and work hard make their own luck. The following excerpt from the introduction to Pauli Murray's *Proud Shoes: The Story of an American Family* recounts her research into her family genealogy, which included slaves, free blacks, some racially mixed family members, and other relatives who were white and socially prominent. Although her detective work took several years and involved both library and field research, her account reflects the problems and successes that all researchers experience.

> My field research had the thrill of detection when the clues panned out. Rigorous discipline was needed for the drudgery of sifting through masses of documentary material in search of one relevant fact or one confirmation of a family legend. The trail of the Fitzgerald family led

me into nearly a dozen localities in several states. It took me into musty basements of old courthouses to pore over dust-silted and sometimes indecipherable handwritten entries in old volumes. I found that each locality had its own captivating legends preserved in family papers; its traditions recorded in pamphlets and privately published little books; its stories printed in almanacs, newspapers, business directories. Almost every place had "the oldest living inhabitants" and their recollections. Most important, almost every locality had its own regional-history enthusiasts, who welcomed me into a fellowship of digging into the past. Some of them gave me expert guidance which improved the efficiency of my research and shortened my labors.

Using Sources to Make YOUR Point

When your hard work does yield a source that has good information and ideas on your exact subject, don't be tempted to let that source take over your paper. If you start stringing together passages from only one or two key sources, you'll be summarizing rather than doing research. You'll be letting the sources tell you what to think, what information is important, or what conclusions to reach. So use the sources to support *your* point. Write your own paper; don't let the sources write the paper for you.

Documenting Your Sources

Documenting your sources is an important part of writing a research paper. Documentation takes place in two stages: first, in the body or text of your paper, you give credit to any material you have taken from your source. Then, at the end of the paper, you include a list of "Works Cited" or "Works Consulted" that gives fuller information about these sources for your reader. If your readers doubt a fact or statistic, they can check your sources for themselves. If your readers want more information, your documentation enables them to track down the sources.

PREPARING YOURSELF FOR THE RESEARCH PROCESS

Writing a research paper involves the same process you used in writing essays. The major difference is that each stage or dimension of the process takes longer. You may spend two weeks just collecting sources, reading articles and books, jotting down ideas, testing your ideas on classmates and friends, and narrowing and focusing your

WARMING UP: JOURNAL EXERCISES

Do at least one of the following journal exercises to help get yourself into a research frame of mind or to discover a possible research subject.

1. Sit down with a family member, friend, or classmate. On a sheet of paper, write down the subject of the most interesting course you are currently taking. Hand the sheet of paper to that person and ask him or her to write down questions for an interview designed to find out *why* you like this course and *what* you like best about it. Then have that person interview you and record your responses. At the end of the interview, discuss your responses. What ideas could you research in order to explain to your interviewer what is interesting about this subject?

2. If you are *not* in the library, try this exercise. Reread your authority list from the journal entries in Chapter 5, "Investigating." Choose one subject from that list. Assume that you are on a scavenger hunt, trying to track down bits of information about that subject *without leaving the building that you are currently in*. Anything is fair game: a dictionary, a textbook, a telephone directory, a telephone, a computer terminal, a friend or roommate, this textbook, your journal, or anything you can observe or remember. You have twenty-five minutes to complete the hunt. Write down all the sources you use and the information you discover from each source.

3. In the library, wander down the stacks, looking at titles of books that might interest you. Choose one volume from the shelf. In your journal, record the basic information about that book: author, title, place of publication, publisher, date. In that book, find *three* specific sources that the author refers to or used to write the book. (If the book does not cite sources, choose another volume.) Does your library have these sources? If so, determine where these sources are located. Ask the reference librarian for help if you need it.

subject. And because you gather so much material, the shaping and organizing are also more demanding. Sometimes you may feel as if you're trying to put forty frogs in a dishpan: By the time you arrange ten, the first four have already jumped out. The revising also takes longer, partly because you have to include your documentation, but partly because the pieces of the paper may not fit together as smoothly as you had hoped. There is really no way to rush research. If writing an ordinary paper is like fixing your lunch, then writing a research paper is like preparing Thanksgiving dinner. You can't microwave a research paper. Good things take time.

The first step in writing a research paper is to *readjust your inner clock*. Initially, you'll think that you're not making much progress. You'll think that you're in a slow-motion movie or that you're trying to jog through butter. Once you readjust your inner clock, set more modest goals, and content yourself with a slower but more persistent pace, however, you've won half the battle. By reducing the pressure on yourself, you'll feel less frustrated when you reach a dead end but also readier to appreciate valuable information when you discover it.

To help you adjust mentally and physically to a new pace and an extended writing process, begin your preparation by making a research notebook, outlining a realistic timetable for the paper, and selecting a documentation format.

Research Notebook

Although many researchers recommend using index cards for recording bibliographic entries and notes, for most shorter research projects (up to twenty pages) a loose-leaf research notebook or a spiral notebook with pockets for additional papers and photocopies may be more functional. Divide your notebook into four sections: research log, bibliography, notes from sources (including photocopies), and drafts and ideas.

The *research log* section of your notebook serves as a scratch pad and log of your research progress. In it you will record what you accomplish during that session, potential references you need to check, reminders to yourself, questions to ask a librarian or your instructor, and notes about your problems, progress, and intended next steps. As you work or when you finish each research session, jot down what you did or need to do. These notes about your problems, progress, questions, and next steps will help you maintain momentum and continuity on your research project. Each time you return to the library or to your research, you can check your notes to see what you need to do next.

Below is an excerpt from student writer Kate McNerny's research log:

4/26

4:30 — 6:00 p.m.

Still working on finding articles. Found the Delbert and Roberta Long article. It has some good stuff. <u>Education</u> is on microfilm, so I learned how to photocopy from microfilm. Of course, just when I had the machine turned to exactly the right page, I discovered I didn't have a nickel for the copy machine, so I had to leave the room (some guy waiting in line looked irritated as I explained I'd be back in a minute). I ran to the change machine, got my nickels and copied the article!

April issue of <u>Parents</u> magazine missing from the shelves. UGH — I hate that.

Question: Do I want to survey students to find out about typical attitudes toward taking foreign languages? What questions could I ask?

Another question: Is this going to be an arguing paper? Is there a controversy? Are there two sides??

Try to find tomorrow: three <u>Education Digest</u> articles on microfilm (L11/E3): Oct. 84, p. 32
Dec. 85, p. 36
Mar. 86, p. 24

Check <u>Education Index</u>.

Remember that 5 - 6 p.m. is a good time to work in the library. Everyone clears out, so I don't have to fight over the microfilm machines.

In the *bibliography* section of your notebook, keep a list of every source you consult, with complete information about each source. Leave space between entries to write additional information, such as call numbers. This list becomes your *working bibliography*. McNerny's bibliography included the following entries:

Long, Delbert H. and Roberta Long. "Toward the Promotion of Foreign Language Study and Global Understanding." *Education* Volume 105 Summer 1985: 366 - 368.

L 11 / . E2 Periodical Microfilm Room

Mayor, Barbara and A. K. Pugh, editors. *Language, Communication, and Education: A Reader*. London: Croom Helm in association with the Open University, 1987.

P / 106 / . L317 / 1987 East Wing stacks

In addition, include in the bibliography section any printouts from computer searches or photocopies of relevant pages from indexes or bibliographies.

In the *source notes* section, leave plenty of pages to record direct quotations, paraphrases of key ideas, and facts from the sources in your bibliography list. Introduce each section with a reference to the author and a short version of the title. After each note, indicate the page number or numbers. One page of McNerny's notes contained the following entries:

Long and Long, *Promotion of Foreign Language Study*

Study by the Longs — group of intellectually gifted 7th graders wrote stories about Soviet children. The 7th graders had acquired many "facts" regarding communism and the Soviet Union, but had many misconceptions, too.

"They expressed fear for the children and thought all schools were military schools with strict rules and harsh punishment. They believed that many soviet children couldn't attend school because they had to work in the fields and ride horse-drawn wagons...." p. 367

Ranwez and Rogers, *Status of Foreign Languages*

91% of Colorado secondary schools the 536 schools responding to the questionnaire offered foreign languages, but 91% of schools responding didn't require any foreign language credits for graduation. pp. 99-100

For your source notes section, make *photocopies* of any valuable source materials. Write author, title, and page numbers on each photocopied source.

In the *drafts and ideas* section of the notebook, jot down brainstorms, looping or clustering exercises, sketch outlines, trial drafts, and examples from your own experience. During a research project, ideas can come to you at any time. When they do, take time to write them down. This section of your notebook serves as a journal devoted solely to your research paper. One example from McNerny's drafts and ideas section records her personal experience with foreign languages:

4/29

I can remember my mom always telling me, "Take French classes, learn how to speak French so that you can go visit your cousins in France some day." At the time (junior high school) though, learning a foreign language was low on my priority list. I did take French classes for two years — but dropped out after my sophomore year and immediately lost any basic competency I might have acquired.

In college, I'd like to take a language again, but it never seems to fit with my schedule. But last year, as my mom had promised, I got the opportunity to visit my cousins in France. For some reason, the fact that I couldn't speak French didn't seem to me like it would be a big problem. That was until I stepped off the train at Gare du Nord in Paris and couldn't find the relative who was supposed to meet me. After frantically searching the entire station several times, I had to break down and ask for help. At the information desk a few completely butchered French phrases escaped my lips — only to be received by an unimpressed, unresponsive station attendant. He muttered something about dumb Americans and then pointed me off towards some unknown destination. Well I survived that ordeal — but at the same time swore to myself that I would never make another trip to France until I could speak the language.

Research Timetable

Before you begin your research, write out a tentative schedule. Your instructor may assign due dates for specific parts of the paper (invention exercises, topic selection, working bibliography, rough draft), but you should make a schedule that fits your work habits and your weekly schedule.

COMPUTER TIP

If you prefer to write on a computer and have access to a battery-operated "notebook" or portable computer, use it as your research notebook. Create separate files for each section in the notebook and then take the computer with you when you do research. After each research session, save your notes on a disk and print them out on hard copy.

If you are accustomed to composing on a computer or at a typewriter keyboard, the notebook computer makes it easier to take notes, draft ideas, and record information during your research. In addition, the final organizing and drafting will be quicker because your sources will already be on file or in the computer's memory.

The following schedule assumes that you have at least a month to work on your research paper. How many days each part takes depends on the amount of time you can work each day. Some days you may have only thirty minutes. Other days you may have several hours. *The key is to do a little bit every day to keep your momentum going.*

Prepare for research: buy and organize a research notebook; set up a timetable; select documentation format.	1–2 days
Choose a subject and narrow it into a well-focused topic. This process begins in the first few days but continues throughout the writing process.	2–3 days
Collect library sources; identify and find unpublished sources; do surveys or questionnaires; conduct field observation; record personal experiences. Evaluate source materials; take notes on selected sources; photocopy sources.	12–14 days
Shape and organize ideas and sources, outline, fine-tune thesis.	4–6 days
Draft ideas as you collect and shape your sources and ideas, but leave a block of time to draft your first version.	2–4 days
Revise your drafts, collect additional information, sharpen your thesis, reshape or outline, cite sources in the text and in the bibliographic list at end, and edit and proofread the paper.	6–8 days

Tailor your schedule to your own temperament and work habits. If you like to work exactly to a schedule or even finish early, design a schedule so you can finish a day or two before the due date. If you are like most writers—you love to procrastinate or you are often up all night before an assignment is due—then use your schedule to set *early* target dates, to get your momentum going. When you finish drafting your schedule, put a copy in the *research log* section of your notebook, so you can check your progress as you work.

Documentation Format: MLA and APA Styles

A final step in preparing for the research paper is to select a documentation style. This chapter illustrates both the MLA and APA styles. If you are writing a paper for the humanities, follow the Modern Language Association (MLA) style set forth in the *MLA Handbook for Writers of Research Papers* (1988). If you are writing a paper in the behavioral sciences, use the American Psychological Association

(APA) style as described in the *Publication Manual of the American Psychological Association* (1984). For some scientific subjects, follow the Council of Biology Editors (CBE) format illustrated in the *CBE Style Manual* (1983). This chapter illustrates only the MLA and APA styles, but all three style manuals are available in most college bookstores.

Leading academic and professional journals also illustrate the documentation styles customary in specialized fields. You may want to consult issues of those journals to determine the exact format for footnotes or in-text citation of sources. *Before you begin doing research, however, select a documentation style* that is appropriate for your subject, purpose, and audience. Then practice on that style as you compile your working bibliography.

RESEARCH PAPER: THE WRITING PROCESS

ASSIGNMENT FOR THE RESEARCH PAPER

Choose a subject that strongly interests you and about which you would like to learn more. It may be a subject that you have already written about in this course. Research this subject in a library and, if appropriate, supplement your library research with questionnaires, interviews, or other unpublished sources of information. Check with your instructor for suggested length, appropriate number or kinds of sources, and additional format requirements. Use a documentation style appropriate for your subject, purpose, and audience.

Choosing a Subject

For this research paper, choose a subject in which you already have personal interest or experience. Start by rereading your journal entries for possible research subjects. Even a personal entry may suggest an idea. If you wrote about how you fainted in the gym during aerobics or weight training, you might research the potential dangers of exercising in high heat and humidity or sitting in a sauna after hard exercise. If you wrote a journal entry about a friend's drinking problem, you might like to read more about the causes and "cures" for alcoholism.

In addition, reread the essays you have written to see whether one of them refers to a possible research subject. If your observing essay was about a tomato, for example, you may want to find out how tomatoes are mass-produced for the supermarket—and why they often look and taste like pink Styrofoam. Your remembering essay may suggest a person, place, event, or custom that you might investigate. Perhaps you could further research the topic of your investigating essay, find more current information about the subject of your explaining paper, or research some specific topic from your problem-solving or arguing papers.

Narrowing and Focusing Your Subject   Once you have a tentative idea, remember that you'll need to narrow it, focus it, or otherwise limit the subject. The topic of alcoholism is too general. Focus your question: "Do beer commercials on television contribute to alcoholism?" "What methods does Alcoholics Anonymous use to help people?" "Has raising the drinking age to 21 reduced the incidence of alcoholism?" Only after you've started your research, however, will you know whether your question is still too broad (you can't begin to read everything about it in just two weeks) or too narrow (in two weeks, you can't find enough information about that question).

Two techniques may help narrow and focus your subject. *You may wish to try these now, wait until you have done some initial reading, or do them several times during your collecting and shaping.*

A *topic cross* uses lists of key terms to focus ideas. In a topic cross, you list, on the vertical axis, key terms related to your subject, from most general to most specific. Then, once you've focused on a level that you think might work for your research, list, on the horizontal axis, similar kinds or examples of topics. Assume, for example, that your general subject is nutrition or diets. Make the vertical axis first: Put the most general subjects or categories at the top, the most specific at the bottom:

Food

Nutrition

Menus

Diets

Vegetarianism

Reducing diets

Reducing diets for joggers

Reducing diets for marathon runners

Choose a topic midway down the list that might relate to your specific interests. Then, for that topic, list on the horizontal axis any examples or similar kinds of topics. If you focus on reducing diets, you might sketch in the horizontal axis as follows:

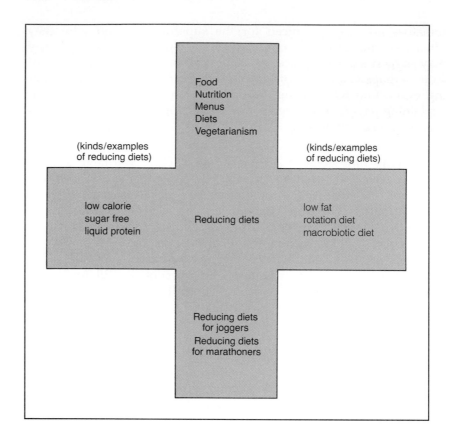

Possibly one of those diets—the low-fat diet—might become the focus of your research. The *topic cross* enables you to "sight in" on a topic as though you were adjusting the cross hairs in a microscope. If your topic is too general, move down the vertical axis. If you are on the right level, brainstorm for other examples you might focus on.

Question analysis is a second narrowing and focusing strategy. The *who, what, when, where,* and *why* questions you use to focus your topic are the same questions that reference librarians use to help you focus your research in the library.

> Who: What group of people are interested or affected?
>
> What: How are key terms defined? What academic discipline is involved?
>
> When: What is the period or time span?
>
> Where: What continent, country, state, or town is involved?
>
> Why: What are possible effects or implications?

Answering these questions about your subject—by yourself, in a group, or with a reference librarian—may suggest new angles, new avenues for research, or subtopics that might lead to a focus for your research paper. As you narrow your topic, you are narrowing and focusing the range of your research in the library. Student writer Kate McNerny, brainstorming with another class member, applied these questions to her subject about foreign language study and came up with the following possibilities.

Foreign Language Study

Who? Ans: I am interested in Americans. Specifically, I want to focus on why Americans should begin learning a foreign language early in school, in grade school, secondary school and college. Learning a foreign language would affect how foreigners see us.

What? Ans: Key terms defined — perhaps what "learning" means. Does it mean just basic speaking competency? Probably. If I could have asked a few simple questions in the Gare du Nord, I wouldn't have felt so stupid. Academic discipline — learning the foreign language is important, but culture is part of it, too. History should teach us about foreign cultures. So should psychology — do the Japanese think differently from the Spanish? Why did the French seem rude and Italians friendly? Do I want to research the psychology of languages? I don't think so.

When? Ans: I really want to know why foreign language studies are currently not emphasized. The 1980's. But what about trends — is it getting better or worse? Are more people learning foreign languages than a few years ago? I don't know.

Where? Ans: In the United States. In my home town. Why is it that in the French schools, children as a matter of course learn several languages while we aren't required to learn any?

Supposedly, we are the "melting pot" for many different languages and cultures, but we don't know each other's languages.

Why? Ans: I can make a long list of the effects:
— We can't communicate when we're tourists.
— We can't read anything printed in their language.
— We don't understand their culture.
— We don't even understand the cultures of the millions of Americans from other cultures.
— We isolate ourselves in businesses, too.

To avoid these effects, I want to argue for stronger foreign language requirements in secondary schools and colleges.

As a result of her question analysis, McNerny decided to discuss both language and culture, to focus on the current conditions, and to recommend that secondary schools require foreign languages. *In any research, however, what you look for and what you find are always different. You will need to modify your focus as you read and learn.*

Collecting

Once you have a tentative subject, a possible purpose, and an audience, you are ready to start collecting information. Collecting data for your research paper will require identifying and locating published and unpublished sources, evaluating your sources and choosing those that are the most appropriate for your needs, and then taking notes on your selected sources. *Remember, however, that finding sources—like writing itself—is an ongoing and recursive process.* You often identify new sources after you have taken notes on other sources. Although you may begin your search in the card catalogue, the on-line catalogue, or the reference section, as you narrow and focus your topic or draft sections of your paper, you may come back and recheck the card catalogue, basic references, periodical indexes, or bibliographies.

Use *informal contacts* with friends or acquaintances as an integral part of your collecting process. Friends, family members, business associates, or teachers may be able to suggest a key question or give you some sources: relevant books and magazine articles, television programs that are available in transcript, or local experts on your subject. One student, for example, was doing research on successful techniques for job interviews. She mentioned her project during a telephone conversation with her father. As it turned out, he regularly interviewed job applicants at his company. The student was able to interview him for specific recommendations. Another student was doing biographical research on television reporter Charles Kuralt. He mentioned his project to his journalism professor who, as it turned out, knew Kuralt personally and gave the student both some personal anecdotes and the titles of several recent articles. Most teachers, in fact, are happy to talk about their field and recommend key sources of information.

Unpublished Sources Although the library may be the main source of information for your paper, other sources can be important, too. You may *interview* authorities on your subject or design a *questionnaire* to measure people's responses. (Interviews and questionnaires are discussed in Chapter 5.) *Phone calls* and *letters* to experts, government agencies, or businesses may yield background information, statistics, or quotations. *Notes from classes, public lectures, or television programs* are useful sources. Use a tape recorder to ensure that you transcribe your information accurately. A *scientific experiment* may even be appropriate. *Unpublished public documents,* such as deeds, wills, land surveyors' maps, and environmental impact statements, may contain a gold mine of information. Finally, don't ignore the most obvious sources: Your room, the attic in your home, or your relatives may have a repository of valuable unpublished data—*private letters, diaries, old bills, or check stubs.*

For her research paper, Kate McNerny decided to conduct an informal survey of attitudes toward foreign languages. She recorded the responses in her "drafts and ideas" section of her research notebook. When she drafted her paper, she used some of these responses in the introduction to her paper.

Q: Should foreign languages be required in Junior and Senior High?

A: (Mindy, 21, student) Yes, I think its a good idea — it would have been more valuable to me than some of the other required classes I took — like P.E.

A: (Jodi, 22, student) No, I had a hard enough time with English. Besides, I don't think I'd ever need to use it.

A: (Roger, 23, carpenter) Yes, I was in Europe last year and missed out on a lot because I couldn't speak any other language. Europeans don't speak English as much as we hear they do, but most of the people I met there spoke at least two languages.

A: (Jim, 49, contractor) No, I've never gone to Europe and never needed to speak another language for any other reason. I had enough trouble getting through other classes.

A: (Carolyn, 51, teacher) Yes, when I was teaching there were few language classes available. But as a reading teacher I can see many ways in which language studies would have enhanced our program.

Primary and Secondary Sources Some sources—accounts of scientific experiments, transcripts of speeches or lectures, questionnaires, interviews, private documents—are known as *primary sources.* They are original, firsthand information, "straight from the horse's mouth." Secondhand reports, analyses, and descriptions based on primary sources are known as *secondary sources.* Secondary sources may contain the same information, but they are once-removed. For example, a lecture or experiment by an expert in food irradiation is a primary source; the newspaper report of that lecture or experiment is a secondary source.

The distinction between primary and secondary sources is important for two related reasons. First, secondary sources may contain errors. The newspaper account may misquote the expert or misrepresent the experiment. If possible, therefore, find the primary source—a copy of the actual lecture or a published article about the experiment. Second, finding the primary sources may make your research document more persuasive through an appeal to character (see Chapter 9). If you can cite the original source—or even show how some secondary accounts distorted the original experiment—you will gain your readers' trust and faith. Uncovering the primary data not only makes your research more accurate, but your additional effort makes all your data and arguments appear more credible.

Library Sources Before you begin collecting information in the library, acquaint yourself with the library itself. If you have not already done so, inquire at the information desk about library tours or tour the library with a friend or classmate. Locate the *reference section; the library catalogue* for books; the *indexes* for newspapers, journals, and magazines; the *microform room;* the *stacks;* and the *government documents* section. Don't assume that because you've used one library, you can immediately start your research in a new library. Remember: Librarians themselves are valuable sources of information. Use their expertise early in your research.

BACKGROUND INFORMATION AND GENERAL REFERENCE Before you consult the on-line or card catalogue or run to the *Readers' Guide to Periodical Literature,* you need a general overview of your subject. Start with an encyclopedia, dictionary, almanac, or biography for background information. Many people associate encyclopedias with their grade-school "research"—when they copied passages out of *World Book* or *Collier's Encyclopedia.* But encyclopedias are an excellent source of basic information and terminology that may help you focus, narrow, and define your subject. Use them as background reading, however, not as major sources.

In addition to the general encyclopedias, there are hundreds of references—one or two might just save you hours of research in the library and lead you directly to key facts or important information on your topic. (You may wish to begin your collecting in the reference room or check there only after you have collected information from other books and articles. Often these references are more valuable *after* you have done some reading on your subject.) Beyond the standard college dictionary or thesaurus, the *Oxford English Dictionary,* known as the *OED,* or *Webster's Third New International Dictionary of the English Language* may help you find key ideas or definitions.

There are also many specialized dictionaries for scientific terms, slang words, symbols, and a host of other specialized vocabularies. If you need facts, figures, or statistics, consult the *World Almanac* or the *Statistical Abstract of the United States.* If your subject is a person, check one of the references that indexes collections of biographies. *Biography and Genealogy Master Index* and *Biographical Dictionaries* reference more than three million biographical sketches.

Bibliographies (lists of books and articles on a specific subject) can also contain a gold mine of information about sources that are possibly useful to you. There are three strategies for finding bibliographies. First, check the *Bibliographic Index.* This work refers to entire bibliographies or parts of books that already have a list of sources related to your topic. Next, check the subject card catalogue. Look either for a subhead for your subject labeled "bibliography" or for specific books that have a bibliography. Finally, check in the books and articles you find. Some contain bibliographies not mentioned in the card catalogue or the on-line catalogue.

The librarian is still the most valuable resource for your research. At some point during your research in the library, probably after you have a focused topic and have collected some sources, talk to a reference librarian. For many writers, asking for help can be really intimidating. To make the process of asking for help as painless—and productive—as possible, try saying something like the following: "Hi, I'm Kate McNerny. I'm doing a research project for my college writing course. My topic is foreign language study in the United States. I'm trying to find information about the current state of foreign language study in the United States and collect some arguments for increasing requirements in secondary schools and colleges. Here's what I've found so far [explain what you've done]. What additional reference books, indexes, dictionaries, or bibliographies might help me in my research?" The resulting conversation may be the most productive five minutes of your entire library research. After you've talked to the librarian once, it will be easier to return and ask a question when you hit a snag.

THE ON-LINE OR CARD CATALOGUE   Most large university libraries have computer access or on-line catalogues to speed the process of locating books and periodicals. If you are unfamiliar with your library's computer-access system, ask the librarian about an orientation tour. A few minutes with a librarian will spare you the frustration of learning by trial and error.

Many libraries, however, still use card catalogues to access to the collection. The card catalogue lists books and other materials in three major categories: *author, title,* and *subject.* if you don't know the author of a book, you may wish to check the title listing; or if you have a bibliography list, you may check by author. In most cases, however, research begins with the *subject cards.* But the question is, what *subject* do you look under? When Kate McNerny went to the card catalogue and looked under "Language," she found several drawers full of cards, with special categories, subheadings, and cross-references. The drawers looked bewildering. On advice from the reference librarian, she checked a standard reference work called the *Library of Congress Subject Headings* (LCSH). It was sitting on a desk next to the card catalogue.

The *Library of Congress Subject Headings* is like the Yellow Pages in the phone book. If you want to find the phone number of a doctor, for example, and you check the Yellow Pages under "doctors," you will probably find a reference that says, "See Chiropractors,

Optometrists, Physicians & Surgeons." Similarly, the LCSH will help you identify the key words and subject headings used by the Library of Congress to classify or cross-reference your subject. McNerny looked in the LCSH under "Foreign Languages" and found "See Language and languages—Study and teaching and Languages—Modern." So she looked under "Language and languages" and found the listings and cross-references condensed below:

Language and languages

Here are entered works on language in general, works on the origin and history of language, and surveys of languages. Works dealing with the scientific study of human speech . . . are entered under Linguistics. Works on the philosophy and psychology of language are entered under Languages—Philosophy, and Languages—Psychology, respectively.

[see also]	sa	Alien labor—language
		Bilingualism
		Children—Language
		Imaginary languages
		Mass media and language
		Music and language
		Sign language
		Women—Language
[also referenced under]	x	Foreign languages
[subheadings]		—Ability testing
		—Foreign words and phrases
		—History
		—Psychology
		—Sex differences
		—Study and teaching
		—Syntax

Then she looked in the LCSH under "Languages, Modern" and found additional entries. From these lists McNerny decided that the subheadings, "Language and education" and "Study and teaching," might contain useful sources. So she went back to the subject card catalogue, looked under "Language and languages" and "Languages, Modern," and copied out (in the *bibliography section* of her research notebook) a list of relevant books for her research question. Below is a subject card for one of the books she found. Although the card has basic information, such as call number, author, title, publisher, and date, it also indicates that this book has a bibliography, illustrations, and is catalogued also under "Manners and customs—Study and teaching."

Sample Subject Card

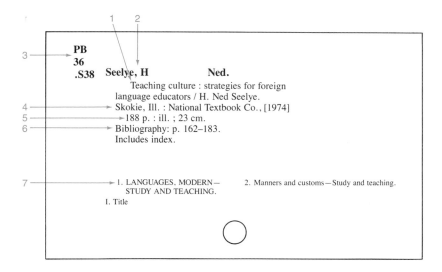

1. The title of the book, as it appears on the title page.
2. The author's name, last name first—sometimes followed by birth and death dates.
3. Library call number used to locate the book on the library's shelves.
4. Publication information: place of publication, publisher, and date.
5. Pages in preface or introduction (if applicable), pages in text, illustrations, height of book in centimeters.
6. Bibliography, index, and other special features.
7. Subject headings and listings.

PERIODICAL INDEXES   Magazines, journals, and newspapers are called *periodicals* because most are published on a daily, weekly, or monthly basis. An *index* is just a list of citations, organized for easy reference. Just as the index of a textbook refers you to topics, ideas, or names in that book, a periodical index refers you to articles published in a certain group of magazines, journals, or newspapers. Periodical indexes, such as the *Readers' Guide to Periodical Literature,* are usually monthly, quarterly, or annual publications that refer to articles published in hundreds of different periodicals.

The library contains hundreds of periodical indexes, each referring to a slightly different subject or group of periodicals. A *general* index such as the *Readers' Guide* refers to approximately two hundred popular magazines. Some libraries even have general periodical indexes listed on computer: *InfoTrac,* for example, draws from more than one thousand current magazines, journals, and current newspapers. A *specialized* index may focus on just one publication, such as *The New York Times Index,* or on just one subject, such as the *Art Index,* which indexes approximately three hundred periodicals in the arts.

Below is a list of frequently used indexes. When you discuss your research project with your instructor or with the reference librarian, ask which indexes will be most helpful for your subject.

- *Applied Science & Technology Index*
- *Art Index*
- *Book Review Index*
- *Business Periodicals Index*
- *Consumers Index*
- *Education Index*
- *Humanities Index*
- *Infotrac*
- *New York Times Index*
- *Psychological Abstracts*
- *Public Affairs Information Service Bulletin*
- *Readers' Guide to Periodical Literature*
- *Social Sciences Index*

When you find an index appropriate for your subject, begin with the most recent volumes and work back in time (unless your subject is a limited historical period). In each volume, you will find entries related to the subject headings or descriptors for your topic. Below is a condensed version of what Kate McNerny found in the *Readers' Guide* entry under "Language and languages":

Language and languages

See also
Bilingualism
College Students—Language
French language
Sign language

Origin

Anthropologist argues that language cannot be read in stones [views

      of Thomas Wynn] R. Lewin. *Science* 233:23–4 Jl 4 '86.

Political aspects

Lingo [W. Safire's On Language column] J. Quinn. *Nation* 242:58–60

      Ja 18 '86

Study and teaching

Should your child learn a foreign language? F. Roberts. il *Parents*

      61:58+ Ap '86

Taking a foreign language could be your ticket to travel—and a

      whole lot more. M. G. Lee. por *Seventeen* 45:44 My '86

ANALYSIS OF SAMPLE READERS' GUIDE ENTRY

Look in the front of most indexes for explanations of abbreviations and for a list of magazines indexed. **Note:** Most citations of articles will not contain all the information necessary to document the source in your paper. When you locate the actual article, write in the bibliography section of your research notebook the above information and *add* the author's *first name* and the *additional pages* of the article, here indicated by the [+] sign following the page citation.

In addition to a general index such as *Readers' Guide* or *Infotrak*, also check a *subject index* for periodicals relating to your topic. The subject indexes, such as the *Art Index, Applied Science and Technology Index, Consumers Index, Education Index,* or *Social Sciences Index,* may direct you to an article in a slightly more specialized magazine or journal that has exactly the information you're trying to find. McNerny decided to check the *Education Index.* Condensed below is what she found under "Languages, Modern."

Languages, Modern

See also
Arabic language
Chinese language
Japanese language
Russian language
Spanish language

Aims and objectives

The case for a national foreign language center: an editorial. R.
D. Lambert. *Mod Lang J* 71:1–11 Spr '87

A review of proposals to strengthen foreign language and
international education. M. Allison. *Foreign Lang Ann* 19:533–6
D '86

Curriculum

The foreign language requirement: an alternative program. K. A.
Demuth and N. B. Smith. *Foreign Lang Ann* 20:67–77 F '87

On the teaching of culture in the FL curriculum. G. F. Westphal.
bibl por (p193) *Can Mod Lang Rev* 43:87–93 O '86

Study

Industry held back by lack of languages [Great Britain] F. Jones.
Times Higher Educ Suppl 707:6 My 23 '86

Strengthening the language requirement at the University of
Minnesota: an initial report. J. D. Arendt and others. *Foreign
Lang Ann* 19:149–56 Ap '86

In addition to finding some articles that were about her exact subject, she discovered several journals devoted entirely to the study and teaching of foreign languages. Browsing in the most recent issues of those journals, she found other articles on her subject.

GOVERNMENT DOCUMENTS The largest publisher in the world is the United States Government Printing Office (G.P.O.). It publishes countless articles, pamphlets, and books on history, government, and law. Many of the publications cover an astonishing variety of everyday topics and are written in nontechnical language for the general public. Your library will probably have a separate government documents section, and the documents librarian can help you gain access to the collection. References such as the *Monthly Catalog of U.S. Government Publications,* the *Public Affairs Information Service Bulletin,* or *American Statistics Index* will help you identify government documents relevant to your subject. Many libraries will have a monthly updated microform called the *Government Publications Index.* Checking under the subject heading "Language and languages—Study and teaching," McNerny found the following entry:

> = Grants to promote foreign language
> programs:-report together with individual
> views . . . (Washington, D.C.?:–U.S.
> G.P.O.-1981) . . .
> SuDoc #Y1.1/8:97–316

With the Superintendent of Documents number (SuDoc) on the last line of the entry, McNerny then asked the librarian to show her how to find the document. Don't hesitate to ask for a librarian's help in the Government Documents section of the library.

BIBLIOGRAPHIC COMPUTER SEARCH   Many library catalogues have been converted to electronic databases, so you may access information about books and journals with a computer terminal. A growing number of standard periodical indexes are also available in database format, and some of these, such as ABI/INFORM, a general business index, have no print equivalent. Your library may have one of the popular databases, such as the *Knowledge Index, DialogOnDisc,* or *INFOTRAC,* which you can use in the library or access with a microcomputer and a modem. Listed below are some other commonly searched databases.

- ERIC (Education Resources Information Center)
- NTIS (National Technical Information Service)
- SOCIAL SCISEARCH (Social Science Citation Index)
- SCI SEARCH (Science Citation Index)
- PSYCHINFO

Check with your librarian to determine which databases are available and whether they are appropriate for your research project.

Evaluating Sources   As you collect both published and unpublished information, you should appraise your sources with a critical eye. Do not assume that every glittering statement you read or hear is valuable; only a handful of the dozens of sources you dig up will be true gold. Some will not relate specifically to your topic; others will be too superficial or too technical. Some will be out of date; others will be biased or simply inaccurate. Evaluate your sources based on the following *criteria:*

Sources should be relevant. The sources you select should be relevant to your subject, your purpose, and your intended audience. If your narrowed topic is still too general, all your sources will look relevant. In that case, narrow your subject even more. Sources must be relevant to your purpose as well. If you are writing an argumentative research paper, you need several sources representing both sides of the issue. If you are proposing a solution to a problem, look for sources describing the problem or the solution. Finally, sources should be appropriate for your intended audience. The articles that Kate McNerny found in *Foreign Language Annals* were more appropriate for her academic audience than was the brief and superficial article from *Parents* magazine.

Sources should be current. As a rule of thumb, look for the most current sources—especially those on scientific or technical subjects. Research on AIDS is more accurate and complete now than it was in 1985. Current articles on turbocharged automobiles should be more informed than those written in 1970. Recent articles on child day-care programs will more accurately reflect current trends. Sometimes, however, older books and articles are important. If you are doing historical research about the Great Depression in the United States, you may want to read key documents from the 1930s. If your subject is Shakespeare, seventeenth-century literary criticism may be as valuable as twentieth-century analyses. In every academic discipline, some sources remain authoritative for decades. When you find that many writers refer to a single source, it may be valuable regardless of its date of publication.

Sources should be reliable. Check for possible bias in an article or book. Don't expect the National Rifle Association to give an unbiased report on gun-control legislation. Don't assume that representatives of right-to-life or pro-choice groups will objectively represent the full range of facts about abortion. Since at least some bias is inevitable in any source, locate and use a variety of sources representing several points of view. If you are in doubt about an author's point of view or credibility, consult experts in the field or check book reviews. *Book Review Digest*, for example, contains references of reviews that may indicate the author's reputation or reliability.

Taking Notes   Taking careful notes from both published and unpublished sources is, of course, fundamental to accurate documentation. When a source appears relevant and useful, do the following:

1. *Record complete bibliographical information about it in the bibliography section of your research notebook* (or in your computer notebook). For *books,* you need authors, editors, title, volume, publisher, place of publication, and year of publication. For *articles,* you need authors, article title, magazine or journal title, volume and number or date, month, and year of publication, and beginning and ending page numbers. As Kate McNerny did in her log, leave a space between each entry to record call numbers or location of document:

> (Book): Simon, Paul. *The Tongue-Tied American: Confronting the Foreign Language Crisis.* New York: Continuum Publishing Co., 1980.
>
> PB/38/.U655 East wing stacks, main floor
>
> (Article): Lambert, Richard D. "The Improvement of Foreign Language Competency in the United States." *Annals of the American Academy of Political and Social Science* March 1987: 9-19.
>
> H1/.A4 On shelf with current issues,
> 2nd floor

If the source is unpublished—such as a telephone conversation, a letter, or a public document in the country courthouse—record all the information about it that your readers will need to identify and consult the source themselves. (See "Documenting Sources" section in this chapter.) For printed sources, remember that the information you copy from a periodical index may be missing key information, such as the author's full name or page numbers for the article. *When you actually find each source, update your bibliographical information.*

2. *Record notes in the "source notes" section of your research notebook.* In the source notes section, identify each entry with the author's name and the title. If your notes fill two or more pages, put the author and title at the top of each page. Write on only one side of each page. Briefly *summarize* the main points made in the source, note specific information useful to you, paraphrase key ideas, transcribe interesting

quotations, and jot down your own brief comments, questions, and memories. Place page numbers immediately following each paraphrase or quotation. Use direct quotation rather than paraphrase when the actual words in the source are more concise, authoritative, or persuasive than your paraphrase might be. *Be sure that direct quotations are accurate, word-for-word transcriptions from the original.*

3. *Photocopy important sources for later rereading and reference.* Make sure all photocopies clearly show author, title, and page numbers. (For some research projects, your instructor may request a photocopy of every source you paraphrase or quote.) If you photocopy several pages, copy the book's title page or the magazine's cover, and staple the copies together. Then you can underline key passages or make notes on the photocopies themselves.

Photocopying has distinct advantages. You can copy the relevant pages of a source so you don't have to lug thirty books home. (Leaving the sources in the library also helps other researchers.) Photocopies are good insurance against losing key information—in case the book or journal is checked out the next time you need it. Photocopies also allow you to reread sources *after* you have read other books or articles; often, on the first reading of a source, you're not certain what is important and what is not. Finally, photocopies allow you to recheck the final draft of your research paper against the source, to make sure that paraphrases, direct quotations, and page citations are accurate. You may save yourself an extra trip to the library to check a page number, a date, or a journal title. To avoid spending unnecessary amounts of money on photocopies, however, always read sources before making copies.

4. *As you read sources and take notes, record your own reactions and ideas in the "drafts and ideas" section of your research or computer notebook.* Be an active reader of your sources. When you agree or disagree with what you are reading, stop for a minute and jot down your ideas. When you think of a comparison, a process, a way to analyze or evaluate something, possible causes and effects, or examples from your own experience, *write out your ideas as completely as you can, right then, while they're fresh in your mind.* Don't get so locked in on taking notes that you forget to record your own ideas. You don't have to collect twenty sources and *then* do a draft; instead, draft ideas *as* you collect information.

Shaping

Once you've collected information for your research paper, you may feel overwhelmed by the task of shaping it into a coherent form. You can assert control over your data, however, and shape them into

Writing is the hardest work in the world not involving heavy lifting.

—*Peter Hamill, journalist*

Writing a book is not as tough as it is to haul 35 people around the country and sweat like a horse five nights a week.

—*Bette Midler, singer, actor, author*

coherent form by reconsidering your purpose and thesis. *Reread your own notes and especially your draft sections from your research notebook.* Then, in the draft section of your notebook, answer the following questions:

Subject:	What is your general subject?
Narrowed topic or question:	What aspect of your subject is most interesting to you now? What question will you answer or explain?
Purpose:	Is your purpose primarily to inform, explain, evaluate, describe a problem and propose a solution, or argue a claim?
Working thesis:	What thesis, claim, or proposal do you want to impress upon your readers?
Audience:	Analyze your audience. How can you interest them in your subject? What aspects of your collected data are most appropriate for your audience?

As you shape, draft, and revise your research paper, you may continue to slightly refocus your topic and question, refine your thesis, or revise your sense of audience.

Shaping Strategies Your goal now is to design some order, sequence, plan, or outline for your research paper. Forcing yourself to write an outline, however, simply may not work. You should have an idea from your previous papers how your writing process works best, but if you're stuck, feeling frustrated, or overwhelmed, try several of the following strategies:

- *Review strategies for shaping* that are appropriate for your particular purpose. If you are arguing for a certain claim, reread shaping strategies in Chapter 9. If you are evaluating something or analyzing a problem and proposing a solution, review the strategies discussed in Chapter 7 or 8.
- *Explain to a friend or classmate* your purpose, audience, and working thesis. Then try to explain how you might proceed.
- *Try freewriting, looping, or clustering* to develop a plan.
- *Reread your notes and drafts* from your research notebook.
- *Take a break.* Let your ideas simmer for a while. Go for a walk. Work on assignments for another course. Go jogging or swimming. Let your mind run on automatic pilot for a while—the information and ideas in your mind may begin organizing themselves into an initial "sketch outline" without your conscious effort.

- *Try branching or treeing your main ideas.* On paper or at the chalk-board, begin with your topic and draw the trunk and main branches of your topics. Try to explain your sketch or chalk-board drawing to someone.

Think of these activities as a circle—begin at any point, work in either direction, repeat them as necessary. When something starts to work, stay with it for a while. If you start to block or become frustrated, go on to the next activity.

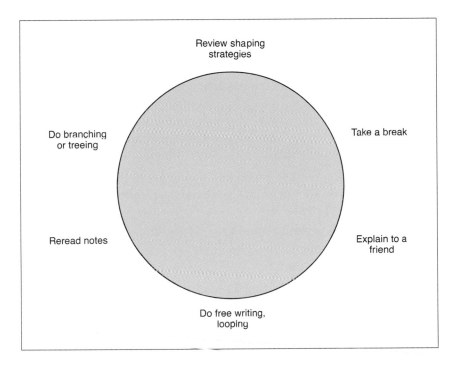

Working Outline   If the shaping activities helped you discover a basic design or plan, translate it into a working outline. If not, you may need to begin drafting in order to discover an outline. Kate McNerny decided to follow a pattern for writing an argument. She modified it considerably as she wrote, but it helped her organize her ideas and source material so she could begin drafting.

Introduction:	Comments-quotations from informal survey-why people feel they don't need to know a foreign language. Mention study on misconceptions of school aged children about Russian children.
I. Narration:	Foreign language studies position in other countries as opposed to U.S.

Mention "glasnost" here?

Example of French and Swedish requirements?
—Statistics on how many Americans are actually competent in another language.

Bill to require a state language?

U.S. position in world as far as power-trade

II. Parition: American students should be required to study a foreign language throughout the 6 years of junior and senior high school. Study of a second language should also be encouraged. Reasons: language, culture, awareness, peace, trade, and business.

III: Arguments: To promote realistic understanding of other cultures

Will help to improve diplomatic relations with other countries-peace cannot be achieved without this.

Change foreigners' attitudes of Americans.

Facilitate international trade and other business.

Enhance quality of education.

Without requirement, no incentive for many students.

IV. Refutation: Not necessary because other countries can speak English (This is more an argument against learning a language, not against a requirement.)

Not essential for quality education.

As requirement, would detract from other important subjects.

Not enough teachers to handle all students—use survey on Colo. schools.

Conclusion: Restate the problems created by current system: Offering 2-3 years of study doesn't lead to competency.

We misunderstand and are misunderstood.

Contrary to popular belief, we are not an isolated country.

A required study of languages will bring us one step closer to global understanding and peace.

Organizing Your Notes With a rough outline as a guide, reread your draft ideas, notes, and photocopies, and label them according to headings and subheadings in your working outline (e.g., Intro; I; Culture; II; Business; III; and so forth). (If you are using a computer notebook, print out all your files and label them.) Before you remove pages from the "source notes" section of your notebook or unstaple photocopied articles or sections of books, *make sure each entry or photo-copy contains the author, title, and page numbers.* Now you are ready to arrange your notes and copies for use during drafting. Organize your notes into groups according to each section of your working outline. Reread each group, deciding which information should come first, in the middle, or last.

Drafting

At this stage of writing a research paper, the most difficult work is behind you. Congratulate yourself—there aren't many people who know as much as you do right now about your subject. You are an authority: You have information, statistics, statements, ideas from other writers and researchers, and your own experiences and observations at your fingertips. As you write, remember that you are communicating *your ideas* and what you have learned. Your sources become the evidence and support for your ideas. Remember that your voice and point of view should unify the information for your reader.

Many writers prefer to start a draft with the first main idea, leaving the introduction until later. As you write, you may discover a quotation, example, or narrative that doesn't fit anywhere else, but would be a perfect lead-in. Or you may already know how you want to start, using an idea that will help organize and direct your thoughts. As you draft, be guided by your working outline and your notes. Avoid copying passages verbatim from your own notebook ideas; instead, reread your notes and express those ideas in language that fits the idea you're working on.

If you get stuck, go back and reread what you have drafted so far or reread the source notes and ideas you have assembled from your notebook and photocopies. Try to maintain your momentum by writing as quickly as possible. Don't be upset if the natural flow of your writing suggests a slightly different order or deviates from your working outline. Consider the new possibility. You may have discovered a better way to shape your material. If you are missing some fact or quotation, just leave a long line and keep writing. Later you can find the source and add the material you need.

Using Sources Proper use of sources requires both creativity and scrupulous honesty. On the one hand, you want to use other people's information and ideas when and where they serve *your* purpose and *your* ideas. A research paper is not simply a long string of people's quotations connected by a few transitions. On the other hand, the sources you cite or quote must be used fairly and honestly. You must give credit for other writers' ideas and information. You must quote accurately, cite your sources in your text, and document those sources accurately.

✳WHAT SOURCES TO CITE   You must cite a source for any fact or bit of information that is not *general knowledge*. Obviously, what is "general knowledge" varies from one writer and audience to another. As a rule, however, document any information or fact that you did not know before you began your research. You may know, for example, that America spends more money on defense than it does on education. However, if you state that the defense budget for the previous year is greater than the total amount spent on education for the past forty years, then cite the source for that fact.

Knowing when you must cite a source for an idea, however, can be tricky. You do not need to indicate a source for *your* ideas, of course. But if you find a source that agrees with your idea, or if you suspect that your idea may be related to ideas from a particular source, cite that source. A citation will give your idea additional credibility: You show your reader that another authority shares your perception.

HOW TO CITE SOURCES   In the text of your research paper, you will need to cite your sources according to either the Modern Language Association (MLA) style or the American Psychological Association (APA) style. **Remember:** Choose *either* the MLA style *or* the APA style and stick with it. Don't mix styles.

According to the Modern Language Association (MLA) style, the in-text citation contains the *author and page number* of your source (Unks 24). No comma appears between author and page number. (If the author is unknown, identify the title and page number of your source. Underline book titles; place quotation marks around article titles.)

According to the American Psychological Association (APA) style, the in-text citation contains *author and date* (Unks, 1985). Use a comma between author and date. If you refer to page number, it should appear after the author and date (Unks, 1985, p. 24). Use a "p." (or "pp." for more than one page) before the page number(s).

The in-text citation (either MLA or APA) refers readers to the end of your paper, where you give complete information about each source in a *Works Cited* (MLA) or *References* (APA) list. For illustration purposes, the following examples use MLA style. See Documenting Sources section (pp. 412–424) for examples of both APA and MLA styles.

Once you have decided that a fact, a paraphrase, or a direct quotation contributes to your thesis and will make a strong impression on your reader, use the following guidelines for in-text citation.

Identify in the text the persons or source for the fact, paraphrased idea, or quotation:

As two foreign language teachers noted: "Like it or not, we are members of a world community consisting of hundreds of nations, and our fates are closely intertwined" (Long and Long 366).

Note: The parentheses and the period *follow* the final quotation marks.

If you cite the author in your sentence, the parentheses will contain only the page reference:

According to Paul Simon, former member of the President's Commission on Foreign Language, the United States should erect a sign at each port of entry that reads, "WELCOME TO THE UNITED STATES—WE CANNOT SPEAK YOUR LANGUAGE" (1).

Use block format (separated from the text by a blank line, indented ten spaces, and double-spaced) for quotations of five lines or more:

Educator Gerald Unks points out two instances in which a lack of language proficiency caused companies to initiate fatal marketing programs.

> When Pepsi-Cola went after the Chinese market, "Come Alive with Pepsi" was translated into Chinese in Taiwan as "Pepsi Brings Your Ancestors Back from the Dead." No Sale! General Motors sought to sell its Nova in South America, oblivious to the fact that "No va" in Spanish means "It doesn't go." (24)

Note: In block quotations, the final period comes *before* the parentheses containing the citation of your source.

Vary your introductions to quotations:

Educator Gerald Unks claims that "only 15 percent of American high school students study a foreign language. Only 8 percent of our colleges require credit in a foreign language for admission (down from 34 percent in 1966)" (24).

"Only 15 percent of American high school students study a foreign language," according to educator Gerald Unks. And the problem is compounded because only 8 percent of our colleges currently have any foreign language admission requirements (24).

The problem is that high school students are not taking foreign languages, and most colleges no longer require a foreign language for admission: "Only 15 percent of American high school students study a foreign language. Only 8 percent of our colleges require credit in a foreign language for admission (down from 34 percent in 1966)" (Unks 24).

Edit quotations when necessary to condense or clarify. Use three ellipsis points or spaced periods (. . .) if you omit words from the middle of a quoted sentence:

> As two foreign language teachers noted, "We are members of a world community . . . and our fates are closely intertwined" (Long and Long 366).

If you omit words from the end of a quoted sentence or omit sentences from a long quoted passage, place a period after the last word quoted before the omission, and follow it with three ellipsis points— for a total of four periods. (Be sure that you have a complete sentence both before and after the four periods.)

> Paul Simon advises us that our nation's lack of language proficiency may have been a partial cause of our disastrous policies in Vietnam:
>
> > Vietnam and the Middle East have taught us that our security position is not solely a matter of dealing with the Warsaw Pact countries or the giants among the nations. Before our heavy intervention in Vietnam, fewer than five American-born experts on Vietnam, Cambodia, or Laos . . . could speak with ease one of the languages of that area. . . . What if—a big if—we had had . . . a mere twenty Americans who spoke Vietnamese fluently, who understood their culture, aspirations, and political history? Maybe, just maybe, we would have avoided that conflict. (9)

Note: The first line is indented five spaces because in the source the quotation begins a new paragraph.

In some cases you may want to change the wording of a quotation or add explanatory words of your own to clarify your quotation. If you do so, clearly indicate your changes or additions by placing them within square brackets:

> As Simon suggests, if only a few Americans knew Vietnamese then "maybe, just maybe, we would have avoided [the Vietnam War]" (9).

HOW TO AVOID PLAGIARISM   Plagiarism is the act of passing off another researcher's or writer's *information, ideas, or language* as one's own. Whether intentional or not, plagiarism is a serious offense. In this class, the result may be a failing grade in both the research project and the course. In the working world, people have lost jobs and presidential candidates have been forced to end their campaigns because they have been caught plagiarizing.

To avoid such disastrous consequences, be honest and give credit to the work of others by carefully documenting *all* facts, ideas, charts, diagrams, and actual phrases or sentences borrowed from your sources. Assume that an accurate quotation from your source would read as follows:

> "Most Americans take it for granted that English is the language of the United States and even imagine that every American speaks it fluently. According to the 1980 U.S. Census, however, 11 percent of Americans come from non-English-speaking homes, and over 1 percent of the U.S. population speaks English not well or not at all. No indicators suggest that these percentages will soon decrease" (Conklin and Lourie 3).

The most blatant form of plagiarism involves using *both* your source's information and your source's language (shown below in italics) without giving credit:

> It is ironic that *11 percent of Americans come from non-English-speaking homes,* and yet most Americans say they will never need to speak a foreign language.

A second form of plagiarism, equally serious, involves giving credit to a source for facts or ideas, but *failing to use quotation marks to indicate that you have borrowed the exact language from the source.* In essence, you are saying that these ideas and facts come from Conklin and Lourie, page 3, but that the language is your own. That, of course, is untrue.

> It is ironic that most Americans take it for granted that English is the language of the United States and even imagine that every American speaks it fluently (Conklin and Lourie 3).

Avoid plagiarism by documenting the passage as follows:

> It is ironic, as two researchers recently pointed out, that "most Americans take it for granted that English is the language of the United States and even imagine that every American speaks it fluently" (Conklin and Lourie 3).

To avoid plagiarism, don't randomly copy out interesting passages. Take accurate notes and transcribe quotations *exactly* as they appear in the source. Either put quotation marks around the exact words of the source, or paraphrase the main ideas in your own words.

Revising

You have been revising your research essay since the first day of the project. You thought about several subjects, but you chose only one. You started with a focus but revised it as you thought, read, and wrote more. You initially tested your ideas in the draft section of your research notebook, but you revised those ideas as you drafted. At this point you are just continuing your revising, only now you have a complete draft to revise.

What makes me happy is rewriting. . . . It's like cleaning house, getting rid of all the junk, getting things in the right order, tightening things up.

—Ellen Goodman, journalist

Start the revision of your complete draft by taking a break. Fix your schedule so you can do something else for a couple of days. When you return and reread your draft, be prepared to be flexible. If there is something missing in your data, prepare yourself to track down the information. If a favorite source or quotation no longer seems relevant, have the courage to delete it. If an example on page 4 would work better as a lead-in for the whole paper, reorder your material accordingly. If the evidence for one side of an argument appears stronger than you initially thought, change your position and your thesis. *Being willing to make such changes is not a sign of poor research and writing. Often, in fact, it demonstrates that you have become more knowledgeable and sophisticated about your subject.*

After you have finished your rough draft, ask friends or class-mates to give you their responses. Accept their criticism gracefully, but ask them to explain *why* they think a certain change would help. Would it help to make your purposes clearer? Would it be more appropriate for your audience? Don't be intimidated and feel that you must make every change a reader suggests. *You* must make the final decisions.

Documenting Sources   Both the Modern Language Association (MLA) and the American Psychological Association (APA) documentation styles require citation of sources in the text of your paper, followed by a Works Cited (MLA style) or References list (APA style) at the end of your paper. Use footnotes only for content or supplementary notes that explain a point covered in the text or offer additional information.

IN-TEXT DOCUMENTATION: MLA STYLE   In the MLA style, give the *author's name* and the *page numbers* in parentheses following your use of a fact, paraphrase, or direct quotation from a source. These in-text citations then refer your readers to the complete documentation of the source in a "Works Cited" or "Works Consulted" list at the end of the paper.

As you cite your sources in the text, use the following guidelines:

If you cite the author in the text, indicate only the page number in parentheses:

> According to Vicki Galloway, Project Director for the American Council on the Teaching of Foreign Languages, a student's horizons will not be broadened by "grammar lectures and manipulative classroom exercises" (33).

If the author is unknown, use a short version of the title in the parentheses:

Most students in the United States would be surprised to learn that the Communist Party in Russia actually sponsors rock concerts (A Day in the Life 68).

If the source is unpublished, cite the name or title used in your bibliography:

In an informal interview, one university administrator noted that funding foreign languages has steadily decreased over the past ten years (Meyers).

If your bibliography contains more than one work by an author, cite the author, a short title, and page numbers. The following examples show various ways of citing a reference to Paul Simon, The Tongue-Tied American:

In The Tongue-Tied American , Simon explains that students can earn a doctorate degree in the United States without ever studying a foreign language (2).

As Simon notes, "it is even possible to earn a doctorate here without studying any foreign language" (Tongue-Tied 2).

In the United States, one can earn a doctorate degree without studying a single foreign language (Simon, Tongue-Tied 2).

Note: Use a comma between author and title but not between title and page number.

If a source has two authors, cite both authors' names in the text or in the parentheses:

A 1984 study sampling 536 secondary schools revealed that 91 percent did not require foreign language credits for graduation (Ranwez and Rodgers 98).

If a source has three or more authors, give the name of the author listed first in your bibliography followed by the abbreviation *et al.,* meaning "and others":

Teachers should integrate the study of history, culture, politics, literature, and religion of a particular region with the study of language (Berryman et al. 96).

If a source has several volumes, precede the page number with the volume number and a colon, as indicated:

Language and grammar can be taught with real-life contexts or scenarios (Valdman 3:82).

If you are citing a quotation or information from a source that itself cites another source, use the abbreviation "qtd. in" for "quoted in" to indicate that you have used an indirect source for your information or quotation. (If possible, however, check the original source.)

As Sue Berryman et al. explain, "The course is developed as a world tour during which time the students take a vicarious trip . . . to become saturated in every aspect of a particular area of the globe" (qtd. in Simon 96).

If you cite two or more authors as sources for a fact, idea, or plan, separate the citations with a semicolon, as follows:

Most recently, two prominent foreign language educators have published plans to coordinate foreign language studies (Lambert 9–19; Lange 70–96).

IN-TEXT DOCUMENTATION: APA STYLE   In the APA style, give the *author's name* and *date* in parentheses following your use of a summary or paraphrase. If you quote material directly, give author's name, date, and page number. (Use "p." for one page and "pp." for more than one page.) These citations will direct your reader to your References list, where you give complete bibliographical information. As you cite your sources, use the following guidelines:

If you do not cite the author in the text, give author, date, and page in parentheses at the end of the citation:

In a recent survey, New Jersey secondary school administrators "rated social studies objectives as contributing most to the attainment of high priority goals, and foreign language as contributing least" (Koppel, 1982, p. 437).

If you cite the author in the text, indicate the date in parentheses immediately following the author's name and cite the page number in parentheses immediately following the quotation:

According to Vicki Galloway (1984), a student's horizons will not be broadened by "grammar lectures and manipulative classroom exercises" (p. 33).

If you cite a long direct quotation (more than forty words), indent the passage five spaces from the left margin. Omit the enclosing direct quotation marks. Place the period at the end of the passage, not after the parentheses:

Educator Gerald Unks (1985) points out two instances in which a lack of language proficiency caused companies to initiate fatal marketing programs:

When Pepsi-Cola went after the Chinese market, "Come Alive with Pepsi" was translated into Chinese in Taiwan as "Pepsi Brings Your Ancestors Back from the Dead." No Sale! General Motors sought to sell its Nova in South America oblivious to the fact that "no va" in Spanish means "It doesn't go." (p. 24)

If you are paraphrasing or summarizing material (no direct quotations), you may omit the page number:

> According to Coxe (1984), many top American businesspeople agree that students who combine some business or economics training with fluency in Japanese have unlimited job possibilities.

Note: Although the APA style manual says that writers may omit page citation for summaries and paraphrases, check with your instructor before you omit page references.

If you have previously cited the author and date of a study, you may omit the date:

> In addition, Coxe points out that many top American businesspeople agree that students who combine some business or economics training with fluency in Japanese have unlimited job possibilities.

If the work has between two and five authors, cite all authors in your text or in parentheses in the first reference:

> Long and Long (1985) refer to two foreign language teachers who noted, "We are members of a world community . . . and our fates are closely intertwined" (p. 366).

> As two foreign language teachers noted, "We are members of a world community . . . and our fates are closely intertwined" (Long & Long, 1985, p. 366).

Note: In your text, write "Long and Long"; in parenthetical citation, use an ampersand: (Long & Long).

If a work has six or more authors, use only the last name of the first author and the abbreviation *et al.* followed by the date:

> Teachers should integrate the study of history, culture, politics, literature, and religion of a particular region with the study of language (Berryman et al., 1988).

If a work has no author, give the first few words of the title and the year:

> Most students in the United States would be surprised to learn that the Russian government has sponsored rock concerts (A Day in the Life, 1988).

If the author is a corporation, cite the full name of the company in the first reference:

> Foreign language study must be accompanied by in-depth understanding and experience of culture (University of Maryland, 1990).

If the source is a personal communication (letter, memo, interview, phone conversation), cite in text but do *not* include in References list (personal communications are not recoverable data):

As Professor Devlin (personal interview, September 21, 1991) explained, "Foreign language study encourages students to see their own language and culture in a fresh perspective."

If you are citing a government document, give the originating agency, its abbreviation (if any), the year of publication, and (if direct quotation) the page number:

Newcomers to a foreign culture should "pay attention to their health as well as their grammar. What the natives regularly eat may be dangerous to a foreigner's constitution" (Department of Health and Human Services [DHHS] , 1989, p. 64).

If your citation refers to several sources, list the authors and dates in alphabetical order:

Several studies (Lambert, 1987; Lange, 1987; Long & Long, 1985) have documented severe deficiencies in America's foreign language preparation.

CONTENT OR SUPPLEMENTARY NOTES   You may use footnote numbers in the text of your paper to refer to a "Notes" section at the end of the paper. If you have an important idea, a comment on your text, or additional information or sources *that would interrupt the flow of your ideas in the text,* you may use that idea or comment in your supplementary Notes section. During her research, for example, McNerny read about the movement to make English the "official language" of the United States. She didn't want to digress in her paper, so she described the controversy in a supplementary note at the end of the paper. Below is a first draft of that note.

Twelve states currently have bills before their legislatures to make English the "official language." Proponents of these bills argue that immigrants need incentives to learn English. Many opponents from ethnic and civil-rights groups believe these bills are racist (McBee 64). If Americans were all educated in foreign languages, these bills would be unnecessary. Americans' ignorance and fear of foreign languages is probably a reason that these bills are so popular.

"WORKS CITED" LIST: MLA STYLE   After you have revised your essay and are certain that you will not change any in-text documentation, you are ready to write your list of sources. Depending on what you include, it will be one of the following:

- A "Works Cited" list (only those works actually cited in your essay)
- A "Works Consulted" list (works cited and works you read)
- A "Selected Bibliography" (works cited and the most important other works)
- An "Annotated List of Works Cited" (works cited followed by a short description and evaluation of the source)

A Works Cited list alphabetically orders, by author's last name, all published and unpublished sources cited in your research paper. If the author is unknown, alphabetize by the first word (excluding *A, An,* or *The*) of the title. The first line of each citation begins at the left margin, and succeeding lines are indented five spaces. As a general rule, underline or italicize titles of books, periodicals, and newspapers, but use quotation marks to enclose titles of newspaper and magazine articles. Use the following abbreviations for missing information (other than an unknown author): N.p. (no place of publication given), n.p. (no publisher given), n.d. (no date of publication given), or N. pag. (no pagination in source). Double space within and between all entries.

Below are examples of MLA style entries in a Works Cited list, organized by kind of source: books, articles, and unpublished sources. Use these as models for your own Works Cited list. For additional examples, see *MLA Handbook for Writers of Research Papers (1988)*.

BOOKS: MLA STYLE

Order the information as follows, omitting information that does not apply:

Author's last name, first name. "Title of article or part of book."
    Title of Book. Ed. or Trans. Name. Edition. Number of volumes.
    Place of publication: Name of publisher, Date of publication.

A book by one author

Abbey, Edward. Desert Solitaire: A Season in the Wilderness. New
    York: Ballantine, 1968.

Other books by same author

———. Down the River. New York: Dutton, 1982.

A book with two or three authors

Conklin, Nancy F., and Margaret A. Lourie. A Host of Tongues:
    Language Communities in the United States. New York: Free
    Press, 1983.

Fairbank, John K., Edwin O. Reischauer, and Albert M. Craig. East
    Asia: Tradition and Transformation. Boston: Houghton, 1973.

[The names of well-known publishers are often shortened to the first key word. Thus, "E. P. Dutton" is shortened to "Dutton"; "Houghton Mifflin Co." is shortened to "Houghton"; and "Harcourt Brace Jovanovich, Inc." becomes simply "Harcourt."]

More than three authors

Donald, Robert B., et al. Models for Clear Writing. Englewood Cliffs:
    Prentice, 1984.

An unknown or anonymous author

Publication Manual of the American Psychological Association. 3rd ed. Washington: American Psychological Association, 1984.

An author and an editor

Austen, Jane. Pride and Prejudice. Ed. Mark Schorer. Boston: Houghton, 1956.

Editor of an anthology

Abbey, Edward, ed. Slumgullion Stew: An Edward Abbey Reader. New York: Dutton, 1984.

Editor

Robinson, Janet O., ed. An Annotated Bibliography of Modern Language Teaching. London: Oxford UP, 1969. ["UP" is abbreviation for "University Press."]

A translation

Sophocles. Electra. Trans. David Grene. Greek Tragedies. Ed. David Grene and Richmond Lattimore. Vol. 2 Chicago: U of Chicago P, 1960. 2 vols. 45–109.

A work in more than one volume

Morrison, Samuel Eliot, and Henry Steele Commager. The Growth of the American Republic. Vol 2. New York: Oxford UP, 1941. 2 vols.

A work in an anthology

Blake, William, "The Tyger." The Norton Anthology of English Literature. Ed. M. H. Abrams et al. 4th ed. Vol. 2. New York: Norton, 1979. 2 vols. 39–40.

[Work appears in volume 2 on pages 39–40.]

Entry in an encyclopedia or dictionary

"Don Giovanni." Encyclopedia Americana. 1982 ed.

Government document

Machenthun, Kenneth M. Toward a Cleaner Aquatic Environment. Environmental Protection Agency. Office of Air and Water Programs Washington: GPO, 1973.

["GPO" stands for "Government Printing Office."]

Government document—unknown author

United States. Department of Health, Education, and Welfare. Infant Care. Washington: GPO, 1972.

ARTICLES: MLA STYLE

For all articles published in periodicals, give author's name, title of article, and name of publication. For magazines, add complete date and inclusive page numbers. For most professional journals, add volume number, issue number if appropriate, year of publication, and inclusive page numbers.

Article in a weekly or biweekly magazine

Gorman, Christine. "Why It's So Hard to Quit Smoking." <u>Time</u> 30
     May 1988: 56.

Article in a monthly or bimonthly magazine

Morrison, Ann M., Randall P. White, and Ellen Van Velsor.
     "Executive Women: Substance Plus Style." <u>Psychology Today</u>
     Aug. 1987: 18–21, 24–26.

Hancocks, David. "<u>Animals from All Over Down Under</u>." <u>Animal</u>
     <u>Kingdom</u> Nov.–Dec. 1986: 50–61.

Unsigned article in a magazine

"Catching a Cold: It's Up in the Air." <u>Science86</u> July–Aug. 1986: 8.

Article in a professional journal

Many professional journals have continuous page numbers throughout the year. The first issue of the year begins with page 1, but every issue after that begins with the number following the last page number of the previous issue. For such journals, give volume followed by the year.

Sady, Stanley P. "Prolonged Exercise Augments Plasma
     Triglyceride Clearance." <u>Journal of the American Medical</u>
     <u>Association</u> 256 (1986): 2552–55.

     (For page numbers over 100, use only two digits for final page
         citation: 2552–55.)

If a professional journal begins with page 1, for each issue, cite the volume, issue, and year, *or* cite the volume, month, and year. In the following examples, the article is in volume 9, issue 1, published in January 1987.

Brodkey, Linda. "Writing Ethnographic Narratives." <u>Written</u>
     <u>Communication</u> 9 (Jan. 1987): 25–50.

Brodkey, Linda. "Writing Ethnographic Narratives." <u>Written</u>
     <u>Communication</u> 9:1 (1987): 25–50.

Article in a newspaper

Pasztor, Andy, and Robert S. Greenberger. "Justice Agency Begins
     Probing Arms Scandal." <u>Wall Street Journal</u> 28 Nov. 1986,
     sec. 1: 3–4.

Unsigned article in a newspaper

"President's News Conference on Foreign and Domestic Issues."
New York Times 20 Nov. 1986: A12–13.

Editorial

Haavind, Robert. "Artificial Intelligence Has a Bad Name."
Editorial. High Technology Dec. 1986: 4.

Unsigned editorial

"Getting Tough with Parking Cheats." Editorial. Chicago Tribune 10
Nov. 1986, sec. 1: 10.

Review

Molotch, Harvey. Rev. of A Cycle of Outrage, by James Gilbert.
Science 15 Aug. 1986: 794–95.

Published interview

Lamm, Richard D. "Governments Face Tough Times." With Robert
Baun. Coloradoan [Ft. Collins, CO] 30 Nov. 1986: B9.

UNPUBLISHED SOURCES: MLA STYLE

For unpublished sources, give relevant information that may help
your reader *identify* or *locate* the source.

Computer software

Microsoft Word. Computer Software. Microsoft, 1989.

Film

Star Trek IV: The Voyage Home. Dir. Leonard Nimoy. With William
Shatner and Leonard Nimoy. Paramount, 1986.

A Recording

LaBelle, Patti. "On My Own." Winner in You. Rec. 1985. MCA
Records, MCA–5737, 1986.

Television or radio program

60 Minutes. CBS. KMGH, Denver. 30 Nov. 1986.

Letter

Ehrlich, Gretel. Letter to the author. 15 Mar. 1987.

Lecture or speech

Gridley, Rita. Lecture on Texas Folklore. U of Kansas. Lawrence, 8
Mar. 1990. [If known, use actual lecture title.]

Unpublished dissertation

Burnham, William A. "Peregrine Falcon Egg Variation, Incubation,
    and Population Recovery Strategy." Diss. Colorado State U,
    1984.

Personal interview

Miller, J. Philip. Personal interview. 9 Sept. 1986.

Pamphlet

Guide to Raptors. Denver: Center for Raptor Research, 1990.

"References" List: APA Style   If you are using the APA style, you
should make a separate list, titled "References" (no underlining or
quotation marks), that appears after your text but before any appen-
dices. Include only sources actually used in preparing your essay. List
the sources cited in your text *alphabetically,* by author's last name. Use
only *initials* for author's first and middle names. If the author is
unknown, alphabetize by the first word in the title (not *A, An,* or *The*).
In titles, *capitalize* only the first word, proper names, and the first
word following a colon. If the entry is more than one line, start the
first line at the left-hand margin and *indent* subsequent lines three
spaces. *Double space* the entire References list.

   Below are samples of APA style entries in a References list. For
additional information and examples, consult the *Publication Manual of
the American Psychological Association* (1984).

BOOKS: APA STYLE

A book by one author

Abbey, E. (1968). Desert solitaire: A season in the wilderness. New
    York: Ballantine.

Other books by same author

Abbey, E. (1982). Down the river. New York: Dutton.

A book with two or more authors

Conklin, N.F., & Lourie, M.A. (1983). A host of tongues: Language
    communities in the United States. New York: Free Press.

An unknown or anonymous author

Publication manual of the American Psychological Association (3rd
    ed.). (1984). Washington, D.C.: American Psychological
    Association.

Note: In titles of books and journals, capitalize the first word, the first word after a colon, and any proper names. (American Psychological Association is a proper name.)

An author and an editor

Austen, J. (1956). Pride and prejudice (M. Schorer, Ed.). Boston: Houghton Mifflin.

A work in an anthology

Chopin, K. (1989). The story of an hour. In E.V. Roberts & H.E. Jacobs (Eds.), Literature: An introduction to reading and writing (pp. 304–306). Englewood Cliffs, NJ: Prentice Hall.

Note: Titles of poems, short stories, essays, or articles in a book are *not* underlined or italicized or put in quotation marks. Only the title of the anthology is underlined.

A translation

Sophocles. (1960). Electra (D. Grene, Trans.). In D. Grene & R. Lattimore (Eds.), Greek tragedies (Vol. 2, pp. 45–109). Chicago: University of Chicago Press.

Note: The APA style usually uses the full name of publishing companies.

Government document

Machenthun, K.M. (1973). Toward a cleaner aquatic environment. Environmental Protection Agency. Office of Air and Water Programs. Washington, D.C.: U.S. Government Printing Office.

Government document—unknown author

United States Department of Health, Education, and Welfare. (1972). Infant care. Washington, D.C.: U.S. Government Printing Office.

ARTICLES: APA STYLE

The following examples illustrate how to list articles in magazines and periodicals according to APA style. **Note:** Do *not* underline or italicize or put quotation marks around titles of articles. Do underline (or italicize) titles of magazines or periodicals. If you cite a volume number, omit the "p." or "pp." before any page numbers.

Article in a weekly or biweekly magazine

Gorman, C. (1988, May 30). Why it's so hard to quit smoking. Time, p. 56.

Article in a monthly or bimonthly magazine

Morrison, A.M., White, R.P., & Van Velsor, E. (1987, August).
Executive women: Substance plus style. Psychology Today, pp.
18–21, 24–26.

Unsigned article in a magazine

Catching a cold: It's up in the air. (1986, July–August). Science86,
p. 8.

Article in a journal with continuous pagination

Sady, S.P. (1986). Prolonged exercise augments plasma
triglyceride clearance. Journal of the American Medical
Association, 256, 2552–2555.

Note: Underline the volume number and do not include "pp." Also,
APA style requires repeating all number digits: Write 2552–2555, not
2552–55 as in MLA style.

Article in a journal that pages each issue separately

Brodkey, L. (1987). Writing ethnographic narratives. Written
Communication, 9 (1), 25–50.

Note: Underline the volume number followed by the issue number in
parentheses.

Article in a newspaper

Pasztor, A., & Greenberger, R.S. (1986, November 28). Justice
agency begins probing arms scandal. Wall Street Journal, sec. 1,
pp. 3–4.

Unsigned article in a newspaper

President's news conference on foreign and domestic issues. (1986,
November 20). New York Times, pp. A12–13.

Note: A12–13 means that the article appears in Section A, pp. 12–13.

Editorial

Haavind, R. (1986, December). Artificial intelligence has a bad
name. [Editorial.] High Technology, p. 4.

Unsigned editorial

Getting tough with parking cheats. (1986, November 10).
[Editorial.] Chicago Tribune, sec. 1, p. 10.

Review

Molotch, H. (1986, August 15). A cycle of outrage. [Review of Gilbert, J., A cycle of outrage]. Science, pp. 794–795.

Published interview

Lamm, R. (1986, November 30). Governments face tough times. [Interview with Baun, R.] Coloradoan, p. B9.

Computer software

Microsoft word. Vers. 5.0 [Computer software]. (1989). Microsoft.

Film

Nimoy, L. (Director). (1986). Star trek IV: The voyage home [Film]. Paramount.

Recording

LaBelle, P. (Performer). (1985). On my own. Winner in you [Album]. MCA Records.

Television or radio program

60 Minutes [Television program]. (1986, November 30). KMGH Denver: CBS.

Lecture or speech

Gridley, R. (1990, March 8). Texas folklore in popular western fiction. Speech presented to the English faculty at the University of Kansas, Lawrence.

UNPUBLISHED SOURCES: APA STYLE

In the APA system, unpublished letters and interviews are personal communications and do not represent recoverable data. Therefore, they should *not* appear in a References list. Do, however, cite personal letters or interviews in your text. (See In-text Documentation: APA Style.)

Editing and Proofreading   Edit your paper for conciseness, clarity, and accuracy of grammar, spelling, and punctuation. See your handbook for assistance in revising errors and improving usage. Check your direct quotations to make sure they are an *accurate, word-for-word* transcription of the original. Make sure your in-text citation of sources is accurate. Proofread both the text *and* the Works Cited section. Finally, have someone else proofread your research paper for typos, spelling errors, missing words, or confusing sentences.

POSTSCRIPT ON THE WRITING PROCESS

As your final entry in your research notebook, answer the following questions:

1. Reread your "research log" section. Compare your initial schedule with your actual progress. What parts of the research paper took longer than you anticipated? What took less time?

2. What was the most difficult problem you encountered while writing the research paper? How did you try to solve that problem?

3. What do you like best about the final version of your research paper? Why? What do you like least? Why?

RESEARCH PAPER: STUDENT WRITING

FOREIGN LANGUAGE STUDY: AN AMERICAN NECESSITY

Kate McNerny

Kate McNerny's final version of her research paper appears below. Her purpose is to persuade students, administrators, and ordinary citizens that learning the language and culture of a foreign country is important, both to people as individuals and to America as a nation. In this paper, she uses facts, information, and her own experience to alert her readers to the seriousness of the problem. She argues that American schools should require students to study at least one foreign language during junior and senior high school.

McNerny follows the MLA style for in-text documentation, supplementary Notes, and Works Cited list. The marginal notations highlight key features of her research paper.

"Why should I learn a foreign language--everyone speaks English!" "I would never use another language--I never plan to leave the United States." "I had a hard enough time learning English!" These are only a few of the excuses people have given for

For her lead-in, McNerny uses quotations she collected in her informal survey.

opposing foreign language studies, and unfortunately they represent the ideas of more than a few American citizens. While other people agree that learning a second language can be

McNerny presents historical background on the problem.

beneficial, they still fail to see it as a necessity. Deep-rooted misconceptions regarding the value of foreign language study exists among Americans. Theodore Huebener's study, <u>Why Johnny Should Learn Foreign Languages</u>, shows how those misconceptions have, historically, led to a decline in foreign language study. In 1940, a committee of the American Youth Commission issued a report labelling foreign language studies as "useless and time-consuming" (Huebener 13). An even more appalling statement came from a group of Harvard Scholars. They suggested that "foreign language study is useful primarily in strengthening the

Ellipsis points indicate omitted material from the source.

student's English. . . . For the average student there is no real need at all to learn a foreign language" (Huebner 14). With such attitudes, it is no wonder that students and administrators ignored

The footnote refers the reader to the "Notes" page for McNerny's comment on the history of the problem.

foreign language programs during the 1940s and 1950s.[1] Even today, in an era of trade with Pacific Rim countries, with Russian *glasnost* or "openness," with increased cultural and economic exchange with China, students in our colleges and high schools are insufficiently educated in foreign language and culture. (1)

Despite promising signs of changes, foreign language study still holds the weakest position of any other major subject in American secondary schools. A recent study of foreign language programs reports that "only 15 percent of American high school

Square brackets in quoted material indicate a word added by McNerny to clarify the sentence.

students study a foreign language. Only 8 percent of [American] colleges require credit in a foreign language for admission (down from 34 percent in 1966)" (Unks 24). Because available programs at the junior and senior high school level are generally limited in variety and scope, only a small percentage of those students that take a foreign language ever become fluent in it. A 1984 study that sampled 536 secondary schools revealed that most offered a foreign language, but 91 percent did not require foreign language credits for graduation (Ranwez and Rodgers 98). In contrast, many countries require all students to learn at least one, and often two, foreign languages. In France, all students must study one modern language throughout their seven years in the lycée (secondary school). During the last four years of lycée, French children must also study Greek or an additional modern language. Swedish children spend almost one third of their secondary school class time on language studies (Huebner 26).   (2)

    The United States cannot continue to lag behind other countries in language capability. As two researchers noted, "We are members of a world community consisting of hundreds of nations, and our fates are closely intertwined" (Long and Long 366). It is time to change attitudes and to recognize that in order to successfully interact with its "world community," the United States must drastically change its foreign language policies. American students should be required to study at least one foreign language throughout their six years of junior and senior high school.   (3)

    School administrators across the country oppose the idea of requiring foreign languages because they cannot see the contribution these studies make to the overall goals of the schools' curriculum. In a recent survey, New Jersey secondary school administrators "rated social studies objectives as contributing most to the attainment of high priority goals, and foreign language as contributing least" (Koppel 437). These officials fail to realize that language studies can add a valuable dimension to a social studies program. Educators can use a combined program to emphasize a global perspective in language and cultural studies. "The world looks and sounds different when one is 'standing in the shoes' of another, speaking another language, or recognizing another's point

In-text citation for a source with two authors

*Notice punctuation for in-text citation: source appears in parenthesis **after** the quotation marks **but before** the period.*

McNerny's thesis

McNerny begins refutation of opposing arguments

of view based on an alternative set of values" (Bragaw 37). This global awareness is crucial in our increasingly interdependent world.[2]   (4)

     School administrators express concern about foreign language study's relevance to curriculum goals, but in addition many students simply fail to see why they will ever need to use a foreign language. I used to belong to that group. I remember my mom always telling me, "Take French classes. Learn how to speak French so you can visit your cousins in France someday." At the time, during junior high, I did take French classes for a while, but then dropped them when my schedule became "too busy." Then, as my mom had promised, I got the opportunity to visit my cousins in France. For some reason, the fact that I couldn't speak French didn't really hit me--until I stepped off the train at Gare du Nord in Paris and couldn't find the relative who was supposed to meet me. After frantically searching the entire station several times, I had to break down and ask for help. At the information desk, a few completely butchered French phrases escaped my lips--only to be received by an unimpressed, unresponsive station attendant. He muttered something about dumb Americans. Then, with a wave of his hand, he gestured toward some unknown destination. I did survive that painful ordeal, but I vowed I wouldn't embarrass myself--and other Americans--again.   (5)

     When Americans travel abroad, they not only face a language barrier, but they may also face culture differences as well. Most foreign language courses today teach culture as well as language because the teachers realize that grammar and language are only a part of the barrier. In his resource book, Teaching Culture, H. Ned Seelye, Director of Bilingual-Bicultural Education for the State of Illinois, cites just one of many examples of culture shock that Americans may face:

McNerny introduces the author, the title of the book, and the author's credentials to lend authority to the quoted passage.

x5 → At a New Year's Eve celebration in an exclusive Guatemalan hotel, one American was overheard telling another. "You see all these people? They're all my wife's relatives. And every damn one of them has kissed me tonight. If another Guatemalan man hugs and kisses me I'll punch him right in the face!" The irritated American was disturbed by two things: the extended kinship patterns of the group and by the *abrazo de ano neuvo* as executed by the men (he did not complain of the female *abrazos*). Both customs--close family ties that extend to distant relatives and the abrazo given as a greeting or sign of affection devoid of sexual overtures--elicited hostility in the American who was bored by unintelligible language and depressed by nostalgia and alcohol. (85)   (6)

In order to prevent such linguistic and cultural misunderstandings, instruction in language and culture needs to begin early. In a recent study designed to reveal what children know about foreign language and culture, a group of intellectually gifted seventh graders wrote imaginative stories about the lives of Soviet children. While the students displayed some knowledge of communism and the Soviet Union, they also expressed serious misconceptions about the day-to-day lives of the Soviet children. The students believed that many Soviet children could not attend schools because they had to work in the fields. Many of the students did not understand that Soviet children could also be happy and enjoy their lives despite the political climate of their country (Long and Long 367). Even if most Americans never travel to another country or need to speak another language, they should be able to understand and appreciate different cultures.   (7)

Recently, Soviet Leader Mikhail Gorbachev's policy of "glasnost" has created a promising change in Americans' attitudes. According to a report in *Time* magazine, Soviet studies are on the

At the end of the quotation, McNerny cites only the page number, since she has already introduced the author. Page number follows the period in a block indented quotation.

McNerny presents arguments for her thesis.

McNerny paraphrases key information from article; she does not introduce the author here because she wants to emphasize the facts and trends rather than his authority.

upswing in the U.S., and interest in languages is following along. At Vermont's Middlebury College, for example, almost 10% of the 1,900 undergraduates are currently majoring in Soviet studies, and a consortium of 18 Northeastern colleges has signed an agreement to exchange undergraduate students with Soviet students from throughout the Soviet Union (Bowen 65). We have known for a long time that suspicion and hatred between countries often grows from the inability to understand each other. The students majoring in Soviet studies or participating in exchanges know that in order to achieve world peace, we must be able to communicate and empathize with our "enemies" as well as our allies. (8)

As a transition, McNerny uses a paragraph hook ("Cultural understanding") to lead into this paragraph on international trade and the following paragraph on diplomacy.

A nationwide language study requirement not only would promote cultural understanding but also would strengthen the United States' international relations in business and diplomacy. International trade is continually increasing in the United States and has created a demand for business people competent in foreign languages. Many top American businesspeople agree that students who combine some business or economics training with fluency in Japanese have unlimited job possibilities (Coxe 194). Company executives simply cannot expect to make efficient, sound decisions in their international markets without understanding and speaking the language of the country they are dealing with (Huebener 45). Educator Gerald Unks points out two instances in which a lack of language proficiency caused companies to initiate fatal marketing programs.

McNerny does not end her paragraph with a quotation; instead, she shows how this evidence supports her point.

When Pepsi-Cola went after the Chinese market, "Come Alive With Pepsi" was translated into Chinese in Taiwan as "Pepsi Brings Your Ancestors Back from the Dead." No Sale! General Motors sought to sell its Nova in South America oblivious to the fact that "No va" in Spanish means "It doesn't go." (24) These examples illustrate that business people need thorough competence in, not just rudimentary knowledge of, foreign languages. (9)

Language proficiency is important not only for business and trade, but also for diplomatic relations. Often, the United States attempts to help countries by showering them with money and technical aid but is unable to deal with their problems on a cultural or psychological level (Huebner 42). Thus, our "good intentions" are poorly communicated and often unappreciated or misinterpreted. "South America denounces 'Yankee Imperialism'; Cuba vilifies us; Panama is sullen. Our European allies are lukewarm" (Huebner 43). The image of the "Ugly American" can be traced directly to our lack of training in foreign language and culture. Ignorance of foreign language by our diplomats has been almost the rule rather than the exception (Huebner 53). If long term language studies become an integral part of America's education systems, we could fill diplomatic positions with people who are linguistically and culturally sensitive to the people of that country. (10)

Even though McNerny has just cited Huebner twice, she cites the source again because this material is taken from a different page.

The need for required language study in the United States is urgent. The solution to the problem requires effort on at least two fronts: making students and school administrators aware that foreign language study is important, and obtaining the necessary funding for new programs. In the last few years, some educators have advocated required foreign language studies in the elementary grades (Jassey 159). Some have called for a reexamination of goals and teaching methods to meet social needs yet fit into the public school system (Galloway 32–35). Most recently, two prominent foreign language educators have organized a "national agenda" for improving language instruction and a national foreign language center to implement that agenda (Lange 70–96; Lambert 9–19). (11)

McNerny begins her conclusion, calling for local and Federal Administrators to support a foreign language requirement.

Although the plans and the strategy exist, often the funds do not. Some funds can be diverted from within school districts, but

the federal government must take some initiative. The current
presidential administration spends endless time and money
developing national defense and supporting business interests.
Since foreign language knowledge contributes strongly to success in
both these areas, it would be practical for the administration also
to support expansion of language studies. Instead, it continues to
cut funding for special programs including language studies centers
and international teaching facilities (Unks 25). Realistically, a
foreign language requirement in junior and senior high school
cannot be initiated without the support of both local school districts
as well as the federal government. Americans must acknowledge
the fact that they are not isolated from the rest of the world.
Successful interaction in the "world community" relies on our
ability, as a nation, to effectively communicate with and
understand people from other countries. Understanding,
communication, and world peace can hardly be achieved without
language competency. (12)

Notes

[1]One of the most disturbing facts is that although Heubener's
study was done in 1961, very little has changed in almost thirty
years. Except for slight changes in statistics, dates, and names of
wars, Americans have remained strikingly insular in their
attitudes toward foreign languages and foreigners.

[2]It is ironic that Americans not only hesitate to take a foreign
language, but they also seem bent on keeping foreign languages
officially "out of sight." Twelve states currently have bills before
their legislatures to make English the "official language." According
to a recent *U.S. News and World Report* article, proponents of these
bills argue that multiple language use threatens to erode English as
a unifying force, that immigrants need incentives to learn English,

*Content notes are
placed on a separate
page and double-
spaced. Use raised
footnote number and
indent first line five
spaces.*

*In her notes, McNerny
includes two ideas that
would have been
digressive in the text of
her paper.*

and that bilingual ballots merely postpone the melting pot process. Many opponents from ethnic and civil-rights groups believe these bills are racist (McBee 64). Americans' ignorance of foreign languages (and the fear that ignorance breeds) is an important cause for the popularity of these proposed "official language" laws.

Works Cited

Bowen, Ezra. "Iron Curtain Raising on Campus." Time 12 Oct. 1987: 65.

Bragaw, Donald H., and Helene Zimmer-Loew. "Social Studies and Foreign Language: A Partnership." Education Digest Dec. 1985: 36–39.

Coxe, Donald. "The Back Page." Canadian Business Feb. 1984: 194.

Galloway, Vicki B. "Foreign Language Study in the 1980s." Education Digest Oct. 1984: 32–35.

Huebener, Theodore. Why Johnny Should Learn Foreign Languages. New York: Chilton, 1961.

Jassey, William. "Aiming for a Foreign Language Requirement." Clearing House Dec. 1984: 159–61.

Koppel, Irene E. "The Perceived Contribution of Foreign Language to High Priority Education Goals." Foreign Language Annals 15 (1982): 435–37.

Lambert, Richard D. "The Improvement of Foreign Language Competency in the United States." Annals of the American Academy of Political and Social Science Mar. 1987: 9–19.

Lange, Dale L. "The Language Teaching Curriculum and a National Agenda." Annals of the American Academy of Political and Social Science Mar. 1987: 70–96.

Long, Delbert H., and Roberta A. Long. "Toward the Promotion of Foreign Language Study and Global Understanding." Education 105 (1985): 366–68.

McBee Susanna. "A War Over Words." U.S. News and World Report 6 Oct. 1986: 64.

Ranwez, Alain D., and Judy Rodgers. "The Status of Foreign Languages and International Studies: An Assessment in Colorado." Foreign Language Annals 17 (1984): 97–102.

Seelye, H. Ned. Teaching Culture: Strategies for Foreign Language Educators . Skokie, IL: National Textbook, 1974.

Unks, Gerald. "The Perils of Our Single-Language Policy." Education Digest Mar. 1985: 24–27.

The works cited list begins a new page. List entries alphabetically according to author's last name. If no author is given, list by first word in the title. Double-space entries.

Indent five spaces after first line or each entry.

Book

Article from a journal with continuous pagination

Article from a monthly magazine

For inclusive page numbers over 100, use only the last two digits in the second page number (366–68).

11 | RESPONDING TO LITERATURE

Berthe Morisot
The Artist's Sister Edma and Their Mother
National Gallery of Art, Washington. Chester Dale Collection

In a film class, you watch Roman Polanski's *Tess*, an adaptation of Thomas Hardy's novel *Tess of the d'Urbervilles*. You decide to compare the film with the novel, focusing on four key episodes: the "strawberry scene," in which Tess meets Alec; the rape scene at night; the harvesting scene; and the final scene at Stonehenge. On the basis of your comparison, you argue that Polanski's interpretation (and the acting of Nastassia Kinski) retains Hardy's view of Tess as a victim of social and sexist repression. □

In an Introduction to Literature class, you and a friend are assigned to work collaboratively on an essay about Eudora Welty's "A Worn Path." You are both interested in how Phoenix Jackson's journey contains images of the phoenix, a mythological bird said to live for five hundred years after which it burns itself to death and then rises from its ashes to become youthful and beautiful again. You draft your essays separately and then read each other's drafts. At that point, you collaborate on a single essay, combining the best ideas and evidence from your separate drafts. Your collaborative essay shows how Phoenix Jackson is characterized by birdlike images, how she calmly faces images of fire and death on her journey, and how her grandson represents her rebirth. □

I hungered for new books, new ways of looking and seeing. It was not a matter of believing or disbelieving what I read, but of feeling something new, of being affected by something that made the look of the world different.

—Richard Wright, *author of* Black Boy

No one else can read a literary work for us. The benefits of literature can emerge only from creative activity on the part of the reader.

—Louise Rosenblatt, *author of* Literature as Exploration

Responding to literature requires that readers participate *imaginatively* while they read a literary work, *reread* to see how the parts of the work relate to the whole, and *share* their interpretations of a piece of literature with other readers.

First, readers must *imagine* and recreate that special world described by the writer. The first sentences of a short story, for example, throw open a door to a world that—attractive or repulsive—tempts our curiosity and imagination. Like Alice in *Alice in Wonderland,* we cannot resist following a white rabbit with pink eyes who mutters to itself, checks its watch, and then zips down a rabbit hole and into an imaginary world.

> Young Goodman Brown came forth at sunset into the street at Salem village; but put his head back, after crossing the threshold, to exchange a parting kiss with his young wife.
>
> —Nathaniel Hawthorne, "Young Goodman Brown"

> As Gregor Samsa awoke one morning from uneasy dreams he found himself transformed in his bed into a gigantic insect.
>
> —Franz Kafka, "The Metamorphosis"

> The morning of June 27th was clear and sunny, with the fresh warmth of a full-summer day; the flowers were blossoming profusely and the grass was green.
>
> —Shirley Jackson, "The Lottery"

Whether our imagination constructs the disturbing image of a "gigantic insect" or the seemingly peaceful picture of a perfect summer day, we actively create the story. Responding to literature does not mean passively reacting to the writer's story. As readers, we should anticipate, imagine, feel, worry, and question. A story is like an empty balloon that we must inflate with the warm breath of our imagination and experience. Our participation makes us partners with the author in the artistic creation.

Responding to literature also requires that readers *reread.* If we read a story or a poem only once, we have misunderstood the whole point of literature. Great literature is worthy of study because the more we reread, the more we learn and discover. If we assume that the purpose of a story is merely to entertain us or to provide a moment's diversion, then we should stick to television sitcoms written for an audience of couch potatoes who want only predictable, unimaginative plots and canned studio laughter.

Rereading requires two distinct but related operations. First, you should *reread for yourself,* to write down your ideas, questions, feelings, and reactions. To heighten your role in creating a story, you should note, in the margin, your questions and responses to important events, main characters, bits of description, and images that catch your attention: "What about the names Hawthorne uses? Is Young Goodman Brown really good? Is his wife, Faith, really faithful?" "I don't understand why Kafka's narrator thinks he is a gigantic insect. Is this happening, or is he dreaming?" "Why does the Shirley Jackson lottery happen on such a beautiful summer day?" Don't just underline or highlight passages. Actually *write* your responses in the margin.

Second, you should *reread with a writer's eye*. In fiction, identify the main and minor characters. Look for and note the conflicts between characters. Mark passages that contain foreshadowing. Pinpoint sentences that reveal the narrative point of view. Use the critical terms (character, plot, conflict, point of view, setting, style, and theme) to help you reread with a writer's eye, to see how the parts of a story relate to the whole. Each critical term is a tool—a magnifying glass that helps you understand and interpret the story more clearly.

In addition to rereading, responding to literature requires that readers *share* ideas, reactions, and interpretations. Sharing usually begins in small-group or class discussions, but it continues as you explain your interpretation in writing. A work of literature is not a mathematical equation with a single answer. Great literature is worth interpreting precisely because each reader responds differently. The purpose of literature is to encourage you to reflect on your life and the lives of others—to look for new ways of seeing and understanding your world—and ultimately to expand your world. Sharing is crucial to appreciating literature.

> Hawthorne doesn't come right out and say that people become disillusioned by experiencing evil. He shows how it actually happens in the life of young Goodman Brown.

> Shirley Jackson's "The Lottery" helps me see that the notion of human sacrifice and the idea of the human scapegoat still exist in our culture today.

Writing about your responses and sharing them with other readers helps you "reread" your own ideas in order to explain them to other readers fully and clearly.

FREEWRITING: RESPONDING TO A SHORT STORY

Read and respond to Kate Chopin's "The Story of an Hour." Use your imagination to help create the story as you read. Then *reread* the story, noting in the margin your questions and responses. When you finish rereading and annotating your reactions, write our your interpretation of the *last line* of the story.

THE STORY OF AN HOUR

Kate Chopin

Kate O'Flaherty Chopin (1851–1904) was an American writer whose mother was French and Creole and whose father was Irish. In 1870, she moved from St. Louis to New Orleans with her husband, Oscar Chopin, and over the next ten years she gave birth to five sons. After her husband died in 1882, Chopin returned to St. Louis to begin a new life as a writer. Many of her best stories are about Louisiana people and places, and her most famous novel, The Awakening, *tells the story of Edna, a woman who leaves her marriage and her children to fulfill herself through an artistic career.*

Knowing that Mrs. Mallard was afflicted with a heart trouble, great care was taken to break to her as gently as possible the news of her husband's death.   (1)

It was her sister Josephine who told her, in broken sentences, veiled hints that revealed in half concealing. Her husband's friend Richards was there, too, near her. It was he who had been in the newspaper office when intelligence of the railroad disaster was received, with Brently Mallard's name leading the list of "killed." He had only taken the time to assure himself of its truth by a second telegram, and had hastened to forestall any less careful, less tender friend in bearing the sad message.   (2)

She did not hear the story as many women have heard the same, with a paralyzed inability to accept its significance. She wept at once, with sudden, wild abandonment, in her sister's arms. When the storm of grief had spent itself she went away to her room alone. She would have no one follow her.   (3)

There stood, facing the open window, a comfortable, roomy armchair. Into this she sank, pressed down by a physical exhaustion that haunted her body and seemed to reach into her soul.   (4)

She could see in the open square before her house the tops of trees that were all aquiver with the new spring life. The delicious breath of rain was in the air. In the street below a peddler was crying his wares. The notes of a distant song which some one was singing reached her faintly, and countless sparrows were twittering in the eaves.   (5)

There were patches of blue sky showing here and there through the clouds that had met and piled above the other in the west facing her window.   (6)

She sat with her head thrown back upon the cushion of the chair quite motionless, except when a sob came up into her throat and shook her, as a child who has cried itself to sleep continues to sob in its dreams.   (7)

She was young, with a fair, calm face, whose lines bespoke repression and even a certain strength. But now there was a dull stare in her eyes, whose gaze was fixed away off yonder on one of those patches of blue sky. It was not a glance of reflection, but rather indicated a suspension of intelligent thought.   (8)

There was something coming to her and she was waiting for it, fearfully. What was it? She did not know; it was too subtle and elusive to name. But she felt it, creeping out of the sky, reaching toward her through the sounds, the scents, the color that filled the air.   (9)

Now her bosom rose and fell tumultuously. She was beginning to recognize this thing that was approaching to possess her, and she was striving to beat it back with her will—as powerless as her two white slender hands would have been.   (10)

When she abandoned herself a little whispered word escaped her slightly parted lips. She said it over and over under her breath: "Free, free, free!" The vacant stare and the look of terror that had followed it went from her eyes. They stayed keen and bright. Her pulses beat fast, and the coursing blood warmed and relaxed every inch of her body.   (11)

She did not stop to ask if it were not a monstrous joy that held her. A clear and exalted perception enabled her to dismiss the suggestion as trivial.   (12)

She knew that she would weep again when she saw the kind, tender hands folded in death; the face that had never looked save with love upon her, fixed and gray and dead. But she saw beyond that bitter moment a long procession of years to come that would belong to her absolutely. And she opened and spread her arms out to them in welcome.   (13)

There would be no one to live for during those coming years; she would live for herself. There would be no powerful will bending her in that blind persistence with which men and women believe they have a right to impose a private will upon a fellow creature. A kind intention or a cruel intention made the act seem no less a crime as she looked upon it in that brief moment of illumination.   (14)

And yet she had loved him—sometimes. Often she had not. What did it matter! What could love, the unsolved mystery, count for in face of this possession of self-assertion which she suddenly recognized as the strongest impulse of her being.   (15)

"Free! Body and soul free!" she kept whispering.   (16)

Josephine was kneeling before the closed door with her lips to the keyhole, imploring for admission. "Louise, open the door! I beg; open the door—you will make yourself ill. What are you doing, Louise? For heaven's sake open the door."   (17)

"Go away. I am not making myself ill." No; she was drinking in a very elixir of life through that open window.   (18)

Her fancy was running riot along those days ahead of her. Spring days, and summer days, and all sorts of days that would be her own. She breathed a quick prayer that life might be long. It was only yesterday she had thought with a shudder that life might be long.   (19)

She arose at length and opened the door to her sister's importunities. There was a feverish triumph in her eyes, and she carried herself unwittingly like a goddess of Victory. She clasped her sister's waist, and together they descended the stairs. Richards stood waiting for them at the bottom.   (20)

Some one was opening the front door with a latchkey. It was Brently Mallard who entered, a little travel-stained, composedly carrying his grip-sack and umbrella. He had been far from the scene of accident, and did not even know there had been one. He stood amazed at Josephine's piercing cry; at Richards' quick motion to screen him from the view of his wife.   (21)

But Richards was too late.   (22)

When the doctors came they said she had died of heart disease—of joy that kills.   (23)

TECHNIQUES FOR RESPONDING TO LITERATURE

As you read and respond to a work of literature, keep the following in mind.

- **Understanding the assignment and selecting a possible purpose and audience.** Unless stated otherwise in your assignment, your purpose is to *interpret* a work of literature. Your audience will be other members of your class, including the teacher.

- **Actively reading, annotating, and discussing the literary work.** Remember that literature often contains *highly condensed experiences*. In order to give imaginative life to literature, you need to patiently reread both the major events and the seemingly insignificant passages. In discussions, look for the differences between your responses and other readers' ideas.

- **Focusing your essay on a single, clearly defined interpretation.** In your essay, clearly state your main idea or thesis, focusing on a single idea or aspect of the piece of literature. Your thesis should *not be a statement of fact*. Whether you are explaining, evaluating, or arguing, your interpretation must be clearly stated.

- **Supporting your interpretation with evidence.** Since your readers will probably have a different interpretation, you must show which specific characters, events, conflicts, images, or themes prompted your response and support your interpretation. *Do not merely retell the major events of the story—your readers have already read the story.*

WARMING UP: JOURNAL EXERCISES

Read all of the following questions and then write for five minutes on two or three. These questions should clarify your perceptions about literature and develop your specific responses to "The Story of an Hour."

1. Describe a work of literature (a poem, short story, novel, or play) that you have read recently. Why did you read it? What did you like best about it? What did you not like about it?

2. On your bookshelves or in the library, find a short story or poem that you read at least six months ago. Before you reread it, write down the name of the author and the title of the work. Describe when you read it last and what you remember about it. Then reread the story or poem. When you finish, write for five minutes, describing what you noticed that you did not see the last time you read it.

3. Find a popular song whose lyrics describe a character and tell a story about that person. Listen to the record and copy down the words. Compare it to Kate Chopin's "The Story of an Hour." Do the lyrics have the basic ingredients of short fiction (character, plot, point of view, setting, style, and theme)? Is it a miniature story? What elements does it lack?

4. Write out the *question* that "The Story of an Hour" seems to ask. What is your answer to this question? What might have been Kate Chopin's answer?

5. Read the Responding to Short Fiction section in this chapter. Review the descriptions of character, plot, point of view, setting, and style. Explain which of these terms and definitions best helps you find *evidence* in "The Story of an Hour" to answer the question you wrote in #4, above.

6. The words "heart," "joy," "free," "life," and "death" appear several times in "The Story of an Hour." Underline these words (or synonyms) each time they appear. Explain how the meaning of each of these words seems to *change* during the story. Is each word used ironically?

7. Write out a dictionary definition of feminism. Then write out your definition. Is Mrs. Mallard a feminist? Is Kate Chopin a feminist? What evidence in the story supports your answers?

8. Kate Chopin's biographer, Per Seyersted, says that Chopin saw that "truth is manifold," and thus preferred not to "take sides or point a moral." Explain how "The Story of an Hour" does or does not illustrate Seyersted's observations.

9. Literature often expresses common themes or tensions, such as the individual versus society, appearance versus reality, self-knowledge versus self-deception, or civilization versus nature. Which themes are most apparent in "The Story of an Hour"? Explain your choices.

PURPOSES FOR RESPONDING TO LITERATURE

In responding to literature, you should be guided by the purposes you have already practiced in previous chapters. As you read a piece of literature and respond in the margin, begin by writing *for yourself.* Your purposes are to observe, feel, remember, understand, and relate the work of literature to your own life: What is happening? What memories does it trigger? How does it make you feel? Why is this passage confusing? Why do you like or dislike this character? Literature has special, personal value. You should write about literature initially in order to discover and understand its importance in your life.

When you write an interpretative essay, however, you are writing *for others.* You are sharing how you and the author worked as imaginative partners in recreating the work. Your purposes will often be mixed, but an interpretative essay often contains elements of *explaining, evaluating, problem solving,* and *arguing.*

- **Explaining.** Interpretative essays about literature explain the *what, why,* and *how* of a piece of literature. What is the key subject? What is the most important event or character? What are the major conflicts or the key images? What motivates a character? How does a character's world build or unravel? How does a story meet or fail to meet our expectations? How did our interpretation develop? Each of these questions might lead to an interpretative essay that explains the *what, why,* and *how* of your response.

- **Evaluating.** Readers and writers often talk about "appreciating" a work of literature. Appreciating means establishing its value or worth. It may mean praising the work's literary virtues; it may mean finding faults or weaknesses. Usually, evaluating essays measure *both strengths and weaknesses,* according to the specific criteria. What important standards for literature do you wish to apply? How does the work in question measure up? What kinds of readers might find this story worth reading? An evaluative essay cites evidence to show why a story is exciting, boring, dramatic, puzzling, vivid, relevant, or memorable.

- **Problem Solving.** Writers of interpretative essays occasionally take a problem-solving approach, focusing on how the reader overcomes obstacles in understanding the story or how the author of a story solved problems in writing key scenes, creating characters, setting a plot in motion, and creating and resolving conflicts. Particularly if you like to write fiction yourself, you may wish to take the writer's point of view: How did the writer solve (or fail to solve) problems of setting, character, plot, or theme?

- **Arguing.** As readers share responses, they may discover that their interpretations diverge sharply from the ideas of other readers. Does "The Story of an Hour" have a feminist theme? Is it about women or about human nature in general? Is the main character admirable, or is she selfish? In interpretative essays, writers sometimes argue for their beliefs. They present evidence that refutes an opposing interpretation and supports their own reading.

Most interpretative essays about literature will use these purposes, either singly or in combination, to focus and direct the essay. Writers should *select* the purpose(s) that are most appropriate for the work of literature and their own responses.

RESPONDING TO SHORT FICTION

Responding as a Reader

Begin by noting in the margins your reactions at key points. *Summarize* in your own words what is happening in the story. Write down your *observations* or *reactions* to striking or surprising passages.

Ask yourself *questions* about ambiguous or confusing passages. Below are examples written by students that illustrate all three kinds of responses.

Summary Comments

Mrs. Mallard is initially paralyzed by the news.

Mrs. Mallard feels her sister will protect her. She weeps in her sister's arms.

From the security of her chair, she stares at life outside her window.

Mrs. Mallard is young, but the lines on her face reveal repression.

Mrs. Mallard now feels "free, free, free" of the bonds of marriage.

News of her husband's death does not kill her, but news of his life does.

Observations and Reactions

Mrs. Mallard has "heart trouble"—possible double meaning.

Although Mrs. Mallard is experiencing shock and grief, outside her window the world is full of life.

The mistaken belief that men and women have a right to impose their will on others—this may be the point of the story.

Joy that kills = monstrous joy.

She does not die of the joy that kills—she dies of killed joy.

Questions

Why does the "storm" of grief come so quickly and then disappear?

She would live for herself: Is this selfishness or just a desire to be free?

Why does Chopin make Mrs. Mallard seem powerless, as though she was overcome by a fever?

Should we admire Mrs. Mallard for wanting her freedom?

Is this the story of an hour or the story of her life?

Reading With a Writer's Eye

After you respond initially and make your marginal annotations, use the following basic elements of fiction to help you *analyze how the parts of a short story relate to the whole.* Pay attention to how setting or plot affects the character, or how style and setting affect the theme. Analysis artificially separates plot, character, and theme, so look for ways to *synthesize* the parts. Seeing how these parts *relate* to each other should suggest an idea, focus, or angle to use in your interpretation.

Character   Short stories usually focus on a *major character*—particularly on how that character faces conflicts, undergoes changes, or reveals himself or herself. *Minor characters* may be flat (one-dimensional), static (unchanging), or stereotyped. To help you analyze character, diagram the *conflicts* between or among characters. Examine characters for *motivation:* What causes them to behave as they do? Is their behavior affected by *internal* or *external* forces? Do the major characters reveal themselves *directly*, through their thoughts, dialogue, and actions, or indirectly through what other people say, think, or do?

Plot   Plot is the sequence of events in a story, but it is also the cause-and-effect relationship of one event to another. As you study a story's plot, pay attention to *exposition, foreshadowing, conflict, climax,* and *denouement.* To clarify elements of the plot, draw a time line for the story, listing in chronological order every event—including events that occur before the story opens. *Exposition* describes the initial circumstances and reveals what has happened before the story opens. *Foreshadowing* is an author's hint of what will occur before it happens. *Conflicts* within characters, between characters, and between characters and their environment may explain why one event leads to the next. The *climax* is the high point, the point of no return, or the most dramatic moment in a story. At the climax of a story, readers discover something important about the main character(s). *Denouement* literally means the "unraveling" of the complications and conflicts at the end of the story. In "The Story of an Hour," climax and denouement occur almost at the same time, in the last lines of the story.

Narrative Point of View   Fiction is usually narrated from either the first-person or the third-person point of view.

A *first-person narrator* is a character who tells the story from his or her point of view. A first-person narrator may be a minor or a major character. This character may be relatively *reliable* (trustworthy) or *unreliable* (naive or misleading). Although reliable first-person narrators may invite the reader to identify with their perspective or predicament, unreliable narrators may cause readers to be wary of the narrator's naive judgments or unbalanced states of mind.

A *third-person omniscient* narrator is not a character or participant in the story. Omniscient narrators are assumed to know everything about the characters and events. They move through space or time, giving readers necessary information at any point in the story. *Selective omniscient* narrators limit their focus usually to a single character's experiences and thoughts, as Kate Chopin focuses on Mrs. Mallard in "The Story of an Hour." One kind of selective omniscient point of view is *stream-of-consciousness* narration, in which the author presents the thoughts, memories, and associations of one character in the story. Omniscient narrators may be *intrusive,* jumping into the story to give their editorial judgments, or they may be *objective,* removing themselves from the action and the minds of the characters. Objective point of view creates the impression that events are being recorded by a camera or acted on a stage.

Reminder: As you reread a story, do not stop with analysis. Do not quit, for example, after you have identified and labeled the point of view. Determine how the point of view *affects* your reaction to the central character or to your understanding of the theme. How would a different narrative point of view change the story? If a different character told the story, how would that affect the theme?

Setting   Setting is the physical place, scene, and time of the story. It also includes the social or historical context of the story. The setting in "The Story of an Hour" is the house and the room in which Mrs. Mallard waits, but it is also the social and historical time frame. *Setting is usually important for what it reveals about the characters, the plot, or the theme of the story.* Does the setting reflect a character's state of mind? Is the environment a source of tension or conflict in the story? Do changes in setting reflect changes in key characters? Do sensory details of sight, touch, smell, hearing, or taste affect or reflect the characters or events? Does the author's portrait of the setting contain images and symbols that help you interpret the story?

Style   *Style* is a general term that may refer to sentence structure, figurative language, and symbols, as well as to the author's tone or use of irony. *Sentence structure* may be long and complicated or relatively short and simple. Authors may use *figurative language* (Mrs. Mallard is described in "The Story of an Hour" as sobbing, "as a child who has cried itself to sleep continues to sob in its dreams"). A *symbol* is a person, place, thing, or event that suggests or signifies something beyond itself. In "The Story of an Hour," the open window and the new spring life suggest or represent Mrs. Mallard's new freedom. *Tone* is the author's attitude toward the characters, setting, or plot. Tone may be sympathetic, humorous, serious, detached, or critical. *Irony* suggests a double meaning. It occurs when the author or a character says or does one thing but means the opposite or something altogether different. The ending of "A Story of an Hour" is ironic: The doctors say Mrs. Mallard dies "of joy that kills." In fact, she dies of killed joy.

Theme   The focus of an interpretative essay is often on the theme of a story. In arriving at a theme, ask how the characters, plot, point of view, setting, and style *contribute to* the main ideas or point of the story. The theme of a story depends, within limits, upon your reactions as a reader. "The Story of an Hour" is *not* about relationships between sisters, nor is it about the doctors' medical malpractice. It *is* an ironic story about love, personal freedom, and death, but what precisely is the theme? Does "The Story of an Hour" carry a feminist message, or is it more universally about the repressive power of love? Is Mrs. Mallard to be admired or criticized for her impulse to free herself? The theme of a story should not be trivialized by looking for some simple "moral." In describing the theme, you should deal with the complexity of life recreated in the story.

SHORT FICTION: PROFESSIONAL WRITING

A WORN PATH

Eudora Welty

Eudora Welty was born in Jackson, Mississippi, in 1909, and earned degrees from Mississippi State College, the University of Wisconsin, and Columbia University. While she was writing short stories during the early 1930s, Welty held jobs with the Works Progress Authority (WPA), a Jackson radio station, and local newspapers. Like Flannery O'Connor and William Faulkner, Eudora Welty wrote stories and novels set in the South. Her first major publication, A Curtain of Green, and Other Stories *appeared in 1941 and was followed by three more collections of short stories. Her novels include* Delta Wedding *(1946) and* The Optimist's Daughter *(1972) which won a Pulitzer Prize. Welty's collection of reviews and essays,* The Eye of the Story *(1978), and her brief autobiography,* One Writer's Beginnings *(1984), provide insight on her fiction and her life.*

It was December—a bright frozen day in the early morning. Far out in the country there was an old Negro woman with her head tied in a red rag, coming along a path through the pinewoods. Her name was Phoenix Jackson. She was very old and small and she walked slowly in the dark pine shadows, moving a little from side to side in her steps, with the balanced heaviness and lightness of a pendulum in a grandfather clock. She carried a thin, small cane made from an umbrella, and with this she kept tapping the frozen earth in front of her. This made a grave and persistent noise in the still air, that seemed meditative like the chirping of a solitary little bird.   (1)

She wore a dark striped dress reaching down to her shoe tops, and an equally long apron of bleached sugar sacks, with a full pocket: all neat and tidy, but every time she took a step she might have fallen over her shoe-laces, which dragged from her unlaced shoes. She looked straight ahead. Her eyes were blue with age. Her skin had a pattern all its own of numberless branching wrinkles and as though a whole little tree stood in the middle of her forehead, but a golden color ran underneath, and the two knobs of her cheeks were illuminated by a yellow burning under the dark. Under the red rag her hair came down on her neck in the frailest of ringlets, still black, and with an odor like copper.   (2)

Now and then there was a quivering in the thicket. Old Phoenix said, "Out of my way, all you foxes, owls, beetles, jack rabbits, coons, and wild animals! . . . Keep out from under these feet, little bob-whites. . . . Keep the big wild hogs out of my path. Don't let none of those come running my direction. I got a long way." Under her small black-freckled hand her cane, limber as a buggy whip, would switch at the brush as if to rouse up any hiding things.   (3)

On she went. The woods were deep and still. The sun made the pine needles almost too bright to look at, up where the wind rocked. The cones dropped as light as feathers. Down in the hollow was the mourning dove—it was not too late for him.   (4)

The path ran up a hill. "Seem like there is chains about my feet, time I get this far," she said, in the voice of argument old people keep to use with themselves. "Something always take a hold of me on this hill—pleads I should stay."   (5)

After she got to the top she turned and gave a full, severe look behind her where she had come. "Up through pines," she said at length. "Now down through oaks."   (6)

Her eyes opened their widest, and she started down gently. But before she got to the bottom of the hill a bush caught her dress.   (7)

Her fingers were busy and intent, but her skirts were full and long, so that before she could pull them free in one place they were caught in another. It was not possible to allow the dress to tear. "I in the thorny bush," she said. "Thorns, you doing your appointed work. Never want to let folks pass—no sir. Old eyes thought you was a pretty little *green* bush."   (8)

Finally, trembling all over, she stood free, and after a moment dared to stoop for her cane.   (9)

"Sun so high!" she cried, leaning back and looking, while the thick tears went over her eyes. "The time getting all gone here."   (10)

At the foot of this hill was a place where a log was laid across the creek.   (11)

"Now comes the trial," said Phoenix.   (12)

Putting her right foot out, she mounted the log and shut her eyes. Lifting her skirt, leveling her cane fiercely before her, like a festival figure in some parade, she began to march across. Then she opened her eyes and she was safe on the other side.   (13)

"I wasn't as old as I thought," she said.   (14)

But she sat down to rest. She spread her skirts on the bank around her and folded her hands over her knees. Up above her was a tree in a pearly cloud of mistletoe. She did not dare to close her eyes, and when a little boy brought her a little plate with a slice of marble-cake on it she spoke to him. "That would be acceptable," she said. But when she went to take it there was just her own hand in the air.   (15)

So she left that tree, and had to go through a barbed-wire fence. There she had to creep and crawl, spreading her knees and stretching her fingers like a baby trying to climb the steps. But she talked loudly to herself: she could not let her dress be torn now, so late in the day, and she could not pay for having her arm or her leg sawed off if she got caught fast where she was.   (16)

At last she was safe through the fence and risen up out in the clearing. Big dead trees, like black men with one arm, were standing in the purple stalks of the withered cotton field. There sat a buzzard.   (17)

"Who you watching?"   (18)

In the furrow she made her way along.   (19)

"Glad this not the season for bulls," she said, looking sideways, "and the good Lord made his snakes to curl up and sleep in the winter. A pleasure I don't see no two-headed snake coming around that tree, where it come once. It took a while to get by him, back in the summer."   (20)

She passed through the old cotton and went into a field of dead corn. It whispered and shook and was taller than her head. "Through the maze now," she said, for there was no path.   (21)

Then there was something tall, black, and skinny there, moving before her.   (22)

At first she took it for a man. It could have been a man dancing in the field. But she stood still and listened, and it did not make a sound. It was as silent as a ghost.   (23)

"Ghost," she said sharply, "who be you the ghost of? For I have heard of nary death close by."   (24)

But there was no answer—only the ragged dancing in the wind. (25)

She shut her eyes, reached out her hand, and touched a sleeve. She found a coat and inside that an emptiness, cold as ice. (26)

"You scarecrow," she said. Her face lighted. "I ought to be shut up for good," she said with laughter. "My senses is gone, I too old. I the oldest people I ever know. Dance, old scarecrow," she said, "while I dancing with you." She kicked her foot over the furrow, and with mouth drawn down, shook her head once or twice in a little strutting way. Some husks blew down and whirled in streamers about her skirts. (27)

Then she went on, parting her way from side to side with the cane, through the whispering field. At last she came to the end, to a wagon track where the silver grass blew between the red ruts. The quail were walking around like pullets, seeming all dainty and unseen. (28)

"Walk pretty," she said. "This the easy place. This the easy going." (29)

She followed the track, swaying through the quiet bare fields, through the little strings of trees silver in their dead leaves, pass cabins silver from weather, with the doors and windows boarded shut, all like old women under a spell sitting there. "I walking in their sleep," she said, nodding her head vigorously. (30)

In a ravine she went where a spring was silently flowing through a hollow log. Old Phoenix bent and drank. "Sweet-gum makes the water sweet," she said, and drank more. "Nobody know who made this well, for it was here when I was born." (31)

The track crossed a swampy part where the moss hung as white as lace from every limb. "Sleep on, alligators, and blow your bubbles." Then the track went into the road. (32)

Deep, deep the road went down between the high green-colored banks. Overhead the live-oaks met, and it was as dark as a cave. (33)

A black dog with a lolling tongue came up out of the weeds by the ditch. She was meditating, and not ready, and when he came at her she only hit him a little with her cane. Over she went in the ditch, like a little puff of milk-weed. (34)

Down there, her senses drifted away. A dream visited her, and she reached her hand up, but nothing reached down and gave her a pull. So she lay there and presently went to talking. "Old woman," she said to herself, "that black dog come up out of the weeds to stall you off, and now there he sitting on his fine tail, smiling at you." (35)

A white man finally came along and found her—a hunter, a young man, with his dog on a chain. (36)

"Well, Granny!" he laughed, "what are you doing there?" (37)

"Lying on my back like a June-bug waiting to be turned over, mister," she said, reaching up her hand. (38)

He lifted her up, gave her a swing in the air, and set her down. "Anything broken, Granny?"   (39)

"No sir, them old dead weeds is springy enough," said Phoenix, when she had got her breath. "I thank you for your trouble."   (40)

"Where do you live, Granny?" he asked, while the two dogs were growling at each other.   (41)

"Away back yonder, sir, behind the ridge. You can't even see it from here."   (42)

"On your way home?"   (43)

"No, sir, I going to town."   (44)

"Why, that's too far! That's as far as I walk when I come out myself, and I get something for my trouble." He patted the stuffed bag he carried, and there hung down a little closed claw. It was one of the bob-whites, with its beak hooked bitterly to show it was dead. "Now you go on home, Granny!"   (45)

"I bound to go to town, mister," said Phoenix. "The time come around."   (46)

He gave another laugh, filling the whole landscape. "I know you old colored people! Wouldn't miss going to town to see Santa Claus!"   (47)

But something held Old Phoenix very still. The deep lines in her face went into a fierce and different radiation. Without warning, she had seen with her own eyes a flashing nickel fall out of the man's pocket onto the ground.   (48)

"How old are you, Granny?" he was saying.   (49)

"There is no telling, mister," she said, "no telling."   (50)

Then she gave a little cry and clapped her hands and said, "Git on away from here, dog! Look! Look at that dog!" She laughed as if in admiration. "He ain't scared of nobody. He a big black dog." She whispered, "Sic him!"   (51)

"Watch me get rid of that cur," said the man. "Sic him, Pete! Sic him!"   (52)

Phoenix heard the dogs fighting, and heard the man running and throwing sticks. She even heard a gunshot. But she was slowly bending forward by that time, further and further forward, the lids stretched down over her eyes, as if she were doing this in her sleep. Her chin was lowered almost to her knees. The yellow palm of her hand came out from the fold of her apron. Her fingers slid down and along the ground under the piece of money with the grace and care they would have in lifting an egg from under a sitting hen. Then she slowly straightened up, she stood erect, and the nickel was in her apron pocket. A bird flew by. Her lips moved. "God watching me the whole time, I come to stealing."   (53)

The man came back, and his own dog panted about them. "Well, I scared him off that time," he said, and then he laughed and lifted his gun and pointed it at Phoenix.   (54)

She stood straight and faced him.   (55)

"Doesn't the gun scare you?" he said, still pointing it.   (56)

"No, sir, I seen plenty go off closer by, in my day, and for less than what I done," she said, holding utterly still.   (57)

He smiled, and shouldered the gun. "Well, Granny," he said, "You must be a hundred years old, and scared of nothing. I'd give you a dime if I had any money with me. But you take my advice and stay home, and nothing will happen to you."   (58)

"I bound to go on my way, mister," said Phoenix. She inclined her head in the red rag. Then they went in different directions, but she could hear the gun shooting again and again over the hill.   (59)

She walked on. The shadows hung from the oak trees to the road like curtains. Then she smelled wood-smoke, and smelled the river, and she saw a steeple and the cabins on their steep steps. Dozens of little black children whirled around her. There ahead was Natchez shining. Bells were ringing. She walked on.   (60)

In the paved city it was Christmas time. There were red and green electric lights strung and crisscrossed everywhere, and all turned on in the daytime. Old Phoenix would have been lost if she had not distrusted her eyesight and depended on her feet to know where to take her.   (61)

She paused quietly on the sidewalk where people were passing by. A lady came along in the crowd, carrying an armful of red-, green-, and silver-wrapped presents; she gave off perfume like the red roses in hot summer, and Phoenix stopped her.   (62)

"Please, missy, will you lace up my shoe?" She held up her foot.   (63)

"What do you want, Grandma?"   (64)

"See my shoe," said Phoenix. "Do all right for out in the country, but wouldn't look right to go in a big building."   (65)

"Stand still then, Grandma," said the lady. she put her packages down on the sidewalk beside her and laced and tied both shoes tightly.   (66)

"Can't lace 'em with a cane," said Phoenix. "Thank you, missy. I doesn't mind asking a nice lady to tie up my shoe, when I gets out on the street."   (67)

Moving slowly and from side to side, she went into the big building and into a tower of steps, where she walked up and around and around until her feet knew to stop.   (68)

She entered a door, and there she saw nailed up on the wall the document that had been stamped with the gold seal and framed in the gold frame, which matched the dream that was hung up in her head.   (69)

"Here I be." she said. There was a fixed and ceremonial stiffness over her body.   (70)

"A charity case, I suppose," said an attendant who sat at the desk before her.   (71)

But Phoenix only looked above her head. There was sweat on her face, the wrinkles in her skin shone like a bright net.   (72)

"Speak up, Grandma," the woman said: "What's your name? We must have your history, you know. Have you been here before? What seems to be the trouble with you?"   (73)

Old Phoenix only gave a twitch to her face as if a fly were bothering her.   (74)

"Are you deaf?" cried the attendant.   (75)

But then the nurse came in.   (76)

"Oh, that's just old Aunt Phoenix," she said. "She doesn't come for herself—she has a little grandson. She makes these trips just as regular as clockwork. She lives away back off the old Natchez Trace." She bent down. "Well, Aunt Phoenix, why don't you just take a seat? We won't keep you standing after your long trip." She pointed.   (77)

The old woman said down, bolt upright in the chair.   (78)

"Now, how is the boy?" asked the nurse.   (79)

Old Phoenix did not speak.   (80)

"I said, how is the boy?"   (81)

But Phoenix only waited and stared straight ahead, her face very solemn and withdrawn into rigidity.   (82)

"Is his throat any better?" asked the nurse. "Aunt Phoenix, don't you hear me? Is your grandson's throat any better since the last time you came for the medicine?"   (83)

With her hands on her knees, the old woman waited, silent, erect and motionless, just as if she were in armor.   (84)

"You mustn't take up our time this way, Aunt Phoenix," the nurse said. "Tell us quickly about your grandson, and get it over. He isn't dead, is he?"   (85)

At last there came a flicker and then a flame of comprehension across her face, and she spoke.   (86)

"My grandson. It was my memory had left me. There I sat and forgot why I made my long trip."   (87)

"Forgot?" The nurse frowned. "After you came so far?"   (88)

Then Phoenix was like an old woman begging a dignified forgiveness for waking up frightened in the night. "I never did go to school, I was too old at the Surrender," she said in a soft voice. "I'm an old woman without an education. It was my memory fail me. My little grandson, he is just the same, and I forgot it in the coming."   (89)

"Throat never heals, does it?" said the nurse, speaking in a loud, sure voice to Old Phoenix. By now she had a card with something written on it, a little list. "Yes. Swallowed lye. When was it—January—two-three years ago—"   (90)

Phoenix spoke unasked now. "No, missy, he not dead, he just the same. Every little while his throat begin to close up again, and he not able to swallow. He not get his breath. He not able to help himself. So the time come around, and I go on another trip for the soothing medicine."   (91)

"All right. The doctor said as long as you came to get it, you could have it," said the nurse. "But it's an obstinate case."   (92)

"My little grandson, he sit up there in the house all wrapped up, waiting by himself," Phoenix went on. "We is the only two left in the world. He suffer and it don't seem to put him back at all. He got a sweet look. He going to last. He wear a little patch quilt and peep out holding his mouth open like a little bird. I remembers so plain now. I not going to forget him again, no, the whole enduring time. I could tell him from all the others in creation."   (93)

"All right." The nurse was trying to hush her now. She brought her a bottle of medicine. "Charity," she said, making a check mark in a book.   (94)

Old Phoenix held the bottle close to her eyes and then carefully put it into her pocket.   (95)

"I thank you," she said.   (96)

"It's Christmas time, Grandma," said the attendant. "Could I give you a few pennies out of my purse?"   (97)

"Five pennies is a nickel," said Phoenix stiffly.   (98)

"Here's a nickel," said the attendant.   (99)

Phoenix rose carefully and held out her hand. She received the nickel and then fished the other nickel out of her pocket and laid it beside the new one. She stared at her palm closely, with her head on one side.   (100)

Then she gave a tap with her cane on the floor.   (101)

"This is what come to me to do," she said. "I going to the store and buy my child a little windmill they sells, made out of paper. He going to find it hard to believe there such a thing in the world. I'll march myself back where he waiting, holding it straight up in this hand."   (102)

She lifted her free hand, gave a little nod, turned round, and walked out of the doctor's office. Then her slow step began on the stairs, going down.   (103)

Questions for Writing and Discussion

1. Which of the following approximates your response(s) to the character of Phoenix Jackson: Surprise that she should be the subject of a story? Anger that no one helps her on her journey?

Boredom that you just read a story where nothing seems to happen? Puzzlement at her apparently senile behavior? Amazement at her determination and courage? Describe any other responses you may have.

2. According to legend, the Phoenix is a mythological bird that lives for five hundred years, burns itself to death, and then rises from its ashes in the freshness of youth to live through another life cycle. What *events, references,* and *images* in the story suggest that Welty's Phoenix Jackson is like the mythological bird?

3. One reader has suggested that during her journey Phoenix encounters twelve obstacles (internal and external) that represent tests, or trials, of her faith and courage. How many of these tests can you find? Does she "pass" each test? What do these tests reveal about her character?

4. In an essay entitled "Is Phoenix Jackson's Grandson Really Dead?" Eudora Welty says, "The story is told through Phoenix's mind as she undertakes her errand. As the author at one with the character as I tell it, I must assume that the boy is alive. As the reader, you are free to think as you like, of course: the story invites you to believe that no matter what happens, Phoenix for as long as she is able to walk and can hold to her purpose will make her journey." Explain how the boy's actual condition might affect your interpretation of the story.

5. Kate Chopin's "The Story of an Hour" and Eudora Welty's "A Worn Path" are both stories about love. By contrast, what does the character and behavior of Mrs. Mallard tell you about Phoenix? What does the character and behavior of Phoenix reveal about Mrs. Mallard?

RESPONDING TO LITERATURE: THE WRITING PROCESS

ASSIGNMENT FOR RESPONDING TO LITERATURE

Choose one of the short stories from this chapter (or a work of literature assigned in your class) and read it actively, reread and annotate the work, and share your responses with others in the class. Then write an interpretative essay. Assume that you are writing for other members of your class (including your instructor) who have read the work but who may not understand or agree with your interpretation.

Collecting

In addition to reading, rereading, annotating, and sharing your responses, try the following collecting strategies:

- **Collaborative Annotation.** In small groups, choose a work of literature or select a passage that you have already annotated. In the group, read each other's annotations. Then discuss each annotation. Which annotations does your group agree are the best? Have a group recorder record the best annotations.

- **Elements of Fiction Analysis.** Reread the paragraphs defining character, plot, point of view, setting, and style. Choose three of these elements that seem most important in the story you are reading. Reread the story, annotating for these three elements. Then freewrite a paragraph explaining *how these three elements are interrelated* or *how they explain the theme.*

- **Time Line.** In your journal, draw a time line for the story. List above the line everything that happens in the story. Below the line, indicate where the story opens, when the major conflicts occur, and where the climax and the denouement occur. For "The Story of an Hour" student writer Karen Ehrhardt drew the following time line.

- **Character Conflict Map.** Start with a full page of paper. Draw a main character in the center of the page. Locate the other major characters, internal forces, and external forces (including social, economic, and environmental pressures) in a circle around the main character. Draw a line between each of these peripheral characters or forces and the main character. For his character conflict map for "The Story of an Hour" student writer Darren Marshall used images from his computer program to surround his picture of Mrs. Mallard.

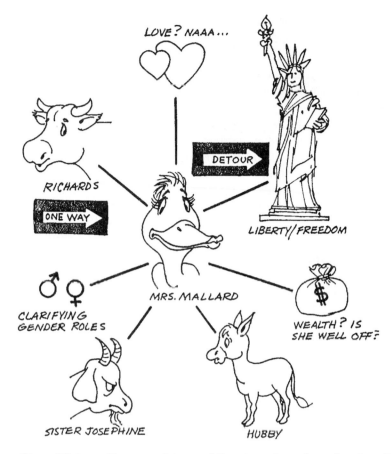

- **Story Picture.** Draw a picture of the story, based on the time line and conflict mapping, that represents the entire story. Use the information from your character analysis, time line, and character conflicts to help you draw a single picture of the complete story. Student writer Lori Van Skike drew a picture for "The

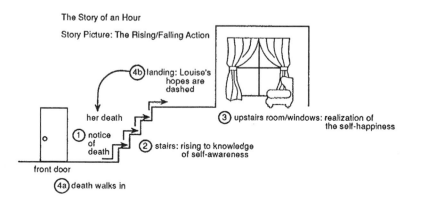

Story of an Hour" that shows how the rising and falling action of the plot parallels Mrs. Mallard's ascent and descent of the stairs.

- **Feature List.** Choose a character trait, repeated image, or idea that you wish to investigate in the story. List, in order of appearance, every word, image, or reference that you find in the story.

- **Scene Vision or Revision.** Write a scene for this story in which you change some part of the story. You may *add* a scene to the beginning, middle, or end of the story. You may *change* a scene in the story. You may write a scene in the story from a different character's point of view. You may change the style of the story for your scene. How, for example, might Eudora Welty have described the opening scene of "The Story of an Hour"?

- **Background Investigation.** Investigate the biographical, social, historical, or geographical context for the story. Locate a biography of the author. How are the major events of the author's life relevant to the story? Read about the historical or economic background of the story. Look at maps or descriptions of the setting for the story. How do these background sources increase your appreciation or widen your understanding of the story?

- **Reconsideration of Purposes.** What idea, theme, or approach most interests you? Will you be explaining, evaluating, problem solving, or arguing? Are you combining purposes? Do these purposes suggest what kinds of information you might collect?

Shaping

Test each of the following possible shapes against your ideas for your essay. Use or adapt the shape or shapes that are most appropriate for your own interpretation.

Explaining Relationships Often interpretative essays analyze how the parts of a story relate to the whole. As you explain these relationships, you should show how key lines or scenes contribute to the portrait of the major character or to the overall theme of the story. Your focus might be on how *plot* or *character conflicts* affect your understanding of the major character, on how the *setting* reflects the theme, or on how *images* reveal character and/or contribute to the theme.

Introduction and thesis: The images in story "X" reveal that the theme is "Y."

First scene or part:	How key images contribute to theme
Second scene or part:	How key images contribute to theme
Third scene or part:	How key images contribute to theme
Conclusion:	

Evaluating If your response suggests an evaluating purpose, you may wish to set up *criteria* for an effective short story and then provide evidence that shows how the particular story does or does not measure up to your standards. Your thesis might be "Story 'X' is highly dramatic because the main character undergoes emotional changes, the character conflicts heighten the tension, and the theme is controversial." (A similar shaping strategy might be to set a *definition* of a hero or heroine and then analyze how the main character fits your ideal definition.)

Introduction and thesis:	Story "X" is highly dramatic.
Criteria #1:	A dramatic short story should focus on a character who changes his or her behavior or beliefs.
	Judgment and evidence for criteria #1:
Criteria #2:	A dramatic story must have striking conflicts that lead to a crisis or a predicament.
	Judgment and evidence for criteria #2:
Criteria #3:	A dramatic story should have a theme that makes a controversial point.
	Judgment and evidence for criteria #3:
Conclusion:	

Arguing During class discussion, you may disagree with another person's response. Your thesis may then take the form, "Although some readers believe this story is about 'X,' the story is really about 'Y.'" In an argumentative structure, you counter opposing interpretations by pointing to evidence in the story and then you support your interpretation with evidence.

Introduction and thesis:	Although some readers suggest that the story is about "X", it is really about "Y."
Body paragraphs:	State the opposing interpretation and give evidence that this interpretation cites:
	State your interpretation and give evidence (description, dialogue, images, points of conflict, incidents from the plot):
Conclusion:	

Investigating Changes in Interpretation   Often, readers *change* their interpretation during the course of responding to a piece of literature. Thus, your main point might be "Although I initially thought 'X' about the story, I gradually realized the theme of the story was 'Y.'" If that sentence expresses your main idea, you may wish to organize your essay following the *chronology* or the *steps* in the changes in your interpretation:

Introduction and thesis:	"Although I initially thought "X," I now believe "Y."
Body paragraphs:	First step (your original interpretation of the story and supporting evidence):
	Second step (additional or contradictory ideas and evidence that forced you to reconsider your interpretation):
	Third step (you final interpretation and supporting evidence):
Conclusion:	

Note: One strategy you should *not* use is to simply retell the main events of the story. A review of the plot is not an acceptable interpretation. Your audience has already read the story. They want you to state your interpretation and then use details from the story to show how and why your interpretation is credible. *In your essay, you will cite events from the plot, but you must explain how or why these events support your interpretation.*

Drafting

To prepare to draft your essay, read through your annotations in the story and gather your collecting and shaping notes. Some writers prefer to write a one-sentence statement of their main idea at the top of the page to keep them focused as they write. Other writers prefer to make a rough outline to follow, based on their adaptation of one of the above shaping strategies. When you begin drafting, you may wish to skip your introduction and start with the body of your essay. You can fill in the introduction after you have written a draft of the essay.

Once you start writing, keep your momentum going. If you draw a blank, reread what you have already written or look at your notes. if you cannot think of a particular word or are unsure about a spelling, draw a line _____ and keep on writing.

COMPUTER TIP: REVISING

When you have finished your draft, you need to revise your main idea or thesis. *The exact phrasing of your main idea or interpretation is crucial.* On the computer, use a block move to copy your conclusion and place it just above your introduction. (You can also use your split-screen function to compare the two paragraphs.)

Concluding paragraph(s):

Introductory paragraph(s):

With both your conclusion and introduction in front of you on the screen, reread them carefully. If you wrote your conclusion *after* you wrote the body of the essay, it probably contains a clearer statement of your main idea. Revise your introduction so it includes the clearest and most concise statement of your interpretation. If you have to move a key sentence from the conclusion to the introduction, do so. You can then revise your conclusion as necessary.

Revising

Use the following guidelines as you read your classmate's drafts and revise your own essay. Be prepared to make changes in your ideas, organization, and evidence, as well as to fix problems in sentences and word choice.

GUIDELINES FOR REVISION

- **Clarify your main idea or interpretation.** Ask your readers to write, in one sentence, the main point of your interpretation. If their statement does not exactly match your main point, clarify your thesis. Your interpretation (not a statement of fact) should be clearly stated early in your essay.

- **Do not give a plot summary.** Your readers have read the story, so do not simply retell the plot. Do, however, give ample evidence. You must also explain how that evidence supports your main point.

- **Support each part of your interpretation with references to specific passages from the text.** Do not be satisfied with one piece of evidence. Find as many bits of evidence as possible. The case for your interpretation grows stronger with each additional piece of evidence.

- **Explain how each piece of evidence supports your interpretation.** Do not just cite several pieces of evidence and go on to your next point. Explain for your reader how the pieces of evidence you cite support your interpretation.

- **Define key terms in your essay.** If you are writing about the hero in a story, define what you mean by "hero" or "heroine." If you are arguing that "The Story of an Hour" has a feminist theme, define "feminism."

- **Signal the major parts of your interpretation.** Let your reader know when you shift to a new point. Use transitions and paragraph hooks at the beginning of body paragraphs.

- **Use the present tense as you describe the events in the story.** If you are describing the end of "The Story of an Hour," write "Mrs. Mallard descends the stairs and learns the 'good news' about her husband."

- **Quote accurately and cite page numbers for each reference.** Double check your quotations to make sure they are accurate, word-for-word transcriptions. Following each direct quotation, cite page references as follows: In the first sentence, Kate Chopin says, "Mrs. Mallard was afflicted with a heart trouble" (415). **Note:** The period goes outside the parentheses. See pages 412 to 414 in Chapter 10 for correct documentation in style.

- **Revise your essay for sentence clarity and conciseness.** Read your essay aloud or have a classmate read your essay. Reduce unnecessary repetition. Use active verbs. Rework awkward or confusing sentences.

- **Edit your essay.** Check your essay for correct spelling, word choice, punctuation, and grammar.

POSTSCRIPT ON THE WRITING PROCESS

Before you turn in your essay, answer the following questions in your journal.

1. Explain what part of this essay (collecting ideas and evidence, focusing on your interpretation, shaping your essay, drafting, or revising) was most difficult for you. How did you work around that problem?

2. What do you like best about your essay? Refer to specific places in the essay (lead-in, thesis, pieces of evidence, ideas, conclusion). Which specific paragraphs did you like best? Why?

3. What did you learn about the story by writing your interpretation? What do you realize now that you did not understand when you first read the story?

4. If you had two more hours to work on this essay, what would you change? Why?

RESPONDING TO LITERATURE: STUDENT WRITING

A WORN PATH

Julia MacMillan and Brett MacFadden

Julia MacMillan and Brett MacFadden collaboratively wrote their essay on the Phoenix imagery in Eudora Welty's "A Worn Path." They drafted their own essays separately and then collaborated on a revision that shared their interpretations and their best textual evidence. Included below are their original separate notes and drafts, their plans for their collaborative revision, and their final revised interpretation. Read their separate versions first, and then see how they collaborated to produce their revised essay.

Rough Drafts

Julia MacMillan

The journey that Phoenix Jackson makes in Eudora Welty's "A Worn Path" is very similar to that made by the mythological phoenix on its way to rebirth. Much of the symbolism and figurative language throughout the story shows the succession of events that parallel a Phoenix-like ending to the old woman.

We can feel, almost from the beginning, that Phoenix's long life is coming to an end. She is described with "the two knots of her cheeks illuminated by a yellow burning under the dark" (289). In only a few more sentences, however, we hear the mourning dove, apparently mourning for Phoenix. The yellow burning under the dark is almost a desperate, final fiery burst in the face of oncoming death.

Her death is also foreshadowed in the mention of a buzzard, watching her from the tall, dead trees. She asks of him, "Who are you watching?" as if she knows it is herself. Further in her journey, upon meeting the white hunter, her impending death as well as her expectation of it are shown. The little bob-white, "its beak hooked bitterly to show it was dead" (262), that the hunter was carrying on his bag quite forcefully shows us her death. The fact that she does not fear, but expects this death is shown when the hunter points his gun at Phoenix, and she "stood straight and faced him" quite fearlessly (263). In not fearing this death and seeming to understand its nearness, Phoenix Jackson becomes more like the bird she is named for.

It is most clearly seen that the author intended her reader to see the Phoenix imagery when the grandson is introduced near the end of the story. On page 264, she "entered a door, and there she saw the document that had been stamped with the gold seal and framed in the gold frame, which matched the dream that was hung up in her head." The gold in this passage seems to represent flame—the flame of her funeral pyre and the dream in her head of perpetuation and reincarnation through her grandson's life. It is even more clearly stated when, once in the doctor's office, she goes into a strange trance, becoming unable to answer the agitated nurse's questions. When finally asked, "He isn't dead, is he?", a "flutter, then a flame of comprehension comes across her face" (265). These flames are symbolic of her death, yet they are caused by her remembering the importance of her grandson's life to her. This life is most precious to her, because it is through her grandson that Phoenix, like the mythological bird, will live again.

Brett MacFadden

In many ways Phoenix Jackson is like the mythical bird she is named after; her physical characteristics, her purpose in life, and her extreme age and nearness to death all support her likeness to the mythological Phoenix.

The Phoenix is a bird of myth that lives for 500 years and then burns itself to death, rising from its ashes renewed and beautiful. Phoenix Jackson in the story "A Worn Path" by Eudora Welty is a very old black woman near the end of her life cycle who takes a long walk through the woods to town in order to get medicine for her ailing grandson. The core story is very simple, and it is because of this simplicity that the reader is forced to look beyond the core for a more complex tale. One of the first clues toward the inner story is the name of the main character, Phoenix. With the knowledge of what a Phoenix is, we can find many clues supporting the idea of the old woman living her life as a Phoenix.

Throughout the short story, words and phrases that describe the old woman might also describe the mythological bird. Her skin is black with a "golden color underneath" (259) and the "two knobs of her cheeks were illuminated by a yellow burning under the dark" (259). Both the golden color and especially the yellow burning are colors of fire, symbolizing the bird's fiery death. A red rag that she wears on top of her head is also another color of flame. Her black, wrinkled skin can be thought of as looking quite like ashes, and assuming that her grandson is a blood relative, his skin should also be the color of charred ash. She is like a fire that is almost out. It is mostly black, but there is the small flicker of flame to show you it is not yet extinguished.

Assuming the reader chooses to believe that Phoenix does in fact have a grandson and he is in fact sick, then the main purpose of her trip is to get the boy his medicine. This idea goes along nicely with the phoenix theme because she is giving everything she has left for the benefit of her grandson. She is essentially burning herself up so that the new person can exist. We can assume from the physical appearance and actions of Phoenix that she is pretty nearly burnt out. Phoenix knows her grandson is the one with the potential now, and so she gives all the effort she has to get him his medicine. Her only wish is to see him rise from his sick bed.

There are many hints to Phoenix's extreme age. At one time she tells herself, "I is the oldest person I ever know" (261), indicating that she has lived longer than most. Another time the hunter that she came across estimated that she was "a hundred years old" (263). Much of the imagery in the story symbolizes her oncoming death. The fact that it is winter can be seen as the winter of her life. Other death images include the big dead trees, the buzzard, the scarecrow she mistakes for a ghost, and the black dog that knocks her into the ditch.

A SINGULAR PERPETUATION

Brett MacFadden

Julia MacMillan

Phoenix Jackson, in the story "A Worn Path," by Eudora Welty, is in many ways like the mythological bird she is named after. Her purpose in life, birdlike characteristics, and nearness to death all support a clear parallel between the character and her namesake. The story is very simple, and because of this simplicity the reader is forced to search for a more meaningful tale. One of the first clues towards the inner story is the name of the main character, Phoenix. With the knowledge of what a Phoenix is, it is possible to find many clues supporting the idea of the old woman living her life as a Phoenix, burning herself out for the benefit of the new bird, her grandson.   (1)

The Phoenix is a mythological bird who after living for 500 years, burns itself to ashes on a pyre, and rises renewed to live another cycle. Phoenix Jackson journeys through the woods to town to get medicine for her ailing grandson. This idea parallels the Phoenix theme, because she is making what appears to be her final journey, in order that her grandson may rise from his sickbed. The legend of the Phoenix is one of singular perpetuation; only one exists in the world. This is shown when she tells the nurses that "We is the only two left in the world" (255). Phoenix is concerned because if both of them were to die, then it would result in the extinction of the species. As much as she worries about him surviving, she is confident that he, like the immortal bird, will survive. Speaking to the nurses again, she says, "He suffer and it don't seem to put him back at all. . . . He going to last" (265–66). As well as his immortality, his birdlike characteristics and dependence on Phoenix for his perseverance are shown when he peeps out of his quilt "holding his mouth open like a little bird" (266). He is her reincarnation, and she is devoted to his successful ascension.   (2)

Throughout the story many words and phrases that describe the old woman might also describe the mythological bird. Her skin is described as black with "a golden color underneath," and the "two knobs of her cheeks were illuminated by a yellow burning under the dark" (259). She wears on top of her head a red rag. Both the "golden color," and the "yellow burning," as well as the red of her rag are colors of fire, symbolizing her approaching death. As she walks, the tapping of her umbrella sounds like "the chirping of a solitary little bird" (259). Her likeness to a bird is evidenced when, in passing a scarecrow in a field, she is frightened, as a bird would be. When startled by a dog, she fell into a ditch "like a little puff of milk-weed" (262). This gives the appearance that she is a light creature, mostly flame and feather. These birdlike characteristics of Phoenix seem to imply that the author intended her to represent the mythical bird.   (3)

The myth of the Phoenix holds that when ". . . its eyes begin to grow dim, it knows that the time of death has come" (Oswalt 239). When we are first introduced to the main character, as well as being old, she is described as having "eyes . . . blue with age" (259). Many images of death, some quite vivid, link Phoenix Jackson's impending death to that of the Phoenix of myth. At one point in her journey she stoops and looks upwards exclaiming, "Sun so high! Time getting all gone here" (260). This clearly indicates her knowledge of her approaching death. Her death is also forshadowed by the mention of several images that bombard us from the dawn of the story. Early on she reflects on the call of a mourning dove—mourning being something done in the wake of death. Later she comes upon a buzzard sitting in a dead tree. She asks of him, "Who you watching?" (261), as if she knows it is herself. Her death is foreshadowed further when walking through a cornfield she happens upon what she perceives to be a ghost. Upon closer inspection, the ghost turned out to be a scarecrow. However, she shows no fear approaching what she thinks is a ghost, which demonstrates that she is comfortable with dying. The black dog that knocks her into a ditch is another vivid image of death. Further in her journey, upon meeting a white hunter, her impending death as well as her expectation of it are shown. The little bob-white, "its beak hooked bitterly to show that it was dead" (262) that the hunter was carrying on his bag quite forcefully shows us her anticipated death. The fact that she does not fear, but expects this death is shown when the hunter pointed his gun at Phoenix, and she "stood straight and faced him" quite fearlessly" (263). In not fearing this death and seeming to understand its nearness, Phoenix Jackson becomes more like the bird she is named for.   (4)

A carefully wrought story, "A Worn Path" is more than a tale of an old woman's formidable journey. It is the rebirth of an age-old myth wrapped in the cloak of conventionality. In examining some of the symbols, allusions, and the underlying legend, we find a well hidden but evident parallel between the lives of the main character and her namesake, the Phoenix.   (5)

Works Cited

Oswalt, Sabine G. <u>Concise Encyclopedia of Greek and Roman Mythology</u>. Chicago: Follett Publishing Co., 1969.

Postscript on the Collaborative Revision

We began this collaboration by reading each other's papers and rereading our own in order to find the strengths and weaknesses of each paper. Then together we combed through each paper, pulling out what we both agreed were our strongest points and compiled these into a thesis. For our thesis, we used the second sentence in the first paragraph: "Her [Phoenix's] purpose in life, her birdlike characteristics, and her nearness to death support a clear parallel between the character and her namesake."

Having decided on a thesis and a rough plan of action, we then went to the computer lab and began writing. At this point, the paper became more difficult because we had to narrow two papers into one and decide what we should omit. For example, Julia's paper discussed the emblem on the doctor's office wall as another symbol of Phoenix's fiery death. After discussing this scene, we decided that the symbolism was not strong enough and should be left out. We both knew each other before deciding to write the collaborative essay, so we were both comfortable around each other and were able to say what we really thought about each other's writing. We knew also that our basic writing styles were opposing. Brett's was concise, while Julia's was more flowing. Our different writing styles had to be combined into one smooth style. We did this by having one person dictate and the other type, which caused an intertwining of our styles by the time the words hit the screen. We had fun working on this paper and learned quite a bit about collaboration in the process. For example, we found it challenging because we had to work on one sentence at a time, making sure each sentence was right before we went on to the next one. This process made the revision take far longer to complete than if it had been done by one person.

QUESTIONS FOR WRITING AND DISCUSSION

1. What are the best ideas or evidence in this essay? Explain at which points you might disagree with the writers' interpretation.

2. Compare MacMillan's and MacFadden's drafts with the final version of their essay. Explain how their interpretation changed as they worked collaboratively on the final version. What did they add to their final version? What did they omit from the earlier drafts?

3. In the final version, MacMillan and MacFadden do not cite evidence from the final part of the story. Explain why the events in town support or do not support the Phoenix parallels.

4. Review the Guidelines for Revision. In the authors' essay, underline sentences that contain the *main idea*, that *define key terms*, that contain *evidence* or support, that *explain* how the evidence supports the thesis, that *signal* major parts of the interpretation, and that contain *accurate* quotations. Based on your annotations, what suggestions for further revision do you have for the authors?

DEATH: THE FINAL FREEDOM

Pat Russell

Following a class discussion of the feminist theme in Kate Chopin's "The Story of an Hour," Pat Russell wrote in his journal, "Is the story a feminist one? No. It is not just about feminism

*but about how people stifle their own needs and desires to accom-
modate those of their mate." In his essay, Russell argues that the
traditional feminist reading limits the universal theme of the story.
As you read his essay, see if you are persuaded by his argument.*

The poor treatment of women and their struggle for an individual
identity is a major underlying theme of Kate Chopin's stories.
Although many regard Chopin's "The Story of an Hour" as a feminist
story, today a more universal interpretation is appropriate. This story
is not about the oppression of a woman, but about how people strive
to maintain the normalcy and security of their relationships by sup-
pressing their own individual wants and needs.   (1)

Evidence in favor of the feminist argument begins with the period the story was written in, sometimes around the turn of the century.
Society prevented women from coming out of the household. Most
women weren't allowed to run a business, and for that matter, they
couldn't even vote. Their most important jobs were wife and mother.
This background sets the tone for the main character's life. In the
beginning we are told Mrs. Mallard has a "fair, calm face whose lines
bespoke repression" (414). There is also evidence that suggests her
husband was ignorant of her ideas and forceful with his own. Chopin
writes: "There would be no powerful will bending her in that blind
persistence with which men and women believe they have a right to
impose a private will upon a fellow creature" (415). In addition, Mrs.
Mallard is described early on as fearful and powerless, and later as a
triumphant "goddess of Victory," indicating her rebirth. These citations suggest that this is a feminist story, but this label limits the
meaning behind the story.   (2)

Many people who are unhappy with their marriages either fail
to recognize their unhappiness or refuse to accept responsibility of it. I
feel sorry for those who don't recognize their unhappiness. However,
it is pathetic to see someone such as Mrs. Mallard hold onto a relationship simply because she doesn't know how to let go. "And yet she
had loved him—sometimes. Often she had not" (415). She continuous-
ly fell in and out of love with her husband until he "died," at which
point she told herself that love didn't matter compared to the self-
assertion "which she suddenly recognized as the strongest impulse of
her being" (415). It is as if she had waited for all of her life for this
moment; she prayed for a long life, when only the day before she had
dreaded it. She wept for him but at the same time compared her husband to a criminal, a man whom she had lived her life for, never once
thinking of herself. But now "there would be no one to live for during
those coming years; she would live for herself" (415). She was lucky in
that she felt "free." Her emotional suppression was over, and she
would no longer have anyone to blame for her unhappiness.   (3)

It is important not only to try to interpret the author's intended meaning of the story, but also to think about what message "The Story of an Hour" has for us today. As a feminist story, the lesson "The Story of an Hour" teaches is one dimensional. Interpreting it as a story about the struggle of all people opens up the possibility of teaching others that selfishness and selflessness are both good, when used in moderation. In Mrs. Mallard's case, correcting this balance became a matter of life and death. In the face of her suppressor, her desperation for freedom forced her to choose death.   (4)

QUESTIONS FOR WRITING AND DISCUSSION

1. With what parts of Russell's interpretation do you agree? (What additional evidence from the story might Russell cite in support of his interpretation?) What ideas or sentences might you challenge? (What evidence from the story might refute those statements?)

2. Write out your definition of feminism. Where does or should Russell explain his definition of feminism? How should Russell clarify his definition?

3. Write out Russell's main idea or thesis. Explain why his thesis is an interpretation and not just a statement of fact.

4. What shaping strategy does Russell use to organize his essay?

5. Write out two other possible titles for Russell's essay. Explain why your alternate titles are or are not better than Russell's title.

APPENDIX:

WRITING UNDER PRESSURE

The main chapters of this text describe purposes for writing and strategies for collecting, shaping, drafting, and revising an essay. These chapters assume that you have several days or even weeks to write your paper. You have time to read model essays, time to think about ideas for your topic, and time to prewrite, write several drafts, and receive feedback from other members of your class. Much college writing, however, occurs on midterm or final examinations, when you may have only fifteen to twenty minutes to complete the whole process of writing. When you must produce a "final" draft in a few short minutes, your writing process may need drastic modification.

A typical examination has some objective questions (true/false, multiple choice, definitions, short answer) followed by an essay question or two. For example, with just twenty-five minutes left in your Western Civilization midterm examination, you might finish the last multiple-choice question, turn the page, and read the following essay question:

> Erich Maria Remarque's *All Quiet on the Western Front* has been hailed by critics the world over as the "twentieth century's definitive novel on war." What does Remarque's novel tell us about the historical, ideological, national, social, and human significance of twentieth-century warfare? Draw on specific illustrations from the novel, but base your observations on your wider perspective of Western Civilization. Good luck!

Overwhelmed by panic, the blood drains from your face and your fingers feel icy. You now have twenty-two minutes to write on the "historical, ideological, national, social, and human significance of twentieth-century warfare." Do you have to explain everything about modern warfare? Must you use specific examples from the novel? Good luck, indeed! Everything you remembered about the novel has now vanished. Bravely, you pick up the pen and start writing down the main events of the novel, hoping to show the instructor that you at least read the novel.

You can survive such an essay examination, but you need to prepare yourself emotionally and intellectually. Some advice from senior English majors who have taken dozens of essay examinations in their four years of college follows. These seniors answer the question, "What advice would you give to students who are preparing to take an essay examination?"

Even though I'm an English major, I'm perfectly petrified of writing impromptu essays. My advice is to calm yourself. Read the question. Study key words and concepts. Before beginning an essay question, write a brief, informal outline. This will organize your ideas and help you remember them as well. Take a deep breath and write. I would also recommend *rereading* the question while you are writing, to keep you on track.

The first step is to know the material. Then, before you begin, read the instructions. Know what the teacher expects. Then try to organize your thoughts into a small list—preferably a list that will become your main paragraphs. Don't babble to fill space. Teachers hate reading nonsense. Reread what you've written often. This will ensure that you won't repeat yourself. Proofread at the end.

Organization is important but difficult in a pressure situation. Well-organized essays do have a tendency to impress the professor, sometimes more than information-packed essays. Organize your notes and thoughts about those notes as you study (not necessarily in a chronological order, but rather in a comprehensible order). Good luck.

Read the question carefully.
Get your thoughts in order.
Write what the question asks, not what you hope it says.
Don't ramble.
Give textual facts or specific examples.
Summarize with a clear, understandable closure.
Proofread.
Keep calm. Your life doesn't depend on one test.

My advice would be first to learn how to consciously relax and practice writing frequently. *Practice!!!* It's important to practice writing as much as possible in any place possible, because the more writing you do, the better and easier it becomes. Also, your belief that it *can* be done is critical!

Know the information that you will be tested over well enough that you can ask yourself tough and well-formed questions in preparation. You should be able to predict what essay questions your professor will ask, at least generally. I always go to the test file or ask friends for sample essay questions that I can practice on. Then I practice writing on different areas of the material.

The common threads in these seniors' advice are to know your audience, analyze key terms in the question, make a sketch outline, know the material, practice writing before the test, and proofread when you finish writing. Knowing how to read the question and practicing your writing before the test will help you relax and do your best.

Know Your Audience

Teachers expect you to answer a question exactly as it is asked, not just to give the information that you know. Since teachers must read dozens of essays, they are impressed by clear organization and specific detail. As one senior says, teachers hate babble because they cannot follow the thread of your argument. They demand specific examples and facts from the text, but they want you to explain how these examples *relate* to the overall question. In a pile of two hundred history exams graded by one professor, the marginal comments repeatedly said, "Reread the question. This doesn't answer the question." "What is your main point? State your main point clearly." "Give more specific illustrations and examples." Keep this teacher in mind as you write your essay response.

Analyze Key Terms

Understanding the key terms in the question is crucial to writing an essay under pressure. Teachers expect you to respond to *their* specific question, not just to write down information. They want you to use your writing to *think* about the topic, to analyze and synthesize the information. They want you to make sense of the information. Below are key terms that indicate teacher's expectations and suggest how to organize your answer.

DISCUSS: A general instruction that means "write about." If the question says "discuss," look for other key words to focus your response.

DESCRIBE: Give sensory details or particulars about a topic. Often, however, this general instruction simply means "discuss."

ANALYZE: Divide a topic into its parts and show how the parts are related to each other and to the topic as a whole.

SYNTHESIZE: Show how the parts relate to the whole or how the parts make sense together.

EXPLAIN: Show relationships between specific examples and general principles. Explain what (define), explain why (causes/effects), and/or explain how (analyze process).

DEFINE: Explain what something is. As appropriate, give a formal definition, describe it, analyze its parts or function, describe what it is not, and/or compare and contrast it with similar events or ideas.

COMPARE: Explain similarities and (often) differences. Draw conclusions from the observed similarities and differences.

CONTRAST: Explain key differences. Draw conclusions from the observed differences.

ILLUSTRATE: Provide specific examples of an idea or process.

TRACE: Give the sequence or chronological order of key events or ideas.

EVALUATE: Determine the value or worth of an idea, thing, process, person, or event. Set up criteria and provide evidence to support your judgments.

SOLVE: Explain your solution; show how it fixes the problem, why it is better than other alternatives, and why it is feasible.

ARGUE: Present both sides of a controversial issue, showing why the opposing position should not be believed or accepted and why your position should be accepted. Give evidence to support your position.

INTERPRET: Offer your understanding of the meaning and significance of an idea, event, person, process, or work of art. Support your understanding with specific examples or details.

Make a Sketch Outline

The key terms in a question should not only focus your thinking but also suggest how to organize your response. Use the key terms to make a sketch outline of your response. You may not regularly use an outline when you have more time to write an essay, but the time pressure requires that you revise your normal writing process.

Assume that you have twenty-five minutes to read and respond to the following question from a history examination. Read the instructions carefully, note the key terms, and make a brief outline to guide your writing.

- Answer *one* of the following. Draw on the reading for your answer. (25 pts)

1. Explain the arguments that the balance of power does and does not work in the nuclear age (discuss and illustrate both sides of the argument). Then take a stand—citing the evidence for your position.

2. Explain the arguments that the United Nations does and does not play a positive role in international relations (discuss and illustrate both sides of the argument). Then take a stand—citing the evidence for your position.

Assuming that you know more about the United Nations, you choose the second question. First, you should identify and underline key words in the question. The subject for your essay is the *United Nations* and its role in *international relations.* You need to *explain* the reasons why the UN does or does not have a positive effect on international relations. You will need to *discuss* and *illustrate* (give specific examples of) both sides of the controversy. Finally, you need to *take a stand* (argue) for your belief, citing *evidence* (specific examples from recent history) of how the UN has or has not helped to resolve international tensions.

Based on your rereading and annotation of the key words of the question, make a quick outline or list, perhaps as follows:

I.   Reasons (with examples) why some believe the UN is effective
   A.   Reason #1 + example
   B.   Reason #2 + example

II. Reasons (with examples) why some believe the UN is not effective
   A.   Reason #1 + example
   B.   Reason #2 + example

III. Reasons why you believe the UN is effective
     Refer to reasons and examples cited in I, above, but explain why these reasons and examples outweigh the reasons cited in II, above.

With this sketch outline as your guide, jot down reasons and examples you intend to use and then start writing. Your outline will make sure that you cover all the main points of the question, and it will keep your essay organized as you concentrate on remembering specific reasons and examples to use in your essay.

JOURNAL EXERCISE

For practice, analyze at least one question from two of the following subject areas. First, underline key terms. Then, in your journal explain what these terms ask you to do. Finally, sketch an outline to help organize your response. If you are not familiar with the topics, check a dictionary or encyclopedia. (Do not write the essay.)

Biology

- Describe the process by which artificial insulin was first produced.
- What is reverse transcriptase and how was it used in genetic engineering?
- Humans—at least most of us—walk on two legs as opposed to four. How might you account for this using a Darwinian, Lamarckian, and Theistic model?

History

- Discuss the significant political developments in the English colonies in the first half of the eighteenth century.

- Account for the end of the Salem witchcraft delusion and discuss the consequences of the outbreak for Salem Village.

Human Development

- Discuss evidence for nature versus nurture effects in human development.
- Contrast Piaget's, Vygotsky's and Whorf's ideas on connections between language and thought.

Humanities

- How and why did early Christian culture dominate the Roman Empire? In terms of art and architecture, discuss specific ways in which the early Christians transformed or abolished the Greco-Roman legacy.

Literature

- Aristotle wrote that a tragedy must contain certain elements, such as a protagonist of high estate, recognition, and reversal, and should also evoke pity and fear in the audience. Which of the following best fits Aristotle's definition: *Hamlet, Death of a Salesman,* or *The Old Man and the Sea?* Explain your choice.

Philosophy

- On the basis of what we have studied in this class, define "philosophy." Taking your major subject of study (for example, biology, history, literature), discuss three philosophical problems that arise in this field.
- Write an essay explaining the following statement. Be clear in your explanation and use specific examples. "Egoism allows for prudent altruism."

Political Science

- Evaluate the achievements of the current administration's policy in Africa in recent years.
- Analyze the role of force in the contemporary international system.

Psychology

- Contrast Freud's and Erikson's stage theories of personality.
- What is meant by triangulation of measurement (multiple methodology)?

Know the Material

It goes without saying that you must know the material in order to explain the concepts and give specific examples or facts from the text. But what is the best way to review the material so you can recall examples under pressure? The following three study tactics will improve your recall.

First, **read your text actively.** Do not just mark key passages in yellow highlighter. Write marginal notes to yourself. Write key concepts in the margin. Ask questions. Make connections between an idea in one paragraph and something you read earlier. Make connections between what you read in the text and what you heard in class.

Second, do not depend only on your reading and class discussion. **Join or form a study group** that meets regularly to review course material. Each person in the group should prepare some question for review. Explaining key ideas to a friend is an excellent way to learn the material yourself.

Finally, **use your writing to help you remember.** Do not just read the book and your notes and head off for the test. Instead, review your notes, *close* your notebook, and write down as much as you can remember. Review the assigned chapters in the text, close the book, and write out what you remember. If you can write answers to questions with the book closed, you know you're ready for an essay examination.

Journal Exercise

Get out the class notes and textbook of a course you are currently taking. Annotate your class notes with summary comments and questions. In the margins, write out the key ideas that the lecture covered. Then write out questions that you still have about the material. Open your textbook for that class. Annotate the margins of the chapter you are currently reading. Write summary comments about important material. Write questions in the margins about material you do not understand. Note places in the text that the instructor also covered in class.

Practice Writing

As several of the senior English majors suggested, practicing short essays *before* the examination will make you feel comfortable with the material and reduce your panic. A coach once noted that every athlete wants to win, but only the true winners are willing to *prepare* to win. The same is true of writing an examination. Successful writers have already completed 80 percent of their writing process *before* they walk into an examination. They have written notes in the margins of their notebooks and textbooks. They have discussed the subject with other students. They have closed the book and written out key definitions. They have prepared questions and practiced answering them. Once they read the question, they are prepared to write out their "final" draft.

JOURNAL EXERCISE

For an up-coming examination in one of your other courses, write out three possible essay questions that your instructor might ask. For each question, underline the key words and make a sketch outline of your response. Set you watch or timer for fifteen minutes and actually write out your response to *one* of your questions.

Proofread and Edit

In your normal writing process, you can put aside your draft for several days and proofread and edit it later. When you are writing under pressure, however, you need to save three or four minutes at the end to review what you have written. Often, you may be out of time before you have finished writing what you wanted to say about the question. At that point, one effective strategy is to draw a line _____ at the end of what you have written, write "Out of Time," and then write one or two quick sentences explaining what you planned to say: "If I had more time, I would explain how the UN's image has become more positive following the crises in Israel and Iraq." Then use your remaining two or three minutes to reread what you have written, making sure that your ideas are clear, that you have written in complete sentences and used correct spelling and punctuation. If you don't know how to spell a word, at least write "sp?" next to a word to show that you think it is spelled incorrectly.

Sample Essay Questions and Responses

The following are sample essay questions, students' responses, and instructors' comments and grades.

HISTORY 100: WESTERN CIVILIZATION   Examination II over Chapter 12, class lectures, and Victor Hugo's *The Hunchback of Notre Dame*

ESSAY I (25 POINTS)   What was the fifteenth-century view of "science" as described in the *Hunchback*? How did this view tend to inhibit Claud Frollo in his experiments in his closet in the cathedral?

An excellent response. Your focus on superstition and heresy along with the specific examples of the roasted mouse, the "Philosopher's Stone," and La Esmeralda's goat illustrate the fifteenth-century view of science and its inhibiting effect. Grade: A

Answer 1

The fifteenth-century view of "science" was characterized by superstition and heresy. In the Hunchback of Notre Dame for example, we see superstition operating when the king's physician stated that a gunshot wound could be cured by the application of a roasted mouse. Claud Frollo, a high-ranking church official, had a thirst for knowledge, but unfortunately it pushed beyond the limits of knowledge permitted by the church. When he worked in his closet on the art of alchemy and searched for the "Philosopher's Stone" (gold), he was guilty of heresy. Frollo read and mastered the arts and sciences of the university and of the church, and he wanted to know more. He knew that if he pressed into the "Black Arts," the Devil would take his soul. And indeed, the "Devil" of passion did. Frollo felt inhibited because many of the experiments he performed would have made him guilty of heresy and witchcraft in the eyes of the church. And this seemed to be the case in almost anything "new" or out of the ordinary. La Esmeralda, for instance, was declared "guilty" of witchcraft for the training of her goat. Her goat appeared to have been possessed by the Devil himself. When in fact, all the girl was guilty of was training the goat to do a few simple tricks. All in all, the fifteenth-century view of "science" was not one of favor, but of oppression and fear. Thankfully, the Renaissance came along!

Answer 2

The fifteenth-century view of science was that according to the Bible. God was the creator of all and as to scientific theory, the

subject was moot. No one was a believer in the scientific method—
however we do find some science going on in Claud Frollo's closet,
alchemy. At that time he was trying to create gold by mixing
different elements together. Though alchemy seems to be the only
science of that time period, people who practiced it kept it to
themselves. We even find King Louis IX coming to Frollo, disguised,
to dabble in a little of the science himself. At this time people were
rejecting the theory of the Earth revolving around the sun because,
as a religious ordeal, God created the Earth and man and they are
the center of all things so there were no questions to be answered
by science, because the answer was God.

Answer 3

According to The Hunchback of Notre Dame, the view of "science"
in the fifteenth century was basically alchemy, that is being able to
turn back metals into gold. Everything else that we would regard
as scientific today was regarded as sorcery or magic in the
fifteenth century. What inhibited Claud Frollo in his experiments of
turning bare metals into gold was that, according to the laws of
alchemy, one needed "The Philosopher's Stone" to complete the
experiment and Claud Frollo was unable to find this particular
stone.

Answer 4

During the period that the Hunchback took place, the attitude
toward science was one of fear. Because the setting was in the
medieval world, the people were afraid to admit to doing some
things that were not being done by a majority of people. The
overall views during that period was to keep one's own self out of
trouble. The fright may be the result of the public executions which
was perhaps Claud Frollo's deterrent in admitting to performing
acts of science which others are uneducated in. Claud Frollo was

Give more examples from the novel and show how the fifteenth-century view actually inhibited *Frollo. Otherwise, generally good response. (Why was creating the Earth such a religious "ordeal"?) Grade: B*

Needs more specific illustrations from the novel. Frollo was inhibited by his lack of scientific method and the censure of the church. Underline titles of novels: The Hunchback of Notre Dame. Grade: C outnumbered in the area of wanting to be "educated" and he kept to himself because he feared the people. He was in a a position that didn't give him the power to try and overcome people's attitude of fear toward science. If he tried, he risked his life.

BIOLOGY 220: ECOLOGY
FINAL EXAMINATION

ESSAY II (20 POINTS)

Water running down a mountainside erodes its channel and carries with it considerable material. What is the basic source of the energy used by the water to do this work? How is the energy used by water to do this work related to the energy used by life in the stream ecosystem?

Answer 1

The process begins with the hydrologic cycle. The sun radiates down and forces evaporation. This H_2O gas condenses and forms rain or snow which precipitates back to earth. If the precipitation falls on a mountain, it will eventually run down the hillside and erode its channel. (Some water will evaporate without running down the hill.) The energy used by water to do its work relates directly to the energy used by life in the stream system. The sun is an energy input. It is the source of energy for stream life just as it is the source of energy for the water. Through photosynthesis, the energy absorbed by the stream is used by higher and higher trophic levels. So the sun is the energy source for both running water and the life in the stream. It all starts with solar energy.

Answer 2

Ultimately, the sun is the basic source of energy which allows water to do the work it does. Solar power runs the hydrologic cycle, which is where water gets its energy. Heat evaporates water and allows molecules to rise in the atmosphere where it condenses in clouds. Above the ground, but still under the effects of gravity,

State your ideas more clearly. Your response doesn't answer the question. Very limited in your examples of science. Grade: D

Good response. Clear focus on the hydrologic cycle, photosynthesis, and solar energy as the source of energy for both the stream and its ecosystems. Grade: A

Very clear explanation of the hydrologic cycle, but response doesn't explain how source of energy for the stream's ecosystems is related, through photosynthesis, to solar energy. Grade: B

water has potential energy at this point. When enough condensation occurs, water drops back to the ground, changing potential energy to kinetic energy, which is how water works on mountainsides to move materials. As water moves materials, it brings into streams a great deal of organic matter which is utilized by a number of heterotrophic organisms. That is the original source of energy for the ecosystems, and also how energy used by water is related to the energy that is used by life in streams.

Answer 3

The actual energy to move the water down the mountains is gravitation pull from the center of the earth. The stream's "growth" from the beginning of the mountain top to the base starts out with being a heterotrophic system. This is because usually there is not enough light to bring about photosynthesis for the plants and in turn help other organism's survival so the streams use outside resources for energy. Once the stream is bigger (by meeting up with another stream), it is autotrophic. It can produce its own energy sources. When the water reaches the base and becomes very large, it falls back to heterotrophic system because the water has become too deep for light to penetrate and help with photosynthesis.

Reread the question. The basic source of energy is solar power. You almost discover the answer when you discuss photosynthesis but after that, you get off track again

Grade: C −

HANDBOOK

"A piece of writing is never finished. It is delivered to a deadline, torn out of a typewriter on demand, and sent off with a sense of accomplishment and shame and pride and frustration. If only there were a couple more days, time for just another run at it, perhaps then . . .

—Donald Murray,
teacher and writer

Section 1
REVIEW OF BASIC SENTENCE ELEMENTS

If you are unfamiliar with grammatical terms, parts of speech, or basic sentence elements, check the definitions and examples in this section.

Section 2
SENTENCE STRUCTURE AND GRAMMAR

This section shows you how to revise common problems such as sentence fragments, faulty parallelism, unnecessary use of passive voice, and lack of subject-verb agreement.

2a Fragments
2b Mixed Constructions and Faulty Predication
2c Dangling Modifiers and Misplaced Modifiers
2d Faulty Parallelism
2e Active and Passive Voice
2f Nominals and "Be" Verbs
2g Subject-Verb Agreement
2h Verb Tense
2i Pronoun Agreement
2j Pronoun Reference

Section 3
DICTION AND STYLE

This section contains tips on making your writing more precise, concise, and effective. You will learn to recognize and eliminate vague words, needless words, clichés, and jargon. At the end of this section, the Usage Glossary explains distinctions between confusing pairs of words such as affect/effect, advise/advice, and amount/number.

3a Vague Words
3b Wordiness
3c Colloquial Language and Slang
3d Clichés and Jargon
3e Sexist Language
3f Denotation and Connotation
3g Usage Glossary

Section 4
PUNCTUATION AND MECHANICS

If you have problems using commas, semicolons, colons, or dashes, this section will help you pinpoint the errors and fix them. The examples show you how to revise comma splices and fused sentences, how to punctuate dialogue, and how to use numbers, apostrophes, italics, and capitals.

The information in this handbook will help you with the final stages of the revising process: editing and proofreading. Most writers and researchers agree that editing and proofreading should wait until the end of the writing process, when you are least likely to interrupt the flow of your ideas. During this final stage, you need to clarify your sentences and correct any errors in grammar, usage, diction, spelling, and mechanics. As you edit, concentrate on polishing the surface blemishes in your writing, but don't get so locked in on punctuation or grammar that you ignore the meaning, the organization, or the development of your essay. Even when you are proofreading, you may find an occasional spot to add another bit of detail, take out a repetitious phrase, or sharpen a transition.

To be a good editor, you need to understand the *conventions* of language and *expectations* of the reader instead of memorizing rules of right and wrong. In fact, the "rules" of grammar, punctuation, and usage may vary from one occasion to the next. A sentence fragment or a substandard usage such as "ain't" may be appropriate for one situation but not for another. Moreover, the notion of "rules" tends to suggest that language is static or unchanging. In fact, the opposite is true: Vocabulary, acceptable usage, even grammatical choices depend on current conventions and expectations. What is acceptable for one occasion or audience may be totally inappropriate for another. If you are not aware of these conventions, all your hard work in collecting, shaping, drafting, and revising may be wasted. A sloppy job of editing can ruin the best of essays.

This chapter describes standard conventions of editing for formal American English usage. As you edit your writing, however, remember that your purpose and audience should be the final guide.

Easy writing's curst hard reading.

—*Richard Brinsley Sheridan, dramatist*

WHY EDIT AND PROOFREAD?

Most writers and readers agree that grammar, usage, spelling, and mechanics are less important than the writer's content and ideas. But writers should realize that readers react not only to the ideas in an essay but also to the clarity, accuracy, and even the surface appearance of the writing. Often writers will say, rather defensively, "Of course there are a few typos and grammar problems in my essay, but readers can still get the message. After all, it's my *ideas* that count." Unfortunately, ideas count only if the reader *gets* them. If the reader falls asleep or becomes irritated by unclear sentences and errors in spelling or usage, the good ideas may never reach their destination.

The man snoozing in his chair with an unfinished magazine open on his lap is a man who was being given too much unnecessary trouble by the writer.

—*William Zinsser, writer and teacher*

Writers who say that surface errors are unimportant are either rationalizing or living in a fantasy world. In the real world, most readers react negatively if writing is not neat, accurate, and readable. If your friend or roommate leaves a scrawled note that says, "I borried your shert for too day—hope you do'nt mind!" you may worry about the "shert"—and look for a new roommate. If your bank statement has misspellings, crossed out numbers, or penciled-in debits, you may change banks in a hurry. If your doctor writes a note saying, "In my opinnion you should have bone serjury immediately!" you may rush to get another "opinnion" before agreeing to "serjury." The medium may communicate the real message: If the medium—your language—is flawed by surface errors, readers may think the message is flawed, too.

Some readers believe that writers who do not edit or proofread are just lazy and do not take sufficient time. Although you need time to polish your writing, effective editing and proofreading are not just a matter of effort or willpower. Rereading your essay ten times will not necessarily resolve all the problems. Editing is often difficult because many of your errors really don't look like mistakes—primarily because *you already know what you are trying to say.* When you reread what you have written, you tend to recall the idea already in your mind instead of reading the words exactly as they are written on the page.

If you live with a roommate, try this experiment. Sit in a neutral corner of the room and look at your desk. It looks relatively clean, right? A few books, papers, and pencils are scattered here and there, but you know where everything is. It has an order. It makes sense. The math book is on the corner of the desk—under the notebook, the sock, and the coffee—just where you left it last night. The psychology book is open to Chapter 4, right underneath the sweatshirt and the lecture notes you're going to study after dinner. Stuff is kind of stacked up, but not really messy. Now look at your roommate's desk. Everything looks disorganized, as if it were dumped upside down from a backpack. You count four books, two spiral notebooks, four dog-eared sheets of paper, one cup of stale coffee, a broken ball-point pen, and a T-shirt. It's a mess, right? And sometimes it really irritates you. *How can your roommate stand to live in such chaos?* But wait. Your roommate's desk has some order to it, too, just as yours does. You just can't see the order for the mess.

Unfortunately, the same is true for writing: In your *own* writing, all you see is the meaning, the order that is in your mind. In other people's writing, you see the errors first and then, only after careful reading, the meaning. The bedrock truth is that readers will more easily see your mess than your meaning. Your writing will be more effective if your readers aren't irritated about your mess that they have had to read through. Errors or surface distractions may even undermine your credibility as a writer. For some kinds of writing—letters of application or essays for classes—the result of a few errors may be more than irritation; you simply may not be admitted, get the job, or get a passing grade.

HOW TO EDIT AND PROOFREAD

The purpose of editing is, of course, to keep language problems from interfering with the ideas or message, to make language work for your purpose rather than against it. Editing usually requires that you read over your work several times, checking for errors and anticipating problems that your readers might have. However, since you literally may not *see* many "obvious" errors, have friends or classmates look over your draft for problems or mistakes. When you use other readers, however, explain your purpose and audience. Then ask them to use conventional proofreading and editing marks to indicate their suggestions. *Remember: Your editors' marks are suggestions.* If they mark errors you've simply overlooked, change the language. But if they mark something that you don't understand, check the appropriate section in this Handbook. If you disagree with their marks or suggestions, ask them to explain *why* they are suggesting the change. *You are responsible for deciding whether and how to make the change.*

Begin your editing and proofreading process for each essay by *reviewing your previous essays.* What problems and errors did your peer readers notice or your teacher mark? If you are keeping a log in your journal of your problems in grammar, usage, punctuation, or mechanics, review your entries. If you typically have punctuation problems and wordy sentences, reread those sections in this Handbook and focus on those specific items as you edit.

To improve your editing and proofreading skills, learn the following proofreading marks and correction symbols.

Proofreading Marks

$\wedge$	Insert comma
embar$\wedge$assing	Insert letter or word
hot tub. $\vee$	Insert quotation marks
south‿bound	Close up
¶	Begin a new paragraph
NO ¶	Do not begin a new paragraph

down his face⊙	Add period
hop|back	Add space
pe(i)ce of pie	Transpose letters
left (will that)	Transpose words
in a ~~large~~ sweat	Delete words
encounter⌣is	Delete punctuation
Los Angelǿs	Replace a letter
deep ~~inhilations~~ breaths	Replace a word
Manure	Use lowercase
friday	Capitalize

The following paragraph by student writer Kenneth Clause illustrates how to use these proofreading marks.

My Home Town, LA Style

It is 11:00 p.m on a chilly friday night. We are travelling South on the 405 freeway and have just entered Los Angeles city limits. A thick, damp fog rolls in from the ocean to blanket the city. Visibility is low. The vehicle discends through a sharp, banked turn and the headlights reveal the first glimpse of "it" looming in the distance. What my weary travelling companion from New York is about to encounter is the most embarassing and horrifying beast known to residents of Los Angelǿs. I break out in a ~~large~~ sweat, realizing there are no exits left will that detour this formation. In a moment of desperation, I step on the accelerator. Perhaps I can speed by this ~~depraved~~ ugly monument so my friend will not notice. Unfortunately, I'm too late. In that instant, he begins howling with laughter. We are suddenly upon it. The headlights reveal a heaping pile of Manure ~~appears~~ with a sign posted on the pinnacle that says, "Welcome to Los Angeles! A town where the grass is greener . . . on the other side of the hot tub." Well, no use in trying to hide any longer. I hit the brakes and pull the car over to the side of the road. Immediately, my jovial friend from New York opens the door and falls to the pavement with tears of laughter streaming down his face. The last thing he expected to see among the palm trees of California was a huge dungheap. The laughter of my merry schoolmate quickly ceases after a few deep ~~inhilations~~ breaths. The foul stench of this revolting glob of dung is enough to make even his pollution-hardened lungs feel weak. Upon my request, we hop|back in the car and head for home. After receiving such a shock to his senses, his only hope for revival a long shower and a price of my dad's hot apple pie.

Editing Symbols

As you edit someone else's draft, use the following symbols to refer the writer to problems discussed in this Handbook. Your instructor may also use these correction marks to guide your own editing. Listed below are some of the most common symbols, with an explanation and reference to the section number in this Handbook.

adj	use adjective, 1c
adv	use adverb, 1c
cs	comma splice, 4b
d	revise diction (word choice)
dm	dangling modifier, 2c
frag	sentence fragment, 2a
fs	fused sentence, 4b
mm	misplaced modifier, 2c
//	revise faulty parallelism, 2d
p	punctuation needed, 4a-j
pn agr	make pronoun agree with antecedent, 2i
ref	pronoun referent problem, 2i
sp	spelling error
sxt	sexist language, 3e
sv agr	subject-verb agreement error, 2g
t	verb tense error, 1d, 2h
trans	needs transition
v	verb form problem, 1d
wdy	wordy—omit needless words, 2f, 3a, 3b
wc	revise word choice

Tips for Editing and Proofreading

1. Review sections of this chapter just before you begin editing. If you need to review basic grammatical terms, begin with section 1. Otherwise, review appropriate parts of sections 2, 3, or 4.

2. Practice your editing and proofreading skills first on others' essays. You will see others' problems much more quickly than you will see your own. Becoming a good editor of their writing will, in turn, help you recognize your own problems more easily.

3. As you edit, look for one problem at a time. Concentrate, for example, just on punctuation, or just on subject-verb agreement, or just on diction or word choice.

4. Have a friend or classmate read your essay aloud. Listen as the person reads. If you notice something that is not clear, stop and revise the sentence. If the reader does not understand what he or she is reading, stop and revise.

5. If you are writing on a computer, reformat and print out your essay, double-spaced, in narrow columns, forty to forty-five spaces wide. Many obvious errors will jump out at you as you reread your writing in a new format.

6. For proofreading, place a ruler or a blank piece of paper underneath the line you are checking. Or if you are proofreading for typos, try reading backward, one word at a time, from the bottom of the page to the top.

Section 1
REVIEW OF BASIC SENTENCE ELEMENTS

This section reviews the names and definitions of basic sentence elements. Other sections in this Handbook use the terms defined and illustrated in this section.

1A SENTENCE STRUCTURE

A sentence is a group of words beginning with a capital letter and ending with a period or other end mark; it has a subject and a predicate and expresses a complete thought. The *subject* is the word or group of words that is the topic or focus of the sentence. It acts, is acted upon, or is described. The *predicate* gives information about the subject: what the subject is, what it is doing, or what is done to it.

[Subject]	[Predicate]
Piranhas	bite!
The McNeils	dig clams at the seashore.
Bubble gum	can cause cancer in rats.

Sentences may contain the following elements: subject (S), verb (V), direct object (DO), indirect object (IO), subject complement (SC), object complement (OC), modifier (M), and conjunction (+).

S   V

Piranhas bite.

S   V   DO +   DO   M

Piranhas attack fish or animals in their waters.

S   V   IO   M   DO

Andrea gave Carlos two piranhas.

S   V   DO   OC

Carlos considers Andrea a prankster.

S   V   SC

Andrea is a prankster.

Subjects may be nouns, pronouns, noun phrases, or noun clauses.

Verbs may be single words *(bite)* or verb phrases *(will have bitten)*. Verbs may be transitive or intransitive; verbs have tense, voice, and mood.

Direct objects can be nouns, pronouns, noun phrases, or noun clauses. A direct object receives the action of a transitive verb. Direct objects usually answer the question "What?" or "Whom?" about the subject and verb.

Piranhas bit [whom?] *people.*

Indirect objects can be nouns, pronouns, noun phrases, or noun clauses. The indirect object answers the question "To whom?" or "For whom?" about the subject and verb.

Andrea gave [to whom?] *Carlos* two piranhas.

Complements occur in the predicate of the sentence following a "to be" or linking verb. Subject complements rename or describe the subject. Object complements rename or describe the object.

SC

Carlos is *upset.*

OC

Carlos named one piranha *Bucktooth.*

Modifiers describe or limit a subject, verb, object, or complement. They may be a single word, a group of words, or an entire clause.

M

Piranhas have a *nasty* disposition.

Conjunctions are words that link words, phrases, clauses, or sentences. The word *conjunction* is derived from a word meaning "join together." (See Section 4a for additional examples of conjunctions.)

- *Coordinating conjunctions* (and, but, or, yet, for, nor, so) join equal sentence elements.

  Carlos is angry, *but* Andrea is laughing.

- *Correlative conjunctions* (both either . . . and, others) also join equal sentence elements.

  Neither Carlos *nor* his aquarium fish are particularly happy about the piranhas.

- *Subordinating conjunctions* (because, since, although, if, until, while, and others) begin many dependent clauses.

  If Andrea plays another joke on Carlos, she may lose a good friend.

1B NOUNS AND PRONOUNS

A *noun* names a person, place, object, or idea. Nouns may be grouped in several classes.

- *Proper nouns* name specific people, places, or things (Abraham Lincoln, Cape Hattaras, Buick).
- *Common nouns* name all nouns that are not proper nouns (cat, ocean, helicopter).
- *Concrete nouns* name things that can be sensed (table, waves, coat).
- *Abstract nouns* name things not knowable by the senses (justice, pity, freedom).
- *Collective nouns* name groups (family, committee, team).
- *Compound nouns* are several words joined by hyphens to form a noun (brother-in-law, commander-in-chief).

A *pronoun* takes the place of a noun. Pronouns must meet three requirements.

- *Reference:* A pronoun must refer to a specific, identifiable word, phrase, or clause. This referent or antecedent occurs within the sentence or in a preceding sentence. (See Section 2j for examples of how to solve problems in pronoun reference.)

  Evelyn has the flu. *She* has missed two classes. [Evelyn is the referent for *she.*]

- *Agreement:* A pronoun must agree with or correspond to the noun that it replaces. A pronoun must agree in person (first, second, or third person), number (singular or plural), and gender (he, she, it). (See Section 2i for examples of how to solve problems in pronoun agreement.)

  Each girl should check on *her* friend. [*Her* agrees in person (third person), in number (singular), and gender (her) with the referent, *girl.]*

- *Case:* Pronouns must take the appropriate case (subjective, objective, possessive).

  Subjective pronouns (I, you, he, she, it, we, they, who) should be the subject or the complement in a sentence.

  They have the flu. [Subject]

  Who is sleeping there? It is *she.* [Complement]

  Objective pronouns (me, you, her, him, whom, us, you, them) should act as objects in a sentence.

  Evelyn gave *me* the flu. [Indirect object]

  Possessive pronouns (my, mine, your, yours, his, her, hers, its, our, ours, their, theirs, whose) show possession.

  I am sick as a dog with *her* flu virus.

Pronouns may be grouped in several classes.

- *Personal pronouns* (I, me, my, mine, we, us, our, ours, you, yours, she, her, hers, he, him, his, it, its, they, them, theirs) refer to people or things:

  She bought a cat for *him.*

- *Relative pronouns* (that, who, whom, which, what, whose, whoever) introduce clauses.

  Whoever fed the cat made a mistake.

- *Interrogative pronouns* (who, whose, what, which, whom) introduce a question:

  Which cat is the mother?

- *Reflexive and intensive pronouns* (myself, yourself, herself, ourselves, and so on) refer back to a pronoun or antecedent or intensify the antecedent:

  She says she paid for the cat *herself.* I *myself* suspect she just found it.

- *Indefinite pronouns* (all, anyone, another, anybody, both, each, few, most, some, several, none, someone, something, such, and so on) refer to nonspecific persons or things:

  Someone will turn up and claim the cat.

- *Demonstrative pronouns* (this, that, these, those) refer to an antecedent:

  On Tuesday morning, I must pay my bill. *That* will be a painful moment.

1c ADJECTIVES AND ADVERBS

Adjectives are modifiers that limit, describe, or add information about nouns and pronouns.

> Secretariat was my *favorite* horse. [Modifies noun, *horse*]

> Even standing still, he looked *dynamic*. [Modifies pronoun, *he*]

Adverbs limit, describe, or add information about verbs, adjectives, or other adverbs, and they complete sentences.

> He won *overwhelmingly*. [Modifies verb]

> The Kentucky Derby was a *very* important victory. [Modifies adjective, *important*]

> On that day, he ran *extremely* fast. [Modifies adverb, *fast*]

> *Fortunately*, he won the Triple Crown. [Modifies whole sentence]

1d VERBS

Verbs are the heart of most sentences. They can set up an equation or definition ("A flotilla *is* a small fleet of ships"). They can describe a state of being ("Fear and confusion *exist* in Lebanon"). They can explain an occurrence ("The players *became* angry at the referee's call") or describe an action ("The candidate *defeated* her opponent"). When sentences communicate clearly, verbs often deserve the credit.

The great variety of verb forms creates a richness in the language. This richness, however, can create confusion. Some verbs are regular; others, irregular. In some cases, combinations of verb tense, voice, and mood may entangle sentences. The following explanations and examples will help you resolve problems in verb forms so that you can communicate precisely and vividly.

Principal Parts of Verbs

Verbs have three principal parts: simple form, past tense, and past participle.

Simple Form (Infinitive)	Past Tense	Past Participle
live (to live)	lived	lived
go (to go)	went	gone

Regular and Irregular Verbs *Regular verbs* form the past tense and past participle by adding -ed or -d to the simple form.

Simple Form	Past Tense	Past Participle
count	counted	counted
dance	danced	danced
create	created	created

Irregular verbs can cause problems because they form the past tense and past participle by changing letters, sounds, or entire words. Check your dictionary to determine if a verb is irregular. If the dictionary gives only two forms *(catch, caught)*, the past participle is the same as the past tense *(caught)*. Below are some examples of the nearly two hundred irregular English verbs.

Simple Form	Past Tense	Past Participle
sing	sang	sung
begin	began	begun
break	broke	broken
drive	drove	driven
sink	sank, sunk	sunk
sleep	slept	slept
read	read	read
eat	ate	eaten
see	saw	seen
slide	slid	slid

Linking Verbs *Linking verbs (is, becomes, seems, looks,* and so on) equate the subject with the predicate, so that the word or words in the predicate rename or describe the subject. Linking verbs create a subject complement (SC)—a word or words that complete the equation.

```
S      V       SC              M
```
Lillian was president of the company. [Lillian = president]

```
S         V        SC
```
The storm seemed threatening. [Storm = threatening]

Auxiliary Verbs   *Auxiliary verbs,* also called "helping verbs," combine with main verbs to show tense, voice, or mood. The verbs *be, do,* and *have* are common auxiliary verbs.

She is running a marathon.   [Auxiliary verb = *is*]

They did enjoy the dinner.   [Auxiliary verb = *did*]

He had left before she arrived.   [Auxiliary verb = *had*]

Tense   *Tense* tells *when* a verb's action, occurrence, or state of being takes place. The six verb tenses in English are illustrated below with the regular verb *create.* The parentheses contain the *progressive* form (*-ing*) to show continual or ongoing action, occurrence, or state of being.

Present: I create   (I am creating)

Past: I created   (I was creating)

Future: I will create   (I will be creating)

Present perfect: I have created   (I have been creating)

The present perfect tense describes actions occurring or conditions existing at an unspecified time in the past and continuing into the present: *I have created several award-winning recipes for chili.*

Past perfect: I had created   (I had been creating)

The past perfect tense describes actions occurring or conditions existing before a specific time in the past: *I had created three different recipes for extra-hot chili before I won my first award.*

Future perfect: I will have created   (I will have been creating)

The future perfect tense describes actions that have already occurred or conditions that will exist by a specific future time: *I will have created a new salsa recipe before the county fair begins.*

Transitive and Intransitive   Many verbs in English can be either transitive or intransitive, depending on the sentence. *Transitive* verbs take objects. As the prefix *trans-* suggests, they carry the action *across* to the object.

```
S       V          DO
```
Myrna developed the film.

S   V   DO

Michael sees the oncoming car.

Intransitive verbs do not take an object.

S   V   M

Myrna developed early. (*Early* is not a direct object; it describes when Myrna developed)

S   V   M

Michael sees in the dark.   (*In the dark* is not a direct object)

Voice   Verbs have *active* and *passive* voice. *Active voice* means that the subject of the sentence performs the action. *Passive voice* means that the subject is acted upon. A passive voice sentence uses a form of "be" plus a past participle. (For additional discussion of active and passive voice, see Section 2e.)

Active voice: Eskimos *build* stone and peat houses.

Passive voice: Stone and peat houses *are built* by Eskimos. [Contains a form of "be" + past participle: *are + built*]

Mood   Verbs have three *moods* that indicate a writer's attitude toward a statement. *Indicative mood* expresses a statement of fact or asks a question. *Imperative mood* expresses commands or directives. *Subjunctive mood* expresses a wish or condition contrary to fact.

Indicative: She has perfect pitch. [Fact]

Why does she sing opera? [Question]

Imperative: Pay attention to the music. [Command]

Turn and face the spotlight. [Directive]

Subjunctive: I wish that I were more talented. [Wish]

If she were to catch a cold, she would not sing on opening night. [Condition contrary to fact]

1E PHRASES AND CLAUSES

Phrases

A *phrase* is a group of related words that does not contain a subject or a predicate.

Prepositional phrase: He wrote *on the computer.*

Noun phrase: A *notebook computer* is handy.

Appositive phrase: The Apple II, *the first popular school computer,* is the Model T of home computers. [An appositive phrase identifies or provides more information about the preceding noun or pronoun.]

A verbal phrase is a group of related words that contains a verbal: an infinitive (to talk), a present participle (talking), or a past participle (talked). There are three kinds of verbals:

Infinitives usually use *to + simple verb;* they function as nouns, adjectives, or adverbs.

Infinitive: *To talk*

Infinitive phrase: He planned *to talk for three minutes.* [Infinitive phrase = direct object]

To listen carefully was his first objective. [Infinitive phrase = subject]

Gerunds are nouns made from the "-ing" or present participle form of the verb.

Gerund: *Talking* got her into trouble. [*Talking* is a gerund. Gerund = subject]

Gerund phrase: *Talking during the lecture* got her into trouble. [Gerund phrase = subject]

Participles are adjectives made from verb forms. As adjectives, they modify a noun or pronoun. They can use either the "-ing" (present participle) or the "-ed" (past participle) verb form.

Participle: *Coughing* students may bother the teacher. [Participle modifies students.]

Whispered conversations may distract students. [Participle modifies *conversations.*]

Participial phrases: *Rustling their papers and snapping their notebooks closed,* they prepare to leave the lecture hall. [Participial phrase modifies *they.*]

Several students, *entranced by the final scene in the film,* write quietly for a few moments. [Participial phrase modifies *students.*]

Clauses

A *clause* is a group of words containing a *subject and a verb.* It need *not* be an entire sentence or a complete thought. Clauses can be independent (main) or dependent (subordinate).

- *Independent or main clause:* A group of words containing a subject and a verb that can stand by itself as a complete thought.

  We drank decaffeinated coffee.

- *Dependent clause:* A group of words that contains a subject and verb but cannot stand by itself as a complete thought.

  Because we drank decaffeinated coffee

- *Subordinate* clauses (sometimes called *adverb clauses*) are dependent clauses that begin with a subordinating conjunction, such as *because, if, although, unless, when, while, since, as, until, before,* and *after.*

  Although I drank coffee, everyone else drank tea.

- *Relative clauses* (also called *adjective clauses*) are dependent clauses that begin with *when, where, why,* or with relative pronouns (*who, that, which, whom, whoever, whomever, whatever*).

  Driving *when you are under the influence of alcohol* may result in a mandatory jail sentence. [Adjective clause modifies *driving.*]

  Free coffee, *which the bar serves after midnight,* is part of a campaign for responsible drinking. [Adjective clause modifies *coffee.*]

  The policeman gave a ticket to the woman *who was driving the red pickup truck.* [Adjective clause modifies *woman.*]

1f ARTICLES, PREPOSITIONS, INTERJECTIONS

Articles

The *articles (a, an, the)* often appear before nouns. Articles are modifiers that limit a noun. *A* and *an* are less limiting than *the.*

> I have *a* plan to solve our problems.

> I have *the* plan to solve our problems. [*The* suggests that the plan is more definitive.]

The article *a* appears before words that begin with a *consonant sound* (not necessarily a consonant): *a* kite, *a* hammer, *a* university, *a* one-sided victory.

The article *an* appears before words that begin with a *vowel sound* (not necessarily a vowel): *an* opening, *an* egg, *an* old shirt, *an* honor, *an* E.

Prepositions

Prepositions (*in, on, up, to, after, by, for, across, within,* and others) usually occur in prepositional phrases with a noun or pronoun that is the object of the preposition.

> *In* the hot sun *by* the edge *of* the water, a small turtle lay perfectly still.

Note that some words can function as either prepositions or conjunctions.

> We will row home *after* lunch. [Preposition]
>
> *After* you finish your sandwich, we will row home. [Conjunction]

Interjections

Interjections (*oh, alas, yea, damn, hooray, ouch,* and others) are words conveying strong feeling or surprise. Interjections occasionally appear in informal writing or in dialogue.

> The Cardinals won the pennant *(yea!)* but lost the World Series *(boo, hiss).*
>
> *Alas,* their hitting was anemic.
>
> "*Oh,* she moped about it for days."

I've noticed a good deal, and there's no bird, or cow, or anything that uses as good grammar as a bluejay. You may say a cat uses good grammar. Well, a cat does—but you let a cat get excited once; you let a cat get to pulling fur with another cat on a shed, nights, and you'll hear grammar that will give you the lockjaw. Ignorant people think it's the noise *which fighting cats make that is so aggravating, but it ain't so; it's the sickening grammar they use.*

—*Mark Twain,* Baker's Bluejay Yarn

Section 2
SENTENCE STRUCTURE AND GRAMMAR

When sentences don't follow standard American English conventions, readers may become aggravated, confused, or simply lost. Some deviations from established conventions barely distract the reader, while others totally scramble the meaning. If "sickening grammar" detracts from your meaning, your readers may react uncharitably. If you write a confusing sentence fragment, some readers will think, "This writer doesn't know what a sentence is." If you have a problem in subject-verb agreement, readers may think, "This writer didn't reread the sentence or doesn't know what the subject of the sentence is." If you write a sentence with a dangling modifier, the reader may think, "The writer doesn't know how comical this sounds." This section will help you avoid those embarrassing problems that confuse readers or invite them to think about your grammar rather than your meaning.

2A FRAGMENTS

Use sentence fragments only for special emphasis. A *fragment* is an incomplete sentence. A fragment may lack a subject or verb, or it may be only a dependent clause. *Test* for sentence fragments by taking the group of words out of the context. If the group of words cannot stand by itself as a complete thought, it is a fragment.

Revise sentence fragments by adding a subject or verb or by combining the fragment with the preceding sentence.

FRAGMENT: I still remember the championship basketball game when I scored forty points. *Breaking the existing conference record.*
        Test: "Breaking the existing conference record" is not a complete sentence. It cannot stand by itself as a complete thought. Combine with previous sentence.

REVISION: I still remember the championship basketball game when I broke the existing conference record by scoring forty points.

FRAGMENT: At home I enjoy many water sports. *Water skiing and sailing, which are my two favorites.*
        Test: "Waterskiing and sailing, which are my two favorites" cannot stand by itself as a complete thought. Revise to make one complete sentence.

REVISION: At home, I enjoy my two favorite water sports, waterskiing, and sailing.

FRAGMENT: She stood in line for four hours in the freezing rain. *To get tickets for the rock concert.*
        Test: To get tickets for the rock concert" cannot stand by itself as a complete thought. Combine with previous sentence.

REVISION: To get tickets for the rock concert, she stood in line for four hours in the freezing rain.

FRAGMENT: After a tough class, I took a long shower, dried my hair, and put on my underwear. Then I walked into the living room. *Because no one was home.* Was I surprised to discover my mother talking to Reverend Jones!
        Test: "Because no one was home" cannot stand by itself as a complete thought. It is a dependent clause or fragment.

REVISION: After a tough class, I took a long shower, dried my hair, and put on my underwear. Because I thought no one was home, I walked into the living room. Was I surprised to discover my mother talking to Reverend Jones!

FRAGMENT: At the end of the game, the frustrated fans began to throw snowballs on the field. *The score being 42–0.*
Test: "The score being 42–0" is not a complete sentence. Change *being* to *is* or *was.*

REVISION: At the end of the game, the frustrated fans began to throw snowballs on the field because the score was 42–0.

For special emphasis, however, sparingly used sentence fragments can be effective. In context, the following are examples of effective sentence fragments:

When the river was dammed almost all of these things were lost. Crowded out—or drowned and buried under mud.

—Edward Abbey

Head off? Decapitation cases are rather routinely handled.

—Jessica Mitford

When I finally did fall asleep, I had that same hideous nightmare in which a woodchuck is trying to claim my prize at a raffle. Despair.

—Woody Allen

Exercise In the following passage, identify all sentence fragments. Then revise the passage to eliminate inappropriate fragments.

(1) Most people think that a library is as quiet as growing grass, but often it is the noisiest place on campus to study.   (2) The worst time being finals week.   (3) Some of the chatter is from people who come to the library just to visit: "How did you like the party Saturday night?"   (4) "Did you get the notes from chemistry?"   (5) The chatter goes on continually, punctuated by coughs, gasps, and giggles.   (6) Just when I start to panic about my calculus examination.   (7) Someone across the table tells a joke, and they all start laughing.   (8) They try to cover their laughter with their hands, but the sound explodes out anyway. (9) Irritating ten other students who are trying to study.   (10) Sometimes I wish the library had its own police force.   (11) To arrest those gabby, discourteous "party people."   (12) I would sit there smiling as they handcuffed these party people and dragged them out of the library.   (13) Ah, the sweet revenge of daydreams.

2B MIXED CONSTRUCTIONS AND FAULTY PREDICATION

Mixed Constructions Occasionally writers begin sentences with one structure and then switch, right in the middle, to another. Revise sentences with mixed constructions by choosing one structure and sticking to it.

MIXED:	Because the repairs were so expensive is why I ended up selling the car.
REVISED:	Because the repairs were so expensive, I sold the car.
MIXED:	By getting behind in math classes is a quick way to flunk out.
REVISED:	Getting behind in math classes is a quick way to flunk out.

Faulty Predication

Sometimes the predicate does not *logically* fit with the subject. Remember that the verb "to be" is an *equals sign.* Revise faulty predication by changing either the subject or the predicate.

FAULTY:	Freestyle ski jumping is where skiers take crazy chances in midair.
	Note: "Ski jumping" is an activity, not a place. It is illogical to say "ski jumping *is* where . . ."
REVISED:	Freestyle ski jumping is a sport that encourages skiers to take crazy chances in midair.
FAULTY:	My dog Noodles is the reason I'm feeling depressed.
	Note: "My dog Noodles" is a specific animal, not a "reason." Missing Noodles, however, could be a cause for depression.
REVISED:	I'm feeling depressed because I miss my dog Noodles.
FAULTY:	Real intelligence is when you can say no to that third piece of chocolate cream pie.
	Note: *Intelligence* is or equals a mental condition, not a *when.*
REVISED:	Saying no to that third piece of chocolate cream pie requires real intelligence.

Exercise   In the following passage, identify sentences with mixed constructions, faulty predication, or both, and then revise them.

(1) After my sophomore year, I intend to transfer to Boston College. (2) Basically, I want to attend a school that has a city environment and a diverse population of students.   (3) I suppose my sister Nadine is a big reason I want to transfer.   (4) She wants me to move closer to home. (5) Also, by attending a city school will enable me to see plays, to visit museums occasionally, and to eat out at good restaurants.   (6) Finally, I'd like to meet all sorts of students.   (7) A good university is when a student can meet people from all walks of life.   (8) Because Boston College has diversity is really why I intend to transfer.

2c DANGLING MODIFIERS AND MISPLACED MODIFIERS

Dangling Modifiers

Modifying phrases must clearly describe, qualify, or limit some word in the sentence. When the modifying phrase occurs at the beginning of a sentence, the word that is modified must appear *immediately* following the phrase. Otherwise, the modifying phrase "dangles" or is logically "unattached" to the sentence. Such sentences are confusing and often comical.

FAULTY: Rushing to get to class on time, my shoelace broke.
          Question: Who was rushing to get to class? The shoelace? Revise by indicating the person immediately after the comma.
REVISED: Rushing to get to class, *I* broke a shoelace.

FAULTY: Flying at 5,000 feet, the cars looked like tiny toys.
          Question: Are the cars flying at 5,000 feet? *Who* is flying at 5,000 feet? Revise by indicating that person immediately after the comma.
REVISED: Flying at 5,000 feet, *I* saw cars that looked like tiny toys.

FAULTY: From birth until the first grade, one parent should be home with the children.
          Question: Does the opening phrase, "From birth until the first grade," modify *parent* or *children?* Revise by placing the appropriate word immediately following the introductory phrase.
REVISED: From birth until the first grade, *children* should have one parent at home.

FAULTY: Sue practiced her freestyle stroke until she knew she could swim faster than Flipper, being a fanatical swimmer.
          Question: Who is the fanatical swimmer—Sue or Flipper? When modifying phrases "dangle" from the *end* of a sentence, revise by placing the phrase next to the word it modifies.
REVISED: Being a fanatical swimmer, Sue practiced her freestyle stroke until she knew she could swim faster than Flipper.

Misplaced Modifiers

Place a modifying word, phrase, or clause immediately before or after the word it modifies. In the following sentences, notice how changing the placement of the word "only" changes the meaning of the sentence.

> Only I tasted grandfather's pumpkin pie. [I was the only one who tasted it.]
>
> I only tasted grandfather's pumpkin pie. [I only tasted it; Pete actually ate it.]
>
> I tasted only grandfather's pumpkin pie. [I didn't taste anything else; I didn't even taste Aunt Margaret's pecan pie.]
>
> I tasted grandfather's only pumpkin pie. [Grandfather made only one pumpkin pie, and I tasted it.]

CONFUSING:	He borrowed a computer from his professor with a faulty memory.
	Question: Who or what has the faulty memory? Place the phrase "with a faulty memory" next to the word it modifies ("computer").
REVISED:	He borrowed a computer with a faulty memory from his professor.
CONFUSING:	The hamburgers have been horrible in the fast-food restaurants that I've eaten.
	Question: Did the writer eat restaurants or hamburgers? Revise by placing the clause "that I've eaten" next to the word it should modify ("hamburgers").
REVISED:	The hamburgers that I've eaten in fast-food restaurants have been horrible.

Exercise   In the following passage, identify sentences with dangling modifiers and misplaced modifiers, and then revise each faulty sentence.

(1) SP302, History of Film, is a worthwhile class to take.   (2) Occurring on Tuesday night from 7:00 P.M. to 9:45 P.M., Professor Hancock teaches the class so that it coincides with dollar movie night at the campus theater.   (3) Normally, a long class would be boring because of the Nod Factor.   (4) However, Professor Hancock keeps everyone awake and entertains the students, being very energetic.   (5) Her lecture on *Citizen Kane* was a particularly good example.   (6) Unfortunately, the film began before she finished her lecture.   (7) Rushing across the stage just as the film was beginning, an electrical cord tripped her up, causing her to lose her balance and fall.   (8) She regained her composure in time to remind us that Orson Welles also wrote and performed

the famous broadcast about the invasion of the Martians on the radio. (9) We certainly were relieved to get that important information!

2D FAULTY PARALLELISM

Repeated elements in a sentence that are similar in meaning or function should be parallel in grammatical form. The parallel form should, in turn, help to emphasize the meaning. Any repeated sentence elements, from subjects and verbs to prepositional phrases, may occur in parallel form.

Parallel clauses:	*I came, I saw, I conquered.*
Parallel adverbs:	He read *slowly* and *thoroughly.*
Parallel prepositional phrases:	She walked *through the archway, across the quadrangle,* and *into the library.*

Identifying and numbering the repeated elements may help you see the parallel elements in a sentence.

	(1) through the archway,
She walked	(2) across the quadrangle
	and
	(3) into the library.

FAULTY: Walking, biking, and automobiles are the three most popular modes of transportation.
Test: Identify and number elements that should be parallel. "(1) *Walking,* (2) *biking,* and (3) *automobiles* are the three most popular modes of transportation." Revise, choosing one pattern for all three elements.

REVISED: Walking, biking, and driving are the three most popular modes of transportation.

FAULTY: Traveling abroad last summer, John increased his social awareness, his cultural knowledge, and overall sophistication.
Test: Identify and number elements that should be parallel. "Traveling abroad last summer, John increased (1) *his social awareness,* (2) *his cultural knowledge,* and (3) _____ *overall sophistication.*" Then revise, choosing one grammatical pattern for all three elements.

REVISED: Traveling abroad last summer, John increased his social awareness, his cultural knowledge, and his overall sophistication.
[or]

REVISED: Traveling abroad last summer, John increased his social awareness, cultural knowledge, and overall sophistication.

FAULTY: There are three commandments for college students: Thou shalt go to class; thou shalt read the text; and be sure to borrow your neighbor's notes.
           Test: Identify and number elements that should be parallel. Since the first and second "commandments" set the grammatical pattern, the reader *expects* the third commandment to take the same "thou shalt" form.

REVISED: There are three commandments for college students: Thou shalt go to class; thou shalt read the text; and thou shalt borrow thy neighbor's notes.

FAULTY: She was angry not only because he was late but also he forgot the tickets.
           Note: Compared or contrasted sentence elements introduced by "either . . . or," "both . . . and," or "not only . . . but also" must be parallel.
           Test: Identify and number elements that should be parallel. "She was angry not only (1) *because he was late* but also (2) _____ he forgot the tickets." Revise to make (1) and (2) parallel.

REVISED: She was angry not only because he was late but also because he forgot the tickets.

Exercise   In the following passage, identify and revise any sentences with faulty parallelism.

(1) Alcohol abuse is a primary cause of spectator violence at college football games.   (2) On average, the police department makes between five and ten arrests at each home football game.   (3) These arrests are for property destruction, public intoxication, and occasionally when students conduct themselves in a disorderly manner.   (4) When spectators consume too much alcohol not only do they hurt themselves but also act obnoxiously toward others.   (5) Following a recent fight, ambulance attendants said that some drunken spectators or "animals" actually pelted them with sod while they tried to assist an injured man. (6) The attendants tried pleading, reason, and shouting, but to no avail. (7) To reduce these ugly incidents and restoring the enjoyment of the game, alcohol should not be sold at football games after the beginning of the second half.

2E ACTIVE AND PASSIVE VOICE

Verbs that can have direct objects (transitive verbs) are in the *active voice* when the subject of the sentence *acts upon the object:*

The wolfhound bit Perry.

Wolfhound, the subject of the sentence, *acts upon the object, Perry.* The arrow shows that in the active voice, the action of the verb *bit* goes forward, toward the object, *Perry.*

Verbs that can have objects (transitive verbs) are in the *passive voice* when *the subject is acted upon.* The passive voice uses a form of *be (is, am, are, was, were, been, being)* followed by the past participle of the main verb (in this case, *bitten*).

Perry was bitten by the wolfhound.

The verb *was bitten* is transitive, but *Perry,* now the subject of the sentence, is *acted upon.* The arrow shows that the action of the verb goes backwards, so that *Perry* receives the action.

Notice the following *differences* between active and passive voice:

The *active voice* sentence, "The wolfhound bit Perry," uses two fewer words than the passive version, its action moves in a normal forward direction, and it clearly identifies the actor.

The *passive voice* sentence, "Perry was bitten by the wolfhound," uses two more words, and it inverts the direction of the action in the sentence. In some cases, the passive voice may omit the *actor* altogether: "Perry was bitten on Friday." In that case, the reader does not know who or what bit Perry.

Active Voice

Usually, active voice is preferable because it is more direct, vivid, and concise than passive voice. Remember, though, that sentences must be judged *in the context* of the writer's purpose, audience, and focus.

Below are examples of passive voice constructions that, in context, may be more effective in the active voice. To change from passive to active, move the actor (often identified in the "by" phrase) to the subject of the sentence.

Passive: Children's unruly behavior cannot be accepted by their parents.
Note: The actor in the "by" phrase is *parents.* Change to active voice by making *parents* the subject of the sentence.

Active: Parents cannot accept their children's unruly behavior. [The active voice version places the actor in the subject of the sentence and has two fewer words.]

Passive: It is argued by the members of our class that the teacher grades too hard.
Note: The *actor* in the "by" phrase is *members.* Change to active voice by making *members* the subject of the sentence.

Active: Members of our class argue that the teacher grades too hard. [This active voice version is more direct and has four fewer words.]

Passive: Under the current proposal, property taxes will be raised $1,000 dollars over the next two years.
Note: The *actor* is not identified in a "by" phrase; however, the *governor* actually proposed the tax increase. Change to active voice by making *governor* the subject of the sentence.

Active: The governor currently proposes to raise property taxes by $1,000 over the next two years. [The active voice version reveals who, in fact, is responsible. It adds information without increasing the length of the sentence.]

Passive Voice

The passive voice is appropriate when the actor is unknown or is less important than the action or the receiver of the action. Use the passive voice in the following situations:

When the actor is unknown.

When her sports car swerved off the road and into the river, Carolyn was killed. [We don't know who or what actually killed her.]

When you want to emphasize that some person or thing is helpless or is a victim.

The small Kansas town was leveled by the tornado.

Our football team was mauled by the Bears, 42–0.

The bag lady was mugged in broad daylight.

When the scientific experiment and the results should be the focus of the sentence or the passage. (Scientific writing typically uses the passive voice to lend objectivity to the findings.)

The first recordings of humpback whales were obtained in 1952 from a U.S. Navy hydrophone installation.

The titration experiment was performed under careful laboratory conditions.

One typical *abuse of passive voice* occurs when writers omit the actor in order to conceal responsibility.

The tuition for nonresident students was increased by $500 for the upcoming academic year.

This sentence, written by university officials, omits the actor or the agency responsible for the change. Since tuition increases are unpopular with students, university officials may have deliberately omitted the responsible actor or agency to avoid confrontation or blame. Careful readers should recognize such deceptive uses of passive voice.

Caution: Don't assume that all verbs that follow the pattern, "be" verb form+ past participle ["was _____ed"], are necessarily passive voice. In the sentence "I was scared," for example, the verb "scared" can be either transitive or intransitive, depending on the context. Only transitive verbs can be either active or passive voice:

Transitive active:	A horrible Halloween mask scared me.
Transitive passive:	I was scared by a horrible Halloween mask.
Intransitive:	At the Cave of Horrors, I was upset and scared.
Transitive active:	The boss fired me.
Transitive passive:	I was fired.
Intransitive:	I was tired.

Test: To distinguish between intransitive and transitive passive, try adding the word *very.* If *very* cannot logically be used, the construction is passive voice.

I was [very] tired. [*Very* works; *tired* is intransitive.]

I was [very] fired. [*Very* doesn't work; *fired* is transitive passive.]

In addition, a good dictionary will indicate whether a verb is transitive, intransitive, or both.

Exercises   Identify sentences containing passive voice. Change passive voice sentences into active voice.

1. People communicate using body movements.
2. A nod, gesture, or a glance can be interpreted by people in several ways.
3. A wave and a smile mean one thing, but a wave and a tear can be interpreted to mean something else.
4. In addition, some people may be irritated by a continual or intense stare.
5. We may also be intimidated by a person who talks to us at very close range.

Read the following passage and identify sentences that are in the active or passive voice. Then determine which sentences should be active voice and which should be passive voice. Revise the passage, leaving sentences as they are, changing active voice sentences to passive, or changing passive voice sentences to active—as appropriate for the context.

(1) Writing on a word processor can transform the act of writing, but only if the writer has some rudimentary typing skills. (2) Unfortunately, many men have a sexist hang-up about typing so that their writing on a computer is inhibited. (3) Traditionally, it has been felt by most men that only females—i.e. secretaries—should type. (4) Only the macho Hemingways and Mailers of the world actually type their own novels and stories. (5) Now, however, many male business executives are caught by conflicting role-images. (6) It is socially acceptable for them to be computer literate, but it is still somehow demeaning to sit at a keyboard and practice the "female" skill of typing. (7) One more example of how notions about sexist roles can hurt men as well as women is thus provided by word-processing.

2F NOMINALS AND "BE" VERBS

Nominals

Nominals (also called nominalizations) are *nouns* created from verbs. Nominals often make sentences less dynamic because they disguise or eliminate the action in a sentence. Frequently, nominals are nouns ending in *-ment, -ance, -ence, -ion,* and *-ing.* Each of the following nominals "contains" a verb: expectation (expect), description (describe), solution (solve), resistance (resist), government (govern), preference (prefer), meeting (meet). *For many purposes and audiences, you can make your writing more vigorous, dynamic, and readable by changing nominals into verbs.*

NOMINAL:	Bill's *expectation* was to win the marathon.
REVISED:	Bill *expected* to win the marathon.
NOMINAL:	The owner's manual contains a *description* of how to adjust the timing.
REVISED:	The owner's manual *describes* how to adjust the timing.
NOMINAL:	On this campus, there exists some *resistance* among students to the tuition increases.
REVISED:	On this campus, students *resist* tuition increases.
NOMINAL:	*Dissatisfaction* with drinking-policy *decisions* is likely to be a major *contribution* to student *objections.*

Note: When repeated nominals obscure the meaning, rewrite the whole sentence, making the primary *actor* the subject of the sentence.

REVISED: Students object to the drinking policy.

"Be" Verbs

"Be" verbs *(is, am, are, was, were, been, being)* are effective for stating *conditions, definitions,* or *concepts.*

Annie Dillard's *Pilgrim at Tinker Creek* is a literary classic.

An "iconoclast" *is* one who destroys sacred images or seeks to overthrow popular ideas or institutions.

Often, however, "be" verbs create static, flat, or lifeless sentences. Where appropriate, make your writing more dynamic by replacing "be" verbs with action verbs.

Eliminate "be" verbs by changing passive voice to active voice, by changing nominals or adjectives into verbs, by selecting a more vigorous verb, or by combining sentences.

"BE" VERB: The classical mythology course that *is* offered by the English department *is* fascinating.

REVISED: The English department *offers* a fascinating course in classical mythology.

"BE" VERB: Star Wars *is* a high-tech defense system that may *be* a major deterrent to global nuclear war.

REVISED: Star Wars, our high-tech defense system, may deter global nuclear war.

"BE" VERB: The driving force for many workaholics *is* their fear of failure.

REVISED: Fear of failure *drives* many workaholics.

"BE" VERB: AIDS *is* a simple but lethal malfunction of the immune system. AIDS *is* a disease that can lead to the physical and mental destruction of its victim.

REVISED: AIDS, a simple but lethal malfunction of the immune system, can *destroy* its victim physically and mentally.

Exercise   In the following passage, identify *nominals* and *be* verbs. Then revise the passage to make the passage more vivid, energetic, and concise by eliminating inappropriate nominals and "be" verbs.

(1) As parents, we know that many young people love to ride motorcycles, motorbikes, and motorscooters.   (2) Today, however, our ten-year-old kids have some attraction to those off-road three-wheelers. (3) Although kids get enjoyment from riding three-wheelers in the hills,

these vehicles can be the cause of serious injury.   (4) Unfortunately, these young drivers—and their parents—do not receive sufficient education from salespeople about the potential dangers.   (5) As a result, some activist groups are in opposition to the sales of all three-wheelers. (6) These groups want regulations for the industry in order to make riding safer for children and adults.   (7) The efforts of these groups to reform the industry are commendable to every responsible parent.

2G SUBJECT-VERB AGREEMENT

A verb must agree *in number* with its subject. Remember: *-s* or *-es* added to a *noun* makes it plural: whale, whales. Adding *-s* to a present-tense *verb* makes it singular: *whales sing; whale sings.*

1. Many agreement problems occur when plural words come between a singular subject and its verb. To correct a subject-verb error, first identify the actual subject and then use the correct verb ending for that subject.

FAULTY:	A list of campaign promises often hurt the candidate.
	Test: Put brackets around any prepositional phrases. The subject of the sentence is never in a prepositional phrase. "A list [of campaign promises] often hurt the candidate." *List* is the subject and *hurt* is the verb. Read without the words inside the brackets and revise verb.
REVISED:	A *list* of campaign promises often *hurts* the candidate.
FAULTY:	This company, with few skilled mechanics and electricians, do not guarantee any repairs.
	Test: Put brackets around the prepositional phrase. "This company [with few skilled mechanics and electricians], do not guarantee any repairs." Read the sentence without the words in brackets and revise the verb.
REVISED:	This company, with few skilled mechanics and electricians, *does* not guarantee any repairs.

2. Two subjects connected by *and* take a plural verb. "The sergeant and his recruits march double-time across the grounds." When two subjects are connected by *or* or *nor*, however, the verb agrees with the closer subject.

FAULTY:	Neither the recruits nor the sergeant know how to march.
REVISED:	Neither the recruits nor the sergeant *knows* how to march.
	[or]

REVISED: Neither the sergeant nor the recruits *know* how to march.

3. Indefinite pronouns *(each, one, either, everyone, neither, everybody, nobody, no one, none, somebody, someone)* usually take a *singular* verb.

FAULTY: Each of the books cost twenty dollars.
            Test: Remove the prepositional phrase: "Each [of the books] cost twenty dollars." *Each* is singular, so the verb should be *costs.*
REVISED: Each of the books *costs* twenty dollars.
FAULTY: Everybody in all three classes are going to see the film.
            Test: Remove the prepositional phrase: "Everybody [in all three classes] are going to see the film." *Everybody* is singular, so the verb should be *is.*
REVISED: Everybody in all three classes *is* going to see the film.

4. A collective noun as a subject takes a singular verb. Collective nouns *(family, committee, audience, class, crowd,* and *army)* usually refer to a single *unit* or *group* of several individuals or elements, and thus they take a *singular* verb.

FAULTY: The audience at the concert whistle its approval.
REVISED: The audience at the concert *whistles* its approval.
            Note: When referring to the action or condition of *several individuals* within a group, use the phrase *the members of* or the phrase *a number of* followed by the plural verb.

            The members of the committee *argue* about the policy.

5. Even when the normal subject-verb order is reversed, the verb should agree in number with the subject.

FAULTY: For such a small dormitory, there is far too many students.
            Test: Put the subject and verb in their normal order: Too many students *are* in the small dormitory. [*Students* is the subject, so the verb is plural: *are.*]
REVISED: For such a small dormitory, there *are* far too many students.

Exercise   In the following passage, revise all errors in subject-verb agreement.

(1) If you have friends or a family member who smoke, I have some suggestions to help this person quit. (2) First, if the family are supportive, try talking openly about the facts. (3) There is a few public service agencies that will provide evidence demonstrating the link between smoking and cancer. (4) Next, investigate this person's behavior: What does this person do just before he or she smokes? (5) To quit smoking, the smoker must disrupt the patterns of behavior that leads to smoking. (6) An inventory of the activities and places that cause a person to smoke provide key information. (7) For example, if the person always smokes after dinner, suggest eating snacks over a two-hour period instead of having a sit-down meal. (8) If he or she always smoke in a certain chair in the living room, change the furniture. (9) Breaking any habit is always easier if you break the entire behavior pattern. (10) Of course, each of these smokers need to want to stop smoking.

2H VERB TENSE

Avoid unnecessary shifts in verb tense.

SHIFT: After they *ate* ice cream and cake for dessert, they *are* ready to relax.

REVISED: After they *ate* ice cream and cake for dessert, they *were* ready to relax.

SHIFT: Peter *ate* dinner before you *had offered* to cook tacos.

REVISED: Peter *ate* dinner before you *offered* to cook tacos.

SHIFT: At one point in the film, Gandhi *gathered* his followers together to discuss strategy. Suddenly, a British general *gave* an order to fire upon them. People then *scurry* around and *try* to protect themselves and their children from the hail of bullets.

Note: For summaries or accounts of artistic works, films, literary works, or historical documents, use the *present tense.*

REVISED: At one point in this film, Gandhi *gathers* his followers together to discuss strategy. Suddenly, a British general *gives* an order to fire upon them. People then *scurry* around and *try* to protect themselves and their children from the hail of bullets.

Exercise   In the following passage, revise any unnecessary shifts in tense.

(1) In Sophocles' play, *Antigone,* two characters are tragic figures: Antigone and Creon. (2) In the play, Antigone faced a choice of con-

science.   (3) Should she be loyal to her family and bury her brother, or should she have been loyal to the state and obeyed the edict of Creon, the King of Thebes?   (4) She assumes that she knew the best way to handle the situation and willfully chooses her own death.   (5) Creon also faced a choice of conscience.   (6) Should he punish someone who has betrayed the state, even if that person is a member of his family? (7) Like Napoleon and General Custer, Creon thought primarily about himself and his public image.   (8) In Creon's case, ego or "hubris" leads to tragic results for the people around him.

2I PRONOUN AGREEMENT

A pronoun must agree in number and person with the noun to which it refers.

FAULTY: One of the scientists signed their name to the report.
              Test: Since the subject is never in the prepositional phrase, put parentheses around the prepositional phrase. "One" is singular, so use the singular pronoun "his" or "her."
REVISED: One of the scientists signed her name to the report.
FAULTY: Each of the students felt cheated on their test.
              Note: *Each* is singular: *their* is plural.
REVISED: The *students* felt cheated on *their* tests.
FAULTY: Everyone brought their gift to the party.
REVISED: Everyone brought *his or her* gift to the party.
              Note: Avoiding sexist language by using "his or her" can be wordy or awkward in some contexts. Rewrite the sentence with a plural subject and plural pronoun.
REVISED: The *guests* brought *their* gifts to the party.

Avoid shifts in person. Avoid shifting between third person *(people, one, they, he, she)* and second person *(you)*.

FAULTY: When *you* come to the party, *everyone* should bring a friend.
              Note: *You* is second person; *everyone* is third person. Revise the sentence, using either second or third person throughout.
REVISED: When *you* come to the party, bring a friend.
FAULTY: A good party should make *people* feel at ease, so *you* can make new friends.
REVISED: A good party should make *people* feel at ease, so *they* can make new friends.
REVISED: A good party should make *you* feel at ease, so *you* can make new friends.

2j PRONOUN REFERENCE

A pronoun should refer clearly and unambiguously to its antecedent.

UNCLEAR: Joan told Bev that her bank account was overdrawn.
             Question: Whose bank account is overdrawn?

REVISED: When Joan discovered that her bank account was over-drawn, she told Bev.

UNCLEAR: If people do not take care of their cats, we should turn them into the humane society.
             Question: Who should be turned in—the cats or their owners?

REVISED: If people do not take care of their cats, we should report the owners to the humane society.

Exercise In the following passage, correct problems in pronoun agreement and reference.

(1) People use the term *best friend* to describe a person who has a special warmth and friendliness.   (2) I still remember when Michelle Martin, one of my best friends, said that they really liked me, too.   (3) I called her my best friend; we stood by each other.   (4) One time at a party, I saw her talking angrily to another woman.   (5) It turned out that she had dated Tom, the guy she was going with at the time.   (6) Each of them felt cheated by their boyfriend.   (7) Before I knew what was happening, they were screaming at each other.   (8) When I tried to stick up for her, she took a swing at me, and so I swung back with my best left hook, popping her in the right eye.   (9) As a result, I was suspended from school for a week.   (10) It just goes to show that when you have a best friend, everyone expects that you'll help them if you can.

Section 3
DICTION AND STYLE

Effective writing hides a curious paradox. On the one hand, good writing contains vivid, showing detail. Good writing does not merely assert that thus-and-so is true; it supports a claim or assertion with evidence. It recreates an experience, shows exactly how the writer feels, or communicates precisely what the writer thinks. To accomplish this, writers *add* specific details, examples, facts, or other data. On the other hand, good writing is also concise. Good writers *take out* vague words, weak verbs, and empty language. Their writing is as lean and sinewy as a long-distance runner. As you edit your writing for diction (choice of words) and clarity of style, therefore, you should

Vigorous writing is concise. A sentence should contain no unnecessary words, a paragraph no unnecessary sentences, for the same reason that a drawing should have no unnecessary lines and a machine no unnecessary parts. This requires not that the writer make all his sentences short, or that he avoid all detail . . . but that every word tell.

—*William Strunk, Jr., author of* Elements of Style

add specific examples but *remove* vague, imprecise language. Your details should be ample, your diction and style spare.

3A VAGUE WORDS

Replace vague words with more specific or concrete language.

1. The following *nouns* are vague or unspecific. Vague nouns encourage writers to *tell* rather than to *show* with specific details or examples. Vague nouns may also lead to wordy and imprecise sentences. In most cases, *replace* the following nouns with more specific words, details, or examples.

thing	factor	aspect
something	situation	difficulty
anything	type	feeling
something	way	beauty
someone	fun	people
some	trouble	deal
area	problem	place
case	field	character
manner	nature	appearance

VAGUE: During their freshman year, students worry about all sorts of *things*. [Be specific: What things?]

REVISED: During their freshman year, students worry about leaving their families, making new friends, and passing their courses.

VAGUE: I have taken courses in the *field* of statistics for two years, and it has changed my *feeling* toward studying in the *area* of mathematics.

REVISED: After taking statistics courses for two years, I no longer hate studying mathematics.

VAGUE: Meteorologists occasionally have a great *deal* of *trouble* in forecasting a *situation* where an upper-level disturbance becomes a *factor* in local weather. [Be specific: What kind of trouble? Be concise: Omit unnecessary vague words.]

REVISED: When an upper-level disturbance affects local weather, meteorologists occasionally miss a forecast.

2. The following modifiers are weak, vague, or unspecific. Replace with a stronger modifier or add specific details.

very	a lot	pretty
really	good	bad
a few	certain	happy
many	nice	much
regular	similar	soon

VAGUE: I *really* liked *certain* classes in high school *very much,* but I just couldn't stand *a lot* of the *really boring* courses. [Be specific: What *certain classes?* Be specific: How or why were they *really boring?*]

REVISED: I really looked forward to learning about the turtles, snakes, and birds in the biology lab, but I couldn't stand just sitting still and practicing grammar hour after hour in French class.

VAGUE: Overall, *The Bill Cosby Show* is *pretty good,* but sometimes it gets *somewhat* unreal. [Be specific: What makes it *pretty good?* What makes it *unreal?*]

REVISED: *The Bill Cosby Show* has entertaining stories about family problems—I still remember the episode when Theo decides he just has to join the Blue Angels—but in many episodes, the family seems to resolve the conflict too easily and simply.

3. The following *verbs* are weak, vague, or unspecific. Where appropriate, replace with more active, energetic, or vivid verbs. When these verbs occur with nominals or passive voice, change to active verbs or active voice. Always test your revision: In your context, is the change more effective, concise, or vivid?

deals with	take	get
involved with	relate to	go
has to do with	make	give

VAGUE: He gets some enjoyment from sky diving.

REVISED: He enjoys sky diving.

VAGUE: Her job deals with collecting rare species of lizards.

REVISED: She collects rare species of lizards.

VAGUE: Jogging along the path, she got involved with a rattlesnake in a serious way. [How exactly was she "involved" with this rattlesnake?]

REVISED: Jogging along the path, she was seriously bitten by a rattlesnake.

Exercise   In the following passage, substitute specific and vivid words or phrases for all vague nouns, verbs, and modifiers.

(1) When I was separated from my girlfriend, I missed her a lot.   (2) Being alone sometimes gave me a pretty empty type feeling.   (3) When I called her on the phone, we talked about all the nice times we spent together, not about all the very big fights we used to have.   (4) Since there was no stress to deal with, we had a fun-filled, long-distance relationship.   (5) I know that one aspect of this relationship will improve the way we get along, now that we're back together.   (6) We always had difficulty talking in a serious manner about our future. (7) Now we are more involved with each other and can really talk about all sorts of things.   (8) For anyone who is having troubles, I recommend this kind of separate situation because, in the long run, the relationship will be much happier.

3B WORDINESS

1. The following wordy phrases can be stated more concisely:

Wordy	Concise
due to the fact that	because
despite the fact that	though
regardless of the fact that	although
at this point in time	now
at the present time	now
until such time as	until
in the event that	if, when
at all times	always
there is no doubt that	doubtless
in a deliberate manner	deliberately
by means of	by
the reason is that	[omit]

2. The following phrases are redundant—they say the same thing twice or repeat unnecessarily.

Redundant	Concise
new innovation	innovation
disappear from view	disappear
repeat again	repeat
reflected back	reflected

circle around	circle
few in number	few
cheaper in cost	cheaper
oblong in shape	oblong
blue in color	blue
consensus of opinion	consensus
important essentials	essentials
resulting effect	effect
cooperate together	cooperate

3. Where appropriate, be more concise by omitting *there is, there are, it is,* and *this is* constructions.

WORDY: There are seven people living in that apartment.
REVISED: Seven people live in that apartment.

WORDY: This is the step that is crucial for getting a job.
REVISED: This step is crucial for getting a job.

4. Some *who, which,* and *that* clauses can be changed into modifying words or phrases.

WORDY: Cheryl Stickfinger, who is the mayor, is accused of embezzling city funds.
REVISED: Mayor Cheryl Stickfinger is accused of embezzling city funds.

WORDY: Then they each wolfed down a banana split that contained 500 calories.
REVISED: Then they each wolfed down a 500-calorie banana split.

WORDY: The police officer, who was frustrated about missing his promotion, started taking kickbacks.
REVISED: The police officer, frustrated about missing his promotion, started taking kickbacks.

Exercise   Revise the following passage to reduce wordiness.

(1) One of the most recent new discoveries in medicine is the so-called diving reflex.   (2) When people fall into water that is icy, their circulation slows down due to the fact that the water is so cold.   (3) In addition, the metabolism of every cell that is in the body slows down, conserving oxygen.   (4) In a recent case, Alvaro Garza, who is eleven years old, disappeared from view underneath the ice for 45 minutes.   (5) When rescuers finally pulled him at long last from beneath the ice, he was unconscious, his body temperature was cold and below normal, and his skin

was grayish-blue in color.   (6) Regardless of the fact that rescuers could find no pulse or heartbeat, they began CPR (cardiopulmonary resuscitation) immediately.   (7) Within a few days, Alvaro began to recover in a steady manner, and soon he was asking for a hamburger and French fries.   (8) Although he may have some lingering effects from his ordeal that do not go away in a short period of time, the unexplainable miracle is that he survived.

3C COLLOQUIAL LANGUAGE AND SLANG

Your audience and purpose should determine whether conversational language is appropriate. In informal or expressive writing, colloquial language (spoken language), slang, or trendy expressions may be vivid and effective. In conversation or informal writing, we may say that something is *cool, hip, gross, weak, sweet,* or *too much,* or we may call a friend *dude,* a skateboarder a *thrasher,* or someone we don't like a *wimp* or *geek.*

In formal writing, however, you should avoid colloquial expressions and slang. Your readers may not know the expressions, they may find some slang offensive, or they may think "gross" is simply too vague to describe what really happened. Slang, in fact, tends to become a shorthand for a whole experience and thus invites *telling* ("This guy was a real geek") rather than *showing* ("Rudolph had messy hair, wore adhesive tape on his glasses, and always had one green and one orange sock sticking out of his polyester pants. He lived out of a forty-pound book pack, watched *Dr. Who* on TV every day, and spoke like William F. Buckley").

3D CLICHÉS AND JARGON

Clichés

Some expressions are so commonly used that they have become automatic, predictable, trite, or hackneyed. They may have been fresh and original once, but now they are as stale as dirty dishwater and about as exciting as a secondhand sock. The expressions in the right-hand column, for example, are so predictable that we can easily guess the missing word.

tried and true	strong as an _____
needle in a haystack	dark as _____
easier said than done	heavy as _____

burning the midnight oil	cold as _____
straw that broke the camel's back	busy as a _____
didn't sleep a wink	happy as a _____
crack of dawn	white as _____
dead of night	quick as a _____
last but not least	blind as a _____
birds of a feather	sober as a _____
hit the nail on the head	tough as _____
face the music	gentle as a _____

Jargon

Jargon is the technical vocabulary of any specialized occupation, field, or profession. In technical or specialized writing, writers should use the vocabulary of their field. In the following passage, the specialized vocabulary (*homeotic, mutant, rudimentary,* and *thoracic*) is entirely appropriate.

> In the cockroach *Blatella germanica,* a homeotic mutant produces rudimentary wings on the first thoracic segment. No modern insect normally bears wings on its first thoracic segment, but the earliest winged fossil insects did!
>
> —Stephen J. Gould, *Hen's Teeth and Horse's Toes*

Jargon, however, is also a generic label for impressive words used for their own sake. Any specialized vocabulary is inappropriate when used not to *inform* an audience but to *impress* an audience with the writer's great intelligence. When writers use jargon inappropriately, they are not communicating—they're showing off.

Below is a jargon-filled parody, in legalese, of the simple, clear sentence, "Have an orange." This passage, by the editors of *Labor Magazine,* appears in Stuart Chase's essay "Gobbledygook."

> I hereby give and convey to you, all singular, my estate and interests, right, title, claim and advantages of and in said orange, together with all rind, juice, pulp, and pits, and all rights and advantages therein . . . anything hereinbefore or hereinafter or in any other deed or deeds, instrument or instruments of whatever nature or kind whatsoever, to the contrary, in any wise, notwithstanding.

Sometimes writers use jargon not to make *themselves* sound impressive but to promote the *subject* they're writing about. We commonly call the result "advertising." Here is a sample of a Nike advertisement for a walking shoe:

Walking. To you, it's a simple matter of putting one foot in front of another. To Nike, it's an entire science.

In fact, we have studied walking in one of the world's leading biomechanical labs. Our own. And as a result, we've designed a technically advanced shoe specifically for the walking motion. The EXW. We built it close to the ground for stability. With a tri-density midsole that supports and centers your foot. A vented toe area for cool comfort. Flex grooves that bend with your foot. And a Nike-Air cushioning system that makes you feel, literally, like you're walking on air.

Now, all this technology may seem a bit much. But try on a pair. You'll see that the EXW doesn't make walking more complicated. It just takes it one step further.

Nike hopes the inflated language and technical jargon in this passage will make you feel better about spending fifty dollars for a walking shoe. "World's leading biomechanical labs," "advanced shoe specifically for the walking motion," "tri-density midsole," "vented toe area," and "flex grooves"—all this jargon does "seem a bit much." We may ridicule such language, but remember that if the advertisement causes us to buy the shoe, the language is appropriate for the audience.

Exercise   In the following passage, replace clichés with fresh, figurative language and eliminate or replace inappropriate jargon.

(1) The television news media in America needs to be reformed.   (2) The bottom line is that serious news has been lost as stations rush to entertain the viewer.   (3) Trying to find an informative story on the evening news is like looking for a needle in a haystack.   (4) The station executives who finalize the programmatic output for the evening news believe that the average American is dumber than an ox.   (5) As a result, viewers see in-depth stories about a sex scandal involving a local politician, but only a few seconds explaining why the stock market is scraping the bottom of the barrel.   (6) Newscasters attempt to maximize their humor by telling jokes that go over like a lead balloon rather than informing the viewer about the latest decision-making process on armament restrictions.   (7) If station programmers actually interfaced with the public occasionally, they would recognize the error of their ways.

3E SEXIST LANGUAGE

Do not use language that unfairly stereotypes people or discriminates against either women or men. Just as you would avoid racist terms you should avoid language that stereotypes people's roles, occupations, or behavior by gender. Sentences such as "A doctor always cares for his patient" or "A secretary should always help her boss" imply that all doctors are men and all secretaries are women. Phrases such as female logic, male ego, emotional woman, or typical male brutality imply that all women are excessively emotional and all men are egotistical brutes. In fact, those stereotypes are not true. If you use sexist language, you will offend your readers. Even more important, your language should not encourage you or your reader to see the world in sexist stereotypes.

1. Avoid words that suggest sexist roles.

Sexist	Revised
man	people, person
chairman	chair, head
businessman	businessperson
policeman	police officer
mankind	humanity
congressman	representative
statesman	politician, diplomat
lady lawyer	lawyer
career girl	professional woman
coed	student
mailman	letter carrier
old wives' tale	superstition

Note, however, that some words that link occupation with gender are still appropriate. Most writers still use *actor* and *waiter* for men and *actress* and *waitress* for women. Other words such as *stewardess* or *seamstress,* however, are often replaced with *flight attendant* or *garment worker.*

2. Be consistent in your use of people's names. If you write *Ernest Hemingway,* then write *Emily Dickinson,* not *Miss Dickinson.* If you write *Mikhail Gorbachev,* then write *Margaret Thatcher,* not *Mrs. Thatcher.* If you write *Lennon,* then write *Parton,* not *Dolly Parton* or *Dolly.*

3. Avoid using the pronouns *he, his,* or *him* when you are referring to activities, roles, or behavior that could describe either sex.

SEXIST: A doctor should listen carefully to his patient.
             Note: Use plural if it does not alter your meaning.
REVISED: Doctors should listen carefully to their patients.
SEXIST: An effective teacher knows each of her students.

Note: You may use *his or her* sparingly, but avoid using the construction *s/he.*

REVISED: An effective teacher knows each of his or her students.

SEXIST: Everyone hopes that he will survive the first year of college.

Note: Often, you can revise the sentence by using first or second person or by omitting the pronoun.

REVISED: I hope to survive the first year of college.

REVISED: All of us hope to survive the first year of college.

REVISED: You hope to survive the first year of college.

REVISED: Everyone hopes to survive the first year of college.

Note: Do *not* mix singular and plural by saying, "Everyone hopes *they* will survive the first year of college."

Exercise Revise the following passage to eliminate sexist language.

(1) Everyone in college now is looking for that special job that will match his talents and yet bring him sufficient income.   (2) Teaching is a low-paying but good career if you don't mind being a professor who spends his life reading papers, getting grants, and serving on committees.   (3) A secretary or stewardess can begin her career with minimal training, but a nurse must dedicate herself to rigorous medical schooling.   (4) In business and entertainment, girls can work right alongside the men.   (5) In the entertainment field, many people dream of being a Bruce Springsteen or a Tina Turner, although most singers don't have Springsteen's talent or Tina's perseverance.   (6) A businessman often works his way up the ladder and becomes chairman of the company. (7) Even staying at home and raising a family is a respectable career for either a man or his wife, though most men simply don't have the temperament to raise children.   (8) Whatever your chosen career, from mailman to congressman, hard work and dedication are the keys to landing and keeping that important job.

3F DENOTATION AND CONNOTATION

The *denotation* of a word is its literal or dictionary definition. Both *house* and *home* refer, denotatively, to a structure in which people live. Many words have, in addition, a *connotation* or an emotional association that can be negative, neutral, or positive. *House* has, for most people, a *neutral* or sterile connotation, whereas *home,* for most people, has a *positive* connotation, suggesting warmth, comfort, security, and family.

Choose words appropriately for their connotative value.

INAPPROPRIATE:	Dr. Aileen Brown, a *notorious* scientist, just received the Nobel prize for her work with superconductors. [*Notorious* people are usually famous for their *misconduct*.]
REVISED:	Dr. Aileen Brown, a *famous* scientist, just received the Nobel prize for her work with superconductors.
INAPPROPRIATE:	Beverly looked at her friend Steve and said, "Why don't you finish your dinner? You need the food— you're already a bit *scrawny* looking." [Steve prefers to think of himself as *thin* or *slim* rather than *scrawny*.]
REVISED:	Beverly looked at her friend Steve and said, "Why don't you finish your dinner? You need the food— you're already a bit *thin*."
INAPPROPRIATE:	Lynn's father told Paul that the apartment was decorated *cheaply* but tastefully. [Paul's feelings may be hurt. He does have good taste in furnishings, and he did the best he could on his tight budget.]
REVISED:	Lynn's father told Paul that the apartment was decorated tastefully but inexpensively.

Exercise The following groups of words have similar denotative meanings but vary widely in their emotional associations or *connotative* meanings. Rank the words in each group from most negative, to neutral, to most positive.

social drinker, wino, lush, reveler, alcoholic, sot, party animal, elbow bender, inebriate, problem drinker, booze hound, bar hopper

scholar, intellectual, four-eyes, walking encyclopedia, geek, savant, bookworm, genius, pedant, bibliophile

thrifty, penny-pinching, frugal, miserly, tight-fisted, cheap, economical, prudent, stingy

steady, loyal, stubborn, firm, unyielding, dedicated, obstinate, devoted

3g USAGE GLOSSARY

This glossary alphabetically lists words and phrases that frequently cause problems for writers. In many cases, writers disagree about the preferred usage in formal writing, so if you are in doubt, check a dictionary such as *The American Heritage Dictionary*, the *Random House Dictionary*, or a guide such as Margaret Bryant's *Current American Usage*.

Since this glossary references only the most obvious usage errors, refer to a standard or unabridged dictionary for items not included.

a, an: Use *a* when the following word begins with a *consonant sound:* a book, a clever saying, a hat. Use *an* when the following word begins with a *vowel sound:* an apple, an old building, an honor.

accept, except: *Accept* is a verb meaning "to receive": "I accept the gift." *Except* is a preposition meaning "other than" or "excluding": "Everyone received a gift except John." Rarely, *except* is a verb meaning "to exclude": "The editor excepted the footnote from the article."

advise, advice: *Advise* is a verb: "I advise you to exercise regularly." *Advice* is a noun: "Please take this advice."

affect, effect: *Affect* is a verb: "The flying beer cups did not affect Dale Murphy's concentration." *Effect* is a noun: "His obvious poise had a calming effect on the crowd." Remember: If you can say, "Th*e* effect," then you are correctly using the noun form. Less often, *effect* is also a verb: "His behavior effected a change in the crowd's attitude."

all right, alright: *All right,* two words, is the accepted spelling. *Alright* is nonstandard, in the opinion of most experts.

already, all ready: *Already* means "by now" or "previously": "The essay was already completed." *All ready* means *completely prepared:* "The paragraphs were all ready to be printed."

a lot: *A lot* is always two words that mean "many." Wherever possible, however, *avoid* using *a lot.* Replace with more specific description. See Section 3a.

among, between: Use *between* for *two* people or things: "Let's divide the cake between the two of us." Use *among* for *three or more* people or things: "We should distribute the winnings among all the players. *Note: Between* is used for three or more items when location or a reciprocal relationship is indicated: "They found the treasure at a point equidistant between the three trees." "Through careful negotiations, a nonaggression treaty was reached between the four nations."

amount, number: *Amount* refers to quantity: "He saved a large amount of food for the winter months." *Number* refers to countable items: "She owned a large number of expensive sports cars."

anyone, any one: *Anyone* is a pronoun: "Anyone who likes Mayan art should hear the lecture." *Any one* is an adjective phrase modifying a noun: "He owns more Mayan art than any one person could possibly appreciate."

bad, badly: *Bad* is an adjective used in the predicate ("After a week of the flu, she looked bad") or before a noun ("She caught my cold at a bad time"). "She felt bad because she had a bad cold." *Badly* is an adverb: "He wrote badly because he had a high fever."

being, being that: *Being* cannot be used as a complete verb. "The seat being taken" is not a complete sentence. *Being that* is nonstandard: "Being that the bus was late, we missed the show." Use *because* or *since:* "Because the bus was late, we missed the show."

beside, besides: *Beside* is a preposition meaning *next to* or *by the side of:* "Peggi sat beside the senator." *Besides* is a preposition meaning *moreover* or *in addition to:* "Besides, the senator likes several people besides George."

can, may: In formal writing, use *can* for ability: "I can take out the garbage." Use *may* for permission: "May I have the honor of taking out the garbage?" Also use *may* for possibility: "If I have time, I *may* take out the garbage."

center around: Illogical: One can "circle around" but not "center around." Replace with "center on" or "focus on": "The controversy focused on the right of the worker to a safe, smoke-free environment."

cite, site: *Cite* is a verb meaning "to quote as an authority or to mention": "She cited Newcastle's blue law, which forbade card playing on Sunday." *Site* is a noun meaning "a place or location": "The church basement was, in fact, the site of Newcastle's first bingo game."

continual, continuous: *Continual* means "frequently repeated": "Most soap operas have continual interruptions for commercials." *Continuous* means "unceasing": "Throughout the broadcast, we heard a continuous buzzing sound."

could of, should of: Nonstandard. Use *could have* or *should have.*

data, media, criteria: The singular forms are *datum, medium,* and *criterion.* In formal writing, use plural verbs and pronouns with the plural noun. "Our data reveal a sharp increase in rapes and assaults since last year." "The media use their own criteria for sex and violence."

different from, different than: For prepositional phrases, use *different from:* "His chili recipe is different from yours." Although "different from" is preferred, sometimes "different than" results in a more concise sentence. "She is a different player than she used to be" is less wordy than "She is a different player from the player she used to be."

disinterested, uninterested: *Disinterested* means "objective or impartial": "As a disinterested third party, Marji resolved our dispute." *Uninterested* means "lack of interest": "We were uninterested in the outcome of the hall elections."

farther, further: *Farther* usually refers to distance: "How much farther are we going to jog?" *Further* refers to additional time, amount, or degree: "Furthermore, if you cannot hire me, I will go further into debt."

fewer, less: *Fewer* refers to numbers or countable items: "Fewer teenagers smoke than a decade ago." *Less* refers to amount ("less sugar") or degree ("less important"): "Teenagers spend less money on cigarettes than they did a decade ago."

hopefully: *Hopefully* means "with hope," or "in a hopeful manner": "Charlene waited hopefully for a letter from home." Most good writers still object to the colloquial usage of *hopefully* (meaning, "I hope," or "it is to be hoped"): "Hopefully, Charlene will get her letter from home." Change to: "I hope Charlene gets her letter from home."

imply, infer: *Imply* means to suggest without directly stating: "The news report implied that the president was seriously ill." *Infer* means to draw a conclusion: "I inferred from the news report that the president was seriously ill." Writers and speakers *imply*; readers and listeners *infer.*

its, it's: *Its,* like *his* or *her,* is a possessive pronoun: "The tree is losing its leaves." *It's* is a contraction of *it is:* "It's your turn to rake the leaves."

lay, lie: *Lay* is the transitive verb (lay, laid, laid) meaning "put" or "place." "Please lay the book on the table." *Lie* is an intransitive verb (lie, lay, lain) meaning "recline" or "occupy a place": "The books lie on the table."

like, as, as if: *Like* is a preposition: "A great race driver is like an opera singer—vain and arrogant." *As* can be a preposition ("His mission as a driver was to demonstrate his grace and courage"), but it can also introduce a clause: "Even at the end of the race, he looked as if he had just stepped off the cover of a magazine."

lose, loose: *Lose* is a verb meaning "misplace" or "be deprived of": "Good detectives never lose their nerve." *Loose* is an adjective meaning "free" or "not tight": "The psychopath got loose by climbing through the ventilating system."

principal, principle: *Principal* as an adjective means "major" or "main"; as a noun, *principal* refers either to a "chief official" or to a "capital sum of money": "The principal of the high school listed as his principal debt the $50,000 he owed on the principal of his house mortgage." *Principle* is a noun meaning "basic truth," "rule," or "moral standard": "He learned the principles of accounting and finance."

quote, quotation: *Quote* is a verb: "I quoted the passage from Thoreau's *Walden*." Do not use *quote* as a noun ("The following quote from *Walden*"); instead, use "quotation," "remark," or "passage": "The following passage from *Walden* illustrates Thoreau's politics."

that, which: *That* always introduces restrictive clauses; *which* introduces either restrictive or nonrestrictive clauses. Some writers prefer, however, to use *that* only for restrictive clauses and *which* only for nonrestrictive. "The hat that has the pheasant feather was a birthday present." The clause, "that has the pheasant feather" restricts, limits, and *identifies* which hat was the present. "The hat, which is nearly ten years old, was a birthday present." The clause, "which is nearly ten years old" is only incidental information; it does not specify which hat was the present.

their, they're, there: *Their* is a pronoun: "She is playing with their tennis balls." *They're* is a contraction: "They're really upset that she didn't even ask." *There* is an adverb or an expletive: "She's practicing over there. There are the tennis balls."

to, too, two: *To* is a preposition: "I am writing to Bev." *Too* is an adverb meaning "in addition" or "also": "You too can write her a letter." *Too* also is an intensifier meaning "very": "Dad expects me to write too often." *Two* is a number: "I have written two times this month."

used to, supposed to: Use the past tense ("used to") not ("use to"): "I used to go there every weekend."

Section 4
PUNCTUATION AND MECHANICS

The purpose of punctuation is to clarify meaning and promote communication. Commas, periods, semicolons, dashes, and other punctuation marks guide readers to the meaning, just as traffic signals, double yellow lines, turning lanes, and one-way signs guide motorists to a destination. The conventions of punctuation create *expectations* in the reader. Just as you are surprised when a car runs a red light and nearly hits you, readers are surprised when writers fail to follow the conventions of punctuation.

Punctuation—or the lack of it—can change the entire meaning of a sentence. In actual conversation, pauses, inflections, intonation, gestures, and facial expressions do the work of punctuation. In writing, however, punctuation must provide these clues.

"Sorry, but I'm going to have to issue you a summons for reckless grammar and driving without an apostrophe."

Read the following sentences. How many different ways can you find to punctuate each sentence? How does each version alter the meaning?

Give the peanuts to my daughter Ella

She said walk quietly

Let's go see the lions eat Marcia.

Sometimes writers unintentionally create confusion by omitting important punctuation. Notice how the appropriate use of commas in the following sentences prevents a possible surprise and clarifies the meaning.

CONFUSING: To keep the pipes from freezing the plumber advised us to run the water all night. [How exactly did the pipes freeze the plumber?]

REVISED: To keep the pipes from freezing, the plumber advised us to run the water all night.

CONFUSING: On the menu for lunch was ham and Sam was doing the cooking. [Is Sam on the menu?]

REVISED: On the menu for lunch was ham, and Sam was doing the cooking.

The guidelines for punctuation and mechanics in this section will help you avoid unintentional problems and clarify your writing.

Review these guidelines as you edit your own and other people's writing.

4A   SENTENCE PUNCTUATION

Much of the confusion about punctuation occurs because connecting words often have similar meanings but they signal different punctuation conventions. A stop sign, a red light, and a blinking red light, for example, all mean that motorists must stop, but each signals a slightly different procedure. In English, *but, although,* and *however* mean that a contrast is coming, but each requires different punctuation.

We won the volleyball game, *but* our best hitter broke her wrist.

Although we won the game, our best hitter broke her wrist.

We won the game; *however,* our best hitter broke her wrist.

Using commas and semicolons to punctuate sentences and clauses requires knowing the three basic types of connecting or *conjunctive* words.

Coordinate conjunctions: "Con/junction" means "join together"; "coordinates" are "equals." A coordinate conjunction joins equals together. The acronym BOYFANS will help you remember the coordinate conjunctions:

B	O	Y	F	A	N	S
but	or	yet	for	and	nor	so

Subordinating conjunctions: A subordinate conjunction joins a dependent or subordinate clause to an independent or main clause. The following are the most common subordinating conjunctions:

after	before	since	until
although	even if	so that	when
as	even though	than	whenever
as if	if	that	where
as though	in order that	though	wherever
because	rather than	unless	while

Subordinating conjunctions change an independent clause (IC) to a dependent clause (DC).

IC

Independent clause: He buys a newspaper.

Add a subordinating conjunction to create a *dependent clause:*

DC
If he buys a newspaper

DC   IC
Complete sentence: If he buys a newspaper, he will see the story.

Conjunctive adverbs: A conjunctive adverb acts as a transitional phrase. Below are the most common conjunctive adverbs.

accordingly	however	meanwhile	still
also	incidently	moreover	thereafter
consequently	indeed	nevertheless	therefore
furthermore	instead	otherwise	thus
hence	likewise	similarly	

If you are uncertain whether a connecting word is a conjunctive adverb, *test* by moving the connecting word to another place in the clause. Conjunctive adverbs *can* be moved; subordinating conjunctions (such as *if* or *because*) and coordinating conjunctions (BOYFANS words) *cannot*.

Conjunctive adverbs can be moved:

>We won the game; *however,* our best hitter broke her wrist.

>We won the game; our best hitter, *however,* broke her wrist.

>We won the game; our best hitter broke her wrist, *however.*

Subordinating conjunctions cannot be moved:

>*Although* our best hitter broke her wrist, we won the game.

>Our best hitter, *although,* broke her wrist, we won the game. [Obviously, *although* cannot be moved to another position in the clause.]

Coordinating conjunctions cannot be moved:

>We won the game, *but* our best hitter broke her wrist.

>We won the game, our best hitter, *but,* broke her wrist. [Moving a coordinating conjunction scrambles the sentences.]

Rules for joining independent clauses (IC) and dependent clauses (DC):

1. Join two independent clauses with a comma and a coordinating conjunction.

   IC,   BOYFANS   IC.

   The pizza is good, *but* the mystery meat is disgusting. [Must have *both* a comma *and* a BOYFANS word]

2. Join two independent clauses with a semicolon and a conjunctive adverb.

IC;   CONJUNCTIVE ADVERB,   IC.

The pizza is good; however, the mystery meat is disgusting.

3. Join two independent clauses (IC) with a semicolon.

IC;   IC.

The pizza is good; the mystery meat is disgusting.

4. Join a dependent clause (DC) to an independent clause (IC) with a comma.

DC,   IC.

Although mystery meat tastes all right, it looks disgusting.

4B COMMA SPLICES AND FUSED SENTENCES

Two common errors in joining independent clauses are the *comma splice* and the *fused sentence* (also called a run-on sentence). Revise by following one of the patterns in 1–3 above.

COMMA SPLICE: [IC , IC] I know that airplanes are safer than cars, I still have a fear of flying.

COMMA SPLICE: [IC , Conjunctive Adverb IC] I know that airplanes are safer than cars, however I still have a fear of flying.

FUSED SENTENCE: [IC IC] I know that airplanes are safer than cars I still have a fear of flying.

REVISED: I know that airplanes are safer than cars, *but* I still have a fear of flying.

REVISED: I know that airplanes are safer than cars; *however*, I still have a fear of flying.

REVISED: *Although* I know that airplanes are safer than cars, I still have a fear of flying.

Exercise In the following passage, correct all comma splices and fused sentences.

(1) For years, scientists have attempted to teach animals to communicate for the most part, their efforts have failed.   (2) In the 1950s, psychologists failed to teach a chimpanzee to speak, the ape was able to grunt only a few words.   (3) In the 1960s, however, a chimp named Washoe

learned the sign language of the deaf.   (4) Washoe came to understand hundreds of words, he used them to communicate and express original ideas.   (5) As it turns out, the great apes have the capacity to learn language, but they cannot speak.   (6) This research proved that humans are not the only animal capable of using language they are, however, the most sophisticated users of language.

4c COMMAS

Commas for Introductory Elements

Use commas to set off most introductory elements.

> Because I broke three flasks, I'm going to have a large bill for chemistry lab. [Introductory dependent clause]

> In the middle of finals week last semester, I became seriously depressed. [Long introductory prepositional phrase]

> Jogging home after classes, I see children playing in the school-yard. [Introductory participial phrase]

> To save money, I often take the bus. [Introductory infinitive phrase]

> Incidently, I hope my roommate will be here this weekend. [Introductory adverb]

Items in a Series

Use commas to separate items in a series (a, b, and c). Generally, use a comma before the "and." In some cases, omitting the comma before the final item in the series may cause confusion:

CONFUSING: She rented an apartment with a convection oven, a microwave, a refrigerator with an icemaker and a garbage disposal. [Does the refrigerator have a built-in icemaker and garbage disposal?]

REVISED: She rented an apartment with a convection oven, a microwave, a refrigerator with an icemaker, and a garbage disposal.

Exercise   Revise the punctuation in the following passage.

> (1) Everyone can have fun outside in the wintertime by following some commonsense rules.   (2) If you are going to be outside for several hours be sure to eat a nutritious meal before leaving.   (3) On cold damp or windy days wear clothes that are warm and dry.   (4) To stay warm protect yourself against moisture that builds up from the inside.

(5) Most experts recommend dressing in layers. (6) The inner layer wicks moisture away from your body the middle layer provides thermal protection and the outer layer protects against rain or wind. (7) Curiously enough most people tend to put on too many clothes, underestimating their body's ability to exercise comfortably naturally and safely in cold weather.

Nonrestrictive Elements

Nonrestrictive modifiers should be separated from the sentence by commas. Always *test* the phrase or clause: If it can be removed from the sentence without changing the meaning, use commas.

NONRESTRICTIVE: Coach Hall, who was invited to the party, celebrated the victory.
Test: The clause, "who was invited to the party," is incidental information. It does not restrict or specify which coach was celebrating. The two commas indicate that removing the clause from the sentence will not change the meaning: "Coach Hall celebrated the victory."

NONRESTRICTIVE: Seattle, which has a reputation as a rainy city, is actually drier than New Orleans.
Test: Remove the clause, and the meaning of the sentence is not altered. "Seattle is actually drier than New Orleans."

NONRESTRICTIVE: Charles, the man in the gray suit, eats fried grasshoppers when no one is looking.
Test: The appositive, "the man in the gray suit," can be removed from the sentence without altering the meaning.

RESTRICTIVE: Demonstrators who hurled bricks were arrested by the police.
Test: The meaning is that *only those* demonstrators *who hurled bricks* were arrested by the police. The phrase *who hurled bricks* cannot be removed from the sentence without changing this meaning. Do *not* use commas to separate restrictive elements.

NONRESTRICTIVE: The class, which was taught by Anne Perkins, met at eight o'clock in the morning.
Note: This sentence says that the class met at eight o'clock, and Anne Perkins was, incidentally, the teacher. (Usually use *which* for nonrestrictive clauses.)

RESTRICTIVE: The class that was taught by Anne Perkins met at eight o'clock in the morning.

Note: This sentence says that *the particular class taught by Professor Perkins* met at eight o'clock. Other classes met at some other time. (Use *that* for restrictive clauses. Do not use commas.)

Unnecessary Commas

Do not use a comma to separate a subject and a verb.

FAULTY: My toughest class of the day, met at eight o'clock.
REVISED: My toughest class of the day met at eight o'clock.

Do not use a comma to separate compound subjects or predicates.

FAULTY: The Dean of Students, and the Chancellor decided to cancel classes. [Compound subject]
REVISED: The Dean of Students and the Chancellor decided to cancel classes.
FAULTY: Because of the heavy snowfall, I stayed inside all afternoon, and popped popcorn. [Compound predicate]

Note: When coordinate conjunctions do not join independent clauses or items in a series, a comma is usually not necessary. (See Section 4a for appropriate use of commas with coordinate conjunctions.)

REVISED: Because of the heavy snowfall, I stayed inside all afternoon and popped popcorn.

Coordinate Adjectives

Use a comma to separate coordinate (equal) adjectives. Test for coordinate adjectives: (1) insert an "and" between the adjectives and (2) reverse the order of the adjectives. If the meaning of the sentence remains unchanged, the adjectives are equal or coordinate.

EXAMPLE: It was a dull dark day.
Test: Insert "and"; reverse adjectives. It was a dull and dark day. It was a dark and dull day. Since meaning of the sentence has not changed, these are coordinate or equal adjectives. Remove the *and* and add a comma.
REVISED: It was a dull, dark day.
EXAMPLE: The car had studded snow tires.
Test: Insert "and"; reverse adjectives. The car had studded and snow tires. The car had snow and studded tires. The meaning of the original sentence is changed; therefore, the adjectives are not coordinate. Do *not* separate with comma.
REVISED: The car had studded snow tires.

Dialogue

Use commas to set off dialogue or direct quotation.
Dialogue:

> "We'll try it," the professor said to me, grimly, "with every adjustment of the microscope known to man."
>
> —James Thurber

Direct quotation:

> The author points out, "One of the effects of embalming by chemical injection, however, has been to dispel fears of live burial."
>
> —Jessica Mitford

Addresses, Dates, Degrees

Use commas to set off addresses, dates, degrees, or titles.

Addresses: What Cheer, Iowa, is his home town.

Dates: On December 7, 1941, the Japanese bombed Pearl Harbor.

Degrees: Randall Beaver, D.D.S., is my orthodontist.

Exercise   Revise the punctuation in the following passage.

> (1) Dinosaurs which have been extinct for millions of years are making news again.   (2) At a meeting of the Geological Society of America in November 1987 scientists announced a startling discovery.   (3) Dinosaurs, that lived 80 million years ago, benefited from an atmosphere that contained nearly 50 percent more oxygen than it does now. (4) Gary Landis geochemist for the U.S. Geological Service and Robert Berner professor at Yale University reached that conclusion after analyzing, air bubbles trapped in bits of amber.   (5) They found that the tiny, air bubbles contained 32 percent oxygen, compared with 21 percent in the modern atmosphere.   (6) When asked whether a decreasing oxygen supply, could have caused the extinction of the dinosaurs, Berner explained "It was a very gradual change, and most organisms easily adapt."   (7) "The large slow-moving dinosaurs probably became extinct" he said "following some cataclysmic, geological, event."

4D PERIODS AND SEMICOLONS

Periods

Use periods at the end of sentences, indirect questions, and commands.

Sentence: The Statue of Liberty was officially rededicated.

Indirect question:	I asked my friend when he was going to stop taking pictures.
Command:	Wait until the ship moves into the picture.

Semicolons

Use a semicolon to join related independent clauses. Remember to test for independent clauses by using a period. If you can use a period and if the sentences are related, you may wish to use a semicolon. Remember, however, that semicolons are usually more appropriate in formal writing.

> Nowadays, says one sociologist, you don't have to have a reason for going to college; it's an institution. His definition of an institution is an arrangement everyone accepts without question; the burden of proof is not on why you go, but why anyone thinks there might be a reason for not going.
>
> —Caroline Bird

> I take a dim view of dams; I find it hard to learn to love cement.
>
> —Edward Abbey

Use a semicolon to separate items in a series that already have internal punctuation.

> We quickly meet the "good guys" of *Star Wars:* Luke Skywalker, played by Mark Hamill; Ben "Obi-Wan" Kenobi, played by Alec Guinness; and Han Solo, played by Harrison Ford.
>
> —Judith Crist

Do *not* use a semicolon to join dependent with independent clauses.

> Harrison Ford played the leading role in *Raiders of the Lost Ark;* which made him an instant star.

4E COLONS AND DASHES

Colons

Use a colon to introduce a list or an explanation. Colons often create formal, structured sentences.

> When you go to the grocery store, please get the following items: two boxes of frozen peas, five pounds of baking potatoes, and a package of stuffing for the turkey.

> There is only one guaranteed method to lose weight: eat less and exercise more.

Usually, a colon following a verb is unnecessary.

UNNECESSARY: The best way to lose weight is: eat less and exercise
               more.
REVISED: The best way to lose weight is to eat less and exer-
               cise more.

UNNECESSARY: I need: peas, baking potatoes, and stuffing.
REVISED: I need peas, baking potatoes, and stuffing.

Dashes

Use a single dash for an abrupt shift. Use a pair of dashes for an interrupting or parenthetical comment. Use a dash instead of a comma,
colon, or parentheses when you want a sentence to have a more informal, colloquial flavor.

> At last a happy thought struck me—I would draw the fish.
>
> —Samuel Scudder

> Indeed, there are moments today—amid outlaw litter, tax cheating, illic-
> it noise, and motorized anarchy—when it seems as though the scofflaw
> represents the wave of the future.
>
> —Frank Trippett

Exercise   In the following passage, insert semicolons, colons, or dashes at the appropriate places. In some cases, there are several ways to
punctuate the sentence correctly, so be prepared to explain your choice.

> (1) Yo-yo dieting the process of repeatedly losing and gaining weight is
> common today.   (2) Instead of changing eating habits and exercise
> patterns, the yo-yo dieter uses three common strategies to lose weight
> taking diet pills, drinking diet liquids, and fasting outright.   (3) The
> yo-yo dieter, however, needs to know the truth about dieting diet cycles
> decrease the muscle-to-fat ratio in the body and decrease the body's
> ability to lose weight during the next dieting cycle.   (4) Quick-fix diets,
> in other words, will lead to rapid weight losses however, they will be
> followed by an even faster weight gain.   (5) Ultimately, crash diets do
> more harm than good the body just wasn't designed to be a yo-yo.

4F EXCLAMATION POINTS
AND QUESTION MARKS

Exclamation Points

Use exclamation points sparingly, for stylistic emphasis.

> I saw the sleek gray-haired manager standing near the dance floor,
> snapping his fingers and smiling. . . . I bet myself that he owned one
> of the few blow-dryers in Moscow. . . . He was watching the growing

success of the only Western-style club in town and thinking: These kids! Right on! Crazy, but I love 'em!

—Andrea Lee

Bicyclists often ride as though two-wheeled vehicles are exempt from all traffic laws. Litterbugs convert their communities into trash dumps. . . . And then there are (hello, Everybody!) the jaywalkers.

—Frank Trippett

Question Marks

Use a question mark after a direct question.

What is your first childhood memory?

Do not combine question marks with commas or periods.

"What is your earliest memory?" she asked me. [Do *not* use a comma and a question mark: "What is your earliest memory?," she asked me.]

4G *QUOTATION AND ELLIPSIS MARKS*

Quotation Marks

Use quotation marks to indicate a writer's or speaker's exact words.

Marya Mannes says, "Woman, in short, is consumer first and human being fourth."

Use quotation marks for titles of *essays, articles, short stories, poems, chapters, and songs—any title that is part of a larger collection.*

"Television: The Splitting Image" is the title of an essay by Marya Mannes.

Use single quotation marks for quotations within a quotation.

James said, "I know I heard her say, 'Meet me outside the east door.'"

Ellipsis Marks

Use ellipsis marks (three *spaced* periods) to indicate material omitted from a direct quotation.

Marya Mannes said, "Woman . . . is consumer first and human being fourth." [The ellipsis indicates that words are omitted from the middle of the sentence.]

Use a period plus three spaced periods to signal either omitted words at the end of a sentence or omitted intervening sentence(s).

Marya Mannes said, "Woman, in short, is consumer first and human being fourth. . . . The conditioning starts very early. . . ."

Punctuation With Quotation Marks

The following guidelines will help you to punctuate sentences with quotation marks:

Periods and commas go *inside* quotation marks.

> According to biologist Julie Earwig, "Penguins are more densely covered with feathers than any other bird—nearly 180 feathers per square inch."

Colons and semicolons go *outside* quotation marks.

> Recent data about the eagle's feathers may revise the old saying "light as a feather": the vaned feathers on a bald eagle weigh more than its entire skeleton.

Exclamation points and question marks go *inside or outside* quotation marks. They go *inside* if they are a part of the quoted material:

> The award for the highest number of feathers, according to Earwig, "goes to the whistling swan with a staggering 25,000 feathers!" [The original sentence ends with an exclamation point.]

They go outside if they are not a part of the quoted material:

> Is it true that, as Earwig claims, "the tiny ruby-throated hummingbird has 940 feathers"? [The original sentence ends with a period.]

4H UNDERLINING FOR ITALICS

Use underlining to indicate words that should be in italics.

Titles: "Down the River" is the most interesting chapter in Edward Abbey's *Desert Solitaire*. [Underline titles of books, magazines, films, paintings, newspapers—any work published separately. Use quotation marks for titles of chapters, articles, or poems—any title that is part of some collection in a book or magazine.]
Exceptions: Do not underline the Bible or titles of legal documents, such as the Deed of Trust or the United States Constitution.

Names: The most famous travel ships used to be the *Santa Maria,* the *Titanic,* and the *Queen Mary.* Now the great ones are the *Apollo* and the *Challenger.* [Underline names of ships, trains, aircraft, or spacecraft.]

Foreign words:	He graduated *cum laude,* while his friend, who barely passed freshman mathematics, graduated *magna cum laude.* "*C'est la vie,*" he thought. [Note, however, that some foreign words (burrito, bourgeois, genre, cliché, junta, and many others) have been incorporated into the language and do not need italics. Consult your dictionary if you are in doubt.]
Words or letters:	*Suppose to* should have a *d: supposed to.* [Quotation marks are also used to indicate italics in handwritten or typed manuscripts.]

Note: Do *not* underline or put quotation marks around the title of your essay when it appears on a title page or the first page of your manuscript.

Exercise Revise the following passage, underlining appropriate words and titles.

(1) Tom Wolfe, author of The Right Stuff, has written a novel about a Wall Street broker in his newest work, The Bonfire of the Vanities. (2) This novel first appeared in twenty-seven installments in Rolling Stone magazine. (3) Wolfe's style has always been au courant, and Bonfire is no exception. (4) This novel features New York characters who run the gamut from drug pushers to the cunning and ambitious young lions of the investment world. (5) It is not a cliché to say that this book is difficult to put down.

41 PARENTHESES AND BRACKETS

Parentheses

Use parentheses () to set off additional information, examples, or comments.

Writing a film review requires that you carefully examine the criteria for your judgment (see Chapter 6).

Outside our lifeboat, let us imagine another 210 million people (say the combined populations of Colombia, Ecuador, Venezuela, Morocco, Pakistan, Thailand, and the Philippines), increasing at a rate of 3.3 percent per year.

—Garrett Hardin

Brackets

Use brackets [ ] to set off editorial remarks in quoted material. Brackets indicate that you, as an editor, are adding comments to the original material.

Original: After you hear my argument, you will reelect Eastwood.

Edited: After you hear my arguement [sic] , you will reelect [Mayor Clint] Eastwood. [As editor, you add information about Clint Eastwood and indicate by using "sic" ("thus it is") that the misspelling, grammatical mistake, or inappropriate usage occurs in the original source and is not your error.]

4J APOSTROPHES AND HYPHENS

Apostrophes

Use apostrophes for contractions, possession, and some plurals.

Contractions: It's too bad you don't agree.

Possession: The wind blew the student's notes across the front lawn. [The notes belonging to one student blew across the lawn.]

                  The wind blew the students' notes across the front lawn. [Several students' notes blew across the lawn.]

                  Your sister-in-law's accident was someone else's fault. [For compounds, make the last word possessive.]

Plurals: The 1980's [or 1980s] were the Yuppie years.

                  Eliminate unnecessary *which's* in your sentences.

Hyphens

Use hyphens for compound words, compound adjectives before nouns, some prefixes, and some numbers. When in doubt, always check a good dictionary.

Compounds: cross-reference; president-elect

Adjectives: a well-known writer; the slate-blue sea; the three-year-old child

                  Note: When the compound adjectives follow a noun, omit the hyphen: *He is a writer well known only in Vermont.*

Prefixes: ex-President Reagan; self-motivation

Numbers: twenty-six; one hundred sixty-five; one-fifth

4k CAPITALS AND NUMBERS

Capitals

Capitalize proper nouns and adjectives, professional titles, principal words in titles of books or articles, and regional locations.

Proper names:	Judson Smith, Atlanta, Los Angeles, Missouri River, English, Swahili, American, Labor Day, Christmas, Hanukah, Wednesday, October [Do *not* capitalize seasons or terms: autumn, spring, summer, fall semester, freshman year.]
Titles:	Senator Kennedy, President Lincoln, Professor Findlay, Associate Dean Natalie Renner, Uncle Don, Father [Do *not* capitalize family titles preceded by a pronoun: my mother, my uncle, our grandfather.]
Titles:	*Gone with the Wind,* "The Short Happy Life of Francis Macomber," "The Triumph of the Wheel," "Star Wars" [Note that some style manuals suggest capitalizing only the first word in a title. If you are citing titles in a bibliography or list of works cited, check your style manual.]
Regions:	the South, the Northwest, the Middle East [Do *not* capitalize directions: traveling east, walking due north.]

Numbers

Conventions regarding numbers vary. Generally, except in scientific or technical writing, spell out numbers of one hundred or less or numbers that require two words or less. If a passage requires many numbers, be consistent in your usage.

> This stadium seats fifty thousand people, but adding the end-zone bleachers increases the seating to fifty-seven thousand. [Hyphenated words count as one word.]

> Our chemistry lecture hall seats 425 students, but only 310 are enrolled this semester in Chemistry 201. [However, at the beginning of sentences, spell out numbers (Three hundred and ten students are enrolled this semester) or rewrite the sentence (In Chemistry 201, 310 students are enrolled).]

Exercise   Revise the following passage for proper use of apostrophes, hyphens, capitals, italics, and numbers. Use your dictionary to help you edit this passage.

(1) The advertisement shows a sky-diver floating down to earth, and the pictures caption says, "I take vitamin supplements every day, just to be on the safe side."   (2) Self styled experts, from your local pharmacist to physicians from the mount Sinai school of Medicine in New York city, encourage the public to believe that vitamins are a cure all.   (3) There are only thirteen known vitamin deficiencies (such as scurvy, which is a Vitamin C deficiency), but nearly sixty percent of the two hundred fifty two american's responding to our questionnaire believed in taking vitamin supplements.   (4) These days, its almost patriotic to take vitamins—even your Mother says, "Dont forget to take your vitamins!"   (5) During the 1980's, vitamins popularity rose an astonishing twenty nine percent, and revenue from vitamin sale's jumped to nearly three billion.   (6) Although sales are generally higher in the west, some Eastern cities such as boston and Philadelphia have also shown dramatic increase's in sales.   (7) If you want to learn more about vitamins, read The Vitamin-Pushers in a recent issue of Consumer Reports.

INDEX

ALPHABETICAL REFERENCE TO THE HANDBOOK